# HAVANA

**REVISED EDITION**

# HAVANA

## TWO FACES OF THE ANTILLEAN METROPOLIS

Joseph L. Scarpaci

Roberto Segre

Mario Coyula

Foreword by

Andres Duany

THE UNIVERSITY OF NORTH CAROLINA PRESS · CHAPEL HILL AND LONDON

Original edition published in 1997 by John Wiley & Sons Ltd.
Revised edition published in 2002 by The University of North
Carolina Press.

This book was published with the assistance of the William Rand
Kenan Jr. Fund of the University of North Carolina Press.

Designed by Heidi Perov
Set in Monotype Garamond and Meta by Eric M. Brooks

Manufactured in the United States of America

The paper in this book meets the guidelines for permanence and
durability of the Committee on Production Guidelines for Book
Longevity of the Council on Library Resources.

Library of Congress Cataloging-in-Publication Data
Scarpaci, Joseph L.
Havana: two faces of the Antillean metropolis / Joseph L. Scarpaci,
Roberto Segre, and Mario Coyula; foreword by Andres Duany. —
Rev. ed.    p. cm.
Rev. ed. of Havana: two faces of the Antillean metropolis /
Roberto Segre, Mario Coyula, and Joseph L. Scarpaci. Rev. ed. 1997.
Includes bibliographical references and index.
ISBN 0-8078-2700-2 (hardcover: alk. paper) —
ISBN 0-8078-5369-0 (pbk.: alk. paper)
1. Urbanization—Cuba—Havana—History. 2. City planning—
Cuba—Havana—History. 3. Havana (Cuba)—Economic conditions.
4. Havana (Cuba)—Social conditions. I. Segre, Roberto, 1934–
II. Coyula, Mario. III. Segre, Roberto, 1934– Havana. IV. Title.
HT384.C92 H387    2002
307.76'097291'23—dc21        2002001050

cloth   06  05  04  03  02    5  4  3  2  1
paper   06  05  04  03  02    5  4  3  2  1

# Contents

FOREWORD BY ANDRES DUANY xv

PREFACE xvii

ACKNOWLEDGMENTS xxi

ONE. History, Geography, and Society 1

TWO. The First Half Century: The Rise of an Antillean
Metropolis 51

THREE. The Havana of January 89

FOUR. Socialist Havana: Planning, Dreams, and Reality 131

FIVE. City Government and Administration: Old and
New Actors 168

SIX. The Hope and Reality of Socialist Housing 196

SEVEN. The Changing Nature of the Economy 234

EIGHT. The Value of Social Functions 260

NINE. Habana Vieja: Pearl of the Caribbean 310

TEN. Havana's Future: Risks and Opportunities 346

BIBLIOGRAPHY 379

INDEX 409

# Figures

1.1. Havana monthly temperature and precipitation  5

1.2. Traces of quarries in Havana's twenty-first-century landscape  7

1.3. Imprint of marine terraces on selected main streets in Vedado  9

1.4. Curvilinear imprint imposed by the waterfront on street pattern of Habana Vieja, ca. 1849  10

1.5. Settlement of *villas* in Cuba, 1512–28  13

1.6. Typical elite carriage in Habana Vieja, early nineteenth century  34

1.7. A view of the boulevard Alameda de Isabel II  35

1.8. Calzada de Vives (Avenida de España), ca. 1954  42

1.9. Havana's land area and population density, 1519–1958  44

1.10. Obispo Street with awnings, ca. 1906  47

1.11. Territorial expansion of Havana, 1519–1958  48

1.12. Centro Habana with its late-nineteenth- and early-twentieth-century construction and design  48

1.13. Havana's fifteen municipalities in 2001  49

2.1. Centro de Dependientes, ca. 1910  61

2.2. Tobacco factories from the nineteenth century  62

2.3. Present-day Plaza de la Revolución  66

2.4. Five aerial views of Havana, ca. 1950  70

2.5. View of Fifth Avenue (Quinta Avenida)  81

2.6. City block design for Habana Vieja proposed by J. L. Sert  85

2.7. Artificial islands with hotels, casinos, and shopping centers, proposed by J. L. Sert  85

2.8. Five functional nodes of Havana  87

3.1. Cuban sugar harvest and value, 1900–1958  92

3.2. The Cuban Electric Company  94

3.3. Industrial plants by province, 1957  103

3.4. Images of Tropical Brewery Park  108

3.5. View of the Vedado skyscrapers  110

3.6. Havana Hilton, renamed the Habana Libre in the early years of the revolution  123

3.7. Hotel Nacional in Vedado  124

3.8. Art deco–style residence built in the 1940s in Miramar  125

4.1. Cuba's foreign trade balance, 1989–98  147

4.2. Value of Cuban fuel imports, 1989–98  147

4.3. The 1971 master plan  157

5.1. Jurisdictional reorganization of Cuban provinces, 1959, 1976  170

5.2. The new federalism in Cuba  191

6.1. Traditional wooden bungalows in Regla  198

6.2. Multiflex module designed by Fernando Salinas, 1969  209

6.3. Modern and anonymous high-rises at Infanta and Monte Streets, built in 1960s  214

6.4. Twin high-rise apartment towers in Vedado  215

6.5. Villa Panamericana  226

6.6. Pedestrian mall at Villa Panamericana  227

7.1. Bicycling in Havana  244

7.2. Industry and manufacturing in Havana, 1996  246

8.1. One new bus style introduced in Havana in the 1990s  270

8.2. A trolley stop, Plaza de Armas, ca. 1950  272

8.3. Major green spaces in Havana  276

8.4. Protest plaza in front of the U.S. Interests Section in Havana  280

8.5. Health care facilities and medical research centers, Havana, late 1990s. 284

8.6. Infant mortality rates in Havana, by municipality, 1993  285

8.7. Leading origins of tourists to Cuba  294

8.8. Tourist "poles," Havana City Province  296

8.9. Driving time from Capitolio building to points in Havana City Province  304

8.10. The Malecón, Havana's "social living room" and seaside promenade  305

8.11. Natural lookout points for panoramic views of Havana  306

9.1. Nineteenth-century image of Havana  311

9.2. Rhythmic sequence of arcades and porticoes facing Plaza Vieja  313

9.3. The underground parking garage at Plaza Vieja  321

9.4. Top of Plaza Vieja's parking garage, 1993  322

9.5. Modern building in Habana Vieja  334

9.6. Land uses in Old Havana, 1992  335

9.7. New buildings in Old Havana  336

9.8. Restored buildings on Calle Obispo, Habana Vieja  337

9.9. Microbrigade project halted  339

9.10. Master plan, Habana Vieja  341

9.11. Organizational chart, City Historian's Office  342

10.1. School of Arts complex, Cubanacán, Havana City Province  360

10.2. Banco Financiero Internacional  364

10.3. Parque Central Hotel at busy intersection of Prado and Neptuno in Habana Vieja  365

10.4. Hotel Meliá-Habana in Miramar, Monte Barreto  366

10.5. Foreign resident condominiums, Miramar  367

10.6. Relative location of Miramar Trade Center  368

10.7. Architectural model of Miramar Trade Center within Monte Barreto development project 368

10.8. One of eighteen business and office complexes at the Miramar Trade Center 369

10.9. Novotel Miramar, anchoring the southern end of Monte Barreto complex 370

10.10. University Martyrs Park-Monument, Centro Habana 372

10.11. Heroes of March 13, Colón Cemetery, designed by Escobar, Coyula, and Villa, 1981–82 373

10.12. John Lennon statue 374

# Tables

1.1. Population of Selected Major Villages in the Antillean Section of the Audience of Santo Domingo, 1574  17

1.2. Population of Cuba, Selected Years, Late Nineteenth Century  27

1.3. Historic Nineteenth-Century "Firsts" in Havana  36

1.4. Public Works Projects in Havana, Commissioned by Miguel Tacón, Governor of Cuba, 1834–1838  38

3.1. Population Growth of Havana and Cuba, 1899–1958  120

4.1. The Contribution of Building Trades to the Gross Social Product  143

4.2. Housing Completion, 1959–1990 (in thousands)  145

4.3. Accomplishments of the Master Plan of 1963–1964  155

4.4. Premises of the First Stage of Updating Havana's Master Plan  163

4.5. Profiles of the Havana *Talleres* (Workshops)  164

5.1. Reorganization of Counties (*Municipios*) in Pre- and Postrevolutionary Havana  171

5.2. Major Urban Planning Laws in Cuba and Havana, 1523–1985  178

5.3. Urban Environmental and Quality-of-Life Problems  181

5.4. Urban Agriculture in Havana, 2000  184

5.5. New Forms of Community Participation  185

6.1. Selected Housing Laws during the First Years of the Castro Government  200

6.2. Prefabricated Panels Used in Cuban Construction  212

7.1. Havana's Labor Force by Productive and Nonproductive Spheres, ca. 1990  243

7.2. Actions to Rehabilitate Cuba's Internal Finances, 1996–2001  249

7.3. Annual Frequency of Distribution of Selected Food Items, 1993 and 2000  251

7.4. Normative Food Distribution per Person through the Ration Book (*Libreta*), Havana, 2000  252

7.5. Average Prices for Selected Food Items in the Peso Market (1989) and the Free Market (January 2001)  253

7.6. Benefits and Detriments of Illegally Self-Employed Workers  254

8.1. Cuba's Ranking in the United Nations' Human Development Index  262

8.2. Selected Data on Services in Havana, ca. 1989 with Selected 2000 Updates  269

8.3. Health Care Facilities in Havana, 1995  282

8.4. New Educational Facilities Placed in and around Havana, 1960s–1970s  288

8.5. Temperature (°C) Comparisons between Selected Florida Cities and Havana  291

8.6. Leading Origins of Tourists to Cuba, 1995–1999  292

8.7. Selected Joint-Venture Hotel Chains in Cuba, ca. 2001  302

9.1. City Historian's Office, Approximate Income and Investment after Decree-Law 143 in 1993  340

9.2. Rehabilitation Works at Old Havana by the City Historian's Office, 1999–2000  343

10.1. Sectoral Assessment of Havana's Physical and Human Resources, 2001  354

# Foreword

This book is an extraordinary document, not least because its subject is a truly great city, perhaps the most interesting in the New World.

La Habana contains the sediment of several failed destinies. It has been the great colonial capital of an enormously arrogant European empire; republican heir to an epic war of liberation; aesthetic playground of an haute bourgeoisie of remarkable refinement; and currently the stage for a revolutionary process unsurpassed in ideological zeal. The passion of the Cuban people has distilled these sequential ideals, giving their capital its uniquely tragic, heroic visage.

On the other hand . . . perhaps not.

Perhaps the greater influence has been that of the international architectural ideologies, washing wave upon wave upon this crossroads of an island. Perhaps the cosmopolitan architects of Cuba have been the dominant influence. After all, the urban conditions of La Habana have contemporary siblings elsewhere. Must we conclude from the evidence that the virulence of architectural ideology overwhelms sociopolitical considerations?

Perhaps there is only one certainty: that the architecture and urbanism of La Habana are superb in an absolute sense. They do not call forth the abeyance that a relativist discourse accords the Caribbean, the provinces, or the Third World.

This is all described by the authors of this book: one a rigorous North American scholar, another himself immersed in the revolutionary process, and the third a roving, skeptical intellectual. Combined, they manage a fascinating presentation from which our own conclusions may be drawn.

To read it, and to visit La Habana, is to become addicted to urbanism.

Andres Duany
Miami, September 2001

# Preface

This book is a work of love. As with all amorous encounters, it has been titil-
lating and taxing, uplifting and unnerving, and fulfilling and frustrating. It
grew out of a deep appreciation for one of the truly great cities of the world.
Regrettably, little has been written in English recently about Havana, except
for several coffee-table books, which are of a very different genre than this
publication. Nonetheless, scholars and residents enamored with San Cristóbal
de la Habana have been writing about its complex beauties in Spanish and
other Romance languages. Few cities in the Western Hemisphere are as rich
in architectural beauty as is Havana. Since 1993, we have tried to describe and
assess the evolution of this place and to assemble our three perspectives into
a single tome, spun, inevitably, into a story conceived by our personal and
professional experiences. At the outset, we realize that some readers will attempt to pigeonhole our epistemological, philosophical, and political approach before reading a word further. Anything written about Cuba, it seems,
creates predetermined positions. To those skeptics, we suggest reading on
with an open mind and heart.

John Wiley and Sons published the first edition of this book in 1997. That
edition sold out in three years, but, for a variety of reasons, Wiley dropped the
World Cities series to which the book belonged, despite the positive reviews
of *Havana* in journals in the fields of geography, architecture, planning, soci-
ology, and economics. Moreover, these peer reviews appeared in leading international English, Spanish, and German publications and led to a Choice
Book Award given by the American Library Association and recognition by
Lingua Franca as an "outstanding urbanography." For these reasons, we were
enthusiastic about updating the book in 2001 and were very pleased that the
University of North Carolina Press shared our interest in developing a new
edition.

In the five years since the first publication of this book, Havana and Cuba
have experienced major transformations. This tide of change brings both new
threats and opportunities to the Cuban capital. New actors such as foreign in-

vestors in tourism, a limited real estate market, and even public utilities have appeared. In each instance, these actors are almost always tethered in some fashion to Cuban state counterparts. Some disrupting new hotels, condominiums, and even shopping malls have introduced mostly banal international architecture that is largely alien to Havana. Even though there are few of them, these new structures have already been publicly criticized because they threaten the city's unique built heritage. Thus, domestic and international capital's search for quick profits now compounds the perennial problem of a city: very little money for maintenance and rehabilitation.

The effects of the dollar as legal tender, coupled with family-scale self-employment, appear in the streetscape as an endless catalog of vendors, kiosks, and homemade signs. In an abrupt departure from the city's past, there are now intimidating high fences that are common in most Latin American cities but have been anathema in Havana. These defensive barriers disrupt the traditional front-yard openness and introduce trends that reflect Latin American soap operas more than something innate to Havana. Indeed, globalization has ushered in new "wealth" in the form of building and residential additions that distort the original character of former upscale residential and commercial districts that we call the poor nouveaux riches. Despite the quick pace of events, if properly handled, these changes portend new resources for the much-needed upkeep of Havana's immense built environment.

We learned from readers of the first edition that they wanted to know who wrote which chapters. At the outset, we state what is obvious: this is not an edited book. We each reviewed the others' drafts and then worked every chapter into a single, collective work. However, given our expertise, it made sense to divide the writing in the following manner. Scarpaci's human geography background led him to write the original drafts of Chapters 1, 7, and 8. Segre's architectural history and housing expertise placed him in good stead to commence Chapters 2, 6, and 9. Coyula's lifelong residence in Havana and work there as a professor of architecture and city planner made him the authority to pen the first versions of Chapters 3, 4, and 5. Of course, we made adjustments, transferring some parts of chapters to others. After reviewing more versions of these nine chapters than we can recall, we then collectively wrote the final chapter. In this edition, we have updated the entire book where appropriate and where information existed.

Our perspectives in writing this book are informed by vastly different life experiences that have produced unique perspectives in approaching a city about which we care deeply. Roberto Segre was born in Milan, Italy, was reared in Buenos Aires, Argentina, and worked most of his professional life in Havana. His writings about architecture in revolutionary Cuba—translated into many languages—are benchmarks about the transformation of socialist Cuba as expressed in the island's built environment. Mario Coyula is the Havana-born author in this project. His voice surfaces in these pages with both expertise and firsthand experience of life in Havana before and after the watershed year of 1959. Perhaps more than his coauthors, Coyula knows well the passion and energy required to see Havana's "two faces." His professional experience as an architect, planner, and professor gives continuity and authority to the work. Joseph L. Scarpaci, a native of Pittsburgh, Pennsylvania, came to Cuba late in his life. He has tried to make up for that handicap by visiting Havana thirty times over the past decade. The only social scientist on the team, he offers, by virtue of his training in human geography and his work in social policy, urban planning, and heritage preservation in other parts of Latin America (Puerto Rico, Chile, Argentina, and Colombia), a comparative perspective in the study of Havana.

The authors began writing this book during what was arguably the most difficult economic time in recent Cuban history. To complicate matters, in 1993 Segre assumed a professorship in Brazil, where he continues to work. The chilling winds of the Cold War between Washington, D.C., and Havana made Scarpaci's trips to Cuba difficult and Coyula's travels to the United States even harder. In the midst of this, Coyula managed to work in a city burdened with power blackouts. As the book shows, many of these problems have abated in Havana, but others have moved in to take their place.

For a city referred to as a "living museum," for better or worse, we chose a busy time in Cuban history to write about its capital city. No sooner would we have a contemporary aspect of Havana down in writing when something would change; a new law, an investment scheme, or forecast led to a revision and updating. Despite this modification, we managed to exchange manuscripts, diskettes, photographs, and slides through the usual assortment of "gee-whiz technologies": E-mail, fax, next-day courier, and the like (though countless friends also lugged our pages back and forth). We have savored those all too infrequent times when we could bridge time and space and pore over our more than one hundred thousand words in the same room. Through it all, we have learned much from one another and hope that our professional and personal backgrounds will cast a net that is broad enough to attract those who do not know Havana at all, and, in turn, we urge them to do so. And to those who are old friends of the city, we hope you reacquaint yourselves with this marvelous place.

We want readers of this second edition to know that our subtitle (*Two Faces of the Antillean Metropolis*) is a simple metaphor that should not be taken too literally, as did some of the readers of the first edition. Our reference was not intended to use 1959 as the criterion to divide the study of the city into two dimensions, into two faces. Such dichotomies are false, as we attempt to make clear. Rather, there are many facets of Havana: capitalist-socialist, modern-traditional, inspiring-depressing, preserved-dilapidated, magical-mundane, and so on. Havana's great appeal lies in the fact that it was not "overbuilt," as often happens in many cities throughout the Americas. Its built stock, although greatly deteriorated, remains, as do the imprints of its occupants of the past and present. The conservation of Havana's built heritage is a great challenge, but it is also a wonderful opportunity to put the city to work so that it might pay its own way and restore its faded beauty.

Our hope is that this book sets readers on their own journeys to explore Havana's many faces and to appreciate its aged charm.

# Acknowledgments

The idea for this book project first grew out of conversations that one of the series editors, Paul Knox, began with Roberto Segre back in 1985. Segre held a Guggenheim Fellowship that year and lectured briefly at Virginia Tech. Over the past decade Knox has done much so that this book could be written, despite the changing composition of the research team. In Cuba, Gina Rey, then director of the Grupo para el Desarrollo Integral de la Capital, was instrumental in providing resources and encouragement, helping the project to take flight. Jill Hamberg in New York has also encouraged its publication. She has offered thoughtful and extensive comments on the project at various times. The errors and misrepresentations, however, are ours alone.

This revised edition owes a great debt to Elaine Maisner, our editor at the University of North Carolina Press, who encouraged us in updating the book and has worked with us patiently.

In what follows we each give special thanks to those who were helpful along the way.

*Joseph L. Scarpaci, Blacksburg, Virginia*

My children, Cristina Alessandra and Michael Joseph, graciously tolerated the interruptions caused by this project. They treated the writing of this book as a younger sibling competing for their father's attention. My wife, Gilda de los Angeles Machín, a *camagüeyana*, naturally looked with suspicion on the attention that Havana consumed. She nurtured, cajoled, and—at times—tolerated the disruptions resulting from the book's unusually long gestation period.

I was able to use a study-abroad program that I coordinate, Urban Design and Planning in Cuba, to "get me into" the field to do much of the research. Cathy Gorman of Virginia Tech's Photographic Services (now Digital Imaging) produced several illustrations with patience and good cheer and helped get the figures and illustrations burned on a CD ROM. Many students and graduate assistants—Mary Ellen Carroll, Robert Moore, Aaron Crum, Scott

Sincavage, David Zellmer, Jill Cavanaugh, Vishal Pujal—helped in research and data manipulation. Jill Hamberg, Wendy Prentice, and Felípe Préstamo reviewed the entire manuscript of the first edition and provided critical feedback. Orestes del Castillo Jr., Armando Portella, Victor Marín, and Roberto González provided comments, data, and references at various stages. I am especially grateful to the Roberto Acosta and Xiomara Hernández families. Thanks also to my in-laws in Cuba: Mery Sosa, Delia Sosa, Dania Cristiá, and René Barrios-Niz. Gilberto and Sabina Vargas have been gracious during my ten years of research in Havana and have offered insights into life in the city. In Trinidad, Cuba, Nancy Benítez and Roberto López ("Macholo") provided invaluable points of reflection about Cuba's built heritage as well as valued friendship.

*Roberto Segre, Rio de Janeiro*

The documentation gathered for the historical analysis of this work was made possible by the position I held as director of Grupo de Investigaciones Históricas de la Arquitectura y del Urbanismo (GIHAU, 1972–82) at the Instituto Superior Politécnico José Antonio Echeverría. I also wish to thank Dr. Denise Pinheiro Machado, then chair of the Programa de Pós-Graduação em Urbanismo, Departamento de Planejamento Urbano, Faculdade de Arquitectura e Urbanismo of the Universidad Federal de Rio de Janeiro, for the generous time she granted me for writing this book. The Conselho Nacional de Pesquisa (CNPq) in Brasilia awarded me a grant to carry out a multimedia project that was related to the work contained in this book. I was also able to complete a study about the evolution of Latin American cities in the twentieth century, a comparative study of transformations in urban space and its cultural meaning, Rio de Janeiro/Havana. I carried out this research between 1994 and 1996.

My wife, Licenciada Concepción Pedrosa Morgado, helped in the compilation of the bibliography. In Cuba, I received support from architects Dr. Eliana Cárdenas; Dr. Rita Yebra; Isabel Rigol, then director of CENCREM (National Center for Conservation, Restoration, and Museum Science); and Francisco Bedoya.

At Rice University, Houston, Texas, Professor Stephen Fox commented on drafts of the first edition, as did Halley Margon and José Kós, both from CNPq, and collaborators on my research team in Rio de Janeiro.

*Mario Coyula, Havana*

Thanks to my grandfather
a forgotten icon to be reborn one day
To my elder son, uprooted before harvest
a void filled with rage and tenderness
To Marta, Miguel, Mariana, and her little sprouts
who carry on my blood and instill my breath
Thanks to those old-fashioned abstractions
family honor courage
fidelity decency
To enduring loves and to others that have faded
To those who back me and those in front
Thanks to the Revolution
for expanding two-thirds of my time
with successes and flaws, which are also mine
To this salty island, long-suffering and rebellious
the homeland sculpted by my ancestors
broken and reshaped again and again
And thanks to my Havana, graceful and crumbling
waiting for this body, already fulfilled
meant to breed new lives
and mourn the same deaths

*A todos, nuestro profundo agradecimiento.*

# HAVANA

# 1

# History, Geography, and Society

> Yet it was something else to stroll through the city. Behind those formidable and sad walls was a world of color and gaiety. A kaleidoscopic juxtaposition of races and ethnic shades of historical stages. In brief, there lay the riches and misery of the capital's face, where foreigners could find what they had left behind in their countries, plus the entertainment and universal vices that characterized Havana's infamous lifestyle.
>
> —Julio Le Riverend, *La Habana: Biografía de una provincia*, 1961

San Cristóbal de la Habana is a beautiful world city where history's hand has left a mark on every corner. For nearly half a millennium, its built environment has shown capitalist grandeur and plunder, as well as the mediating successes and failures of socialist planning. Havana is unique in many ways, and this book explores those defining features.

The city defies most of the conventional schemata that classify cities by their shape or skylines. Urban geographers and literary scholars (Cabrera Infante 1991, 300–301), for instance, are intrigued by its polycentric structure. Its lack of a discernible center, central business district, or some semblance of a core is noteworthy, as are the many changes in the location of the center over time. *Habaneros* lack a consensus about where *el centro* might be; references to it form part of the daily parlance among commuters, cyclists, and bus riders. More perplexing is that while the debate over defining Havana's central region is relatively new in the city's historical geography—arising only this century—the wandering of the city's former centers has left vestiges of an urban landscape. What the built environment reflects is rich in architectural and social history, making it inviting even for a novice to "read" the built environment as if it were text (Segre, Cárdenas, and Aruca 1981). Havana was on its way to developing a skyline of steel-and-glass towers, but that process ended abruptly. Understanding why that is so speaks volumes about the history of both Havana and Cuba (Segre and Baroni 1998).

The discourse about Havana, like Cuba in general, is often emotionally and intellectually charged, depending on the "lenses" one uses to interpret the city. Marxist students of the city, for instance, claim that public spaces had become "decommodified" under socialist rule; that is, Havana was isolated from market forces that produce nonessential consumer goods and prestigious private shops, restaurants, and clubs. That characterization was accurate from the early 1960s until the 1990s. In response to the collapse of the former Soviet Union, however, the Cuban government legalized the circulation of the U.S. currency and limited private markets. This new direction of economic development is called the "Special Period in a Time of Peace" (or simply "Special Period") and is changing the face of Havana significantly. Despite the reintroduction of a market economy, many architects and urban designers consider Havana to be a city of eclectic and decentralized neighborhoods that are joined by roads, public services, and urban culture. Regardless of the perspective, San Cristóbal de la Habana is undeniably a modern, world-class city. Its cultural landscapes, art, theaters, universities, public institutions, and Afro-European roots distinguish it from the world cities of Europe, Latin America, and North America. The urban historical geography of Havana invites the reader to experience the delights and intrigues of its spaces, buildings, natural settings, and the transformation of its social content.

The aims of this chapter are modest considering the arduous task implied by its title: to identify the forces behind nearly five hundred years of urbanization in Havana (Carley and Brizzi 1997). Accordingly, the approach is broad, selecting key points in history and urban geography to anchor the chapters that follow. The chapter begins with a survey of pre-Columbian Cuba and the level of material culture that Columbus may have seen in 1492. The settlement of Havana over the next three centuries follows, calling attention to significant historical events that tied Havana to the Spanish colonial economy.

A central argument is that Havana served first as a transfer point for wealth coming from other Spanish colonies and subsequently from the rest of the island. Generating little wealth of its own, the island did not develop a formidable resource base until the sugar boom of the nineteenth century. Although

Havana has always had a large service economy (today it has just one sugar mill), it benefited from the wealth generated by sugar barons throughout the island (Marrero 1975a, 1975b).

In the latter half of the chapter, attention turns to the spread of the city. Havana's fortifications included a vast network of forts, castles, and watchtowers (Segre 1968a). Ultimately, a wall was erected between the seventeenth and eighteenth centuries, only to be torn down in the mid-nineteenth century. The rise and fall of the walled city marked both Havana's urban growth and its political challenge to Spain about serving as its American warehouse. In the first half of the nineteenth century, Havana no longer grew at a leisurely pace that could be contained in the colonial core. The city spilled over the crumbling walls and pushed west and south. A service economy tied to agriculture, not industry, filled Havana's coffers and enabled an ambitious governor, Miguel Tacón, to lay out a template of public buildings and a street plan that ushered Havana's urbanization into the present century. Last, the chapter offers a glimpse of twentieth-century Havana, enticing readers to pursue those themes more fully in the chapters ahead. In brief, the urban historical geography of Havana identifies the nuanced transitions of a city originally designed and ruled by the Spanish, modernized by the United States, and, ultimately, governed by a centrally planned Cuban government. We begin with the physical backdrop and the dawn of European conquest.

## The Physical Context

Cuba is the largest island (114,524 square kilometers) in the Antilles archipelago. It is three times as large as Hispaniola, nine times larger than Jamaica, and twelve times the size of Puerto Rico. Straddled to the north by the Florida Straits, to the south by the Caribbean Sea, to the east by the Windward Passage, and to the west by the Gulf of Mexico, Cuba's main island is complemented by more than 1,600 small islands and keys. Cuba spans 1,250 kilometers from east to west at its maximum and has median width of roughly 100 kilometers.

More than half of the island's topography is plain; the rest is in mountains and hills. Cuba, like the 2,400-kilometer stretch of the Greater Antilles, is linked tectonically with the eastern flank of the Yucatán Peninsula. Mountain-building processes from the Cretaceous period were associated with the plate tectonic movements of North and South America and produced Cuba's mountains. Eastern Cuba is both the most rugged area of Cuba and the oldest core region in the Caribbean. Its deeply folded and dissected Sierra Maestra range is in the southeastern corner of the island. West of the city of Santiago de Cuba is the highest elevation of the island, Turquino Peak, at 2,005 meters (6,570 feet). Other orographic features include the Escambray Mountains in south central Cuba, near the colonial city of Trinidad. Another range, the Sierra de los Organos in the western part of the island, can be seen from western points of the province of Havana and on a clear day from Havana city when arriving by airplane.

Western Cuba and the areas surrounding Havana are composed mostly of Cretaceous limestone that has produced a karstic topography of caves, caverns, underground streams, and resistant surface remnants known technically as monondocks (called *mogotes* locally). Despite more than two hundred bays and 5,746 kilometers of coastline along the main island, the bays of Havana, Matanzas, Mariel, Nuevitas, Santiago de Cuba, Cienfuegos, and Nipe are the only major deepwater ports. The preponderance of the island's limestone base makes for acidic soils that, coupled with heavy precipitation, can lead to the leaching of valuable soil minerals and nutrients. In addition, Cuba is well endowed with extensive nickel reserves, discovered in the twentieth century. Nickel ranks as Cuba's fourth or fifth export, depending on prevailing market conditions. Copper, iron, cobalt, and manganese are also found, but in smaller quantities. Although in 1993 a record of 1.1 million tons of oil were extracted in Cuba—some twenty-two times larger than production levels of the late 1950s—the island only satisfies about 10 percent of its consumption demands (Portela 1994, 6; Rivero 1994, 7).

Located just within the northern limit of the Tropic of Cancer, Cuba exhibits a classical wet-dry tropical climate. Average monthly temperatures always exceed 18°C (72°F), with heavy summer rains produced from convection. The maximum temperature ever registered officially in Havana by the National Observatory was 35.8°C in May 1923, though there was an unofficial reading of 42°C in Sagua de Tánamo in 1927. The minimum temperatures for Havana hover around 10°C in the winter months, though Rancho Boyeros in southern Havana registered 0°C (32°F) during a cold wave in 1939. A long dry period ensues in the winter months, and a short dry season prevails in the summer. These pronounced wet-dry periods produce a savanna landscape with distinct drought-resistant (xerophylic) species (Marrero 1981b, 70–73).

Havana receives an average of 45 inches of rain per year, with pronounced

FIGURE 1.1. Havana monthly temperature and precipitation

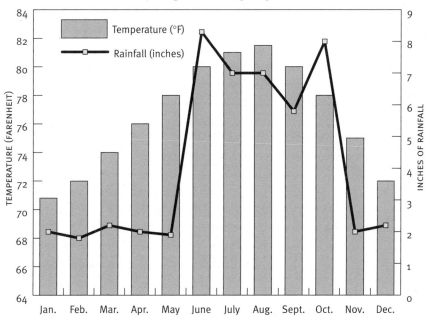

convectional downpours in the warmer months (May–October) and dry weather between December and April. Havana's location (23°N, 82°W) on the Straits of Florida exposes it to the prevailing northeast trade winds. Havana's average monthly temperatures range from 27°C (81°F) in July and August to 22°C (71°F) in January and February, with an annual average of 24.5°C (76°F) (Wernstedt 1961, 33).

The coastal plain surrounding Havana yields to rolling hills as one moves inland. Enhanced with large water supplies, the city of Havana is drained by two principal rivers: the Almendares, between Vedado and Miramar municipalities on the north shore, and the Luyanó, draining much of the southeastern corner of the city before emptying into Havana Bay. Numerous freshwater reservoirs (*embalses*) provide the city with most of its water. New wells are sought in a large aquifer, El Gato, lying outside the city proper. Other minor water resources provide Havana and the rest of the island with only limited hydroelectric energy.

Because Cuba is a long and narrow island with rapid precipitation runoff, its water resources are threatened by saltwater intrusion. Of the hundreds of catchments for fresh water, only about 15 percent are larger than 200 square kilometers (77 square miles). As a result, one of Cuba's gravest environmental concerns is the provision of fresh water for cities, industry, and farms. Noncyclical periods of drought brought devastating consequences to cities and agriculture in 1964–66, 1970–71, 1973–76, and 1986–87. Cuba's extensive underground water resources, however, compensate for rapid runoff and supplied 6.5 billion cubic meters (1.7 trillion gallons) in 1994. Underground water lies in basins that require pumps and costly fossil fuels for its distribution. Overuse of these underground sources aggravates saltwater contamination.

The island's total water resources appear to be underutilized because of the relatively high energy costs in pumping the water. Perhaps half of Cuba's water may be polluted, although the industrial slowdown of the 1990s may have limited pollution sources (Díaz-Briquets and Pérez-López 2000). The gravest environmental threat to the drinking water in Havana comes from the saltwater intrusion in the South Havana Aquifer, the city's main source of drinking water. Estimates are that the water table has fallen about 30 percent, and seawater has invaded some well fields ("Cuba's Water Resources" 1995). As if these problems were not sufficiently daunting, an estimated 55 percent of the water pumped through Havana is lost through leakage (Pérez and Fernández 1996). We discuss water problems more fully in Chapters 5 and 10.

Geologists describe the northernmost shores of Cuba, including those around Havana, as a region that is in a "process of emergence." This means that between Mariel Harbor, 30 kilometers west of Havana, to Matanzas Harbor, some 100 kilometers east, a gradual rising of the landmass has contributed to small, sandy beaches. Differential erosion produced from the rise and fall of water levels during the last ice ages has carved out a moderately scarped coastline, characterized by marine erosion that leaves rock outcrops and fine-sand beaches. For centuries, these rocks have provided the city's builders with ample limestone that could be crushed and used for *mampostería*, a building block made of compacted rubble. Quarries operated at many of these sites until as recently as the early twentieth century (fig. 1.2), and the remnants of one are still visible at the base of the Hotel Nacional and the Malecón (Havana's oceanfront promenade) in the Vedado section of Havana. A series of well-defined marine terraces from which these outcrops derive is evident along this stretch of shoreline (Marrero 1981a, 59).

The marine terraces produced by the sea's recent rising and falling have shaped the layout and settlement of Havana. A series of capes and escarpments—still quite visible despite landscape modification—characterizes the

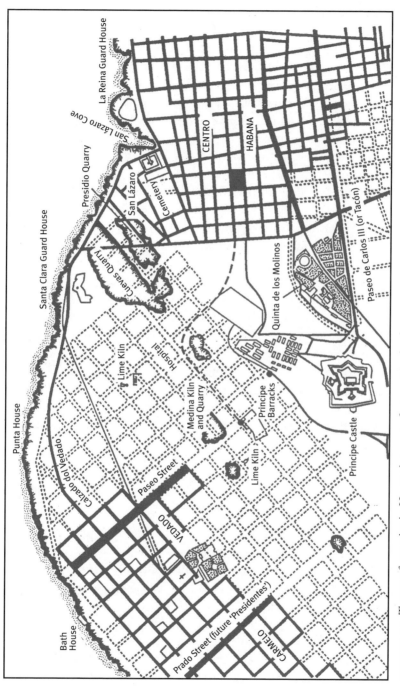

FIGURE 1.2. Traces of quarries in Havana's twenty-first-century landscape

main settlements, neighborhoods, and roads of contemporary Havana (Tingle and Montenegro 1923). Old Havana (Habana Vieja) sits on a cape on the western side of the bay. The cape is a structural remnant of a marine terrace. In Vedado, one can easily walk inland (e.g., south) from the oceanfront along the Malecón—preferably along Paseo Avenue or Presidentes Avenue because of their gardened pedestrian medians—and encounter a series of these gentle platforms. Línea Street, about five blocks from the Malecón, marks the first separation between the coastal level and the first prominent escarpment. Seven blocks farther along, one arrives at Twenty-third Street, which marks the beginning of yet another marine terrace (fig. 1.3). In fact, the entire city's irregular grid twists and turns to accommodate the marine terraces, resistant outcrops, and low-lying areas prone to flooding and occupied by swamps. Old Havana's oval shape stems from the curvature of the bay and the construction of roads running parallel to the shore. Although the "grid" of the old city resembles the perpendicular principles of modern street design, the curvilinear imprint imposed by the waterfront has endured nearly five hundred years of urbanization (fig. 1.4). The original roads of the city—called *calzadas*—still exist, and the *calzadas* of Infanta, Monte, Luyanó, Cerro, and Diez de Octubre follow either the hilltop ridges or lowlands of the marine terraces. It is precisely this irregular grid depicted in figure 1.4 to which Carpentier (1966, 51) attributes "the primordial, tropical necessity of playing hide-and-seek with the sun, laughing at its surfaces, exposing shaded areas, and fleeing from the torrid announcements of twilight, with an ingenious proliferation of awnings draped across the streets." Such an irregular design of early Havana represented a victory of medieval ideas held by the colonizers over the abstract theories of the Renaissance that had not yet made their way to the city planning guidelines of the Laws of the Indies (Segre 1974).

## The Pre-Columbian Setting

On October 28, 1492, Christopher Columbus allegedly remarked when he saw Cuba that it was "the loveliest land ever beheld by human eyes." Like most of the indigenous peoples in the Caribbean, the early inhabitants of Cuba had not developed the high material culture of large cities or the monumental structures found in Mesoamerica or in the Andes. Columbus found three culturally distinct indigenous groups in Cuba: Guanajatabeyes, Siboneyes, and Taínos. The Guanajatabeyes represented about 10 percent of Cuba's

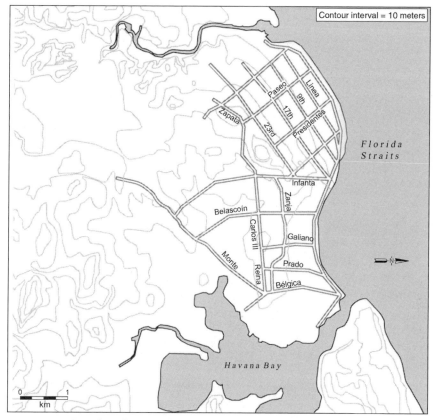

FIGURE 1.3. Imprint of marine terraces on selected main streets in Vedado

indigenous population; located in the western part of the island—ethnically related to native people on Hispaniola—they were perhaps the oldest population (ICGC 1979, 9). They were cave dwellers and hunters and gatherers and exhibited the lowest level of material culture. Sustenance derived from turtles, fish, and plants found in the natural landscape. Of a notably higher material level, the Siboneyes were scattered about all parts of the island. However, they were not agriculturists and lived in caves until the arrival of the Taínos, who forced them into servitude. Originally nomadic when they arrived in Cuba, the Siboneyes later established small villages along the coast and rivers (Portuondo 1965).

The indigenous population clustered mainly in the eastern central portions of the island and resided in straw and palm-thatched dwellings called *bohíos*, a term still used today to describe small huts and shacks in the Cuban country-

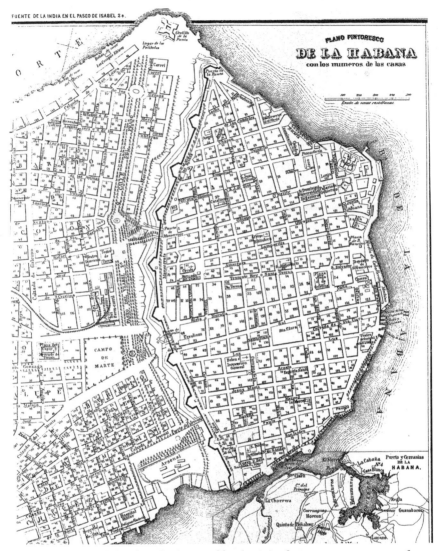

FIGURE 1.4. Curvilinear imprint imposed by the waterfront on street pattern of Habana Vieja, ca. 1849

side. Taíno settlements were structured around a central plaza, and the Taínos preferred higher elevations with fertile soils and potable water nearby. Although they were not numerous, the Taínos modified the pre-Colombian landscape more than other indigenous groups, and they left the Spaniards with numerous place-, flora, and fauna names that form part of contemporary Cuban culture (West and Augelli, 1966; Rallo and Segre 1978; Marrero 1981b, 143–44).

Details on the pattern and process of Amerindian settlement and culture defy easy reconstruction. None of the indigenous cultures had a written language, and the European conquest decimated most of them quickly. Archaeological reviews of middens, village sites, and burial caves, as well as scattered writings from early settlers and explorers, provide most of what we know about these people. Alexander von Humboldt, the German naturalist who visited Cuba in the early nineteenth century, placed the native population of Cuba at 1 million. West and Augelli (1966), however, argue that such a figure must have included Hispaniola, Cuba, and Puerto Rico. Rallo and Segre (1978) reviewed contemporary anthropological and historical records in Cuba and give a much smaller figure. Given the swamps, mountains, and dense vegetation in certain parts, it is unlikely that more than 300,000 persons occupied the island in 1492, and the minimum was probably 50,000. This range is corroborated by the *Atlas demográfico de Cuba*, which estimated about 112,000 aborigines on the island at the time of conquest (ICGC 1979, 9).

The native population clustered in villages, called *bateyes*, that were concentrated on the coast, near the mouths of rivers, and in the hills rising above swampy areas. The *batey* was not laid out in a strict grid system as were most Incan, Mayan, and Aztec settlements in Mesoamerica and Andean America. Social, climatic, and technological factors dictated native architectural styles. Huts were erected on stilts using palm-tree leaves as building materials. Structures not on wooden stilts had earthen floors. Although the use of the palm leaf in building construction protected them from intense tropical heat and torrential downpours, early settlers soon learned that it transferred many parasitic diseases (Rallo and Segre 1978, 10).

## The Settlement of Havana: "A Lemon Not Worth Squeezing"

Between 1500 and 1515 an expedition of about three hundred men, headed by explorer and governor Diego Velázquez de Cuéllar, searched the island for mineral wealth. They founded seven original settlements—military outposts actually—called *villas*: Baracoa (1512), Bayamo (1513), Trinidad (1514), Sancti Spíritus (1514), San Cristóbal de la Habana (1514 on the southern coast and then in 1519 on the northern coast), Santiago de Cuba (1515), and Puerto Príncipe (1514 but later moved inland to Camagüey in 1528). The *villas* would determine in good measure the subsequent urbanization of the island by controlling trade and production in their hinterlands (fig. 1.5). Each received a loosely defined area of jurisdiction. At the time of settlement, however, their relative locations were less than desirable in many respects. In some cases, the *villas* were settled because there was a small indigenous settlement that could be evangelized. In others, the existence of a navigable river or a deep harbor proved attractive, as did proximity to fertile soils, healthy sites (i.e., removed from swamps), and potable water. Only two of the original settlements — Camagüey and Santiago — were founded on good harbors, and the former's location on the Nuevitas Bay later shifted inland. Baracoa and Trinidad were situated on small bays that were actually next to much deeper and navigable harbors that were overlooked at the time. The historical resiliency of these original settlements is noteworthy because they have survived into the present (Díaz-Briquets 1994, 173). In 1509, Sebastián de Ocampo docked in what is now Havana Bay to repair his small fleet while circumnavigating the island. His expedition dispelled Columbus's contention that Cuba was a continent. However, he did not settle there, and two false starts would mark the path to Havana's present site (Fernández Figueroa 1993).

Havana was first located on the Broa Inlet, just off the Gulf of Batabanó, on the southern coast of Cuba, on the Caribbean Sea. The fifth of the seven *villas*, the settlement on the Broa Inlet was directed by Pánfilo de Narváez, who was acting on the orders of Governor Velázquez. It is believed that this was Hernán Cortés's last stop in the Caribbean on his first voyage to conquer Mexico. However, the unhealthy environs and the shallow port forced the settlers to relocate. In 1519 the *villa* of Havana moved to the northeastern shore of the island, almost due north, on the Florida Straits. Although the precise location of this original settlement is unknown, it is believed to have been founded along the shore of a small river that the Indians called Casiguagua (later renamed Almendares by the Spanish). Reasonable estimates place the settlement near the mouth of the Almendares, along the Ensenada de la Chorrera. The location was considered ideal because of the fresh water of the Almendares, but that advantage was outweighed by its vulnerability to rising seas and the lack of a sheltered harbor. Shortly thereafter, in late 1519, the *villa* was again relocated, this time to the western side of a large deepwater bay, a few kilometers east of the Almendares site. There, on a flat cape adjacent to a large deepwater bay, Havana Bay (Bahía de la Habana), is where the city of Havana has been for nearly five hundred years. Legend has it that the location of the young *villa* was sanctioned when both a mass and a town-council meet-

Havana, 1519
Havana, 1514
Sancti Spíritus, 1514
Trinidad, 1514
Puerto Principe, 1516
Puerto Principe, 1515
Camagüey, 1528
Bayamo, 1513
Baracoa, 1512
Santiago de Cuba, 1515

FIGURE 1.5. Settlement of *villas* in Cuba, 1512–28

ing were held under a large ceiba tree (kapok or silk-cotton, g. *Bombax*). A commemorative neoclassical monument, El Templete, was built in 1828 to commemorate the city's founding and still stands on the southern side of the Plaza de Armas in Habana Vieja (Segre 1996b).

Obscurity surrounds the origin of the city's name. Some claim that it is a derivative of the Spanish word *sabana* (savanna or prairie). Others speculate that it comes from a defunct northern European port, Havana, a name possibly derived from the Anglo-Saxon word "haven." The refuge that the bay affords residents from tropical cyclones lends credence to that interpretation. Still others contend that western Cuba was ruled by an indigenous cacique, Habaguanex. The Spanish spelling muddles the term further because the letters *v* and *b* are pronounced similarly. Regardless of its etymology, all that is certain is that the city's patron saint, Christopher, remains the guardian of travelers.

The discovery of the Bahamian Channel made San Cristóbal de la Habana a key transshipment point in the commerce between the Old World and the New. This new and important city refurbished Spanish ships carrying gold and silver originating from Mexico and South America. Ships sailing in either direction naturally called there for supplies or sought refuge if followed by enemies. Although Havana became a mere temporary holding place for the Spanish fleet, it nonetheless brought the city both geomilitary significance and modest wealth. The Spanish-Caribbean route staked out by the Spanish fleet was called the Carrera de Indias (Indies Route), which was actually a set of maritime routes that united Spain with her colonies (Segre 1990; Marrero 1976).

In 1561 Spain issued a royal decree that sanctioned and regulated with great precision the movement of its fleet. Two fleets carrying goods from Seville (via the port of Cádiz, Spain) would leave each year. The first would set sail for Mexico in April and would include ships stopping in the Greater and Lesser Antilles as well as Honduras. A second convoy would depart Seville in August, bound for Nombre de Dios (Panama), Cartagena, and Santa Marta (Colombia) and other ports on the mainland (terra firma). Havana was clearly privileged by its relative location in this hemispheric trade pattern, earning the nickname Llave del Nuevo Mundo y Antemural de las Indias Occidentales (Key to the New World and Bulwark of the West Indies; see Arrate 1762). Transshipments from Cartagena and Portobelo, Trujillo and Puerto Cortés, and Veracruz carried wealth extracted from South America, Central America, and Mexico, respectively (Marrero 1956).

Havana's role in assisting Spain to fight the forces of nature and pirates became essential to the motherland's economic and political might. Jacques de Sores attacked and burned Havana in 1555. Spain authorized Havana to function as the sole port to engage in commerce in 1558. It was then decided to build the La Fuerza fortress (1558–77), the first military stone building in Latin America. The Italian engineer Juan Bautista Antonelli designed the coastal defensive system. Two main fortresses still flank the entrance of the bay: Tres Reyes del Morro (1589–1610) and San Salvador de la Punta (1589–1600). The network also includes a series of small sentry towers between La Chorrera and Bacuranao (Weiss 1972). The Cuban port could both harbor and supply ships with essential provisions during their 1,700-league (and at least seventy-five-day) journey between Seville and Nombre de Dios (Panama) and Veracruz (Mexico). The fleet took advantage of the shifting trade winds between winter and summer. No major port was as close to the Gulf Stream—the major force carrying ships eastward—as Havana. The fleet would try to leave the New World between April and June to avoid hurricanes, and the ships would often dock in Havana to wait out bad weather (Sánchez-Albornoz 1974, 82–83). One description of the armed convoy that would accompany Spain's merchant ships comes from Bartolomé Carreño, who in 1552 set out for the Antilles from Seville. He documented four large boats with a 250- to 300-ton capacity and two smaller ships with an 80- to 100-ton capacity that could carry 360 soldiers. The convoy would escort the merchants to the Caribbean, at which point the ships would disperse to their various destinations. In the meantime, the bulk of the convoy would head off to Havana, where it would dock and use the colonial port as general headquarters for combing adjacent waters in pursuit of pirates and corsairs (Marrero 1956, 123).

In the early sixteenth century, gold deposits in Cuba had proved more bountiful than in Puerto Rico (Wright 1927; Hardoy and Aronovich 1969). Local Indians in Cuba were forced to pan for gold and work the few operating mines. Spanish treatment was brutal, and the constant insurrections by the Amerindians, coupled with infectious diseases, led to the rapid demise of the native people. Panned gold came out of the Arimao, Escambray, and Holguín Rivers. Important gold mines were La Mina, close to Havana, and one near Bayamo. Following the general wave of Spanish settlement from east to west throughout the Greater Antilles, the search for gold and settlement in Cuba also moved from the eastern to western ends of the island. Havana remained subordinate to Santiago de Cuba as a political and economic power until the locus of Spanish power shifted from the Caribbean to Mexico. With the shift, Havana became important as a strategic gateway between the continent and the Caribbean settlements. The initial number of Spaniards in Cuba probably hovered around three hundred but then reached a maximum of three thousand between 1518 and 1520; these were the early years of gold exploration and settlement in the hinterlands surrounding the seven *villas*. However, the population "dropped sharply as the colonists followed Cortés and others to the greener pastures of the mainland" (West and Augelli 1966, 66).

When Cortés left Cuba en route to Mexico in 1519, he took the largest collection of gold ever mined and processed in a single year in Cuba: 104,000 pesos (Marrero 1956, 232). By 1547, gold production had virtually ceased in Cuba (Wright 1916b). The island of Hispaniola supplied Spain with most of its Caribbean sugar. In response to its poor terms of trade, colonists in Cuba sought out alternative markets, including clandestine trade with French, Dutch, and English ships. In the mid-sixteenth century, when authorities in the Canary Islands received permission from the Royal Crown to dispatch ships directly to the Indies, maritime commerce between Havana and the Canaries increased dramatically. Records show that Canarian wine was in great demand in Havana because of the scores of ships that would dock there. Still, the influence of the Sevillan monopoly over sixteenth-century Cuba was great, and the island's economy was, in the words of Wright (1916a), "a lemon not worth squeezing."

If eastern Cuba possessed the economic and political clout of the island during the first half of the sixteenth century, changing political and economic winds moved westward during the rest of the century. Santo Domingo would lose some of its importance as Mexico and other economies on terra firma gained in importance. Havana benefited from this shift in economic power, and its ample bay protected merchant ships from menacing northerly winds (*los nortes*). Havana dominated maritime routes in the Gulf of Mexico, the Straits of Florida, and the Yucatán Channel and was akin to Tangier, which guarded the Straits of Gibraltar in the Mediterranean Sea. Although the concentration of gold-laden ships passing by the northern shores of Cuba would create a breeding ground for corsairs and pirates, Havana would become the "Key to the Indies" and a collection point for ships carrying American treasures to Spain. Havana's significance in Antillean maritime trade led the Audiencia de Santo Domingo in 1553 to transfer Cuba's governor's office from Santiago de Cuba in the east to Havana in the west (Marrero 1956, 118–21).

The swift elimination of the indigenous people of Cuba created a demand for slave labor. Slavery in Cuba dates from 1513, when Amador de Lares obtained permission to bring four Africans from neighboring Hispaniola. Within a decade some three hundred "prisoners" began working the Jagua gold mine in Cuba (Williams 1994, 22). Carabalí and Bantu peoples along the Congo River constituted the largest share of Africans in Cuba, but they would not occupy a strategic role in the island's economy until the eighteenth century. Even though sugarcane was introduced in Cuba in 1523, it lacked export value and was not pursued as a major crop for another two centuries (Rallo and Segre 1978, 17).

In contrast to the more casual style of the French, English, and Dutch, who came to the Caribbean a century later, the conquistadores evolved a unique system of land usage, land tenure, and colonial administration (Peyrerea 1929). The first *audiencia* (colonial administrative region) in the New World was that of Santo Domingo, founded in 1511. It consisted of a rosary of islands: Puerto Rico, Hispaniola, Jamaica (until 1655), Cumaná, and Margarita. By 1574 the dispersed territory claimed only thirty-two settlements, comprising about 1,654 residents, or *vecinos* (García-Saiz 1990, 261). Although Havana remained the principal settlement of Cuba in 1574, it was an intermediate-sized settlement compared with the rest of the Spanish Antilles (table 1.1).

Havana developed a few essential public works to sustain its development. Its vital position in supplying the crews and passengers of the Spanish fleet introduced new pressures to satisfy the fleet's demand for fresh water. Originally, the small *villa* met its freshwater needs with a small cistern replenished by rainwater. In 1550, the Havana *cabildo* (town council) issued a proclama-

TABLE 1.1. Population of Selected Major Villages in the Antillean Section of the Audience of Santo Domingo, 1574

| COUNTRY/VILLAGE | POPULATION | COUNTRY/VILLAGE | POPULATION |
|---|---|---|---|
| *Cuba* | | *Hispaniola* (continued) | |
| Baracoa | 80 | El Cotuy | 17 |
| Bayamo | 80 | Azua | 15 |
| La Habana | 60 | Puerto Plata | 15 |
| Higüey | 19 | | |
| Santiago | 3 | *Jamaica* | |
| | | Puerto Príncipe | 46 |
| *Hispaniola* | | Vega | 11 |
| Santo Domingo | 500 | | |
| Santiago | 70 | *Puerto Rico* | |
| Concepción de la Vega | 60 | San Juan | 200 |
| Puerto Príncipe | 46 | San German | 50 |
| Monte Christi | 30 | Arecibo | 30 |

*Source*: García-Saiz 1990, 261.
*Note*: Early census figures counted only Spanish males and discounted women, children, Indians, and Negro slaves as well as transient merchants and sailors.

tion to increase Havana's water supply by bringing water from the Almendares River, 9 kilometers to the west. Such a grand public works project dominated civic and political discourse in Havana throughout most of the late sixteenth century.

The main problem, though, was how to finance the project. Original estimates placed the cost of the project at 5,000 pesos, then later at 8,000 ducats (gold coins). In a novel move, the Havana *cabildo* requested special permission to establish a local tax (*echar sisa*). In addition, Philip II authorized an "anchoring fee" in Havana Bay to finance the construction of a canal (*zanja*, and called the Zanja Real, or "Royal Canal") connecting the small *villa* to the Almendares River (Zanja Street, running through Vedado and Centro Habana, retraces much of the original course). This ambitious project marked the first major water supply built by Europeans in the New World. By 1562, however, records showed that many ships were reluctant to dock at Havana's port because of the high fee and instead opted for the port of Matanzas, 100 kilometers east. Havana lost out not only on the anchoring fee but also on the economic multipliers of supplying the ships.

In late 1562 the fee was lifted, and a novel municipal fund-raising venture ensued on two fronts. One was a sliding tax scale based on personal income; the wealthiest *habaneros* paid 50 ducats, while the most destitute paid a single ducat. A second way was a "sin tax" levied against three basic products: wine, soap, and meat. In truth, two-thirds of the "canal tax" (*sisa de la zanja*) derived from the sale of wine. The project opened in 1592, and by 1600 its construction costs had been fully recovered (Marrero 1956, 152).

The cumulative effect of completing this major aqueduct in 1592, coupled with Havana's transshipment functions, convinced King Philip II of Spain to grant Havana its official title as a "city." Havana had already completed the requirements of the standard Spanish grid layout as carefully documented by the planning guide, the Law of the Indies. As a "legitimate" city in the Spanish empire, Havana thus qualified to adopt a coat of arms as part of its new status. Characteristically, the coat of arms reflected the significance of the city's absolute and relative location. Three castles in the official city seal denote the city's great fortresses and garrisons—Fuerza, Morro, and Punta—under which lies a golden key. The key represented Havana's ability to "unlock" lands and seas in the Caribbean, continental America, and the Old World. Colonial rulers in Mexico welcomed Havana's status as a royal city. Veracruz was the only decent Gulf port available to the Spanish in Mexico, but its harbor entrance was marred by a series of islets described by mariners as "a pocket full of holes." Thus, Mexico welcomed Spanish investment in Havana, which to some extent served as a port for all of Mexico. In fact, so important was Havana to Mexico's prosperity that Mexico provided Cuba with a permanent and open credit line. Access to this capital was especially useful when the island lacked minted coins or required provisions and matériel for naval and military defense (Santovenia 1943).

Havana would become the most heavily fortified city in the Americas, even though for most of its first century it was just a small port. Its unlit streets were perilous at night. Harlotry flourished, and with that came syphilis. Havana ranked as one of the most nefarious towns in the West Indies despite its impressive forts and veneer of military discipline. Along with youth came styles of design and governance adopted from other kingdoms. Spain was a new political entity when Havana was established. Only three decades earlier had it managed to shake off the yoke of Moorish domination, which had ebbed and flowed across the Iberian Peninsula since the eighth century. Moorish influence as well as Italian, Greek, and Roman styles influenced the early Spanish towns throughout the Americas, and Havana was no exception. However, it would take centuries before a distinctively Cuban or Havanan architecture and urban design emerged, and then those origins would be subject to great intellectual debate (Amaral 1994).

A systematic effort to circumscribe the city with a protective wall did not begin until 1674. In 1767, the entire wall was finally completed. As discussed in Chapter 9, the walls came down in the 1860s, and today there are only a few scattered remnants at the edge of Habana Vieja. The largest stretch is the Puerta de la Tenaza (built between 1674 and 1740), on Egido Street, one block south of the train station (Estación Central de Ferrocarriles), in the southern part of the old town. The contemporary traveler cannot avoid seeing the vestiges of Havana's fortresses situated on prominent hills and points in the center of the city. Except for Cartagena de las Indias, Colombia—with 70 percent of its colonial wall intact—perhaps no other city in the New World holds so many relics of a past military landscape.

The second paradox is that Havana kept few of those riches it fought so hard to protect; wealth merely passed through its ports. Only a small elite manifested any semblance of affluence. The relative location of Havana gave salience to its role as colonial entrepôt and would continue to exert powerful influences for centuries to come.

To compensate for its role as an intermediary agent in foreign trade, colonial Havana turned to the land for its survival. Spanish authorities established a land-distribution system (*mercedazgo*) for their loyal servants. The land (*mercedes*) was defined by first establishing a central point, which was used to delineate a radius. This became the loosely defined circular border for each *merced*. Over time and with the subdivision of property, these circular land plots would overlap and leave a distinct imprint in the Cuban landscape. The Havana *cabildo* granted 148 *mercedes* between 1552 and 1601 in order to satisfy the port's demand for meat and produce. Havana was, moreover, the only Cuban settlement that registered the granting of *mercedes* during this period, thus underscoring its importance in the local and interhemispheric contexts (Pérez de la Riva 1946).

## Havana in the Colonial Hierarchy

The geopolitical organization of the Audiencia de Santo Domingo was subdivided into archdioceses. The Archdiocese of Santo Domingo (1511) covered the entire island of Hispaniola (1511); San Juan (1511) encompassed the island of Puerto Rico. Cuba's archdiocese (1522) was divided between Santiago in the east and Havana in the west, and Venezuela (1531) was split between Coro on the coast and Caracas in the mountains. The Atlantic coast of Florida held scattered fortresses with the exception of the formidable castle in St. Augustine. The dominant classes in the archdioceses imported wine, oil, wheat, tools, arms, furniture, and utensils from Spain. Only the poor Spanish settlers used such indigenous tools as wooden chairs, clay and wooden utensils, hammocks, and poorly spun cotton clothing. Colonists relied on horses, which became a valued commodity for expeditions and armed warfare, even though the settlement was evidently less engaged in warfare than elsewhere in Spanish America.

The seven original *villas* in Cuba reflected the authority of the church, the army, and the *cabildos*. Although each of the *villas* had a main plaza, the original town design was irregular and sporadic. Cuban *villas* obeyed more the whims of the topography or the original settlers than any guidelines imposed by the Law of the Indies. Neither did they reflect planning and zoning ordinances promulgated by the Spanish government during the sixteenth century. Coastal *villas* such as Havana built their plazas on the waterfront, while the land-based *villas* situated the plazas in the middle of the buildings and houses (Duverger 1993a). The only type of residential segregation was between the white Spanish population, settled around the plaza, and the indigenous population, who settled behind the Spanish.

The Audiencia de Santo Domingo suffered endemic problems between 1573 and 1750. It was beleaguered by pirate raids and hurricanes. As gateway to Spanish America, it was less interested in preventing the Lesser Antilles from being occupied by non-Spanish powers and more concerned with refurbishing ships coming and going from Seville and terra firma in Mexico and South America. Thus, by the late sixteenth century the Caribbean Sea was no longer a "Spanish lake" but a commercial body of water traversed by African slaves and French, English, Dutch, and Danes engaged in business transactions, most of them illicit and "dirty" in nature (García-Saiz 1990, 262).

Santo Domingo was by most accounts the "first" city of Spanish America, at least until the latter part of the sixteenth century. Havana lacked the institutional structures and ceremonial buildings that colonial towns of importance boasted. Santo Domingo, however, showcased a cathedral, a hospital, and convents and churches run by the most important religious orders (Pérez Montás 1998).

By the 1600s, primacy in the Spanish Antilles had shifted to Cuba. Its main urban center, Havana, became a commercial and defensive enclave as well as a crucial node in trade between the "metropolis" (Spain and the rest of western Europe) and territories in the New World. Sir Francis Drake's sacking of

Santo Domingo left in its wake a path of ruin and burned buildings. Palm (1955) contends that Drake's looting of Santo Domingo in 1586 sealed its fatal demise and cast it merely as a provincial city, despite its status as capital of the Audiencia de Santo Domingo and its university. Drake later postured offensively at the entrance to Havana Bay but decided not to attack. Instead, he sailed to St. Augustine, Florida, which he destroyed, and then on to Roanoke Island, North Carolina, to rescue survivors of Sir Walter Raleigh's ill-fated colony (Roberts 1953). Havana's rising prominence was not reflected by the city's stately buildings until the eighteenth century. A Jesuit church located on the old Plaza de la Ciénaga (now Plaza de la Catedral) was built in 1749. The original cathedral, Parroquial Mayor, situated on the Plaza de Armas, was demolished.

Although San Cristóbal de la Habana prospered from Santo Domingo's loss of political and economic power, it was never characterized in the sixteenth to eighteenth centuries as a city of great splendor. (Havana would have to wait until sugar profits in the late eighteenth century and first half of the nineteenth found their way into the city's *calzadas*, parks, promenades, and new elite neighborhoods such as Cerro and the early Vedado. Only then would wealth situate Havana among the truly beautiful cities of the Americas.) British threats on Havana were a decisive factor in the city's development, and they placed great demands on the island's mines. Artillery for Morro and Punta Castles were forged from Cuban copper mines, and most of it was supplied from the Bacuranao copper mine near Havana. After 2,000 *quintales* (92,000 kilograms) of copper was forged from the Bacuranao mines, newer deposits were sought out in eastern Cuba, near Santiago de Cuba.

Emphasis on Havana's economic and geopolitical significance did little to stimulate the arts in the sixteenth century. It was not the official capital of the island (Santiago was) and thus lacked the few privileges that came with such status. During the first half of the sixteenth century, governors would divide their time between Santiago and Havana, "while the Crown in its dilatory way refused to admit that the new town was becoming the real center of Cuba's activities" (Roberts 1953, 11). On the broader stage of the Antilles, Havana played the role in the west that Santo Domingo still played in the middle.

Tropical heat and humidity were unkind to the relatively small collections of oil paintings and outdoor sculptures in colonial Cuba. Insects, particularly termites, took their toll on picture frames, wooden crucifixes, wooden carvings, and other colonial artwork. Although many native woods withstood termite damage, those fine woods are now rare. Contemporary homes in Havana have imported furniture made from non-termite-resistant wood that show the consequences of using exotic woods.

Wood products contributed much to Havana's early colonial economy before the demand for sugar led to quick deforestation in the early nineteenth century. The shipbuilding trades figured among some of the first industrial activity in Cuba, and Havana was an ideal location because of its maritime traffic. In the latter half of the sixteenth century, shipbuilders in Havana sought out *ácana*, *guayacán*, oaks, and mahogany for their strength and water resistance. So strategic was Havana's shipbuilding industry to the Spanish Crown that it enacted a royal decree in 1620 that authorized the free cutting of all trees in Cuba whose wood would be destined for shipbuilding. The governors of the island (Menéndez de Avilés, 1568–73; Texeda 1589–94; Valdés 1602–8) took pride in both the size and quality of galleons built at the Machina shipyard located at Alameda de Paula Street along the waterfront of Havana Bay (Marrero 1956, 308). The Spaniards also used these hardwoods for carving ornamental keepsakes, termite-resistant building construction, and furniture making. Even today one can appreciate the likeness between the colonial ceilings of Santa Clara Convent in Habana Vieja and the ceilings of other historic structures and an inverted ship hull. Unfortunately, as Havana's role increased as a major refurbishing port for Spanish fleets, so too mounted pressures on the island's resources. Deforestation around Havana resulted from farming, lumbering, ranching, and urban sprawl (Marrero 1981b, 165).

Havana, like most colonial Spanish cities, has a semiregular grid related to the subsequent Law of the Indies. Sartor (1992–93) describes the irregular layout as "organic" and closer to the medieval towns of Europe than the formal grid plan found in most Latin American cities. Placing La Fuerza fortress on the Plaza de Armas disrupted the usual pattern of locating important buildings of the church (*iglesia*) and government (*cabildo*) on a single town square. As we discuss in the following chapter, this gave rise to the dispersal of city functions to other town squares and characterized Havana's polycentric nature. Plaza de Armas held the major military institutions, Plaza de la Catedral was home to the church, and the commercial activities concentrated around Plaza Vieja, while Plaza de San Francisco handled mainly foreign trade (Segre 1994c).

If the sixteenth century in the economic history of the European conquest of the New World was "Spain's century" (Herring 1966; Pendle 1978), then Havana played no small part in helping the Iberians secure that position.

France, Holland, and England would not seriously erode Spain's power until the defeat of the Spanish Armada in 1588 and the sacking of Cádiz by the English in 1596. Those three European powers had secured colonies in the Caribbean, and they would use them to launch raids against Cuba. Cuba's bilateral relations with non-Spanish powers in the Caribbean swung from illegal contraband trade at one extreme to sustained naval and land warfare at the other. The vicissitudes of prosperity and warfare have led Pichardo-Moya (1943) to refer to the seventeenth century as Cuba's "Middle Ages." Under the last of the Habsburg kings (Philip III, 1598–1621; Philip IV, 1621–65; and Charles II, 1665–1700) who ruled Spain in the seventeenth century, Cuba was subjected to the mercantilist policy of a closed sea and trade (*mare clausum*). This meant that the island could not receive foreign ships, merchants, or colonists (Barnou 1951). Spain's three hostile maritime rivals—Holland, France, and England—drew up a "Friendship Line" that consisted of the meridian of longitude running through the Azores (28°W) and the parallel of latitude noted by the Tropic of Cancer (23.5°N).

On January 4, 1762, George III of England declared war on Spain, and the strategic data gathered by Admiral George Knowles, recast in a military plan drawn up by the duke of Cumberland, would be used to gain control of Havana. Advances in munitions and artillery made El Morro vulnerable. A fleet of British ships—possibly the largest that had ever sailed into the Caribbean at that time—easily outmaneuvered the Havana militia, which counted on nearly twenty-seven thousand soldiers and sailors and nearly as many residents. Part of the British fleet sailed to the west of the city and feigned a landing near the Almendares River. The Spanish dispatched a goodly number of men to that point. Meanwhile, the other part of the British fleet—acting on the keen data of Admiral Knowles—landed east of El Morro. The British gambled on securing the ridge above the eastern side of the bay, across from the walled city. The logic here was that Havana would be rendered useless if the ridge above it was not secured. The gamble paid off handsomely for the British. Within six weeks, the "Key to the New World" had been finally unlocked by a non-Spanish power (Thomas 1998).

The flag of Saint George flew over the island of Cuba for the next six months, during which time the *habaneros* proved to be ornery and uncooperative. Sir George Keppel, earl of Albermarle, headed the British occupation. A normal amount of war booty was extracted, and a fair amount of tithes were taken from the *cabildo*, the church, merchants, and the elite. On February 10, 1763, France, Spain, and England signed a peace treaty in Paris. In what has been considered one of the most curious deals struck during the colonial wars in the Americas, Cuba was exchanged for Florida. Back in England, William Pitt the Elder argued fiercely against the treaty, contending that, with Havana, "all the riches and treasures of the Indies lay at our feet" (Williams 1994, 94). Pressure from sugarcane growers in what was then an "English" Jamaica, who disdained competition, led to the swap. Florida, though, was little more than a low-lying sandy peninsula that afforded the British only a contiguous colony along the Atlantic seaboard (Kuethe 1986).

The fall of Havana to the English and a natural disaster brought four notable accomplishments to Havana's city planning and design. First, there was an official designation of neighborhoods in Havana following a particularly late arriving hurricane in October 1768. The storm, Hurricane Santa Teresa, exposed the vulnerability of many residential structures. Two quarters resulted: La Punta in the northern section of the walled city and Campeche in the south. Each quarter held four barrios (neighborhoods or districts). La Punta contained Estrella, Monserrate, Dragones, and Angel barrios. Campeche contained Santa Teresa (named after the storm), San Francisco, Paula, and San Isidro. Physical inspections of roofs were carried out, and royal-palm-bark thatching was ordered replaced by flat Moorish masonry roofs or tiles. Second, a public street-lighting system was established. Third, modest changes to the colonial design followed. After the wall was completed in 1740, traffic from within became a problem. Only two gates to the city existed: one connecting La Punta and a second near the center of the rampart. By 1773, five additional gates had been constructed, much to the relief of local merchants. Last, to remedy the city's strategic vulnerability shown from the war with England, a fortress was built on La Cabaña ridge, and construction of Atarés and Príncipe fortresses began around 1774. However, it was not Spain that would finance this project. Instead, the viceroyalty of Mexico donated some $14 million to the project (Roberts 1953, 55).

The island's defeat at the hands of the British led indirectly to a sugar boom after 1763 (Moreno Fraginals 1964). A strict system of militia recruitment and training went into effect, and planter-officers exacted commercial privileges in exchange for their military services. The combined effect was to establish institutional structures conducive to capitalist expansion and production. Reform programs put in place by Charles III facilitated the growth of the sugar industry, and Havana served as a major center for exports, banking, and commercial services. When in 1791 a slave revolt led by Toussaint L'Ouverture in St. Dominigue (Haiti) threw the French colony into a devastating twelve-year war against the homeland, Haiti lost its position as the world leader in sugar production.

Cuba profited from Haiti's economic decline. From 1793 onward, Cuba prospered from unrestricted commerce with all countries except enemy nations. Neutral trade lent access to the profitable markets of the United States, which was positioning itself as a leading shipping power that traded wood (for packing crates) and fuel with Cuba, as well as flour from its bountiful milling operations. By 1815, an island population of six hundred thousand placed Cuba "on the threshold of world leadership in sugar production" (Kuethe 1986, 175), and Havana had become the locus of power in this rising sugar empire.

Sugar, though, could not reign supreme without abundant and cheap labor. Until the late 1700s, the ratio of African slaves was relatively low in Cuba compared with Jamaica, Haiti, Trinidad, and Curaçao. However, the collapse of the French colony St. Dominigue in 1791 placed Cuba in a position to increase sugar revenues for the Royal Crown, and the rate of slave importation rose markedly in the following decades. Wealthy French fled to Cuba and exerted strong influences in coffee and sugar production around Cienfuegos, Nipe, Banes, and Nuevitas, all of which were founded about this time.

In the closing years of the eighteenth century and the start of the nineteenth, Cuba was poised to receive immigrants who wished to visit or move to Cuba. Nearly thirty thousand people came from Santo Domingo following a slave insurrection there. When Louisiana was transferred to France in 1803, many Spaniards left, and Havana was their port of entry into Cuba. The Spanish colonial government issued a decree in 1817 that greatly encouraged land ownership by foreigners. South America sent to Havana thousands of Spanish-speaking peoples who fled the devastation of the Independence Wars that swept the continent. The first census of Cuba conducted by the marquis de la Torre in 1774 showed an island population (probably greatly undercounting slaves) of only 171,620 inhabitants—1.5 habitants per square kilometer—after two and half centuries. By 1861, though, Cuba's sugar production had spread, and the population had grown by 816 percent to 1.4 million. During its peak years of growth following the Haitian revolution and the immigration of French and Haitians, Cuba averaged an annual rate of growth of 3.4 percent between 1792 and 1817 (Marrero 1981a, 144–45). Population increase driven by agricultural production meant an increase in the immigration of African slaves and, in the mid-nineteenth century, Chinese indentured workers. Thus, the white population, constituting 56 percent of the island's total in 1774, dropped to 42 percent in 1841. An 1845 decree on the importation of slaves caused a rise in the white population to 54 percent in 1861.

Cuba's expanding sugar industry unleashed a new demand for labor. Using slave labor was becoming harder as Britain attempted to interrupt slave shipments between Africa and the New World. Cuban sugarcane growers, however, were always in search of slaves to replace their exhausted laborers. A relatively unpopulated island that had been settled by Europeans and African slaves for three centuries began to increase population steadily. The Cuban government even tried buying Indians from the Yucatán Peninsula as slaves. Spanish regulations also included a campaign to promote Chinese immigration. Between 1847 and 1860 nearly forty-eight thousand Chinese entered Cuba (Niddrie 1971, 98).

The Havana Asiatic Company (Compañía Asiática de La Habana) brought over most of the Chinese coolies, who settled among the sugarcane communities between Havana and Matanzas and around the towns of Cárdenas and Colón. Contract labor of Chinese workers in Cuba, as in Peru and Mexico, was "hardly distinguishable from slavery" (Sánchez-Albornoz 1974, 150). Havana today still has vestiges of a small Chinatown near the Capitolio building, though intermarriage and out-migration since then have left a relatively small population of pure Chinese in Havana. A small though well-preserved Chinese cemetery remains in Havana, near the large Colón Cemetery in Vedado. Although some Native Americans from the Yucatán Peninsula also immigrated in the mid-nineteenth century, their contribution to the national population stock was minor. The 1899 census classified 67 percent of the population as white and 33 percent as "colored," including Chinese (Gobierno de Cuba 1899).

Cuba's national population fluctuated greatly during the latter half of the nineteenth century because of the long periods of war between Cuba and Spain (table 1.2). Whereas the first half of the nineteenth century registered rapid population growth, Cuba actually lost population during the latter half of the century. In 1887, Cuba registered 1.63 million residents, but by the end of the Independence Wars (discussed in the next chapter) in 1898, the island had 60,000 fewer inhabitants. Marrero (1981a, 149) calculates an annual loss of 0.3 percent during the warring 1887–99 period.

Rapid population growth in early-nineteenth-century Cuba meant a larger labor pool for its agricultural production and more wealth for Havana. The slave trade in the Caribbean was largely concentrated in Cuba, and more than 387,000 black slaves entered the island between 1800 and 1865, despite Spain's

TABLE 1.2. Population of Cuba, Selected Years, Late Nineteenth Century

| YEAR | POPULATION |
| --- | --- |
| 1861 | 1,396,530 |
| 1877 | 1,521,684 |
| 1887 | 1,631,687 |
| 1899 | 1,572,797 |

*Source*: Gobierno de Cuba, 1899.

abolition laws of 1845. It was common among even modest white, Creole, middle-class *habaneros* to have several slaves. Bells were not used in summoning slaves within the home. Rather, the master's family would merely yell, for the slaves lived conveniently in entresols (mezzanines). White Creoles (Cuban-born Spaniards) and *peninsulares* (Spaniards born in Spain) were expected to maintain a Negro mistress within the home, and he was not all that concerned about hiding these sexual antics. Bastards from Creole fathers and black mistresses usually were granted freedom and the family surname when they reached adulthood.

## The Rise and Fall of the Walled City

The walling of colonial Havana was a long process, not only because of the great amount of labor and raw materials required for the public work but also because of the decision-making process leading up to its approval. It seems to have become a key point of public discussion following the attack of the French pirate Jacques de Sores in 1555. Alternatives to encasing the city included placing barricades at the ends of the streets. Juan Bautista Antonelli's nephew, Cristóbal de Roda, argued against the walls, claiming that the city had a sufficient network of fortresses (Weiss 1996).

The building of the wall sealed Havana's status as a link in Spain's mercantile system. An erratic flow of funds from Spain delayed construction, and building did not commence systematically until 1663 and ended some eight decades later. Havana's bulwark fortress consisted of walls set in a polygon made up of nine bastions. Parapets and escarpments pulled the walls together with an exterior moat. The northern end of the walled city was anchored by La Punta Castle, and San Francisco de Paula grounded the southern end.

When construction began, the ramparts encased a larger area than had been settled. Well before the completion of the wall, the town exceeded its limits. When the final stone was laid in 1740, the original design had not been faithfully erected. It failed to include a covered passageway and a moat around the entire wall. In the end, the walled city consisted of 56 streets, 179 blocks, 5 plazas (Catedral, Armas, Vieja, San Francisco, and del Cristo), 14 churches and convents, 2 hospitals, 6 military barracks, and 1 jail (Roberts 1953, 41).

The elite of colonial Havana used key social spaces to flaunt their status. One prominent display was the outing in the family coach just outside the walled city. This was particularly important for the well-off women of Havana. At the end of the eighteenth century, the Alameda de Paula along the bay was *the* place with the greatest amount of street life, especially on days when dances and *retretas* (impressive displays and evening military parades) were held. Although some men strolled there, women usually remained in the *carruajes*. The *paseo en carruaje* (for carriages) had acquired greater importance than the *paseo a pie* (for pedestrians). With the creation of the Tacón Theater and the widening of the Paseo Extramural in the 1830s, the coach *paseos* became more common as the elite sought recreation outside the crowded conditions of the walled city. New customs such as theater, cafés, traveling carnivals, and the carriage stroll brought the well-off *habaneros* outside the confines of the walled city. They served, furthermore, as a creation of popular space where rich and poor could see the differences between Spanish lifestyles and those of the island (Le Riverend 1992).

Ways of life and land uses in Havana in the early nineteenth century were at cross-purposes. On the one hand, provisions, animals, and light industries that were essential to the survival of the *villa* when it was a frontier town held less importance in the 1800s. Beasts of burden and all kinds of carts and carriages made the streets of the walled city nearly impassable. More than two thousand horses and mules kept in Old Havana undermined public hygiene. Street congestion resulted from the more than two thousand two-wheel carriages (*volantas*), open horse-drawn carriages (*quitrines*), and other passenger and cargo carts and wagons (Chateloin 1989). On the other hand, much of the city had grown beyond the old ramparts as the fear of corsair and pirate attacks waned, and the livelihood of the city's residents moved into services outside the original core (Pérez Beato 1936). Epidemics and infectious diseases compounded the misery in parts of the walled city, and the cholera outbreak of 1833, which took three thousand lives, was particularly tragic. Water quality was also poor; between 1592 and 1835, the potable water came from the Zanja Real, which required constant upgrading and maintenance (Marrero 1956, 1981a).

By 1860, Havana's role in the world economy had changed its land use and urban morphology, giving rise to a well-defined commercial district outside the walled city. New elite neighborhoods, more thoroughly discussed in Chapters 2 and 3, originated from sugar wealth. At that time there existed outside the walled city ten furniture stores, six clothing stores, five leather shops, five cafés, six hardware stores, four china shops, three pharmacies, and a handful of tailor shops, tea shops and restaurants, barber shops, print shops, and even a store devoted exclusively to Asian merchandise. When the walls came down in the early 1860s, Havana had outlived its role as a mere warehouse of Mexican and Peruvian wealth; it had emerged as an economic power in its own right.

## Design and Style in Colonial Havana

The classic Spanish architectural elements of cut stone and lumber arrived relatively late in the Cuban colony. Abundant clay soils favored the use of brick and adobe construction materials. Even the first public buildings in the *villas* used the indigenous construction method of thatched leaves and stalk covered with a layer of mud and clay. When "Spanish" architecture did take hold, it reflected a strong Moorish influence. Interior patios remain today in Havana that are similar to designs found in Tunis, Alger, Seville, Granada, and Cádiz.

The transition from baroque to neoclassicism also arrived relatively late in Cuba, and there is some dispute about whether it even took hold (Sánchez Agusti 1984). Even though the baroque style was beginning to decline in Europe in the 1740s, it did not arrive in Cuba in full force until the beginning of the nineteenth century. Local stone, with its wide grain and hollow cavity, did not lend itself easily to baroque decoration. The development of European building styles in Cuba was limited, as military engineers were responsible for most of the major projects in Havana. Trained to solve technical problems and affiliated with the asceticism of classical tradition, these military engineers were unaccustomed to the decorative ways of baroque architecture. In addition, the craftsmen and slave builders obtained their experience in military construction, which they then applied to civic buildings. That explains the limited presence of decoration as shown by the smooth curves of the Segundo Cabo (Intendente) Palace. (A similar problem is discussed in Chapter 9 regarding the loss of building trade skills because of the prefabrication of socialist housing.) Thus, the type of stone was a determining factor in the predominant style of architecture of the nineteenth century (Weiss 1972).

Other political and ideological factors also interfered with the transition from baroque to neoclassical. Neoclassicism was associated with rationality and the French Revolution, at least in its early phase. Cuba, though, was relatively conservative as a Spanish colony (at least until the later-eighteenth- and early-nineteenth-century awakenings brought on by the stirrings of a Cuban independence movement and the example set by Haiti). Havana's entrance into neoclassical design was facilitated by Bishop Espada, the influential organization the Economic Society of Friends of the Country (Sociedad Económica de Amigos del País), French immigration to Cuba via Haiti, and the intelligent government of Carlos III in Spain. The outlying suburb of Cerro received the bulk of this new, neoclassical design in the first half of the nineteenth century. Iron was used in versatile and whimsical ways typical of the baroque style and made the use of wood obsolete in verandas and balustrades. Greco-Roman styles were also used widely in Havana through neoclassical buildings and homes. Neogothic architecture also appeared, and the Villanueva Station was perhaps the city's finest example (Weiss 1966).

Colonial residential structures were equally simple. Old Havana's initial homes were merely huts (*bohíos*) made from wooden slats, wattle, and guano. These structures were later improved with walls of broken stone cemented by plaster (*mampostería*) or a combination of buttresses, mud walls, and tiles (Weiss 1972, 1978). Such precarious structures were highly susceptible to fire, which swept through colonial Havana often. *Habaneros* built more stone structures after the French torched Havana in 1538. Even in the nineteenth century, most buildings were only of one story, and in cases of two-story buildings, the ground floor was most often used for retailing. Windows did not have glass. Instead, heavy iron bars on the street side covered them, and occupants used wooden shutters on the inside. Few houses had basements because of the miry soil, which was polluted by sewage. Wood, not stone, characterized the sixteenth-century city. Buttresses, beams, doors, joists, trusses, and railings were made of high-quality wood, which covered the island.

Havana is remarkable today because of its broad *portales* (arcades or arched colonnades), which reflect the influence of Basque immigrants from northeastern Spain. In the era of the *villas*, retail trade took place in the plazas, near the coast, in open-air markets and makeshift wooden kiosks. In the seventeenth century houses were built out of various block mixtures (*albañilería,* which used cementing materials such as crushed limestone, fruit juices, and oxen blood, mixed with brick or shattered stone), with wooden roofs and tiles, and formed one- or two-story structures. The owner of the house occasionally used or rented out the street-level floor for retail trade and often lived on the second floor. The Laws of the Indies proclaimed that the colonial cities of Latin America would "surround the plaza" and that the four main streets emanating out from them would have "*portales* for the comfort of passer-bys" (Aruca 1985, 25; our translation). The *portales* were added on to the Havana buildings located on town squares around the beginning of the seventeenth century. In the eighteenth century, so important were the *portales* that homes were classified as either having or lacking them (Aruca 1985, 25).

In the early nineteenth century, Havana's elite drew on French culture for ideas and models to emulate (López Segrera 1972). *Habaneros* danced and dressed like the French elite even before the immigration of French and Spanish residents who had resided in Haiti and Louisiana. The minuet, moreover, was danced only by the aristocracy in Cuba. With the arrival of these new immigrants and their servants, French music became so popular that Spanish and Cuban music was played with a distinguishing French touch.

One venue for disseminating this French influence was the Academia de Música de Santa Cecilia, which was founded in 1816 with the financial support of the Sociedad Económica de Amigos del País. French artists arrived in Havana and influenced local painters. They included Garneray (1807) and Vermay (1817). The latter founded the San Alejandro Painting Academy in 1818. In literature the romanticism of Heredia illuminated local readers and writers. The surge in elite admiration of the French could even be seen in the interiors of Havana's upper-class houses, which were decorated in French style. The Aldama Palace, which was the most important neoclassical residential building in Cuba, illustrates this. Even the quintessential Cuban habit of drinking coffee derived from the French.[1] The slave rebellion in Haiti was a major catalyst in bringing the practice of coffee drinking to Cuba.

---

1. Culture and economy in Havana were interwoven in essential ways. The social value placed on coffee consumption led to an increase in coffee production. At the beginning of the nineteenth century, Cuba was exporting 50,000 arrobas (Spanish weight of 25 pounds) of coffee beans, and by 1830 production reached 2 million. Half of that production was consumed on the island, and half was exported. By 1840, the railroad precipitated the substitution of coffee around Havana for sugarcane. But the production and consumption of coffee increased. Drinking coffee replaced the practice of sipping chocolate among the affluent, and cafés like those found in

## Tacón: The Neoclassical Appeal

The nineteenth century marked a watershed period of independence movements and change in Latin America. In the Caribbean, however, the sugar-oriented economies remained isolated from the *independendista* fervor on Mexican and Central and South American soil. While the Creoles in Cuba strongly resented the disproportionate power exercised by the *peninsulares*, they feared even more the downturns in the sugar economy. Haiti's independence movement unleashed violent uprisings of Negro slaves against plantation owners, the reports of which were fresh in the minds of white Cubans. Thus, "they considered a Spanish colony preferable to a black republic," even though Spanish rule was "appallingly corrupt" (Pendle 1978, 119).

Governor Miguel Tacón's main charge from 1834 to 1838 was to keep Cuba a Spanish colony, and improving Cuba's economy and image was one way to achieve that goal. Tacón wished to make Havana a symbol of urban modernity, which at the time was identified with neoclassicism. This modern drive embraced sobriety, order, righteousness, straight avenues, and open spaces for the new middle class. Tacón's elder brother, Francisco, was the Spanish ambassador in Washington, D.C., and there is speculation that the young capital's layout by L'Enfant might have influenced Governor Tacón's urban reforms (Chateloin 1989). Governor Tacón had a rivalry with the influential Creole Count Villanueva (Pérez de la Riva 1963), which greatly benefited Havana.

Tacón also wanted to bring law and order to the Cuban capital. His police force had to meet minimum weekly arrest quotas. Illegal slave trade was allegedly snuffed out, even though he is said to have profited from kickbacks and direct revenues for certain slave trading that he condoned. In Havana, though, he began an erstwhile beautification process. Beginning with reno-

---

Europe appeared. The first café was opened on the Plaza Vieja within the walled city in 1772, and it would become an important gathering place in the nineteenth century. It was originally called Café de Tavern but was renamed Café de la Taverna. Other cafés followed: in 1804 the Café de los Franceses opened on the Campo de Marte (just outside the walled quarters), and the Café de las Copas was opened on Oficios Street (within the walled city). This is where early separatist thinkers met. The Café de la Dominica on Obispo Street (1812) and Café de la Paloma (1825) were also popular meeting places for the elite, foreign travelers, and the early revolutionaries who sought independence from Spain (Chateloin 1989, 31–32). The role of cafés as public gathering places has all but disappeared in contemporary Havana.

vating the Captain General's Palace in the Plaza de Armas, he added a neo-classical marble portico over the main entrance door, which faced the town square. Tacón recognized that the town jail—a locally unwanted land use in today's vocabulary—was not desirable in its location, so he moved it to a less central position near the Punta Castle, where a small portion still remains.

The Prado boulevard, at that time called the Alameda (literally, a poplar-lined street), was redesigned with trees on both sides. It was renamed Paseo de Isabel II and became the principal avenue for afternoon rides in thickly decorated carriages (*volantas*) carrying rich women. The *volantas* were elabo-rately designed with leather hoods and brass buckles, and the insides were decorated by imported fabrics and even small Persian rugs (fig. 1.6). Such outings in carriages were of great social value among upper-class women (Barclay 1993, 179).

Although these carriage outings lasted just two hours, it was often the only time that aristocratic women could get out of the house. As "their only means of escape," it contributed to a distinctly gendered, spatially defined, and class-specific use of space in nineteenth-century Havana.

Tacón's chief contribution to altering the urban shape of Havana was yet to come. The western suburbs during his reign were little more than a few scat-tered houses outside the city walls. He built a wide boulevard running directly west of the walled city, naming the main section Carlos III. This broad exten-sion (fig. 1.7) was the continuation of Paseo de la Reina, which was later re-named Avenida de Bolívar. This new monumental avenue commissioned by Tacón took on his name (Paseo de Tacón), which later became Carlos III and ultimately Salvador Allende under the Castro government. Carlos III ran to Príncipe Castle and passed the beautiful grounds of the Spanish governor's summer residence, called La Quinta de los Molinos. Even today, remnants of the city's first aqueduct—the Zanja Real of 1592—trickle through the botan-ical gardens on those grounds where stone mills (*molinos*) used to grind to-bacco leaves into *rapé*.

Tacón set out to clean up much of the riffraff—thieves, assassins, and va-grants—and generally ruled with an iron hand. Clamping down on gambling led him to raid illegal gaming houses, especially in the small town in the south-eastern corner of the bay, Regla. The backwater village had become notorious for cockfighting, smugglers, and illicit gambling (Barclay 1993, 172). He cen-sored many of the presses permitted by his predecessors and did his utmost to exclude Creoles from sources of power. The colonial governor understood all too well the value of maintaining a slave-driven sugar economy and would

**THE VOLANTE.**

FIGURE 1.6. Typical elite carriage (*volanta*) in Habana Vieja, early nineteenth century (Courtesy of Library of Congress)

not tolerate any of the revolutionary fervor spreading throughout Spanish America.[2]

A favorable sugar market financed public works and city beautification programs during Tacón's administration. When he took office in the 1830s, sugar was selling for 8 *reales* per arroba; five years later it had risen to 11.25. In 1832 a steam-powered barge with four huge nets reaching a depth of 9 meters was used to clean debris in Havana Bay. In 1830, just five years after the invention of the steam locomotive, formal proposals were launched in one of

2. Yet despite his seeming penchant for law and order, Tacón was not above barter and negotiation. A well-known tale of his administration includes the establishment of a fish market by Francisco Marty, by all accounts a crafty merchant. In exchange for showing Tacón how contraband was run through the island, Marty won exclusive rights to build and operate the fish market. Similar "deals" were struck with other entrepreneurs.

FIGURE 1.7. A view of the boulevard Alameda de Isabel II. The Tacón Theater is to the left and the Paseo del Prado is in the background. This series of broad monumental roads, beginning with the Paseo de Tacón, was designed by Ramón de la Sagra.

the island's colonial government branches to finance a railroad project. Tacón would mediate between aristocratic Creole factions who wanted English capital and technology to finance the project and Tacón's council of advisers, who were pressured by the sugar aristocracy (Moreno Fraginals 1976). It is now clear that Tacón's short administration in the 1830s was part of a larger set of historic "firsts" in Havana in the nineteenth century that gave the city a special place in Cuba, the Caribbean, and Latin America (table 1.3).

If Havana owed her fortune in the nineteenth century to her port and relative geographic location, then surely the second most essential factor was the railroad. Its construction permitted the expanse of sugarcane planting without fear of losing precious sugar content while cut cane lay waiting for horse-cart transport to sugar mills. The railroad compressed both time and space and in so doing contributed to the wealth of the capital city. Appropriately, then, train stations mirrored the forms common in the United States and England, where train technology had originated. The Villanueva Station in Havana had a striking symmetrical appearance. Two curved beams were sup-

TABLE 1.3. Historic Nineteenth-Century "Firsts" in Havana

| YEAR(S) | HISTORIC "FIRST" |
|---|---|
| 1794 | Use of first steam engine |
| 1818 | McAdam road-paving system employed |
| 1819 | First regular steam-engine route in Latin America established between Havana and Matanzas |
| 1834–38 | Urban planning reforms under Governor Miguel Tacón |
| 1837 | Rail service between Havana and Bejucal, 35 kilometers south of Havana. Cuba becomes sixth country—even before Spain—to establish railroad |
| 1837 | Ferry service in Havana Bay between Habana Vieja and Regla |
| 1848 | Gas-fired public lighting system employed |
| 1849–50 | Italian Antonio Meucci invents the telephone (he called it the "talking telegraph," or *telégrafo parlante*) in Havana. He later works with Alexander Graham Bell. U.S. Supreme Court recognizes Meucci as inventor after his death. |
| 1851–55 | Telegraph service established |
| 1862 | Animal-drawn tram car service begun |
| 1874–93 | Albear Aqueduct |
| 1881 | Telephone service developed in Havana |
| 1890 | Electric public-street lighting |
| 1897 | Cinema arrives. First short feature film shot in Havana, 1898–1902 |
| 1898–1902 | First automobiles arrive. Malecón expansion begins |
| 1901 | Electric street-car system inaugurated |

*Source*: GDIC 1990.

ported by six Doric columns. Though the railroad was of English construction, the planners, stockbrokers, engineers, and superintendents were American (James 1959).

With growing coffers under his control and a prosperous economy before him, Governor Miguel Tacón turned his gaze toward the city of Havana. For nearly three hundred years Havana had been designed, planned, built, and lived in strictly from the perspectives of military strategists and powerful religious orders. Tacón admired the works of Pierre L'Enfant and used them as a model for his Havana. However, whereas L'Enfant used the topography of Washington, D.C., to locate key monuments on prominent hills that served as pedestals for his monuments (e.g., the Capitol building on Jenkins Hill and the White House at a right angle from there), Tacón failed to consider the role of local topography in Havana. Indeed, his idea for Havana was merely to adopt the axes that L'Enfant had used to connect Washington. In doing so, Tacón has been criticized for "breaking out of the urban scale" and "perpetuating not only isolated Havana architectural works, but also [for] being a redesigner of urbanism" (Chateloin 1989, 92; our translation). Unlike L'Enfant, who used open spaces as "state squares" throughout Washington, D.C., Tacón used them as places to display military prowess.

Some of Tacón's projects were ostentatious and symbolic. Among these was a magnificent theater house with a beautiful exterior framed by Doric columns that carried both his name and a thousand-light chandelier. There was also a notable increase in shantytowns on the city's outskirts that held the indigent, thieves, assassins, army deserters, freed slaves, and beggars. Many urban improvements had mixed results politically and pragmatically. On the one hand, numerous streets were widened or resurfaced. Obispo and O'Reilly Streets were paved from the port to Monserrate. On the other hand, some of the improvements were ineffective. The thoroughfare just outside the wall to the west of the city—now Monserrate-Egido Avenues—could accommodate only about 10 percent of the nearly twenty-seven hundred carriages in the city in the late 1820s (Chateloin 1989, 95).

Tacón's grandest project advanced the Parisian example of straight and wide boulevards like those built under Napoleon III and his prefect, Baron Haussmann. It entailed the widening and extension of Carlos III westward. The project was resented by the Creoles of Cuba, more for its symbolism than its practicality. It marked an authoritarian stamp of colonial power across the Havana landscape, and its maximum utility would not fully be realized as a transportation artery until decades later. Tacón's other accomplishments included a slaughterhouse, public lighting, fire squad, siren system, sinkhole filling, and street sign campaign, among many others (table 1.4).

## Sugar and Tobacco: Nineteenth-Century Havana

When the walls came down in the 1860s, Havana had already broken out of the confines of the walled city, although most of the commerce clustered around the old plazas. Some commercial activity was evident outside the walled city, as were residential areas, warehousing, and some retail shops. The

TABLE 1.4. Public Works Projects in Havana, Commissioned by Miguel Tacón, Governor of Cuba, 1834–1838

| YEAR(S) | PROJECT | LOCATION | PRESENT STATUS |
|---|---|---|---|
| 1834–35 | Santo Cristo market | Inside wall; on Teniente Rey Street | No longer exists |
| | Tacón market | Outside wall, on Plaza de Vapor, between Aguila, Dragones, San Luis Gonzaga and Galiano | No longer exists; a park stands there today |
| | Fish market | Walled city on Desembocadura del Puerto, near the cathedral | No longer exists; land occupied by other works on Avenida del Puerto |
| 1835 | Road paving, street signs, sewer lines, sinkhole filling | Inside and outside walled city | Some street signs still visible |
| | Repairs to San Juan de Díos Hospital | Walled city, on block flanked by Aguilar, Habana, Empedrado, and San Juan de Díos | No longer exists |
| | Remodeling governor's house | Walled city, facing Plaza de Armas | Museum of the City today |
| 1836 | Campo de Marte | Outside walls near Paseo Extramural | Part of Fraternity Park near Capitolio |
| | Tacón jail | Outside walls, at end of Paso Extramural (Prado, today) | Demolished in 1939, though chapel remains |
| 1836–37 | Enhancing Galiano Bridge | Outside walls | Does not exist |
| | Tacón's rest home and gardens | Outside walls | Known today as Quinta de los Molinos and Botanical Gardens on Salvador Allende Street |
| | Neptune Fountain and dock repairs | Walled city | Fountain moved to Vedado, in Gonzálo de Quesada Park, but was recently removed |
| | Widening of Paseo Extramural | Outside walls; in 1840 renamed Isabel II | Officially "Paseo José Martí" but popularly called "El Prado" |
| | Paseo de Tacón | Outside walls | Called Carlos III later |
| | San Luis Gonzaga Street | Outside walls | Known later as Reina |

TABLE 1.4. (continued)

| YEAR(S) | PROJECT | LOCATION | PRESENT STATUS |
|---------|---------|----------|----------------|
| 1837–38 | Carabineros' jail | Walled city | No longer exists |
| | Monserrate Gate | Entrance through wall | Walls torn down |
| | Tacón Theater | Outside wall | On corner of Prado and San Rafael, next to Hotel Inglaterra |

*Source*: Greatly modified after Chateloin 1989, 209–12.

economic hub of Havana, though, was concentrated along the streets of Ricla (now Muralla), Teniente Rey, San Ignacio, Obispo, and O'Reilly. This retail activity grew thanks to the sugar trade, which had made the port of Havana, already a major harbor, one of the most important in the world. Muralla Street served as a major warehousing center, displaying silks, china, silverware, and other goods. Only the street of Jesús del Monte had any significant retail trade beyond the colonial core (Aruca 1985).

Nineteenth-century Havana was greeted with relative prosperity and even splendor. By 1790, Havana and its suburbs held about 44,000 residents on an island of 273,000 (Roberts 1953, 61). That same year marked the printing of the first newspaper in the colony, *Papel Periódico de la Habana*. Sugar destined for the United States filled city coffers with unprecedented tax revenues, some of which went to public works projects. In 1845, for instance, El Morro Castle received its present-day beacon, which is perhaps the most widely recognized symbol of the city. For many years it bore the name "O'Donnell 1845" in honor of the Spanish governor, Leopoldo O'Donnell. Prosperity from sugar also led to urban sprawl, and in 1862 the inevitable happened: the city government authorized the piecemeal destruction of the colonial walls, which had outlived their utility. In their place would come new buildings, streets, and city blocks, creating the Murallas neighborhood, with monumental palaces and tobacco factories (Venegas 1996).

Moreno Fraginals (1976, 172–73) offers one interpretation of Cuba's nineteenth-century economic history that situates Havana's growth in national and international frameworks. He dismisses the notion that Cuba was exclusively a monocultural and dependent sugarcane producer for the external market. Instead, he contends that between 1815 and 1842 Cuba distributed its exports among the United States, Spain, England, Germany, France, Russia, and the Low Countries, as well as smaller markets. Cuba's economy grew by

4.0 percent per year between 1815 and 1842, while the value of sugar exports rose by only 2.6 percent. This meant a relative increase in the island's overall economic performance and suggests that Cuba was not the monocultural sugarcane exporter as many have claimed.

Cuba alone could not exercise decisive political pressure to produce economic advantages for itself. In the latter half of the nineteenth century, however, it increased its sugar exports to the United States. The United States also increased its imports of processed honey, rum, coffee, leaf and processed tobacco, copper, wax, and precious woods. The core of Cuba's export economy, though, was composed of sugar, honey, and rum, and these passed mainly through the port of Havana. Not only was the island the leading exporter of sugar and coffee during this period, but it also led the world in copper exports. The three key agricultural export goods—sugar, honey, and rum— originated on slave-worked plantations.

Underlying Moreno Fraginals's theorization of the sugar-driven stages of economic development during the nineteenth century is the concept that slavery was incompatible with mechanization. The traditional sugar mill complex (*ingenio*), representing early sugar-processing techniques and traditional technology, was greatly challenged in the late nineteenth century and early twentieth by the new *centrales* (modern steam-fired mills), most of which were built by U.S. investors. Bergad (1989) disagrees with the basic tenet of Moreno Fraginals, arguing instead that economic dependence and monoculture were controlled mainly by Cubans. In his study of sugar production in Matanzas Province (sharing its western border with Havana Province), Bergad (1989, 336, 338) concludes, "There were no foreign villains here, ransacking the local economy and repatriating profits to their countries of origin. . . . Dependence was created by Cubans responding to their own carefully defined class interests."

The introduction of new technology aided Cuba's insertion in the world economy as a producer of tropical agricultural products. In 1837, a rail line connected Havana and the town of Bejucal, just south of the city. Cuba thus became the first Spanish-speaking nation in the world to introduce the railroad. Modest improvements in technology facilitated Cuba's trade with the rest of the world. Sugar plantings spread throughout Havana's hinterland in the early 1800s. Rail connections spread beyond the first Havana-Bejucal line and enabled Cuban planters to settle in provinces adjacent to Havana (Le Riverend 1960). The first generation of Havana sugar growers entered Matanzas in the early nineteenth century because "the exhaustion of soil and forest reserves in Havana province led them to seek new territory for sugar production" (Chomsky 1994, 226).

The Ten Years' War (1868–78) between the Cuban colony and Spain interrupted the importation of legal (contract labor with Haitians and Jamaicans) and illegal (African slaves) workers in the sugar economy, which remained essentially labor-intensive. Abolition in 1878 threatened traditional sugarcane production in Cuba, as did competition from European beet sugar. Many old planters gave up or sold their *ingenios* and sought new investment opportunities in Havana and Santiago de Cuba (Moreno Fraginals 1964). Just as this new economic restructuring was unfolding, the War of Independence in 1895–98 shattered it. U.S. investors would move in and build large *centrales*, shape the Cuban economy well into the next century (Chomsky 1994, 227), and solidify Havana's role as the island's service center and gateway to the world economy.

As with most Latin American cities, the planning and zoning of colonial Havana were satisfactory until the mid-nineteenth century (Hardoy 1992, 21) but proved to be too restrictive to accommodate rapid urbanization. The building codes laid out in the Ordenanzas de la Construcción de 1862 (Building Codes of 1861) gave the colonial city a unique look (discussed in Chapter 4). This meant carefully monitoring even the smallest design of new buildings and road networks. As a major building code and planning mandate, the Ordenanzas were quite progressive for their day and left an indelible mark on Havana. Roads were classified in a hierarchy, and a neoclassical style was imposed on the porticoes, which contrasted with the commanding baroque style of the walled city. First-order roads were called *calzadas*, whose width could not be less than 25 meters (90 feet). *Calzadas* Zapata, Puentes Grandes, Güines, Cristina, Monte, Cerro, Galiano, Belascoaín, Jesús del Monte (later called Diez de Octubre), and Infanta still exist today, adding *calzada* to the roadway nomenclature of *calle* (street) and *avenida* (avenue), which form part of contemporary Havana's road names. These *calzadas* were typically lined on both sides with *portales* (fig. 1.8), which gave access to stores at the ground level, with dwellings above. Such a pattern was important in shaping the look of the city beyond the old walled city (the *extramuros*), but in the historic core, *portales* were confined to the buildings surrounding the main plazas. Secondary roads, deemed the *ordenanzas*, would also have porticoes at the expense of land lots if necessary. Sidewalks and promenades outside the walled city were wider and longer and recommended for a pedestrian's protection from the tropical sun (Segre and Baroni 1998).

FIGURE 1.8. Calzada de Vives (Avenida de España) in Jesús María neighborhood, southwest of Habana Vieja, ca. 1954. Covered sidewalks (*portales*) straddle both sides of Havana's *calzadas*. *Portales*, dating from the nineteenth century, are a feature of the contemporary city.

The colonnaded portico is Havana's trademark. By the late 1880s, Vedado designed its building fronts with deep setbacks and the rhythmically positioned colonnades (Livingston 1996). So pronounced was the construction of these porticos in neighborhoods such as San Lorenzo, Cerro, Diez de Octubre, and Centro Habana that the entire city has been referred to as the "City of Columns" (Carpentier 1982). Not all primary and secondary roads, however, were shaded by porticoes. When used, however, they joined visual elements above the sidewalks and symbolized the economic power and social position of Spanish and Creole merchants in the city. Colonnaded porticoes also adorned luxurious palaces, as well as theaters, hotels, and tobacco factories. The Independence Wars interrupted the city's development and brought decay during the last decade of nineteenth century. It was not until the American presence in 1898 that this decline was arrested (Alvarez Tabío 2000).

## Population Density and Land Area, 1519–1958

Havana's growth over four and a half centuries of urbanization is closely tied to the availability of land through annexation or new settlements. If we assume that population density averages are inversely linked to the quality of life, we can then infer about general patterns related to the quality of urban life over time. Two distinct patterns can be gleaned from the six historical periods shown in figure 1.9. First, as discussed in the next chapter, the end of Cuba's Independence Wars increased the available land in metropolitan Havana appreciably. Between 1899 and 1924, Havana's land area—through annexation and the opening up of new lands to the west and south—increased nearly fourfold, from 800 to 3,000 hectares. By 1958, the land area nearly doubled, reaching 5,000 hectares.

A second discernible pattern shows widely ranging population density, defined here as the number of persons per hectare. Curiously, the peak periods of high-density settlement emerged in the seventeenth (1601–1750) and nineteenth (1831–99) centuries, when persons per hectare reached 330 and 312, respectively. These data complement the narrative descriptions of the very crowded conditions (for animals and people) discussed previously. With the tearing down of the colonial walls in the 1860s, the expanse of new suburban additions, and the relocation of the city center to Centro Habana, the population density fell by 35 percent, from 312 persons per hectare (1831–99) to 200 (1900–1924).

Between 1924 and 1958 the population density increased to 280 persons per hectare, yet it was still below both the seventeenth- and nineteenth-century peak periods. The overall pattern points to a low population density over time, with a slow, low-density suburbanization at the urban edge replacing massive densification in the city center. The low-density amenity of contemporary Havana has prevailed in the 1990s and has given the city a quality of life uncommon in other Latin American world cities, including Mexico City, São Paulo, Rio de Janeiro, and Buenos Aires.

## A Glimpse into the Twentieth Century

With the end of Spanish colonial rule in 1898, the old city fell into severe decay. U.S. authorities embarked on several projects during their occupation of the island between 1898 and 1902. Perhaps the most influential in the plan-

FIGURE 1.9. Havana's land area and population density, 1519–1958

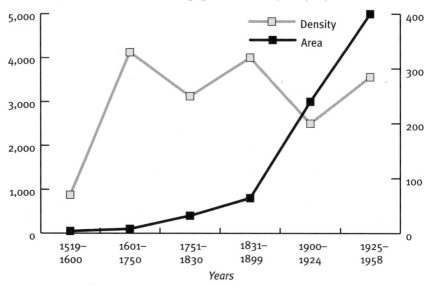

ning and design fields was extending the Malecón—the waterfront boulevard now passing through Vedado and linking Habana Vieja with Miramar—from the northern edge of the old city (González 1993). This eased the establishment of summer homes for the elite in points west of San Lázaro neighborhood and allowed automobiles easier access into the sparsely settled bedroom communities of Vedado and Miramar. If the suburbanization of the city to the west and the south marked the gradual decay of the old city, this turn-of-the-century construction continued the linear network of porticoes, so characteristic of nineteenth-century Havana.

Independence from Spain in 1898 replaced a second-class world power (Spain) with a first-class power (the United States). The island was lightly populated, with only 1.5 million inhabitants in 1900, about the size of Havana in 1970. One-fifth of the nation's sugar production was concentrated in nineteen sugar mills owned by U.S. businesses, in which some thirteen thousand tenant farmers labored. The long period between harvest and planting, on the one hand, and the lengthy growing season, on the other, left thousands of seasonal rural workers unemployed throughout most of the year. Urban migration—especially to Havana—would spring from this idle labor and create slums and shanties around the city edge. The urban poor also sought housing in the more dilapidated structures of the old walled city. In classic fashion, the low-income "invasion" of the colonial core produced a "succession" of migrant groups who would occupy the housing stock of the generation before them (Park, Burgess, and McKenzie 1925).

On the eve of the twentieth century, Havana was, as at so many times in its past, a paradox (Le Riverend 1992). Pockets of great wealth contrasted with abject penury and environmental ruin. General Leonard Wood of the U.S. occupation forces remarked that Cuba was the "new California . . . a brand new country" and set out to open up investment there (Pérez 1988, 121). At the same time, though, Havana had all the decadence that the revolution would find half a century later: more than two hundred brothels were registered in Havana, most in the old city and in the industrial sectors near immigrant neighborhoods.

By 1898, Spain had made few improvements in the city's infrastructure beyond the accomplishments of Governor Tacón six decades earlier. Havana Bay was especially polluted: "Between Morro Castle and its neighbor across the way, La Punta, the vessels steam into that bay, foul with four hundred years of Spanish misrule and filth, where three hundred years of the slave trade centered, and into which the sewers of a great city poured their filth" (White 1898, 134). Raw sewage pouring into the harbor was not diluted and became most unpleasant during the summer months, producing a "festering mass . . . fronting the whole sea wall and throwing a stench into the air which [had to] be breathed by everyone on shipboard" (White 1898, 134–35). If it was this bad for the tourists, then the residents of Regla and Habana Vieja and those downwind from the trade winds were constantly exposed to the bay's wrath.

The twentieth century would not significantly modify the look of the city or the Afro-Spanish imprint of its population. Chapter 3 argues that the city's most significant buildings both qualitatively and quantitatively were constructed in the twentieth century, but for the most part they would blend into the city's beige, low-lying skyline. The early decades of the twentieth century would also vary the ethnic composition of Havana as the city accepted refugees and migrants fleeing war-torn Europe and the breaking up of colonial empires. The dissolution of the Ottoman Empire, for instance, sent thousands of *turcos* into the major Atlantic seaports of Latin America. Havana was no exception, and it accepted thousands of Jews, Greek Orthodox, and Arabs.

Cuba had been one of the friendliest and most welcoming host countries for Jews in the Americas (Levine 1993, 7). Perhaps because Cuba had a small indigenous population, foreigners had always been prominent on the island.

In 1900 fewer than 1,000 non-Spanish Europeans lived in Cuba, but by 1917 there were 5,619 (Levine 1993, 2). Jews were authorized to enter Cuba in large numbers for the first time in 1881, but they could not practice their faith openly until after the Spanish-American War. Moreover, some American Jews who fought in the war remained in Cuba as part of an expatriate community. They founded the first synagogue in 1906, the United Hebrew Congregation. Some Jewish peddlers — Askhenazic and Sephardic — acquired enough capital to set up shops along Sol, Muralla, Bernaza, and Teniente Rey Streets. Both eastern European and Sephardic Jews ghettoized themselves in these Habana Vieja neighborhoods at least until the Second World War, and they rarely interacted, except at the Jewish market (Levine 1993, 293–94). Muralla and Sol Streets housed many Jewish retail activities during much of the twentieth century.

By 1900, Habana Vieja had developed a special residential flavor that went beyond the traditional breakdown of Spaniard, white Creole, mulatto, and black. Historically, Andalucians, Castilians, and Extremeños were the regional Spanish groups that predominated during the founding of Cuba. After the first century of conquest, they became a minor migration stream to Cuba. Instead, Galicians (*gallegos*), Asturians (*asturianos*), Basques (*vascos*), and Canary Islanders (*isleños*) prevailed, especially in the eighteenth and nineteenth centuries (Moreno Fraginals 1995). Popularly, Cubans referred to all Spanish immigrant groups as *gallegos*. Even though Europeans north of the Pyrenees who migrated to the island were not numerous, Cubans referred to central Europeans and Jews as *polacos*; all Turks, Lebanese, and Syrians were called *turcos*; and all Asians were referred to as *chinos*. Americans were simply called *americanos*; *gringo* was not commonly used in Cuba (Johnson 1920).

The Havana of 1900 contained three distinct parts: "Old" Havana (the old quarters behind the walls), "New" Havana (parts of Centro Habana, Vedado, and Cerro), and "Suburban" Havana (new developments in points west and south). Old Havana consisted of tightly packed structures of adobe, mortar, rubble, stone, and plaster construction. Streets remain narrow there as a carry-over from the days of needing to defend against attackers and to keep the streets cool by stretching awnings above them (fig. 1.10). Old Havana may not have looked much like Andaluz in Spain, but it was clearly the daughter of Seville, Málaga, Cádiz, and Córdoba. The effect was enhanced by the yellowish umber and related pastel shades adorning its walls.

The demarcation of an "Old" from a "New" Havana depended on both form and function. Older quarters held less desirable attributes: low lying,

FIGURE 1.10. Obispo Street with awnings (*toldos*), ca. 1906
(Courtesy of Library of Congress)

prone to flooding, close to industrial zones, and overwhelmed by the stench
of the bay. These less desirable neighborhoods include parts of Regla, Habana
Vieja, Cerro, and Atarés. If social class distinctions characterize the demarcation of the old from the new, so does the location of economic activity. The
amount and location of commercial establishments before and after 1900
changed significantly (Llanes 1988). Around 1880, nearly two of three commercial establishments were located in the area that had previously been
walled. Forty years later, nearly that same percentage of commercial establishments (70 percent) had shifted to areas beyond the walls (Aruca 1985, 26).

During the first decades of the twentieth century, Havana expanded more
rapidly than at any other time in its history (Santovenia and Shelton 1964)
(fig. 1.11). Outside the old town lay "New" Havana, with regularly laid out
and wider streets than its colonial predecessor. Designed for the automobile
though still retaining the Mediterranean Spanish style of light-colored buildings (mostly khaki), New Havana (or Centro Habana) spreads westward
(fig. 1.12). It begins along the Prado, where fine mansions from the turn of

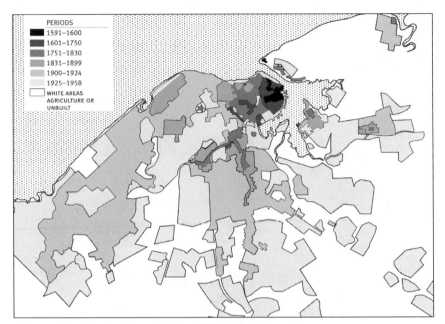

FIGURE 1.11. Territorial expansion of Havana, 1519–1958

FIGURE 1.12. Looking westward across Centro Habana (foreground) with its uniform late-nineteenth- and early-twentieth-century construction and design (Photograph by Roberto Segre)

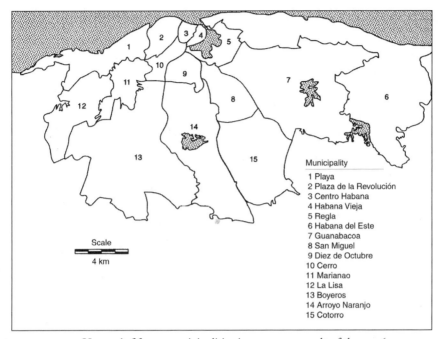

Municipality

1 Playa
2 Plaza de la Revolución
3 Centro Habana
4 Habana Vieja
5 Regla
6 Habana del Este
7 Guanabacoa
8 San Miguel
9 Diez de Octubre
10 Cerro
11 Marianao
12 La Lisa
13 Boyeros
14 Arroyo Naranjo
15 Cotorro

FIGURE 1.13. Havana's fifteen municipalities in 2001 as a result of the 1976 jurisdictional reorganization

the century remain. When the city crept into this part a hundred years ago, it left behind the colonial administrative buildings and churches. In their place were built modest middle-income housing, schools, retailing, and convent hospitals. New Havana moves along the Malecón up to the Vedado district. Its western boundary ends with the University of Havana on Aróstegui Hill. Built between 1908 and 1932, the university is flanked by the Quinta de los Molinos. Príncipe Castle and Atarés Castle, respectively, mark the western edge of New Havana and denote the historical limit of the city's archaic defense system.

Suburban Havana would become more American than Spanish, leaving behind an Old World architectural style (see Chapter 3). The wealthy and the middle class would stake out neighborhoods in the west and the south, respectively. Miramar in the west would house the twentieth-century elite, while the middle-income groups staked out Víbora, Luyanó, and Santos Suárez as their claim (fig. 1.13). As Chapters 2 and 3 show, these areas were designed to accommodate automobile travel for the city's middle- and upper-income groups, who commuted from Miramar, Country Club, and Nuevo Vedado prior to the revolution. The city's new suburban landscape would hold a few modern buildings that stand out like high-rise curios, but the overall effect of Havana's charm softens these iron and glass intrusions.

Twentieth-century Havana would acquiesce to U.S. economic powers. Nevertheless, not all its planners and designers would hail from the north. The influence of beaux artes came with J. C. N. Forestier, and the modern movement (1920s and 1930s) arrived in Cuba through Le Corbusier and the Congrés International de Architecture Moderne (CIAM) (Duverger 1994). Currents of avant-garde surfaced among scores of Cuban architects and planners. Not all twentieth-century city governments were corrupt, but the prerevolutionary city would dote on ceremonial projects at the expense of essential sites and services (Chapters 4, 5, 6, and 8). The United States would invest heavily in areas formerly coveted by the Spanish, and it would often meddle behind the scenes in political dealings. Both its economic prowess and political shenanigans would keep the Cuban people from attaining the sovereignty they had sought during the long wars of independence in the nineteenth century. The twentieth century would also be a time of preservation—a time of accommodating urban growth with the built environments of the past—not always by design, and more often by default.

# The First Half Century
## The Rise of an Antillean Metropolis

> Havana is a city of unfinished works, of the feeble, the asymmetri-
> cal, and the abandoned. Since the time we were kids, we've been
> coming across tenement houses daily where cans are piling up and
> the garbage is becoming increasingly worldly and more diverse.
> —Alejo Carpentier, 1939

## Postwar Modernity in the Colonial City

The U.S. Army snatched victory from the Cuban patriots in 1898. American forces found a dispersed city made up of a central core (Habana Vieja) surrounded by small suburban and rural settlements. Havana was depressed and lackluster, vastly different from its heyday of the sugar booms before the colonial wars. As the century drew to a close, Havana was being pulled in two opposing directions. One was shaped by social and economic powers that wanted to make Havana a modern city. The other was an attempt to slow the quest for political power that accompanies economic might. Spain had long been preoccupied with a useless and fratricidal Cuban war. It sought to preserve its last colony in the Americas, "the Pearl of the Caribbean," or at least cling to an antiquated vision of what the Spaniards thought that might be.

Cuba's Independence Wars (1868–78, 1879–80, 1895–98) had paralyzed virtually all building construction and destroyed an economy that had flourished since the end of the eighteenth century (Moreno Fraginals 1995). Unlike other independence wars in the Americas, Cuban patriots were vastly outnumbered by Spanish troops. The "enemy" had been equipped with the most modern means of communications, transportation, and weapons. Adding paramilitary troops—Spanish volunteers and Cuban guerrillas—to the regular forces, Spain unleashed some 600,000 soldiers against the Cuban troops (*mambises*) on an island with 1.5 million inhabitants. By comparison, Spain sent fewer than 100,000 soldiers and militiamen against the fourteen Spanish colonies during the first part of the nineteenth century, and General Simón Bolívar warred with only 25,000 Spaniards. The former thirteen colonies of the United States, moreover, fought against just 50,000 British soldiers (Anon. 1935).

These wars devastated Havana in several ways. Wealthy Creole landowners and Spanish merchants had tried to launch new construction on a monumental scale beyond the old walled city along Monserrate Street in the last half of the nineteenth century (Venegas 1990). Such projects included palatial residences, theaters, and huge cigar factories that rivaled contemporary models found in mainland Latin America: Mexico, São Paulo, and Buenos Aires. A few isolated new buildings, however, could not undo the precarious living conditions of the city's almost one-quarter of a million residents, most of whom were crowded within 10 square kilometers (Duverger 1993b). Squalor, unhealthy living conditions, and deficient roads and infrastructure characterized the setting of the masses (Le Riverend 1992).

Urban poverty was exacerbated by the settlement efforts of the Spanish Liberating Army. Under the charge of Captain General Valeriano Weyler, the Spanish tried to force the rebelling rural population into designated towns and cities (a process that was known as *reconcentración*) where they could be more easily contained. Nearly one hundred thousand people were resettled in Havana, where they lived in improvised shelters called *yaguas*. Clustered at the city edge, these shantytowns were ravaged by epidemics of typhus, dysentery, cholera, and German measles (Poumier 1975). Rural uprooting and forced urban migration quite possibly marked the beginning of contemporary urban marginality in Latin America (Alvarez Estévez 1988).

The first measures taken by the U.S. administration in Cuba between 1898 and 1902 were to establish basic infrastructure to ensure the growth of a modern city. The United States introduced at least five major public works projects. First, it completed a network of water mains throughout the city. Second, it expanded the networks of electric streetlights, telephones, and natural gas. Third, comprehensive systems of sewage and garbage collection were established. Fourth, extended street paving ended many pitted dirt roads and would later satisfy the demands of a small number of automobile owners. Fifth, the electric streetcar replaced the horse-drawn tram running through the new neighborhood of Vedado and was gradually extended through the inner city and some suburbs (Bens Arrarte 1956). At the same time, there were advances in building materials. Tile, cement, and architectural adornment factories were developed to accommodate the building frenzy during the early years of the republic (De las Cuevas 1993). Havana, introverted and drawn toward the bay and terra firma, increased its potential to develop more of the oceanfront through the extension of the Malecón. Curiously, though the seaside promenade has come to symbolize Havana, it was introduced fairly recently in the city's history.

Following the war, U.S. business interests moved quickly to monopolize urban services. Cubans and Spaniards set aside the rancor of the bloody Independence Wars and delved into real estate development and land speculation. More than half a million immigrants arrived in Cuba during the first three decades of the twentieth century. Real estate markets absorbed the growing numbers of new immigrants and their businesses. Almost one out of three (29.6 percent) of the 660,958 immigrants—mostly from Spain—settled in Havana. As a result, the city doubled in size by 1925, with a population of just over half a million (Roig de Leuchsenring 1952). Its land base increased to 116 square kilometers in 1923 from 95 square kilometers only four years earlier (Le Riverend 1992, 243). In the face of changing times, the confining colonial shell of the city was left behind.

## Havana Expands Its Borders

The 1898 map of Havana (Martín Zequeira and Rodríguez Fernández 1993, 1998) shows the compact yet successive rings of expansion by the nineteenth-century city. At the century's end, Havana's western edge reached Calzada de Infanta Street. New growth stretched between the bay to the east and the ocean shoreline to the north, forming a semiregular grid plan of city blocks and streets. The traditional main arteries of the city—the *calzadas*—connected Havana to a broad hinterland to the south where new neighborhoods developed (Zardoya 1999). The districts of Cerro, Jesús del Monte, and Puentes Grandes were more loosely defined and dispersed than the confining colonial core. It was only a matter of time before outlying villages and towns would be drawn into Havana's metropolis: Guanabacoa, Regla, and Casablanca to the east, Santiago de las Vegas y San Francisco de Paula in the south, and Marianao to the west.

Urbanization to the east of the colonial core of Havana had long been impeded by Havana Bay. Several proposals were put forth to link the eastern areas of Havana, including one to build a massive iron bridge across the bay (Valladares y Morales 1947). That plan was discarded in 1914, and road networks fanned out elsewhere, especially to the west and southeast. Their courses were determined by the preexisting transportation lines—the railroad and electric streetcar paths—and the location of social groups, which were becoming increasingly segregated and stratified. Residential segregation was particularly acute along the sea-breeze-filled oceanfront districts of Vedado, Miramar, and Country Club. The wealthiest *habaneros* resided in these districts, while the surrounding hills served as territory to the small bourgeoisie and a nascent proletariat.

Although Havana's building codes and regulations were unevenly enforced, they helped to preserve a homogeneous style of new construction during the first decades of the twentieth century. As noted in Chapter 1, the Building Codes of 1861 dictated the use of columnar *portales* in both central and residential areas (Segre and Baroni 1998). This ensured uniformity of construction well into the present century. Many master plans for the city were put forth, including those by Raúl Otero (1905), Camilo García de Castro (1916), Walfrido de Fuentes (1916), and Pedro Martínez Inclán (1919) (Préstamo 1995). However, these plans were rendered defenseless against crude land speculation by landowners who held on to large tracts of land or sold them off in piecemeal fashion. Wealthy Cubans and Spaniards controlled the housing market through the sale of spacious suburban estates that later would be converted to compact *repartos* (subdivisions).

Not all landowners at the city's edge sold out immediately: Dionisio Velasco y Sarrá, owner of several kilometers of eastern shoreline property, waited until the 1950s to build new "bedroom communities" ("Análisis del mercado de la vivienda" 1955; see Chapter 3). A good number of landowners, though, made a name for themselves through large-scale suburban expansion. These included the entrepreneur Zaldo y Salmón, who promoted Ensanche de la Habana (the Almendares district, in 1914); José Manuel Cortina initiated recreational facilities at Playa de Marianao (Marianao Beach) in 1916; Antonio González de Mendoza and Pedro Pablo Kohly established Alturas de Almendares (Almendares Heights) in Marianao; and Enrique Conill reserved a strategic tract of land in the southwest that covered the area from Príncipe Castle at the edge of Vedado to the mechanic shops of Ciénaga. Conill's holdings enabled him to get an edge on the ambitious residential project at Loma de los Catalanes, where the Plaza de la Revolución is currently located.

## Housing Styles and Social Diversity

Havana is one of the most architecturally diverse cities in Latin America. Its variations range from the housing stock of the wealthy to the many functions of its central districts. The first decades of the twentieth century witnessed distinct settlement patterns that would shape the evolution of Havana's neighborhoods. The upper bourgeoisie of Spanish origin would gradually abandon the prebaroque and baroque colonial mansions in the compact core to take up residences at the summer homes of Cerro (Quintana 1974; Weiss 1996). Housing tastes and construction changed with this move to the suburbs. No longer would the elite opt for the *casa almacén* (warehouse mansion), which consisted of a sugar, tobacco, or coffee warehouse on the ground floor; a middle floor (entresol or mezzanine) held the offices or slave quarters, and the top floor was occupied by the master and his family. The layout centered on a large interior courtyard. In place of the *casa almacén* stood lighter, modern housing with its characteristic colonnade: a gallery of neoclassical columns surrounding the house (Llanes 1999; García Santana 1999; Lobo Montalvo 2000). The architectural origin of this design can be traced to the *portales* found on mansions located in town squares or facing open spaces, typified by the monumental Aldama Palace. Another new feature of the nineteenth-century home was a generous green space between the building and both the street and neighbors' houses. Architectural individuality nestled within a natural landscape marked the end of the neoclassical Spanish style of a large home occupying an entire city block.

Spanish heritage also meant an aversion to waterfront construction, leaving an abundance of shoreline properties for future residential development. Such a disdain for waterfront properties, to paraphrase Juan Pérez de la Riva (1946, 1975), stemmed from Cuba's being surrounded by "enemy waters" on all sides throughout its history. The wealthy Creoles preferred placing their mansions in the district of Cerro. However, working-class intrusion diluted the social "purity" of Cerro. Residents in clusters of working-class neighborhoods who worked in the nearby arsenal, factories, and the port also sought housing in Cerro. Another drawback of Cerro was that its undulating landscape produced an irregular pattern of streets and blocks. Many Cerro merchants and landowners who suffered economically during the wars of independence were forced to sell their lands to offset losses. Parceling lands created small lots for nonelites, thereby interrupting Havana's urban and social geography.

Two large country farms in the western edge of the city were subdivided in 1858. These farms ran along the coast from the city's edge at Calzada de Infanta to the Almendares River (Roig de Leuchsenring 1964). Engineer Luis Iboleón Bosque surveyed these two farms—El Carmelo and Vedado—which were owned by Domingo Trigo, Juan Espino, and the count of Pozos Dulces (Izquierdo and Quevedo 1972; see also fig. 1.2). Approximately four hundred city blocks composed of 100-meter sides marked the first broad and systematic layout of Havana's grid pattern. Unlike the irregular colonial pattern, the residential streets of the western suburbs were 16 meters wide. For the first time in Cuba, streets were lined by trees in *parterres* (tree-lined corridors of lawn between the curb and the sidewalk). The Cerro upper-class type of dwelling—neoclassical detached villas—was transferred to this new, better-looking neighborhood fronting the sea. The initial *reparto* (township), El Carmelo, was continued with El Vedado and then with Medina. Each reflected the same urban design. In time, they came to be known as El Vedado. Because of its size and advanced urban design, El Vedado (or simply Vedado, in English) is possibly the best piece of colonial planning in Cuba. The Independence Wars almost paralyzed construction in the last third of the nineteenth century except for a brief peace period in the 1880s. Therefore, the eclectic villa from the 1920s period dominates the architecture in El Vedado. Despite its elegant aura, El Vedado was socially mixed, with a wide spectrum of dwellings that ranged from spectacular mansions to humble tenements that were disguised behind classic facades. The mixture was under the rule of the upper class, who dictated the look and the patterns of behavior in public spaces (Coyula 1999c). Spacious tree-lined boulevards of Paseo, Línea, Calle 23, and Avenida de los Presidentes served as major thoroughfares through the new district (see figs. 1.2 and 1.3).

These new boulevards gave distinction to neighborhoods and were anchored by public squares (one of which is the site of the John Lennon sculpture dedicated in late 2000). Zoning laws mandated 5-meter building setbacks (mostly for houses) from the street, creating a buffer of green space called the *carmen*. Buildings had to meet the 4-meter-wide portal requirement on the ground floor. The new grid pattern standardized lot sizes, which in turn facilitated the orderly sale of suburban houses. Street-sign nomenclature consisting of letters and numbers reinforced this geometric pattern (Rama 1985) with its design elements borrowed from the suburban Garden City style. Perhaps coincidentally, the new grid pattern wove green spaces into the city's traditional fabric as Ildefons Cerdá had proposed for Barcelona in 1859 (Coyula

1991a; Segre and Baroni 1998). Through the rest of the nineteenth century, these lands were gradually settled, and wooden gingerbread-style bungalows dotted the landscape. By 1894, only 30 percent of these lots had houses on them (González Manet 1976). Later, roughly from the time of the republic (after 1902) until the 1930s, luxurious eclectic houses filled in the remainder of the neighborhood. Most of the residences were built by the nouveaux riches during the prosperous "fat-cow" (*vacas gordas*, or prosperous) years (1914–20) when sugar prices soared.[1]

Great wealth in Cuba prompted a surprising outpouring of architectural styles by professionals such as Leonardo Morales, Raúl Otero, Eugenio Rayneri, and Govantes y Cabarrocas (Alvarez Tabío 1989, 2000). Several contributing factors ushered in this flurry of design and construction. One was the return of Cuban capital that had been temporarily deposited in the United States for safekeeping during the wars of independence. Placed back into circulation on the island, this capital found its most profitable outlets in real estate and building construction. Another factor was that the U.S. government required repayment on its war loan that was used to pay the pensions and salaries of Cuban retired officers from the Independence Wars, many of whom built spacious houses in Vedado (Ibarra 1985, 1992). Property was subdivided and sold by cash-strapped landowners. Rises in sugar prices on the world markets during World War I also increased the circulation of hard currency on the island. These factors led to a building boom.

Once Vedado filled up and the Almendares River was bridged at Quinta Avenida and Calle 23, the private automobile entered into wide use. Suburbanization spread to Marianao, particularly the district of Miramar. New construction in this corner of Havana became more segregated. Design features in Miramar came from Cuba and abroad. City building codes were greatly relaxed. The Anglo-Saxon concept of the Garden City exerted a strong appeal at this time. The city's fabric opened up and spread out to Country Club, which resembled the winding layout of Riverside in suburban Chicago. These new places embraced the Garden City ideas of Frederick Law Olmsted and his work in Illinois that allowed the affluent to live in neatly landscaped suburban enclaves. These became the defining features of Havana's wealthy outskirts.

1. During this time powerful entrepreneurs and socialites such as the marquises de Avilés, Josefina García de Mesa, Ernesto Sarrá, Juan Gelats, José Ramón del Cueto, Catalina Lasa, Juan Pedro Baró, Condesa de Revilla-Camargo, and Pablo González de Mendoza built magnificent homes in what is today called Vedado (Martín Zequeira and Rodríguez Fernández 1992).

Unlike its sister Caribbean cities of San Juan, Puerto Rico, and Santo Domingo, Dominican Republic, Havana did not relinquish its compact nature during its period of urban growth early in the century (Segre 1994c). Newcomers to Havana did not settle in unspoiled areas. Spanish immigrants, a new urban proletariat, and the lower-middle-class workers, for example, settled in the well-established Centro Habana, the Calzada de Monte, and Jesús María neighborhoods. Houses were modest in scope, typically two-story structures called "twins" (*gemelas*). The house was set deep inside the block along a narrow gallery. It marked a stylistic transition from the colonial style to the republican home era. Long gone were the massive, unadorned walls of the colonial core with their limited entrances and exits. In their place were windows and doors framed by highly decorative classical ornamentation that combined with the vibrant facades of houses. The fronts of these buildings blended together by means of the filigree ironworks covering doors and windows. This design spread to the neighborhoods of Santos Suárez, Luyanó, and Víbora in a process that changed the look of residential structures from the compact block model of the traditional grid pattern to the freestanding cottage-style home (Llanes 1985, 1988, 1993).

The first apartment buildings appeared in the center of the city as well by 1910. Interspersed with these new styles were tenement houses, slums, and shantytowns. According to Diego Tamayo in 1904, there were 2,839 *solares* (older subdivided houses converted into tenements for the poor) that housed 86,000 people in a city of about a quarter of a million inhabitants (cited in Llanes 1978). *Solares* lacked the most elementary of conveniences and suffered greatly from overcrowding (Bay Sevilla 1924).

The government acted slowly and superficially when housing the urban poor. As the administration of President José Miguel Gómez set out to build workers' housing, it proved to be more of a publicity stunt than a real solution. For example, of the 2,000 houses planned for Pogolotti neighborhood in Marianao, only 950 units were completed in 1913 after three years of construction. Each unit was to be a semidetached house (two homes per structure) with a wooden covered porch at the front. The final construction lacked storm sewers and used flimsy materials. Not surprisingly, the housing stock deteriorated quickly, and Pogolotti soon turned into a slum, notorious for outbreaks of infectious diseases (De Armas 1975; De Armas and Robert 1975).

## Symbols and Allegories of Political and Economic Power

The new republic displayed its prowess and made its presence felt through the functions it executed. The two decades spanning the administrations of Presidents Tomás Estrada Palma (1902–6) and Mario G. Menocal (1913–21) defined the location of government offices of the young republic. Other prominent forces were vying for strategic locations to represent their constituents. These included new economic actors: banks, insurance companies, and firms in the hands of U.S., Spanish, and Cuban investors. Old peninsular elites held on to the more traditional cultural symbols of power but only temporarily. Early republican governments set up their offices at the Captain General's Palace on the Plaza de la Catedral but later abandoned the site because the quarters became cramped. Beyond the old "ring" of Habana Vieja, the administrations of the new republic diffused national icons through the construction of prominent landmarks: the fire station (Cuartel de los Bomberos, 1910), the Presidential Palace (1919), the national Capitol (Capitolio, 1929), and the high school (Instituto de Segunda Enseñanza, 1929). "Functional" buildings built by U.S. engineers included the Central Train Station (Estación Central de Ferrocarriles) in 1912 and the Customs House (Aduanas) in 1914, bringing closure to the distinctive ring of buildings around Habana Vieja that is visible today (Leff and Menocal 1996).

Early in the twentieth century, the compact layout of the narrow colonial streets and the old-fashioned and quiet interior courtyards of the Habana Vieja houses were slowly replaced by modern buildings that rose above the prevailing building heights of just a few stories (*La Habana* 1919). Within just twenty years, high-rise government office buildings, warehouses, shops, and even a stock market building called the Lonja de Comercio (1909) broke through the sleepy landscape of the historic core (Rallo and Segre 1978). The automobile was especially unkind to the city's old quarters. The atmosphere was described this way: "Traffic is bedlam . . . and overflows and crashes against the walls and smashes into doors and bludgeons the street corners. It is invasive and noisy like a fat and disgusting river spilling over its banks and sweeping everything away. . . . It feels like we are entering a savage beehive" (Mediz Bolio 1916, 42; our translation).

Since the end of the nineteenth century, the social life of the Creole elite tended to concentrate on an axis defined by where the Campo de Marte (to the west of the old city) and the Prado (originally known as Isabel II) meet and the Aldama Palace was built. The nation's main theaters (Nacional,

Payret, Irijoa, Politeama, and Alhambra) and the nation's first tourist hotels (Inglaterra, Plaza, Telégrafo, and Sevilla Biltmore) were located in this area. With the advent of the republic, the axis acquired an essential spatial dimension for socializing: Parque Central (Central Park) held the new monumental buildings tied to the competition between the state, private initiatives, and Spanish communities. In this setting emerged the Manzana de Gómez (1894–1917), the first shopping arcade of European style with offices on the upper floors. Of course, the politicians and the Spanish community could not miss out on this social setting. Along the Prado, as in Vedado, majestic mansions were built, including the homes of the U.S. consul Frank Steinhart (1908) and President José Miguel Gómez (1915) (Alvarez Tabío 1989; Rodríguez 1998).

Despite the disappearance of colonial power, the *peninsulares* (Spaniards born in Spain) held on to significant economic power until the crisis of 1920, which definitively sealed the hegemony of U.S. capital (Ibarra 1992). Havana's urban scale revealed itself at two territorial dimensions: the center and periphery. Areas adjacent to Parque Central held cultural and recreational centers of regional Spanish groups. Not to be outdone by the classic monuments of government, these Spanish ethnic groups erected the Centro de Dependientes (1907; fig. 2.1), Centro Gallego (Galician Center; 1915), Casino Español (Spanish Country Club; 1914), and the Centro Asturiano (Asturian Center; 1927). Buildings with neobaroque interior spaces of uncommon dimensions gave definition to a public life dominated by rituals handed down from the ostentatious practices of the motherland. Hospitals and medical clinics of mutual-aid societies prolonged the neoclassical repertoire of buildings with colonnades. Spaniards from different regions and provinces formed mutual-aid clinics such as Benéfica, Covadonga, Dependientes, and Purísima Concepción (Presno 1952), which took up residence on the edge of Havana on what were once neighboring farms that were let go by the local aristocracy during the Independence Wars.

If Havana's primary commercial center functioned in neighborhoods adjacent to the colonial town squares, then its second one was close by. Large tobacco factories such as La Meridiana (1880), Barces y López (1886), José Gener (1882), and Calixto López (1886) appeared on the outskirts of the original colonial ring. Tobacco factories employed thousands of manual laborers from adjacent neighborhoods just beyond the old city walls. This light industry peaked during the first decade of the twentieth century and reaffirmed its prominence by occupying such a central place. Behind the Capitolio (1929) there existed from the nineteenth century the Partagás Tobacco

FIGURE 2.1. Centro de Depedientes at Prado and Trocadero Streets, ca. 1910. Built in 1907, the large (3,871 square meters) social club contained a gym, billiard hall, and library, as well as drawing, music, and dance schools. It could accommodate 5,000 couples and was typical of the grandiose social clubs built during the early years of the republic. (Courtesy Universidad de La Habana, Departamento de Historia del Arte)

Factory, and in front of the Presidential Palace (Palacio Presidencial; 1920), just off the Prado, was La Corona (built by the American Tobacco Company in 1902) (see fig. 2.2; Venegas 1989).

Palatial residences representing Cuba's bourgeois power were located so close to these factories that it made Havana unique in Latin American urban

FIGURE 2.2.
Tobacco factories
from the nine-
teenth century
still operating
today, behind the
Capitolio building
(Photograph by
Roberto Segre)

planning and design circles (Bühler-Oppenheim 1949). However, the symbolic axis of republican power was interrupted by working-class neighborhoods in Habana Vieja and Centro Habana. By the turn of the century, it was
too late to use radical slum-eradication measures as were taken in Paris half a
century before. Those plans would have expelled the poor from these areas as
was done by Haussmann in Paris. They would have also wiped out the "gray"
spaces of the "non-existent" city and converted them, as was done in Paris, to
income-stratified neighborhoods (Aymonino 1965). It became indispensable
for wealthy *habaneros*, on the one hand, to seek refuge in the exclusive suburbs
and, on the other, to grant the poor proximity to striking landmarks in the city
center.

# The Mirror of Progress in the Caribbean's Nice: Havana, 1920–1935

The economic crisis of 1920 paralyzed building construction in . Sugar fell from 20 cents to 3 cents a pound (Le Riverend 1965). This downfall introduced the "lean cow" (*vacas flacas*) days of Cuba's economic history. While the recession forced many Spanish and Cuban firms into bankruptcy, it marked a decided upturn for U.S. businesses. From 1925 until the world stock market crash of 1929, U.S. businesses invested $1.5 billion in Cuba, equaling just over one-quarter of all investment in Latin America during that period (Acosta León and Hardoy 1971). This was the era when the great "sugar barons" emerged in the eastern provinces of the island. Foreigners controlled 78 percent of the island's arable land, and the United States consumed 50 percent of Cuban sugar (Le Riverend 1966). It was in this setting that the 1925 unveiling of the monument honoring the sunken SS *Maine* took on symbolic meaning. The SS *Maine* mysteriously exploded in Havana Bay in 1898 and helped the United States justify its "intervention" in the final days of the Cuban independence war against Spain. The dictator Gerardo Machado, closely tied to foreign economic interests, also took power in 1925.

Until Machado's overthrow in 1933, and with the enthusiastic help of the minister of public works, Carlos Miguel de Céspedes (known as the Tropical Haussmann), the Cuban government invested its own money, as well as loans drawn on U.S. banks, to modernize Havana. In doing so, Cuba's economy became even more closely tied to the United States than in the past, as did a growing number of Latin American countries at that time. Cuba's unique Latin American role, however, was consecrated with the holding of the Sixth Pan-American Conference in Havana in 1928. President Calvin Coolidge's attendance at the conference highlighted the significance the meeting held for both U.S. foreign policy and business interests. At that time Havana possessed half a million residents, covered 102 square kilometers, received 70 percent of Cuba's imported items, and welcomed 250,000 tourists per year (Soto 1977). This is why Pedro Martínez Inclán sought to make Havana the "Nice of America," even if it meant first becoming the "perverse Pompeii of the Caribbean" (Martínez Inclán 1925).

In the *années folles* of more prosperous and earlier decades, the city center offered many first-rate hotels: the Plaza (1908), Sevilla Biltmore (1908–23), Saratoga, Lincoln, Central, and Isla de Cuba, as well as the older "classic" hotels (Inglaterra, Plaza, and Pasaje). In the 1920s, though, more luxurious and sophisticated ones were being built in Vedado. These included three landmark properties: the Hotel Nacional (built by McKim, Mead, and White in 1930), located on the Malecón, which would stand as the insignia hotel of Havana; the Palace (1928); and the Presidente (1927). The latter two were situated on the gardened Avenida de los Presidentes.

Havana in the 1920s was rife with contradiction. Parts of its street plan were fragmented and disorderly. Its building stock consisted of deteriorating colonial structures and a precarious infrastructure as well as a new wealthy class (in Vedado and Miramar), a petite bourgeoisie (Víbora and Lawton), and a proletariat (Jesús María and Cayo Hueso). Solid masonry houses contrasted with light wooden structures in different neighborhoods. Few wooden structures withstood the terrible hurricane of 1926. Yet this was an image of Havana far removed from the ostentatious Caribbean capital envisioned by Céspedes and Machado (Sambricio and Segre 2000).

Some of the main problems identified by urban planners were the lack of green areas and a poor road network incapable of handling the increasing automobile traffic. At least since the late nineteenth century, an idea circulated that would make Serrano Avenue a limited-access road to link the Captain General's Palace at the Plaza de la Catedral with the periphery (Roig de Leuchsenring 1964). Walfrido de Fuentes (1916) also argued for the widening of some main streets in Habana Vieja—Cuba and Lamparilla—to relieve vehicular congestion. In the 1920s the engineer Amado Montenegro revived the idea of "the Great Havana Road" (La Gran Vía de La Habana) in expectation of the imminent population increase. Finally, Martínez Inclán, in his book *La Habana actual* (1925), envisioned a network of twenty-six avenues to resolve the city's transportation problems.

The problems of the city's center were foremost in the urban planning debates of the day. Although Martínez Inclán supported strengthening the complex of monuments around Parque Central, it became clear that government buildings needed to be relocated in the suburbs. This would provide an impetus for subsequent urbanization. Deliberating on land use and determining the location of new public buildings were internal affairs; only a small cadre of politicians and professionals debated the advantages and disadvantages of different sites and designs. The Cuban people, of course, had little say in the matter.

In 1923, a group of engineers (Raúl Otero, Camilo García de Castro, Enrique J. Montoulieu, and Martínez Inclán) concluded that properties around Loma de los Catalanes (Catalans' Hill), which belonged to Enrique Conill, would be designated for a government-buildings complex. By late 1925, the chief of parks and streets of Paris, J. C. N. Forestier, had arrived in Havana to assess the site development. His entourage included a team of French designers (Eugene E. Beaudoin, Jean Labatut, Theo Leveau, Louis Hietzler, M. Sorugue) who were contracted by the Cuban minister of public works to draft the city's master plan (Segre 1992b). Forestier, who had visited Buenos Aires only a few years before to consult on green spaces (Novick 1991), was already well known in Cuba. Both the government and Cuban elite had made the acquaintance of Forestier in 1918 when President Mario G. Menocal appointed him to design the park around La Punta fort at the northern edge of the old city. Wealthy landowner Enrique Conill—who sponsored Forestier's visit to the island—had also introduced him to his circle of friends and business associates. Beginning in 1925, Forestier and his associates worked with a group of architects for the next five years. Their objective was to link metropolitan Havana's dispersed places into a harmonious land-use plan. Although Forestier's team of Cuban architects Raúl Otero, Emilio Vasconcelos, and J. I. del Alamo was not completely successful in reaching its goals, its master plan helped to define the unique classical and tropical beauty of Havana.

One aspect that set Forestier apart from the practice of urban planning was that he belonged to the Parisian school of civic art headed by the core of designers Marcel Poéte, Henri Prost, and Eugéne Hénad. Theirs was not necessarily a rigid academic approach to urban design that entailed merely applying preconceived schemata. Rather, it embraced some of Haussmann's ideas about the importance of road networks. This meant connecting the ship terminal, the Central Train Station, the Plaza Cívica, and the Hotel Nacional by a network of diagonal streets and round points. This road plan emphasized functional needs (integrating the city's road system) and symbolic iconography (accentuating prominent landmarks). To carry out this plan, Forestier and the minister of public works flew over the city in a small aircraft, just as Le Corbusier had done. This air reconnaissance confirmed the thesis posited by the Cuban team: the new monumental center—the Plaza Cívica—should be located at the hill, Loma de los Catalanes, which lay midway between the old and new middle-class neighborhoods (fig. 2.3).

The new master plan executed by the binational team emphasized Havana's natural setting. It incorporated the rolling topography, the lush tropical vegetation, and the enduring presence of the ocean. The French master perceived both the present and future dimensions of the city in his beltways, traffic circles, and spokelike road networks. He even sensed that Havana Bay

FIGURE 2.3. Present-day Plaza de la Revolución, looking south-southeast on Avenida Paseo. Parades and important public ceremonies are held in this area. It is anchored by the obelisk José Martí Monument (center) and flanked by government ministries and other public buildings. The Ministry of the Armed Forces Building (MINFAR) is visible to the left (east). (Photograph by Joseph L. Scarpaci)

would only temporarily impede the city's spread eastward. Perhaps because of his European training, Forestier was unwilling to give attention to the automobile if it meant sacrificing tree-lined pedestrian spaces. Instead, he accentuated the roles of royal-palm-lined avenues and pedestrian malls to protect *habaneros* from the scorching tropical sun. Promenades adorned with flowerbeds and thick shade trees were used wherever possible. The Prado best illustrated these landscape-architecture principles.

Forestier, however, did not have a crystal ball. Just as he could not anticipate the role of the automobile, neither could he foresee the role of the bus or truck, the introductions of which were encouraged by U.S. sugar interests. Thus, he gave considerable importance to the railroad station at the expense of these newer modes of transportation. President Machado's approval of the Central Highway (Carretera Central) to link provincial capitals was as much to satisfy U.S. commerce in Cuba as it was for national businesses. In the end, Forestier's plans were cut short by the depression of 1929 and the popular uprising of 1933, which toppled Machado, followed by the 1935 coup d'état led by Sergeant Fulgencio Batista (who would return as self-appointed president in the 1950s). Graft and strong-arm tactics ultimately pushed through the Central Highway project, with little concern about the costs or consequences for the Cuban people (Bens Arrarte 1931). Despite all this, Forestier's work in landscape architecture left an indelible mark on the city.

## Tropical Landscapes and Classical Monuments

Havana's image can be characterized by four successive architectural languages whose synthesis contributes to the city's personality: (1) popular architecture, (2) early baroque styles in the colonial monuments of Habana Vieja, (3) academic codes of design imposed during the first three decades of the twentieth century, and (4) the International Style built in the new central areas (La Rampa in Vedado) and the suburban neighborhoods. Nevertheless, the greatest visual presence in Havana is the widespread classical structures used as much by modest and anonymous builders as by name designers on some of the city's landmarks. Alejo Carpentier devised a separate classification system and enlisted what he called a "Third Style": that which has no style (Alvarez Tabío 2000). This "Third Style" is "the process of symbiosis, of amalgams, of transmutations, both in the architectural and the human" (Carpentier 1974a, 12). We must add to that the ecological conscience of Forestier and his associates, who were determined to strike a balance between nature and the built form. In the 1930s, these designs would become the capital's defining features (Duverger 1994).

In the first two decades of the twentieth century, Havana strengthened its Caribbean character by the compactness of its center, evidenced by the relationship between the building grid and the light building facades. Toward the end of the 1930s, the classical designs had become "tropicalized" by the colonnade passages along the streets and avenues of Havana. The social life of the bustling city enlivened as neighborhoods became racially and socioeconomically integrated, except, of course, in the elite quarters. Recognizable design features made their mark, including the gable, spire, entablature, talamon, and caryatid. Even today, these elements are visible along the central streets of San Lázaro, Galiano, Belascoaín, Reina, and Infanta. They even surfaced in what was then the remote settlements along the *calzadas* of Monte, Cerro, Diez de Octubre, Puentes Grandes, Luyanó, and Güines (Cárdenas 1991; Fernández 1990; Llanes 1993; Martín Zequeira and Rodríguez Fernández 1993). The porticoes that first appeared in the nineteenth century became an integral part of the city. Even today, city dwellers circulate under the shade of the portico, and street vendors huddle there to sell their wares. The latter foreshadowed the rise of the "informal" economy that would spawn in these same places (Chailloux 1945). Adjacent to these shaded corridors were the retail stores and the corner grocery stores (*bodegas*) frequented by mixed social classes.

The French landscape architect understood the different social spaces of the city and the ways in which Habana Vieja and the rest of the city contrasted. If the small scale of the colonial core represented an introverted segment cut off from the rest of Havana—the solitude and silence imposed by the walls—then the expanding metropolis required broad new perspectives (Kavafis 1978). Forestier was sensitive to the meaning of open spaces as a means of framing the city's monuments and also as a stage for the casual stroller who could ponder the aesthetic beauty created by the tropical landscape (Labatut 1957; Benjamin 1962). The interaction between classical beauty and the encompassing natural landscape constituted one of the essential premises in redesigning the social areas in the city center (Forestier 1928). Landmarks, argued Forestier and his disciples, were not to be autonomous and isolated objects but rather should interact with spaces near and far. This premise is verified in Havana with the concentration of six essential focal points built in the late 1930s:

1. Parque de la Fraternidad, a rhythmic expansion of the Ionic order of the Capitolio building
2. Avenida de las Palmas (or Avenida de las Misiones), which frames the Presidential Palace
3. La Avenida de la Universidad, which was supposed to be a nexus between the Plaza Cívica and Colina but which was never executed. Such a union would have been important because the university's design atop a hill parallels the Acropolis in Athens as a temple of knowledge, though filtered through the model of Valhalla by Von Klenze (Gelabert-Navia 1994).
4. The gardens surrounding Principe Castle, which are terraced from the tops of the hills down to Paseo de Carlos III
5. The Maine Monument, whose property extends the gardens of the Hotel Nacional down toward the Malecón (Otero 1940)
6. The Prado, the city's "living room," with its green "roof" creating a

serene space for the casual stroller who can appreciate such symbolic
historical structures as the dome on the Capitolio and the composed
and colossal Morro Castle (Cabrera Infante 1992)

The streets and avenues configure the fabric of the city's central districts
and blend its identity into a collective unit. Forestier's work defined the city's
edge that separated architecture from nature. The first element valued in separating the two was the waterfront and the creation of an exterior "side" of
the city that would renew Havana's long-standing look within, away from the
ocean. This meant allowing a sizable setback of buildings away from the
water. Beginning with the port—the "reception hall" for tourists arriving by
ship—this waterfront edge of the city wound along the Malecón. From there,
it passed successive parks and monuments. Several kilometers west of the
port, the water edge meets the Avenida de los Presidentes and Avenida Paseo
in the Vedado. Forestier envisioned the city's "water edge" to continue westward until the beaches of Marianao, and the Malecón would serve as the city's
seaside thoroughfare.

Having just returned from Buenos Aires, Forestier envisioned the Malecón
as the same grand boulevard that he built in the Argentine capital in 1924, the
Costanera. The Costanera is a wide shore-walk avenue running along the Río
de la Plata extending from downtown Buenos Aires to the northern suburbs
of Palermo. It is adorned with gardens, parks, and tree-lined promenades in
the classic landscape design so typical of Forestier. However, crude land speculation and environmental disregard made the extension of the Malecón beyond the Vedado impossible. The Almendares River, separating Miramar
from Vedado, marked an edge to the city and forced urbanization to points
south. As we discuss in Chapter 3, the festive beer gardens of the two large
breweries along the banks of the Almendares served as the city's "green
lungs." By the 1950s, twentieth-century urbanization, partly shaped by the
French master's work decades before, had left an indelible stamp on Havana
(fig. 2.4).

Forestier's plan faithfully followed the attributes of the beaux arts styles. It
also shared in less pronounced ways the features of Garden City, the English
and German hygienists, the U.S. City Beautiful movement, and the function-
alist theories of Le Corbusier. His plan was perhaps the last attempt to safeguard the "human" dimension of Havana and achieve an equilibrium between
practical needs, private initiative, and state control, while maintaining continuity and coherence in the built environment. Even though only isolated

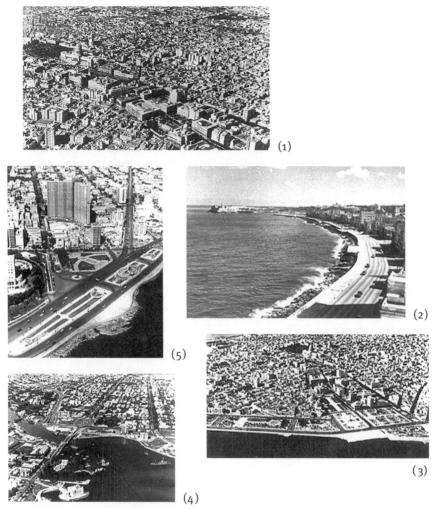

FIGURE 2.4. Five aerial views of Havana, ca. 1950: (1) the "ring" of Havana between Habana Vieja and Centro Habana, seen from the north-northeast looking south-southeast; (2) the Malecón in Centro Habana, seen from the west looking east; (3) aerial view of the "ring" of Havana from the entrance to the bay, seen from the northeast looking southwest; (4) mouth of the Almendares River between Vedado and Miramar, before the tunnel connected Línea Street with Fifth Avenue (Quinta Avenida) in Vedado and Miramar, respectively (note the presence of the old bridge, with still-standing "Iron Bridge" [Puente de Hierro] upstream [south, at left of bridge]); (5) view of the Malecón in Vedado looking southwest with Focsa building upper center, Maine Monument on Malecón, middle right, and part of Hotel Nacional visible, middle left.

remnants of Forestier's designs survived, they helped Havana to come of age and assume the expressive codes of modernity (Segre 1994b, 1994d).

While the designs of Forestier did much to beautify the city, there were still plenty of neglected pockets. State policies directed mostly at the wealthy did little to alleviate the precarious living conditions of the poor, most of whom were devastated by the 1926 hurricane. A succession of misfortunes aggravated the welfare of Havana's poor in rapid succession: the 1929 stock market crash, the ensuing Great Depression, and the decline of sugar exports to the United States. U.S. exports dropped from 50 percent of the island's production in 1925 to 28.6 percent in 1932 (Le Riverend 1966). Both urban unemployment and migration to Havana shot up in response to the global crisis. The latter led to a dramatic increase in squatter settlements on the outskirts of Havana.

In light of this crisis, all the government did was extol a single, public-funded, and proletariat housing project. The project, Lutgardita, was constructed in the midst of light industries such as paint, tannery, and oil factories. Although this working-class housing project designed by Evelio Govantes and Félix Cabarrocas was only half-heartedly received by the dictator Machado in 1929, it marked one of the first experiments of its kind in Latin America (Fernández 1987). The workers' housing complex was situated near Rancho Boyeros Avenue on the road to the airport and consisted of one hundred freestanding residences. The units were comparable to the models proposed by the European and Latin American "Commissions of Low-Cost Housing" and were well endowed with sites and services. Lutgardita, built in 1929 and clustered at the city's southern edge, included a school, kindergarten, hospital, theater, and shops. Its Spanish colonial architectural style conferred a romantic populist image that suggested balance and social well-being, aspects far from the reality of the urban poor (Segre 1994c).

## Breaking Up the Urban Image and Expanding the Periphery, 1935–1950

Until the 1930s, the state's role in urban planning concentrated on building classical monuments and landmarks. Government authorities had uncritically adopted a model of urban planning that was based on defining and constructing a hierarchy of monuments symbolizing middle-class power. These attributes molded Havana's image as a cosmopolitan city ready to be launched into modernity. More important, such symbolism covered up the very real and precarious conditions of its past. Neither the millions of dollars of loans from U.S. banks nor the radiant shine of its granite and marble buildings could hide the age of Havana's old plastered walls. The growth of the urban poor, moreover, encroached on Havana's exclusive suburban neighborhoods. With the overthrow of Machado in 1933 and the ensuing political crisis that lasted until the 1940s, so too ended the good old days of Cuba's belle epoque.

This convulsive political and economic situation would limit Havana's growth until 1940, when World War II produced a windfall of profits for Cuban sugar. Two presidential administrations benefited from strong sugar prices: Fulgencio Batista (1940–44) and Ramón Grau San Martín (1944–48). President Grau San Martín established the Sugar Differential, a tax added to sugar sales to help finance public works projects. U.S. interests invested heavily in light industry at a time when most of Latin America was experimenting with import-substitution industrialization. In Cuba, light industry was located on the outskirts of Havana. Sugar-derived prosperity and burgeoning new industries demanded an increase of labor in Havana. The need for labor, moreover, made suburban areas grow faster than the central city. While Havana's population grew 45 percent, from 837,670 inhabitants in 1943 to 1,216,762 ten years later (Pérez de la Riva 1965), the core urban counties within the city (*municipios*) increased by only 17 percent during the same period, from 676,376 to 787,765 (Roig de Leuchsenring 1964).

Forestier's plan had enhanced internal road traffic in the city's residential districts and improved local and regional tourist routes. The Central Highway facilitated the spread of the metropolitan area toward the southeast and the suburban neighborhoods of Diezmero, San Francisco de Paula, Cotorro, and San José de las Lajas. The highway also promoted westward expansion through Marianao, La Lisa, Arroyo Arenas, Punta Brava, and Bauta. These westward and southeastern throughways served as sites for new industries and working-class residences. The new airport to the south of Havana and the extension of Rancho Boyeros Avenue brought the development of small factories throughout Calabazar, El Cano, and Santiago de las Vegas (Le Riverend 1992). Besides these radial axes, peripheral beltways to get around the city also became necessary. Avenida del Puerto facilitated the shipping of imported goods toward Vía Blanca and the Central Highway with further connections to Rancho Boyeros through Santa Catalina, Lacret, and Avenida de Acosta.

Emphasis on transportation networks also had an international counterpart during this time. Cuba participated in the Pan American Highway projects by running a ferry service from Florida and the Yucatán. The Habana-Pinar del Rio Highway marked Cuba's contribution to the Atlantic-Caribbean branch of the Pan American Highway.

Within this flurry of road building and economic activity, local professionals returned to plans of action focusing on fragmented and isolated patches of the city. José Luis Sert's whirlwind tour through Havana en route to the United States in 1939 served as a rallying point for vanguard architecture and debates in urban planning. The 1940 constitution went into effect in the first year of the elected Batista government (1940–44) and included articles concerning urban and regional planning, industrial zones, and low-cost public and private housing. In 1942, Pedro Martínez Inclán headed up an academic and policy forum concerned about urban affairs and planning (Patronato Pro-Urbanismo). The impetus of the forum, which was a precursor to a national commission on similar issues, came from the works of such luminaries as the Frenchman Gastón Bardet, who lectured throughout Latin America, and the Austrian Karl Brunner, who resided for a long time in Chile and Colombia (Eliash and Moreno 1989; Violich 1987).

On the heels of these initiatives, the Ministry of Public Works created a number of work groups in 1943. Their task was to modernize the obsolete urban laws and define the limits of the growth of the city. Proposing urban dispersion and establishing satellite cities in metropolitan Havana received support from the Anglo-Saxon notions of the Garden City (Bens Arrarte 1960a–c). Finally, Pedro Martínez Inclán introduced his "Havana Charter" (Carta de La Habana) at the 1948 First National Architecture Conference. Martínez Inclán's plan was a direct transposition of the "Athens Charter," but his version included the peculiarities of the Caribbean city, which had previously been ignored (Rossi 1966; Munford 2000).[2]

Ramón Grau San Martín's government (1944–48) carried out the largest urban plan by the state in the first half of the century (San Martín 1947). For the first time ever, urban and regional planning authorities designed a pragmatic master plan for Havana and the provincial capitals of Pinar del Río, Matanzas, Cienfuegos, and Santiago de Cuba. After long and heated debate,

---

2. The Athens Charter was a seminal document resulting from the Fourth International Congress of Modern Architecture (CIAM in French), held in 1933 on a boat that traveled from Marseilles to Athens. It was dedicated to town planning and included the experiences of thirty-three cities. Standards identified in its pages became the driving force behind the modern movement, up to the 1960s.

the academic project of Forestier was finally put to rest. In its place rose the executors of the new master plan: the architects José R. San Martín, minister of public works, and Luis Dauval Guerra, general director of architecture. Drawing on Franklin Delano Roosevelt's New Deal, their efforts absorbed idle rural laborers who were unemployed in "dead time" (*el tiempo muerto*, that period between planting sugarcane and harvest). Despite the habitual detouring of funds and the deals struck by politicians in office, the public works projects that materialized did modernize the city, especially at the outskirts. Other key works entailed modernizing the port facilities, upgrading the water and sewage systems, building new roads, creating parks and gardens, and building houses, schools, and hospitals. Bens Arrarte (1956) estimated that city public works projects averaged $80 million annually during the government of Grau San Martín.

This first wave of modernizing Havana left the major features of the city undisturbed. In fact, expansion at the city's edge merely continued some of the city's defining traits. This is evident in the types of housing and public buildings designed by the state architectural offices. The use of such styles as monumental-modern, Spanish colonial, proto-rationalist, and art deco merely echoed in the suburbs many of the designs of the city center (Rossi 1966). The proliferation of apartment buildings was not associated with the huge isolated complexes of the Congrés International d'Architecture Moderne (CIAM). Instead, Havana's flurry of construction conserved the homogeneous layout of city blocks, limited building heights to four stories, and continued the porticoes along the city's main thoroughfares. The traditional Spanish interior courtyard (patio) reappears in the form of the *cortijo* model, evident throughout the Caribbean by means of the Spanish colonial style used widely in California and Florida. The small single-family houses in the suburban neighborhoods, with their flat Mediterranean-style roofs, front porches, and simple art deco decorative details, have little in common with the central-city landmarks.

## The Brevity of the Welfare State

The government began addressing the lack of basic social services in squatter settlements without neglecting ongoing projects of a "loftier" nature. Projects concerned with defining central Havana continued, including works tied to the Plaza Cívica and the Pro–José Martí Central Commission initiated at an

Inter-American design competition. Despite difficulty in finding support for the project, the architect Aquiles Maza and the sculptor Juan José Sicre won the design competition in 1942 (Pereira 1985). In 1953, a year after he led the military coup d'état, Fulgencio Batista started building the monument, but he replaced the first-prize winner's design with that of the second-place finalists: Jean Labatut, Raúl Otero, and Enrique Luis Varela (Noceda 1984).

Identifying the backgrounds of the social and political groups that define the landmarks of Havana reflects broader structural profiles of Cuba. When Machado fell in 1933, the generation of soldiers headed by Sergeant Batista, himself from a modest middle-class background, managed things from behind the scenes. These officers had little interest in the Plaza Cívica project, which was, from its inception, a project supported and valued by Havana's core elite. Rather, from that moment of support for a new multifunctional core, the army focused on the Columbia military base in Marianao. Several housing projects and public monuments to be built at the periphery supported this new multifunctional core: Plaza Finlay (1944), the Military Hospital (1940), and the maternity hospital Maternidad Obrera (1939). These works expressed notions of a peripheral centrality compared with the standing built hegemonic structures. Future master plans would neglect this kind of peripheral centrality.

Cuba pulled out of the depression of the 1930s thanks to a rise in sugar prices, which in turn steered private construction into a strong phase. In 1939, investment in private housing stood at $9 million, but by 1946 it had risen to $36 million (De Armas and Robert 1975). A rent-control law was passed in 1939. It favored landlords and addressed the demand for more housing brought on by migration into Havana. These new communities required hospitals and schools. Even today, most of the schools and hospitals in the city date from the 1940s. Other larger projects of the late 1930s and 1940s included the children's antituberculosis sanitarium, La Esperanza; La Benéfica clinic; Las Animas hospital; and the high schools Institutos de Segunda Enseñanza, which were located in Víbora, Marianao, and Vedado (Weiss 1947, 1966, 1973). A zoo was also built in Nuevo Vedado. Architectural styles of the day were influenced by prominent foreign styles: the functionalism of New Deal public buildings from the United States coupled with rationalism and art deco from Europe.

Although Havana experienced a spate of public construction, it did little to enhance the condition of housing among the neediest *habaneros*. The quality and quantity of low-income housing progressively worsened, as shown by the proliferation of tenement houses (*casas de vecindad, solares,* and *ciudadelas*).[3] Infamous squatter settlements of the era were Las Yaguas, La Timba, Cueva del Humo, and La Tambora, among others. Unevenly dispersed throughout the city, this destitute population—the majority of them black or mulatto—reached upwards of three hundred thousand *habaneros,* or about one-third of the city's residents.

The first appearance of a popular housing complex, built according to the features of European rationalism, emerged. However, as with two previous state-funded demonstration projects—Pogolotti (1910–13) and Lutgardita (1929)—it was a token showing of public welfare. In 1944, the government of Grau San Martín developed the Barrio Residencial Obrero de Luyanó (Luyanó Workers' Residential Neighborhood) pilot project in Reparto Aranguren. Using lands just south of the bay that were sandwiched in between industrial complexes, architects Pedro Martínez Inclán, Mario Romañach, and Antonio Quintana worked on the project, which originally entailed fifteen hundred houses, eight four-story apartment complexes, and sites and services that included a market, school, sports field, and senior citizen center. This was a significant project because the architects involved were pioneers in the Cuban modern movement. Generous amounts of green spaces were interspersed throughout the complex. At the 1947 official inauguration of the complex, however, only 177 houses and some of the sites and services had been completed (López 1987). Barrio Residencial Obrero de Luyanó represented the only example of working-class housing built during the first half of the century under republican governments, and it was designed according to the canonical principles of the modern movement.

## The Sad Joys of Tourism in Havana

Havana in the 1950s, with its paradoxical effervescence, marked a time of intense adherence to modern architecture and planning. Most professionals acritically adopted the International Style disseminated from the United States. There remained, however, a group of professionals who questioned the loss of Cuban identity and experimented with new ways to express the

---

3. Of the many variables that go into classifying the collective housing for the poor in Cuba, the number of rooms per structure is perhaps the least controversial. A *casa de vecindad* consists of homes or buildings with twelve rooms; the *solar* held about twenty to thirty rooms, and *ciudadelas* more than one hundred. Precarious housing is discussed in more detail in the next chapter.

country's cultural legacy of urbanism (Quintana 1974). The venue for this new voice surfaced in the 1953 public debate, the Plaza Cívica Forum. It served as a sounding board for a broad range of politicians, intellectuals, urban planners, and architects about the present and future of Havana (Segre 1975).

The United States invested heavily in Cuba throughout the 1950s. Le Riverend (1966) estimated an average annual investment of $713 million during the decade. Most of the U.S. moneys were targeted for light industry and the service sector. The products and brand names in Havana at that time read like a list from any U.S. telephone directory or stock sheet: soft drink bottlers (Coca Cola, Pepsi Cola, Canada Dry, Royal Crown), pharmaceutical companies (Abbott, Parke-Davis, Squibb), paint manufacturers (Sherwin Williams, Glidden, Du Pont), and tire makers (U.S. Rubber, Good Year, Firestone) (Gutelman 1967; Aranda 1968). U.S. retail chain stores of the day, Ten Cents, Sears and Roebuck, and Woolworth (Pérez 1975; Pino-Santos 1973), appeared throughout Cuba's major cities.

Havana was internationally renowned as a tourist destination since at least the 1930s, and its image was heightened in the 1950s. Since the fall of Machado, organized crime from the United States increased its operations in Havana. Notorious figures such as Charles Lucky Luciano, Santos Trafficante, and Meyer Lansky were perhaps the best known, as were their commercial dealings in Havana after World War II. Representatives of the large organized "families" divided themselves among the zones of influence along a strategic triangle of U.S. tourist and gambling centers: Las Vegas, Miami, and Havana. Organized crime also controlled gambling (legal and illegal), narcotics, and prostitution. As we discuss in the next chapter, the Batista government of the 1950s participated in these lucrative businesses through its approval of concessions and licenses and the construction of multimillion-dollar tourist complexes. Tourism in the Caribbean, established by multinational firms along the Miami–Havana–San Juan axis, centered on Havana's unique features. In the early stage of modernity, the Central Business District reaffirmed the compact form and retained the centrality of its residential areas (Fernández 1990). However, the unitary image of Havana began to unravel in the 1950s.[4] High-rise office buildings and apartment complexes located in high-rent areas permanently transformed the city's landscape (Segre 1985b).

4. Until the 1940s, Cuban architecture and city planning vacillated between the dynamics of the European vanguard and the functional efficiency of the United States. A cast of European maestros flocked to the United States before World War II: Ludwig Mies van der Rohe, Walter Gropius, Richard Neutra, Marcel Breuer, and José Luis Sert. Gropius, Sert, and Neutra visited

The Hispanic flavor of the Antillean capital city became progressively diluted through the spread of single-family houses, like those in the United States, increasingly located farther away from the city center as the result of improved roads. A fictitious aura of rapid progress invaded the lifestyle and replaced the slow Caribbean rhythm of Havana. Street life diminished and even disappeared in some quarters as air-conditioning beckoned folks into cooler buildings. Department stores proliferated in the city center—Fin de Siglo, El Encanto, and Flogar—and quickened the decline in street vendors and traditional storefront retailing. Although the traditional *bodega* (small, mom-and-pop corner grocer) remained in working-class neighborhoods, supermarkets and shopping centers began to appear in the more affluent sections of Vedado and Miramar. These included La Rampa and La Copa, as well as the Ekloh chain on the main thoroughfares of Forty-second and Forty-first Streets in Miramar, Seventeenth Street in Vedado, and Twentieth Avenue in Nuevo Vedado.

These new retail centers offered economies of scale and variety in high-income neighborhoods. The more contemplative way of life found in open-air bars and outdoor cafés, protected by the shade of large trees or under the awnings of downtown shopping galleries, was offset by the counters of bars and fast-food corners of department stores. Boogie, fox trot, and feeling (*filin*) displaced the traditional rhythms of the *danzones* and cha-cha-cha that had sounded in public spaces. Much of the impromptu local music and dancing under the sun faded into the crimson darkness of nightclubs and cabarets. At the city's edge there survived a smattering of local culture and theater, designed mainly for the nighttime entertainment of U.S. tourists. There, the Tropicana cabaret and its "fiery mulattas" (*mulatas de fuego*) became the lewd symbol of Havana in the 1950s (Cabrera Infante 1971).

## A Metropolis of Three Million

By the 1950s, the great Antillean city had reached its long-sought dream. The nation's 1958 population stood at 6,548,300, while Greater Havana registered 1,361,600, Metropolitan Havana held 1,272,300, and the city of Havana housed 813,300. Growth rates between 1950 and 1958 for the three areas reg-

---

Havana, and Neutra built a magnificent house in 1956 for Alfred Schulthess, the Swiss Nestle's manager in Cuba. Their influence directly and indirectly led to many International Style and postrationalist buildings and developments in Havana's city centers and suburbs.

istered 20.8 percent, 19.4 percent, and 12.4 percent, respectively. Although the city occupied only 0.3 percent of the total area of the country (47,846 hectares, or 478 square kilometers) and 8.5 percent of the province of Havana, one of five Cubans and one of every three urban dwellers were *habaneros*. Havana in the 1950s, therefore, exhibited the classic features of a primate city (whereby the largest city is several times larger than the second city). It was 6.4 times larger than Santiago de Cuba, the nation's second largest city, and 9.4 times larger than Camagüey, the third largest city. Whereas Metropolitan Havana constituted 76.1 percent of the provincial total, Santiago de Cuba contained only 9.2 percent of its provincial (Oriente) population.

The spatial differentiation of Havana varied considerably. The symbolic administrative and commercial center occupied 4.9 percent of the metropolitan area (2,350 hectares) and possessed the greatest population density, ranging from an average of 399 persons per hectare to a maximum of 800 per hectare. This latter high-density area comprised the blocks between Belascoaín, Galiano, and the Malecón. The remainder of the urban agglomeration consisted of 15,000 hectares (32 percent of the city's area) and the peripheral zones with close to 13,000 hectares. Here at the city's edge the population densities dropped off dramatically to 40–54 hectares in Marianao and 7 hectares in Boyeros and La Coronela. Such irregularity in the population distribution meant maladjustment in several functional relationships in the city, such as the location of housing in relation to services, work, and recreational areas. A crude translation of this spatial irregularity is that more than a million hours were "lost daily" in commuting time within the city. The clustering of great concentrations of industries and services led to disparities among municipalities. The municipality of 10 de Octubre, for example, with 391,342 residents, lacked industrial and service installations, while Boyeros (120,000) was equipped with industries, factories, laboratories, hospitals, and services that were on a metropolitan scale (Segre 1974).

Havana's primacy also surfaced in statistical tabulations other than population data. The city generated 52.8 percent of the nation's industrial output—including the processing of sugar—and 75 percent of the national total without sugar's contribution. Eighty percent of Cuba's imports came through the Port of Havana, as did 60.7 percent of its everyday consumer goods. The 1953 breakdown of the labor force revealed a prevalence of tertiary-sector workers: 41.9 percent worked in services, 20 percent in industry, and 17.9 percent in commerce (see also Chapter 7). Primarily a city of consumption, Havana absorbed 38 percent of all wages, 35 percent of domestic commerce, and 49 percent of services. Practically every sector of the economy revealed the concentration of the nation's services and functions in Havana. The capital held 40.7 percent of all hospital beds and 45 percent of all public health personnel. There were 13.9 beds per 1,000 residents in Havana, while Matanzas had only 5.9 beds per 1,000 (see Chapter 8). Nearly two-thirds of the nation's hotel beds, university students, and high schools were concentrated in the capital, as were three-quarters of Cuba's professional labor force and 90 percent of its architects (Garnier 1973).

Despite the concentration of the building trades in Havana, the housing conditions of the poor and the overall urban services of the city were quite tenuous. Almost half of the housing stock was in bad condition, and 6 percent of the population lived in shantytowns (see Chapter 6). Havana had only 1.1 square meters of green areas per inhabitant even though standards based on its climate recommended 18 square meters (see Chapter 8). Havana lacked about one-third of the water required daily—about 80 million gallons, which would have complied with the normative guideline of 140 gallons per person needed to meet all domestic and industrial needs (Rallo and Segre 1978). As with other Latin American cities (López Rangel and Segre 1986), two mirrors reflected the urban image. The wealthy one showed the daily glow of a beautiful seaside landscape defined by the Malecón and the thick vegetation of the houses, parks, and gardens along Quinta Avenida (Fifth Avenue in Miramar; see fig. 2.5). The poor reflection was opaque and somber, as evidenced by the growing deterioration and crowding of Habana Vieja, *solares*, and *cuarterías* (dilapidated rooming houses). It included the squalor of the port area and the industrial back-bay quarters as well as the precarious houses of the proletariat located along the winding roads that linked Havana with the center of the island.

A group of professionals took measures to solve these visible and mounting contradictions. Never before had urban affairs and planning been so intensely debated in Havana. The pioneer work of Pedro Martínez Inclán (1883–1957) is noteworthy. He became the chair of Urban Planning at the University of Havana. Since 1925 he had argued forcefully for the need to use a master plan leading to balanced growth for Havana (Martínez Inclán 1925, 1946, 1949). His doctrine, at first connected to the French academic tradition and later attached to the Le Corbusier school of the CIAM, was furthered by colleagues and students who played an active role in the theoretical formulations of this interdisciplinary group.[5]

5. Among the many we note Alberto Prieto, Eduardo Montoulieu, Manuel de Tapia Ruano, Eduardo Cañas Abril, and Nicolás Quintana. The visit of José Luis Sert to Havana in 1939 cre-

FIGURE 2.5. View of Fifth Avenue (Quinta Avenida) in Reparto Miramar, taken from the Clock Tower, ca. 1921 (From American Photo Studios, Havana, The Tropical Paradise of the West Indies)

The decision of the government of Fulgencio Batista to build the José Martí Monument in the Plaza Cívica in Havana generated bitter controversy. Personal and political motives made Batista award the design to the second-place team headed by Enrique Luis Varela (Tejeira-Davis 1987). Its design was exhibited and provoked heated discussion in a forum organized by the Institute of Architects (Colegio de Arquitectos), the principal professional organization of Cuban architects. Despite the triumph of the traditionalists who finalized the academic and monumental image of the Plaza Cívica through such structures as the Martí Monument, Palacio de Justicia, and the National Library, a new group of professionals arrived on the scene.[6]

ated a contingent of Cuban loyalists to the CIAM and opened contacts between Cubans and European maestros; Walter Gropius (1949), Richard Neutra (1945), and Joseph Albers (1952) passed through Havana and gave lectures. In the wake of this interest arose a series of meetings debating urban problems: the First National Conference of Architects (1948), the celebration as of 1950 of the World Day of Urbanism (November 8), the Eighth Pan-American Conference of Architects (1954), and the First National Planning Conference (1956).

6. This group was made up of architects such as Eduardo Montoulieu, Mario Romañach, Nicolás Quintana, and Jorge Mantilla, all of whom were connected with Sert, Gropius, and Neutra. They joined the workings of the government in the National Planning Board (Junta de Planificación) established in 1955. The board would oversee the development of multimillion-dollar

Multinational interests in the hospitality industry were addressed by preparing countries for massive international tourism throughout the Caribbean. Once the tunnel was completed underneath Havana Bay, the city could begin expanding to lands east of the city that for four centuries had remained inaccessible. To accommodate the perceived image of a new metropolis of three million inhabitants, the Junta Nacional de Planificación contracted the office of Town Planning Associates, which included José Luis Sert, Paul Lester Wiener, and Paul Schulz (Bastlund and Sert 1967).

Latin America in the 1950s was one of the last bastions left untouched by the urban planning theorists of the CIAM. Significant projects related to CIAM ideas were launched throughout the region: Sert and Le Corbusier's plan for Bogotá (1951), Lucio Costa's idea for Brasília (1957), and Antonio Bonet's project (1957) for the Barrio Sur neighborhood of Buenos Aires (Gutiérrez 1983). Havana's project of 1956 joined this list, with each of these plans sharing the Le Corbusieran models associated with the Athens Charter. In general, these models emphasized a hierarchy as the guiding component in urban projects, as shown by

1. the five principal roads used by Le Corbusier in Chandigarh, India;
2. the presence of a hegemonic political-administrative center;
3. the separation of social functions (residential areas, government complexes, industrial zones); and
4. the breadth of green areas and the layout of housing in strips and isolated clusters.

Nonetheless, Havana exhibited several unique characteristics that were defined not by theory or concepts but by dominant economic forces. These powers revealed themselves through landowners, major "Mafia" projects, and politicians backing certain businesses (Ramón 1967).

This blend of economic might shaping Havana in the 1950s appeared in the treatment of political-administrative spaces. It culminated with the design of the "modern" enclave, the Plaza Cívica, which interrupted the road system established by the Martí Monument and the imposing Palacio de Justicia. Toward the Quinta de los Molinos (the former summer retreat of the colonial governor, located between Vedado and the Plaza) and the Colina Universitaria (University Hill, home of the University of Havana in Vedado), a series

---

tourist projects in Havana, the beach resort of Varadero, the colonial town of Trinidad, and Isla de Pinos (Isle of Pines, today Isle of Youth, Isla de la Juventud).

of new buildings were constructed: National Theater (1958), General Comptroller's Office (Tribunal de Cuentas) (1953), Ministry of Communications (1954), Ministry of Public Works (1960), bus station (1949), and Havana City Hall (Ayuntamiento de la Habana; 1960). Another complex of government structures or a presidential palace would not have been necessary because the 1950 arrangement was adequate.

Batista, however, sought refuge from the political and social tensions of the city, especially, perhaps, because of the attack on the Presidential Palace that nearly cost him his life in 1957. He supported the idea of creating a new governmental growth pole near Habana del Este that, if completed, would have marked the fourth and final "center" of Havana's polycentric design. Land between the Morro Castle and the Cabaña fortress would have afforded him space that was distant from the latent aggressiveness of the city yet would allow him direct contact with the exclusive areas of the bourgeoisie who would soon settle in Habana del Este. With the recent inauguration of the tunnel under Havana Bay came an expected boom in residential areas along the coast. In this context surfaced a potential real estate bonanza for the powerful landowner Dionisio Velasco y Sarrá, who subdivided his land and placed Miguel Gastón in charge of its development. Gastón, in turn, solicited alternative development and design proposals from the U.S. firm of Skidmore, Owings, and Merril and the Italian architect Franco Albini.

José Luis Sert's plan under consideration by the Batista government anticipated considerable population growth. The most widely criticized aspect of Sert's plan for Havana centered on changes in the Malecón and the transformation of the city's historic old town. In the plan he contradicted the basic concepts of his book, *Heart of the City*, in which the traditions of people and their lifestyles, and the use of styles that conform to the social history of a city, were paramount. For example, substituting the homogeneous waterfront, with its low-lying buildings, colonnades, and eclectic architecture, for a series of high-rise hotels and apartments would have violated premises of harmonious and historically sensitive design. City blocks in the old quarters would have been reconfigured with parking lots (fig. 2.6). Although Havana would ultimately be spared this assault, San Juan, Puerto Rico, and Santo Domingo, Dominican Republic, did not fare as well. The proposal for redesigning Havana was even more audacious than its Caribbean sisters because it contemplated building in the Straits of Florida an "artificial island" of hotels, casinos, and businesses (fig. 2.7). The design was a banal parody of the Cité des Affaires in the Río de la Plata as envisioned by Le Corbusier in the master plan of Buenos Aires (Le Corbusier 1947). Did the island possess symbols like the ones assumed by the Cartesian skyscrapers envisioned by the great master? Were these ideas born out of imperative functional necessity? These questions were not the real intentions of the design but were, instead, driven by financial gain. Widening the Malecón and creating a marine platform meant driving up land values and padding the personal checking accounts of government officials.

Sert's proposal was certain to have devastated Havana's historic center. Its dialectical homogeneity—recognized much later as a World Heritage Site designated by UNESCO in 1982, praised for its narrow streets with modest colonial houses and pretentious eclectic buildings that were adorned by the tranquil flavor of its plazas—would have been lost. Although Sert's plan would have conserved a few isolated landmarks, it would have radically altered the profile of Havana. Modern limited-access highways and wide streets with artificial town squares and parking garages were to infringe on the traditional colonial grid. Practically all the existing construction would have been demolished or radically altered to accommodate this new plan (Wiener, Sert, and Schulz 1960). With surgical precision, the poor in the old quarters would have been expelled. Industrial satellite towns with workers' housing were envisioned.

A scenic setting for tourist activities had also been included in the design. Along Cuba and Havana Streets—the main thoroughfares of the center of Habana Vieja—were to be high-rise offices and retail and hotel complexes, which would have replaced the dilapidated colonial blocks. In all, the new design represented a hypothetical Hollywood revival of porticoes and interior patios whose ascetic modernity reflected the Venturian axiom that "less is a bore." This was a design with an abstract and reductionist configuration, remote even from the ironic and caustic realism of the masterminds at Disneyland, who could have created infinite versions of "a romantic evening" in Havana.

A perceptive error also existed in Sert's plan regarding the habits and customs of the popular masses of Havana. He had proposed a strip of single-story housing to envelop the city like "upholstery," as did the original plan for Chimbote, Peru (Donato 1972). In the end, Havana could have been deprived of the extroverted street life typical of Caribbean cities. Last, although they were designed with very different criteria, the Plaza Cívica and Habana del Este projects assumed symbolic and geographic significance.

The negative features of Sert's plan notwithstanding, some of its proposals were consciously or unconsciously included in urban design and planning

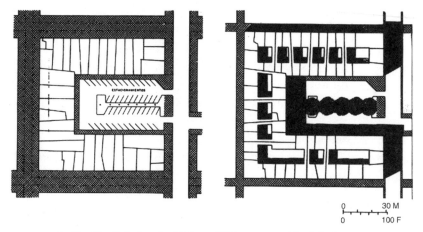

FIGURE 2.6. City block design for Habana Vieja proposed by J. L. Sert
(From Wiener, Sert, and Schulz 1960, 62)

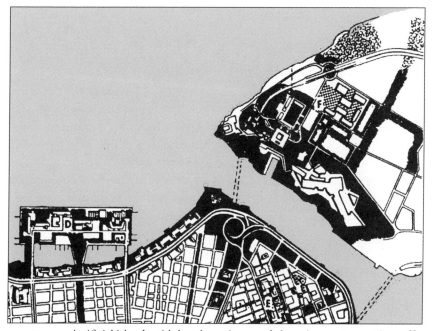

FIGURE 2.7. Artificial islands with hotels, casinos, and shopping centers set just off
the Malecón, proposed by J. L. Sert (From Wiener, Sert, and Schulz 1960, 62)

projects after 1959. The first came in the form of a new shape of the city that would include the bay not just as a boundary but as a central element of a city that both surrounded and enveloped it. In addition, the traditional urban sprawl to the south and west became multidirectional, retaking lands that had been unsettled to the east of the bay. This radial focus required a road network connecting the old areas with newer ones. It entailed the lengthening of the spokelike road system and some of the proposed beltways, most of which were carried out in the 1960s. Sert's ideas also materialized in the system of green spaces. They possessed a certain flexibility that integrated different neighborhoods and took advantage of open spaces. This made the expensive expropriation of private lands unnecessary. The city's peripheral areas succumbed to planning regulations, not only the road systems but also the typologies of orthodox rationalism and proposals for low-cost housing. Sert's plan should be interpreted within its historical context and the spirit of modernity. Cuban architects and planners, trained in that same spirit, would have done something similarly iconoclastic in the early 1960s had the revolution's priorities not quickly turned away from Havana.

## Polycentric or Eccentric?: The Urban Nodes of Havana

It is difficult to characterize the urban morphology of Havana. On the one hand, it shares few of the features present in North American models of urban structure. The Concentric Zone Model (Burgess 1925), Sector Model (Hoyt 1939), and Multiple Nuclei Model (Ullman and Harris 1945) make certain assumptions about land use that do not apply to Havana. These include the flat topography, equal distribution of transportation and land costs, and the changing nature of suburban transportation in the U.S. city, especially the role of the automobile and the highway system joining suburbs and downtown. Moreover, the Latin American urban land-use models by Griffin and Ford (1980) or Bähr and Mertins (1982) fail to capture the noneconomic forces that have shaped Havana's nearly five hundred years of urbanization.

Figure 2.8 identifies five recognizable nodes or centers in Havana's contemporary landscape: (1) the Colonial Center (1519–1898); (2) First Republican Center (1902–30); (3) Second Republican Center at the Plaza Cívica (1930–58); (4) Third Republican Center (1956) proposed by José Luis Sert; and (5) a Complementary Center consisting of residences, hotels, and nightclubs. These functional nodes reflect myriad political and economic forces

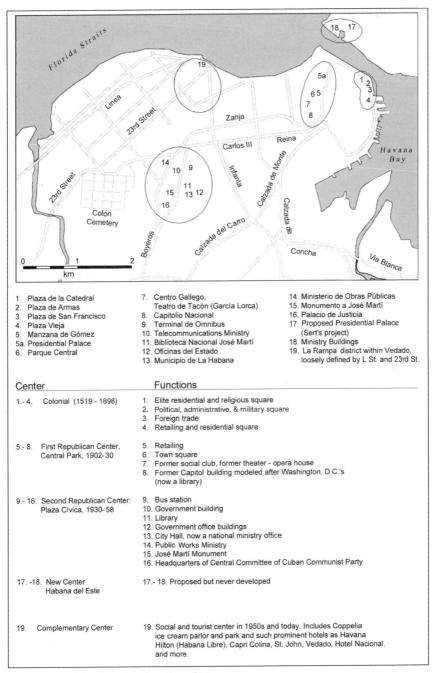

1. Plaza de la Catedral
2. Plaza de Armas
3. Plaza de San Francisco
4. Plaza Vieja
5. Manzana de Gómez
5a. Presidential Palace
6. Parque Central

7. Centro Gallego,
   Teatro de Tacón (García Lorca)
8. Capitolio Nacional
9. Terminal de Omnibus
10. Telecommunications Ministry
11. Biblioteca Nacional José Martí
12. Oficinas del Estado
13. Municipio de La Habana

14. Ministerio de Obras Públicas
15. Monumento a José Martí
16. Palacio de Justicia
17. Proposed Presidential Palace
    (Sert's project)
18. Ministry Buildings
19. La Rampa district within Vedado,
    loosely defined by L St. and 23rd St.

| Center | Functions |
|--------|-----------|
| 1.- 4.   Colonial (1519 - 1898) | 1. Elite residential and religious square<br>2. Political, administrative, & military square<br>3. Foreign trade<br>4. Retailing and residential square |
| 5.- 8.   First Republican Center,<br>Central Park, 1902-30 | 5. Retailing<br>6. Town square<br>7. Former social club, former theater - opera house<br>8. Former Capitol building modeled after Washington, D.C.'s<br>(now a library) |
| 9.- 16.  Second Republican Center:<br>Plaza Cívica, 1930- 58 | 9. Bus station<br>10. Government building<br>11. Library<br>12. Government office buildings<br>13. City Hall, now a national ministry office<br>14. Public Works Ministry<br>15. José Martí Monument<br>16. Headquarters of Central Committee of Cuban Communist Party |
| 17. -18.  New Center<br>Habana del Este | 17.- 18. Proposed but never developed |
| 19.   Complementary Center | 19. Social and tourist center in 1950s and today. Includes Coppelia<br>ice cream parlor and park and such prominent hotels as Havana<br>Hilton (Habana Libre), Capri Colina, St. John, Vedado, Hotel Nacional,<br>and more. |

FIGURE 2.8. Five functional nodes of Havana

that have left their indelible mark. Throughout this book, we will refer to these polycentric or, perhaps, "eccentric" centers of Havana, as well as their attendant buildings, landmarks, town squares, and land uses.

Little survived of Sert's dream for Havana. It was a delirious vision because it contemplated grandeur in a city that, on the one hand, would have held ostentatious casinos, gigantic shopping centers, and luxurious skyscrapers. On the other hand, it was also submerged in misery and exploitation. With its population growth held constant, the city preserved the history of its built environment, the semblance of a memory, the richness of its ambiance, and the complexity of its neighborhoods (Dunlop 1999). From 1959 onward, the city's prospect would radically change, and Havana would become the only "museum" in Latin America's first wave of modernity (Sambricio and Segre 2000).

# 3

# The Havana of January

At last, we are in the midst of all the chaos that has come from the
breaking up of Cuba, with all its confusion and sense of inferiority
over these last 30 years. . . . On the one hand, fear, surprise, per-
plexity. On the other, desperation!

—José Lezama Lima, *Diario*, September 11, 1957

When the revolution triumphed on January 1, 1959, Havana could only be described as a small "big" city that had come to dominate an underdeveloped island. Despite Havana's glittering appearance, the rest of Cuba was not exempt
from the external dependency forces that afflicted Latin America. A single
product (sugar) and one principal market for exports (the United States)
characterized the Cuban economy. Extensive agricultural production was
split between a latifundium system in the eastern half of the island and the
*minifundia* in the west. A well-known litany of underdevelopment traits also
besieged Cuba: unemployment, weak industrialization, a deficient infrastructure, low technology, and poor educational and health indicators (García Pleyán 1986). All these features were evident in Cuba's towns and cities as well as
the internal structure of Havana.

This profile of underdevelopment stemmed from a fundamental contradiction between the public and private use of the territory and resources. Several bipolar development profiles resulted. The original conflict between
Cuba (colony) and Spain (metropolis) continued during the neocolonial relationship with the United States and typified the classic trade imbalance between core and periphery nations (Cardoso and Faletto 1979). Perhaps the
most striking bipolar features were the geographic schisms between rural and
urban and between inner city and suburban. Profit and land speculation drove
urban development. Little concern was given to the quality of the natural en-

vironment, the rational use of human and material resources, or social and spatial segregation. Public services and infrastructure that did not lend them- selves to profitable ventures went underfinanced. In brief, the nation faced weaknesses in infrastructure and structural distortions.

The shining face of Havana and a disproportionate investment in luxury goods masked the harsh economic reality that touched even those lucky enough to hold a steady job. Uneven access to a relatively deteriorated public school system produced limited occupational and social mobility for rural workers, small farmers, and the chronically unemployed (Barkin 1974, 195).

Annual per capita income improved only slightly during the twentieth century. In 1902 it stood at $200; in 1959 it had crawled up to $374. Disaggregating annual income by workers revealed a dismal mid-1950s figure of just $91 for rural workers (ACU 1957). Income distribution was skewed by the top 10 percent of wage earners accumulating 38.5 percent of all income. Geographic disparities were also apparent, including the differences between the eastern and western halves of the island as well as between Havana and the rest of the island. Even within Havana income differentials prevailed, as evidenced by the gap between middle- and upper-income groups as well as within the "invisible" city of the proletariat and subproletariat (Segre 1978).

Despite these income distribution inequities, Cuba's underdevelopment differed from that in the rest of the Third World. If the gross national product, industrialization, and educational levels gave Latin America a higher standard of living when compared with Asia and Africa, then Cuba and Puerto Rico warranted special note. Both islands were fairly Europeanized because of Spanish colonial rule, which lasted until 1898, almost a century longer than the rest of Spanish America.

Cuba attracted a steady stream of migrants from the Old World after its formal independence from Spain. Between 1902 and 1912, two of three immigrants to Cuba hailed from Europe. Havana maintained levels of European immigrants well above the 30 percent mark during the first half of the twentieth century, although many migrants ultimately settled in the island's interior during the sugar-boom years. Like Puerto Rico, Cuba displayed strong economic and cultural influences from the United States, dating from the nineteenth century. This U.S. sway was greater in Cuba than other parts of the world (Manitzas 1974). By 1959, the United States had $1 billion invested and controlled 40 percent of the island's sugar production, 90 percent of electric utilities and telephones, and 50 percent of railroads. It also had significant interests in mining, oil refineries, rubber by-products, livestock, cement, and tourism and a quarter of all bank deposits. Eighty percent of Cuban imports came from the United States. Cuban currency (the peso) established in 1915 was evenly exchanged for U.S. dollars. That dollar was so commonplace in Havana during the 1950s that people would receive change in dollars when they made minor purchases in pesos.

Cuba obtained 80 percent of its foreign earnings from exports. As a monocultural producer and agro-exporting nation, it remained perennially vulnerable to external "shocks," slight market shifts, and natural disasters. That the price of sugar governed Cuba was evidenced by the popular slogan "Without sugar, there's no country." From sugar harvests that averaged 5.3 million tons during the 1950s, the United States would purchase 2.8 million tons at above-market prices. Sugar prices varied greatly during the first half of the twentieth century, as did the revenues in the public treasury (fig. 3.1). Oscillating prices made planning difficult. Reliance on a single buyer was made clear by the U.S. sugar quota and a menacing political and military influence that led to two U.S. military interventions in the early twentieth century. The United States extended its control in the 1950s by allowing the repudiated Batista dictatorship to hold power, which later generated public resentment and consolidated support behind the revolution in the late 1950s. The exodus of upper-class and many middle-class Cubans during the early years of the Castro government also helped to consolidate the revolution.

To be sure, sugar was king in the 1950s. It took up half of the arable land and required a quarter of the labor force. Consequently, the labor force suffered from seasonal fluctuations during the much feared "dead time" between planting and harvest, when thousands of workers could not find work. It also meant relying on importing goods that could have been produced in Cuba. Foodstuffs amounted to 22.2 percent of all imports. Although three-quarters of foodstuffs could have been produced nationally, pressures from U.S. producers who sought access to the Cuban market for their products blocked domestic production (Consejo Nacional de Economía 1958). This classic situation of economic dependency (Cardoso and Faletto 1979) led to a trade deficit that by 1958 had reached $43.5 million. Fidel Castro remarked as early as 1953 that "except for a handful of food, wood, and textile industries, Cuba is still a raw-material factory" (Castro 1984b, 44; our translation).

This monocultural sugar production and bondage of economic dependency minimized the chance of "multiplier effects" or spin-off industries. The work force suffered the most from this malaise. In 1958, the average unemployment rate was 16.4 percent, to which could be added 30.2 percent of un-

FIGURE 3.1. Cuban sugar harvest and value, 1900–1958

deremployed workers. The situation worsened at the end of the sugarcane harvest (*zafra*), when 20.5 percent of the labor force became completely unemployed, as opposed to 9.1 percent unemployment during the peak of the harvest (Consejo Nacional de Economía 1958).

Nevertheless, Cuban monoculture had its own unique features. Sugar production was more capitalist than feudal, as shown by the social relations of production among workers (Moreno Fraginals 1978). In the early 1950s, agricultural workers accounted for 63 percent of the labor force. This made them more "modern," and their aspirations were distinct. On the one hand, land ownership consisted of corporate and absentee landlords instead of the nearly feudal patriarchs that reigned elsewhere in Latin America (Manitzas 1974). On the other hand, the Cuban latifundium was like any other in Latin America: crops were extensively produced, almost half of the land remained idle, and the twenty-eight largest producers of sugarcane controlled a fifth of the arable land.

Local Cuban (*criollo*) industry was small and backward, not very productive, and concentrated mainly in manufacturing. This backwardness could be explained by the small size of the potential national market and the proximity of large U.S. producers. In its search for stability, the economy of the nation's capital focused on the real estate market, or else Cuban capital was invested overseas. Well-known multinationals found Havana to be a friendly and profitable market (fig. 3.2). The Cuban government also wielded considerable power in the economy even though industries were neither nationalized nor created by the state (Manitzas 1974). By the end of the 1950s, 52.8 percent of Cuba's industrial production had concentrated in Havana and employed a fifth of the economically active population that worked outside the sugar industry. The sugar industry had its own settlement and production system, which included more than 150 sugar mills (*centrales*) throughout the island. These included the sugar plantations and ancillary installations (*bateyes*) that formed agro-industrial complexes in the countryside.

These contradictions and inequalities created a unique type of urban system compared with industrialization and urbanization in the North Atlantic countries, but it was fairly common in Latin America. Jorge Hardoy describes the system this way: "[Cuba was] a fragmented nation . . . that neither understood nor felt its major national problems. . . . Urbanization, as a process, and the city, as an ecological space, reflected social forces, levels of technical competence, and external ties. In Cuba, like in the rest of Latin America, urbanization did not result from industrialization" (1974, 286; our translation).

Underdevelopment forces notwithstanding, Cuba's gross national product (GNP) ranked in the upper quartile of Latin American countries. Other standard measures attested to Cuba's relative prosperity in the 1950s: the ratio of physicians to population (1:420 in Havana), automobiles (1:20 nationwide), televisions (which arrived in 1949, before many European countries imported them), and other consumer durables. Employed urban workers were relatively well paid compared with rural workers, who lacked schooling, medical care, and decent housing. Cuba's level of urbanization, moreover, was high and had been evolving since the nineteenth century. In 1898, 28.5 percent of all Cubans lived in cities with twenty thousand inhabitants or more; the same figure for the United States was just 23.8 percent (Hamberg 1986). In 1958, with Cuba's population at about 6.5 million, almost one of three Cubans (32 percent) lived in cities with more than fifty thousand people ("Habana 1" 1971).

Cuba had one of the higher per capita incomes in Latin America: $345. Only Venezuela, Argentina, and Uruguay surpassed this level (Jiménez 1998). The cost of living during the 1950s was the lowest in Latin America, though by the end of the decade it began to rise. Consumption of goods was also very high. For example, Cuba ranked third in Latin America in the consumption of meat, among the four top in shoes, second in newspapers and radios, and

FIGURE 3.2.
The Cuban Electric Company
(Photograph by Roberto Segre)

number one in television sets and television stations. With 960 physicians per inhabitant, it ranked first in Latin America (Jiménez 1998).

The housing rental market was widespread. In 1953, three-fifths of all nuclear families and three-quarters of all Havanans paid rent on their primary residence. Housing conditions in the countryside were deplorable. Many Cubans at that time spent up to a quarter of their wages on rent (UIA 1963). Although tenants' rights legislation existed in Cuba and was fairly progressive for that time, such laws were overlooked or weakened by administrative corruption (Alonso 1950). In short, prerevolutionary housing was rife with strong contradictions such as "drastic differences of living conditions between city and countryside and among social classes and within urban areas, long-standing rent control coexisting with high rents, and an established 'right to occupancy' along with widespread evictions" (Hamberg 1986, 588).

Underdevelopment was concentrated unevenly in rural areas throughout the island, manifesting itself in various ways. The eastern region was particularly disadvantaged. For example, there was only one physician for every 2,550 residents (see Chapter 8 for the contemporary scene). Nationally, four-fifths of all rural dwellings were *bohíos* (thatched huts), fewer than 3 percent had running water, and two-thirds had earthen floors. Even though the majority (87 percent) of the national urban housing stock had electricity, fewer than half of all homes were connected to a proper waste-disposal system. In addition, less than half of the housing stock was connected to water mains, and even fewer had hookups to sewers that were in compliance with the law. In 1958, 1.4 million dwellings were below acceptable standards. Even in Havana—the most prosperous Cuban city—6 percent of the population lived in dismal shantytowns (Fernández Núñez 1976). Nevertheless, these figures were relatively low compared with other Latin American countries (Hamberg 1990).

## The Political Framework: Antecedents to January's Revolution

Dependency in Cuba resulted in part from an irrational use of material and human resources. It generated frustration and irritation in a people who, despite their characteristic nonchalance, had periodically risen up to shake off their oppressors. The Batista military coup d'état in 1952 unleashed a response that quickly bypassed a traditional political opposition that was demoralized by corruption and the status quo.

Opposition to Batista broadened as it incorporated young people who lacked political-party affiliation. This was the case of the Revolutionary Directorate (Directorio Revolucionario) at the University of Havana. The Directorate was headed by a young architecture student, José Antonio Echeverría, who was killed in a confrontation with state security forces on the campus of the University of Havana after a student-led attack against the Presidential Palace on March 13, 1957.

Other opposition movements disassociated themselves from traditional political parties, as did Fidel Castro when he was a young lawyer. Castro headed a leftist splinter group that broke away from the Orthodox Party and whose members were initially inspired by an opposition senator, Eduardo Chibás. Dramatically, the senator committed suicide during a live radio program one year before Batista's coup d'état. This splinter movement later took the name "26 de Julio," after the date of the unsuccessful 1953 assault against the Moncada barracks in Santiago de Cuba. The student movement centered at the University of Havana, an important impetus in ousting the dictatorship, was significant for many reasons. Two are particularly germane to our discussion of Havana as a world city. One is that the University of Havana was arguably one of the finest institutions of higher learning in Latin America. A second reason is that it is located at one of the highest elevations in Havana ("University Hill," or Colina Universitaria) and since the 1920s had been the site of numerous student protests. Its central location just a few blocks from the heart of the Vedado tourist district served to disseminate news reports of violent conflicts between students and police.

The Moncada attack was the first notable action in a short but whirling struggle of urban and mountain guerrilla fighters. In both settings, the 26 de Julio movement was at the vanguard and progressively earned the support of the rest of the country, including such unlikely partners as members of the upper class and the old Communist Party. The movement ended triumphantly on January 1, 1959, with the taking of the city of Santa Clara—strategically important because of its size and location in the middle of the island—and the total collapse of the Batista regime amid an impressive explosion of public celebration.

Following this popular victory, there remained a series of social justice issues that the revolutionary government had to address. Perhaps the most crucial challenge was the critical situation of the poor, which Fidel Castro addressed during his trial for attacking the Moncada. In his now well-celebrated speech, "History Will Absolve Me," he said: "The problem of land tenure, the problem of industrialization, the problem of housing, the problem of unemployment, the problem of education and the problem of health care; we have here six concrete points to which our efforts will be directed, with resolve" (Castro 1984b, 43). Nevertheless, both critics and sympathizers of the revolution agree that Cuba in 1959—especially Havana—possessed a physical, economic, and social infrastructure relatively well developed compared with most socialist movements that would later come to power in Africa and Latin America. This would support the revolution immeasurably.

## Havana: Structure and Infrastructure

Havana city in the twentieth century was composed of counties. In 1959 there were 1.27 million people in the city proper and 1.36 million when adjacent counties (*municipios*) were added to include the metropolitan area. Clearly the primary city of Cuba, Havana was six times larger than the second city of the nation, Santiago de Cuba ("Habana 1" 1971). The city covered 478 square kilometers (186 square miles). It is still shaped like the fingers of a hand, with radial arteries extending from the western and eastern edges of the bay in the central part of the metropolis. Several of these "fingers" follow the old routes of *calzadas* and the Central Highway (Carretera Central) as well as the more recently built bypasses of the 1950s: Calle 100, Vía Monumental, and Autopista del Mediodía.

## Islands within the City

The coherence of Havana's shape and skyline was affected not only by a poor secondary-road network and pockets of speculative subdivisions but also by natural barriers and large complexes that functioned as enclaves within the urban fabric. The port, the city's raison d'être, had become an ambiguous element in Havana. It both joined and separated the city functionally and socially. It was a spectacular landscape for tourists as they passed through the narrow strait at the mouth of the bay. The colonial forts of El Morro and La Cabaña cradle the bay as one enters by ship. To the left (eastward) sits the small settlement of Casablanca clinging to the side of a hill that is crowned by the dome of the Observatory. Off to its side sits the enormous white-marble statue, the Christ of Havana, erected in the 1950s. To the right (westward) runs the seaside promenade of Avenida del Puerto, designed by the French landscape architect J. C. N. Forestier (see Chapter 2) as part of his uncompleted master plan for Havana (1926–28).

Shaped like a bag with the narrow straits forming its top, the bay opens toward the south while the center of Havana falls off in the distance, only to be replaced by another interesting colonial settlement, Regla. Twentieth-century industrial installations surround the town today much as they did in the 1950s (see Chapter 7). The 65-hectare Belot oil refinery that belonged to Esso, Shell, and Texaco and the dockyards are readily apparent. So too are the power plant, Burrus grain towers, and a fertilizer plant. At the southern tip of the old walled city a compact string of docks and warehouses block the view of the water from Havana's first promenade, Alameda de Paula, dating from the late 1700s.

This was the heart of the city's trade and industry. Ocean vessels, loading cranes, and cargo were part of the constant traffic that included ferry boats running between Old Havana and Regla and Casablanca. Occasionally, the ferry that transported vehicles and passengers from Key West arrived at Hacendados dock, as did the steamship *Florida*, which regularly sailed between Miami and Havana. Curiously, the Key West–Havana route was the same distance (140 kilometers) as that separating Havana from the famous and spectacular beaches of Varadero. The human landscape of this 1950s dockside setting included a wide cast of characters: longshoremen, truck drivers, taxi drivers, local residents, tourists, office workers, beggars, sailors, and a colorful array of local bar patrons and prostitutes.

If we were to continue along this north–south traverse through Havana Bay in the 1950s, we would find other large industrial complexes, shipyards, rail yards, and roads. In the midst of this lay Cayo Cruz (Cross Key) with its gigantic heap of garbage. The old gas plant Melones (1870), the Tallapiedra power plant (1890), and Paso Superior railroad yards of Vía Blanca were also in full view. Just beside it ran the elevated railroad tracks that led from the great passenger station (1912) that blocked the possibility of completing a "greenbelt" encircling Old Havana along the strip where the city walls once stood.

The trade winds blowing through this southern portion of the bay carried factory smoke and the stench of rotting garbage to the nearby poor communities of Luyanó, Atarés, and the southern part of Habana Vieja. When the winds blew exceptionally hard, the foul smell and soot even reached Chaple Hill in southern Diez de Octubre, which was settled in the 1920s by middle- and upper-middle-class families. Ironically, many had chosen these higher elevations for their once clean air that helped in treating respiratory ailments. By the 1950s, however, the air had become thick with pollutants.

Air travel became popular and widespread by the 1950s. However, the new look of southern Havana, meant to be viewed from the air, had not been beautified the way that Forestier had envisioned it in the 1920s, when most visitors arrived by sea (Laprade 1931). The existing airport at Boyeros in southern Havana was not well connected to the city center. Situated on fertile agricultural lands that were prone to periodic flooding, the area lent itself to other land uses. Moreover, the airport sits on top of the Vento aquifer, which is still one of the main sources of water for *habaneros*. Airline traffic endangers the nearby settlements of Boyeros and Calabazar.

Havana's only other airport in the 1950s was Columbia military base, located in the west near the ocean, but it was generally off limits for commercial use. Some commercial activity did, however, take place at Columbia. This was carried out by Aerolíneas Q (Q Airlines), which was associated with contraband activities under the direction of military brass. The Columbia base had been built by U.S. troops earlier in the twentieth century and was, essentially, the de facto center of power in Cuba in the 1950s. This was yet another "island" in Havana, with its large military and hospital complexes and affiliated military-base centers of privilege. Although in 1959 it was turned into Ciudad Libertad (Liberty City)—a large educational complex—Columbia represented the military's intervention between the wealthy and the downtrodden. In practical terms, the Columbia base disrupted the road networks between the old downtown center of Marianao and the nearby upper-class neighborhoods on the strip along the coast, including the upscale Country Club Park, now called Cubanacán.

## Housing and Urban Structure in the 1950s

By 1959 Havana was a metropolitan area that held two different cities. One was composed of the inner districts (roughly including the present counties [*municipios*] of Habana Vieja, Centro Habana, and Plaza). The grid pattern gave the area the kind of coherence found in other Spanish American cities. The cityscape had several nodes such as parks, traffic circles, and landmark buildings. Another city within 1959 Havana contained a seemingly endless number of subdivisions leading out to the southeast, south, and west.

The grand axis of the Malecón and Quinta Avenida spectacularly linked the financial and commercial center of Havana with its affluent western neighborhoods, from which residents could easily get to downtown Havana—Parque Central, for instance—in less than a twenty-minute car ride. Upper-class housing in Miramar and adjacent areas initially consisted of eclectic—and later some art deco, neocolonial, and many modern—villas that were adorned with front porches and wonderful tropical gardens (Sambricio and Segre 2000). Despite their proximity, working-class neighborhoods to the south were poorly linked by the road network. This is where the rest of the city lived: an array of social classes including lower middle, working, less affluent white collar, and the urban poor. This expansion at the city's edge included tiny pockets of the poor and shanties constructed outside the crowded city center.

If the class structure in this southern area was diverse, so too were the types of dwellings. Common house styles were the petite bourgeoisie single-family structures of Lawton, Santos Suárez, Víbora, Casino Deportivo, La Sierra, and Almendares, among many others. There were other modest copies of affluent homes that were interspersed among two- to four-story apartment buildings. Alongside this "presentable" city defined by standards of middle-class decorum existed a dismal side of Havana. Substandard and speculative housing was shamefully hidden behind classicist facades and tucked away among the compact blocks of Centro Habana, Cerro, and Habana Vieja. These neighborhoods, moreover, had long suffered from land speculation, densification, and physical decay. Deterioration was most acute in the living quarters that were formerly occupied by well-off *habaneros*. Although the housing stock was shabby, these districts maintained their traditional retail, financial, and historic-center functions.

The Havana of 1959 held several types of slum housing. As mentioned in the last chapter, one type was the *cuartería* (a dilapidated rooming house). It evolved from the old baroque, neoclassical, and eclectic mansions of Habana Vieja, Centro Habana, Cerro, and Vedado (Chailloux 1945). Another was the *ciudadela*, a tenement house composed of one or two stories of rooms alongside an interior courtyard. This interior space held elementary collective services (laundering, toilets, showers, trash bin, and access to a spigot) and—by default—social activities such as makeshift playgrounds and places for chatting and dancing. Each family—ranging from a few members to several dozen depending on the space of the structure—occupied its own room. Both the *cuartería* and *ciudadela* reflected broader social changes whose qualitative impact modified the image of the inner city.

The *pasaje* was another type of low-income housing scattered about the city center. Literally a "passage" or "alley," the *pasaje* was a variant of the *ciudadela* that often intersected with two streets, one at each end. Both the *ciudadela* and the *pasaje* combined another type of housing: the *accesoria*. This arrangement consisted of a string of one-bedroom apartment[s] in the lower story of the house that could be accessed directly from the street and was typically followed by a row of rooms found in the *ciudadela*, with access through the long, narrow inner court.

Shantytowns, known locally as *barrios insalubres*, formed a part of the pre-revolutionary Havana landscape. Some of the more infamous shanties of 1958 were Las Yaguas, Llega y Pon, and La Cueva del Humo. More often than not, they were prone to flooding, poorly accessible and steeply sloped, located next to noxious facilities, or just plain unhealthy. Shantytowns arose at the city's edge, where Havana grew incrementally, and some were eventually surrounded by formal, legalized construction. These peri-urban shanties became the first points of contact for rural migrants to Havana. They were fed by migratory streams from small towns, villages, and the Cuban countryside. Shantytowns symbolized the widening social stratification and quality-of-life gap between the Havana elite and the rest of Cuba (Ortega 1996).

Not all squatters came directly from outside the city. Many found themselves in shantytowns on the rebound after failing to secure stable work that would allow them to live in more central areas with better services. In that way, the stock of human capital in the shantytowns remained more marginalized than residents in *ciudadelas* and *cuarterías*, and not just spatially. Social and occupational mobility was also limited, perhaps more than any settlement in Havana.

Altogether, this mass of dispossessed people raises the question of the accuracy of the 1953 census, which reported 59.8 percent of the population working in the tertiary sector (Comité Cubano de Asentamientos Humanos 1976). One reason for the potential undercount is that the "service" category should have been disaggregated (retail, wholesaling, food services, self-employment, banking, public sector). More significant, however, is that the employment data failed to reflect part-time work, seasonal labor, underemployment, and what is now widely called the informal sector (de Soto 1989). It was in these tenuous labor markets where most of the shantytown residents earned a marginal or substandard living, which forced them to live in the grim side of the city. Accordingly, the census counted only 6.2 percent of the city's labor as working in the construction industry. It is likely that this figure did not represent temporary workers and includes what Marx would call the "reserve army of labor." This surplus labor kept wages low in what was actually a dynamic sector of the economy. Another "invisible" segment of the labor force toiled as domestic workers (cooks, maids, chauffeurs, gardeners, handymen, and messengers). Informal employment was especially important for poor women whose work choices were limited and who declined to beg or to prostitute themselves. It was not uncommon for middle- and lower-middle-income families to hire one, two, or even three maids (*criadas*) for 25 pesos monthly plus meals. This revealed the development of a broad sector of marginal (informal sector) activity. Thus, it is more accurate to speak of a lumpen proletarianization of the city rather than tertiarization (e.g., increase in services) ("Habana 2" 1973, 11). Put another way, the service category represented only one segment of the economy of 1958, and it left out a significant part of the labor force.

## Industrial Output and Physical Structure in the 1950s

The 1950s brought industrial growth to Havana in the form of light industry (including textiles, food processing, and cosmetics) and the vibrant construction sector. The shipyards, oil refining, electrical power, and gas generation were concentrated in the port area and its immediate surroundings.

Two large axes moved increasingly farther away from elite residential districts. One spread out southeastward along the Carretera Central and included San Francisco de Paula and Cotorro; a steel mill was located in the latter. This industrial strip extended beyond the metropolitan limit to Cuatro Caminos and, beyond that, to San José de las Lajas. The other concentration included a great southern axis that ran along Calzada de Rancho Boyeros and led to the airport. Both axes departed from an industrial strip, Vía Blanca, which ran along the southern part of the bay and included parts of Cerro. Here, as in Centro Habana and Habana Vieja, small mixed-use tracts of industries, workshops, residences, and warehouses also emerged.

The 1957 Industrial Directory revealed that 3,500 non-sugar-mill factories produced more than 10,000 different products. Of that amount, 2,340 (69 percent) factories produced items that the Industrial Directory considered to be important because of their vertical or horizontal linkages with other components and products. Only 107 (3.1 percent) factories employed more than 100 workers, 830 (23.7 percent) factories employed fewer than 5 workers, and the remaining 937 factories (73.2 percent) employed between 6 and 99 workers (Marrero 1981b, 311). In line with patterns of industrial location in most Latin American cities (Gwynne 1986), the largest percentage of all factories were located in the province of the capital city.

The current location of industry (discussed in greater detail in Chapter 7) and light manufacturing has not changed considerably since the 1950s because the socialist government has promoted development in provincial towns and the countryside. During the last five years of the Batista government, three-fourths of the total value of both residential and commercial construction was built in the capital and Havana's neighboring districts. However, only 1 percent of the new housing was built by the state. Data from the Havana Province Institute of Architects (Colegio Provincial de Arquitectos de La Habana), which documents only those projects directed under its affiliates' charge, reveal that between 1951 and 1955, there were 19,205 licensed construction projects valued at $30.1 million. In 1956, 3,841 construction projects were launched, which included 7,994 housing units worth $60.3 million (Maribona 1957).

FIGURE 3.3. Industrial plants by province, 1957 (From Marrero 1981a, 312)

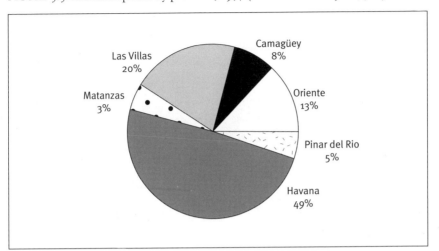

## ROAD NETWORK

Two tunnels built during the 1950s under the Almendares River between Vedado and Miramar greatly improved Havana's road network. One tunnel, consisting of two one-way segments, connected Línea Street with Miramar and Marianao in 1953, and the other extended from the Malecón to Quinta Avenida (Fifth Avenue) in 1959. Another tunnel project was completed in 1958 starting from Morro Castle, under Havana Bay, to the tip of Habana Vieja near the beginning of the Prado. It hooked up with an excellent highway, the Vía Monumental, which would have given rise to great speculative development of lands east of the city if the revolution had not triumphed. Instead, public housing in large apartment complexes, walk-ups, and high-rises was erected here and in many other areas of socialist Cuba beginning in the 1960s (see Chapters 4 and 6).

On a regional scale, the 1950s saw the connection of Havana with two major coastal highways that connected two important ports: one connected Matanzas, 100 kilometers to the east, and the other, Mariel, 45 kilometers to the west. Forty kilometers beyond Matanzas was the tourist center of Varadero, which would receive considerable investment in tourism. Although Varadero, Trinidad, and the Isle of Pines were studied by the brand-new National Planning Board (created in 1955 and discussed in the last chapter) as possible sites of development, the thrust of development continued to center on Havana.

Other roads, new or expanded, such as Avenida 31 in Marianao and the highway, Autopista del Mediodía, lent themselves to upgrading for military purposes because they eased machinery and troop movement to and from the Columbia Military Base and the air base in San Antonio de los Baños. Many streets were repaired, and others were widened using the previous lanes of the extensive streetcar network. Electric streetcar transportation began in Havana in 1901 and was discontinued in 1950 under the purported benefit of "modernization" and "development." The decision more likely aimed to make way for the sale of automobiles, buses, and fuel than it did to enhance "modernization and development." Even though the road network was incomplete, it was one of the few planning projects proposed and carried out by the Batista government.

CLEAN AND DIRTY WATER

Chapter 1 noted that Havana holds the historic honor of inaugurating in 1592 the first European-built aqueduct in the Americas. The city's water system was further enhanced with the Albear aqueduct, an engineering masterpiece started in 1858 and officially completed in 1893. It earned a Gold Medal at the World Exposition in Paris in 1889, two years after Albear's death. These historic landmarks notwithstanding, by the twentieth century Havana's water system had become a nemesis for the city's mayors, even though a new aqueduct, Aguada del Cura, was added in 1927. In fact, the besieged administration of one municipality led to one mayor's suicide in the 1940s. This dramatic act cautioned the subsequent mayor to mind the city's water problems more closely and to build the next, so-called third aqueduct that improved the water supply for the middle and southern areas of the city. To the new aqueduct of Paso Seco (1950) two new fields of wells and waterlines were added, Coscu-lluela (1954) and Ariguanabo (1958).

In the 1950s several important water mains were finished joining the capital with the new Cuenca Sur (Southern Watershed Basin). As a result, the overall volume of water for Havana increased appreciably, even though it had to be drawn from sources each time more remote from the city and more costly to pump. Those investments served the ambitious development projects of Havana at the expense of the neglected inner-city areas. The sewage system, inaugurated in 1913, was designed for about six hundred thousand users, which was double the existing population. By the 1950s, it was servicing one million people in the old municipal limits of Havana. This service area covered the present-day counties of Habana Vieja, Centro Habana, Cerro, Diez de Octubre, Plaza, and the oldest section of Miramar. The rest of the metropolis used septic tanks or else discharged runoff and raw sewage directly into rivers, streams, and canals.

## OPEN SPACES AND RECREATION

Despite Havana's tropical location, it was not a very "green" city by the end of 1958. There was about 1.1 square meters of designated green space per resident, and it was unequally distributed throughout the city. Most of the green spaces were in the well-off neighborhoods of Country Club, Miramar, Vedado, and Nuevo Vedado, as well as a few middle-class districts that included Víbora and Santos Suárez. An area as heavily populated as Centro Habana, with its traditional business district, was practically without open spaces in either public or private (courtyards and patios) places. This produced a textbook case of an urban "heat island," wherein Centro Habana averaged nearly 1°C warmer than the rest of the city.

A modification to the Laws of the Indies in 1573 stipulated normative guidelines about the layout of the colonial Spanish American city. Among its mandates were the use of certain colors to keep temperatures down (i.e., increased albedo levels or solar reflection) and draping narrow streets with canvas to ensure shade, both practices growing out of the Sevillian tradition. In this type of urban pattern, greenery—also inherited from Mudejar tradition—adorned the interior courtyards (patio) of the major homes. Shaded galleries gave cool relief to residents doing household chores. Larger traditional homes of the affluent had plants, shrubs, and trees in the patios, but greenery among the poor was reduced to a few flower pots. With the gradual abandonment and subdivision of the old colonial mansions, tenants used patios to build rooms to accommodate new occupants or add bathrooms and kitchens. Although the growing city continued to follow the same grid plan, the height of buildings increased dramatically, reducing patios to small courtyards that were not much more than simple openings for ventilation ducts.

Outdoor green spaces adjacent to residential neighborhoods first appeared outside the old colonial core in the elegant neighborhood of Cerro, which was built in the first half of the nineteenth century. Aristocratic country houses of the period were called *quintas*. These were neoclassical villas with front *portales* and gardens. So lush were the gardens that some really became tropical parks. Even better examples of open areas surfaced in Vedado during the last half of the nineteenth century. One-hundred-meter-sided blocks in Vedado were accentuated with *parterres*: tree-lined corridors of lawn between the curb and the sidewalk. In front of homes there was a 5-meter-wide swath of garden, coupled with a 4-meter-deep colonnade at the ground floor level that standardized, broadened, and cooled the Vedado landscape. Vedado building regulations instituted rules about the separation of homes and in doing so ended the use of the dividing walls that characterized Habana Vieja and Centro Habana. Not only were the Vedado lots larger on average than their inner-city counterparts, but zoning regulations stipulated that one-third of each lot had to be left uncovered (Llana 1983). These design features added much to a natural cooling process in the tropical heat (Coyula 1999c).

Miramar replicated many of Vedado's building codes and setback requirements. Property lots were even larger than in Vedado. In some of the older districts of Miramar, there was a building code that was unique in all of Havana. It required a 1-meter-deep green strip (garden) between the sidewalk and the property line in addition to the traditional *parterre*. However, this norm did not lead to establishing "green tunnels" through which pedestrians could walk, protecting themselves from the sweltering heat. It was not that the planners and residents did not believe this was a good idea; they simply acknowledged the fact that most residents did not walk a lot. Moreover, the nouveaux riches of the district did not wish to obstruct the views of their pretentious homes.

Public open spaces in the colonial districts of Havana were concentrated along the *paseos* and plazas, like Alameda de Paula and the Plaza de Armas. The latter, however, was not always tree-covered. Initially, it was an open and dusty expanse designed to accommodate military exercises. Significant tracts of public open spaces in the 1950s actually consisted of long-standing parks and promenades such as the axis made up of Paseo del Prado (originally called Isabel II), Parque Central (Central Park), the gardens surrounding the Capitolio, the India fountain, and Parque de Fraternidad (Fraternity Square).

One type of influential public space during the first half of the twentieth century, not only in Havana but throughout towns and cities on the island, was the so-called republican-style park. This consisted of an entire city block adorned with trees and interior sidewalks, two of which crisscrossed the park diagonally. It also contained lampposts, cast-iron-legged benches, and a central element that took many forms: a fountain, commemorative sculpture, kiosk, pergola, or band stand. The republican park functioned as a multiple use urban node for children, adults, and the elderly, where parties and periodic markets could be held. In short, the republican park breached Havana's grid-pattern layout of buildings by providing character, utility, and cool shade to the city's many neighborhoods.

For the most part, the unbuilt spaces separating the major thoroughfares that allowed the city to spread were not used to extend vegetative cover throughout the city. Perhaps the only exception was along the banks of the Almendares River, the city's major freshwater stream. Spectacular vegetation consisting of immense *algarrobo* trees (carob tree, *Ceratonia siliqua*) entangled by spectacular vines in a theatrical scenery that resembled a haunted forest and nurtured by a unique microclimate could be found in El Bosque de la Habana (the Forest of Havana) along the west bank of the river and near two beautiful limestone cliffs separating Kohly from Nuevo Vedado—both middle- and upper-middle-class neighborhoods. This was the setting in the 1940s of a colorful mythical character known as "Tarzan of the Forest." First land speculation and then a lack of control on how the area was used greatly reduced its acreage. However, in the early 1960s, part of the remaining area was upgraded to become Almendares Park (see Chapter 8).

Adjacent to Almendares Park and to its south were the gardens of the old Tropical Brewery, Jardines de la Tropical (1912), also along the banks of the Almendares River. Even farther south was a rival brewery, Polar, which also boasted beer drinking in a cool park protected by lush riparian vegetation. In the European tradition, the breweries promoted their beers in beautiful beer gardens (fig. 3.4). Not only was the tree canopy of Tropical Gardens a novelty, but it was also well known for its whimsical ferro-cement architecture. Pavilions and small structures in the park displayed a strong, early-twentieth-century Catalan Modernisme influence and motifs of sea life and vegetation.

Popular afternoon outings on the evenings of saints' days as well as other celebrations were held at these river parks, always accompanied by lots of beer and frequently organized by one of the dozens of immigrant associations from different corners of Spain. As discussed in the next section, these Spanish associations were numerous, and they afforded their affiliates with a wide array of services in the form of beaches, casinos, schools, home economics courses, hospitalization, and other medical services. Many cemeteries in Havana have pantheons for such groups, and several of the pantheons at Colón Cemetery (1871–86) have considerable artistic value, placing this necropolis at top world-class level.

FIGURE 3.4. Images of Tropical Brewery Park (From Habana, Cuba: Ciudad del Encanto, La Habana Edición Jordi, ca. 1927)

## Beaches, Casinos, and Clubs: To Each His Own

The switch from a Havana heavily influenced by Spain to one of U.S. domination also surfaced in the leisure activities of *habaneros* and their social organizations in the 1950s. The change not only was apparent in the names used (the Spaniards preferred the names "Centro" and "Casino" in theirs, while those of U.S. influence opted for "Clubs") but also corresponded to certain nuances among social strata. The inner city of Havana housed large buildings where these social organizations used the gyms, billiard rooms, and reading rooms and hosted dances and parties. These functions took place in ad hoc eclectic palaces such as the Centro Gallego (1915) and Centro Asturiano (1927) in front of Parque Central. Paseo del Prado contained the smaller yet impressive palatial structures of the American Club and Casino Español as well as facilities of Basque, Catalan, and Andalucian associations (Rodríguez 1998).

At the beginning of the Malecón (intersection with Prado) was the Union Club, with its stone-carved caryatids along the facades. In the same tradition of social clubs in the heart of the city were the Vedado Tennis Club and the Lyceum Lawn Tennis Club. These three clubs had predominantly Cuban membership. The Vedado Tennis Club, for example, was founded in 1902 and was composed of patrician members, which gave rise to the nickname the "Marqueses" in the press and sports circles. So prestigious and powerful was the Vedado Tennis Club that it persuaded the public authorities to build a special ocean access for its canoes that went underneath the Malecón in the 1950s, during the final completion of the seaside promenade.

The gamut of options and social sectors served by clubs was quite broad. Just west of the mouth of the Almendares River was the Casino Deportivo (Sporting Club), whose clientele hailed from the middle and lower middle classes and which was frequented by the wealthy Jewish community of Havana. Farther west was the Club de Ferreteros (Hardware Clerks' Club) for employees in the commercial sector. The Club de Profesionales followed with membership from middle- and upper-middle-class backgrounds. Farther along were the Balneario Universitario (University Bathing Resort) and the Copacabana; the latter had both a clubhouse and a hotel, as did the Comodoro. Continuing westward one would find the Miramar Yacht Club, whose members were upper middle class. In the 1950s that club demolished its interesting wooden clubhouse and replaced it with a modern yet banal building. Moving in the same direction we come across the Club Cubaneleco, designated for employees of the Compañía Cubana de Electricidad, which, despite its name, was a transnational U.S. company. The Compañía moved its recreational facilities to the former Swimming Club when it sold its old clubhouse in the Vedado to accommodate the huge Focsa building, one of the new "skyscrapers" of Vedado in the 1950s (fig. 3.5). Finally, this westward string of social clubs was capped off with the Balneario Hijas de Galicia (Daughters of Galicia Beach Resort), part of the large Galician colony in Cuba.

Following the Galician facility (always moving westward) there was a string of social clubs on the artificial and half-moon-shaped beach of Marianao. The first one was the Círculo Militar y Naval, which sported a new building thanks to General Batista. Marianao beach also held the pseudo-Mudejar building of the Balneario de la Concha, which was not technically a social club because one had to pay for each visit. At the opposite end of the social ladder, yet right next door to the Balneario de la Concha, stood the prestigious Habana Yacht Club. This club, founded in 1886, was the oldest beach resort and club in

FIGURE 3.5. View of the Vedado skyscrapers. Most of the city's buildings that break through the six-floor-height norm are clustered around the Hotel Nacional in Vedado, with the exception of the pediatrics hospital (originally designed as the Bank of Cuba) seen at the back of the image on the right, in Centro Habana. (Photograph by Joseph L. Scarpaci)

Cuba. It was also the nation's most exclusive club; new members had to be relatives of a current member.

The Habana Yacht Club was the principal relic of the patrician *criollo* class and managed to withstand the impoverishment inflicted by both the Independence Wars and the Great Depression of the 1930s (Tabares del Real 1971). Unlike the Vedado Tennis Club, the "Yacht" (as it was widely called) combined elements of social snobbishness with a more familylike atmosphere enhanced by the allure of the beach. By the 1930s or so, the Yacht had displaced the "Tennis" as the pillar of social status among Havanan country clubs. The Tennis, on the other hand, had relaxed its admission standards in its quest to draw the best young athletes to its facilities. Over time it regressed into a place for quick tennis or squash matches within an ambiguous aura of elegance and decadence.

The Casino Español followed the Habana Yacht Club on Marianao's crescent beach. Wealthy Spanish-immigrant merchants, at the insistence of their wives, used the Casino Español to marry their daughters into "good" families. The beach ended with the Club Náutico, whose members were high-salaried white-collar workers and homeowners in the neighboring residential subdivision of the same name. Both the subdivision and the beach club had the same owner. South to the crescent beach of Marianao, and ironically separated by a squatter settlement, was the Country Club de la Habana. The wealthiest Cubans and Americans frequented the club, which was surrounded by a beautiful golf course. Farther to the west lay the waterfront properties of the Havana Biltmore Yacht and Country Club, also, of course, consisting of upper-class members. Except for the Balneario Universitario and La Concha with their open admission policies, only white people belonged to these country clubs. Because of the loose tropical definition of a "white person," the more lax a club's position on the racial composition of its members, the less affluent its members tended to be.

The wealthiest *habaneros* belonged to more than one club, using each according to its location and profile. The relative locations of these facilities also provided distinct attributes. The Tennis, for instance, with its central location in Vedado, was a great place for a quick game of squash, a shower, and a drink before returning to work in the afternoon. The Yacht was more appropriate for a tranquil weekend outing with the entire family, while the "Country" was ideal for closing a big business deal with a rich American client after a round of golf. Social prestige was also attached to spending particular holidays at certain clubs: New Year's Eve at the Tennis, the Tea Party on Christmas Day at the Yacht, and the magnificent formal dance, Baile Rojo, at the Country (Alvarez Tabío 2000).

Five of the main country clubs held sporting events: the Yacht, Vedado Tennis, Biltmore, Miramar, and Casino Español; they formed the Big Five. Later, they were joined by Profesionales to make up the Big Six. These clubs competed among themselves and with certain American groups such as in the dual swimming meet in Atlanta. Physically, Marianao Beach exhibited the futile hypocrisy of class divisions: although the buildings of these clubs were guardedly separate from one another on land, its members shared the same ocean and the same vices. Even when leaving the clubs with their hair still wet, many would cross paths with one another at the roller coaster ride at the Coney Island amusement park, pool halls, bars, and cabarets. Some of the men would run into other club members just by crossing Quinta Avenida, where they would sneak off to the *casas de citas* with mistresses or prostitutes.

Contrasts also appeared in other ways. When Batista tried to join the exclusive Yacht Club, he was rejected in the secret, ancient Roman-style voting with white and black marbles. Eventually the slightly less demanding Biltmore admitted him. As a token of gratitude, Batista gave the Biltmore a splendid marina whose value exceeded all the club's combined assets.

The appropriation of waterfront properties by the elite took place east of the capital as well, but mostly for second homes at a fine, natural beach. In the 1950s there emerged an elegant new subdivision called Santa María del Mar, located west of the small town of Guanabo (a popular free-access beach) and east of the private beach of Tarará. Guanabo existed as a remote vacation spot beginning in the 1930s, when, for a middle-class family, getting there was a bit like going on a safari expedition. The excursion required taking a streetcar to the Avenida del Puerto and then crossing the bay by ferry to Casablanca. From there the family would board the old electric train whose rail line was inaugurated in 1916 to connect Havana to the Hershey sugar mill and finally reaching Matanzas (this is now the oldest electric train of its type still operating in the world). The family would disembark at the crossroads of a small hamlet, Campo Florido, and from there travel by rickety *fotingos* (1928 Fords) to the beach. Vacationers had to carry or buy enough drinking water to last them several days or even months. Lodging at Guanabo consisted then of a few dozen zinc-roofed cottages. There, in the serenity of the wilderness, a child rising before dawn could witness the mysterious egg laying of a giant sea tortoise.

## Havana: Sun, Sea, and Sin

Prostitution contributed to a sordid dimension of Havana in the 1950s. Tourism, social inequality, low education levels, machismo, and the deeply ingrained double standards of the Catholic bourgeoisie sustained the city's sex industry. The cheapest place in the city to secure commercial sex was in the sordid brothels along Pila Street in irascible Atarés. Closer to the city center, though, especially around the port, cheap sex was readily available. San Isidro Street catered largely to sailors and an underworld of shady characters found in most ports, as did Picota, Paula, Conde, and, ironically, Damas (Ladies) Streets. By the 1950s, long gone were the days when San Isidro was the pinnacle of such elegant vice and decadence portrayed by the nostalgia of Alberto Yarini y Ponce de León. The story consists of a well-educated young pimp with a highbrow last name who was killed in 1910 in a street fight over a French prostitute.

The most notorious district was the strip between Habana Vieja and Centro Habana that adjoined the commercial center. It was framed by the Paseo del Prado, Neptuno, San Lázaro, and Galiano. By extension, it was known by the name of the street where the real character of the neighborhood was concentrated: Colón. Another brothel zone adjoined the commercial center, but it was farther south along Zanja Street in Barrio Chino (Chinatown). The latter district captured the market of men who would come to and from the pornographic movie house, Shangai. A neighboring city block, the Plaza del Vapor at the end of Galiano Street, was composed of an entire market where prostitutes were exchanged like any other commodity. The plaza was demolished in 1960.

The neighborhood of La Victoria, so called because prostitution started there at the end of World War II, was located southwest of the Plaza del Vapor around Xifré Street, where Calzada de Infanta met Paseo de Carlos III. This area was near another huge market named after the same Spanish king. Last, another well-established area of prostitution in the 1950s was situated between Centro Habana and Vedado, very close to La Rampa, along the streets of Marina, Hornos, and Vapor. In this area was the notorious house of Marina, considered one of the "finest" in Havana in the 1950s. Taken in their entirety, these red-light districts occupied about 50 hectares of the central city.

The Havana of the 1950s was promoted as both a tropical paradise and a place to gamble, where the tourist was tempted to "sin in the sun." Tourist developers were not timid about marketing Havana's decadence; it was not a mere appendage to the sand-and-beach scene, as the following excerpt from a promotional magazine of the day reveals:

Close your eyes and visualize this scene: Night—a magical night with sky and velvety midnight blue scattered with a thousand glittering stars; low in the east the moon, incredibly large and golden.

A warm breeze tantalizingly scented with the intoxicating perfume of strange, exotic tropical flowers.

Music, warm sensuous, entrancing with Latin rhythms which set the blood to stirring and the feet to tapping.

Glamorous, lissome Latin lasses, black-eyed señoritas, languorously, enticingly swaying as they glide over a polished floor in a smooth rumba.

The bright excitement of gaming tables, the whir of the roulette wheel, the age-old chant of the croupier.

A dream you say? A dream that only the rich man can make come true?

How wrong you are! This is the night-time in Havana . . . the "Paris of the Americas." (Cited in Williams 1994, 47)

Lurid offers of sex ran the spectrum of price ranges, comfort, and discretion. At the low end was quick oral sex in a dark hallway or fornication standing up in a vacant lot whose entrance was often protected by strips of hanging bed sheets. Of course, the conventional bordello staffed by numerous women was also an option. Prostitutes working out of their own homes and apartments forced many a neighbor to place signs on their doors that read "Don't Bother: Family House." Hustlers, called *fleteras* (runners), worked the streets to direct prospective clients to run-down seedy hotels with which they were affiliated.

At the upper end of the business were bars such as the Mambo Club. These were exclusive and discreet bars, somewhat remote from the city center. Clients could reserve time, space, and high-priced women. Another tropical invention was the *posada*, where a couple could clandestinely meet for a few hours (an institution still in vogue in Latin America). The cheaper ones were located in the inner city and thus were pedestrian oriented. In the suburbs, a couple could drive up to a discreet facility and disappear behind a garage door. Once inside, they could not be seen by curious customers or even the clerk; transactions would be carried out through a drop box or dumbwaiter system. The full array of "troops" in the commercial sex industry — street walkers, expensive call girls, pimps, street hustlers, and others — would move into a "state of alert" when a U.S. war ship arrived in port. To many Cubans, the photographs of drunk sailors hanging from the statue of José Martí in Parque Central served as humiliating memories of those visits. Regrettably, even though these episodes occurred forty years ago in Havana, the debasing smell of the trafficking of flesh would reappear like an opportunistic virus among the educated and self-employed street hustlers (*jineteras*) of the 1990s.

## Culture, Education, and Health Care

Cultural life in Havana showed sustained growth in the 1950s. Since at least the nineteenth century, Cuba had always held within Latin America a rather high level in the arts and humanities (see, for example, the *Journal of Decorative and Propaganda Arts, 1875–1945*, no. 22). Paradoxically, this profile existed within a country characterized by institutional crisis, public and private corruption, public indifference about "high culture," and a lack of state support for the arts (Rodríguez Feo 1994; Hart 1979).

Major artistic talents included the painter Wifredo Lam and the novelist Alejo Carpentier. Unfortunately, even they had to emigrate to escape the suffocating setting in which they—the island's best and brightest—could not make a living off their artistic and literary forte. The upper class for the most part spent little money on artistic symbols of status, preferring instead bad copies of works bought in Europe as souvenirs or pretentious portraits made by mediocre local artists. Some upper-class Cubans, however, did have notable collections of art, such as those held by Oscar Cintas or Joaquín Gumá, count of Lagunillas, and the wealthy patrons of the arts, María Luisa Gómez Mena and the Falla-Gutiérrez family. Many national writers subsidized the publication of their own books and poetry and wound up giving them away to friends.

In 1954, Batista made a lame gesture toward reviving the arts. He created the National Institute of Culture, headed by a dandy named Guillermo de Zéndegui, whose most notable accomplishment was to eliminate the national subsidy of the world-renowned Ballet Nacional de Cuba. A joke that circulated sotto voce among the upper class reflected this prophetic association of elitism, superficiality, and uncouthness with the arts. The imaginary setting goes like this: a nervous Batista seeks advice from his brand-new director of the National Institute of Culture about an upcoming special exhibit of the *Mona Lisa*. Looking for an easy way out, the ill-trained de Zéndegui tells the president to pause in front of the painting, take two steps back from the work, and exclaim admiringly: "Such a face! What an expression!" [¡Qué cara! ¡Qué gesto!]. The next day when the exhibit opens, Batista follows Zéndegui's advice but confuses the word "face" (*cara*) with "hell" (*carajo*) and exclaims: "What the hell is this?" [¿Qué carajo es esto?].

The lack of institutional support notwithstanding, Cuban art in the 1950s found outlets wherever it could flourish and express itself. The important literary magazine *Orígenes* went out of business, but it was replaced by *Ciclón* and later by *Isla*. The national press also increased the quality and breadth of its coverage of cultural events. In that same decade, a group called Los Once (the Group of Eleven), composed of young artists devoted to abstract expressionism, was founded. Cuban music became celebrated throughout the Americas, and a new style, *filin* (Hispanicized from "feeling"), was added to the Cuban repertoire of mambo, cha-cha-cha, and other popular musical styles. Another organization, Sociedad Nuestro Tiempo, covertly allied with the outlawed Communist Party (Partido Socialista Popular), labored in promoting theater and classical music. The Havana cultural scene also benefited from painting exhibitions and art cinema at the University of Havana promoted by revolutionary students.[1]

Even though Havana enjoyed a disproportionate concentration of health and educational services compared with the rest of Cuba, public services did not meet the needs of most *habaneros* in terms of both quality and quantity. Politicians and the press frequently commented on the dire situation of public schools, but with little apparent resolve. Nonetheless, the greatest problem was the scarcity and bad condition of the schools themselves. The caliber of the teachers was generally satisfactory. As a consequence of the poor quality of public education, private schools catered not only to the wealthy but also to the working classes that earned steady incomes. Cuba's large number of parochial schools was noteworthy because, unlike most Latin American countries, Catholicism was not deeply rooted in Cuban society, though it was by far the prevailing religion. Catholic schools existed according to purchasing power and religious orders and, of course, were segregated by gender.

Like the social clubs described previously in this chapter, there was an unspoken social hierarchy of private schools in Havana. For the upper bourgeoisie, for example, there were the all-boys schools such as the Jesuit-run Colegio de Belén, where Fidel Castro studied, and the Colegio de La Salle, directed by brothers of that same order. Nuns ran the all-girl schools of Merici Academy and Sagrado Corazón. Administrators and even teachers of most of these schools were Spaniards, French, or Americans, with minor contributions from Cubans and Latin Americans.

Those Cuban families who did not care for a Catholic education, or simply wished to improve their children's English, sent them to private schools such as Ruston or Phillips. The 1950s was also a time when Protestant schools, such as Candler College, which combined religion and English, increased en-

1. In addition to Lam and Carpentier, a host of stellar personalities occupied the artistic scene, including the writers José Lezama Lima, Nicolás Guillén, Onelio Jorge Cardoso, Enrique Labrador Ruiz, José Z. Tallet, Cintio Vitier, Eliseo Diego, Mirta Aguirre, Jorge Mañach, Lydia Cabrera, and Virgilio Piñera. The visual and graphic arts scene involved René Portocarrero, Carlos Enríquez, Mariano Rodríguez, Amelia Peláez, Agustín Cárdenas, and Luis Martínez Pedro. The fields of dance and music contributed the ballerina Alicia Alonso and the musical composers Harold Gramatges, Ernesto Lecuona, Ignacio Villa (Bola de Nieve), Benny Moré, Dámaso Pérez Prado, Enrique Jorrín, César Portillo, and José Antonio Méndez. Cuban architecture boasted the contributions of Max Borges, Mario Romañach, Frank Martínez, Nicolás Quintana, Miguel Gastón, and Antonio Quintana. Historical continuity materialized in the 1960s when many young artists from the previous decade reached their maturity, even though some worked and lived outside Cuba.

rollments. The social prestige of these schools was extensive and covered a gamut of social groups and markets. Ungovernable students or those with little talent simply changed from one school to the next, based on the tolerance level and financial need of the receiving institution. With very few exceptions—such as the huge complex built *ex profeso* by the Colegio de Belén (today the Instituto Técnico Militar)—most schools, even the finest ones, had used converted houses until the 1950s. With hindsight, this would suggest that the quality of teaching depends more on the demands and skills of teachers than classroom amenities.

Higher education in Cuba before the revolution of 1959, like health care and public education, was concentrated in the capital, except for the newly established Universidad de Oriente in Santiago de Cuba and the Universidad de Las Villas in Santa Clara. The University of Havana, founded in 1728, had a long tradition of participating in national life and excelled in the fields of medicine and law. Its campus had been relocated at the turn of the century from Havana Vieja to a commanding location similar to that of the Acropolis. The entire complex was enclosed by a huge wall interrupted by the main entrance of the campus: a grand set of stairs fanning down to the street from a quad of buildings encased by Greco-Roman columns. A statue titled *Alma Mater* anchors the stairs at the top. The design of the monumental stairs is similar to that of Columbia University in New York City but is better framed by two strips of smaller, lateral stairs.

At the back of the campus of the University of Havana stood the Calixto García teaching hospital, where medical students conducted their residencies. In the 1950s the hospital served as a refuge for students who fled from an invading police force that theoretically could not violate the constitutionally sanctioned right of university autonomy and nonintervention in campus affairs. Surrounding the University of Havana campus were the administration building (*rectorado*), library, Aula Magna (Great Hall), and the departments of Law, Natural Sciences, Chemistry, Social Sciences, Physics, Pharmacy, Education, Electrical and Civil Engineering, and Architecture. In other corners around the campus one could find the stadium and the Quinta de los Molinos (former Spanish governors' summer residence), in which the Agronomy Department resided, as did Arts and Sciences, Philosophy, and the schools of Dentistry, Medicine, and Veterinary Sciences.

This section of Havana was full of ancillary services and retailing such as cafés, academic preparation and tutoring centers, and student boardinghouses to accommodate students from an array of socioeconomic back-grounds and different parts of Cuba. A well-known boardinghouse was the so-called *bombonera* (literally, a candy store), where well-groomed young women from wealthy families lodged. Services spread the influence of the university over a considerable area, ranging from Calzada de Infanta, Paseo de Carlos III, Avenida de los Presidentes, and Calle 23 and from San Lázaro turning on L Street as the main axis. In the mid-1950s the police dared to enter this zone only in large numbers, ready to engage in combat with stu-dents who at that point not only threw back rocks but also fired guns.

The Universidad Católica de Villanueva emerged in the late 1940s in the el-egant Biltmore subdivision. It exhibited a clear class spirit that aimed to raise college education to a higher-quality level similar to what had previously oc-curred in primary and secondary schools. In doing so, its goal was to be both morally and socially convenient for the upper classes. It also offered respite from the continuously tumultuous political scene of the University of Ha-vana, beset by closings, demonstrations, and strikes. Despite its intentions, Villanueva carried relatively little weight in the national academic arena, not only because of its high tuition but also because its faculty and the quality of its students could not match its two-hundred-year-old counterpart on Uni-versity Hill. In 1952, for instance, graduating students at the Colegio de Belén could be advised by their guidance counselors to go study with the lay faculty at the University of Havana instead of the Universidad Católica de Villanueva. Such advice reflected not just objective academic criteria but also the aristo-cratic disdain of the Spanish Jesuits at Belén and their dislike of the newly ar-rived American Augustine faculty at Villanueva.

Medical care mirrored the class-ridden inequities and conflicts present in education. Despite the concentration of medical care personnel and facilities in Havana, there was a great demand for medical care outside the strictly fee-for-payment market. This demand was to a large extent absorbed by mutual-aid societies that were often aligned with regional Spanish immigrant groups (see Chapter 8). In the 1950s, about half of the medical care delivered in the city of Havana was provided by these mutual-aid societies. For the middle class, these societies provided comprehensive medical care for a remarkably low monthly premium. A dense network of neighborhood pharmacies was as widespread as the corner grocer. The poor, though, resorted to charity care, tried to pay for private services, or simply did without medical care.

## The Growth of the Capital

The spread of the metropolitan area during the first half of the twentieth century produced a fragmented array of private subdivisions and properties. Private initiative almost exclusively created this urbanization, without any unifying structure. There was little coordination with neighboring lots or among local jurisdictions. Most architects lacked a deep appreciation for urban design and planning. Suburbanization in the 1950s did not follow the mandates of a master plan. Streets started and ended randomly, and there was little concern about linking subdivisions and municipalities with other parts of the city. Thus, the area, with its different neighborhoods and subdivisions, reflected very different city-planning attributes and social classes. A good indicator of this was the use of Spanish versus English place-names. Older parts of the city drew on the city's traditional, indigenous, and natural landmarks. Generally, the newer and more affluent sections of metropolitan Havana were located in the west. In Marianao and points west, a preponderance of upscale place-names characterized the newer suburbs that prospered in the second quarter of the century. Named after famous individuals or simply foreign (i.e., non-Spanish) names, these neighborhoods included Kohly, Country Club, and Floral Park. Another set of neighborhoods was situated at slightly higher elevations (*alturas*, meaning "heights," as in Alturas de Belén, Alturas de Coronela, Alturas de Miramar). These communities were a bit remote from the center of town, but they afforded its residents slightly lower temperatures and more sea breeze in a pre-air-conditioned Havana. Granted, many of these new neighborhoods had "climate-controlled" homes by the 1950s, but the new subdivisions provided access to resident-owned houses and isolation from the run-down city center. The higher elevations also implied a sense of prestige for being located "above" the rest of the city. Still other names carried chic or European labels: Havana Biltmore, Nuevo Biltmore, La Playa (Beach), Playa Miramar, and Club Náutico. Others simply carried the name of the owner of the land or the developer, such as Embil, De Beche, Parcelación Zayas, or Querejeta.

Havana's crude birth rate in 1958 was fairly high (21.3 live per births per 1,000 population), even though it was less than in rural areas (28). High fertility levels in the capital probably resulted from rural and small-town immigrants who were driven by unemployment and misery. Thus, Havana's proportion of the national population rose from 19.8 percent in 1943, to 21 percent in 1953, to 20.9 percent in 1958 (table 3.1).

TABLE 3.1. Population Growth of Havana and Cuba, 1899–1958

| YEAR | HAVANA | CUBA | HAVANA'S PERCENTAGE |
|------|--------|------|---------------------|
| 1899 | 235,981[a] | 1,572,797[b] | 15.0 |
| 1907 | 302,526[a] | 2,048,980[b] | 14.8 |
| 1919 | 363,506[a] | 2,889,004[b] | 12.6 |
| 1931 | 728,500[c] | 3,962,344[c] | 18.4[c] |
| 1943 | 946,000[c] | 4,778,583[c] | 19.8[c] |
| 1953 | 1,223,900[c] | 5,829,029[c] | 21.0[c] |
| 1958 | 1,361,600[a] | 6,548,300[a] | 20.9 |

*Sources*: (a) "Habana 1" 1971; (b) *Anuario Demográfico* 1989; (c) CEE 1983.
*Note*: Population data for Havana in the 1931, 1943, and 1953 censuses refer to the former municipalities of the present city of Havana (Ciudad de la Habana) and have been adjusted to reflect the present city of Havana. Percentages, where no source is indicated, are calculated by the authors.

The new and growing city of the 1950s had increased 5.7-fold between 1898 (population 240,000) and 1958 (1.36 million in Greater Havana). By the triumph of the revolution, one of five Cubans lived in Havana. The capital grew in the 1940s and 1950s at the fastest rate in the nation owing to an upgraded road network and improved automobile and bus transportation connecting Havana with the rest of the country. Although population growth had been fairly sluggish around the turn of the century, it shot up with the frenzied high-price sugar years discussed in the previous chapter (called "*vacas gordas*," or "fat cows") until it reached 560,000 residents by 1925. Population growth stabilized during the Great Depression but then continued in the postwar period. Contributing to this growth was a broadening job market in the metropolitan area, including light industry on the city's outskirts, the construction industry, and suburbanization (Segre 1978). Havana experienced an astounding growth of 43.9 percent (415,600) between 1943 and 1953. It grew by an average annual growth rate of 2.6 percent during this same period, versus the national rate of 2.19 percent. Between 1953 and 1959, the respective annual growth rates for the capital and nation were 3.0 percent and 2.3 percent ("Habana 1" 1971). Within the capital city, though, population growth at the city's edge was 75 percent greater during 1953–59 than in the city center. It was not until 1966 that Havana's overall growth rate would fall below the national level ("Habana 2" 1973).

Suburban developments spread along the western side of the Almendares

River and southward to the Alturas de Miramar and Kohly. When that prime realty became occupied, newer homes were built to the west in Playa, which shared a boundary with the most affluent areas: Country Club (now Cubanacán), Biltmore (currently Siboney), and Alturas de Biltmore (now Atabey). These latter two were completed in the 1950s. During that same decade, land speculation around the Civic Center led to the creation of Nuevo Vedado along the eastern shore of the Almendares River.

High-priced condominium construction increased the density of the central districts. Part of this central-city revitalization by the elite took place in Vedado, which in the 1950s still retained its prestige as an elegant neighborhood (Entenza y Jova 1953). In Cerro, however, where elite neoclassical residences sprang up earlier than in Vedado, such residential allure had already disappeared by that time. While westward elite suburbanization ensued, the Condominium Law (Ley de Propiedad Horizontal) of 1952 allowed the wealthy to resettle in parts of the central district (Bugeda Lanzas 1954). Elite housing along the ocean was not new, having begun in the 1920s with the opening up of Miramar. However, the 1952 law enabled structures greater than six stories to be built along the Malecón in Vedado, permanently transforming the city's skyline. These same buildings are still standing along a strip of land from the Malecón in Vedado and inland several blocks.

This type of oceanfront land speculation was bound to deprive the city not only of prime public space and panoramic views but also of cooling sea breezes. This calamity was indirectly avoided by the 1959 revolution, as it stopped land speculation. The revolution also brought to end the 1955–58 master plan by José Luis Sert (see Chapter 2) to establish a great artificial island with hotels and casinos just off the shores of Centro Habana. His plans were supported not only by the island's elite but also by the gangster-driven investment of Meyer Lansky and Santos Trafficante, who were portrayed in Francis Ford Coppola's film *The Godfather II.*

The city's vocation as a tourist center was too strong not to leave some imprint on the landscape. The 1950s ushered in a new wave of modern-style hotels throughout the bustling Rampa section of Vedado: Habana Riviera, Havana Hilton (fig. 3.6), Capri, St. John, Vedado, Flamingo, and Colina.[2] Hotels

---

2. The Havana Hilton has been a major city landmark since it was built in 1958, if only because of its size. It became the Habana Libre in the early years of the revolution, then the Habana Libre-Guitart (after a Spanish investment group) between 1993 and 1995, and then again the Habana Libre in 1996. Chapter 8 discusses more fully the recent wave of Spanish investment in Havana's tourist industry.

were built in the western edge of the city and extended as far west as Barlovento (today the Hemingway Marina), including Comodoro, Copacabana, and Chateau Miramar. These facilities, directed mainly at the U.S. tourist market, contrasted with the more stately and elegant hotels of a bygone era: Hotel Nacional (fig. 3.7), Hotel Sevilla, and Hotel Plaza. The Hotel Nacional would occupy a prominent role in Havana's landscape because of its premier location on a bluff overlooking the ocean. As Vedado grew and became the premier tourist district of Havana, the Hotel Nacional came to anchor the area around Malecón and Twenty-third Street. The lively strip starting there is known as La Rampa (literally, "the slope," because it was one of the few steep hills in the city center).

These hotels supported an extensive network of internationally recognized ancillary services. More to the west and right by the Belén school, the Tropicana cabaret was among the most widely recognized tourist haunts and was satirized in Guillermo Cabrera Infante's celebrated book *Three Trapped Tigers* (*Tres Tristes Tigres*). As the story begins, the emcee dutifully recognizes the club's celebrated visitors. After introducing a famous movie star, he then presents a U.S. businessman, first in English, then in Spanish, to the local patrons:

> I would like to welcome some old friends to this palace of happiness. . . . Less beautiful but as rich and as famous is our very good friend and frequent guest of Tropicana, the wealthy and healthy (he is an earlier riser) Mr. William Campbell, the notorious soup-fortune heir and world champion indoor golf and indoor tennis (and other not so mentionable indoor sports — ha ha ha!). Mr. Campbell, our favorite playboy! Lights (Thank you Mr. Campbell), lights, lights, lights! Thanks so much, Mr. Campbell! (*Amableypacientepúblicocubanoes Mister Campbell elfamosomillonario herederodeunafortunaensopas.*). (Cabrera Infante 1971, 5)

There were restaurants, such as Sloppy Joe's Bar, La Bodeguita del Medio, El Floridita, and the Terraza de Cojímar, whose patrons included Ernest Hemingway and other celebrities (Fuentes 1987). The array of culinary options was indeed surprising for a Caribbean city of such modest size. French, Italian, Basque, Andalucian, Cantonese, Jewish, and North American fare was available, not to mention the more modestly priced hamburgers (*fritas*) and oyster kiosks. These popular stands carried the ubiquitous sugarcane juice, *guarapo*, and Cuban coffee called *tres quilos* (literally "three cents," its price). A small and attractive theater, Auditorium, featured some of the greatest figures in the world's classical music scene. Auditorium was located in front of

FIGURE 3.6.
Havana Hilton (in background), built in 1958 and renamed the Habana Libre in the early years of the revolution. Many American cars of the same era still circulate throughout the city. (Photograph by Joseph L. Scarpaci)

Parque Villalón and the elegant café El Carmelo, on Calzada Street. Seedier places existed too, ranging from the questionable bars of Playa de Marianao (where the popular local band El Chori and film star Marlon Brando could be found) to the squalid pornographic theater, Shangai, located in Havana's Chinatown.

## Havana's Built Cultural Heritage and Architecture in the 1950s

The modern movement in architecture sheepishly made its appearance in Cuba in the 1940s (Rogers, Sert, and Tyrwhitt 1961). It arrived as art deco was waning, and it initially coexisted with the short-lived modern monumental movement (fig. 3.8). It was not until the 1940s that the modern movement took firm hold in Cuban cities, especially Havana (Rodríguez 1996). The rationalist codes of the modernist European masters—Le Corbusier, Gropius, Neutra, Breuer, and, most of all, Mies—had arrived in Cuba from the United

FIGURE 3.7. Hotel Nacional overlooking the Malecón and the Florida Straits in Vedado. Built in 1930, it was closed for more than two decades during the revolution, but then it was modernized in the early 1990s and reopened. (Photograph by Joseph L. Scarpaci)

States in a steady procession. This detour through the north gave the Cuban version influences such as Wright's organic architecture, the purist minimalist style of the magazine *Arts and Architecture*, and pseudocolonial touches mixed with influences from the California mission style springing up in American suburbs.

The Latin American vanguard in architecture at the time—mainly contemporary Brazilian and Mexican architects, along with the works of Carlos Raúl Villanueva of Venezuela—had strong influences in Cuba. Latin American styles and movements afforded younger Cuban architects a competing paradigm for shaking off the growing commercialism in Cuba (Segre 1970a, 1970b). This meant synthesizing the international with the Cuban, a process that some Cuban architects had pursued in the 1940s. Not surprisingly, the modern movement had a different impact in the United States than in Cuba. In the United States, most projects built in this style were relegated to industrial complexes and prominent downtown office buildings. In Havana, the modern movement played a formidable role in shaping the look of entire residential districts.

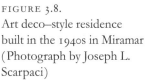

FIGURE 3.8.
Art deco–style residence
built in the 1940s in Miramar
(Photograph by Joseph L.
Scarpaci)

Yet most buildings erected in Cuba in the 1950s were done without an architect. At one extreme, the poor worked on their homes (self-help construction), while the affluent lived in high-rise condominiums that were designed by builders who would simply find an architect to "sign off" on the proper paperwork. It was not uncommon, for instance, to see such practices take place during a friendly domino game in the Colegio de Arquitectos (Institute of Architects).

Perhaps the most striking feature of Havana's built environment in the 1950s was that there was little demolition and substitution of its existing urban fabric, as the upper class preferred to move out from neighborhoods threatened by congestion and social mixture rather than demolish and build anew in the same place. Havana was spared devastating hurricanes for the most part, and it was not exposed to earthquakes, which are so prevalent in Mexico, Central America, Peru, or Chile (Lezama 1994; Scarpaci 1994). The net effect was to preserve a valuable stock of buildings that spanned the city's historical periods, architectural styles, and social classes. Although UNESCO declared Habana Vieja and the adjacent fortresses in 1982 a World Heritage Site, a greater cultural value perhaps rests with the enormous stock of twentieth-century buildings. A visual appreciation of the different historical periods of construction appears in the three-dimensional model of Havana on display at the Grupo para el Desarrollo Integral de la Capital in Miramar whereby distinct periods of construction are represented using a color-coded scheme. The ochre-colored buildings symbolize those that were erected between 1900 and 1958. These buildings, which hail mostly from an architectural period called "lean cow" architecture, are characteristic of eclecticism.

The bulk of this construction took place in the first three decades of the twentieth century. It is a design much simpler than the ostentatious decorations of the great eclectic architecture found among major single projects. Because this "minor Eclecticism" extended into large sectors of the city, it was more of a determinant in shaping the look of Cuban cities including Havana than the valuable built heritage composed of prebaroque, baroque, and neoclassical buildings (Coyula 1987). Thus, the cultural heritage of Havana's built environment sets it apart from most Latin American cities. It is unique in its physical and temporal expanse and in the variety of marked architectural styles that survive today. Although many of the city's buildings have deteriorated over four and a half centuries, Havana displays an impressive record of building construction. Its wide array of styles includes the important modern movement of the 1950s and the introduction of brutalism at the decade's end. Nevertheless, this valuable built stock had not been conserved, and some of it had been abandoned. Before the 1959 revolution, preservation was limited to a few passionate connoisseurs who concentrated on a few buildings rather than entire neighborhoods. Private patrons sponsored historic preservation, but there was no support from the government, the general population, or even the average architect.

The financial center of twentieth-century Havana remained in Habana Vieja. Large banks, the stock market (*bolsa de valores*), and attorneys' offices formed a tropical imitation of Wall Street. Modest skyscrapers that could have easily been found in Chicago or New York had appeared by the 1950s. A floating day population of office workers and shoppers filled the district's streets, as did faithful clients from a bygone era who routinely shopped at the once European-like stores along Obispo Street. Those shoppers refused to patronize the growing retail centers nearby that were anchored by U.S.-like department stores on Galiano and San Rafael Streets. The wares of the Jewish merchants along Muralla Street attracted shoppers looking for bargains. Yet alongside this humming retail and service activity, the sordid and progressive degeneration of Habana Vieja could not be hidden.

In the 1940s the main commercial center moved nearby, west of the old city, along the portico-adorned street of Galiano. Streets intersecting with Galiano, such as San Rafael and Neptuno, were also important retail centers. The European-style shops and small storefronts were replaced with "modern," U.S.-style department stores. The new, larger retail outlets catered to as many tastes as income groups, and their products were differentiated by both quality and the social prestige brought by the department store's location. The flashing window displays of El Encanto, a leading department store that was destroyed in 1961 by arson in support of the imminent Bay of Pigs invasion, contrasted with the modest but well-stocked items found in the department stores along Calzada de Monte.

By the 1950s, the "center" of Havana could no longer be described as either linear or nodal. Instead, it had spread across several commercial subcenters. A common and inexpensive evening activity was to stroll through the streets, window-shop, and browse through the stores. The center encapsulated the concept of "city": to residents who lived fairly close to the city center, to speak about "going shopping" (*ir de tiendas*) meant "going to Havana."[3]

This area of Centro Habana still held the lion's share of the commercial activity of the 1950s despite competition from another new center, La Rampa, located just 2 kilometers west in Vedado. Although La Rampa had very few stores, it contained many restaurants, clubs, cafeterias, and offices. Centro Habana remained the city's commercial district and survived after the revolution, despite its visual deterioration. By the late 1960s, some shops were haphazardly being converted to housing units, while others closed. The overall quality and variety of merchandise dropped quickly, too. Family dwellings originally located over the stores were not kept up and became run down. These

---

3. The busy intersection of Galiano and San Rafael Streets earned the nickname "the Corner of Sin." "Respectable" gentlemen would frequent stores where attractive female store clerks worked, and, allegedly, the prestige of a store was determined by the attractiveness of its clerks. This district was a popular socializing place for young people in the 1950s.

changes notwithstanding, the region characterizes many noteworthy features of a city center.

La Rampa developed quickly between 1947 and 1958—with some streetscape improvements in 1963 and the construction of a fine and often neglected exhibition pavilion, Pabellón Cuba—as a transition zone between Vedado and Centro Habana. La Rampa was popular because it was close to upper-income homes in Vedado and Miramar. It boasted a distinctive modern flavor and a mixture of functions and land uses: movie houses, theaters, art galleries, restaurants, cafeterias, offices, bars, and parks. These locational attributes complemented the cosmopolitan flavor of a large cluster of hotels, which Centro Habana sorely lacked.

In the early 1950s construction began on the much contested Plaza Cívica (Civic Center) with its public spaces and monumental buildings that housed only the state bureaucracy (Estévez 1953). To many professionals and ordinary citizens, though, the design carried symbolism that was too obvious and imposing. Building this amorphous and heavy complex, just a kilometer from La Rampa, put an end to Forestier's plan for a land reserve to be part of the proposed Parque Metropolitano. In the end, the Plaza Cívica project left only about one-quarter of land originally designated for the park.

At least three problems—design, semiotics, and contract bidding—plagued the Plaza Cívica project from the outset. The Palacio de Justicia (Justice Palace; José Pérez Benitoa, architect; 1957), a prominent element in the plan, was a structure of mastodonic proportions. Transformed in the late 1960s as the Palacio de la Revolución, it looked like a Creole rendition of a classic-modern Mussolinesque building in L'EUR 42 (Esposizione Universale di Roma, 1942). At its side stood the lamentable monument to Cuba's national hero, José Martí. Ironically, the obelisk from the Martí Monument was a copy of a Schenley Whiskey advertisement that appeared in the 1939 World's Fair in New York. These two structures—the Palacio de Justicia and the Martí Monument—depict the authoritarian and hierarchical view held by the promoters of these plans. Land preparation and contract tendering were mired by dirty back-room deals involving land speculation, kickbacks, and payoffs from a corrupt state apparatus. The obvious correlation between this Fascist-like architecture and town planning, on the one hand, and the hundreds of men and women killed and tortured by the Batista regime, on the other, stands as a painful reminder of the dirty side of Havana in the 1950s.

# The Inherited City: The Dawn of 1959

The revolution inherited an abnormally large capital city of a small underdeveloped nation. The nation both resented and admired Havana. Cuba was situated relatively high on the Latin American development scale and even more so within the Third World (Ginsberg 1961). Havana was the most important city in the Caribbean basin and among the most attractive in the Americas. Its economy displayed a decidedly tertiary character with a vocation for services, especially tourism. All this was situated in a favorable setting with the bay, shoreline, and its expansive eastern beaches.

Havana in 1959 was a sprawling, low-rise city. Urban sprawl had absorbed neighboring settlements that at the same time managed to maintain their character. This cultural patrimony covered the city's architectural history: prebaroque, baroque, Spanish colonial, art noveau, eclecticism, art deco, modern monumental, neocolonial, rationalism, organic architecture, and brutalism. At the same time, this heritage represented both an important cultural and utilitarian value and highlighted the presence of a broad middle and lower middle class that aspired to live within the norms of bourgeois decorum.

If Havana was a unique collection of the island's architectural and economic history etched into its built environment, it was also a city of great contradictions. Rich and poor, beautiful and ugly, modern and old, lazy and pragmatic—all these faces were apparent from practically any vantage point. To be sure, Havana was *criolla*, but with a greater Spanish and American influence than other Spanish American capitals. Social classes were clearly differentiated, but more by their economic status than by birth. Racial discrimination closed access to social and occupational mobility for blacks and created slums. On the other hand, discrimination lessened somewhat in matters of art, music, and poetry; most of those media conjured up images of an exotic, dark-skinned tropical sensuality. Miscegenation (*mestizaje*) found a popular outlet for the syncretic Afro-Cuban cults, consensual unions, and vernacular humor (*choteo*).

The central districts of Havana displayed high-population densities and a curious mix of physical and social diversity. High-order services such as banking and tourism at times gave this area a veneer of social integration. However, that pretense disappeared in the low-population densities and open spaces of elite suburban communities. The cost of a quieter lifestyle meant losing the noisy yet vital mixture of Havana's urban culture. Havana's traditional centers were actually a chain of connected districts that were supported by growing yet well-defined secondary centers pushing out toward the city limits.

Havana was a city of disproportions in the way it looked, its open spaces and work sites, and its services. Havana exhibited inequalities between its center and periphery as well as with urban and social decay that had begun in the most congested central areas. It was an attractive, fascinating city while also cynical, a bit laid back, and gullible. Havana awoke expectant that first day of January.

# Socialist Havana

## Planning, Dreams, and Reality

> One hears about the end of history, the end of ideology, and even
> the demise of architecture. . . . Maybe these outcomes will come
> about through the miraculous resurrection of a superior man, phi-
> losophy, and architecture.
> —Luis Lápidus, *Patrimonio y herencia del siglo XX en Cuba*, 1995

## The Magic of Change

The year 1958 ended with a chain of takeovers by the Rebel Army. On December 31 the important city of Santa Clara fell to the 26th of July Movement
and the Directorio Revolucionario. The dictator, Batista, after celebrating
the new year with champagne, shamelessly fled in an airplane with a small
band of his rogues. More than almost the decade of the 1950s came to an end
on January 1, 1959 (Coyula 2000b). Cuba, and indeed Havana, had reached a
watershed that separated two important periods: that before and after the triumph of the revolution.

Havana in 1959 had changed in ways unforeseen a decade before. Central
districts had increased in density with building subdivisions and the reconstruction of improvised lofts and attics. Curiously, this population was attached to its dilapidated dwellings and neighborhoods because the revolutionary laws stopped evictions and mandated that residents of tenement
houses not pay rent.

The elite corners of the city also changed. Elegant neighborhoods such as
Miramar were almost completely abandoned by their owners. Bourgeois mansions were converted into schools and dormitories for thousands of children
on scholarships who marched in orderly lines along Fifth Avenue, imitating
the marches by the light-blue-shirted worker militias. Even the lobby of the

old Havana Hilton (renamed Habana Libre) lost its flashy doorman who wore a feathered helmet. In its wake, the lobby had become a sort of bubble-roofed town square "whose vitality and movement shined throughout its rounded area and even became a festive and commemorative symbol of the entire city" (Segre 1989, 62; our translation). The most diverse characters rubbed elbows there, while the Malecón, just a few blocks from the Habana Libre, was silhouetted by black antiaircraft guns pointing upward.

One coffeehouse, El Carmelo de Calle Calzada, briefly hosted a social mosaic of patrons who flocked to it to enjoy the best ice cream in the city. From this would emerge the famous Coppelia ice cream that gave rise to the Coppelia parlor discussed in Chapter 8. Former members of the Yacht Club and Vedado Tennis who had not yet gone into exile would sit at their regular tables. Proud waiters would look pejoratively at the new clients who were dressed in clothing purchased at the low-quality stores along Monte Street. Those shabbily dressed patrons arrived mesmerized at this Havana "Mecca" of such elegant consumption and *dolce far niente*, located across the street from the most beautiful "park" (actually, a one-block city square planted with trees, the so-called republican park) in Vedado. This was the setting of Alejo Carpentier's novelette *El Acoso*. Here, too, gathered balletgoers, who would heatedly comment on the fine points of a ballet *foueté* while they observed with snobbish curiosity the latest vestiges of the Creole upper class or become comically alarmed by the extemporaneous nature of a bearded rebel soldier with hand grenades hanging from his belt.

The casting of this new collection of social characters was enriched by a group of young readers of the cultural supplement *Lunes de Revolución*. These youth were ardent fans of the recently created Cinemateca and would sit there discussing recent recitals of poems by the Chilean poet Pablo Neruda. Only a few tables would separate them from the balletgoers, and they might ostensibly turn their back toward them, for they were deemed silly and superficial. These young intellectuals would be enthralled over the next film of Tomás Gutiérrez Alea, and they would inevitably call him by his nickname, Titón (Titan), to impress those who might be eavesdropping. As the evening progressed, an elite group coming from a midnight concert at the Auditorium would cross the street after having heard the vibrant piano and the hoarse voice of the well-known Bola de Nieve. Seated at yet another table at the café one could find Cuban writers and friends who might have frequented the Casa de las Américas, such as Edmundo Desnoes, Lisandro Otero, or Ambrosio Fornet, quietly chatting with the Argentine writer Julio ( Peruvian author Mario Vargas Llosa.

Aside from the well-known street character "el Caballero c "Gentleman from Paris"), other famous people also frequen The preposterous Marquesa aggressively pan-handled while the minded Juan Charrasqueado would guard his alluring figure underneath a large Mexican sombrero, while singing *corridos* (tunes) for the legendary Rebel Army *comandante* Efigenio Ameijeiras. Another *comandante*, Rolando Cubelas, displayed his splendid reddish beard in the same place where just two years earlier a clean-shaven Cubelas had conversed with his friends from Vedado Tennis. This impossible mixture of people, confined to some 300 square meters, encapsulates what Graham Greene had in mind when he said that Havana was a place where anything could happen.

During the first months of the revolution, crowds who supported the accelerated political changes expressed their gratitude by displaying signs that read "Gracias Fidel." A wide spectrum of citizens shared this exuberance, ranging from a slum dweller in the center of the city, to a public employee in a government ministry, to university students, agricultural workers, waiters, and even the owner of a sugar mill ("Informe Central al XIV Congreso de la Central de Trabajadores de Cuba" 1978).

The euphoria of the postrevolutionary period, however, was short lived. In the same way in which the democratic-bourgeoisie revolution changed quickly to a socialist revolution, the confiscation of misappropriated goods and property of the *batistianos*, landholders, industrialists, and merchants signaled deep structural changes ahead. According to estimates made by the U.S. government, the value of North American property confiscated in Cuba amounted to $1.85 billion. Of the 5,911 officially received claims made by the United States, 86 percent of that total value was held by thirty-eight businesses or corporations. If we add to this the property of Cubans who subsequently became U.S. citizens—which was the pretext of the Helms-Burton bill for tightening the U.S. embargo in 1996—the figure would reach approximately $7 billion more (Pita 1995). Ricardo Alarcón, the current president of the National Assembly, claims that the figure might actually be hundreds of billions of dollars. The enormous discrepancy further underscores the difficulty in sharpening the accuracy of these estimates and the great weight that those nationalizations had in financing the early social benefits provided by the revolution.

## The First Revolutionary Laws

Law 35, enacted on March 10, 1959, lowered rents by 50 percent. That law transferred from landlords to salaried workers and farmers about 15 percent of the national income (Chaffee 1992). In April, land-use regulations were implemented and were complemented on December 23, 1959, by Law 691 (see also table 6.1). This law, also called *solares yermos* (vacant lots), established a very low and fixed price of 4 pesos per square meter for urban land. In doing so, it ended land speculation (Fernández 1996). In May 1959 the First Agrarian Reform Law expropriated the holdings of large plantation owners (*latifundistas*). Most of these large landowners were absentee landlords who rented their lands to those who worked them. The new law established a maximum property size of just 402 hectares, a limit that would be further reduced in 1963 to 67.1 hectares by the Second Agrarian Reform Law. As a result, state control increased to 70 percent of all arable lands.

In addition to these measures, other state actions changed the island during the first year of the triumph of the revolution (Séneca 1976). They included intervention in the Cuban Telephone Company (actually North American), the lowering of electrical utility rates, the creation of National Revolutionary Militias, and the opening up of public beaches and private clubs, all of which created a considerable uproar. However, these actions moved in tandem with a campaign of support for national industry and other declarations that reaffirmed the "Cubanness" (*lo cubano*) of the revolution. A climate of confusion grew among the Cuban bourgeoisie, who believed that the United States would ultimately intervene to thwart efforts by the young revolutionaries. By July 1959, however, the more conservative Cubans in the new government had been removed from important positions. The very wealthy, preceded by the small Jewish community, began accepting the idea of emigration in the hope that it would be a short one.

The second year of the revolution would be like the first. In August 1960, thirty-six sugar mills and North American oil refineries were nationalized. In October of that year banks and more than three hundred large firms also suffered the same fate. During this same period, the Committees for the Defense of the Revolution (Comités para la Defensa de la Revolución [CDR]) were established at the neighborhood level throughout the island. Private schools were taken over by the state, and religious education ended even though the churches were kept open. Some parents, fearing the loss of legal custody of their children, sent them alone to the United States. These youngsters became a part of Operation Peter Pan, and many of them never returned to see their family.

Meanwhile, the climate of internal confrontation escalated. The middle class, ideologically divided, increasingly opted for exile or blended a mixture of anguish and hope that would ultimately carry as much weight as reason. The opposition resorted to help from the United States, hoping to create a base for the invasion of the island. Brigade 2506 invaded the Bay of Pigs (Playa Girón) in April 1961. Acts of sabotage in the city such as the burning of the famous Havana department store El Encanto were tied to the anti-Communist uprising in some rural parts of Cuba, principally in the Escambray mountains in south-central Cuba.

Although we discuss housing in greater detail in Chapter 6, it will be useful to identify briefly its status in the early years of the revolution and its relationship with state planning. The Self-Help and Mutual Aid program began in 1960 as a way to find solutions for the eighty thousand housing units that were in poor condition. Construction was managed by the Ministry of Public Works, while the Ministry of Social Welfare carried out the social research and mobilized the population. This program began with the eradication of the Manzana de Gómez neighborhood in Santiago de Cuba. Officials in the capital cleared the large shantytowns of Llega y Pon, Las Yaguas, and La Cueva del Humo as well as the notorious Carreño Building just 50 meters away from La Rampa (Menéndez 1992). These residents were relocated in five new complexes in the neighborhoods of Perla, Martí, and Zamora. Many families continued being taken care of after their relocation. The new housing complexes contained between 100 and 150 units and included a school and medical clinic. Each family volunteered twenty-four hours weekly for work, and the unemployed received small stipends (Fernández Núñez 1976).

This program was quickly abandoned, and the Ministry of Social Welfare was dissolved in 1961. Critics of Self-Help and Mutual Aid had charged since the beginning of the program that it maintained social marginality by relocating entire communities, creating little stability, low productivity, and poor-quality construction. Data on the number of neighborhoods that were eradicated and housing units built through this means vary among authors: 4,700 units would include the eradication of 33 shantytowns with 20,000 residents (Segre 1989). Others (Hamberg 1986) place the figure at 40 neighborhoods; yet another (Fernández Núñez 1976) documents some 400 units. The differences in these figures reflect not only the lack of data at a time when the present seemed to last forever but also different foci and opinions among officials and scholars (see also Hamberg 1994). Taken in its entirety, this uncertainty adds even more to the curiosity some thirty-five years later about what might have occurred had the program continued.

The truth, it would seem, is that this strategy of dealing with Havana's housing and planning problems offered possibilities that were not taken full advantage of because the same measures were not consistently used (Baroni 1994a, 1994b). Planning gave little importance to social work and exaggerated the role of centralized programs that supposedly had solutions that could be repeated and generalized everywhere. Ironically, despite the early evidence regarding new technologies, little opportunity was actually provided for their experimentation.

If the eradication of Havana's shantytowns is to be commended, it is important to note other problems that appeared in its aftermath. Immigrants from the rest of the island as well as those who were displaced within the city of Havana lacked adequate housing. Havana's historic attraction drew to it rebel soldiers, farmers who were welcomed in their homes by *habaneros* as part of a state-sponsored campaign, and others who occupied the homes of those who left the island. Havana also received the families of thousands of Cubans who earned scholarships and who had come from the provinces to study in the city. In this way, neighborhoods such as El Romerillo and La Corbata, located near the Columbia military base, developed. The neighborhood of Atarés, located on the slopes of the old colonial castle, also attracted immigrants, as did La Güinera, located near an important hospital.

## The Physical Framework and Population: Change and Continuity

The reuse of the elegant newer places such as Country Club, Miramar, Kohly, and Nuevo Vedado—practically vacated by the bourgeoisie—generated a situation of privilege for their new residents. Newcomers to these former elite neighborhoods benefited greatly once these districts were identified as a "frozen zone." This meant that it served as a housing reserve for high-level government officials, schools and dormitories, dignitaries, foreign experts, and diplomats. What changed the class character most, aside from the schools, was the assignment of housing to low-income people (Hamberg 1994). Nonetheless, the level of physical segregation by different socioeconomic groups that the revolution had inherited slowly dissipated.

Since the 1959 revolution, the neighborhoods in which the ruling class had resided have lost their charm. Isolation, physical and social deterioration, and difficult accessibility by vehicles plague these neighborhoods. Central city functions have also changed. With the cautious opening of market forces, the Miramar neighborhood is once again adapting itself to major changes. The old boardinghouses, mansions, and shelters that were used for students who had scholarships back in the early years of the revolution are now being refurbished with hard currencies. Revitalization efforts strive to accommodate new business offices and joint-venture operations even though the traditional commercial center (Centro Habana) shows empty stores and precariously adapted housing in substandard buildings.

Land use in Miramar still includes the presence of embassies and housing for foreigners, some Cuban government officials, and ordinary citizens. Some former servants of the upper class remained in Miramar illegally despite the area's being designated as Zona Congelada (frozen zone) with a very tight control over the housing stock. However, there is an unprecedented surge in retail outlets for Cuban and foreign shoppers with hard currency (the so-called *diplotiendas*), as well as new joint-venture offices (Scarpaci 1996a). High-level Cuban government officials and research centers coexist with those who moved into empty dwellings in the 1960s and 1970s. One can still find among this latter group many of the workers and home attendants who worked in the student boardinghouses. These include the well-known *tías* (literally "aunts," but actually they were maids) and caretakers who initially occupied the back garages and maids' rooms of their former employers and then eventually took over the entire mansions. Relatives from the countryside joined them later and lived in the many rooms of these spacious homes. In this regard, Miramar has become the Havana neighborhood with the greatest change since the triumph of the revolution. The beautiful image of Fifth Avenue (Quinta Avenida) has been kept practically the same, though there is less automobile traffic today than in 1958. Although traffic has declined, an increase in the number of bicyclists who tenaciously pedal through the city has compensated for this loss. Although Fifth Avenue is a four-lane road with a central raised promenade shaded by trees that could make up for the best bikeway in Havana, cyclists, large buses, and parking are not allowed, probably for security reasons, as government motorcades often use the road. In the early 2000s, more cars are moving through Miramar, mostly related to the new dollar economy that has clustered there. New Japanese, Korean, and French cars are displacing the ancient American gas-guzzling ones and the Russian-made Ladas and Moskvichs.

## A Revolution in Stages

Five stages characterize urban and regional planning since the triumph of the revolution: 1959–63, from the First to the Second Agrarian Reform Law; 1964–70, from the Second Agrarian Reform Law to the Great Harvest; 1971–75, the Great Harvest to the First Five-Year Plan; 1976–86, the Five-Year Plans; and 1987 until the present, the Process of the Correction of Mistakes and the Special Period. We briefly highlight these stages as they apply to Havana.

### LAND FOR ALL, LAND FOR NO ONE: 1959–1963

The first stage witnessed the seizure of power by the most radical sectors of the revolutionary movement, and the socialization process accelerated through the nationalization of the means of production and the Agrarian Reform Laws. During that period both economic and military aggressions were unleashed against Cuba. Chief among these events were the Bay of Pigs Invasion, the Cuban missile crisis, the uprising of anti-Communist guerrillas in the Escambray Mountains (the "cleansing of Escambray") and other areas, and the North American blockade. Bellicose actions like these spurred investment in Cuba's military, and defense assumed a high priority. The suspension of the sugar quota and shipments of petroleum from the United States in retaliation for Cuba's nationalizations were offset by aid and trade from the Soviet Union. This began a profound change in the Cuban economy that would last some thirty years. Not only did this lead to economic and political repercussions throughout the country, but it also included cultural changes. Although Spanish names prevailed, many children were named Yuri or Vladimir instead of American names such as Frank and Johnny that were common before the revolution. After the collapse of the Soviet Union, these names were one of the few remainders of a thirty-year lapse of close economic, political, and ideological ties. A new generation of impossible names has taken over, the Misleidys and Ihosvanys that correspond to loud music and colors and distortions of the traditional streetscape. Revolutionary Cuba's initial development strategy was profoundly rural oriented. It focused on quickly eliminating the inherent inequality between city and countryside. Development projects during this first stage included the construction of 26,000 units of housing, highway paving in remote areas, and the construction of schools and medical facilities in the countryside. Approximately 150 new rural villages were built in the early 1960s, initially by the efforts of the Rebel Army (1959–60) and later by the Rural Housing Department (Viviendas Campesinas) at the National Institute of Agrarian Reform.

National policy during this stage attempted to overcome Cuba's historical dependence on monoculture and a single market. This was to be achieved through a program of agricultural diversification and accelerated industrialization. Both goals were tied to the social objective of eliminating unemployment. However, many of the new jobs were not always in productive activities. That fact, coupled with the effects of centralizing government, created a structural framework that had negative outcomes.

In 1962, the first annual economic plan was enacted, and so began the field of physical planning. The initial task of physical planning concentrated on locating agricultural investments and restructuring state farms. Physical planners conducted preliminary studies for creating new regions throughout Cuba. One year later, Havana's first master plan was executed and became the first ever in revolutionary Cuba.

## WITHOUT SUGAR THERE IS NO HOMELAND: 1964–1970

During the second stage, planners attempted to review critically the excessive optimism of the previous phase. Between 1959 and 1963, planning did not take into account the scarcity of materials or financial and human resources. Rising costs in the defense field and the lack of support infrastructure (road networks, ports, warehouses, electrification) had been impediments. As a result, the second stage directed efforts toward creating infrastructure and finding ways to increase development potential. Agricultural production, especially sugarcane, topped the list. It was in this realm that Cuba had historically been the major world exporter. There was no denying the veracity of a popular phrase among the bourgeoisie during the republican period: "Without sugar there is no homeland." Agricultural and food-processing industries entered the state's priority list, as did investments for warehouses, energy production, port installations, fertilizers, and cement for the building trades.

Despite the sobering realism that supposedly would correct the previous excess of optimism, the second stage was also overwhelmed by the search for quick results. This philosophy was guided by the metaphor of the turnpike model—a limited access beltway—that assumed that the best road to reach a destination is not necessarily the most direct (Hamilton 1992). The 1964–70 period prompted a great debate about the way to construct socialism: Should it be gradual or in successive stages? Should Cuba follow the theoretical premises derived from the French economist Charles Bettelheim, which were supported in Cuba by orthodox Marxist and Soviet advisers and the countries of Eastern Europe? Bettelheim favored a "market socialism" based on self-financing state firms as a way to obtain an objective material base that could sustain the social justice agenda of the revolution.

A more radical line of action focused on the inequalities that a policy of material rewards in the production system might create. This line of thinking held that the production system could indeed increase in a way that would appeal to the collective interests of Cuban workers through moral incentives. Such a perspective entailed a highly centralized government overseeing a state budget that would allocate resources by a plan and not by following the laws of the marketplace. This vision required the creation of "the new man" espoused by Che Guevara in his book *Socialism and Man in Cuba*. Che's work reflected his interest in the Chinese experience and how it could be interpreted by the revolutionary Cuban vanguard. His treatise also included the realistic conclusion that low economic productivity in Cuba would not create sufficient components to be used as material incentives for workers. In the end, Fidel Castro chose a third path that incorporated some of the ideas of Bettelheim and Guevara (Castro 1965a, 1965b; Boorstein 1968; Bettelheim 1969).

In 1968, the revolutionary offensive eliminated the rest of commerce and services that still remained in private hands. This was the time of the Agricultural Command Post (Puestos de Mando de la Agricultura). In this model, administrators, technicians, workers, housewives, and students dressed in rural workers' clothes would leave Havana to work in the countryside. It was in this setting that the Havana Greenbelt (Cordón de La Habana), an ambitious belt of more than 10,000 hectares of fruit trees, pigeon peas, and coffee, began. These lands would feed the capital. To carry out the Greenbelt project, lands were purchased from scattered farmers, and hundreds of new homes were built for them using Sandino technology (lightweight prefabricated structures with walls of columns and small concrete panels). Each unit was equipped with small self-consumption lots: the microplans. This was the epic of "special plans," "extraplans" and "microplans," which sometimes became more important than the overall development plan. In some cases, the new settlements included a mere thirty or so housing units.

Despite the great promotion of the volunteer project, these efforts did not have proportional outcomes. The pigeon peas, for example, were rejected even by livestock, and the enormous Greenbelt project produced a system of only about thirty small reservoirs, a few areas of fruit production, some coffee plants, and an indeterminate amount of "maybes." Underlying this Havana Greenbelt development was an implicit antiurban settlement. Cities were viewed as parasitic and corrupt places. That view prevailed even in the new rural towns built during the revolutionary period. The climax of this deurbanization process was reached when the giant mobilizations of the sugarcane cutting campaign ensued in the late 1960s. These efforts culminated with the targeted goal of a 10-million-ton sugarcane harvest in 1970. During this massive harvest the cities were practically empty. By 1970, the Cuban economy had become entirely state owned, except for 30 percent of agricultural land.

The 10-million-ton sugar harvest (La Gran Zafra) became a symbol with which the faith of the revolution could be measured. Such a sentiment was expressed with the slogan "10 Million Are on Their Way!" [¡Los Diez Millones Van!]. Those who had discrepancies with the 10-million-ton goal were foreign specialists who had analyzed the world sugar market. They had predicted with uncanny precision that the harvest would fall short by some 1.5 million tons. This exact amount of shortfall had also been predicted by the Cuban minister of sugar, Orlando Borrego. Such a precise forecast increased the professional prestige of the experts in the New York firm Czarnikow-Rionda and also brought bittersweet consolation to one Cuban who soon thereafter became a former minister.

## FROM THE GREAT HARVEST TO THE
## FIRST FIVE-YEAR PLAN: 1971–1975

The third period searched for a harmonious balance between the government and mass organizations. It strengthened the state apparatus through a process of institutionalization. Efforts for economic planning were redoubled, as were economic controls that culminated with the First Five-Year Plan. This period also strengthened the role of the Communist Party of Cuba and the nation's unions.

Building efforts received a great impulse with the creation of the Social and Agricultural Development Group (Grupo de Desarrollo Social y Agropecuario [DESA]) and the Agricultural Development (Desarrollo Agropecuario [DAP]). The Microbrigade movement was created by Fidel Castro himself during this time as an alternative mode of building construction that could complement the lack of public housing units. *Microbrigadistas* also aimed to train and bring back skilled construction workers into the building process and to reduce the excess number of workers at factories and clerical jobs. Groups of employees from a work center would set out for two or three years to build housing for themselves and for their fellow workers; the center would maintain their salary, and the state would supply them with land, material inputs, equipment, and tools and provide technical advice (Angotti 1989). From an annual production of only five thousand units built in 1970, the Microbrigade movement had completed twenty thousand new units in 1975. However, the production model of houses employed by state firms remained wedded to the panacea of high-tech solutions and included IMS technologies (imported from Yugoslavia), a Sliding Scaffolding Model, and the Great Panel 70. One outcome of these building efforts was that the surge in construction produced a marked increase in the gross social product (GSP) during this period (table 4.1).

Even though the construction industry's contribution to the GSP was great, it was difficult to measure the full amount of investment that went into construction. Some experts believed that it was disproportionately large in relation to the end result. It is important to note that the large investment that went into a national network of prefabricated materials plants also created a commitment to use that kind of technology. The results were mixed: not only were the built units rigid and monotonous, but they were also costly and dependent on specialized inputs. When ideas were proposed to transfer these projects to remodeling inner-city areas, such as what occurred in the Havana neighborhood of Cayo Hueso, the results were even worse. New big buildings disrupted the layout of the city and interfered with social networks already in place. Central city residents, moreover, had a set of cultural values all their own, deeply attached to a low-rise/high-density urban pattern.

Efforts at centralization required a search for supposedly valid national models that could adapt to the Cuban reality. Construction solutions originally crafted for one situation were repeated and converted into a generalized model. This happened with the Girón prefabrication model. It was used massively in the construction of secondary schools in the countryside (ESBEC, discussed more fully in Chapter 8). About five hundred such schools were built during the period. Nevertheless, some good projects appeared using Girón, such as the Lenin or the Volodia schools in Havana—a demonstration that mental prefabrication is the real threat. Later, the Girón model was extended to hospitals, hotels, and even housing units and at times was often a rather forced solution. Ironically, the same Microbrigades became rather in-

TABLE 4.1. The Contribution of Building Trades to the Gross Social Product

| YEARS | CONTRIBUTION (%) |
| --- | --- |
| 1961–65 | 1.9% per year |
| 1966–70 | 3.9% per year |
| 1971–75 | 10.0% per year |

Source: Data from García Pleyán 1986.

fatuated with prefabrication without understanding the potential of simpler, local technologies and flexible processes of self-construction that were much more akin to the work of Microbrigades.

Of the 212,000 housing units built in Cuba between 1971 and 1975, only 40 percent were built by the state. Put another way, of the 19,000 units built per year, half were erected by the Microbrigades (Hamberg 1986). Planners tried to solve the housing problem through state-directed construction. Conserving the existing housing stock held low priority, which resulted in a qualitative, functional, and visual deterioration of the central parts of Havana. In cases of severe deterioration, occupants were transferred from buildings on the verge of collapse to sturdier structures.

At the end of the period, the First Congress of the Cuban Communist Party was held in 1975. Preparations for the congress included beautification efforts in prominent areas of Havana. These efforts were orchestrated through a program called Urban Revitalization carried out by the Department of Architecture and Urbanism of the city of Havana. The use of large murals, called Super Graphics, and other elements of urban landscape architecture formed key components of this revitalization campaign (Coyula 1985a). The process of institutionalization throughout Cuba would become the most important activity of the subsequent stage, and the preparations had already begun.

## THE INSTITUTIONALIZATION OF CUBAN SOCIALISM: 1976–1986

From the outset, the fourth stage concentrated its efforts on the creation of People's Power (Poder Popular) organizations, the divisions of the Central Administration of the State (Oficinas Administrativas Centrales del Estado [OACE]), and the System of Economic Planning and Management (Sistema de Dirección y Planificación de la Economia [SDPE]). A new constitution replaced the one from 1940, which in its day was one of the most advanced in the world (Cuba 1976). In the economics sphere the central task became import-substitution industrialization, which meant creating exportable funds and satisfying national consumption. During the First Five-Year Plan (1976–80) state investment reached $11 billion. The emphasis on education that had been instigated in the previous stage also continued. Beginning with the Second Five-Year Plan (1981–85), tourism became a principal development focus in Havana.

Housing construction increased during this period. To the surprise of many, the Eleventh National Conference on Housing and Urbanism held in Santa María del Mar in 1984 revealed that the production of housing units by the population through self-help was practically double that of state firms (Estévez 1984). From an average of 50,000 housing units per year, only 16,400 were built by the state. Eleven years later, one study (Pérez 1995a) showed that Havana fared dismally compared with housing construction elsewhere in Cuba.

While state construction efforts continued the multifamily prefabricated mid-rise apartment building designs, self-help efforts received support from local governments and workplaces (especially in the interior parts of the country). At the same time the role of the Microbrigades was reviewed, and the sale of construction materials to the general population increased appreciably. Building preservation efforts also rose. For example, between 1973 and 1983 the budget for state companies in charge of housing maintenance increased fivefold, while the sale of building materials increased tenfold. However, the figures distort the frequent diversion of state resources to other prioritized programs. Regarding the sale of building materials to the general population, for example, many materials purchased for repairs were really used to build new housing or expand existing units.

In December 1984 the General Housing Law was approved. It confirmed and expanded the property of tenants through a rent-payment system. The new law allowed Cubans to rent rooms and regulated inheritances, swapping (*permutas*), and the sale of homes and lots. The 1984 law also opened the possibility of establishing housing cooperatives to work with self-help housing in construction, remodeling, and expansion. Because the law was approved reluctantly, it fell victim to certain fatal prejudices; some of its stipulations—such as those that pertain to cooperatives—were not well instrumented, and still others, such as the ability to sell and sublease, were suspended. We explore these and related housing issues in Chapter 6 and more recent events (from 1997 to 2002) in the final chapter.

TABLE 4.2. Housing Completion, 1959–1990 (in thousands)

| | STATE-BUILT HOUSING | % OF TOTAL | PRIVATE INITIATIVE HOUSING | % OF TOTAL | TOTAL |
|---|---|---|---|---|---|
| Cuba | 495 | 28 | 1,330 | 72 | 1,770 |
| Havana | 99 | 32 | 211 | 68 | 310 |

Source: Pérez 1995b.

## THE CORRECTION OF MISTAKES AND THE SPECIAL PERIOD: 1987

The fifth period corresponds to a crisis in Cuba's socialist model of development and marks a watershed as well as a search for new solutions for the nation's problems. Although normally the "Correction of Mistakes" and "Special Period" are analyzed separately, for purposes of brevity we combine them here. Based on the errors made by the Eastern European socialist models, the objective of this period was to preserve the Cuban socialist ideology and stabilize the country and the economy. In Cuba, however, greater weight is now being given to material incentives and the self-financing of state companies than was the case during the final stage of Eastern European socialism in the late 1980s. Prior to the Special Period, the opposite policy of prioritizing moral incentives created a generalized dependence and a growing reliance on the Council of Mutual Economic Assistance (discussed in Chapter 7). The overall well-being of the population increased notably with a state parallel market where one could purchase goods and food in addition to those provided by the state through the ration book. Previously, such items were considered luxury goods. However, this model based on material incentives was quickly modified. Ironically, the harshest critics did not attempt to polish or improve the rewards system but rather opted to abandon it.

Criticisms by technocrats and pessimists came quickly when the state decided to invest in nonproductive enterprises. For example, Microbrigade housing and health care clinics had no economic basis to sustain them. While perestroika spread in the former Soviet Union, 1987 in Cuba marked a time when moral incentives and conventional directives would be returned to state leadership. The Third Five-Year Plan should have covered 1986–90, but it was postponed and ultimately eliminated because of the obvious effects brought on by the breakup of the European socialist field and its dire effects on the Cuban economy.

The so-called Process of the Correction of Mistakes (*proceso de rectificación de errores*) began turbulently through a series of investments in housing construction and services that overwhelmed the cautious initial forecasts made by economists, who were soon labeled as "technocrats." The Microbrigade, accused ten years earlier of being unproductive, was revitalized and expanded to create the "social brigade." It incorporated neighbors from a specific area instead of workers who came from a workplace. From this point on, Microbrigade efforts were also largely used for the construction. The focus turned to building on empty lots in the central city or where buildings had been demolished. No longer were its efforts devoted to the construction of new neighborhoods and towns. Microbrigade efforts had often been used in the past for the construction of social projects such as hospitals, medical clinics, day care centers, sports and recreational complexes, and the new convention center occupied by ExpoCuba at the city's edge. Its efforts were also used in the construction of facilities for the Pan American Games of 1991 held in Habana del Este and Santiago de Cuba. For many *microbrigadistas* the delay, brought on by a scarcity of inputs, was demoralizing. After the games many of the workers occupied the Villa Panamericana (a common practice in the Cuban building sector through the Microbrigades). For many other *microbrigadistas*, the delay caused by the priority given to this and similar public works projects proved fatal when combined with the scarcity of building materials, especially when their own buildings remained half built.

One of the most dramatic consequences of Cuba's attempts to balance its economy in the international arena in the early 1990s, after the demise of European socialism, was the appearance of a hard-currency market alongside the national currency. The purchasing power of the Cuban peso, which had long been pegged to the U.S. dollar before 1959, was greatly devaluated in the early 1990s. Inflation skyrocketed, and essential materials became scarce as pressures mounted to ensure full employment, which otherwise had little productive results. This translated into a vicious cycle that was altogether demoralizing. As late as 1989, the Soviet bloc trading arena had provided Cuba with 85 percent of its foreign trade, and it did so with favorable prices that were subsidized by the bloc. The collapse of that market, coupled with Cuba's lack of capital, credit, and energy, sent shock waves throughout the Cuban economy and society. Moreover, it was aggravated by the persistent U.S. blockade. By 1991, imports and exports had been cut to almost half the 1989 levels, and while the economy bottomed out in 1993 and showed modest growth in the late 1990s, it still remained behind levels of 1989 (fig. 4.1). Petroleum imports,

FIGURE 4.1. Cuba's foreign trade balance, 1989–98 (From "Foreign Trade, 1989–1998," in *Cuba: Handbook of Trade Statistics* [Washington, D.C.: CIA, 1999])

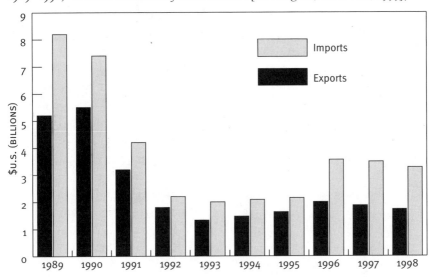

FIGURE 4.2. Value of Cuban fuel imports, 1989–98 (From *Cuba: Handbook of Trade Statistics* [Washington, D.C.: CIA, 1999])

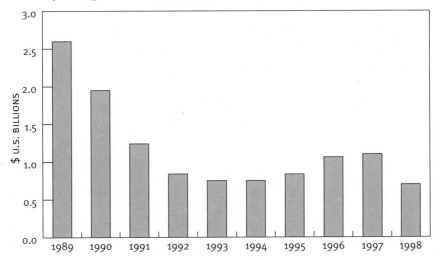

the primary source of energy in Cuba, faced a drastic reduction in the 1990s. For instance, 13 million tons of imported petroleum in 1989 fell drastically to just 6 million in 1990. Fuel imports plummeted from $12.4 billion in 1989 to $750 million in 1994 and hovered roughly at that level for the rest of the decade (fig. 4.2). In light of this economic downturn, the withdrawal of Soviet aid and trade, and a perception that the United States would attack the island, the revolutionary leadership declared in 1990 that Cuba was in its first phase of the "Special Period in a Time of Peace." Though the economy had improved somewhat by 1996, the label remained in force even in 2001.

One strategy for coping with the economic problems of the Special Period has been to allow a gradual opening whereby foreign investors are allowed to participate in joint ventures with the Cuban government. A total of 240 agreements have been signed between the Cuban government and foreign firms as of July 1996. These agreements include forty-three nations and span thirty-four areas of the Cuban economy. An estimated 143 other projects were under negotiation at that time. Despite the passage of the Helms-Burton Law, which threatens to prosecute foreign companies doing business in Cuba, twenty-five new associations were signed in the three months following the passage of the law (Prensa Latina 1996).

A second strategy is to encourage the flow of funds from family members abroad, which up until this period had been looked down on. Tourism, biotechnology, and the pharmaceutical industry are now emphasized in Cuba to generate foreign exchange (see also Chapters 7 and 8). All of this takes place in a market in which moral incentives must prevail because few workers share in profits, which instead accrue to the state or joint-venture operations. Because of the lack of capital and access to credit from international organizations (partly because of U.S. pressure to discourage such lending), the situation has become increasingly difficult in Cuba and has exacerbated problems of scarcity.[1]

---

1. Throughout Cuba, but especially in Havana, efforts to generate hard currency accentuated differences between Cubans who have access to dollars and those who do not. Scarcity of basic foods, a large portion of which used to come from the Soviet bloc, began to affect the physical health of the Cuban people in 1993. The Cuban public health system had received international acclaim as an accomplishment of the revolution, even by the most ardent opponents. In 1993, the government was forced to provide massive doses of multivitamins to its 11 million residents to compensate for an unbalanced diet. In the 1990s, and for the first time since the crisis in the beginning of the 1960s, food displaced housing as the number one social problem among the Cuban people. Further improvement in food supply, though mostly at very high prices, brought back housing as the main problem in the late 1990s.

The immediate effects of disinvestment were disastrous. Agriculture and construction were practically paralyzed because of the lack of imported resources such as petroleum, fertilizers, pesticides, fodder, machine repair parts, steel, building components, and semiassembled products. Lacking such materials exposed the vulnerability of a socialist development model that was very dependent on external resources. Under the scrutiny of the world market, these vulnerabilities exposed ecological, social, and cultural problems.

Several measures implemented in 1993 tried to arrest the crisis. Central among them was the ability of self-employed workers to earn a living in retail trades. In the agrarian sector, most state lands were turned over to cooperatives in order to create Basic Agricultural Production Units (Unidades Básicas de Producción Agropecuaria [UBPA]). A highlight of this agricultural reform was the reopening in October 1994 of the Free Farmers' Market (Mercado Libre Campesino), which had previously been harshly criticized by Fidel Castro. In its present reincarnation, the new name is the Agricultural Markets (Mercados Agropecuarios). Like the industrial markets opened just before them (which included the sale of most items except food), the Agricultural Markets also sell goods at very high prices (see Chapter 7). Problems of scarcity, limited production, and high prices arose as the government attempted to capture circulating hard currency and pesos (Carranza, Guitiérez, and Monreal 1995). However, the efforts seem to have paid off: since 1994, inflation has fallen, and the black market exchange rate of 120–130 pesos to the U.S. dollar had fallen to 20–25 in mid-1996.

Although the major objective of the government's attempt to reinsert Cuba into the global economy has been to provide stability and earn hard currency, much of the Cuban population does not fully understand the process. In some cases, the government's actions seem rather ad hoc. *Habaneros* coped tenaciously with daily problems such as frequent power outages during the summer of 1993 and the exodus of many northward-bound rafters (*balseros*) in the summer of 1994. Public discontent reached its pinnacle with the first large public demonstration on the Malecón on August 5, 1994, although that may be a single, isolated event.

The state's attempt to improve international and national finances in 1994 has been more coherent. Prices have increased, many goods previously provided free of charge have been eliminated, some taxes have been established, and the time period for repayment of debt has been shortened. At the end of 1994 the minister of finances and prices, José Luis Rodríguez, presented a possible solution to the National Assembly. He proposed the Law for the

State Budget of 1995, which, compared with 1994, sought to cut the deficit by 69 percent. This law also entailed a 56 percent reduction in state central government subsidies for local prices. It was hoped that such a strategy would create a budget surplus in some provinces. In 1995 the budget increased by 4.4 percent in education, 1.9 percent in health, 5.5 percent in science and technology, and 4.1 percent in housing and community services.

Also forecast in 1995 was an alarming increase of 13.1 percent in social security expenditures, where a deficit of 679.5 billion pesos was expected. Only employers make social security contributions. However, it has become painfully clear that a full employment labor policy and retirement payments maintained throughout thirty-five years will place great fiscal pressure on the state. Demographic pressures on the aging population will worsen this situation: women can retire at fifty-five years of age and men at sixty. Worker contributions to their own individual retirement funds are now under review. Not much different from the social security debate in the halls of the U.S. Congress in 1995, the idea of increasing individuals' contributions to their retirement funds has been controversial in Cuba. Trade unions are especially concerned about having more of their already low wages diverted to social security payments, especially when many of the self-employed are thought to be getting rich. The idea has been indefinitely postponed regarding state workers, despite a major conference held by Cuba's organized labor in April 2001.

## Physical Planning: A Star Is Born

Physical planning in Cuba began at the national level in 1962. In 1959 several construction projects were started in new rural communities, cooperatives, and state farms. The projects remodeled quarters for sugarcane workers at the *bateyes* (small settlements around the sugar mills). The Rebel Army Corps of Engineers, directed by Captain Oriente Fernández and later by *comandante* Julio García Oliveras, was in charge of these early initiatives. In addition, at that time, the National Institute of Savings and Housing (Instituto Nacional de Ahorro y Vivienda [INAV]) built several small suburban neighborhoods as well as the landmark projects at Habana del Este.

The leadership of Urban and Regional Planning in Cuba first emanated from the Office of Physical Planning, located in the Ministry of Public Works. It later became the Institute of Physical Planning (Instituto de Planificación Nacional [IPF]) from the Central Planning Board (Junta Central de Planificación [JUCEPLAN]). Initially directed by René Saladrigas, the institute played an important role in reorganizing national territory for state agricultural production. Since its offices were in the capital, planners decided to do the planning for Havana Greenbelt (Cordón de La Habana), but this was transferred in the late 1960s to the Agricultural Command Outpost (Puesto de Mando Provincial de la Agricultura), located near the village of Nazareno, just south of Havana.

Under the energetic management of Cecilia Menéndez, Nazareno became a teaching center for regional planners in the last two years of their studies.[2] An average day's work ended at seven o'clock in the evening for the planners when they were not pulling "all-nighters." (Nazareno was turned into an HIV-positive sanatorium in the late 1990s.) Among the projects designed by these groups were the new rural communities of Ceiba del Agua and Valle del Perú, designed by Mario González, Mario Coyula, and others.

Planning was directed from the Agricultural Command Outposts (Puestos de Mando), which were frequently visited by Fidel Castro and other revolutionary leaders. These outposts symbolized a rejection of the city and stemmed from the ideology inherent in the rural guerrilla warfare in the Sierra Maestra. Guerrilla fighters assumed important leadership positions in the new government and therefore had a different mentality than the underground urban fighters. The guerrilla fighters' rejection of the conventional methods and institutions of governance and their disdain for a bureaucracy that was characterized mostly by clean-shaven light-skinned men created conflicts. Employees at the Puesto de Mando would board buses and trucks at cosmopolitan La Rampa in Vedado neighborhood, clad in a "rural" uniform composed of gray khaki pants and shirts, black boots, and shapeless straw hats. On the other hand, high-rank officials (*dirigentes*) set off from the same place but in their Alfa Romeos, which had been recently imported from Italy to offset the lack of U.S. car imports and keep the state apparatus running.

The IPF laid out in the 1970s a system for siting investments and productive services. These criteria were included in the National Physical Plan, provincial plans, urban master plans, and Urban Forecast System and Project Zones for the year 2000 (García Pleyán 1986). By the end of the 1970s, the emphasis had shifted from regional planning for spatially reorganizing rural areas to urban planning.

2. The first urban and regional planners in Cuba were architects, but later they included geographers, economists, engineers, and sociologists (demographers).

creation of the People's Powers in 1977, that planning structure
place until 1995. At the national level, regulatory and locational
e made by the IPF in order to balance regional and investment
al-level decision making was made by provincial planning departments (Dirección Provincial de Planificación Física [DPPF]), which per-
tained to local governments. Plans and projects for provinces, regions, zones,
cities, and towns were also overseen by the People's Power committees at the
provincial level. Last, the municipal offices of Architecture and Urbanism
(Departamentos de Arquitectura y Urbanismo [DAU]) exercised control over
construction, gathering information and statistics and adjusting the plans to
meet local conditions (García Pleyán 1986). In recent years, these municipal
offices have attempted to decentralize the execution of the master plans and
control over local land use. This resulted in considerable agility at the plan-
implementation phase, but with it came the cost of making important decisions vulnerable to the shortsightedness of local authorities (García Pleyán
1994).

## THE FIRST HAVANA MASTER PLAN: 1963–1964

Under Batista in the 1950s, planning had been bolstered by the work of José
Luis Sert, Paul Lester Wiener, and Paul Schultz in order to form a team of
Cuban architects that contained such well-known professionals as Mario Ro-
mañach and Nicolás Quintana. This new plan was created by architects, the
Cuban planner Mario González, and the Colombian Luis Espinosa.
González also worked on subsequent master plans for the capital and became
one of the most recognized planners in the country.

The 1963–64 plan addressed many of the problems of Havana that until
that time had been dealt with by the efforts of six independent municipalities.
Each political division had had its own mayor and separate municipal agencies. Planning projects were spotty and idiosyncratic. Broad metropolitan-
based planning problems could not be effectively resolved.

Through this plan Havana's political and administrative functions began to
be treated as a metropolitan entity. The master plan created six regions in
order to provide greater physical and social coherence to planning endeavors.
Each region had its own center in order to give it an identity and also to reduce commuting. This objective, however, was not carried out despite considerable efforts. Occasionally, persistent political barriers did not allow for
some territories to receive uniform services and infrastructure.

This master plan took effect when the city had just 1.5 million inhabitants. One of its objectives was to decrease the rate of population growth. In those days the capital city had an annual natural increase of twenty-three thousand residents, as well as seventeen thousand immigrants from the interior of the country (González 1993). Some planning strategies of the master plan redistributed maritime and port activities as well as noxious industries to points elsewhere in Cuba. This shift also involved the development of appropriate infrastructure to support those economic activities. Decentralization slowed the rate of Havana's population growth, which also declined as a result of environmental, sewage, and transportation problems.

The 1963–64 master plan recommended a reduction in population density in the central areas of Havana. Although this was not achieved, the rate of new housing construction declined, and no coercive measures were employed to prevent migration to the capital. The effect was to worsen the quality of the central areas of Havana. Physical deterioration accelerated because of little routine maintenance, especially of streets and buildings, which needed repair and painting, respectively.

The plan gave considerable importance to the environmental quality of the capital, and it examined the sources of air pollution originating around Havana Bay: refineries, the gas plant, and the garbage dump at Cayo Cruz (a small island or key). The dump would be replaced in the early 1970s by a sanitary landfill at a new location near Calle 100, very close to the new José Antonio Echeverría University campus (Ciudad Universitaria José Antonio Echeverría [CUJAE]), named after the revolutionary architecture student leader killed in 1957. The scarcity and poor distribution of green space in the city prompted proposals to increase the prerevolutionary ratio from 1 square meter per resident to 18 square meters per resident. The latter figure was finally achieved in the 1970s. From the first master plan arose the idea of the Metropolitan Park (Parque Metropolitano). It took advantage of open spaces and tree-covered areas along the banks of the Almendares River. Metropolitan Park connected with the Havana Greenbelt through a network of parks. The most remote of those parks—Lenin, the Botanical, and the new zoo— were created in the 1970s. Metropolitan Park, however, was postponed until later, even though it was centrally located and of great importance for the city and the Almendares River (see "Leisure Time, Green Spaces, Sports, and Religion" in Chapter 8).

The delay in creating Metropolitan Park stemmed from the considerable water pollution along the Almendares River and the presence of several nox-

es and shantytowns along its banks. Another factor was the per-
policy preference to carry out completely new projects in non-
eas. Therefore, new projects were free of preexisting built envi-
social conditions. One result of this strategy was that Havana
residents had to travel considerable distances to the parks located along the
southern edge of the metropolitan area. An initial allure in traveling to the
parks was to buy chocolates and cream cheese that could not be bought at the
corner grocer.

Because of the delay in starting Metropolitan Park, its lands became threatened by industrial, military, and squatter-housing activities. Husillo Dam was
partially destroyed in 1990 in order to build a canal for a flood control and
drainage system. The demolition seriously affected the historic and environmental value of this area, and the canal failed to solve the flooding problem.
Administrative changes in 1994 brought new hope for completing the park,
but progress has been slow. On the other hand, this project has carefully incorporated ecologically sound and participatory methods. When ultimately
completed, it will showcase how sustainable landscape problems become opportunities.

Other important aspects of the plan analyzed the loss of water through the
city's poor network of aqueducts and water mains. It also addressed the excessive water consumption of inappropriate technology and deficiencies in
the public transportation system. To confront these problems, the master
plan proposed the creation of functional areas according to zoning principles,
which until then had been accepted without any serious questioning (table
4.3).

Thirty years after the first master plan, the principal author (González
1993, 15) analyzed some of its main weaknesses:

- A lack of baseline data
- Poor analysis of infrastructure network except for the water mains
- Housing located in industrial development zones on top of the Vento
  Watershed Basin
- Imprecise delineation of functional zones
- Weakness of the proposed road structure
- A lack of team work in settings dominated by architects
- Little imagination about the city and not taking advantage of the
  functional and aesthetic attributes of Havana's more attractive areas

TABLE 4.3. Accomplishments of the Master Plan of 1963–1964

---

1 Zones of large-scale housing construction in Habana del Este (Bahía, Guiteras, and especially Alamar); Boyeros (in-filling in Altahabana and to a lesser extent Fontanar, Mulgoba, and Panamerican); Central Highway (Cotorro); and La Lisa (Ermita–San Agustín).

2 Industrial zones and warehouses. Habana del Este (Berroa) and La Lisa to the west.

3 The port area (Puerto Pesquero, new terminals of container loading and unloading)

4 Major road networks including beltways.

5 The zone of influence surrounding Plaza de la Revolución.

6 The historic core of Habana Vieja (old walled city). This proposal, conducted with the First National Landmark Commission, was the forerunner of the study that culminated in 1975 with the first master plan for that zone and its subsequent designation as a World Heritage Site in 1982.

7 The location of new cemeteries and garbage dumps.

8 The spatial organization of the city (groups of 1,000–2,000 inhabitants; microdistricts of 6,000–8,000; districts of 25,000–30,000; and regions of 100,000 and more. Focus influenced by the principles of the International Congress of Modern Architecture (CIAM), British urban planners such as Abercrombie and Korn, and Soviet planners.

9 System of green areas with different levels of parks (metropolitan, regional, district, and local) that correspond with new urban spatial organization. A large part of this green area was planted by massive mobilizations, mass organizations, and state workers.

10 New political administrative division that divides metropolitan Havana into a single administrative entity for the entire city, with six regions. The government organized along with those two levels—metropolitan and regional—a smaller unit called the sectional levels. It kept the name of the control and inspection boards (JUCEI) used in the early years of the revolution. In addition, administrative subdivisions were added: districts and microdistricts, which were used exclusively for planning studies and site plans.

---

*Source*: González 1993.

## THE MASTER PLAN OF 1971

This new plan was prepared by a team of architects in the Institute of Physical Planning, among them Max Baquero, Eusebio Azcue, and the Italian Vittorio Garatti (fig. 4.3). This project also included the participation of other specialists such as demographers, sociologists, geographers, and civil engineers. Such professional diversity coupled with what was learned from the previous plan produced a document that had scientific, technical, and cultural criteria that were missing from the previous one. It was also influenced by the ideas of Fidel Castro as expressed in speeches of the day. The plan projected that by the year 2010 Havana would have an estimated population of 2.3 million inhabitants. In general the plan kept the principal approaches of the

1963–64 guide, correcting some of their weaknesses and building on some of their strengths.

The road network was much better organized and incorporated an important element: a transportation node south of the bay that would connect the major passenger and cargo flows to the rest of the city. It was also to include buses and railroads. However, this important node was not developed, and the new docks on the southern part of the bay were never completed. The railroad did not receive the priority that was expected. What little investment was earmarked for the road network was diverted elsewhere. The 1971 road plan detailed an image of the city with special attention to landscaping roads and major thoroughfares. It was not implemented, however.

Years later, at the beginning of the 1980s, other urban landscape projects took place along major roads and promenades of the city. One of the most important was the arrival of the airport. However, several of these projects were only partially carried out during the late 1980s. An important road was the east-west highway that would have helped to remove cargo traffic from the center of the city. On the other hand, there was an ambitious program of highway construction. Highway projects were almost always built disproportionately large, such as the eight-lane national highway (Autopista Nacional). This program was also left unfinished, and the national highway never connected with the ring around the port area (see fig. 2.7).

The 1971 plan analyzed the polycentric character of the capital and proposed to reinforce a set of secondary centers. If the revolutionary offensive of 1968 against small businesses provided a great boost to the revolution, it also had the unintended outcome of deteriorating the quality of the city's major centers. This occurred when local commercial establishments were readapted as housing units, almost always of an improvised nature and of very low quality. With this came problems of building maintenance in the central areas as well as a dearth of a variety in products and services.

Nonetheless, the range of this planning focus and the new awareness of the city's problems helped give special planning attention to these areas. The 1971 plan emphasized both shopping areas and services as well as workplaces and housing. In particular, the housing program received considerable attention because of the Microbrigades. Another achievement of the plan was the location of housing zones near production, teaching, and research centers. The 1971 plan also maintained the policy of creating special planning districts as outlined in the previous plan, and it maintained the concept of creating industrial microdistricts that were compatible with residential areas.

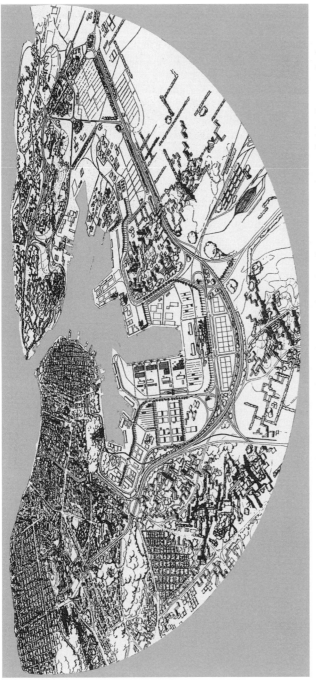

FIGURE 4.3. The 1971 master plan. This plan gave special attention to enhancing the transportation and shipping terminals around Havana Bay. A detail of the proposed design is shown here. (Drawing by Vittorio Garatti; from *Arquitectura/Cuba* 341, no. 1 [1973]: 67 and facing map insert; courtesy of the Instituto de Planificación Física)

Another activity that received considerable attention in the 1971 plan was the development of the port. As noted above, the southern part of the bay was targeted for the most modern technology for managing ships and maritime cargo. Two proposed terminals, one for containers and another with four piers, were completed, but it was not until 1995 that an Italian cruise ship company restored a passenger terminal in Habana Vieja. The 1971 planning focus, though, marked an important step toward freeing up and using the traditional dock areas that blocked the view of the water all along the southern half of the old walled city. Although residents of Habana Vieja welcomed these revitalization efforts, planners did not have the power to implement plans.

During this time Habana Vieja became very fashionable because of visits by Fidel Castro and foreign gentry. Throughout the same area there operated as many as six agencies and national commissions dedicated to preserving Havana's built heritage. For example, three branches of the government as well as UNESCO worked to save Plaza Vieja. Perhaps the greatest support for historic preservation and restoration came in 1982, when UNESCO declared Habana Vieja and the network of colonial forts a World Heritage Site (see also Chapter 9). That accomplishment notwithstanding, efforts continued to be focused on buildings and public spaces that held significance for the country but were also both costly and time consuming to preserve. Many of these revitalization efforts produced museums, cultural centers, and restored buildings, but they lacked a comprehensive vision to address serious environmental problems and to incorporate the concerns of the local residents. The City Historian's Office has played a leading role, and since 1993 it has enjoyed a special status that has allowed it to multiply its work and become self-financed.

The principal defect of the 1971 plan was that it did not study Havana's relationship with its hinterland. It also proposed massive housing construction in the southern part of the capital that threatened the Vento Watershed Basin (González 1993). That watershed is vital because it supplies about 50 percent of the capital's current demand for fresh water. Construction of ExpoCuba on top of the aquifer assured visitors prestigious accommodations, but at a site too removed from the center of Havana. As we shall see later, the Special Period took care of that problem in its own way.

## THE MASTER PLAN OF 1984

This plan had a projection to the year 2030. It was an ambitious work, consisting of twelve volumes of reports that were drafted in the Provincial Physical Planning Office. A team of sixty-seven Cuban professionals and technicians and fourteen foreign advisers (mostly Soviet) participated in the project.[3] Both the scope and the depth of the work surpassed those of previous master plans. In 1984, Havana had a population of 1.9 million residents and a growth rate of 2.3 percent per year. This plan analyzed the city in relation to the neighboring province of Havana. It covered aspects such as population, settlement systems, road and transportation networks, agricultural production, recreation, and tourism.

The scope of the plan covered a long period—forty-five years—and attempted to assure that the most basic needs of Havana were not overlooked. However, for practical reasons, the plan specified only certain details until the year 2000. The technical basis covered two broad fields: an analysis of current situations and a development forecast and proposal. In time, more detailed planning was carried out.

This 1984 master plan studied several alternatives for the capital, such as a concentric ring, an east-west alignment, and three variants on these two themes. The east-west alternative posed more problems than the concentric ring in terms of departing from the historical evolution of the city. It did, however, offer several advantages. These included balancing metropolitan-wide needs but also respecting the traditional centers (a common problem in most cities where the center remains fixed as the city expands), preserving the Vento Watershed Basin, avoiding problems posed by the airport, maintaining the fertile agricultural lands to the south of Havana, and assuring a steady food supply (e.g., truck farming) for the capital. Another advantage of the east-west plan was that expanding toward the east of the city meant that lands not well suited for agriculture would be used. The eastern sector would be "cleansed" by the prevailing trade winds, which would help rid the city of air pollution from points around the bay. Those breezes would also complement the natural beaches along the eastern part of Havana, which remained a major recreation source for *habaneros*.

Theoretically, the plan included parallel east-west strips running from the

---

3. The Cuban team was headed by Gina Rey and also included Joel Ballesté, Mario González, Marta Lorenzo, Enrique Fernández, José M. Fernández, Rosa Oliveras, and others. Norald Nercesián headed the group of foreign advisers.

shoreline toward the south that would be devoted to recreation, housing, and light industry, respectively. This idea was similar to the linear-city planning of Soria y Mata for Madrid and Miliutin in Stalingrad. The 1984 plan envisioned a system of central places composed of a major downtown area and five subcenters within five urban regions.

Because of the basic linear structure, three large road networks running parallel to the coast were proposed. One of them, the east-west highway, was outlined in studies before the 1984 plan, and construction commenced on the western portion of the road in 1989. A major feature of this plan was to incorporate for the first time in Cuba a system of legal guidelines that had originated from the old Building Ordinances of 1861. National and provincial government agencies were consulted in addressing environmental concerns. For the first time in Cuba, the plan was approved by the Executive Committee of the Council of Ministers in May 1984.

Despite these novel features, important aspects were not sufficiently addressed. This included gathering community input in a few cases but not consistently throughout the entire planning process (Taller 1995). Nor was there a search for a coherent image of Havana. With hindsight, it is safe to say that the plan paid a great deal of attention to how the city would be at the end of the period without paying enough attention to the processes that should lead to that form. Similarly, little importance was given to sustainable development principles, the role of the neighborhood in a large city, and the creation of "urban" culture.

## The 1990 Updating of the Master Plan

This plan was projected to the year 2010 by a team of thirty-seven professionals and technicians.[4] At this time Havana had a population of 2.1 million inhabitants, and the scheme anticipated a population of 2.3 million inhabitants. The 1984 plan was thoroughly revised, drawing on the successes and failures of the plan over the previous seven years. The new scheme also identified environmental concerns that had traditionally been overlooked. The planners believed that the previous plan had overstated the territorial expansion of the city and therefore chose to "compact" Havana by filling in open

---

4. Personnel from the Physical Planning Department of the province were headed by Aracelis García, Rosa Oliveras, and Jorge Carlos Diez.

spaces within the city's limits. Smaller service centers received greater attention in the 1990 plan than the previous one, in which large centers became the main functional points. However, despite the rationale of this focus, those subcenters did not materialize, not only because of the lack of resources but also because of the lack of enthusiasm for carrying out the plan (Pérez 1996).

The spectacular collapse of the socialist camp, which Fidel Castro called the *desmerengamiento* (dissolution), made clear the intrinsic vulnerability of the model. Havana was dependent on a budget by the upper echelons of the Cuban government that did not have the proper means for allocating such resources. It also became clear that little attention had been given to land values; nor was there balance between material versus moral rewards. Planning had become the victim of top-down decision making and provided few incentives for planners and other technicians.

By 1987 an ambitious construction phase brought on by the Process of the Correction of Mistakes intended to cover up many of Havana's problems. A group of young architects tried to ride on this surge to renovate the ailing Cuban architecture. Their work mostly lacked a proper fitting into local surroundings, and they affiliated themselves with the postmodern movement, which was already falling into disfavor in North America and Europe (Coyula 1993b). Their efforts focused on tourist projects, initially the construction of new hotels and later on the rehabilitation of existing ones. Another benefit to Havana was the strong growth in the construction of scientific research centers and pharmaceutical plants throughout Havana, especially in the area that came to be known as the "western scientific pole."

These programs, like tourism, aimed to generate hard currency in order to keep the country functioning. The actual construction phase, however, belonged to a new organizational form called the *contingentes* (work crews). Unlike the Microbrigades, the *contingentes* were composed of professional builders who worked overtime but were also paid for their work. Nonetheless, the productivity and quality of their work remained low; their work style was directed more toward the finished product than quality (Hamberg 1994, Chapter 20).

In 1992, the same team that had revised the master plan in 1990 focused its efforts on the plan, and it did so with a more clearly defined territorial focus. What determined this new approach was a consideration of the circumstances brought on by the Special Period. Thus, the first stage was concerned with the different alternatives proposed for the country to deal with the reduction of fuel. The study was much more decentralized than any previous plan. The city was divided among six hundred study zones. Considerable importance was given to the fifteen county (*municipio*) offices of the Provincial Department of Architecture and Urbanism. In the past, these municipal offices had merely collected data. This new focus, though, placed great emphasis on local potential and created 93 Popular Councils in Havana in 1990, which were later increased to 102. The Popular Councils are government entities with more administrative power than a delegate. This latter representative is elected from a district and serves as an intermediary between the constituents and higher levels of government (see Chapter 5). Significantly, though, these Popular Councils do not have their own funds for making investments.

The premises for updating the master plan (table 4.4) brought a new focus for urban planning in Cuba, one that sought greater sustainable development and public participation. This philosophy began to take shape among different fields and professions that were influenced by the scarcity brought on by the Special Period. To that can be added a new appreciation of the spatial, functional, bioclimatic, and cultural patterns of the city such as traditional materials and techniques used in construction. The movement was initially limited to a few professionals who were dedicated to the theory and practice of architecture and planning and the conservation of national landmarks.[5]

## The Workshops of Neighborhood Change: A Havana Experience in Participatory Planning

The Comprehensive Workshops for Neighborhood Change (Talleres de Transformación Integral del Barrio [TTIBS], or *talleres*) were begun experimentally in 1988 by the Group for the Comprehensive Development of the Capital (Grupo para el Desarrollo Integral de la Capital [GDIC]) in three Havana neighborhoods. They targeted areas with dire problems: Atarés and Cayo Hueso in the central zones, where most buildings were substandard and overcrowded, and La Güinera in the southern edge of the city, which was a shantytown without streets or roads. The experience continued to grow, and by the end of 1995 there were nine neighborhood workshops. The workshops

5. These professionals included Sergio Baroni, Eliana Cárdenas, Mario Coyula, Carlos García Pleyán, Mario González, Isabel León, Luis Lápidus, Rosendo Mesías, Isabel Rigol, Eduardo Luis Rodríguez, Angela Rojas, Fernando Salinas, and Roberto Segre, among others.

TABLE 4.4. Premises of the First Stage of Updating Havana's Master Plan

1   Prioritize the most deteriorated areas of the city both for planning and for specific action.

2   Emphasize home repair, services, and infrastructure.

3   Decentralize planning and building to match local conditions.

4   Execute the work in stages, commencing with the least ambitious ones.

5   Take better advantage of local labor resources.

6   Promote job creation close to where people live.

7   Reintroduce traditional building techniques and materials and in general favor the use of appropriate technology.

8   Recycle leftover building materials.

9   Encourage the participation of the local population in each stage: planning, implementation, construction, and maintenance.

*Source*: González 1993.

are composed of interdisciplinary teams consisting of between three and eight persons that often include architects, sociologists, engineers, and social workers. Usually, a person with organizational abilities who works and lives in the neighborhood is elected. The workshops seek an overall improvement of the physical condition of their neighborhoods as well as the welfare of the residents. Goals are defined after local needs are studied and an inventory taken of materials installations, offices, housing, and professionals that can be used within the local community.

Even though each workshop has its own goals, four general aspects are employed by each: (1) the improvement of the condition of housing, (2) the development of the local economy, (3) the education of children and youth, and (4) the development of neighborhood identity. The approach is based on the principle of not displacing the current population and finding solutions for current residents. In other words, the decision making moves from the grassroots level to the state. Workshops cooperate with various Cuban and foreign institutions that advise the Consejo Popular de Barrio (see Chapter 5) in both the built environment and the socioeconomic sphere. As such, these organizations provide much needed support to local government (Coyula, Cabrera, and Oliveras 1995).

From the start it became evident that the workshops would require their own sources of income for working in the neighborhoods. They experimented with several local initiatives, such as the production of building materials and tapping into tourist potential. Other routes included collaboration

TABLE 4.5. Profiles of the Havana *Talleres* (Workshops)

| NO. | WORKSHOP NAME | COUNTY | YEAR STARTED | POP. SERVED | PRIMARY GOALS AND ACTIVITIES |
|---|---|---|---|---|---|
| 1 | Cayo Hueso | Centro Habana | 1988 | 37,600 | Upgrading tenement houses, social work with elderly, teaching vocational trades to youth, computer & music courses |
| 2 | Pilar-Alarés | Cerro | 1988 | 23,200 | Upgrading tenement houses, social work in women's self-esteem workshops, revival and development of sociocultural values at the community center |
| 3 | La Güinera | Arroyo Naranjo | 1988 | 24,000 | Environmental education for teenagers and children, solid-waste recycling, neighborhood design, and sociocultural development at the community center |
| 4 | Pocitos-Palmar | Marianao | 1989 | 28,400 | Cultural and educational community outreach, home repair |
| 5 | Pogolotti | Marianao | 1990 | 22,700 | Reviving local traditions, home construction, help in developing Metropolitan Park, youth and elderly social work |
| 6 | Zamora-Cocosolo | Marianao | 1990 | 32,600 | Upgrading tenement houses, sociocultural work, and sports programs with children and teenagers |
| 7 | Santa Felicia | Marianao | 1990 | 17,700 | Educational and cultural work with children and teenagers, reviving local traditions, home repair |
| 8 | Alamar-Playa | Habana del Este | 1990 | 28,600 | Developing a sense of residential belonging, sociocultural work |
| 9 | Los Angeles | Marianao | 1996 | 14,600 | Reviving local traditions, sociocultural development in community centers, neighborhood design, social work with children, teenagers, and elderly |
| 10 | Libertad | Marianao | 1996 | 22,300 | Environmental cleanup and education, cultural promotion, community participation projects |
| 11 | Príncipe | Plaza | 1996 | 23,600 | Sociocultural promotion, neighborhood design |
| 12 | El Canal | Cerro | 1996 | 20,700 | Reviving local traditions, sociocultural and educational work |
| 13 | La Ceiba-Kohly | Playa | 1998 | 28,700 | Reviving local traditions, sociocultural work with children and teenagers, community participation projects |

TABLE 4.5. (continued)

| NO. | WORKSHOP NAME | COUNTY | YEAR STARTED | POP. SERVED | PRIMARY GOALS AND ACTIVITIES |
|---|---|---|---|---|---|
| 14 | Buenavista | Playa | 1998 | 31,200 | Improving public spaces, sociocultural work with children and teenagers, community participation projects |
| 15 | Alamar Este | Habana del Este | 1998 | 35,800 | Sociocultural work with children and teenagers, developing a sense of residential belonging, research on neighborhood |
| 16 | Párraga | Arroyo Naranjo | 1998 | 21,000 | Sociocultural work with children and teenagers, reviving local traditions |
| 17 | Balcón de La Lisa-Arimao | La Lisa | 1998 | 17,300 | Sociocultural work with children and teenagers, community outreach |
| 18 | Vedado-Malecón | Plaza | 1998 | 21,000 | Sociocultural work with children and teenagers, elderly |
| 19 | Cubanacan-Náutico | Playa | 1998 | 13,900 | Sociocultural work in targeted neighborhoods |
| 20 | Jesús María-Tallapiedra | La Habana Vieja | 2000 | 30,355 | Home improvement, environmental cleanup |

Source: Grupo para el Desarrollo Integral de la Capital. 2001. *Talleres de transformación integral del barrio: Una experiencia de desarrollo comunitario en la Capital.* Havana: GDIC.

with foreign nongovernmental organizations (NGOs) and even Cuban NGOs, whose resources were used mainly for strengthening the productive and service activities that could help generate revenues for the communities.[6] By the mid-1990s, ten NGOs had financed projects that provide the workshops with tools and building materials for repairing slum tenements and recycling solid waste (Coyula, Cabrera, and Oliveras 1995).

6. The existence of truly independent NGOs in Cuba is controversial. Gillian Gunn documented what she has identified as numerous nongovernmental organizations in Cuba. However, the question of true autonomy from the government is not clear. Raul Castro delivered a very controversial report on March 23, 1996, to the Central Committee of the Cuban Communist Party. He emphasized that the Cuban concept of civil society is not the same as that in the United States, and he claimed that some foreign NGOs in Cuba "attempt to undermine the economic, political and social system freely chosen by [the Cuban] people . . . [and] whose only aim is to enslave [Cuba]" (Castro 1996, 32). Raul Castro's remarks stem from the official Cuban reaction that many international and Cuban NGOs ideologically undermine the revolution through the controversial Torricelli Track Two law in the United States, which provides sanctions against Cuba while also promoting cultural exchanges.

By early 2001, the number of TTIBs had increased from the initial three in 1988 (Atarés, Cayo Hueso, and La Güinera) to twenty (table 4.5). This experience was promoted by the GDIC looking for a more decentralized and participatory planning from the bottom up. The GDIC sited neighborhoods that had historically been excluded, both socially and economically. The basic idea was to break down the enormous problem of a big city into smaller units whose residents could assess and attempt to solve their own problems. By late 2000, nearly half a million persons were covered by TTIBs. The GDIC supplies the TTIBs with advice, training, exchange of experiences among them, and some collaboration projects with foreign NGOs, but emphasis is placed on avoiding a paternalistic relation. An Advisory Council and a Consultant Council for the TTIBs bring together experts from many different agencies and organizations.

Legally, though, the workshops are subordinate to the municipal governments administratively and cannot be considered NGOs. Nonetheless, they support the neighborhood Popular Councils through their full-time staff for the social and cultural work in the community. The workshops also afford continuity of work after changes in the elected delegates. These councils, composed of delegates elected by their constituencies plus other local actors, were created in Havana in 1990 as a better way to reach the grassroots level. A key planning tool has been the Community Strategic Plans in each workshop. These plans incorporate state agencies, organizations, and the local population. Some common issues in these plans are the improvement of the housing stock and sanitation, recovery of local traditions, reinforcing the sense of local identity and esteem, strengthening the local economy (including urban agriculture), and integrating local actors into neighborhood development. More than 470 actions are proposed in these plans, and by the end of 2000, around 50 percent had been completed.

The experience with the workshops has been acknowledged both in Cuba and abroad. It was selected as one "Best Practice" at the Istanbul (Turkey) Habitat Summit in 1998. One workshop in particular, La Güinera, received in 1995 one of the fifty awards from the United Nations for the most successful community development projects in the world.

In addition to preparing the working document of the GDIC, *Estrategia* (Strategy), and collaborating with the workshops, another major task of the GDIC has been the building of a large three-dimensional architectural model of the city. This scale model (1:1,000) was begun in 1988, and the exhibition hall in which it is displayed was designed by Orestes del Castillo Jr. It was opened to the public in June 1995. The model (called the "City Model," or Maqueta de la Ciudad) uses three colors to designate the historical development of Havana: colonial (sixteenth to nineteenth century), republican (1900–1958), and revolutionary (1959 to the present). The scale model is not just a beautiful and interesting artifact for visitors but a tool that can help cement the relationship between Havana and its residents. It aims to encourage an appreciation for the city's layout, design, and growth and to promote geographic literacy. Its chief applied use evaluates the impact of new projects around surrounding areas. For example, when large buildings or complexes are proposed, a scaled model of the project can be placed on the larger *maqueta* to assess how well the proposed structures blend in with the surrounding area. As we shall show in Chapter 8, though, a large Spanish joint-venture hotel was built on the Malecón in Vedado. Unfortunately, it was not previously tested on the model to see how well the project would "fit" into that part of the city.

## Planning: The Long and Winding Road

Planning in socialist Havana revealed at least five key features. First, the city counts on an abundant supply of trained professionals. Although architects and engineers dominated planning in the 1960s and 1970s, many other professionals now participate. Second, decision making has slowly moved from high levels of national government to both metropolitan and neighborhood sources. Third, some political goals have added to the perennial lack of resources in partially derailing the essential features of several of Havana's master plans. Implementation of plans in the past decade has been interrupted by the effects of the Special Period. Fourth, the economic viability of local projects and municipal agencies is necessary for local planning projects to be carried out successfully. As we discuss in the next chapter, the ability for Havana to generate its own resources — without relying strictly on funds approved at the national level — is intricately tied to the success of local land-use planning, economic development, and zoning. Finally, as decision making slowly devolves from the upper echelons of national government, Havana's municipalities will increasingly face the challenges posed by an emerging market. This presents both risks and opportunities for local governments, a point we return to in Chapter 10.

# 5

# City Government and Administration

## Old and New Actors

The centralizing project that meant incorporating the entire population within a few institutions was able to work under a model in which goods and services were centrally distributed and with the help of a canon of equity and equality. For a while, at least during part of the Revolution, that was accompanied by a prosperity that produced a sense of shared well-being.

— Hugo Azcuy, *Estado y sociedad civil en Cuba*, 1995

## Antecedents to the Government Structure in Havana

Cuba's colonial and semicolonial past molded the nature of city government during the republican period, which began with independence in 1902 and ended with the triumph of the revolution in 1959. The two constitutions enacted in 1901 and 1940—the latter considered to be one of the most advanced in the Americas—gave an important role to municipal governments. These city administrations were headed by a mayor supported by a body of town council members who had deliberative functions. Initially, these town council members elected the mayor directly, but beginning in 1908 that charge passed to direct electoral vote by the people for a period of two years (Dilla, González, and Vincentelli 1993). Throughout the twentieth century, Cuba's city governments faced the same challenges that other Latin American city governments faced during that time: a high level of dependence on the national government for funding (Scarpaci and Irarrázaval 1994). Such dependence continued during the revolutionary period, which weakened the power of local government vis-à-vis the national government.

The right to vote was manipulated by a corrupt political apparatus. The coup d'état of 1952 further eroded the already precarious role of municipal governments.[1] Despite the general subordinate role played by Cuban municipalities, the mayor of Havana had always been considered the second most important political figure of the country, after the president of the republic. The distribution and weight of these municipalities were also quite uneven. For example, around 1951 there were 126 municipalities in Cuba, but 26 of them were located in the province of Havana, the equivalent of 1 in 7 municipalities in the entire country (Dilla, González, and Vincentelli 1993). Havana Province included all the territories that encompass present-day Havana City Province (created in 1976) and Havana Province, minus a small part that at that time belonged to Pinar del Río (fig. 5.1).

With the triumph of the revolution in 1959, the central government named commissioners to cover the functions of municipal governments provisionally. In 1961, the commissioners created Coordination, Administration, and Executive Boards (JUCEIS) to coordinate and control policies and national laws and to collect and transmit information about their territories to the national government. These boards were established after a meeting with representatives of political and mass organizations, from which a permanent committee was elected. If the board was a step toward the decentralization of the island's governance, the provinces benefited more than the municipalities, since local governments had little authority over local services. In the capital, JUCEIS were established in each of the former municipalities, and Havana's counties were reorganized (table 5.1).

Seeking even more decentralization, Local Power (Poder Local) was established in 1966. According to Fidel Castro, the objective of Local Power was to reinforce the role of mass organizations, especially political organizations (Castro 1977). In 1965, the political institutionalization of the process had been completed, led by the constitution of the Communist Party of Cuba (Partido Comunista de Cuba [PCC]) and its first Central Committee (Castro 1980). Poder Local was established in each municipality and was made up of an executive committee, its president, two secretaries, and ten delegates that were elected in meetings by the population. The delegates were held accountable to their electorate, but the president was elected by members of the PCC

---

1. The hierarchy of settlements is similar to that in the United States: in ascending order of size, the normal sequence is towns, cities, municipalities, and provinces (roughly the equivalent of states, but in size only, not in jurisdictional function). We use "county" and "municipality" interchangeably. Havana City Province (Provincia Ciudad de La Habana, which is separate from the surrounding Havana Province, or Provincia de La Habana) consists of fifteen municipalities, shown in figure 1.13.

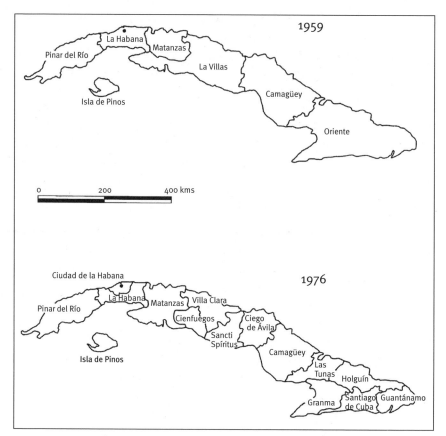

FIGURE 5.1. Jurisdictional reorganization of Cuban provinces, 1959 and 1976

in the area. At the national level, they created the coordination of Local Power.

Also created during this time was the Metropolitan Administration of Havana. As we discussed in the previous chapter, the first master plan of Havana (1963–64) recognized a continuous urban area that had assimilated older municipalities. Subordinate to that administration were six regional administrations, but the territory and name—La Habana, Diez de Octubre, Marianao, Guanabacoa, Boyeros, and Habana del Este—changed according to the historical, economic, and social features of the municipality.

In the mid-1970s Cuba began an open "complex modernization, decentralization, and democratization process involving the political and state system that has been called the *process of institutionalization.* Such a system was

TABLE 5.1. Reorganization of Counties (*Municipios*) in Pre- and
Postrevolutionary Havana

| PRE-1959 NAME | POST-1959 NAMES |
|---|---|
| La Habana | Habana Vieja |
| | Centro Habana |
| | Plaza |
| | Cerro |
| | Diez de Octubre |
| Mariano | Marianao |
| | Playa |
| | Lisa |
| Regla[a] | Regla |
| Guanabacoa | Guanabacoa |
| | San Miguel del Padrón |
| | Habana del Este (part) |
| Santa Maria del Rosario | Cotorro |
| | Arroyo Naranjo (part) |
| Santiago de las Vegas | Boyeros |
| | Arroyo Naranjo (part) |

[a] Despite its small size, Regla has a strong tradition of local pride and history that had to be respected
when officials tried to change its political boundaries.

closely related to the implementation of a new plan of placing Cuba favorably
in the Soviet economic system" (Dilla, González, and Vincentelli 1993, 29;
our translation, original emphasis). That process responded to criticisms of
errors produced by a rigid and highly centralized government and planning
process.

The institutionalization process included a new political and administrative
division. Stages were identified by the System of Economic Planning and
Management (SDPE) to regulate the national economy. A legal socialist framework was created that included the promulgation of the new constitution in
1976 and a revitalization of political and mass organizations, especially among
labor unions (Castro 1978). Institutionalization intended to augment democratization, with an electoral system of indirect vote at the national, provincial,
and municipal levels and direct vote only at the lower constituency level.

Another problem in the capital was the relationships between municipal
government and enterprises that were nationally administered and that worked
directly with the government ministries. The municipalities looked to the
Cuban Communist Party as arbitrator whenever bottlenecks in decision mak-

ing occurred. This process isolated municipal governments from their functions as a political and ideological administrative body attendant to local governance (González 1995).

A premise in government administration is that information is power and that sharing it also means the beginning of shared power. The lack of information makes it difficult to engender a public debate on issues, as is evident in the relationship between grassroots assemblies and higher levels of government. Dialogue such as this is almost always confined to very concrete and immediate issues and rarely enters into the depth of problems, much less their causes. Recent work published in Cuba by Canadian scholar August Arnold (1999) shows the multiple levels of government engagement that are often required so that local residents can resolve relatively minor planning and land-use conflicts.

This weakness threatens municipalities. As Dilla observes, "[Municipalities] crudely confront the risk of returning functions without powers, and beneficiaries of a decentralization of poverty. . . . The insertion of Cuba in the world market or its integration into regional markets will inevitably produce a fragmentation of national economic space" (1995, 70; our translation). On the one hand, state companies hold considerable power. On the other, local governments possess few resources and cannot raise their own funds. This creates conflict and resentment. This ongoing tug-of-war occurs in a rapidly changing local context in which the final goals of local planners cannot be well defined. New economic players appear on the scene: cooperatives, self-employed, local economic development projects financed by foreign non-governmental organizations (NGOs), and joint ventures. In this context the popular organizations in Cuba "should become vehicles of pluralist expression, and not simply transmission fan-belts extending from political centers. . . . Such a relationship assumes mechanisms of negotiation and implementation . . . in order to achieve an effective integration of local society" (Dilla 1995, 72; our translation).

Until the constitutional reform of 1992, the municipal assembly elected an executive committee composed of professional members (dedicated full-time to public administration) and nonprofessionals who held other jobs. Because professional members were each responsible for overseeing different administrative divisions, they gradually turned into virtual representative agents and administrators of those agencies. In other words, they served as judge and jury. This duality bound the municipal assembly members into a counterpart for the interest of the electorate and the region they served. It also committed them to working with successful programs and, perhaps even more frequently, with the errors and deficiencies of the government agencies.

Deputies of the National Assembly were elected through direct vote by the population with the legal reforms of 1992. Although data are scarce, one report by Amnesty International stated, "Fourteen percent of the last election's ballots were ruined, the highest percentage ever, and the only way of showing protest where the voting is obligatory and a single party is running" (Joe 1995, n.p.) Nonetheless, the reforms also meant keeping a lack of effective territorial representation given that candidates could be elected in places where they did not reside. It also applied the principle of "closed candidacy" whereby votes were made in blocks. Actually, those deputies do not represent their territories or their electorates and often times do not even know them.

With the creation of Poder Popular, the capital earned the rank of province, becoming one of fourteen that made up the country (plus the special municipality of Isla de la Juventud, which was the Isle of Pines but had changed its name based on the suggestion of Fidel Castro). At the same time, the provincial assemblies were made up of provincial delegates elected by municipal assemblies at the ratio of 1 delegate per 10,000 residents, or a fraction greater than 5,000 in a municipality. At the time of the July 1995 elections, 29,131 candidates ran for office for some 14,229 delegate seats among the 169 municipalities in Cuba.[2] In Havana, there were 3,224 candidates, of which 26.7 percent were actual delegates. The Provincial Assembly of the City of Havana had 215 delegates (Lee 1995b).

If Poder Popular has enhanced participation by the people in government, it has also set limitations. Provincial governments and other large cities often consume resources and make decisions at the expense of municipalities. The results have been severe in many cases. On the one hand, the smallest Cuban municipality has just 7,000 residents, while half the population resides in municipalities with more than 100,000 residents (García Pleyán 1995b). In the capital, the municipality of Diez de Octubre has practically 240,000 residents, and just two of the fifteen municipalities in the city of Havana Province have less than 100,000 residents. On the other hand, the base delegates serve as communicators of problems without either the resources or the decision-

2. Since 1976, elections have been competitive at the local level. By law, there must be at least two candidates, and there is no official party slate. Often, party members run against each other, but candidates do not have to be members of the Cuban Communist Party. At least half of the representatives to the National Assembly are delegates directly elected to municipal assemblies. This is similar to the notion of "at large" delegates found in other political systems who represent specific geographic areas.

making ability to solve them. This has eroded delegates' credibility, a phenomenon that is somewhat unjust if one considers the tremendous amount of effort made by people who are not paid for their work and who must also maintain a regular job on the side.

To address this problem, representatives of administrative agencies were invited to neighborhood meetings (that is, "rendering account meetings"). In these venues, the delegates respond to their constituents in question-and-answer sessions. However, this process has become somewhat perfunctory. Over time, it became apparent that government agency representatives only infrequently attended meetings, and just like the delegates, they rarely had any way to solve problems. In each new electoral process, there has been an effort to reduce the size of the *circunscripciones* (election districts), which in turn increases the total number of delegates. Improving the delegate-to-population ratio meant sixteen hundred on average in the capital. In one meeting of the provincial presidents of Poder Popular at the end of 1995, the secretary of the National Assembly called for greater flexibility in provinces in order to professionalize full-time delegates given Cuba's new free-market initiatives (Lee 1995b). However, none of these measures got to the root of the problem: the lack of resources and real decision-making power for the delegates.

The initial confusion between elected government and administrative responsibility began to be resolved in 1993 when Executive Committees (Comités Ejecutivos) were replaced by the Administrative Councils (Consejos de Administración) with clearly defined tasks and relationships. Hence, an attempt was made to delimit the functions of representative government. Nevertheless, resources have continued to be centralized at the national level, and budget allocations continue to be quite small at a time when local governments attempt to compete with national priorities in the midst of a terrible economic crisis. Until recently, Havana (and Cuban) municipalities lacked their own revenues. In other words, municipal governments responded to local problems without financial resources for resolving them. Since the advent of self-employment in 1993, counties have had some discretion in generating revenues through the licensing of self-employed workers. Because there are no local property taxes paid to the government—a practice common in the market economies—Cuban municipalities largely depend on the national government for their budgets. Peters and Scarpaci (1998) found that in Centro Habana one market selling goods in pesos and containing more than one hundred kiosks of self-employed workers had generated the equivalent of thousands of dollars a year in revenues for the municipal government based solely on their daily fees for renting a spot in the market. At the same time, community participation continues to perform weakly despite the establishment of the Popular Neighborhood Councils (Consejos Populares de Barrios) in Havana, which increased from 93 original entities in 1990, to 102 in 1995, and 103 in 2001.

Despite its name, therefore, Poder Popular in fact has little power and even less community participation. Paradoxically, some attempts by the central government to help these organizations have actually hurt instead. In 1994, in light of the alarming number of problems in the capital such as sanitation removal, a national-level commission was created to "help" the work of local government. The logical solution would have been to transfer resources to pick up more garbage systematically. This style of work merely highlights the weakness of local government. In the end, Havana implements orders from higher levels of government. Unfortunately, the national level of government thinks it is being useful. Gestures of help become diluted until there is a new campaign of activism in order to carry out another set of directives.

By the early 1990s, it had become widely evident that there were contradictions between the political-administrative structure of Havana city and the needs of the people. In Marxist terms, these contradictions could serve as catalysts to foster necessary changes. Ideological imperatives prevail. Changes should be implemented cautiously so as not to jeopardize the overriding objectives of building socialism, yet they should occur rapidly enough to avoid economic and moral deterioration to the point of no return. Authorities also wish to safeguard the social achievements reached since 1959. Decentralization and participation seem to be pivotal points for such an ordered transformation. Decentralization, though, should not be seen only as administrative deconcentration (e.g., opening a local branch of national-level government agency).

Decentralization in many countries has been used to cover up a host of administrative, social, and political problems. Dismantling the welfare state in market economies has been carried out by privatization and deregulation (García Pleyán 1995b, 82; Scarpaci 1989, 11). Cuba's challenge is how to carry out decentralization in the Cuban context: Should it merely allow for the economic and political survival of the socialist project? Alternatively, will decentralization turn out to be administrative deconcentration, lacking the means for representing the people's and localities' interests? Clearly, city government must tap into local resources and participation. Achieving that goal requires that higher levels of government share power. Traditionally, power sharing in

Cuba has been viewed suspiciously and as a political concession. However, concessions may be perceived as a loss of credibility among national ministries that traditionally have been identified as the essence of the revolution (Roca Calderío 1973; De Armas 1975). Power sharing among government agencies that have enjoyed absolute and indisputable political, ideological, military, and administrative enforcement is virtually unknown in revolutionary Cuba. Nevertheless, its implementation cannot come too soon for the residents of Havana.

Self-governance and the role of civil society will have to be strengthened if Havana is to be decentralized yet retain elements of its socialist project. This will entail creating a new consciousness in which "the decentralization and socialization of power derives from an essential principle for the development of Cuban socialist democracy that includes attaining a pluralism that recognizes the diversity and autonomy of the participants of the decentralization project" (García Pleyán 1995b, 143; our translation).

## Neighborhood Popular Councils

Neighborhood Popular Councils began in 1988. They grew out of a need to compensate for the reduced number of municipalities following the 1976 political and administrative reorganization of the country. At first, the councils were confined to rural Cuba and had uneven levels of community participation. A few small scattered communities in Havana City Province (Campo Florido and Las Güásimas) implemented Consejos Populares. Santiago de Cuba and Camagüey Provinces installed "districts" (*distritos*) in urban areas. Unlike the Consejos Populares, which focused on community participation, these districts sought to enhance public administration. Positive results among Consejos Populares in the capital led to the passage of a law in 1990 that sanctioned the councils in other cities. Article 104 of the constitution was reformed in July 1992 and stipulated the functions of the Consejos Populares de Barrios such that, by 1995, 1,454 councils had been created in 97 percent of the nation's neighborhood electoral districts (CEA 1995; Lee 1995b).

Consejos Populares are composed of delegates from the same neighborhood electoral district; the delegates, in turn, elect a full-time representative to preside over the body. Representatives from grassroots and mass organizations such as the Cuban Federation of Women (Federación de Mujeres Cubanas [FMC]) and the Committees for the Defense of the Revolution

(Comité para la Defensa de la Revolución [CDR]) also form part of the local councils. In addition, the Consejos Populares include a representative from the Communist Youth Union (Unión de Comunistas Jóvenes) but not from the Cuban Communist Party. Representatives from local retailing, manufacturing, and government offices also participate in the councils, as do representatives from hospitals, schools, and research centers. Sectoral government agencies that are now subordinate to municipal government have membership in the local Consejo Popular. These representatives come from housing, education, culture, architecture and urban planning, public works, and other sectors.

Transformations such as those outlined above make the Consejos Populares, the newest entity within the system of Poder Popular, the ones most in touch with local concerns. In Havana, though, the average size of each area under the jurisdiction of a council (about twenty thousand people) is still too large for effective dialogue between council delegates and local constituents. The area covered by each Consejo Popular, moreover, does not always coincide with historical neighborhood boundaries. In the neighborhoods in which a Comprehensive Workshop for Neighborhood Change operates (the so-called *talleres* discussed in Chapter 4), there are reports that Consejos Populares benefit from the distribution of the *talleres*, but there has been no systematic evaluation of these contributions.

## Land-Use Enforcement in Havana and Urban Planning Discipline

Since the end of the 1980s, various criticisms have been put forth about the lack of coordination in the planning and the decision making for Havana's master plans. As described in several chapters throughout the book, this gap between planning and implementation can be seen when the historical image of the city is compared with what is now happening to Havana's built environment. Urban land-use regulation links planning to land-use implementation. In order to achieve efficient city management of land use, Havana planning authorities require, among other instruments, a clearly defined set of enforceable laws.

Havana's urban planning laws are steeped in the city's rich history and date from the early period of conquest. The Law of the Indies of 1523 and its reformulation in 1674 allowed hundreds of uneducated soldiers to settle Cuban cities as well as hundreds of cities elsewhere in Latin America (table 5.2)

Urban land-use regulations in Havana have emanated from more than a

TABLE 5.2. Major Urban Planning Laws in Cuba and Havana, 1523–1985

| LAW | YEAR | BRIEF DESCRIPTION |
| --- | --- | --- |
| Leyes de Indias | 1523, 1674 | Instruction about platting newfound settlements |
| Ordenanzas Municipales | 1574 | General rules about urban land use |
| Ordenanzas para la Zona de Extramuros | 1817 | Land use regulation in areas outside of the walled city |
| Ordenanzas de Construcción para la Ciudad de La Habana y los Pueblos de su Término | 1862 | Comprehensive building and design codes respecting such elements as the colonnaded galleries (porticoes) on the main streets (*calzadas*) |
| Ordenanzas y de Policía Urbana | 1881 | Specified regulatory powers for building and housing inspectors In Havana |
| Nuevas Ordenanzas de Construcción de la Plaza Cívica | 1963 | Updated land-use and building and design codes of 1862 |
| Reglamento de Ornato e Higiene de la Ciudad | 1977, second version in 1989 | Updated public health, sanitation, and waste removal regulations |
| Regulaciones Urbanísticas | 1985 | Standardized land-use planning regulations and zoning for the fifteen municipalities of Havana |
| Plan Director para La Habana Vieja | Early 1980s but fully implemented in late 1990s | Administered by the City Historian's Office. Includes both selected commercial redevelopment in northern and central Habana Vieja (especially the principal town squares) and residential enhancement in the neighborhood of San Isidro, in southern Habana Vieja (see Chapter 9) |

hundred government agencies. Since the mid-nineteenth century, regulations were designated as royal orders, laws, decree-laws, law decrees, resolutions, and collective and institutional resolutions. Between 1859 and 1959 more than eight entities passed laws for Havana, and between 1959 and 1993 another fifty laws and regulations were issued (Fernández 1995), an average of more than one law or regulation per year, of which there have been more than seventy versions.

Havana's fifteen municipalities, moreover, have each issued their own Urban Land-Use and Zoning Regulations (Regulaciones Urbanísticas) (Rodríguez and Cabrera 1995). Although the technical quality of the legal framework of city governance in Havana is quite high, Havana remains vulnerable to serious problems. Urban disorder is tolerated, as evidenced by inappropriate land uses and unauthorized building projects, all of which serve as a cruel mirror that reflects the most serious problem: a lack of citizen discipline. In this sense, aggressive acts against the urban tree canopy, historically undervalued, serves as a barometer for the city's problems. The situation becomes even more alarming with the recent arrival of new economic activities, including real estate. These economic transformations have been ushered in quickly because of the need for foreign capital. Land-use regulations and ordinances ostensibly exist and were created to reconcile discrepancies over land uses (García Pleyán 1995a; Scarpaci 1996a). However, they will now have to be reformulated because of the strong foreign presence in order to deal more effectively with outsiders who "were thought to be forgotten but once again are sneaking around" (Coyula 1995; our translation).

As pressure brought on by unsatisfied needs of *habaneros* increases, the topic of a "legal residence" has officially entered the government's agenda for action. During his rather acerbic intervention at the National Assembly at the end of 1995, Fidel Castro referred to the "illegal ones," lamenting the lack of cooperation among Havanan residents in denouncing them. Castro remarked: "Havana receives the punishment it deserves yes, they and the immense number of easterners [residents originating from the eastern part of the island] and other provinces that are now here. . . . The water network is insufficient, the electrical network telephones all of it insufficient. I've heard it said that in the municipality of Havana [there are more than] thirty thousand illegal residents and that isn't one of the largest estimates" (Castro 1995; our translation). Currently, the annual net gain from migration to the capital is about eleven thousand persons, a figure that pales in comparison with the situation in other capitals of large cities in Latin America. Nonetheless, that figure masks the fact that annually about twenty thousand people leave Havana, many of them young skilled workers, while about thirty thousand individuals migrate to Havana. Many illegal residents are unemployed and leave their provinces in eastern Cuba. Because of their "eastern" origin and "homeless" status, Cubans refer to them colloquially as *palestinos* (Palestinians).

## Urban Environment and Public Participation

Cuba paid little attention to environmental protection for almost two hundred years, and only recently has it begun to assess the impact of urbanization, agriculture, and industry on its environment (Díaz-Briquets and Pérez-López 2000). The enactment of Law 33 on January 10, 1981, marked a first step in environmental regulation. Just twenty-five pages in length, Law 33 purportedly covers regulations from the "principles of the Cuban Communist Party concerning the environment." As such, the law is heavily steeped in rhetoric and ideology and has very little in the way of verifiable policies and procedures. The law even goes so far as to claim that there is "wise use of natural resources by communist countries versus the indiscriminate use of natural resources by the Capitalistic World" (Barba and Avella 1996, 35–36; our translation). To be sure, environmental problems are grave in Havana and elsewhere in Cuba (Collis 1995).

A rapid overview of the major urban environmental problems in Cuba shows natural variation among cities and towns and even within similar neighborhoods. Despite that heterogeneity, the following features characterize some of the urban environmental challenges.

Table 5.3 identifies an entire range of environmental problems and speaks to the wide array of ailments that afflict the home, the neighborhood, and the entire city. It is noteworthy that food procurement is now the number one social problem, dislodging housing as the longstanding number one concern. Housing, however, poses serious challenges because of its generally rundown condition and improvised repairs. Air and noise pollution in Havana are serious problems, though cooling sea breezes tend to alleviate the former problem somewhat. Public transportation runs inadequately and is highly polluting.

Havana has not remained completely idle in the face of these environmental challenges. Public and private solutions surface often. Some are quite innovative and others more conventional. For example, local building materials and construction techniques have improved in recent years. This means that they are less wasteful and dependent on fossil fuel inputs and allow for greater resident participation. The massive use of the bicycle has rapidly transformed the urban landscape. As is noted in Chapter 8, the number of bicycles has increased more than tenfold from a 1990 baseline of about seventy thousand. Several bike lanes and bike paths now run through Havana, including an iron bridge (Puente de Hierro) over the Almendares River. Related economic activities include mechanical and tire repair, a cycle bus that takes cyclists from one side of the tunnel under Havana Bay to the other, and a series of baskets and racks on bicycles for carrying cargo and passengers. New innovations include the so-called *teteras*, which are simple bronze-threaded screws that

TABLE 5.3. Urban Environmental and Quality-of-Life Problems

| |
|---|
| • Food and basic article scarcities |
| • Low quality of housing |
| • Poor quality watersheds |
| • Noise pollution |
| • Flooding |
| • Thin vegetative cover |
| • Insufficient public transportation |
| • Scarce household fuel |
| • Poor waste removal service |
| • Heavily littered public spaces |
| • A deficit of public services (now reaching prioritized sector of health and education) |
| • Distortions in the urban image of the city |

*Source*: Coyula, Uriarte, and Cruz 1995; modified and updated, authors' fieldwork, 2001.

screw on to the rear axle of the bicycle and serve as footrests for passengers on the back seat. Credit for these innovations is divided between public agencies—groping for solutions to major urban problems—and resourceful citizens just trying to survive.

Other proactive measures in the realm of environmental planning surfaced in the late 1990s. The city has seventeen protected areas, eleven of which are located in eastern Havana; all are degraded by human activity. The disposal of garbage improved with the rehabilitation of the Cayo Cruz (Cross Key) dump sites in the southern part of Havana Bay. The fuel and spare parts shortage in the Special Period forced the opening of many scattered dump sites to reduce transportation. Three other dump sites were also closed and rehabilitated, but eighteen more are still waiting. There has been little improvement in reuse and recycling, also unnecessarily increasing the amount of waste to transport and dispose. Monitoring the city's environment was restarted in 1999. Air pollution figures were higher than the maximum accepted in sedimented dust and sulfur dioxide, but not in ammonia and soot. Although Havana is favored by the sea breezes that sweep away foul air, diesel exhaust from passing trucks and buses is a problem.

A special council (Consejo Provincial de Cuencas Hidrográficas) was created for Havana in 1997 for the management of several important watersheds: (1) the Almendares-Vento Basin, with the Almendares River Basin and the

Vento underground aquifer that still supplies almost one-fifth of the city's demand by gravity; (2) the Havana Bay Basin, including the river basins of the Luyanó and Martín Pérez, as well as that of Tadeo Creek; (3) the East Basin, with the rivers Cojímar, Bacuranao, Tarará, Itabo, and Guanabo, plus the seashore where they end (and where a fine strip of beaches is); and (4) the West Basin, with the Jaimanitas and Quibú Rivers plus the seashore where they end. Pollution is worst at the Almendares, Luyanó, Martín Pérez, Cojímar, and Quibú Rivers and at the bay, whose closed baglike shape slows water renovation. Yet the condition improved in the late 1990s, as several polluting factories were closed and others were forced to rehabilitate their preliminary cleaning systems. Oil spills from bay refineries have also been reduced, but illegal wastewater connections to the storm water drains pouring into the bay are very difficult to fight. Many studies have been carried on by the Institute of Research on Transport (Instituto de Investigación del Transporte [IIT]) and the State Group for the Cleaning, Conservation, and Development of the Havana Bay, with help from the United Nations Development Programme (UNDP) and other international agencies. Havana Bay oxygen levels rose from zero, and marine life is already returning to a bay once feared for its sharks.

Abandoned lots in Cuban cities, Havana in particular, are increasingly being used as organic and community gardens cared for by local residents. Many ecologically sound alternatives appeared, forced by scarcity, such as bicycling and organic farming. A search for nonpolluting methods of agricultural production was combined with the need to avoid dependence on imports. Government agencies at many levels encourage the use of biological and natural enemies for plagues, covering more than 800,00 hectares of plantations in Cuba by late 2000 (L. Rodríguez 2000). Nevertheless, unused land suitable for agriculture amounted to 2,600 hectares in 1997.

Urban agriculture in Havana is among the best in Cuba. The food crisis of the early 1990s triggered urban agriculture, and it became a modest way to improve the diet by self-help, community efforts, and state-paid workers within the city fabric. This new "urban agricultural labor force" serves as an alternative to conventional large farms that are distant from the capital. It also promotes a more environmentally sound approach to farming that relies on recycling and composting waste while reducing the use of costly and polluting chemical fertilizers and pesticides. In the end, it encourages a much needed environmental awareness at the grassroots level. By late 2000, there were almost 9,000 hectares and 22,088 persons dedicated to urban agriculture in Havana. Specifically, urban agriculture in Havana takes on the following aspects:

- Vegetable gardens, formerly known as *"huertos populares,"* are tended by neighbors, not by regular state-paid workers. They are now subdivided into *"parcelas"* (lots) and *"huertos intensivos"* (intensive gardens).
- *"Organopónicos populares"* (community organic gardens)
- *"Organopónicos de alto rendimiento"* (high-yield organic gardens) are tended by workers paid by the state. They include 8 hectares tended by government agencies to feed their own employees.
- *"Autoconsumos estatales"* (state-run gardens for self-consumption)
- *"Campesinos,"* or farmers' cooperatives, clustered at the city edge

Table 5.4 summarizes related attributes of this new city farming as it was in 2000.

Surplus produce can be sold in the open market, and technical advice is provided by the state. More than twenty-eight thousand families in Havana take advantage of these gardens. Animal waste, fertilizer, and other organic inputs are being used on state agricultural lands to bolster agricultural output. Lands previously considered to be marginal—often at the city edge—have come into production because of the Special Period. Alternatives for garbage pickup now include tractors and carts pulled by animals. Slowly, the mentality of recycling is taking hold among *habaneros* (Hernández 1994).

There is still little environmental culture in Havana among both the citizenry and authorities. This lack of concern over the environment bodes poorly for Havana in the near future given that it will confront considerable scarcities. Excuses for not becoming more environmentally aware include a degree of mental inertia and the defense of previous positions held by governments. Perhaps even more dangerous is the trend that began at the end of 1995 among certain official circles—provoked by indexes either real or perceived about a slight economic recuperation—to return to the old ways of doing things and working in the environmental realm. For instance, there is now some discussion about returning to the old program of new housing made out of large prefabricated panels (see Chapter 6) and of using only petroleum-based chemical fertilizers that require high energy inputs.

Interest in the concept and practice of environmental sustainability has moved beyond academic circles and the initial narrow focus on environmental conservation. Traditional environmental thinking has elaborated interna-

TABLE 5.4. Urban Agriculture in Havana, 2000

| TYPE OF PRODUCTIVE ORGANIZATION | AREA (HECTARES) | NUMBER OF WORKERS |
|---|---|---|
| *Huertos populares*: | | |
|   *Parcelas (7,944)* | 1,030.14 | 16,869 |
|   *Huertos intensivos* | 87.26 | 663 |
| *Organopónicos populares* | 66.98 | 672 |
| *Organopónicos de alto rendimiento* | 19.10 | 340 |
| *Autoconsumos estatales* | 3,086.00 | 2,044 |
| *Campesinos* | 4,489.00 | 1,500 |
| Total | 8,778.48 | 22,088 |

*Source*: Preliminary returns from a research project coordinated by Kary Cruz, "Evaluación de la agricultura urbana como componente de la economía local en dos zonas de La Habana," sponsored by the Fundación "Antonio Núñez Jiménez / La Naturaleza y el Hombre," forthcoming.

tionally accepted ideas about the possible existence of sustainability. Widely accepted concepts and practices include a new regard for variety and diversity, the interdependence among elements in a system, the carrying capacity of a particular ecosystem and its regenerative potential, the multiplicity of functions that each element plays, and the idea that various elements in an ecosystem can fulfill the same function. That Cuba is a poor, small, isolated island with a mostly urban population suggests that it is logical to extend these principles of sustainability to the natural and social environment and to the economy as well (Scarpaci and Coyula, forthcoming).

A perennial challenge in environmental defense — and Havana is no exception — is that communities often find it difficult to focus on invisible, short-term inputs when other daily needs remain unsatisfied. Cuba, like many other countries, would benefit greatly if it could develop an economic model and a use of the built environment that is viable and rational (Coyula, Uriarte, and Cruz 1995, 1–2). Resources required for that kind of development not only can come out of macroeconomic structures but must also derive from a real and stable family and community economy. The neighborhood can serve as the basic unit of the homeland. In Havana, community participation in the socialist project has been essentially one of mobilization. A variety of new forms of community are evident in Havana, most of which were practically unheard of just a decade ago (table 5.5).

TABLE 5.5. New Forms of Community Participation

| TYPE OF ORGANIZATION | DESCRIPTION |
| --- | --- |
| *Consejo popular* | Continues conventional verticalist approach but focused on a smaller geographical unit with direct feedback by residents |
| Mass organizations | Although strongly tied to the state, contributions from the membership play a greater role |
| Quasi-state organizations | Examples include Comprehensive Workshops for Neighborhood Change (Talleres de Transformación Integral de Barrios). See text. |
| NGOs | United Nations, church, and foreign donor–supported groups picking up slack from diminished role of Cuban government |
| Community organizations | Traditional, private philanthropic organizations that existed in Cuba. Example: Liceo de Regla, created in 1879 and devoted to civic work. |
| Grassroots organizations | Volunteer groups that do not overlap with state agencies or mass organizations. Included are agricultural groups and hog ranchers. |

## Change or Semblance of Change?

Even though the capital is the most productive place in the country, the income it generates is generally not reinvested into it in a way that is proportionate to its level of contribution. One exception is the restoration project of the historic center of Habana Vieja under the management of the Office of the City Historian (see Chapter 9). That office has a special company, Habagüanex, that turns profits on several businesses operating in Habana Vieja and then reinvests some of those resources in the old quarters.

The special funding arrangements for historic preservation and conservation in Habana Vieja are unique in Havana City Province. The rest of the province municipalities do not have such revenue-generating projects. Rather, they receive their budget and material resources from the national budget, which is usually approved, with very little changes, at the end of the year by the National Assembly. The province also receives a corresponding amount of revenue from its fifteen municipalities. Revenues cannot be readjusted or redirected to other areas except when explicitly stated by the national government. In 1986 the municipalities tried to decentralize municipal budgets in the hope of moving toward self-financing. This meant giving the municipality a percentage of the taxes that it had collected in its jurisdiction and a greater flexibility to transfer funds between different accounts without altering the total budget. The essence of the problem of housing, for example, is not allowing local governments to generate their own revenues and to receive funds equitably from the national government. In the main, however, the problem is that surpluses cannot usually be used to purchase building materials because there are no materials assigned for this purpose. Municipal governments do not have the administrative power to obtain materials. Pressure brought on by the economic change in the 1990s forced municipal governments to look for new ways to fill in the gaps left by the withdrawal of centralized planning. One solution is Intercompany Cooperation Councils (Consejos de Cooperación Interempresarial), which oversee coordination of companies but in a market context (González 1995).

Fixed budgets designated for city and county governments in Cuba have always fallen well below the needs of those entities, even during the relatively prosperous bonanza years when exchanges between the Eastern European bloc and Cuba were at a high mark. Even today, the budget allocation to city and county governments almost never fulfills budgetary needs and can be expected to cover only salaries at 100 percent.

The budget situation has worsened during the Special Period and is now begrudgingly accepted as a given by most of the young people in Cuba, who know no other form of government-service delivery. This situation has two aspects. On the one hand, community participation has lost much of the energy and enthusiasm it held in the 1960s. Many formulas for promoting community participation have become mechanical and no longer justify the amount of effort required to employ them given the results of community projects. On the other hand, there is an organizational structure, coupled with a tradition, that is capable of turning out large mobilizations that could yet again become active with clearly visible objectives that interest the residents of Havana (Coyula, González, and Vincentelli 1993). Alternatively these mobilizations could gain greater credibility and take on a protagonist role within civil society, clearly a segment of Cuba that is gradually becoming more empowered in a post-Soviet era (Gunn 1995).

Public administration in Havana is now concerned with efficiency as never before since the advent of the revolution. In order to keep the budget deficit manageable, it is necessary to increase the efficiency of state firms that continue to be the weakest point in the Cuban economy. The government's decision not to shut down large numbers of state firms that were not profitable was a humane gesture. Nonetheless, it makes the country's economic recovery more difficult and continues to be the principal reason for excess cash in the economy, contributing to inflation. Many college-educated professionals, poorly paid, are earning less now in real terms than they did in 1959 (Chauvin 1996). The government, therefore, is indirectly supporting unprofitable state firms. Those same professionals, however, may forget the cost of the education they received as well as the free medical care that all Cubans enjoy. Rising unemployment, moreover, may erode the modest gains of the free market and will cast more university graduates into the unemployment lines. One of the most dramatic pay raises took place throughout Cuba in the late 1990s, when police officers received a major increase. In Havana, the average cop on the beat earns just over 700 pesos monthly (about U.S.$32), surpassing physicians and teachers. In the end, however, instead of dealing with the daunting task of feeding 11 million mouths, it seems more practical to look for a way to find work for 22 million arms so they can feed themselves.

## The Arrival of the Dollar

Since the arrival of foreign investment, the establishment of a dual economy, and the legalization of the dollar, Havana once again reveals contrasting sides. At one extreme are those who have access to dollars or sell goods and services at exorbitant prices in the informal market. In August 1996, twenty-three money-exchange houses operated in Havana. The new private Cuban corporation, CADECA S.A., contemplates opening two hundred similar houses throughout Cuba over the next few years. Cuban vice president Carlos Lage reported on July 23, 1996, that the Cuban peso had increased its value sixfold in the past two years, removing 250 million pesos from circulation during the first semester of 1996 (InterPress 1996a). Between 1998 and 2001, the exchange rate between the Cuban peso and the U.S. dollar held steady at about 22 but reached 26 in 2002.

At another extreme are those who subsist precariously on fixed salaries and who rely on the meager Cuban peso. Old mansions in the "frozen zones" of Miramar and Vedado are increasingly being converted into offices of joint ventures and state businesses that transact in dollars. The main purpose of these stores is not to increase the options available to *habaneros* but rather to capture the greatest amount of hard currency in order to finance the continuation of the prevailing socialist system. This is reflected in the name of a chain of stores that carries the bureaucratic name TRDS, whose initials stand for stores for recovering hard currencies (Tiendas de Recuperación de Divisas). That name itself assumes that hard currency captured by inflated prices (usually 240 percent above cost) morally belongs to the state.

These new dollar-gathering retail activities coexist in the former fancy neighborhoods with embassies, the homes of labor organizational leaders, and illegal residents (many of the last are remnants of the former caretakers who occupied the homes in the 1960s, as discussed in Chapter 6). When schools and boarding houses were massively converted for schoolchildren around the country who had received scholarships, these neighborhoods changed markedly, and the changes in the 1990s rivaled the transformation of those same neighborhoods in the 1960s. Miramar is still structured along an axis—the famous Quinta Avenida—that retains the same status symbol it held in 1959. Its traditional landscaped green areas, carefully pruned trees, and manicured hedges endure. Although the landscape architecture has not varied over these past forty years, small neon signs that timidly break through this carefully groomed landscape are on the rise. Restaurants, cafés, bars, stores, boutiques, pastry shops, gasoline stations, and a whole spate of foreign firms including Benetton, Meliá, and ING Bank have recently located there. This new retail "glow" symbolizes a kind of rebirth amid a setting of abandonment and a fading gleam of former bourgeois Havana, pointing to Cuba's timid foray into capitalism. Moreover, these dollar-run stores allow the state to tap into the estimated $800 million to $1 billion sent to Cubans from family and friends overseas.

While part of the new dollar economy allows many Cubans to purchase food that is unavailable through the state ration book (*libreta*) as well as basic products such as clothes, household goods, and consumer durables, a new social class is on the rise. A new elite occupies the public spaces of Miramar. These new actors are not the elegant yuppies jogging or the nouveaux riches speeding along in their BMWs. Instead, one can see the ostentatious new rich of Cuba—*macetas*—joy-riding in their restored Chevrolets of the 1950s and hear rock and roll or salsa blaring from their car speakers as they drive to the dollar-only shops. Donning only their gaudy T-shirts, these new rich are unprecedented in socialist Havana. Other new actors in Havana's streets include *jineteras* (prostitutes) and lecherous Spaniards, Italians, or Canadians driving around in rented Nissans, Hyundais, and Toyotas in search for cheap sex. Havana's new "sexual tourism" is gaining notoriety in Europe especially as it is more accessible than its competition in faraway Thailand.[3]

These exploits transpiring in Miramar contrast with the large traditional peso-operated stores of Centro Havana. Buildings across town remain under-utilized or closed by a lack of merchandise, the advanced stage of deteriora-tion of the buildings, or houses that are precariously adapted to a low level of habitability elsewhere in the city. Miramar seems far removed from life of the rest of *habaneros*. This new investment in Havana is complemented by the ubiquitous ambulant vendors who proliferate like mushrooms around the city. These self-employed peddle their improvised products in open-air mar-kets, parks, and galleries in the old commercial districts and in front of the empty stores.

## Foreign Investment and the Changing Look of Havana

In September 1995, Law No. 77 passed by the National Assembly broadened the legal and institutional framework for foreign investment. This law substi-tuted Decree-Law 50, approved as the Cuban-Foreign Economic Association Law of February 1982. Decree-Law 50 required the Ministry of Foreign In-vestment and Economic Collaboration (Ministerio para la Inversión Extran-jera y la Colaboración Económica [MINVEC], formerly known as Comité Es-tatal para la Colaboración Económica [CECE]), to work on trade with the Soviet Union and the now defunct socialist countries of the Council of Mu-tual Economic Assistance (CMEA) as the maximum Cuban government entity in charge of business opportunities with foreigners. The Ministry of Foreign Investment and Economic Collaboration monitors business operations and defines the ways in which foreign investors, both companies and individuals, can do business in Cuba. The law establishes certain guarantees for investors and defines the authorized ways of investing: joint ventures, international economic associations, and a completely foreign capital firm.

This ministry also deals with financial contributions and assessment as well as the approval and supervision of applications for investment, the banking system, conditions of import and export, the taxation system, custom tariffs

3. Unfortunately, these new sexual exploits are noted on several sites of the World Wide Web. Home pages are posted and maintained by European travelers who "share" their tips about working with Cuban prostitutes, brothels, and pimps.

and accounting, insurance, the control of information, and the financial registry (Núñez 1996). Foreign capital and joint-venture matters bypass municipal and provincial government and are dealt with directly by MINVEC, which operates at the highest levels of national government (fig. 5.2). In the process, a new federalism is emerging in Cuba in which the national government replaces local decision making and indirectly sets up new employment opportunities and lifestyles for civil society.

Establishing a business in Cuba involves an elaborate chain of approval and review. Included within MINVEC is a firm called Grupo Negociador (Business Group), which establishes the conditions between a foreign partner and Cuban private or state agencies. The firm assesses how to fulfill the terms of agreement and analyzes future business negotiations established by the government. The governmental agencies also have their respective business associates and promotional firms that define the scope of a potential enterprise and the formal details of the project. The project must also be submitted to other agencies such as the Banco Nacional de Cuba, the Ministry of Finances and Prices, the Ministry of Work and Social Security, the University of Havana, and other research centers (Núñez 1996). If the project receives a positive evaluation by MINVEC, then, according to its size, it goes on for review by the Executive Committee of the Council of Ministers or to a special governmental commission for further analysis and final approval. If the project is approved, the Chamber of Commerce inscribes the business in the Register of Economic Associations. The legal framework defines the reach of the businesses as determined by the Law of Foreign Investment, the Tax Law, the regulation of employment and pay, tariff regulations set by customs authorities, and other regulations put forth by ministries and Cuban firms.

There are two predominant forms of associations in practice today: the joint venture and the international economic association. However, the new law of September 1995 allowed the total foreign capital firm to exist without the participation of a Cuban counterpart. The joint-venture firm acts as a single company and has a legal status that is different from that of the participating entities. Both parts put up a certain amount of capital or equity for the new company. Normally, this type of association is a long-term agreement (about twenty years). The international economic association generally employs small projects that are of medium-term duration. This is a contractual form that does not require obtaining legal status in Cuba, and all its legal aspects are established within a contract. Another arrangement used mainly in mineral and oil prospecting is the risk investment (*inversión a riesgo*). A practice

FIGURE 5.2. The new federalism in Cuba: state, civil society, and the market

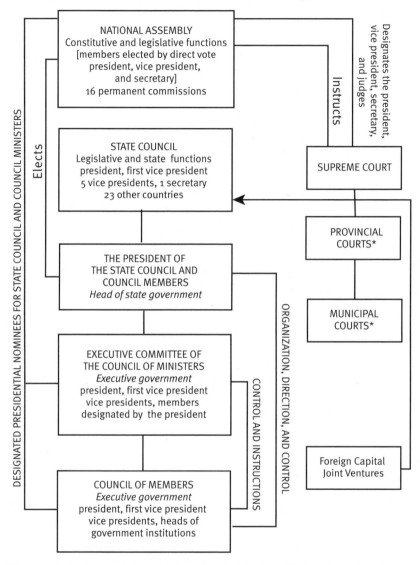

\* The presidents, vice presidents, and judges of provincial and municipal courts are elected by the respective assemblies. The fifth article of the constitution states that the Cuban Communist Party is the supreme force for the direction of the state and civil society.

commonly carried out in the tourism sector is the participation of a foreign firm in the administrative management of hotels. Also recently created are free port zones in three ports and a network of in-bond warehouses that are not subject to custom tariffs (InterPress 1996b). Among these zones is the large district of warehouses in Habana del Este, known as Havana In-Bond. Officially, the new law only excludes foreign investment of sectors of national security, health, and education (Núñez 1996).

A system of taxes was approved by Law 73 in 1994 and consists of three elements: taxes, tax rates, and payments. For foreign investment, that law established a tax of 30 percent over net profits and a 25 percent tax on the salaries and wages of Cuban workers. Any Cuban employed by a foreign company or joint venture cannot be contracted directly by the foreign firm. Rather, that person must be hired through a state agency called ACOREC, which receives the salary in dollars and then pays the Cuban half that amount in pesos. The firm must pay, in addition, taxes for the right to use land, transportation, natural resources, and the airport.

Cuba's banking system centers around the Banco Nacional de Cuba, which must approve any foreign financial operation in Cuba. Firms or individuals can open accounts in Cuban banks, and there are two banks that function with hard currencies: Banco Financiero Internacional (BFI) and the Banco Internacional de Comercio S.A. (BICSA). The only foreign bank with a branch office in Cuba is ING Netherlands, but it cannot disburse money. It accepts Visa and MasterCard credit cards as long as they are not issued by U.S. banks (Núñez 1996).

Since the legalization of the dollar in July 1993, Cubans can now exchange foreign currencies at banks and hotels. The U.S. dollar has become the currency of operation for state enterprises. The dollar circulates in transactions involving a broad range of products and services that are in short supply or else operate within the peso economy. Significantly, this includes food products. The Cuban government operates five chain stores that aim to "capture" hard currency: Tiendas Panamericanas, Tiendas Caracol, operated by the Ministry of Tourism and Hotels; Tiendas TRD, managed by the Gaviota tourist group (see Chapter 8); Tiendas Universal, directed by Cubanacán; and Tiendas CUBALSE, run by a corporation of that same name. Foreign companies may distribute their products directly to these five stores. At the end of 1995 there were 212 foreign economic associations operating in Cuba with a total capital of $2.1 billion (about half of all investments in the country) (Núñez 1996).

## New Actors in City Administration: Real Estate in Havana

Among the most recent investment opportunities for foreigners is the real estate market, with special interest in Havana. Cubalse, Habagüanex, and Eproyiv are the Cuban facilities that serve as joint real estate enterprises. The actors in this real estate process have changed quickly because of an initial inadequate institutional design. A few years ago, early interest by some real estate investors was not properly addressed. Given Cuba's thirty-odd-year closure to the private market, it was not surprising that Cuban state agencies had little understanding of basic urban, economic, and financial aspects of the real estate market (Núñez 1996). On several occasions, promises were made to foreign firms without counting on the prior approval of the administration of physical planning and architecture (Planificación Físcia y Arquitectura), which controls urban land use and building permits. Municipal authorities in Havana were also kept out of the decision-making process.

Real estate investment in Havana—like joint ventures elsewhere in Cuba—tends not to interest Cuban authorities unless the projects are large. This is unfortunate because a myriad of small and medium investments would be appropriate for Havana, since they are the kinds of operations that have historically built the city. They could help the city not only create employment for displaced workers but also save thousands of local properties, many of which are on the verge of collapse. A new real estate market could also provide a central location for the street vendors who—despite the important role they play in satisfying unmet demand in the marketplace—nonetheless interfere with traffic, destroy green areas, and introduce visual blight in the urban landscape. On the other hand, a broadened and decentralized revitalization would be more stable and less vulnerable to economic pressures than another investment scheme that would depend on a few large foreign investors. In other words, this is related to the need of strengthening the urban economy from below. Havana's economy requires productive activities other than just self-employed workers. History shows that the city's economy moves slowly between stages of retailing. It is hoped that Havana will not have to wait another few centuries to develop a full range of retail activities (Coyula 1995, 4–5).

It appears that maintaining a dollar-based real estate market for Cubans will have to wait until the present demand by diplomats, workers from foreign companies, businesspersons residing in Cuba, and other foreigners is satisfied. Havana's urban real estate market could be broadened in the near future with commercial office space and hotel-support facilities for tourism such as marinas. Second homes for retirees who live abroad might also be considered, including eventually the return of elderly Cuban Americans who wish to retire in Havana.

Real estate activities bring both risks and opportunities. On the one hand, they might well represent the arrival of much-needed capital that will allow the city to generate wealth that could be reinvested back into it. On the other hand, a speculative market could destroy what is actually the most attractive feature of the city—its noncommercialized landscape and multilayered built fabric—and convert Havana into just another tourist spot (Coyula 1995). The title of the very successful animated feature-length film by Juan Padrón, *Vampires in Havana* (*Vampiros en La Habana*), could become a portrait of a painful reality if the terrible need for capital pressures Cuban authorities to do just that. In that case, the city would be defenseless and succumb to a new form of piracy.

## Havana Continues

After his participation in the First Physical Planning Seminar in Havana, in 1971, the well-known U.S. urban designer Kevin Lynch formulated interesting questions in his favorite book, *What Time Is This Place?* He pondered what physical changes in Havana can be seen to express the deep economic, political, and social changes that had occurred (Lynch 1972). At that time, new construction in the capital was restricted, and the buildings that the revolution inherited seemed to be able to weather all forms of deterioration. Those transformations were subtle and perhaps more appropriately labeled as changes in function and in users. However, Lynch's well-trained eye detected those trends and anticipated challenges that awaited Havana. As this chapter has shown, these changes are risky and underscore the new relationship between a highly centralized form of government and the new actors on Havana's streets: foreign investors.

In the mid-1980s, investment required for rehabilitating Havana was estimated at between $10 billion and $14 billion. The figures were staggering, and inevitably they triggered the question: How much is this city worth? The capital represents an enormous investment accumulated over twenty generations. Contributions to the city are material and monetary ones as well as energy and housing, which translate into great artistic, historical, functional, and environmental value. Each input has strong economic implications (Vázquez

Raña 1993). The conservation of these values and the development that Havana requires to become a new regional leader seem possible only to the extent that the city itself can finance those changes based on what it can rationally extract from its own resources. Such a perspective requires a fair appraisal of Havana without losing the city to disuse and without deforming, selling, mortgaging, or giving it away (Coyula 1995).

Havana has survived several critical tests in its long history, and some of them appeared at the time to be fatal. It has been beaten but has retained its composure. Without doubt, complicity for its dilapidated state must be shared because, layer by layer, a thick web of relations has been sewn that extends beyond the facades of its buildings. The city reaches out to pedestrians hurrying through its streets; they do not have to raise their head to see if the old companion of their dreams is stubbornly there—peeling, crumbling, distorted by salt and water yet incredibly alive and useful. A city that no longer is what it was and that continues to reinvent itself. Havana always, forever our Havana. *La Habana siempre, siempre nuestra Habana.*

# The Hope and Reality of Socialist Housing

Environment unifies society, individuals, and their surroundings. Life stems from an environmental system that incorporates the past, the present and the future through remembrances, reality and imagination.

—Fernando Salinas, 1984

Housing is the social mirror of a city. If monuments define outstanding elements of the cultural landscape, then the residential stock reflects the social contradictions of the city (López Castañeda 1963, 1971). The complexity of habitat stems from the ongoing tensions between affluence and poverty. Flying over any underdeveloped city of the world, one immediately notices the suburban green spaces of the wealthy or the high-rises at the city's edge. Beyond that, there appear ad infinitum the small homes of the middle class and densely settled apartment complexes that derive from speculative housing markets. Throughout the metropolis, one can see the atomization and the disorder of squatter settlements strung along the periphery or buried in the interstices of the inner city. Here lies the clear evidence of the ever present poverty of the Latin American city.

Havana in the 1950s was no exception to this pattern. The trail of luxurious residences that started at the beginning of the century in Vedado and Miramar continued westward along the coast. There in succession came the neighborhoods of Reparto Náutico, Country Club, Flores, Siboney, and Coronela, until reaching the town of Santa Fe. In the area of Jaimanitas there were Flores and Barlovento. The housing designs ranged from extended tile roofs covering flowered and California-style chalets to the first images of the International Style, consisting of light structures and transparent glass surfaces (Serraino and Shulman 2000). The industrious middle class and young entrepreneurs occupied the axis along Rancho Boyeros—a road that linked the airport with city center—with small cottages nestled in green areas. This pattern was evident in the neighborhoods of Santa Catalina and El Sevillano and rose to a greater population density in Altahabana, gradually tapering off to the remote suburbs of Fontanar and El Wajay. Finally, rather modest and nondescript houses lined up in straight rows along the Central Highway to the southeast. Mantilla, Diezmero, San Francisco de Paula, and Cotorro formed this strip of working-class housing, which were mixed in with factories (fig. 6.1).

Once the tunnel under the bay was opened, expansion toward the east—although incipient and controlled by finance and real estate companies—ensured that large-scale developments could not be easily subdivided into small suburban developments. Habana del Este, the largest conceived development in the late 1950s, sparked interest in the U.S. firm Skidmore, Owings, and Merril and the Italian architect Franco Albini because of its lucrative potential. Although these large-scale projects were never executed, a few single-family residential structures such as in Vía Tunel and Bahía were built in the areas surrounding Habana del Este.

This kind of suburbanization contrasted with the traditional Hispanic layout of rectangular blocks along a continuous grid. Comparisons between poor suburban neighborhoods and the middle class show that even among individual housing typologies, few traditional attributes persisted such as the continuous *portal* along the building front. The chalet, on the other hand, was more of an organic design associated with higher-income *habaneros* who were eager to capture the romantic realm of nature. In the process of breaking up the city's traditional design and layout, there was also an increase in high-rise apartments in Centro Habana and Vedado (García Vázquez 1968; Garnier 1973; Durán 1992). Beginning with the 1952 Condominium Law, the construction of upscale high-rises accelerated (Segre 1985b). At that time there was a strong infusion of foreign capital due to the high rates of return in Havana's real estate market. For instance, between 1941 and 1953 the real estate market in Havana absorbed 28 million pesos annually, whereas between 1953 and 1958 the figure reached 60 million pesos annually out of a total of 72 million invested nationwide (Acosta and Hardoy 1972). If the foreign housing models from abroad favored individual high-rise structures for the bourgeoisie, then the collective imagination of most *habaneros* clung to the freestanding home and garden.

FIGURE 6.1. Traditional wooden bungalows characterized modest housing built in the first half of the twentieth century. This structure is located in Regla. (Photograph by Joseph L. Scarpaci)

Speculative investment in the 1950s explains what would appear to be arbitrary suburban subdivisions. They were isolated and mostly disconnected both from one another and from Havana's existing street pattern. In some cases these suburban enclaves lacked basic infrastructure such as sewers, street lights, and gas. Moreover, they unnecessarily expanded Havana's metropolitan area. Much of the new suburbanization in the 1950s lay outside the cities' political borders and was therefore exempt from Havana's master plan.

Political corruption permeated real estate. Aesthetic norms or urban design was not used to control development on the outskirts. Fierce speculation and higher land and rental values drove the middle class to suburbs increasingly farther from the downtown areas. Havana's suburbanization had little to do with professional architecture, whose parameters were set by formally trained individuals. Instead, anonymous builders erected homes like any other consumption good.

Small construction companies built the predominant model of 1950s housing: single-family residences. Companies and brand names such as Gallo rice; Colgate toothpaste; Candado soap; Lavasol, Rina, and Fab laundry detergents; and *El País* newspaper sponsored contests that gave homes to lucky consumers who purchased their products. The prototypes of these homes repeatedly surfaced in television spots, newspapers, and magazines, which in turn molded the popular "taste" associated with the ambitious middle-class home. These houses looked like small, pink boxes with their porches in the front, attached garages, and pitched roofs. The suburban Havana "dream house" created in the 1950s survived several decades of the socialist revolution and remained present in the minds of many *habaneros* in the 1990s.

## Creativity and Innovation in the Early Housing Initiatives of Havana

The housing problem was strongly evident in Fidel Castro's well-known Moncada declaration, which he delivered at his defense for attacking military barracks in 1953 (Castro 1964). Precarious rural living conditions, the rapid increase in tenements, slums, and shantytowns in Havana, and the exorbitant rents charged for apartments and houses were a call to enforce the laws of the 1940 constitution. Although many of these housing laws had been on the "books" for more than a decade, Castro underscored the fact that the constitutional guarantee of housing to every Cuban had not been enforced by the Batista regime (Fernández Núñez 1976).

From January 1, 1959, onward, the revolutionary government defined three basic principles of its urban and rural housing policy. First, it ended speculation on land and housing. Second, it favored low-income Cubans burdened by high rents. Third, it immediately started building housing for workers and farmers. The first two principles annulled rental payments for those living in substandard housing, and it waived rent for those who could not afford monthly payments. A series of important laws in the first two years radically altered Cuba's housing situation (table 6.1). Overall, these actions defined housing in socialist Cuba. Only landlords had to sell their rental properties to tenants, with the state acting as intermediary. At times, the state paid additional compensation to former landlords in the form of lifetime annuities for low- and moderate-income people. All but the biggest landlords received full compensation. Homeowners could keep their homes no matter how large or well situated, including a second house for recreation. However, the units left by those emigrating became state property. The price of these former rental dwellings was set for twenty years. In many cases, rent was reduced by up to 50 percent by Law 135. A fee of 10 percent of gross income was charged only

TABLE 6.1. Selected Housing Laws during the First Years of the Castro Government

| LAW NO. | DATE | PURPOSE |
|---------|------|---------|
| 26 | January 26, 1959 | Suspend legal action against those who could not pay rent or mortgages or were threatened by evictions |
| 135 | March 10, 1959 | Lower rents by 50 percent |
| 691 | December 23, 1959 | Establish the forced sale of empty lots and their price |
| 892 | October 14, 1960 | Urban Reform Law: A complex doctrine defining the nation's housing policies |

*Source:* Segre 1989.

for newly assigned units, which included newly built dwellings or those that came into the state's hands because of death without heirs or people leaving the country (Hamberg 1994).

Cuba's housing policy in the 1960s was unprecedented in Latin America because for the first time land speculation and profit making on urban land and housing had ended. The laws also ended the prevailing price structure by fixing a flat rate of 4 pesos per square meter for all lots, regardless of whether they were in the much coveted downtown areas or in a distant suburb. Once the cost of urban space was economically leveled, the private sector gradually lost interest in real estate and housing. In 1960, private construction slowed down considerably, and most building projects under way rested in the state's hands. Although large construction and construction materials firms were nationalized in the first few years, private building initiatives continued at a slow pace until 1968. Significantly, all land was not nationalized, and there were relatively few "forced sales" under the housing laws of the 1960s. Small building projects, especially for individual homeowners, continued in Havana during the early to mid-1960s and again in the 1980s.

The new revolutionary government tackled the problems of racial and social segregation produced by the urban land market of the past and began mixing different economic and social strata of Havana in order to alter radically the makeup of the city's neighborhoods. Of course, the out-migration by a large Cuban bourgeoisie freed up part of the city's housing stock, thus easing the need for new housing. Slowly, a migrant stream from the eastern provinces consisting of workers, small farmers, and veterans of the fight against Batista began occupying this housing.

Although the revolutionary government implemented a series of key laws in its early years, there were also signs that it failed to act on other problems in the housing sector. Many of the mansions formerly occupied by those who had emigrated abroad were left to the domestic servants who had previously worked there. These former servants brought friends and family members — many from outside Havana — to live with them. In other cases, emptied mansions that were initially used as schools and dormitories for students on scholarships were occupied after regular school hours by persons who had taken care of the students. As a result, there were striking cases of neglect and abuse of some of Havana's most symbolic and ornate homes. As population increased and pressure for housing mounted in the city, so too did the rate of self-help housing and state construction (CED 1976; Comité Estatal de Construcción 1977; Coyula 1985a, 1985b). Even though these strategies were conceptually valid for coping with Havana's housing problems, they also had the unintended effect of driving down the environmental quality of certain neighborhoods (GDIC 1991, 1994). Witness, for example, the spontaneous and inadvertent "ruralization" of the city spawned by self-help housing. Such construction ran against the state's official policy that supported multifamily housing. Even during the past three decades, there has been much anonymous and low-quality construction built simply to provide shelter for those who resided in the former garden suburbs of Havana. It was not until the 1980s that a group of planners and designers in the central government took interest in establishing an urban design and architectural identity for Havana's neighborhoods.

The revolutionary government directed its housing policies during the first two years toward three fundamental objectives: (1) to eradicate shantytowns, (2) to construct new housing, giving preference to apartment complexes, and (3) to devise technical and building solutions to compensate for the lack of building materials resulting from the U.S. embargo against Cuba that was imposed in 1961. This tripartite policy produced results. The largest shantytowns in the central areas of Havana as well as in the suburbs (Plaza de la Revolución, Boyeros, Marianao, Diez de Octubre) were eliminated. Single-story housing complexes were built with lightweight prefabricated walls and roofs, oftentimes erected by the occupants themselves. This production system was called "self-help and mutual aid" (see also Chapter 4). Self-help housing at that time was increasingly common throughout Latin America (Oliver 1970). Significant legislation in this area consisted of Law 86 (February 17, 1959), which created the National Institute of Savings and Housing (Instituto Nacional de Ahorro y Vivienda [INAV]).

The National Institute of Savings and Housing was directed by the mythi-cal Pastorita Núñez, a small woman with short hair and large blue eyes that stood out against the olive-green uniform that she regularly wore since the days of armed struggle in the Sierra Maestra. Her demeanor was forged within the Orthodox Party. She inherited the inflexible ethic of the party's charis-matic founder, the opposition senator Eduardo Chibás. Pastorita quickly cre-ated a team of architects headed by Cesáreo Fernández, who designed and built several housing complexes. Among them is the well-known Unit No. 1 of Habana del Este (whose name was later changed to Ciudad Camilo Cien-fuegos). Within Havana her team also built the subdivisions (*repartos*) of Capri, Embil, Bahía, Juan Manuel Márquez, and Residencial Wajay. Each of these contained groups of multifamily mid-rise buildings such as the complex of four-story buildings (an INAV height limit) located near the Plaza de la Revolución and many other isolated structures that served as in-filling within the city.

Pastorita's success derived from a very simple method that was curiously abandoned later: guarantee the quality of the design without trying to alter the project's technical features. At the same time, various private builders bid on the construction project. The bidding was carefully supervised by young ar-chitects, engineers, and Pastorita herself. She monitored the amount of build-ing materials they used and the costs of these projects. Taking advantage of her short demeanor, Pastorita would enter the huge concrete tubes stored on the work site and surprise workers who had scatted off to catnap. The quality that came out of these efforts, in terms of both design and construction, made this a model in socialist Cuban urbanism.

In just two years of existence, INAV launched enthusiastic and diverse projects in its construction of almost ten thousand housing units throughout the island, six thousand of which were erected in Havana (INAV 1962). New state agencies spearheaded construction along with small private-sector firms, which at that time were still permitted. The institute awarded contracts to small firms with money that the state obtained from the National Lottery. Building designs included detached or semidetached houses that were one or two stories high, as well as the typical four-story apartment complex. High-rise structures built in Habana del Este were an exception to this national pattern.

The early years of the revolution witnessed a short but intense period of housing construction. The establishment of the Board of Technical Research within the Ministry of Public Works brought together the search for practical solutions and the use of local resources. In particular, this included the struc-

tural use of brick roof vaults and stackable prefabricated building components (D'Acosta-Calheiros 1964). Even though a large share of this experimental construction was located at the outskirts of Plaza de la Revolución
(former Plaza Cívica, or Civic Square), a notable project consisting of three
residential structures was built in the Tallapiedra neighborhood of Jesús María
in 1960. The project was built by Fernando Salinas and embodied some of the
most important conceptual ideas in revolutionary housing and architecture at
the time. Salinas's project contributed to the debate surrounding contextualism, which had not yet surfaced in Cuba at that time; nor had questions taken
hold about CIAM doctrine (which undervalued the link between the traditional layout of the city with new buildings). Salinas argued against the routine
and mundane designs that prevailed during earlier years of the revolution. He
tried, within the limited material means available, to build a new complex in
the heart of the older quarters of the city.

## The Metaphor of the Ideal City

If the essential premises of socialist utopia seek to create improved material
and spiritual levels of a society, then one of those premises must be to make
that utopia a reality. In such a political project, however, the built environment
need not necessarily represent new revolutionary urban design. Although
such utopian designs were apparent in the works of Boullée and Ledoux before the French Revolution and the October Revolution, the situation in
Latin America is different. In urban design and architecture, both the Mexican and Cuban revolutions adhered more closely to the traditional heritage
cast by the bourgeoisie than the revolutions in Europe.

Three neighborhood units of Habana del Este were proposed, but only the
first unit was built. Each symbolized the urban utopia of the Cuban revolution, and Units 2 and 1 merit a brief discussion here. Unit 2 expressed dreams
far removed from Cuban reality. Designed by Fernando Salinas and Raúl
González Romero for one hundred thousand inhabitants, Unit 2 portrayed
the massive scale found in the works of Le Corbusier, the organic styles that
had been handed down by Frank Lloyd Wright, and the light exterior shells so
typical of the works of Pier Luigi Nervi and Félix Candela. Unit 1, though,
differed markedly. Constructed under the auspices of INAV for a capacity of
twenty-three hundred units and eight thousand residents, its inspiration for
design came from the blocks of apartment buildings in Vedado.

Salinas and González Romero conceived a residential structure whose symbolic and expressive importance surfaced in public buildings and outdoor spaces. The detailed curvilinear structures and the green areas complemented the monuments that identified a search for a renewed intensity in human relations: the church of "all religions" or the convention center that serves as the main urban point. Unit 1, the least equipped with social services, did not improve on prerevolutionary architectural design.[1]

With the exception of the area around the Plaza de la Revolución with its four-story height limitations discussed above, INAV built small housing complexes throughout various parts of the city. The population density of Habana del Este played a symbolic role because Cuban society before the revolution had begun to use urban spaces in the east to prepare for a suburb for the wealthy. Luxurious homes were to be built there along with shopping centers, hotel complexes, business headquarters, and government buildings, all of which were based on fairly complex and sophisticated engineering, architectural, and design principles (see Chapter 2). With the onset of the revolution, however, a new humanistic perspective in Cuba's housing policies changed the speculative aspect of the housing market in Habana del Este by giving priority to the neediest. This change in thinking was associated with new spaces, new forms of thinking, the availability of resources, the traditional lifestyles of the residents, and the expectations of the future residents.

Habana del Este also unified the team work of specialists, architects, and engineers. A team-work approach to housing and planning proved a welcome tonic to the isolated and individualistic method of residential construction building of previous decades. Habana del Este also afforded Cuban professionals a venue for expressing some of the theoretical ideas in vogue in the 1950s.[2] The project revealed some of the essential features espoused by the CIAM: alternating between high (ten-story) and low (four-story) buildings,

1. The architectural team working on Unit 1 included Roberto Carrazana, Reynaldo Estévez, Mario González, Hugo D'Acosta-Calheiros, Eduardo Rodríguez, Mercedes Alvarez, and the engineer Lenin Castro. Unit 1 represented the best examples of sprawling apartment complexes for the middle stratum of Havana society. Unit 1's residential composition reflected the leading design principles of the United States and Europe regarding site planning that departed from the existing city grid.

2. The neighborhood-unit concept outlined by Clarence Perry in the United States, the British New Towns, the satellite cities of Scandinavia, and the post–World War II experiences in the Soviet Union and Eastern Europe all became eligible models from which Cuba could pick and choose. Latin American ideas then available in Cuba included those that appeared in Oscar Niemeyer's magazine *Módulo*. His proposal was validated by the examples displayed at the Fifth International Congress of International Architects held in Moscow in 1958 (UIA 1958).

green belts that separated housing from major thoroughfares, a hierarchical road system, the separation of pedestrians and vehicles, diverse sites and services, and a wide array of social services (education, culture, arts, public health). These principles were to be employed in a wide range of scales, from the basic neighborhood unit to the community center. Even though there was no significant question about the validity of the neighborhood-unit concept at that time, new complexes fell victim to the segregating functional character, such as the "bedroom community" idea, which was a by-product of the functional zoning outlined by the Athens Charter (Carta de Atenas).[3]

The high-rise structures of Habana del Este did not go beyond the formal schemes applied in the well-designed modernist buildings in the 1950s: the high-rise Focsa building, the Seguro Médico building, or the Naroca building. Low-rise units that reflected the Italian models of those years were more refined than these high-rises. Even those blocks that were raised on stilts, gently curved and with halls that were placed halfway between floors to create more privacy, were all smaller units that challenged the reductionism of the purist parallelepiped scheme, a heritage of Ludwig Hilberseimer. Through a design based on 45° angles, the alternating of open and closed areas created a succession of spaces and interior places at a pedestrian scale. Such design was far removed from the Cartesian scheme that had been widespread in earlier decades. Despite some degree of freedom in design, the uneven training of project leaders and the use of craft construction methods produced incoherence among some of the buildings and grounds.

Expanses of urban spaces and the scale of parking lots (derived from models used in the First World) generated open spaces that were not compensated for by sufficient population densities. Because sports complexes were specialized and used occasionally, they failed to engage the community. While providing an important social and political function in the revolution, sports complexes had little "personality," and they consumed too much space. Even though Habana del Este became the main paradigm for many years, that model ultimately ceased because of the perception by housing officials and the Cuban leadership that mass state-built production of a few housing block prototypes was the only way to meet the accumulated housing needs. Moreover, the economic difficulties in subsequent decades made such projects dif-

3. Valid alternatives in the 1960s included the architects of Team X (Peter and Alison Smithson, Giancarlo de Carlo, George Candilis, Aldo Van Eyck, and others). Although the writings of Kevin Lynch, Christopher Alexander, and Jane Jacobs also served as potential models for Cuban professionals, that influence came much later and only influenced a few.

ficult. As Fidel Castro affirmed at the close of the Seventh Congress of the International Union of Architects (1963): "You could say that this unit [in Habana del Este] is ideal from our point of view [because of] the construction, the urban housing . . . but also because it is the type of construction that was beyond our economic means. . . . And so, naturally, we don't construct those large buildings anymore. We now try to find variety in other forms, but not by erecting tall buildings" (Segre 1970a, 110; our translation).

## Dialectical and Participatory Technology

The flurry of building construction in Havana was short lived. Upon completion of the large complexes near the Plaza de la Revolución and Habana del Este, the economic pressures from the U.S. blockade stopped the construction of similar structures. An acute awareness developed among the hundreds of architects present at the Seventh Congress of the International Union of Architects (UIA 1963) about the economic limitations facing Cuba. This was a time when aid from the socialist bloc did not exist, and the revolution opted to devote its building resources to cities in the interior and the agricultural sector. Building up provincial towns also aimed to stem the tide of migration to Havana.

Until 1970, state construction in Havana was mostly confined to the building of a few prototypes. To some extent, the demographic pressure on Havana was less than in other parts of the country because of the large numbers of Cubans who emigrated from the capital, thus freeing up vacant units. Aid to Havana was not forthcoming because of the decadent reputation of the city created by the former ruling classes and a sense of disdain they left among the revolutionary leadership. A large part of the Havana population that had been let go from the revolutionary offensive against "bureaucratism" and small private businesses (1968) was absorbed by the Greenbelt (Cordón de La Habana) campaign, an agricultural plan for truck and garden farming located in the hinterland of Havana, where sleepy small towns and agricultural communities served hypothetically as a moral alternative to the urban lifestyle (see Chapter 4).

The highly centralized Ministry of Construction in Havana was the locus of technical and design decision making for the entire country. Few architectural designs associated with research and pilot projects were built in the mid-1960s (Machado 1960). Creative and innovative projects existed, but they contrasted sharply with the low-quality construction built by the state and the private sector. Since high-rise construction was halted, Havana's 1950s skyline was hardly altered. Although the character of Havana's neighborhoods was preserved during this time, a process of physical deterioration also began. Paint, building materials, and skilled labor fell into short supply.

In conceptual terms, housing policy was based on three premises. One was that construction initiatives were confined to the existing building stock or model rural structures (a rectangular dwelling with a front porch). The second premise was that standardized housing designs of the Ministry of Construction's Urban Housing Department would be confined to four-story apartment complexes or detached, semidetached, or row houses for rural areas. A third premise related to the experiments about unique features of the housing unit, building techniques, occupant participation, and site planning (Machado 1969).

The use of the "cell" panel in Cuba was, to paraphrase the Chilean Cristián Fernández Cox (1990), part of the "appropriate technology" movement. The Venezuelan Fruto Vivas (1983) was inspired by this movement to develop two kinds of lightweight prefabricated panels during his stay in Cuba: the Camilo and Van Troi. Although these panels were easy to handle, the Ministry of Construction (Ministerio de Construcción [MICONS])—preoccupied with the unattainable goal of industrialized construction (Bode Hernández 1972)—was not fully convinced of their utility. As a result, Fruto Vivas's (1966) plea for a "construction harvest" of massive housing projects that would draw on laborers who had finished the sugarcane harvest was ignored. If this idea formulated in 1965 were understood by leaders in the construction industry, it would have avoided the improvised architectural solutions used in the Microbrigade starting in 1970. In the latter, resident participation formed a key ingredient and was supported by Fidel Castro in 1970. At the same time, the ideas put forth by Hugo D'Acosta-Calheiros and Mercedes Alvarez were not well received. They had proposed the application of lightweight asbestos-cement materials for flexible-design residential complexes throughout the city (Segre 1989). Significantly, the use of asbestos in Cuba is indiscriminate and is not subject to strict control.

Fernando Salinas was one of the few Cuban professionals who articulated broad design concepts with individual units. As the program chairperson of the Seventh Congress of the Union of International Architects, he knew firsthand the experiences of Third World countries, which allowed him to develop a theoretical architectural foundation (Véjar 1994). Departing from the notion that the housing unit is primarily a cultural construct, he defined the dialectical character of a structure according to the changing economic conditions. These factors include its variation and transformation and whether residents participate in both the building and design phases of construction. Salinas also gave special importance to building maintenance, whether carried out by the state or the housing owners, a factor that had so greatly contributed to the precarious image of Havana during the 1960s and 1970s (Segre 1985b).[4]

Salinas built a prototype housing unit in the suburb of Wajay, 18 kilometers southwest of Havana. He employed the Multiflex system, which had been developed by his students at the School of Architecture at the University of Havana. At a meeting of architectural schools organized by the International Union of Architects (UIA) in Buenos Aires in 1969, the design earned an award. The Multiflex system consisted of a support structure, formed by a central column, that held up a 6 meter by 6 meter panel. The simplicity of both elements allowed for the growth of any given structure in all horizontal directions and independence between the structural forms and the interior spaces. The support structure was a key stabilizing factor. It could be made through traditional artisan methods of pouring concrete on the site, or panels could be precast in factories (fig. 6.2). The rest of the housing unit was based on a careful study of each functional element, including the most basic biological needs and the cultural values and habits of each family. Equipping the interior of each unit was integrally tied to the exterior panels. The unit was designed to allow for changes according to a country's economic conditions and those of its occupants. During the first stage of construction the available materials might be, for example, concrete, tile, wood, and bagasse. But once new factories were built, the interior panels could be built out of an asbestos-cement mixture with a covering of PVC, steel, enamel steel, or aluminum. All pieces were interchangeable and easy to assemble. Multiflex design allowed residents to acquire the building materials best suited to their needs. Salinas's prototype in Wajay proved that the dream could become reality, that the cre-

4. Together with Roberto Segre, Salinas helped refine the concept of "environmental design" employed in many developing countries. This concept enlisted some of the ideas of the Bauhaus school of the 1920s. In Europe the developer was able to control for the interaction of different scales of design, but in Latin America the piecemeal implementation of designs, the impact of complex and diverse cultures, and economic inequality made "open" solutions difficult or nearly impossible. Because urban housing stems from interactions between professional and popular "know-how," Salinas and Segre's "environmental design" approach recognized that urban housing is the product of professional knowledge and spontaneous community initiatives.

FIGURE 6.2. Multiflex module designed by Fernando Salinas, in the Havana suburb of Wajay, 1969 (Photograph by Roberto Segre)

ative imagination would have spiritually and materially enriched the daily life of the community. Nevertheless, the model was ultimately scrapped by the Ministry of Construction. In light of the Special Period, there is hope that Salinas's dreams might be used in an uncertain future.

At the end of the 1960s the first attempt arose to resort to high-rise housing in the central areas of Havana. Along the Vedado waterfront, an area characterized by high-rises built for the bourgeoisie in the 1950s, the architects Antonio Quintana and Alberto Rodríguez built a seventeen-story experimental prototype based on the precedent set by the buildings of Habana del Este. Two basic premises guided this design. First, structural walls and slabs defined the housing units, which were subdivided internally by light elements (*siporex*) that defined functional activities. Second, the continuity of the design had to be ensured. Doing so meant integrating the purist volumes of the apartment complexes into a continuous grid. The banks of elevators and staircases complement the sidewalks and roadways that create the internal traffic system. The model, inspired by the French experiences of Grenoble-Echirolles and Toulouse-le-Mirail and the English cases of Sheffield and Thamesmead, was not applied in subsequent residential high-rises built with the slip mold system.

## The Stark Utopia of Prefabricated Housing

From its beginnings, the Cuban socialist economy had aspired to scientific and technical advances (Mesías and Morales 1985). Assumed by political leaders to be an essential tool to move society forward, changing the dire conditions of the masses also entailed the contributions of urban planners and architects. When Vladimir Lenin put forth electrification as a goal of the Soviet state, the pioneers of constructivism (Vesnin, Melnikov, Leonidov, Chernikov, Golossov) created early images about how those socialist images might materialize (Segre 1985a). In the housing sector, these consisted of light metallic structures and thin tensors that braced the building complexes and that were crowned by antennas on the roofs.

The Cuban revolution did not escape the illusion of attaining technological progress as one of its loftiest goals and as a means of escaping underdevelopment (Castro 1970). Ernesto "Che" Guevara affirmed this sentiment in a well-known talk before Latin American students in 1963 (Segre 1970a). Cuba's technological progress was based in good measure on European models of advanced construction. Cuban housing policies embraced the notion that socialism is equivalent to public housing and prefabrication (Castex 1986).

Even though the aspirations of the socialist revolution in the housing realm were understandable given the unsatisfied needs of a population with limited resources, it turned out that its solutions were unable to satisfy those needs in the short period stipulated by the Cuban leadership. Cuba's post-1959 urban design and architectural history reflects a heightened concern for meeting deadlines, a scarcity of material resources, and a disregard for the immediate past. Both positive and negative factors prevailed in this short history. On the one hand, professionals should have anticipated solutions more suited to Cuban reality in order to, as Fernando Salinas often told his students, "make more with less." Implementing housing projects received little attention. Bureaucratic and political deadlines to complete housing projects all too often centered around national holidays or artificially defined construction phases. In the end, many of the buildings turned out to be superficial and shoddy and were ultimately finished by the more traditional building construction methods than the capital-intensive prefabricated methods originally envisioned.

It was in this context that the unleashing of industrial and prefabricated housing construction succumbed to the same pitfalls found in Eastern Europe. Over time, it became abundantly clear that the acritical adoption of foreign technological models was, in many cases, inappropriate to local conditions. Moreover, importing these models stifled the chances for their success because they were often at odds with the proposed design. Manufacturing prefabricated materials not only used local industry but also meant keeping a careful eye to ensure a steady flow of building materials, labor and materials (Salinas 1963b). All these ambitious activities related to a First World industrial production system became insurmountable contradictions in Cuba's own uneven development (Guselnikov 1976).

The U.S. embargo against Cuba in the 1960s was the key factor forcing Cuba to seek a new formula that drew on local resources instead of building methods used before the revolution. To that end, construction components and techniques had to minimize technical inputs. Housing units made of light shells and vaults sprang up throughout the island. These elements were used in schools, health care clinics, markets, and sporting complexes in new housing developments (Segre 1989). A second step toward prefabrication coincided with Hurricane Flora in 1963, which inflicted heavy damage on the eastern provinces. The Soviet Union donated a large-panel factory that was built in Santiago. These panels were widely used in the construction of apartment complexes. Housing projects in Santiago's José Martí district built with these panels shortly thereafter were supposed to house seventy-two thousand residents. From that time onward, the Ministry of Construction organized its plans around prefabrication, abandoning traditional craft methods of construction (Bode Hernández 1972). This entailed experimenting with a variety of building systems based on European and Canadian construction methods. Those foreign models were reinterpreted somewhat and adapted to local conditions (table 6.2).

Fidel Castro reaffirmed from the mid-1960s onward that Cuba could be completing one hundred thousand housing units a year by 1970. His hope was buoyed by the construction of panel factories across the island. Significantly, that was also the same year of the much touted 10-million-ton sugarcane harvest (Arrinda 1964; Castro 1978). That goal notwithstanding, the impossibility of carrying out this ambitious housing project produced a major production crisis. By 1970, the state was only completing four thousand housing units a year (Fernández Núñez 1976). Prior to that time, high technology had never been able to outproduce traditional building methods, nor did it surpass self-help housing production. For example, in 1976, prefabricated construction constituted only 23 percent of all units, while state-directed traditional artisan methods were used in 50 percent of all completed units (Estévez 1977).

TABLE 6.2. Prefabricated Panels Used in Cuban Construction

| TYPE | ORIGIN | BUILDING HEIGHT |
|---|---|---|
| Large Panel IV | Cuban version of large French panels (e.g., Camus, Coignet) | 4 stories |
| IMS (Serbian Materials Institute) | Yugoslavian | Up to 12 stories |
| Slip Mold | Scandinavian | Up to 18 stories |
| Large Panel 70 | Scandinavian | 4–5 stories |
| LH (*losa hueca* or slab core) technology | Canadian | 4–5 stories |

*Source*: Adapted from Machado Ventura 1976.

The push toward the 10-million-ton sugarcane harvest required all of the nation's available technical, human, and scientific resources. Even though both the sugar and housing goals failed, the 1970s became a time of reaffirming industrial development as a cornerstone of the socialist revolution. In tandem with this push toward industrialization in the housing sector, there was, ironically, widespread use of traditional artisan construction by the Microbrigades. This alternative method formed part of Cuba's economic planning and its political institutionalization process. The First Congress of the Cuban Communist Party in 1976 affirmed this principle. The government stated clearly at the congress that it should fill the vacuum in building construction created by the ruralist approach of the 1960s. Housing assumed an important symbolic presence in the city, matching the availability of social services, schools, and recreational facilities. Some of the more noteworthy projects are the José Antonio Echeverría University campus, the Lenin Vocational School, Lenin Park, and the Botanical Gardens and Zoo, which were located at the city's edge (see Chapter 8). High-rise public housing on the outskirts of Havana not only countered the presence of similar structures in Vedado but also became reference points for the revolution's modernization efforts in Havana. These high-rise structures spread to the most unlikely and remote corners of the city. The twenty-story high-rise housing in Havana during the first decades of the revolution paralleled in many ways Stalin's location of seven skyscrapers in Moscow at the end of the Second World War (Segre 1985a). The enduring nature of Soviet power had been reaffirmed by victory over barbarian Nazi forces. Soviet planning sought to show new features and rights of the unfolding socialist society.

Cuba, too, reaffirmed the equality of land values in the city and rejected the persistent association in capitalist societies between architectural style and social class. The twenty-three high-rises under construction in Metropolitan Havana in 1974 were distributed among the municipalities of Centro Habana, Plaza de la Revolución, Habana del Este, and Diez de Octubre. In 1982, the mayor of Havana proposed to Fidel Castro that sixty-four buildings be built as part of a special plan for high-rise structures. Euphoria about the perceived economic outlook for the nation's economy influenced the proposal, which had no way of predicting the collapse of the Soviet Union and the restructuring of Cuba's economy. In some cases, these buildings were sited in open areas, with little concern about blending in. In other locations, the unremarkable high-rises aggressively ruptured the flow of nineteenth-century *portales*, whose distinctive character was accentuated by historicist decorations of the early twentieth century. Perhaps the most dramatic instance of architectural and urban design insensitivity by designers and planners appeared at the intersection of Calzada de Infanta and Calzada de Monte, popularly known as the Tejas corner. There, two modern and nondescript structures (fig. 6.3) arose on what was one of the most significant corners in the city's history (Coyula 1992). Similar buildings appeared elsewhere in Havana (fig. 6.4).

Although prefabricated housing has kept costs down, it has disrupted the traditional fabric of the city. Other hidden costs, including energy, equipment, maintenance, and social disruption—pointed out by some visionaries—were very evident after the economic crisis of the *periódo especial* of the 1990s. In Alamar, the Microbrigades constructed traditional craft or artisan housing. In Vedado, the LH (*losa hueca*, or slab core) housing system was used. Other new housing spread from the Plaza de la Revolución and penetrated older areas such as Cayo Hueso in Centro Habana. At least two factors account for the cosmopolitan character of these new structures. First, little information existed about the criticisms of these types of buildings, the CIAM theories, and the International Style. Second, there was a short, intense flurry of construction that was out of step with most twentieth-century housing. Thus, there was relatively little time for assessing its critical outcomes. Prototypes in Havana were mechanically and faithfully reproduced according to the original European designs. The absence of balconies, awnings, eaves, and bright colors contributed to the gray, drab look of Havana's newer housing. This bland appearance is evident in the structures built in the Plaza de la Revolución during the 1970s and 1980s, giving them an anonymous look that disregards any contextual reference. A high degree of abstraction places the structures out of step in both place and time.

FIGURE 6.3.
Modern and anonymous
high-rises at Infanta and
Monte Streets (known as
La Esquina de Tejas) built
in the 1960s, intruding into
this historic neighborhood in
Centro Habana (Photograph
by Roberto Segre)

Socialist housing in Havana was similar to the many complexes that existed in Eastern Europe—Prague, Budapest, Sofia, Dresden, Stalingrad, and Moscow—and in some ways to those in the market economies of France, West Germany, and England. The spaciousness of these apartments as built in Cuba made them superior than the speculative housing units built by the bourgeoisie before the revolution. The technical quality of the prefabricated panels used would have placed the real cost of the final units out of the reach of the occupants had it not been for the low and state-subsidized rent. The gap between the real cost and the low fixed monthly rents (10 percent of gross income) created a financial deficit that the state was unable to remedy. That the housing model of finance and construction was not financially viable became readily apparent once the Soviet bloc severed aid to the island, and Cuba had to resort to its own (hard currency) resources. Many projects begun in the 1980s had to be halted, remaining unfinished and gradually decaying in the 1990s.

The 200-meter-long strip used in housing near the Plaza de la Revolución changed the scale of housing design in Havana. In many respects, it was out of step with the kind of social spaces that drew a community with this level of population together. Also discordant was the lack of attempts to blend traditional architectural styles with large socialist complexes. Clusters of new buildings in Cayo Hueso seemed more like a malignancy than a holistic at-

FIGURE 6.4.
Twin high-rise apartment towers in Vedado, just one block off the Malecón. Although each unit has a balcony, the buildings were designed for individual air-conditioning units, which have all since been removed. (Photograph by Joseph L. Scarpaci)

tempt to rebuild deteriorated neighborhoods (Coyula 1992). Housing projects failed to take full advantage of good ideas such as Le Corbusier's *pilotis*. This idea places sites and services on the ground floor. Such services might have included bars, cafés, shops, and restaurants. Indeed, having included these uses would have energized city life. The area's maintenance was deficient and failed to draw on residents for routine upkeep. Residents were alienated from these new architectural projects because of the educational or class differences among them, as well as the lack of a sense of identification with this state-sponsored property.

## The Microbrigade: Precarious Design and Social Content

In the 1970s the housing debate in Latin America centered around two alternative approaches: large housing complexes built by the state and smaller self-help housing (Pradilla 1982). Large housing complexes were still built in some countries, such as Mexico, Argentina, Colombia, and Brazil. Successive military regimes in Argentina tried to alleviate the mounting social pressure for adequate shelter. A series of diverse residential housing complexes for low-income residents, including Lugano I/II, Ciudadela, Villa Soldati, and Piedrabuena, reflect that need for shelter (Segre and López Rangel 1982). At the same time, economists, sociologists, urbanists, and architects confronted the problem of "marginal settlements" as one of the most important elements of the Third World city.

Responses to the housing crisis varied. In Chile, the government of Salvador Allende (1970–73) began a program for the urban poor who lacked adequate shelter. This program was also associated with a high level of political mobilization among those poor who stood to profit from state housing initiatives (Castells 1974; Scarpaci, Gaete, and Infante 1988). In other countries (Peru, Venezuela, Colombia) squatter settlements were manipulated in order to distance the housing solution from community participation, which was associated with political and ideological commitments.[5]

The solution put forth by Cuba in the 1970s represented yet another housing alternative in Latin America. Cuba decided to confront its housing demand by using a mixture of state resources and the active participation of the future residents of the new housing units (Coyula 1990, 1991a, 1991b). Several factors led to this solution. First, prefabricated housing revealed technical differences. Second, prefabrication was costlier than traditional methods (Castex 1986). Third, traditional construction workers were demobilized because in the 1970s they lacked resources. Individual housing solutions, it was felt, created several problems. They increased housing construction and remodeling by users in various parts of Havana, which dispersed housing and resources across the city. In this scenario, housing quality and standards could not be ensured, producing an atomization of the state's housing efforts (Herrera 1976; Izquierdo and Liz 1984). To offset that outcome, Cuba tried to integrate resources and to draw on community strengths. Although the state produced cement-product factories irregularly, by the early 1970s it had invested heavily in these facilities. This made it easier to distribute building in-

---

5. Local specialists and foreigners (Jorge Enrique Hardoy, Marcos Kaplán, Emilio Pradilla, Jordi Borja, Eduardo Caminos, John F. C. Turner, Charles Abrams, William Mangin) conducted research and issued concrete proposals. In particular, the work by Turner in Lima's *barriadas* served as a hypothetical control model for spontaneous squatter settlements in other Latin American cities (Turner and Fichter 1972).

puts not only among government building projects but also among people who desire to repair or expand their homes (Junta Central de Planificación 1976).

The state supplied building materials and designated where the units were to be built. Future tenants or users organized themselves in Microbrigades that consisted of thirty-three workers who built five-story apartment houses with thirty apartments as designed by the architects of the Ministry of Construction (Segre 1984). The Microbrigade was formed within a workplace (e.g., factories, ministries, commercial establishments, schools), which gave them a unique focus.

Urban residents in Latin American countries who lack shelter are expected to build their own housing during their free time after the eight-hour work day (Livingston 1990). Sociologists, geographers, and economists have critiqued this policy by default as a form of double worker exploitation because the free time of laborers should not be used for self-help construction, since the state or landowner ultimately will gain ownership (Rodríguez, Riofrío, and Welsh 1973). The Cuban proposal, however, solved two problems at the same time. The first was the excess of employees in state companies that lost economic control over profitability and efficiency. A second problem was related to the disappearance of artisan labor skills. The Microbrigade consisted of workers from a given workplace who labored full-time on a particular project while the rest of the workers at the original workplace covered the tasks abandoned by their comrades. Thus, activities at the construction site and workplace could be easily coordinated. At the same time, on weekends, all workers could join in "voluntary work" in order to increase the pace of construction.[6]

Participation in the Microbrigade was voluntary and did not necessarily mean the immediate delivery of housing. The apartments that were built belonged to the worker collective, factory, or state agency. Once the structure was completed, the workers would then decide how to allocate some of the

6. Two key factors triggered various degrees of enthusiasm for Microbrigades among North American and European scholars such as Tom Angotti, Tony Schumann, Richard Hatch, Jill Hamberg, Kosta Mathéy, and Julián Salas. One point in their favor was that because apartment complexes served as the basic unit in the spatial organization of housing, it could be coordinated by urbanists, architects, and builders. This model went against the existing system of suburban expansion and spontaneous single dwellings at the city's edge. As a result, it departed from the longstanding curse of not being able to control the technical or aesthetic dimensions of "marginal" constructions found in *favelas, callampas, pueblos jovenes, villas miserias,* and other squatter communities in Latin America. A second attribute was that Microbrigade housing held social and political value.

housing among the members of their work crew and which members should receive priority (Mathéy 1992b, 189). The government held a firm principle: prioritizing the collective over individual interest. During the second half of the 1980s, in the "Correction of Mistakes Period," this very principle led to the creation of social Microbrigades that worked largely at rehabilitating structures. In particular, they focused on schools, hospitals, day care centers, family physician centers, senior citizen centers, and other nonresidential structures (Hamberg 1994; Mathéy 1994).

In December 1970, Fidel Castro outlined the structure and organization of Microbrigades in the national meeting of heavy industry. He created the first Microbrigade in Havana, and in the first semester of 1971, he defined the various relationships and responsibilities of other organizations that would support this new entity. That same year, more than 1,000 workers were assigned to build 1,154 housing units in Plaza de la Revolución, Altahabana, Rancho Boyeros, Alamar, Reparto Bahía, San Agustín, and La Coronela. In just two years, a labor force had been consolidated throughout Cuba that included more than 1,000 Microbrigades. In 1971, 12,715 workers made up 444 Microbrigades. By 1975, 30,000 workers constituted 1,150 Microbrigades that completed 25,600 housing units, in addition to a plethora of nonresidential (e.g., social) projects. By 1983, the movement had built 100,000 units nationwide (Hamberg 1986, 1990, 1994). With hindsight, it would have been logical to have built new residences and new workplaces. That was not possible, however, because of the scarcity of available land and because the fragmentation of work projects would have decreased the output of completed units by scattering these initiatives across the city. Co-locating work and residence was also difficult because most households have more than one member working outside the home, and they usually work in different places.

Housing projects in Havana in the 1970s were clustered in three large areas and were located in districts that had the greatest number of industrial and service-sector workers. The east Havana area was well endowed with a good road network, as well as sewage and electrical services. As noted above, this is where the bourgeoisie in the 1950s had planned suburban subdivisions. The areas included Alamar (130,000 residents) in Habana del Este municipality; in the south, along an axis with Rancho Boyeros, was Altahabana (110,000 residents); and in the west was San Agustín (35,000 residents). The theory underlying the Urban Reform Law (table 6.1)—the standardization of rent—was carried out in the numerous buildings that proletarianized the edges of the city (Carneado 1962; CEE 1983; Chaline 1987). This notion brought uniformity to the images and streets in Havana's suburbs. It was not by chance that the artist Antonio Eligio Tonel would create, as a symbol of the urban land-scape, a sculpture—*El Bloqueo* (1991)—set on a map of the island made up of cement blocks. The haphazard nature of urban design wiped out the positive aspirations for a social environment with aesthetically meaningful shapes and spaces.

Now that a quarter of a century separates the original Microbrigade initia-tive from today, there is little doubt that on balance the Microbrigade efforts were positive conceptually and socially. The quality of suburban Havana's apartment complexes is infinitely superior to the self-help housing found elsewhere in Latin America, and even some other apartment complexes in Cuba. For example, these housing units are larger than those in socialist East-ern European countries. Suburban Havana apartment complexes also include a generous amount of light and air, as well as large green areas surrounding them (even though the landscaping and maintenance have deteriorated). Clearly, these apartment complexes are a homage to Le Corbusieran precepts.

In planning terms, however, the experience is not considered exemplary in Latin America and the Caribbean because it was divorced from the architec-tural and design concepts and models in the region. There were no contextu-alist notions about the traditional city, nor was there much concern about the natural landscape surrounding these complexes. In addition, a debate emerged over the effects of breaking the city into socialist housing quarters given the strong capitalist inheritance of Havana. Had there been nonpollut-ing light industry and jobs in Alamar that could have drawn a female labor force, the singular function of the neighborhood might have changed. In essence, the capital continued its "bedroom communities."

The early 1970s were a dogmatic period. The revolutionary government employed rigid institutional structures and processes in architectural projects and cultural life, peaking with the First Congress of Education and Culture in 1971. It gave rise to the so-called *quinquenio gris* (gray five-year term), which actually lasted the entire decade and affected many architects, artists, and writ-ers (Campuzano 2000). Varying from the norms or otherwise reinterpreting orders from centralized authority was not permitted. An abstract sense of im-portance was given to collective interests, which made it nearly impossible to present alternative ideas. Working in teams was virtually impossible. Unfortu-nately, this meant that state organizations were not able to share and partici-pate in new urban projects. This may explain why urban spaces in Alamar can best be characterized as depressing. Elements of this poor design remain today and can be noted throughout Havana. Each service, such as retail, education, health care, recreation, and industry, was restricted to a specific and isolated building. Little concern was given to integrating these buildings with others. The presence of almost one hundred thousand residents in Alamar would have justified the construction of a major civic center, a central space in the community for recreation, cultural functions, and events for the youth of the settlement. Neglecting social spaces for young people was a particularly glaring oversight because they represented a large segment of Alamar's population. Instead, isolation created a sort of "no man's land." Large expanses of green areas and the impersonal nature of prefabricated structures are so far removed from the dynamism and gay spirit of Cubans. While the International Style and modern movement were being criticized and when Team X was creating new spaces to promote social interaction in different parts of the world, Cuba was replicating tired, old schemes. The end result was a style of construction and housing that was far removed from what a "real" socialism was capable of producing (De la Nuez 1990; Segre 1968b, 1994b).

As the original impulse brought on by Microbrigades languished in the early 1980s, so too did the pace of construction in Havana. Unlike professionals and practitioners with specialized training in the building trades, key officials in other state agencies had grave doubts about the real benefits of Microbrigade initiatives. A spate of ongoing projects had made it increasingly difficult to distribute resources and technology equitably. From the downturn in the 1980s onward, an uneven rhythm of construction came to a complete halt. Long delays and erratic starts and stops increased the costs of many construction projects. To this must be added the higher salaries of workers over time. These salaries did not correspond to the actual position of the construction worker but rather to the original workplace to which she or he belonged. Specialized technicians intervened constantly to correct errors made by unqualified workers. In the end, this produced a series of poorly finished buildings.

A lingering Microbrigade problem was retaining experienced workers in construction crews. Upon finishing an apartment complex, many of those same workers occupied them, as was premised in the initial Microbrigade idea. However, despite worker and party organizations encouraging workers to keep on working in the construction sector after they had secured their own housing, many decided otherwise. Nonetheless, many workers did sacrifice, and their adherence to the revolution's long-term goals came at the expense of immediate material rewards (e.g., housing). Out of a dedicated construction labor force arose "contingents" (*contingentes*, work crews) that carried out ambitious social projects in the late 1980s and infrastructure works in tourist complexes and places outside Havana.

The dynamism of the 1970s and 1980s produced divergent outcomes in Havana's housing sector. Housing censuses in 1981 and 1983 included the self-built housing sector and showed that about two-thirds of the housing stock constructed since 1959 was self-built (Estévez 1984). Figures were derived by subtracting from the total figure of state-made dwellings and an estimate of losses by collapse and demolition. Some professionals struggled for the application of an "artistic integration in the personalization of mass production" (Alvarez Tabío 1994b, 18; our translation). Attempting to rescue visual and symbolic identity in Cuba's housing complexes, artists and graphic designers creatively painted buildings with large murals, called supergraphics (*supergráficas*), that faded in the Caribbean sun and rain. Construction of schools, houses, factories, agricultural centers, and other sites depended on prefabrication and was far removed from high-quality designs. Such structures were based on function without form and a negation of architecture as a cultural expression. Nevertheless, some fine prefabricated buildings were built at that time, such as the Lenin and Volodia schools in Havana and the Máximo Gómez in Camagüey. These buildings proved that rigidity has more to do with bureaucracy and the lack of talent than with technology. Plans executed by Microbrigades did not take advantage of the implicit possibility of alternatives: "typical" projects fell victim to facilism, norms found nationwide, and a deeply ingrained bureaucratization of problem solving. In turn, architects became mere construction laborers, without any positive consequences for buildings and designs. Poorly finished buildings reflected little attention to details and technical specifications.

## Back to the Traditional City

In 1980 a generation of painters, writers, artists, sculptors, and architects known as the "founders" began a new movement. They differed markedly from the utopian and rigid images of the generation before them. Theirs was a world that no longer consisted of issues in "black and white." They had witnessed the disintegration of socialism in the former Soviet Union and Eastern Europe, from the fervent early years of the Cuban revolution (Vega Vega 1963) to the downward spiral of the Cuban economy in the 1990s. In the wake of those events stood a unipolar world where market mechanisms had gained unprecedented influence. As the twentieth century ended, a gamut of philosophical and aesthetic ideas took hold. The "founders" verified the existence of a "real" society that was still far from their ideal. This philosophy allowed room for goals and incomplete projects to coexist. For example, there are now schools in the countryside, while *solares* and *cuarterías* in Habana Vieja persist. In debunking the "myth of the new" (Segre 1994d), there is also a rethinking of traditional housing solutions. This new way of thinking could not have emerged had it not been for the fall of the Berlin Wall and the dissolution of the Soviet Union in 1989, which hurt the Cuban economy.

In the mid-1990s several influences had led to a gradual return of construction in the city. First, the value of the historic centers and their protection—particularly after UNESCO's declaration of Habana Vieja as a World Heritage Site—gave salience to conserving the built environments of bygone eras (see Chapter 9).

Second, the squalor of social spaces in peripheral settlements obliged inhabitants to use the traditional city centers.

Third, there was an ongoing debate at that time among architects about housing complexes and what the future of Havana's center might be. A 1984 conference titled the "International Seminar of City Architecture" set the stage for thinking about these different issues. The thrust of this thinking centered around the fixed and limited number of options available to cities in the 1970s. Those options became further limited in the 1990s: the building needs of Havana could no longer be ignored.

Fourth, economic analyses about the high cost of infrastructure in suburban areas are foremost in planning and design circles. For example, it is now widely accepted that the contiguous areas of Havana should retain pockets of open areas for future construction.

Fifth, decentralization of economic and political decision making has brought about greater freedoms and initiatives to provincial and municipal governments (Padrón Lotti and Cuervo Masoné 1991). For architects, decentralization has meant the creation of Architectural Departments (Direcciones de Arquitectura) in the municipalities of Havana. These departments include young architects with diverse backgrounds; they differ greatly from their predecessors, who were subject to the controls of the Ministry of Construction.

Sixth, the passage of the General Housing Law of 1984 (Ley General de la Vivienda) enabled permanent residents of state structures to assume ownership of their units. This law created incentives and a sense of belonging that improved the maintenance of many of Havana's buildings (Dávalos Fernández 1990).

Seventh, the 1986 Correction of Mistakes Period brought not just new housing construction but also many social projects. In Havana, projects such as day care centers, schools, clinics, and hospitals stemmed from this initiative (Mathéy 1992a).

Eighth, a planning and advising unit in Havana's government, Grupo para el Desarrollo Integral de la Capital, provided a new decentralized forum for coping with Havana's housing problems.

Ninth, Havana has been characterized by general deterioration and an overall lack of maintenance. Although the state has been unable to provide all the necessary building materials, some of this deterioration is due to ad hoc building initiatives taken on by residents (Estévez 1977). Although self-help housing lacked technical and aesthetic controls, between 1981 and 1983 that sector completed seven units per one thousand inhabitants in Havana versus the state's production of two units per one thousand (Gomila et al. 1984).

Finally, Havana in 1987 exhibited an ailing housing sector, even before the Special Period. The city still had 55,000 people in housing that was deemed so precarious that they were slated for the first available housing. Of this group, a few thousand were lodged in shelters (*albergues*, or temporary residences for those who had lost their housing). In addition, 213,000 *habaneros* resided in tenement houses (*ciudadelas*) and another 50,000 lived in shantytowns (*barrios insalubres*). In all, some 357,000 lived in substandard housing (Castro 1964, 1987).

Although some of the utopian ideas of the 1970s were criticized because they were not practical and suited to Cuba, some of these same conceptual ideas of that era were successfully employed. The ideas of Fernando Salinas, for instance, were reapplied in university research and the housing construction sector.[7] In the late 1980s and early 1990s, it became quite apparent that the search for creative and scientific housing solutions in the Third World

---

7. Salinas mentored a cohort of young professionals at the university who came to be known as the "Generation of the 1980s" (Generación de los 80). These professionals (Francisco Bedoya, Daniel Bejerano, Rosendo Mesías, Juan L. Morales, Emma Alvarez Tabío, Eduardo L. Rodríguez, Raúl Izquierdo, Rafael Fornés, Jorge Tamargo, Orestes del Castillo Jr., Emilio Castro, and José A. Choy, among others) were responsible for some of the first public housing initiatives. These efforts were developed by the municipal Popular Power not based on prefabrication but with the contextual features of local surroundings (Segre 1992b; Alvarez Tabío 1992). For an example of the work in Atarés, a rundown back-bay neighborhood basically ignored before and after the revolution, see Ortega (1996).

would require some of Salinas's premises. These new housing concepts included the application of economic principles in building construction; notions of growth and change; economic upkeep; flexibility; variety in housing styles; and a dialectic vision of nature, philosophy, society, and culture to accommodate the architectural forms inherent in the complex reality of the century's end (Salinas 1967).

In the 1980s, housing officials in Havana developed creative ideas and proposals that were not solely focused on the historic district. Architectural designs at the municipal level now used design teams who produced blueprints for new and rehabilitated buildings that blend in with their surroundings. Such an approach is far removed from the formal and preconceived ideas of past years, when experimentation was impossible (Baroni 1992–93). Despite the fact the municipality of Centro Habana was not part of the UNESCO-declared World Heritage Site, it turned out to be one of the areas of greatest interest among designers. Centro Habana has good environmental quality and potential even though many of its buildings are rundown (Bedoya 1992). Only a handful of high-quality rehabilitated and new construction projects occurred in the 1980s.

Other municipalities began projects as well. In Marianao, Daniel Bejerano tried to direct the housing units toward the interior of lots. In Diez de Octubre, Oscar Hernández laid out repetitive and geometric styles. A thesis project by Rosa M. Salinas proposed an entire neighborhood called Nuevo Miramar (1988). It served as an alternative to the traditional checkerboard street layout. Located on the empty lands of Monte Barreto in Miramar, her project stood directly in the area of hotel and tourist development of the municipality of Playa and tried to balance spaces for locals as well as tourists. It invalidated formalism, not only by the isolated blocks that were acritically used in the city but also by emphasizing social relations and functional uses of neighborhood spaces.

Young architects and designers who embraced postmodernism were harshly criticized by professionals such as Sergio Baroni, Mario Coyula, Ramón Gutiérrez, Carlos González Lobo, and Rogelio Salmona. Postmodernism, a hegemonic model imported from the industrial North Atlantic countries, failed to provide a uniquely adapted alternative for Cuba. Critics contended that architects fell into the trap of trendiness and were lulled into this style by reading foreign journals and following trends that were alien to Cuba.

The two largest housing projects of the 1980s were Las Arboledas (1984) and Villa Panamericana (1991), the latter embracing the playful mixtures of postmodern designs (figs. 6.5 and 6.6). However, both projects reflected different paths regarding the rigidity of site planning that had prevailed in the revolution's earlier years. In the case of Las Arboledas, a group of Cuban and North American architects directed by Huck Rorick, and with the initial collaboration of Salvador Gomila, the urban designer Peter Calthorpe, and the landscape architect Ken Kay, designed a microdistrict of twenty thousand residents within Altahabana (Rorick and Gomila 1984). Conceived as part of a new kind of apartment complex with formal construction and spatial variations, this new microdistrict achieved variation by using plazas and winding pedestrian malls and emphasizing dense tree-covered areas to break up road networks. This kind of project tried to tighten the relationship between rational composition and the natural environment. Works such as these were theoretically informed by the ideas of Christopher Alexander and his "design by patterns" principles. The pace of construction slowed during the Special Period, and by mid-2000, only around two hundred dwellings had been finished.

In contrast, the Villa Panamericana complex closed the stage of large residential complexes in Havana and relied on postmodern design to break up the formal layout of buildings. The Villa Panamericana suffers from superficial facades, cornices, and gables and a site plan that evokes a return to the grid pattern with the use of streets, avenues, parks, and town squares. The architect Roberto Caballero and a team of professionals from the Housing Division within the Ministry of Construction projected the image of Havana in an open space on the city's outskirts between the Habana del Este project and Alamar.

Despite the precarious aestheticism and the isolation of the Villa Panamericana from the capital, the complex represents a new part of the city's bedroom communities. It is also a significant improvement in the quality of life for its residents. Although part of the complex remains off limits to most Cubans, the presence of porticoes, retail activities for pedestrians, and tree-lined axes throughout the center of the complex does facilitate social integration. This remedied a longstanding complaint about the "cold" images of many housing complexes built during the revolution. Instead, this project drew from the traditional city, with its clear grid of streets lined by buildings that are closer to one another and have small shops on the ground floors, creating a vibrant streetscape. The complex is appealing, even if the individual architecture of its buildings is rather banal. This demonstrates that good urban design is more important than good architecture. By 2001, however, the com-

FIGURE 6.5. Villa Panamericana. This complex, constructed for the athletic events of the same name and completed in 1991, proved to be a costly housing project. Workers who built the project received priority in securing housing there. The low density and mixed designs of the buildings contrast with public housing built in the early years of the revolution. (Photograph by Joseph L. Scarpaci)

plex reflected a lack of maintenance, and the original landscaping in the buildings' courtyards was in poor condition. At the same time, retailing and street life are not as vibrant as in the traditional neighborhoods of Havana.

The Villa Panamericana grew out of the economic, technical, and planning forces behind the 1991 Pan American Games held in Havana and other parts of the island. Moreover, the project did not flourish because of the disruption of relations between Cuba and Eastern Europe that ushered in the Special Period.

## Housing Trends at the Dawn of the New Millennium

By the end of the twentieth century, Havana had a housing stock of 579,000 dwellings, with 78 percent classified as Type I (the best). Housing stock is classified in three groups: good (242,000 dwellings), fair (133,000), and bad (104,000), of which around 60,000 should be replaced in the last group. The

FIGURE 6.6.
A broad, tree-lined pedestrian mall accented by playful tile designs runs through the middle of the main street of Villa Panamericana. (Photograph by Joseph L. Scarpaci)

overall makeup of the city's housing stock has improved in quality because of the incorporation of new dwellings and the collapse of the worst. Around 1,000 dwellings suffer partial or total collapses every year, mostly after storms. Substandard dwellings in Havana include 7,012 *ciudadelas* and *cuarterías* (collective houses, one family per room) and 186 *barrios insalubres* (shantytowns) and *focos insalubres* (small squatter settlements). Together, they amount to nearly 90,000 inhabitants, but this bad housing condition does not necessarily imply social marginalization. Almost all dwellings have water and electrical service, and 40 percent are covered by the old sewers and storm water systems dating from 1913. There are an average of 3.4 persons per family, with 1.16 families per dwelling. Detached houses represent around 40 percent of the stock but cover the larger area. The area dedicated to housing covers 300 out of the city's 360 square kilometers of urbanized territory. This territory contains

14,000 city blocks, with half a million lots. The total area of Havana's metropolitan territory is 723 square kilometers (Dirección Provincial de Planificación Física 2000).

The Special Period also affected housing, as heavy-panel prefabrication plants producing very few different types of apartment buildings nationwide were paralyzed. High-rises, once seen as a symbol of development, were stopped. Construction with local materials called for a housing typology more sensitive to the physical and social context, also allowing more participation for future occupants (Bancrofft 1994). Most of the new housing projects were constructed at the periphery, and little building or repair work occurred in the inner city. Even these new housing tracts were not properly served by utilities and social services, also lacking local jobs. This helped to preserve the urban fabric and the built heritage but worsened the quality of life because of overcrowding and bad structural and sanitary conditions in many dwellings in the older parts of Havana. Makeshift additions and transformations — including the conversion of former stores into very poor dwellings — compounded the perennial lack of paint. Collectively, then, these factors diminished the urban image and streetscapes. As slightly more people gained economic power in the second half of the 1990s (largely due to the decriminalization of and access to dollars), distortions became bigger and irreversible. Striking colors and high fences, often chain-link, cheapened the look of what had been aging gracefully over different historical periods. These images of the built environment may be just the tip of the iceberg, reflecting deeper social and cultural changes (Coyula 1998).

In 1992, the Group for the Comprehensive Development of Havana called for the First Workshop on Housing Policy. The procedures recommended a decentralization of management with a stronger participation of local governments, community organizations, and local residents. The use of alternative technologies and local resources to substitute imports was encouraged. A top priority was given to those housing programs meant to stabilize the labor force for important economic projects. A housing program using low-consumption building techniques and materials, Viviendas de bajo Consumo, was a result of this workshop. But the quality of design, building materials, and construction proved to be so low that the changes actually increased the costs by making uncomfortable, short-lived structures (González 1997). For instance, to cut costs, the numbers of windows was reduced or even substi-tuted by mortar-block jalousies, forcing residents to spend energy in electric fans and artificial lighting. On the other hand, construction of poor-quality dwellings in valuable urban sites also meant underusing an irreplaceable resource such as land.

The Second Workshop of Housing Policy provided guidelines for the 1996–2000 period: to improve quality, even at the expense of quantity; to raise the population density and give a higher priority to the conservation of the existing stock than to the construction of new dwellings (something that had been systematically recommended since the 1970s, with little results), and to give more support to self-help programs, which during several decades had not been considered in the allocation of building materials. The period closed with an average of 50,000 dwellings per year, also improving quality: units in the upper layer rose from 24 percent in 1996 to 53 percent in 1999, while those in the bottom layer dropped from 33 percent to 1.6 percent. Conservation actions of the housing stock, combining state and self-help, increased from 130,000 to 300,000; and rehabilitation grew from 36,000 to 68,000. A third workshop in 1999 identified some problems: the production of building materials was well short of the needs, as was the number of emergency actions on buildings that had passed beyond their life expectancy but were still inhabited. The economic approach to construction issues was not enough, and the plants that once produced heavy prefabricated panels were not converted to make lighter and more flexible components (Coyula 2000c). The pace of construction of utilities (needed to support the new housing complexes) fell behind, thus continuing with another traditional flaw.

The housing plan for 1996–2000 sought to add 400,00 dwellings to the existing stock: 250,000 new and 150,000 by rehabilitation. These figures reflect contributions by both the state builders and self-help workers. Between 1997 and 1999, 141,400 dwellings were built in Cuba: 47 percent by the state (including several ministries, plus local governments), 18 percent by cooperatives, and 35 percent by self-help. Conservation and rehabilitation also increased in 1999, with 295,000 actions (51 percent by the population). However, the housing deficit persists, and quality remains a problem, especially in conservation and self-help projects. By late 2000, the General Housing Law was modified by Decree-Law No. 211: control on swaps (*permutas*) was tightened by the municipal housing departments, which also assumed control over issuing licenses for self-help housing, while the municipal Physical Planning Departments continued to issue licenses for state-built housing and kept control over the fulfillment of urban codes and regulations. This reorganization was prompted by the proliferation of individuals—mostly renting rooms to foreigners—who made oversized additions to their dwellings in order to serve more guests. Similar irregularities entail those who trade a nice dwelling for an obviously worse one, getting money under the table in the exchange. Both trends are considered negative by housing authorities because in a socialist country—the logic goes—dwellings should not be a commodity. An extreme case surfaced in 2000 at the boundary between two western neighborhoods, formerly upper- and middle-upper-class Miramar and lower-middle-class La Sierra. A foreigner coverted a single-family house owned by a Cuban into a small hotel with fourteen bedrooms and bathrooms. Consequently, authorities confiscated the property. The incident fueled a campaign prosecuting excessive remodeling, additions, and illegal renting.

Between 1994 and 1999, 27,573 new dwellings were built in Havana. Conservation and rehabilitation programs also increased. An estimated 4,760 tenements and 2,453 apartment buildings benefited from this activity. The state sold building materials to more than 188,000 families. Construction of new dwellings, however, has been mostly directed to large families at the expense of maintaining and rehabilitating the existing stock. Internal migrations into Havana had increased during 1992–96, but Decree No. 217 from April 22, 1997, was passed to stop that flow. The inner districts of Havana have actually lost some 22,000 inhabitants who have been relocated to the city edge between 1995 and 1999.

There is some evidence that Havana's population is decreasing. In 2000, it was estimated at 2,185,076, and by 2005 it may drop to 2,168,404. This trend, combined with an increasing life expectancy, contributes to a disturbing fact: the population of Havana is aging. From an economic point of view, this means that fewer people of working age will have to produce enough to pay pensions for more and more retirees; but on the other hand, fewer new dwellings will be needed (Dirección Provincial de Planificación Física 2000).

Despite the most recovery in the late 1990s compared with the worst years of the Special Period, housing remains the biggest problem in Havana at the outset of the new century. Housing never received the same priority as health and education, two programs in which Cuba has excelled even compared with developed countries. Building new dwellings has consistently received more attention and resources than the conservation of the existing stock. Construction materials have always been scarce, so supplies went mostly to support state brigades' and Microbrigades' projects. Therefore, few resources made their way for self-made repairs and additions. Not acknowledging the potential of self-help also contributed to the bad quality of those works, although the Arquitecto de la Comunidad (Community Architect) program, promoted nationwide by the Cuban nongovernmental organization (NGO) Habitat-Cuba in 1994, supplied the population with professional advice.

Early in the millennium, it has become commonplace to identify global problems that create local difficulty. Socialism hypothetically represented a challenge to triumphant neocapitalism. The hopes of that task were dashed with the collapse of the socialist camp, which exposed the social and economic problems of broad strata of the world's populations—problems that are far from being resolved. The reality is most drastic in developing countries where the chance to overcome these problems is hindered by a lack of resources. Increasingly, a wealthy minority distances itself from a poor majority. In Africa, for example, elementary subsistence cannot be achieved for many communities because of drought, famine, and the spread of AIDS. Housing deficits plague many other developing countries.

The crisis in Cuba in the 1990s was unexpected and therefore traumatic. Cubans had become accustomed to a gradual increase in their general well-being and expectations. For example, possessing world-class free public health and educational systems came to be badges proudly worn by the revolution and the Cuban people. A uniform, albeit somewhat bland, diet for Cubans of all social strata was actually something formerly associated only with First World countries. These public social services and food distribution systems, however, had been possible only because of the aid from the more "developed" socialist countries.

When that support collapsed in 1989 or so, the welfare state fell into crisis, and the state was transformed from an entity that could provide everything to one that could provide little. Cubans had come to expect certain rights and services and felt that the state had specific obligations. During the 1960s and 1970s, few asked about the origins of resources that had maintained socialist Cuba at a standard more akin to levels in the developed world than to the penury associated with many Latin American countries (Díaz Acosta and Guerra 1982; Estévez and Pereda 1990). Similarly, few raised concerns about squandering resources on certain imported goods. Perhaps the most important outcome of the Special Period has been the reflection on and analysis of the serious problems created by past mistakes.

Architectural, urban design, and planning fields have not been unscathed during the Special Period. Cuba contained the kind of technocratic bureaucracy common to industrializing countries. As such, it was far removed from local concerns and needs. A schematic and paralyzing dogmatism in Cuba made it impossible to differ from top-down assessments of housing needs and solutions. Instead of soliciting as many solutions as possible to the island's housing needs, top authorities and government agencies foreclosed options. That artisan or craft systems never coexisted with prefabrication is evidence of the narrow approach employed in socialist Cuba. Decisions about housing never emphasized the concept of "dialectics," so frequently used in the writings of Cuban scholar and urbanist Fernando Salinas. This meant that gradual solutions pegged to the resources of housing occupants were not applied. Instead, government officials became obsessed with turnkey projects that entailed turning over spacious, large-scale, and fully equipped housing units (Zschaebitz and Lesta 1990; IPF 1992). Clearly, this was a goal beyond the means of a poor country. Although the revolution resolved the basic housing problems of a majority, it also marginalized a significant minority.

Expensive oil imports weakened housing construction because fuel is a key input in building-materials manufacturing and distribution. Oil shortages paralyzed prefabricated housing production. The building efforts, therefore, shifted to the more deteriorated parts of Havana and drew on local residents' labor. At the same time, research was conducted on the conditions of *solares* and *cuarterías* in the central areas of the city. The Faculty of Architecture at the University of Havana, in collaboration with the Technical University of Hamburg, Germany, conducted a technical study in Atarés neighborhood (Ortega 1993). Atarés is a poor and predominantly Afro-Cuban neighborhood in the back-bay district of Havana. This project revealed the creativity of residents in finding innovative solutions that catered to household needs. The *barbacoa*—a mezzanine or loft in units with high ceilings used to create a sleeping space or second floor—is used to relieve crowding and open new living space.

Economic limitations imposed since 1991 have again eliminated the term "aesthetics" from the vocabulary of Cuban architects. New challenges returning to the forefront of the housing scene consist of making housing less expensive, building "low-energy" housing that draws on local materials and sun-dried clay bricks that can be assembled manually and without fossil fuels. Herein lie those basic elements of so-called sustainable development. Under this form of building construction, between 1992 and 1994, 17,500 housing units were built nationwide (Bancrofft 1994).

Havana remains one of the most beautiful Latin American cities whose value resides in its magnificent landmarks, the homogeneity of its street plan, the exuberance of its parks and plazas, and the transparency of its galleries and colonnades. Because of the persistence of its mixture of styles, Rigau and Stout (1994) have called Havana "the City of Alchemy." Even though Havana has been gutted and left unpainted and abandoned, it remains a living testimony of the many societies that inhabited and enriched it. Despite the severe crisis that plagues Havana, the city affords both culture and shelter and will remain the concrete symbol of daily life.

# 7

# The Changing Nature
# of the Economy

One has to laugh because [our economists] did not go to Harvard to study capitalist economics but went to the former socialist camp . . . which does not exist any more, and I ask myself what use do we have for socialist economics under the current conditions. . . . Now there are 1000 schools of political economy [in Cuba]; whenever three or four economists get together, they found a school and have a formula to solve our problems.

—Fidel Castro, closing speech to meeting celebrating the
40th anniversary of the attack on Moncada Barracks,
*Granma*, July 28, 1993

Consumer societies are not the solution. Political chicanery is not the solution. The capitalist democracy is not the solution. We can adopt some economic measures, but they should not lead us astray.

—Fidel Castro, impromptu interview with reporters, July 1995

One of the most notable changes in the global political economy of the 1990s was the collapse of the socialist camp headed by the Soviet Union. In Cuba, these tectonic shifts in the global political plates created fuel shortages, severe food rationing, power blackouts, transportation crises, and even "cracks" in the once venerable system of health and education (Stix 1995). We have referred to this economic quagmire throughout the book as the "Special Period" (Período Especial en Tiempo de Paz), following the official nomenclature used by the Cuban government. The Cuban government has implemented five strategies to address the Special Period:

1. To increase the staple-foods production by shifting displaced workers into agriculture, increasing arable lands, and reducing reliance on chemical fertilizers.

2. To return to the levels of total rationing of consumer goods (food, clothing, durables) in the 1960s.

3. To lessen oil consumption through rationing public utilities, scheduling blackouts, and reducing industrial production and the use of tractors, private automobiles, and buses. This includes burning sugarcane bagasse to run the sugar mills.

4. To seek out foreign investment through joint projects in order to increase hard currency revenues for the national government.

5. To implement selected structural reforms and market mechanisms that will reinsert Cuba's economy into the world market and create more market conditions internally. This includes reducing the excess of circulating money (pesos and dollars) and attracting workers into private-sector jobs.

This chapter examines these issues in the context of Havana's changing economy during the Special Period. It begins with a review of trends in the national economy from the mid-1980s until 2001. This serves as a backdrop to understand the free fall in which the Cuban economy found itself in the mid-1990s and its gradual climb back to 1989 levels. The latter half of the chapter shifts to the impacts this economic restructuring has had on Havana. The focus is on the emerging free-market private activities that illustrate the nature of Havana's changing economy. The chapter concludes with some reflections on Cuba's transition to socialism and the implications it has for other Third World economies.

## Interpreting the Cuban Economy

The centrally planned economy of Cuba is mainly state owned. Since the 1959 revolution, it has departed little from its dependence on foreign trade and agriculture. Until the Special Period, sugar had traditionally provided nearly three-quarters of total export revenues, and, despite the breakup of the Soviet Union, Cuba still exports about half of its sugar crop to its former republics. The economic malaise afflicting the island has not always been there. According to macroeconomic indicators, Cuba, like many Latin American countries, showed continuous improvements between 1940 and 1980. In the 1980s, though, Latin America and the Caribbean's overall gross national product (GNP) fell by 8.3 percent. However, "among Latin American countries, only Chile, Colombia and Cuba managed to grow" (Gilbert 1994, 33). From 1980 to 1985, the real per capita gross domestic product (GDP) in Latin America had fallen at an average annual rate of 1.7 percent for nineteen countries, excluding Cuba. In contrast, the constant price per capita of Cuba's GSP (gross social product; roughly the equivalent of the GDP) increased annually at an average rate of 6.7 percent. Zimbalist (1989) estimated the real annual Cuban industrial growth between 1965 and 1985 at 6.3 percent, a "very healthy, if not impressive, rate of growth and [it] stands out in sharp relief when compared to the growth experience in the rest of Latin America." Although there are reasons for skepticism (method of calculation, data comparability, Soviet subsidies), the data from the 1980s offer prima facie evidence of impressive economic performance. The economic growth is especially noteworthy because the early 1980s marked the beginning of the infamous "lost decade" in Latin America when the quality of life was quickly being eroded as a result of inflation and structural readjustment policies (Weil and Scarpaci 1992). Before assessing Havana's economy, we must first understand how the performance of the national economy can be measured and tracked over time.

To be sure, there is considerable debate about deciphering Cuban statistics. A number of scholars have questioned whether the Cuban economy is even comprehensible. Others are more sanguine (Brundenius and Zimbalist 1985a, 1985b, 1985c). They argue that once scholars attempt to understand conventions used by the Council of Mutual Economic Assistance (CMEA), the economic data yield "fathomable statistics." Failing to familiarize oneself with CMEA methods can lead to a misinterpretation and distortion of the Cuban economic reality. Worse still, it can leave a tabula rasa for imposing political prejudice (Brundenius and Zimbalist 1989, 2).

These debates raged well before the Special Period. Today, the island sorely lacks even contemporary socioeconomic figures and other basic information. For example, no telephone directory had been published for Havana between 1982 and 1996, mainly because of the cost of paper. A Mexican joint partner helped in the publication of the 1996 directory. The statistical yearbook (Anuario Estadístico de Cuba) was last published in 1989. As a result, economic data must be garnered from interviews, secondary sources, and surrogate measures of production and commerce. Conventional interpretation is made difficult by this dearth of information.[1]

1. Unless otherwise noted, sources here stem from our fieldwork and primary data gathered in Havana.

Analysts working with total output of the Cuban economy use the GSP, which differs from the Western GDP in two fundamental ways. The GDP includes value-added and nonproductive services, while the GSP assesses gross value and excludes nonproductive services. Although the conversion of the GSP to GDP for purposes of comparability varies yearly, in the 1980s the GSP of Cuba was about 20 percent less than the comparable GDP figures for the economy's output (Brundenius and Zimbalist 1989, 12–13).

Since the late 1980s, the economy has declined considerably. In 1990, estimates in the decline of Cuba's GSP ranged between 4 and 7 percent. As the crisis of the Special Period accelerated the following year, so did the range of the estimate in GSP decline, between 15 and 27 percent, though it narrowed to between 7 and 15 percent for 1993 (Mesa-Lago 1994, 8). The ensuing economic problems stem from at least three factors. One is the deemphasis of material incentives in the workplace and the abolition of informal produce markets. Although those policies were reversed in 1994–95, they had been attributed to a decade-long drop in economic productivity (Del Aguila 1992). Second, as noted above, the collapse of the former Soviet Union interrupted considerable price subsidies, foreign aid, and an estimated three-hundred-odd industrial and public works projects that were in production. Third, the continuation of the U.S. blockade has increased the cost of many consumer and industrial goods that could no doubt be secured more cheaply if imported from the United States and not through third countries (Bahamas, Panama, Canada, Jamaica, Mexico, and Venezuela). The blockade also deprives the Cuban economy of a lucrative U.S. tourist trade. However, Cuba is expanding its tourist market greatly (see the next chapter).

For decades the CMEA had provided preferential trade agreements among signatory partners, of which Cuba was a member. The CMEA was a rather small, isolated market whose "backbone" was the Soviet Union. Member nations—especially Cuba, Vietnam, and Mongolia—received preferential treatment because of their "developing nation" status (*The Statesman's Yearbook, 1982–83* 1982, 52). That meant that the Soviet Union would buy Cuban sugar at prices three times the going rate, and Cuba would receive discounted oil in return. These favorable terms of trade allowed Cuba to satisfy about 90 percent of its energy needs (Mesa-Lago 1994, 1). Cuba had the highest dependency rate of trade among CMEA members (84 percent), of which 70 percent alone was with the Soviet Union. In 1989 Cuba received $6 billion in economic assistance, bringing the island's debt to $24 billion. Merchant vessels from the former Soviet Union and Eastern Europe carried about 85 percent of Cuban foreign trade in 1990. Imports from the former Soviet Union plummeted by 70 percent in 1990 alone (Zimbalist 1993, 408). By 1992, vessels from the Cuban merchant marine could handle only 20 percent of total trade volume; Eastern European and Russian vessels now require hard currency for their services (Mesa-Lago 1994, 7).

If the dissolution of the CMEA is the proximate cause of Cuba's current predicament, it is unclear how Cuba can arrest its crisis. One consequence of the unraveling of the Soviet bloc is that Cuba is trying to reinsert itself into the global market during the most dire economic period since the 1959 revolution. Three possible reasons may explain why this has been so difficult for Cuba. First, its sugar harvest has fallen to record lows, from a high of about 9 million tons in the late 1970s to around 4 million tons in 2000. The ramifications are many because sugar is the primary generator of hard currency. Inability to generate hard currency prohibits Cuba from purchasing sufficient oil, fertilizer, machinery, pesticides, and other agricultural inputs. Food production and the quality and quantity of tobacco products have also declined. The externalities derived from the collapse of Soviet aid are multiple and negative: low sugar production and harvest-displaced workers in the labor force, many of whom collect unemployment compensation.

Second, those managing the reemergence of market-driven endeavors in Cuba may not hold the micro- and macroeconomic training required to steer the nation through these difficult times. Political appointments may be a compromise between orthodox hard-liners and reformers.

Third, it is unclear whether the economic reforms outlined in July 1993 (discussed below) will actually propel Cuba to sustainable market reforms. Cuban leaders may not understand market economics and may retain the notion that they can direct the transition to socialism. Alternatively, they may have a good grasp of market mechanisms but may wish to give the impression within and outside Cuba that the government is still in control of a sustainable socialist project (Skidelsky 1996; Mesa-Lago 1994, 71).

The national labor force is estimated to include about 3.5 million workers. Organized labor is affiliated with the only government-approved labor federation: the Workers' Central Union of Cuba (Central de Trabajadores [CTC]). It has 2.9 million members and serves as an umbrella organization for seventeen member unions (Del Aguila 1992). In 1989, the overall unemployment rate was pegged at 6 percent and 10 percent for female employment. Unemployment rose during the early 1990s, and by May 1996 the CTC estimated at the seventeenth congress of their organization that Special Period had created an unemployment rate of 7 percent, which could rise to 13 percent ("Official Says Cuban Unemployment Is 7 Percent" 1996). As the Cuban government downsizes its state bureaucracy, the private sector is expected to absorb displaced workers (Carranza, Gutiérrez, and Monreal 1995). By April 2001, the CTC estimated that unemployment stood at 7 percent nationwide ("Unions in Cuba" 2001).

At this point, it will be useful to recall some of the contours of Cuba's planning system (Chapter 4) because of its important role in the nation's economic system. Five-year development plans have served as Cuba's economic maps throughout most of the revolution. They are executed at the national and provincial levels. In keeping with the revolution's efforts to empower regional governments, the original six provinces of Cuba (Pinar del Río, La Habana, Matanzas, Camagüey, Las Villas, and Oriente) were increased to thirteen in 1976.[2] These provinces are Camagüey, Ciego de Avila, Cienfuegos, Ciudad de La Habana, Granma, Guantánamo, Holguín, La Habana, Las Tunas, Matanzas, Pinar del Río, Sancti Spíritus, and Santiago de Cuba. Before the revolution, higher education, for instance, was confined to Havana; Santiago de Cuba and Santa Clara were the only other cities with a university. Since the revolution, many provinces boast a university and major hospital. The revolution has created a kind of hybrid model of regional development that combines elements of Growth Pole Theory (in which secondary regional cities serve as the "motors" of development and point of investment around their designated hinterland) and a commitment to socialist ideals that have decentralized education and health service into the island's interior. It was common to find as many as 150 bateyes (shabby workers' settlements) around sugar mills before the revolution (Slater 1982).

Deviations from national and provincial five-year plans are most apparent by the rise in new foreign investment and the islands of capitalism they create (Pérez-López 1994b). Although radical for an economy embracing socialism, these "reforms," sanctioned by the Fourth Congress of the Communist Party in October 1991, are all too common in other developing countries. The message is simple: Cuba is "open for business." American entrepreneur Lee Iacocca visited Havana in July 1994, and, according to one journalist, media magnate Ted Turner "frequently shows up" there (Bardach 1995). Fidel Castro would welcome U.S. investment under certain conditions and has long held that position. Currently, Cuban officials actively court corporate Amer-

2. Isla de Juventud (formerly Isle of Pines) is considered a "special municipality."

ica. They target consumer products, manufacturing and tourism companies, and agricultural firms. Although U.S. firms cannot conduct business with Cuba, many are formulating plans for tapping the Cuban market of 11 million. Havana, for instance, would profit from investment in biotechnology (Goodrich 1993; Collis 1995), medical equipment, textiles, asbestos-cement pipes, leather products, and building restoration (*USA Today*, December 27, 1994). Although many U.S. companies have signed memorandums of understanding with the Cuban government, the passage of the Helms-Burton bill in 1996 will deter any U.S. investment in the near future.

Cubans jest about the "second conquest" of the island when they refer to the surge in Spanish investment. Havana is the target for much of this investment. A Spanish conglomerate refurbished the former Havana Hilton between 1993 and 1995. The hotel, which was built in 1958 by Conrad Hilton, is one of the city's landmarks. Although at least $100 million of Spanish investment has generated employment in the construction industry in recent years, most building materials, furniture, wiring, glass, and plaster come from other countries, depriving the city of the usual kinds of economic multipliers and horizontal integration among the building and home-furnishing trades. Within the first ninety days of operation, the hotel management of the Habana Libre renamed the hotel the Habana Libre-Guitart (reflecting the name of the Spanish investment group) and reduced the hotel's workforce from twelve hundred to four hundred.

Although new investment holds promise, Cuba is still not a sanctuary for "safe investment." In 1996, the *Economist Intelligence Unit* ranked Cuba 116th out of 129 countries regarding investment safety. Tourism, though, remains a reliable commodity the Cubans can market (Espino 1993; see also Chapter 8). Risky investment notwithstanding, companies investing in Cuba are Western Mining (Australia), Sherritt (Canada), ING Bank (Netherlands), Grupo Domos (Mexico), Unilever (United Kingdom/Netherlands), Labatt (Canada), and Pernod Ricard (France).

## Changes in Havana's Economy

Political directives have targeted the countryside and provincial capitals for the bulk of investment since 1959. Rural investment served as a counterweight to the traditional emphasis on Havana. Havana has not held more than 21 percent of the nation's population since the outset of the revolution. This stems from a direct policy to avoid urban primacy and resource concentration in the capital city. Fidel Castro stated early in the revolution that Cuba needed a "minimum of urbanism and a maximum of ruralism" (Eckstein 1977, 443). Reversing the trend of more than four hundred years of urbanization was difficult. The 1970 census reported that Havana Province held 38 percent of the nation's industrial employment, while Oriente held only 23 percent of all industrial workers, even though its provincial population surpassed Havana's. Although these regional disparities are striking, Slater (1982) contends that examining spatial rather than class differences may well obfuscate important structural problems of the Cuban revolution.

Socialist Cuba deliberately curtailed growth in Havana. Unlike other primate cities in Latin America, Havana has not been the voluntary destination of thousands of rural and secondary-city migrants, thus averting the usual shantytowns and problems of hyperurbanization associated with this migration stream (though some shanties have existed during the revolution). For instance, when the revolutionary government seized office in 1959, Havana and Lima, Peru, had populations of comparable size. Since then, Havana's population has doubled, while Lima's has increased sevenfold. Notably, Havana lacks the shanties that line the Rimac River in Lima; the few shanties that do exist are located in less prominent places. Several reasons account for Havana's unique position as a Latin American primate city. First, the elimination of the private rental market and the illegality of squatting have curbed voluntary migration. Second, housing exchanges in Havana are mostly done with "For Swap" signs (Se Permuta) and confined mainly to destinations within the city. Potential buyers and sellers gather in the afternoons during the workweek on the pedestrian boulevard, Prado, to arrange deals. Third, employment and housing are controlled by the government, though Cubans find ways to get around these obstacles. Although government regulation characterizes Cuban housing and employment, unlike in the former Soviet Union, residence permits are not required in Cuba. Last, and perhaps most important, food-ration books are used in local state-run food stores (*bodegas*) to secure food staples at subsidized prices.

Despite efforts to control population growth in Havana, a recent poll conducted on the island showed that Havana is still the major migration destination. Since 1990, migration to Havana has escalated on par with the worst economic crisis in recent history. In the 1980s, Havana received a steady flow of between 10,000 and 12,000 immigrants annually. By 1993 there were 13,000, which rose to 17,000 in 1995 and an estimated 27,000 immigrants in

1995. The survey, called the National Poll of Internal Migrants and carried out by the Center of Demographic Studies (Centro de Estudios Demográficos [CEDEM]), found several factors generating migration to Havana. Professor Beatriz Erviti of CEDEM remarked that "the most frequent motive for movement was family related, basically because of marriage or divorce, to improve living conditions and movements due to employment reasons or State made decisions."

As the nation's capital, the city of Havana (population 2.2 million) serves as the major government and service center of the island. In the early 1990s, more than 80 percent of the nation's imports and exports passed through its ports. The most recently available data show a labor force of 939,400 (table 7.1), with slightly more than half of the city's labor force working in the productive sphere. Industry, construction, and transportation are the largest sectors. Industry (22.6 percent) is concentrated mostly in food processing and pharmaceuticals, while construction and transportation each employ 8.7 percent of the labor force.

One trend is that it is likely that the nonproductive sphere has increased since 1990, probably surpassing the productive sphere. Fuel shortages and power outages force industry to slow production, as does the lack of hard currency for purchasing imported raw materials.

Another unfolding pattern is that in 1995 the construction and transportation industries suffered from fuel shortages. In 1986 buses accounted for 86 percent of motorized transport; in contrast, automobile trips—never a significant mode of transportation—accounted for just 6 percent. Roughly 50 percent of all bus routes have been eliminated, consolidated, or cut back, making lengthy waits at crowded bus stops a multihour endeavor. Workers in construction and transportation have been displaced elsewhere, remain under- or unemployed, or form part of the new self-employed labor pool. In the wake of this transportation crisis has come a huge increase in bicycles. In 1990, *habaneros* used their roughly 70,000 bicycles for recreation and sport. By 1993, there were 700,000 bicycles, mostly purchased from China, which were being used for commuting.

In late 1995, estimates placed the figure at 1 million bicycles (fig. 7.1). The Chinese models Phoenix and Flying Pigeon sell on installment plans for 60 pesos for students to 120 pesos for workers; in deflated real dollars in 1995 this would range from about U.S.$2 to $6. The externalities generated by bicycle imports and use mean less air pollution in Havana, greater commuting time for workers, and a proliferation of private-sector bicycle repair and park-

TABLE 7.1. Havana's Labor Force by Productive and Nonproductive Spheres, ca. 1990

| SECTOR | WORKERS (THOUSANDS) | % |
|---|---|---|
| Agriculture | 90.0 | 0.9 |
| Industry | 211.6 | 22.6 |
| Construction | 82.2 | 8.7 |
| Transportation | 1.3 | 7.4 |
| Commerce | 102.9 | 11.0 |
| Other productive spheres | 13.0 | 1.4 |
| Total productive sphere | 500.9 | 53.3 |
| Services | 45.0 | 4.8 |
| Science and technology | 20.1 | 2.1 |
| Education, culture, and art | 105.8 | 11.3 |
| Health, sports, and tourism | 67.8 | 7.2 |
| Finance, administration, and other | 199.8 | 21.3 |
| Total nonproductive sphere | 438.5 | 46.7 |
| Total labor force | 939,400.0 | 100.0 |

Note: These data have probably changed during the Special Period, and they reflect at least two trends. Column totals do not always add up exactly due to rounding.

ing services (Scarpaci and Hall 1995). Increased cycling, however, also carries costs. For example, in 1995 the National Revolutionary Police and the Ministry of Public Health reported 2,175 bicycle accidents in Havana alone and 479 traffic fatalities involving bicycles nationwide ("Facts and Statistics" 1996b).

The proportion of Havana's population working in agriculture has also likely increased. Neighborhood gardens have proliferated everywhere, but it is difficult to determine whether workers who tend to those gardens would be counted as agriculturists (Roca 1994). Intensification of truck farming has also increased in the southern portions of the municipalities of Boyeros, Arroyo Naranjo, and Cotorro, departing from a Third World pattern of decreasing peri-urban agriculture (Browder, Bohland, and Scarpaci 1995). Urban "husbandry"—once outlawed and subject to stiff fines and incarceration—now flourishes, and cattle rustlers in the mid-1990s removed 10,000 animals each year from Cuban farms (Napoles 1996a). In addition, in the mid-

FIGURE 7.1. Bicycling in Havana. Rush hour after an early morning rain at the Puente de Hierro over the Almendares River, between Vedado and Miramar. (Photographs by Joseph L. Scarpaci)

1990s, balconies throughout Havana held many chicken coops, and goats were found in yards, as were makeshift sties for piglets. However, these practices had diminished by 2001 as the circulation of the dollar spread. For decades, pork was unavailable in the city of Havana mainly because of a fever and subsequent infection among swine. A secondary reason was that it was destined for tourist consumption in such typical dishes as roasted pork "Cuban style" (*lechón asado*) and private livestock has been strictly controlled and even outlawed at various times. Cuban economic development analysts and officials herald the rise in domestic livestock as a sign of local creativity, but public health officials fret over the unsanitary conditions (personal interviews, Ministerio de Salud Pública, June 15, 1994). In the main, though, these examples underscore the likely decline in the proportion of workers in the productive sphere. Along with that shift has been a rise in black market (informal) activities and a new urban "subsistence" economy that is difficult to measure.

While the traditional calculation of the socialist GSP separates wage labor into productive and nonproductive spheres, at no time did statisticians or economists envision "self-employment" as a major category before the 1990s. The Special Period has no doubt cast thousands of *habaneros* into "services" and "tourism." Service categories charge in both pesos and dollars and include such low-order retail activities as beauty shops, shoe repair, massage therapy, spiritual advice, and home restaurants called *paladares*. These food establishments cater to both tourists and local Cubans with dollars (mainly from remittances sent by relatives or revenues from new self-employment). The once clandestine restaurants serve meals perhaps at one-third the rates posted in the city's finest tourist restaurants; a lobster dinner, salad, and beer can be purchased for $12–15 in a *paladar* versus $25–35 in tourist facilities (discussed in more detail in Chapter 8). Many of the supplies come from pilfering state warehouses or violating fishing laws. Taken in its entirety, the composition of the Havana labor force has increased in the nonproductive sphere as the city enters into a new mixed economy.

## Industrial Location in Havana

While we have argued that the 1990 figure showing that 22.8 percent of Havana's workforce labors in industry has probably dropped in the 1990s, the city's industrial infrastructure reveals distinctive patterns of geographic concentration. Although the "bottoming out" of the Cuban economic free fall in the mid-1990s is promising, it is still difficult to determine with precision full employment and output data by sector (Ciudad de La Habana n.d.; Poder Popular n.d.). In this section, therefore, we briefly identify the major patterns of industrial location in the capital.

Three major concentrations of industrial activity (light manufacturing, petrochemical, and warehousing) characterize Havana's industrial geography (fig. 7.2). First, the back-bay areas of Regla, Luyanó, and Guanabacoa constitute the central area of industry. This is the historic core industrial center, complete with oil refinery and petrochemical industries visible from the eastern edge of Habana Vieja, looking to the south and southeast. Rail yards and a large array of now aging warehouses make up this industrial landscape.

A second industrial cluster is found along the southeastern railroad line passing through San Francisco de Paula, Cotorro, and Cuatro Caminos. Light industry in the form of food processing, pharmaceutical packing houses, and some light manufacturing is distributed along the railroad corridor and the Central Highway (Carretera Central). Buildings and infrastructure here date from the prerevolutionary period, with a few new additions.

A third and less clearly defined concentration of industry in Havana is strewn along a southwestern and western axis running from José Martí Inter-

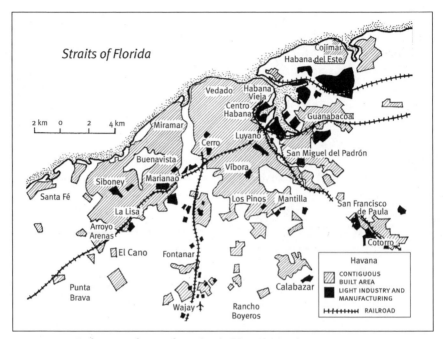

FIGURE 7.2. Industry and manufacturing in Havana, 1996

national Airport northward into the west-central core of the metropolitan areas. Here, too, light industry lies adjacent to a major rail line entering from the west and ending at Havana Bay. The concentration is especially strong at the southern edge of Metropolitan Park.

Havana lacks the industrial concentration that characterizes other Latin American capitals such as Mexico City, Buenos Aires, Santiago, and the Lima-Callao metropolitan area. These cities contribute more than 50 percent of the total national industrial output (Gwynne 1986, 82). Cuba's close relationship with the former Soviet Union and Eastern Bloc nations allowed for a great number of manufactured goods to be imported. Although the concentration of industry in Havana in the 1950s was intense, more than thirty years of attempting to build up provincial industrial production in Matanzas, Santiago de Cuba, Holguín, and other secondary cities has lessened the industrial imprint on Havana. Indeed, the only sign of heavy industry output outside the back-bay area is the utility plant in Tallapiedra and the gas plant at Melones, along the southern rim of the bay. These facilities cast a steady heavy plume across Centro Habana and the Capitolio building. Until the Soviet-initiated construction of a nuclear reactor at Juraguá (outside the south-central city of Cienfuegos) develops cheap energy for industrial production, it is unlikely that Havana's geographic pattern of industrial production will change any-time in the near future (Rohter 1996). A strong residential and service sector characterize the Cuban capital.

Cuban economists are studying the role that industrial production will play in a new globalized economy. Marquetti (2000) argues that the greatest po-tential for industrial growth rests on increasing internal production and con-sumption of Cuban industrial products. Now that market-based business practices and training are increasing in Cuba and the state is loath to support unprofitable agencies, industrial production for the Cuban market seems to be a logical industrial policy to pursue. Related to that, Cuban economist Pedro Monreal (personal communication, March 4, 2001) suggests that Cuba's greatest specialty marketing niche on a global scale might be flexible, special-ized industrial production, especially in the automotive and capital goods in-dustry. He contends that Cuban industry has displayed remarkable creativity and adaptability in manufacturing parts for automobiles and agricultural ma-chinery. Whether the industrial parts are for Soviet tractors that have been discontinued or 1949 American-made Plymouths, Cuban industry displays the attributes of specialized and flexible industrial production.

Parallel developments on the industrial and export fronts have also taken place. On June 3, 1996, the State Council (Consejo de Estado) passed Law Decree 165, which will establish new duty-free zones and industrial parks in the capital, the ports of Cienfuegos and Mariel, and possibly Santiago de Cuba. These duty-free zones consist of territory in Cuba that will not have a resident population. The law will allow duty-free imports and exports to flow through these enclaves. Industrial, business, agricultural, technological, and service activities will be carried out there. In Havana, land next to the José Martí International Airport in Rancho Boyeros will be the site of a new duty-free and industrial park (InterPress 1996b). In 1999, Havana opened a new airport terminal to accommodate international tourism, which in turn freed up two other terminals to attend to commercial imports and exports.

## Socialist Collapse and Capitalist Promise?

The tenacity of the *habaneros* in the face of the city's economic free fall reveals itself at several levels. Their ability to overcome food shortages, power outages, public transportation problems, and other obstacles is evident on each city block. Everyone is trying to survive: bureaucrats, lower-rank party leaders (*dirigentes*), schoolchildren, retirees, college professors, manual laborers, and bus drivers. In the daily parlance of the *habanero*, this means *resolviendo* or *solucionando* (problem solving or "making ends meet"), even if it implies breaking the law. Before July 26, 1993, possession of the dollar was illegal for all Cubans except diplomats. In addition, some forms of self-employment existed since 1977. The number and types of work have changed, however. For example, in the 1970s, most men had to be "disabled" (e.g., get a medical certificate stating they could not hold down their regular jobs) to work in the private sector. "Moonlighting" had also been permitted in the evenings or on weekends. For the most part though, the private sector was very small before the Special Period.

Even before the 1993 market reforms, many Cubans had stashed away dollars for use on the black market. So desperate was the government for dollars or other convertible hard currencies that Fidel Castro announced in his now famous July 26, 1993, speech the possibility of opening checking accounts in dollars. At the same time, more than 150 types of occupations were operating outside state control by mid-1996, and most can charge in dollars after securing the proper license and remitting the appropriate taxes (Lee 1996a). By August 1996 several taxes had been implemented to rehabilitate Cuba's internal finances (table 7.2).

Restructuring the economy has brought about deep changes in socialist Cuba. What had been illegal, relatively small, and clandestine until 1993 was suddenly legal and overt. Attendance at work and schools has fallen off from levels of the mid-1980s, though no reliable data exist to assess its magnitude. Street hustlers, money launderers (generally called *maceteros* or *bisneros*), pimps (*jineteros*), and prostitutes who work the tourists increased notably (Elinson 1999). Prior to the Special Period, Cubans approaching tourists for a pen, chewing gum, or a coin would be scolded by passersby or, worse yet, detained by police if they persisted. State-run stores offered basic wares to the masses, even if they were low-quality products from Czechoslovakia, China, Vietnam, or North Korea. This new "economic liberty" carries externalities (e.g., noneconomic costs) in the forms of delinquency and street crime (cf. Klak 1994), though they pale in comparison with the kinds of problems found in U.S. cities or the rise of organized crime derived from the thawing of communism in Moscow. Havana was heralded during the first decades of the revolution as being one of the safest cities in the Americas, even by

TABLE 7.2. Actions to Rehabilitate Cuba's Internal Finances, 1996–2001

- Graduated hard-currency personal income tax
- Graduated local-currency personal income tax
- Vessel or property ownership tax
- Tax on earnings from businesses associated with passenger and cargo transportation
- Income taxes for vendors in agricultural markets

*Source*: Authors' field research.

harsh critics of the regime (Mesa-Lago 1994, 12). Petty theft and assaults are no longer isolated, random events in Havana. Today, the state-run shops for Cubans are barren, and the streets of the city—with their poverty, prostitution, shabby buildings, and begging—increasingly resemble other Latin American cities.

Black market activities proliferate, and it is difficult to obtain soap, toothpaste, shoes, spare electrical or automotive parts, extra coffee, or fresh meat and poultry without investing time in going from market to market, house to house, or contact to contact. Almost every household has someone who devotes time to checking out black market activity and the new state-sanctioned markets springing up around the city.

## Food and Food Production in Havana's Economy

The nation's economic bind brought on by the Special Period has placed food at the head of the list of Cuban household needs, replacing the longstanding concern over housing (Hamberg 1994). Despite some free-market tinkering with private food markets between 1980 and 1986 (Rosenberg 1986), the Cuban government scuttled market-regulated mechanisms for distributing, selling, and preparing food. In 1995, though, numerous food-preparation occupations and restaurants were legalized.

The state rationing system has been in effect in Cuba since 1961. Over time, the kinds of goods available have changed, depending on Cuba's main trading partners and prevailing economic conditions. At present, most staple food products are covered by the rationing system. Rationing is documented by the booklet, the *libreta*. Each Cuban household receives one for buying highly subsidized products at *bodegas*. By law it must be turned in or modified within ten days of the death of a household member, hospitalization, old-age institutionalization, incarceration, or leaving the country.

The *libreta* lists the age composition of the household by these cohorts: younger than 2, 2–6, 7–13, 14–64, and 65 years and older. Nonfood items are supposed to include fuel (kerosene, preheated kerosene, liquid gas, charcoal, firewood), laundry soap, body soap, cigarettes, rum, and beer. *Bodegas* post prices on a chalkboard, along with the period in which the price is valid and note whether the product is available.

In October 2000, we documented prices at several *bodegas* in the municipalities of Plaza de la Revolución, Centro Habana, and Habana Vieja in Havana City Province. Our aim was to compare the frequency of the annual distribution between 1993 (the worst of the Special Period) and 2000 (a time of marked economic improvement). The trend reveals that meat is rarely allocated and that cooking oil allocations have fallen drastically. Eggs and vegetables from farmers' markets are also less available (table 7.3).

Although the normative distribution of food per person would appear to approach a reasonable diet, the distribution of food through the state ration system is uneven. Many scheduled items do not appear for months and then suddenly show up. Moreover, there is no guarantee that all households assigned to a *bodega* will get their allotment. Rather, supplies are allocated on a first-come basis (table 7.4).

Food distribution by the state has since 1993 been complemented by a free-market system that operates in dollars. Although dollars are not available to all Cubans, those who have access to them through remittances or working in a dollar-based economy such as tourism can purchase food staples. Table 7.5 reveals how expensive food has become between 1989 and 2001.

In the mid-1980s, before the present liberalization of the agricultural and food markets, Cuba had tinkered with private farmers' markets. However, like the *paladares* at the outset, these markets were closed because it was believed that middlemen were acquiring too much wealth too quickly. Thus, until late 1994, farmers' produce had to be secured through tightly controlled state outlets. As of March 1996, there were approximately 1,479 agricultural cooperative units in Cuba, of which 486 (one-third) reported a profit ("Facts and Statistics" 1996a). These cooperatives are permitted to sell their goods to the new Agricultural Markets (Mercados Agropecuarios), though it is likely that two-thirds of those noted above are not making their state quotas (*acopio*)—a prerequisite for selling goods in the private market. For a variety of reasons, therefore, most cooperatives provide few inputs to Havana's legal food markets.

TABLE 7.3. Annual Frequency of Distribution of Selected Food Items, 1993 and 2000

| PRODUCT | 1993 | 2000 |
| --- | --- | --- |
| Cooking oil | 10 | 4 |
| Body soap | 4 | 4 |
| Laundry soap | 5 | 5 |
| Detergent | 4 | 3 |
| Beef | 2 | 3 |
| Chicken | 3 | 4 |
| Fish | 23 | 11 (mostly canned) |
| Eggs | 27 | 18 |
| Ground beef–soy meal | 8 | 5 |
| Farmers' market items (potatoes, tomatoes, plantains, and others) | 97 | 27 |

*Source*: Authors' field research.

Cubans who are unable or unwilling to seek fruits, meat and poultry, and vegetables through that outlet have no recourse but to turn to the black market.

Here lies a deep contradiction in the new market reforms, and one for which Cuban authorities have few facile replies, which in part reflects the complexity of the matter. Put differently, the Cuban government has commodified basic foods and household staples in a way that is not only unprecedented in the forty-two years of the revolution but anathema to a social system based on common ownership of the means of production (Callinicos 1991; Forbes and Thrift 1987). The rise of inequality has been acknowledged by Cuban leaders as a major problem stemming mainly from the Special Period. Both the decriminalization of dollars and the legalization of many black market activities allow the Cuban government to resolve its foreign exchange problems (Pastor and Zimbalist 1995, 709).

## Cuba's New Entrepreneurs:
## Small-Scale Capitalism in the New Economy

Since the advent of more than a hundred self-employed trades in 1993, the number of Cuban self-employed workers has fluctuated. In late 1993, about

TABLE 7.4. Normative Food Distribution per Person through the Ration Book (*Libreta*), Havana, 2000

| PRODUCT | QUANTITY | FREQUENCY | PRICE (PESOS) |
|---|---|---|---|
| Rice | 6 lbs. | 1 per month | 0.25/lb. |
| Beans | 20 oz. | 1 per month | 0.32/lb. |
| Chickpeas | 4 oz. | 1 per month | 0.18/lb. |
| Sugar (white) | 3 lbs. | 1 per month | 0.15/lb. |
| Sugar (brown) | 3 lbs. | 1 per month | 0.10/lb. |
| Coffee (mixed) | 2 oz. (1 pkg.) | 2 per month | 0.10 x package |
| Salt | 1 lb. | 1 per month | 0.10/lb. |
| Soap (bath) | 1 unit | 5 per year (approx.) | 0.25/unit |
| Soap (laundry bar) | 1 unit | 5 per year (approx.) | 0.20/unit |
| Detergent (liquid) | 1 bottle | 3 x year (approx.) | 3.60/bottle |
| Lard | 1 lb. | 4 or 5 per year | 0.40/lb. |
| Crackers | 1 lb. (approx.) | 1 per month (approx.) | 0.63/lb. |
| Toothpaste | 1 tube | Every other month | 0.65/tube |
| "Head cheese" (*mortadella*) | 1 lb. | 3 or 4 per year | 3.00/lb. |
| Frankfurters | 1 package | 3 per year (approx.) | 1.50/package |
| Beef | 1 lb. | 2 or 3 per year | 0.70/lb. |
| Chicken | 1 lb. | 8 or 9 per year | 0.70/lb. |
| Bread | 1 roll | daily | 0.05/roll |
| Fish (canned) | 2 cans | monthly | 2.00/can (in tomato sauce) |
| | | | 1.70/can (natural) |
| Fish (fresh) | 2 lbs. | (none in 2000) | 0.45/lb. |
| Eggs | 12 units | monthly | 0.15/unit |

*Source*: Authors' field research.

15,000 self-employed workers (called *cuentapropistas*) had formally registered with the government. By January 1996, the figure had just surpassed the 200,000 mark, and it steadily fell to about 165,000 workers by April 1998 (Peters and Scarpaci 1998). Cuban officials contend that the decline in self-employment seems to reflect increased competition from state companies and the natural market forces. In early 2001, the figure was about 151,000

TABLE 7.5. Average Prices for Selected Food Items in the Peso Market (1989) and the Free Market (January 2001)

| PRODUCT | 1989 (PESOS) | 2001 ($U.S.) |
|---|---|---|
| Milk (liter) | 1.00 | 1.25 |
| Yogurt (liter) | 1.00 | 1.05 |
| Lard (lb.) | 2.40 | 2.50 |
| Cheese (lb.) | 4.00 | 2.60 |
| Sandwich bread | 1.00 | 1.00 |
| Fish | 0.45 | 0.45 |
| Pork | 1.00 | 1.00 |
| Mutton (lb.) | 1.00 | 1.00 |
| Eggs | 0.10 | 0.10 |
| Black beans | 0.40 | 0.40 |
| Cooking oil | 2.00 | 2.15–2.40 |
| Marmalades | 2.50 | 2.50 |
| Shampoo | 2.00 | 2.00 |
| Hand soap | 0.40 | 0.45 |
| Body soap | 0.50 | 0.50 |
| Detergent (lb.) | 1.00 | 1.00 |

*Source*: Authors' field research.

workers, whose total contribution to the GDP is about 1 percent. Economy Minister José Luis Rodríguez stated in February 2001 that the government had no intention of phasing out self-employment ("Cuba's Self-Employed Continue to Dwindle" 2001), despite a myriad of challenges that illegal self-employed workers face (table 7.6).

In 1998, Peters and Scarpaci (1998) conducted one of the first comprehensive studies of self-employed workers in the Cuban capital. They surveyed 152 *cuentapropistas* who came from every occupation: former college professors, retired gym teachers, accountants, medical technicians, journalists, veterinarians, and others from every walk of life. Not surprisingly, these entrepreneurs had considerable work experience (mean age forty-three), were well educated (average twelfth-grade schooling), and had a relatively high income of 743 pesos per month. As such, they were earning 165 percent of the then net income of Cuban physician (450 pesos) and 347 percent of the then aver-

TABLE 7.6. Benefits and Detriments of Illegally Self-Employed Workers

*Benefits*

• Avoiding licensing fees and bureaucratic snares (health inspections)

• Fewer corruption payments to public officials

• Evading labor laws

• Evading taxes

*Detriments*

• Fear of fine and incarceration
 (social deviant, counterrevolutionary or dangerousness [*peligrosidad*] charges)

• Police shakedowns and confiscation of food, beverages, and wares
 (tables, chairs, cassettes, televisions, stereos, etc.)

• Inability to advertise widely

*Source*: Authors' field research.

age Cuban salary (214 pesos). Moreover, this income came after having paid an average of 41 percent tax as a percentage of operating profit.

The authors anticipated that high taxes and harassment by inspectors would be the principal challenges faced by self-employed workers. Interestingly, 27 percent identified supplies (cost and availability) and 13 percent indicated taxes as their top business challenge. In addition, nearly one-third (32 percent) said that they had no major challenge (Peters and Scarpaci 1998, 7). While self-employment seems to offer an alternative to state employment or working for a joint-venture operation, the government seems unlikely to allow the figure to rise beyond the 150,000 level of workers.

## The Nature of Work in Today's Havana

The transition to socialism has perennially been plagued by several structural impediments. Marx gave neither a blueprint for socialism nor a description of socialist society when he theorized about how capitalist conditions would engender a transition to socialism. Sandinista Nicaragua showed clearly that the revolution took hold differently in the Sierra than on the coast (Vilas 1989; Wall 1990). Contemporary Vietnam—with a population six times larger than Cuba's—is aiming to position itself in the global market without abandoning some of its socialist principles. Other lessons about Third World transitions to socialism since the end of World War II are insightful in understanding Havana's economy and Cuba's present crisis.

First, autarky is not a development option for peripheral Third World economies, especially small socialist ones (Fitzgerald 1986; Stallings 1986). How to combine growth and distribution in such a social transformation (economics) and how to establish representative forms and viable participation (politics) remain perennial questions (Fagen 1986). The recent experiences of Vietnam and China suggest that the inclusion of an important capitalist sector in a mixed economy, whereby the state controls surplus and decisions about accumulation, may be one way the transition to socialism can be accomplished. At the very least, socialist economies would originally guarantee close to full employment, regardless of the fluctuations of the global market. As Fagen (1986, 257) noted before the collapse of Soviet aid and trade:

> The more fully the money economy has permeated the society, the more politically unacceptable even a relatively low level of unemployment becomes. This is why policies of (sometimes artificially constructed) full employment make so much sense at the outset of the transition, even though they may violate economic rationality. . . . The Cuban revolution is instructive: for more than a decade there was . . . no significant unemployment in Cuba. . . . At the outset Cubans (wisely) decided that the political and social costs of open unemployment were greater than the economic costs of full employment.

As noted above, unemployment in early 1996 was officially 7 percent, but it could be much higher.

Second, small internal and regional cooperation markets for most socialist nations (Sandinista Nicaragua, 1979–89; Cuba; Grenada under Maurice Bishop's New Jewel Movement, 1979–83; and Chile under the administration of Dr. Salvador Allende, 1970–73) may prove to be insurmountable obstacles to the transition to socialism (Wall 1990). Cuba aims to replace its former CMEA partners with reorganized Caricom nations. It is among twenty-five sovereign nations and fifteen colonies slated for membership in the Association of Caribbean States (Whitefield 1994).

Third, state ownership alone cannot define a socialist production model. Centralized planning politicizes the economy. It constrains market signals in the form of prices and seeks to keep producers from being motivated only by self-interest (Brundenius and Zimbalist 1989, 141). Deep changes must also take place in the labor process—bringing in worker participation—and in mass participation in forging state policy. The Cuban state labor force, however, is targeted for downsizing. In 1996, 4.6 million Cubans worked in the government, cooperative, and private sectors, and about 600,000 to 800,000 of them collected a full salary even while working half-time or less. Pedro Ross, secretary-general of the CTC, estimated that in 1995, 60 percent of the "surplus" workers let go from the public sector shifted to other jobs, 20 percent were working in temporary positions, and the rest were collecting 60 percent of their salary at home. This translated into an official unemployment rate of about 7 percent (Acosta 1996c) in 1996, a figure roughly the same in 2001. The new "rationalization plan" aims to slash inefficient, state-run industries. Carlos Lage, then a major economic decision maker, planned on cutting about one-fifth of all state workers ("Survey Havana" 1996), an objective that was largely met. The implications these layoffs portend for Cuba's social relations of production are unclear.

A perennial debate among development scholars and economists concerns the weight given to "getting prices right" (Chowdhury and Kirkpatrick 1994; Brundenius and Zimbalist 1989; Pérez-López 1994b; Mesa-Lago 1994). The debate takes different disguises: monetarism versus structuralism; liberalism versus Friedmanism; orthodoxy versus heterodoxy; nationalization versus private enterprise; and so on. Cuba's apparent transition from socialism to points beyond shares many of the structural problems of import-substitution industrialization (ISI) in Latin America from the 1950s through the 1980s. Under ISI, political pressures and union demands led to the extension of tariffs on imported goods from overseas and protectionist laws that stifled competition, innovation, and worker productivity (Cardoso and Faletto 1979; Nochteff 1984; Gwynne 1986; Jenkins 1987; Kay 1994). By extension, Cuban dependency on Soviet aid may have led to the kinds of structural problems facing countries that operated under ISI (Mesa-Lago 1988).

On a more practical level, the use of taxation is important and controversial in Havana. In early 1996, taxes in pesos increased in 144 out of 162 private jobs. Some taxes rose more than 100 percent and even more in 1996. Time will tell if these increases will deter private work in Havana because taxes are too high. To be sure, revenues are needed to run the city's public service and sustain the socialist model. Self-employed workers, moreover, may be forking over as much as 41 percent of their operating profits as tax to the Cuban government (Peters and Scarpaci 1998).

Cuba's transition to a postsocialist economy not only imposes the semblance of market mechanisms and pricing in Havana but also has led to a drop in morale among workers. The moral incentives for worker productivity do not seem as relevant as they once were and perhaps were more closely tied to material rewards than previously thought. Gone are the halcyon days when altruism, abnegation, sacrifice, and discipline produced a "revolutionary conscientiousness" and when "critical thinking" was discouraged (Medin 1990; Fuller 1985; Bengelsdorf 1985). Workers pose an even more basic question: Why go to work at all?

At least six fundamental disruptures confront the *habanero* worker:

1. The production process suffers from a lack of inputs, ranging from books and paper in the office to raw materials in the factory.
2. Extra hours are needed daily to acquire basic food supplies for the household. Work carries an opportunity cost previously irrelevant in the socialist workplace.
3. Public transportation has been decimated, and the physical cost of cycling takes a toll on worker productivity.
4. The socialist workplace traditionally provides lunch for all workers. Now the lunch meal does not always come. Missing the midday meal leads to worker slowdowns, and those who walk and bicycle often leave for home around 1:30 or 2 P.M. and do not return to work in the afternoon.
5. The revolution has now stated officially and categorically that it is acceptable to purchase what were formerly labeled "nonessential consumer goods." In the best of days, pesos purchased little beyond the mere essentials of needs.
6. *Habaneros* see the demonstration effect of workers who have access to dollars from tourism, black market work, or remittances. Those who lack such access must find sufficient solace in the realm of "moral incentives" to continue working in lower-paid state jobs.

## Havana: ¿Adónde Va?

Since 1993 a host of private-sector self-employed ventures have proliferated in Havana and elsewhere, albeit with erratic "stops" and "gos," as the Cuban government defines and redefines what can only be described as a new type of *criollo* Keynesian economics. To some Cuban analysts, there is a way out of

Cuba's quagmire, and its formula sounds much like those drawn from neo-classical economics. One envisions the following: "a new economic structure [that is] less dependent on a single product, with very active international tourism; hundreds of joint-venture firms and associations and dozens of manufactured goods and agricultural products being exported; this could be Cuba's outlook at the end of the century" (Figueras 1994, 181; our translation). Although few observers within and outside Cuba would dispute the value of such a prospect, the economic and policy constraints placed on the simplest of enterprises beg the question about whether such a prospect for the year 2000 was realistic. An increase in government regulation to equalize income distribution may dampen all self-employed enterprises (Alonso 1995; Locay 1995). As Pastor and Zimbalist (1995, 705) note, "The recent spate of halfhearted measures . . . has likely worsened distributional inequities, distorted incentives, and failed to improve the macroeconomy."

## Work and Economy in the Twenty-first Century

Distortions in Havana's economy stifle the kinds of multiplier effects we might envision in a less restrictive setting. Taxes, stop-and-go signals about illicit enrichment, and little experience with the private sector constrain the fledgling new market economy. At the national level, Cuba lacks what the Chilean business community calls *transparencia*: clarity about norms, regulation, and information that is not controlled by cumbersome laws. Like De Soto's (1989) description of pre-Fujimori Peru, state regulations may hinder more than help Cuba's fledgling cottage industries. Nonetheless, newly expanding private jobs are slated to absorb workers being let go from the public sector. Even the military has dramatically cut its personnel and spending levels by downsizing and by trying to satisfy domestic demands for goods and services (Walker 1996).

The template of the city's industrial and manufacturing activities has changed little since the 1950s. Service industries, especially government work and tourism, will likely characterize the nature of work in the Cuban capital well into the next decade. While it is perhaps not surprising that the defining features of a market economy have not yet taken hold, future research should monitor the evolution of the changing nature of work in Havana. For the near future, at least, the nature of work in Havana will continue to reflect the shocks caused by Cuba's reinsertion into the market. Indeed, the most difficult part of the Special Period had ended by 2001. Tourism and globalization, coupled with broad dollar and black market economies, define the nature of work in the Cuban capital in ways that were unthinkable only a few years ago.

# 8

# The Value of Social Functions

In this country, all amateurs seek to become professional artists. That is the truth. In addition, everyone wants to become a college graduate. We were forced to impose restrictions on this. Everybody wants to be an intellectual in this country. This is a vice created by the Revolution itself, by the universities.

—Fidel Castro, April 30, 1996

There are many ways to assess social welfare and the quality of life. In the index for human development elaborated by the United Nations Development Programme (UNDP), Cuba increased its international position in 1995 by ranking 72nd among 174 countries and classifying among those nations with a "median level" of human development. Three fundamental variables produced that index: life expectancy, educational attainment, and gross national product (GNP). With a life expectancy of 75.3 years in 1992, Cuba had surpassed even countries considered to have a high index of human development in Latin America (e.g., Argentina, Chile, and Uruguay). Cuba placed among the thirty most advanced nations in the world in this regard, with the index of .84 over a base of 1.0. The literacy rate for adults was 95.7 percent, and the school enrollment rate for people under twenty-four was 66 percent. Cuba's real gross domestic product (GDP) per capita was $3,110 in 1995, less than Belize ($5,623) or Panama ($6,029). Chile leads Latin America with $6,115, which is still quite low compared with the $26,977 figure for the United States (United Nations Development Programme 2000).

Although the Special Period chipped away at the quality of life in the 1990s, Cuba managed to increase its status in the United Nations rankings. In the most recent data available (*Human Development Report 2000*), Cuba ranked 84th of 174 nations studied by the UNDP. Its position placed it behind such sister Latin American nations as Barbados (24), Bahamas (33), Argentina (35), Antigua and Barbuda (29), Chile (31), and Uruguay (38); all these nations scored in the "high human development" category. Table 8.1 shows Cuba's relative location in the "medium human development" category; half a dozen nations in the hemisphere placed slightly ahead of it within the same category. However, the United Nations' instrument classified Cuba with a higher human development index than Belize, Panama, Venezuela, Jamaica, Peru, Paraguay, the Dominican Republic, and many other Latin American neighbors.

Despite this relatively good news about the quality of life in Cuba, some problems—many discussed throughout this book—have recently appeared. A report from the Forensic Medicine Institute of Havana published in March 1995 reported that 2,500 Cubans committed suicide in a one-year period. This incidence of suicide—225 for each 1 million persons—is twice the U.S. rate (128 per million). Not surprisingly, more young people than old people kill themselves, as do more men than women. Cuba's suicide rate makes it the highest of all countries in the Western Hemisphere (Aroca 1995). The rapid erosion of the material well-being of the population—brought on by the Special Period—probably plays an important role in explaining this statistic. At the same time, though, it is noteworthy that the accuracy of Cuban statistics is probably greater than those of other Latin American countries where vital rates registration is not as developed as in Cuba and Roman Catholic values lead to an underreporting of suicides.

In this chapter, we examine selected dimensions of the quality of life in Havana. Specifically, we review three types of services: health, education, and leisure. Cuba has staked out a special position in these fields. Few countries in the world have such comprehensive health care coverage as in Cuba. Before the revolution, Cuba clearly boasted relatively high levels of life expectancy and literacy, and Havana held world-class tourist attractions. These benefits, though, were not equally enjoyed by all Cubans. Significant gains in life expectancy and literacy have been achieved since 1959.

Divided into six main parts, the chapter begins with a review of the distribution of social functions in Havana. The second section examines transportation, roads, and retailing. We then present a brief summary of Cuba's health care system. Data on the location and utilization of Havana's clinics and hospitals are presented next, followed by a discussion of the city's health care resources. In the third section, we turn to Cuba's and Havana's educa-

TABLE 8.1. Cuba's Ranking in the United Nations' Human Development Index

| HDI RANK | LIFE EXPECTANCY AT BIRTH (YEARS) 1998 | ADULT LITERACY RATE (% AGE 15 AND ABOVE) 1998 | COMBINED PRIMARY, SECONDARY, AND TERTIARY GROSS ENROLLMENT RATIO (%) 1998[a] |
|---|---|---|---|
| *High human development* | | | |
| 1 Canada | 79.1 | 99.0[c] | 100 |
| 2 Norway | 78.3 | 99.0[c] | 97 |
| 3 United States | 76.8 | 99.0[c] | 94 |
| 4 Australia | 78.3 | 99.0[c] | 114[d] |
| 5 Iceland | 79.1 | 99.0[c] | 89 |
| 6 Sweden | 78.7 | 99.0[c] | 102[d] |
| 7 Belgium | 77.3 | 99.0[c] | 106[d] |
| 8 Netherlands | 78.0 | 99.0[c] | 99 |
| 9 Japan | 80.0 | 99.0[c] | 85 |
| 10 United Kingdom | 77.3 | 99.0[c] | 105[d] |
| 30 Barbados | 76.5 | 97.0[e,f] | 80 |
| 33 Bahamas | 74.0 | 95.5 | 74 |
| 34 Czech Republic | 74.1 | 99.0[c] | 74 |
| 35 Argentina | 73.1 | 96.7 | 80 |
| 37 Antigua and Barbuda | 76.0[e] | 95.0[e,f] | 78[c] |
| 38 Chile | 75.1 | 95.4 | 78 |
| 39 Uruguay | 74.1 | 97.6 | 78 |
| *Medium human development* | | | |
| 47 St. Kitts and Nevis | 70.0[e] | 90.0[e,f] | 79[c] |
| 48 Costa Rica | 76.2 | 95.3 | 66 |
| 49 Croatia | 72.8 | 98.0 | 69 |
| 50 Trinidad and Tobago | 74.0 | 93.4 | 66 |
| 51 Dominica | 76.0[e] | 94.0[f,h] | 74[c] |
| 54 Granada | 72.0[e] | 96.0[e,f] | 76[c] |
| 55 Mexico | 72.3 | 90.8 | 70 |
| *56 Cuba* | *75.8* | *96.4* | *73* |
| 58 Belize | 74.9 | 92.7 | 73 |
| 59 Panama | 73.8 | 91.4 | 73 |
| 65 Venezuela | 72.6 | 92.0 | 67 |
| 67 Suriname | 70.3 | 93.0[e,f] | 80 |
| 68 Colombia | 70.7 | 91.2 | 71 |
| 74 Brazil | 67.0 | 84.5 | 84 |

| GDP PER CAPITA (PPP US$) 1998 | LIFE EXPECTANCY INDEX | EDUCATION INDEX | GDP INDEX | HDI VALUE | GDP PER CAPITA (PPP US$) RANK MINUS HDI RANK[b] |
|---|---|---|---|---|---|
| 23,582 | 0.90 | 0.99 | 0.91 | 0.935 | 8 |
| 26,342 | 0.89 | 0.98 | 0.93 | 0.934 | 1 |
| 29,605 | 0.86 | 0.97 | 0.95 | 0.929 | −1 |
| 22,452 | 0.89 | 0.99 | 0.90 | 0.929 | 9 |
| 25,110 | 0.90 | 0.96 | 0.02 | 0.927 | 1 |
| 20,659 | 0.90 | 0.99 | 0.89 | 0.926 | 15 |
| 23,223 | 0.87 | 0.99 | 0.91 | 0.925 | 4 |
| 22,176 | 0.88 | 0.99 | 0.90 | 0.925 | 6 |
| 23,257 | 0.92 | 0.94 | 0.91 | 0.924 | 1 |
| 20,336 | 0.87 | 0.99 | 0.89 | 0.018 | 13 |
| 12,001[f,g] | 0.86 | 0.91 | 0.80 | 0.858 | 9 |
| 14,614 | 0.82 | 0.88 | 0.83 | 0.844 | −1 |
| 12,362 | 0.82 | 0.91 | 0.80 | 0.843 | 3 |
| 12,013 | 0.80 | 0.91 | 0.80 | 0.837 | 3 |
| 9,277 | 0.85 | 0.89 | 0.76 | 0.833 | 9 |
| 8,787 | 0.83 | 0.90 | 0.75 | 0.826 | 9 |
| 8,623 | 0.82 | 0.91 | 0.74 | 0.825 | 9 |
| 10,672 | 0.75 | 0.86 | 0.78 | 0.798 | −7 |
| 5,987 | 0.85 | 0.85 | 0.68 | 0.797 | 18 |
| 6,749 | 0.80 | 0.88 | 0.70 | 0.795 | 7 |
| 7,485 | 0.82 | 0.84 | 0.72 | 0.793 | 5 |
| 5,102 | 0.85 | 0.87 | 0.66 | 0.793 | 27 |
| 5,838 | 0.78 | 0.89 | 0.68 | 0.785 | 13 |
| 7,704 | 0.79 | 0.84 | 0.73 | 0.784 | −3 |
| 3,967[i] | 0.85 | 0.89 | 0.61 | 0.783 | 40 |
| 4,566 | 0.83 | 0.86 | 0.64 | 0.777 | 25 |
| 5,249 | 0.81 | 0.85 | 0.66 | 0.776 | 14 |
| 5,808 | 0.79 | 0.84 | 0.68 | 0.770 | 3 |
| 5,161[f,g] | 0.76 | 0.89 | 0.66 | 0.766 | 9 |
| 6,006 | 0.76 | 0.85 | 0.68 | 0.764 | −3 |
| 6,625 | 0.70 | 0.84 | 0.70 | 0.747 | −16 |

TABLE 8.1. (continued)

| HDI RANK | LIFE EXPECTANCY AT BIRTH (YEARS) 1998 | ADULT LITERACY RATE (% AGE 15 AND ABOVE) 1998 | COMBINED PRIMARY, SECONDARY, AND TERTIARY GROSS ENROLLMENT RATIO (%) 1998[a] |
|---|---|---|---|
| 79 St. Vincent and the Grenadines | 73.0[e] | 82.0[e,f] | 68[c] |
| 80 Peru | 68.6 | 89.2 | 79 |
| 81 Paraguay | 69.8 | 92.8 | 65 |
| 83 Jamaica | 75.0 | 86.0 | 63 |
| 87 Dominican Republic | 70.9 | 82.8 | 70 |
| 91 Ecuador | 69.7 | 90.6 | 75 |
| 96 Guyana | 64.8 | 98.3 | 66 |
| 104 El Salvador | 69.4 | 77.8 | 64 |
| 113 Honduras | 69.6 | 73.4 | 58 |
| 114 Bolivia | 61.8 | 84.4 | 70 |
| 116 Nicaragua | 68.1 | 67.9 | 63 |
| 120 Guatemala | 64.4 | 67.3 | 47 |
| *Low human development* | | | |
| 150 Haiti | 54.0 | 47.8 | 24 |
| 170 Burundi | 42.7 | 45.8 | 22 |
| 171 Ethiopia | 43.4 | 36.3 | 26 |
| 172 Burkina Faso | 44.7 | 22.2 | 22 |
| 173 Niger | 48.9 | 14.7 | 15 |
| 174 Sierra Leone | 37.9 | 31.0[e,f] | 24[c] |
| *All developing countries* | 64.7 | 72.3 | 60 |
| Least developed countries | 51.9 | 50.7 | 37 |
| Arab States | 66.0 | 59.7 | 60 |
| East Asia | 70.2 | 83.4 | 73 |
| East Asia (excluding China) | 73.1 | 96.3 | 85 |
| Latin America and the Caribbean | 69.7 | 87.7 | 74 |
| South Asia | 63.0 | 54.3 | 52 |
| South Asia (excluding India) | 63.4 | 50.5 | 47 |
| Southeast Asia and the Pacific | 66.3 | 88.2 | 66 |
| Sub-Saharan Africa | 48.9 | 58.5 | 42 |
| Eastern Europe and the CIS | 68.9 | 98.6 | 76 |
| OECD | 76.4 | 97.4 | 86 |

| GDP PER CAPITA (PPP US$) 1998 | LIFE EXPECTANCY INDEX | EDUCATION INDEX | GDP INDEX | HDI VALUE | GDP PER CAPITA (PPP US$) RANK MINUS HDI RANK[b] |
|---|---|---|---|---|---|
| 4,692 | 0.80 | 0.77 | 0.64 | 0.738 | 2 |
| 4,282 | 0.73 | 0.86 | 0.63 | 0.737 | 7 |
| 4,288 | 0.75 | 0.84 | 0.63 | 0.736 | 5 |
| 3,389 | 0.83 | 0.78 | 0.59 | 0.735 | 15 |
| 4,598 | 0.76 | 0.79 | 0.64 | 0.729 | −5 |
| 3,003 | 0.75 | 0.85 | 0.57 | 0.722 | 17 |
| 3,403 | 0.66 | 0.88 | 0.59 | 0.709 | 1 |
| 4,036 | 0.74 | 0.73 | 0.62 | 0.696 | −13 |
| 2,433 | 0.74 | 0.68 | 0.53 | 0.653 | 2 |
| 2,269 | 0.61 | 0.80 | 0.52 | 0.643 | 4 |
| 2,142 | 0.72 | 0.66 | 0.51 | 0.631 | 4 |
| 3,505 | 0.66 | 0.61 | 0.59 | 0.619 | −24 |
| | | | | | |
| 1,383 | 0.48 | 0.40 | 0.44 | 0.440 | −7 |
| 570 | 0.30 | 0.38 | 0.29 | 0.321 | 1 |
| 574 | 0.31 | 0.33 | 0.29 | 0.309 | −1 |
| 870 | 0.33 | 0.22 | 0.36 | 0.303 | −16 |
| 739 | 0.40 | 0.15 | 0.33 | 0.293 | −9 |
| 458 | 0.22 | 0.29 | 0.25 | 0.252 | 0 |
| | | | | | |
| 3,270 | 0.66 | 0.68 | 0.58 | 0.642 | — |
| 1,064 | 0.45 | 0.46 | 0.39 | 0.435 | 00 |
| 4,140 | 0.68 | 0.60 | 0.62 | 0.635 | — |
| 3,564 | 0.75 | 0.80 | 0.60 | 0.716 | — |
| 13,635 | 0.80 | 0.93 | 0.82 | 0.849 | — |
| 6,510 | 0.74 | 0.83 | 0.70 | 0.758 | — |
| 2,112 | 0.63 | 0.54 | 0.51 | 0.560 | — |
| 2,207 | 0.64 | 0.49 | 0.52 | 0.550 | — |
| 3,234 | 0.69 | 0.81 | 0.58 | 0.691 | — |
| 1,607 | 0.40 | 0.53 | 0.46 | 0.464 | — |
| 6,200 | 0.73 | 0.91 | 0.69 | 0.777 | — |
| 20,357 | 0.86 | 0.94 | 0.89 | 0.893 | — |

TABLE 8.1. (continued)

| HDI RANK | LIFE EXPECTANCY AT BIRTH (YEARS) 1998 | ADULT LITERACY RATE (% AGE 15 AND ABOVE) 1998 | COMBINED PRIMARY, SECONDARY, AND TERTIARY GROSS ENROLLMENT RATIO (%) 1998[a] |
|---|---|---|---|
| High human development | 77.0 | 98.5 | 90 |
| Medium human development | 68.9 | 76.9 | 65 |
| Low human development | 50.9 | 48.8 | 37 |
| High income | 77.8 | 98.6 | 92 |
| Medium income | 68.8 | 87.8 | 73 |
| Low income | 63.4 | 68.9 | 56 |
| World | 66.9 | 78.8 | 64 |

Source: Column 1: unless otherwise noted, interpolated on the basis of life expectancy data from United Nations. 1998. *World Population Prospects, 1950–2050: The 1998 Revision*. Database. Population Division. New York. Column 2: unless otherwise noted, UNESCO (United Nations Educational, Scientific, and Cultural Organization). 2000. Correspondence on adult literacy rates. January. Paris. Column 3: unless otherwise noted, UNESCO (United Nations Educational, Scientific, and Cultural Organization). 2000. Correspondence on gross enrollment ratios. February. Paris. Column 4: unless otherwise noted, World Bank. 2000. Correspondence on unpublished World Bank data on GDP per capita (PPP US$) for 1998. Development Economics Data Group. February. Washington, D.C. Columns 5–9: Human Development Report Office calculations; see the technical note for details.
Note: HDI=human development index; the HDI has been calculated for UN member countries with reliable data in each of its components, as well as for two nonmembers, Switzerland and Hong Kong, China (SAR).
[a] Preliminary UNESCO (United Nations Educational, Scientific, and Cultural Organization) estimates, subject to further revision.
[b] A positive figure indicates that the HDI rank is higher than the GDP per capita (PPP US$) rank, a negative the opposite.

tional profiles. Special attention is given to the state's policy of building up education services outside the capital city. The fourth section discusses the many venues of tourism in Havana: international, national, health care, and ecotourism. A final section examines Havana for *habaneros*. We identify Havana's natural and cultural resources that afford its residents with recreational outlets for their leisurely pursuits. Sports in the Revolution is also a key process in the socialization process, and Havana holds a good share of the nation's finer sports facilities.

We begin with an overview of the geographic distribution of selected social functions that characterize Havana.

| GDP PER CAPITA (PPP US$) 1998 | LIFE EXPECTANCY INDEX | EDUCATION INDEX | GDP INDEX | HDI VALUE | GDP PER CAPITA (PPP US$) RANK MINUS HDI RANK[b] |
|---|---|---|---|---|---|
| 21,799 | 0.87 | 0.96 | 0.90 | 0.908 | — |
| 3,458 | 0.70 | 0.73 | 0.59 | 0.673 | — |
| 994 | 0.43 | 0.45 | 0.38 | 0.421 | — |
| 23,928 | 0.88 | 0.96 | 0.91 | 0.920 | — |
| 6,241 | 0.73 | 0.83 | 0.69 | 0.750 | — |
| 2,244 | 0.64 | 0.65 | 0.52 | 0.602 | — |
| 6,526 | 0.70 | 0.74 | 0.70 | 0.712 | — |

[c] Human Development Report Office estimate.

[d] For purposes of calculating the HDI, the value of 100.0% was applied.

[e] UNICEF (United Nations Children's Fund). 1999. *The State of the World's Children 2000.* New York: Oxford University Press.

[f] Data refer to a year or period other than that specified in the column heading, differ from the standard definition, or refer to only part of the country.

[g] Heston, Alan, and Robert Summers, 1999. Correspondence on data on GDP per capita (PPP US$). University of Pennsylvania, Department of Economics, Philadelphia. March.

[h] UNICEF (United Nations Children's Fund). 1996. *The State of the World's Children 1997.* New York: Oxford University Press.

[i] As GDP per capita (PPP US$) is not available for Cuba, the subregional weighted average for the Caribbean was used.

## The Dispersal of Social Functions

One of the most significant aspects of Havana in the revolutionary era is the emphasis placed on social versus individual concerns. Highly centralized planning determines the location of schools, hospitals, sports complexes, industries, and housing. For reasons we have put forth throughout this book, the built environment has been practically unaltered throughout four decades, except for demolitions brought on by natural causes or structural reasons. Despite the prevalence of what has come to be known as the "myth of the new" (Segre 1994d), most new construction—in the form of gigantic complexes of public housing—has been built outside the traditional fabric in semirural and previously unoccupied areas beyond the old city edge.

On the one hand, this pattern of siting public housing at the periphery is typical of the previous "modernization" plans for Havana. The plan of Martínez Inclán, the design of Forestier, and the ambitious project of Sert (Segre 1996a) envisioned an expanded city developed around the bay, straddled by equal areas to the east and west (see Chapters 2 and 4). On the other hand, there is a rupture between the "capitalist" and "socialist" image of the city. In the capitalist realm, planners prioritized the functional spaces of the bourgeoisie, thereby ignoring the "gray" areas of the proletariat. In the socialist phase, the operative paradigm sought to dissolve the economic and cultural differences among social groups. Just as Marx and Engels dreamed about joining town and country, Havana would form a seamless urban fabric. Accordingly, it was not by chance that in 1976 the territorial limits of Havana City Province expanded to roughly equal parts of urban and rural lands (see fig. 5.1).

Table 8.2 provides a descriptive summary of the city's education, health, and other services. Although the data are from 1989, they provide some insight into the kinds of services that prevailed until the Special Period. Some changes would be evident in 2001 if the data were available. For instance, the number of movie theaters and bus routes has diminished (Scarpaci and Hall 1995). In contrast, the number of health clinics has increased from seventy-four to seventy-nine, while the expanse of green areas has remained constant.

## Transportation, Roads, and Retailing

New buses incorporated into the urban public transportation system have only been able to replace those buses that were in the worst condition, thus improving quality in the service. Nonetheless, the number remains very low, 565 compared with 2,200 in 1989. Passengers per day also decreased in the same period, from 4.5 million to fewer than 600,000. The number of routes has decreased from 164 to 95 (plus seven lines of Metrobus). Metrobuses are awkward-looking Cuban-made buses driven by a giant truck, and because of a hunchback profile they are popularly called *camellos* (camels).[1] They pack up to 220 passengers and, though uncomfortable, have been able to ease the

---

1. A popular joke compares the experience of riding a fully packed *camello* to the "Saturday night film" shown on Cuban television (almost always American B-class thrillers extensively copied because the U.S. embargo forbids normal trading between the two countries): sex, violence, and dirty language.

TABLE 8.2. Selected Data on Services in Havana, ca. 1989 with selected 2000 Updates

| SERVICE | COMPONENTS | | |
|---|---|---|---|
| Education | Day-care centers | 405 | |
| | Primary schools | 510 | |
| | Secondary schools | 165 | |
| | Pre-university preparatory centers | 15 | |
| | Adult education centers | 71 | |
| | Vo-tech high schools | 37 | |
| | Higher education | 65 departments/programs, 68,514 students | |
| Health | Hospital beds | 25,000 | |
| | Medical research institutes | 12 | |
| | Policlinics (primary care) | 74 | |
| Culture | Movie theaters | 89 | |
| | Museums | 43 | |
| | Cultural centers | 25 | |
| | Libraries | 25 | |
| | Theaters | 16 | |
| | Bookstores | 53 | |
| Open Space | City parks | 4.11 sq. meters per inhabitant | |
| | Neighborhood parks | 0.88 sq. meters per inhabitant | |
| | City sports areas | 0.16 sq. meters per inhabitant | |
| | Neighborhood sports areas | 1.08 sq. meters per inhabitant | |
| | All green and sports areas | 10.41 sq. meters per inhabitant | |
| Transportation | City buses | 2,200 | 2000: approx. 600 |
| | Number of routes | 164 | |
| | Daily bus passengers | 4,500,000 | 2000: 600,000 |
| | Automobile ratio | 36 per 1,000 | 2000: approx. 37 |
| | Kilometers of railway | 293 | |
| | Kilometers of streets | 3,500 | |

*Sources*: GDIC, 1990, 19; year 2000 updates, authors' field notes.

transport deficit, as their numbers increased from 110 in 1995 to 150 in 1999 (fig. 8.1).

The critical transportation situation has forced the extensive use of bicycling. Cycling rose in the early 1990s from around 70,000, mostly used by youngsters for recreation, to almost 1 million in 1994, actively used for everything. Bicycles often carried one passenger on a back grill, his or her feet resting in homemade bronze rods added to the back wheel. The city government established 50 kilometers of separate lanes for bicyclists, and "*bici-taxis*" covered with a small canvas and carrying two passengers have become the Cuban version of the Chinese rickshaw. A shuttle was created to transport bicycles

FIGURE 8.1. One new bus style (*camello*) introduced in Havana in the 1990s (Photographs by Joseph L. Scarpaci)

safely through the bay tunnel, and a special bike lane parallel to Vía Blanca allows bicyclists to ride to Playas del Este, the fine 11-kilometer strip of beaches in eastern Havana.

Safety has been one major problem with bicyling because of the lack of lights and helmets, as well as the lack of a street culture among bicyclists. In the late 1990s the use of bicycles had decreased because Cuban-made bicycles lacked spare parts, and there was a slight improvement in the public transportation system.

Driving bicycles has become more difficult and dangerous as more cars run through the streets. Although the minimum gasoline quota for private car owners has long been eliminated, cars circulating in the Cuban capital are owned mostly by state or joint-venture corporations. Cycling safety is compromised by potholes, especially along the bike lines that are next to the curbs. A commission has been created to study ways to encourage bicycling. Another study is being made by the Institute of Research on Transport (Instituto de Investigación del Transporte [IIT]) about the eventual use of trolley buses, which were a common feature until the early 1950s (fig. 8.2). Havana would benefit from a transportation source that would lower the air pollution by diesel fumes from buses and trucks and the increased conversion into diesel engines of old American cars from the 1940s and 1950s. The number of cars doubled between the 1940s and early 1980s. In 1994, there were 20.8 cars per a thousand inhabitants, and in 1998 the figure rose to 37. This growth was mainly due to new cars from corporations and joint ventures that belong to the so-called emerging (dollar) economy. Although not yet a widespread problem, this trend poses a future threat because there is no reliable public transportation system to reach the new "center" of the dollar economy in the former upper-class neighborhood of Miramar and points farther west. Therefore, reliance on automobiles will increase to reach these points of the city.

One telling trait of Havana is the absence of new symbolic and monumental functions that blight the landscapes of both capitalist and socialist cities. Aggressive "socialist realist" monuments, so common in other socialist cities, are not part of Havana.[2] The only exception is a giant bronze head of Vladimir Lenin tucked away in the remote Lenin Park, south of the city.

Reducing internal consumption in the early years of the revolution practically emptied the department stores in the city center and deterred an increase in retailing for decades. For a long time, the only large office-building complex in socialist Havana was the Ministry of Agriculture on Rancho Boyeros Avenue. In the late 1990s, a powerful state corporation operating in dollars, CIMEX, restored the Sierra Maestra building in Miramar to house its headquarters there. Consequently, the move left vacant many Miramar mansions that CIMEX had used for years. That practice reflects a very practical policy and reverses the normal practice of state agencies occupying and readapting housing for commercial or governmental purposes. Such practices had de-

2. Busts of José Martí are found throughout Havana and the rest of Cuba's towns and cities. However, our discussion focuses on the modern, social realist architecture that prevailed in Eastern Europe and the Soviet Union up until 1989.

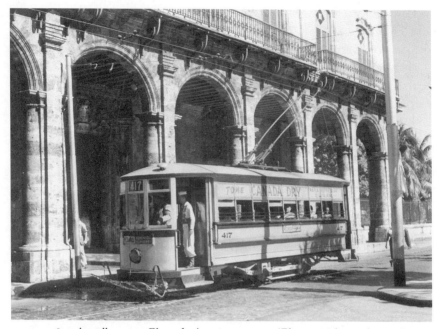

FIGURE 8.2. A trolley stop, Plaza de Armas, ca. 1950 (Photographer unknown)

prived the city of fine residential property, led to building modifications, and introduced distortions in neighborhoods.

Sprawling supermarkets, shopping centers, and malls have not prevailed during socialist rule, except in isolated cases in which these properties had been inherited from the prerevolutionary era. Instead, shoppers use their ration books (*libretas*) to purchase goods at corner grocery stores (*bodegas*). In the 1980s, the number of *bodegas* decreased as the state tried to replace them with state "supermarkets," which would reduce the number of distribution points and keep costs down. However, these supermarkets differed from their U.S. counterparts in that they were not meant to stimulate the sale of nonessential goods. Many supermarkets ended up with internal subdivisions or separate stores and sections that were more suitable for the distribution of rationed goods than nonessential items. As a result, the new supermarkets have become a collection of several "*bodegas*" under a single roof. Customers are now forced to walk longer distances to the new stores. State companies have converted some unoccupied *bodegas* to residential dwellings. These conversions from commercial to residential use are often done precariously, distorting the image of the city at street corners, which are highly visible parts of

Havana's urban design. Over time, though, many occupants of these prime corner locations have begun to offer very elementary services as self-employed workers (*cuentapropistas*).

A surge in the dollar economy and the need to supply foreigners and diplomats living in Cuba created "segregated" stores in Miramar that, for most *habaneros*, are difficult to reach. These stores gradually extended to more central areas of Havana since dollars were legalized. This increased Havana's retail network, which in 1999 had 4,388 units for dispensing nonprocessed food, including 1,461 restaurants, cafeterias, and food stands (kiosks), and 353 stores selling industrial products. Of these, only around 2,000 were in good condition. Because of the great amount of resources needed to restore this network—particularly dense and concentrated along the traditional *calzadas* of the inner city, equaling about 20 linear kilometers of former storefronts—kiosks have been favored. This gives rise to a contradiction. When a new kiosk is placed in front of an empty or underused store to sell, it underscores what could be sold in the unused establishment. Kiosks also create visual blight in some places and even impede the flow of pedestrians. They also add to noise pollution, since some seem to "give away" loud music free.

One disturbing type of construction is a chain of state-run Rápido fast-food restaurants, which are characterized by unimaginative colors (e.g., "ketchup" red and "mustard" yellow) as well as loud music. The chain has done in Havana what McDonald's is not allowed to do in Barcelona. Perhaps because red and yellow are also the colors of the Spanish flag, an odd element has been added to these fast-food outlets: a pitched thatch roof, serving as a symbol of the Cuban peasant's straw hat. Aesthetically, though, the modification adds little to the restaurants. This is one example of how the dollarization of the economy and the globalization of retailing surface in the Cuban capital.

Even though the socialist state created a huge apparatus for administration and control, the empty spaces inherited from the Batista era were sufficient to house the revolutionary government. For instance, the headquarters of the Cuban Communist Party and most high levels of government reside in the former Justice Palace. This huge building is part of a larger political-administrative center created in the mid-1950s, Plaza Cívica, renamed Plaza de la Revolución. Another large group of government offices now occupy the site of former private businesses in the traditional city center. In this sense, comparing Havana with Moscow, Beijing, Hanoi, or Bucharest reveals the difference in the referential system of socialism. Havana lacks monuments of revolutionary heroes perched on gigantic pedestals; Herculean, white Greek marble temples; and broad boulevards anchored by Versallean palaces (Scarpaci 2000a).[3]

Political, social, and economic events gradually eroded the barriers that separated parts of Havana well before state-directed construction projects had begun. Between the Bay of Pigs invasion in April 1961 and the Cuban missile crisis a year and half later, U.S. tourism disappeared completely from Cuba, as did most of the members of the island's wealthy class. Luxury hotels reduced prices to a minimum, which allowed the local population to frequent them. Private hospitals and schools were nationalized and opened to the public free of charge, without regard to race or class. Sophisticated clubs located along the beach (see Chapter 3) became workers' social centers managed by trade unions. Radical changes produced strong social mobilizations throughout Cuba that broke the traditional segregation of class-specific social functions.

The La Rampa district in Vedado exemplifies this change. Exclusive recreational and hotel facilities had traditionally characterized the area. After the revolution, mass organizations, student groups, and workers' organizations heavily used the area (see Chapter 3). Reina Mercedes Hospital once stood on the corner of L and Twenty-third Streets in Vedado. It was leveled with the intention of building a commercial building, and in the early years of the revolution, the Association of Tourist Agents held a convention there. In 1967, though, it was turned into a park and ice cream parlor called Coppelia (Curtis 1993), which we discuss in greater detail below.

A love-hate relationship with the United States characterized part of the revolutionary Cuban utopia. Despite the longstanding political antagonism between the two countries, more cultural models adopted in revolutionary Cuba came from the United States than the Soviet Union. A disproportionate emphasis has been placed on road transportation in Cuba's transportation network even though the island lacks petroleum reserves and has a dense system of rail lines. The latter network, derived from sugar production, could have easily been refurbished to accommodate passenger travel. Only during the Special Period did the government try to switch from freight to passenger rail service. Eager to join Havana with the rest of the country, shorten distances, and overcome the squalid conditions of the Central Highway, built in

---

3. There are, though, monuments to nineteenth-century independence fighters along the Malecón. We refer to the absence of such revolutionary figures from the 1950s as Fidel Castro, Ernesto "Che" Guevara, and Camilo Cienfuegos. This contrasts with numerous revolutionary monuments of heroes found in the cities of Vietnam or North Korea.

1930, the revolutionary government invested heavily in highway construction in the late 1960s and 1970s. Two preliminary highway projects bequeathed to the revolution—the Monumental Highway to the east and Mediodía Highway to the west—turned out to be too narrow. The outer limit of the southern part of the city was joined along Calle 100 in Boyeros municipality with Monumental Highway in Habana del Este. The highway to Güira de Melena and the Autopista Nacional—eight lanes in certain sections—connected the country to the outer edge of Havana, the latter linking Matanzas and Pinar del Río Provinces, to the east and west, respectively. Who would have imagined in those heady, optimistic years three decades ago that the highways Cuba so sacrificed to build would be empty today? Nonetheless, indestructible Fords and Chevrolets trod steadfastly along the nation's nearly empty highways.

Today, Havana has approximately 2,600 kilometers of roads, including 572 major roads. However, many are narrow and not connected (United Nations 1995a, 97). Numerous smaller streets accompanied the web of major roads that connected the traditional city with the hinterland. Road building during the early years of the revolution changed the scale and landscape of Havana. Unlike the linear tourist paths that still prevail today (defined by the axes of Barlovento and Miramar in the west; Vedado and Habana Vieja in the central part; and the beaches of Brisas del Mar in the east), new spaces opened up south of the beaches for recreation and industry. Southeast Havana Province well demonstrated those new land uses: Agricultural Command Posts (Puestos de Mando de la Agricultura; see Chapter 4) located in the Nazareno and Menocal hills and the Escaleras de Jaruco. Unassuming recreational facilities (campgrounds, really) were built on the shores of dammed lakes in Havana City Province (La Coca; Zarza in Habana del Este; Bacuranao in Guanabacoa; and Ejército Rebelde in Arroyo Naranjo).

Four major green spaces in the southern and southwestern parts of the city—Lenin Park (Parque Lenin, 670 hectares), National Zoo (Zoológico Nacional, 400 hectares), the National Botanical Garden (Jardín Botánico Nacional, 650 hectares), and the Metropolitan Park (Parque Metropolitano, 700 hectares, still under construction)—afford *habaneros* outdoor recreation opportunities (fig. 8.3). These green areas are the "lungs" of the city besides possessing other ornamental and aesthetic functions. Since 1959, the ratio of green areas per inhabitant rose from 1 square meter to 8 square meters in 1984 (Dirección de Planificación Física 1984).

Coastal areas around Havana still held a privileged position in the 1960s, perhaps because they had been taken away from the bourgeoisie. Gradually,

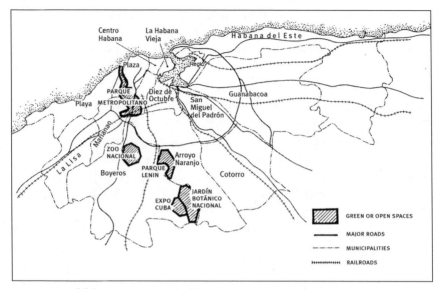

FIGURE 8.3. Major green spaces in Havana

though, modest tourist complexes for Havana families appeared on the beaches of El Salado, Bacuranao, El Mégano, and Arroyo Bermejo. The urbanization of Tarará, formerly a small beach resort with a mixture of both fine and unpretentious single-family homes (see Chapter 3), converted the town into a recreational center for children. In a few spots along the coast arose public housing complexes such as in Habana del Este and, in the west, Reparto Flores in Playa Municipality, which was designed for foreign advisers and professionals from European socialist countries.

The 1970s witnessed a major planning effort to thin out the population. It entailed using extensive agricultural lands in Arroyo Naranjo and Boyeros municipalities to the south of Havana and the Havana Greenbelt discussed in previous chapters. Lenin Park, the National Botanical Gardens, and the National Zoo were clustered within a 1,600-hectare strip. Without a doubt, this was the most important plan undertaken during the revolution in Havana because of the quality of the design, the care taken in integrating it into the natural landscape, and the commitment of both skilled and unskilled labor. The project enlisted the help of a prestigious team of specially selected architects.

For two decades, millions of persons have enjoyed these carefully planned installations. Principal among them is the 735 hectares of Lenin Park, whose installations opened in 1971–72. The park hosts a generous array of services (cafeterias, restaurants, including the luxurious Las Ruinas restaurant, an amusement park, and cultural and sporting events) (González and Cabrera 1996). Lenin Park has been a primary source of weekend recreation for the residents of the capital, though the restaurant charges in dollars, and its fare lies beyond the purchasing power of most *habaneros*. In a city that had previously lacked green areas and recreational facilities on a metropolitan scale, these complexes added a new dimension to the available leisure options. Sadly, though, the current economic crisis has greatly curtailed the use of the park because of a lack of fuel for buses and private automobiles. In 1996, it became commonplace to find several tour buses full of Europeans and Canadians waiting outside Las Ruinas restaurant during a weekday with few Cubans among the crowd seated at the tables inside—a rare sight just a few years earlier. That these facilities are now underutilized by *habaneros* speaks to the distance between socialist dreams and concrete reality. The quiet and nearly abandoned open Amphitheater in Lenin Park was originally equipped with the most advanced sound and lighting technology of the day and was designed by the sculptor Sandú Darié (Segre 1989, 148).

Today, the coastal axis of recreational spaces has again risen to the forefront of leisure activity, with its attendant emphasis on hotel construction in Miramar. The Malecón seaside promenade, originally designed as a limited-access thoroughfare, has become the social "living room" for the city's youth (Pons 1994). It affords teenagers and young people easy bicycle access and the constant beauty of tropical waters and serves as the backbone of *carnaval* celebrations. The Office of the City Historian, with international cooperation, has made possible the restoration of this rich architectural complex, considered to be the "Gateway to Havana" (García et al. 1998).

## Health Care

Havana traditionally enjoyed a plethora of health care services compared with Spain's other holdings. Within the island of Cuba and what was then Spanish Florida—ceded to England in 1763—Havana benefited as the largest recipient of hospitals from the establishment of the first one in Havana in 1539 (Hospital Antiguo) until the nineteenth century. The sugar boom of the nineteenth century produced a spate of hospitals elsewhere on the island. In the main, though, Havana held a large concentration of hospitals during its colonial rule (Mena and Cobelo 1992).

There is no doubt that prerevolutionary Havana possessed a high level of both state and private medical services. Labor unions and Spanish medical care institutions had endowed Havana with a broad network of facilities that were called *quintas de salud* in the suburbs, literally "health farms" but actually large complexes of buildings—often occupying one or more city blocks— that were part of old country estates. However, the prerevolutionary system failed to include low-income and even some moderate-income *habaneros*. Medical facilities were concentrated along the Centro Habana–Vedado–Marianao axis and the *quintas de salud* in Cerro. Medical services that were available to the poor and working classes lacked specialty care. Wealthy Cubans merely traveled to the United States for tertiary care.

Today, Cuba's health care system is world renowned, and health ideology is a defining characteristic of the Cuban revolution (Feinsilver 1993, 1994, 1995). A significant exodus of the nation's medical personnel during the early years of the revolution prompted the Castro government to prioritize physician training. As a result, Cuba was virtually able to place a physician "on every block." Universal health care that is free of charge to all Cubans has helped lower Cuba's mortality and morbidity levels. Before the onset of the Special Period, the state directed about one-quarter of its budget to health care. Health care in Cuba—especially in the capital city—is delivered in hospitals, clinics, schools, and the workplace.

Like most capital cities throughout the world, Havana contains a relative abundance of resources. It has approximately 25,000 hospital beds, which is about half of the nation's total stock of 54,028 (Del Aguila 1992). By 1989, Havana had 74 primary health care clinics (*policlínicos*) and 12 health care and medical research centers (GDIC 1990, 19). Four years later, the number of health care clinics had increased to 79 (MINSAP 1994), despite the hardship of the Special Period. In 1990, the crude birth rate of Havana was 15.1 per 1,000 inhabitants, and its crude death rate was 8.2. Life expectancy in 1990 stood at 74 years of age and rose to 75.5 in 1999, one of the highest figures of any Latin American city (González 1999). By 1984, Cuba had already boasted the greatest life expectancy of any Warsaw Pact nation, and its infant mortality rate was the second lowest (after the former East Germany) (Feinsilver 1993, 28). In 1989, Havana's infant mortality rate was 10.7 infant deaths per 1,000 live births (GDIC 1990, 18). By 1999, Havana's infant mortality rate fell to about 7.0 (González 1999).

Planning measures keep check on runaway rural-to-urban migration, producing a net migratory increase of just 10,000 per year in Havana while the natural annual growth amounted to 14,000 (GDIC 1990, 18). Migration and natural growth added 24,000 new residents in Havana in 1989, for an overall annual rate of growth of 1.16 percent. Although migration to the capital is controlled by planners, laws, and a restrictive housing market (see Chapter 6), in 1995, 35 percent of all Havana residents were born outside the city ("Facts and Statistics" 1996a). The city's low rate of growth is full of implications for planning, housing, and social services, especially compared with other Latin American cities where rates of growth are at least twice as high.

Symbolism in revolutionary Havana plays a key role in promoting socialism, and health care is a weighty part of that symbolism. Although the well-known symbols of the city include the Morro Castle, the Capitol building, and the Martí Monument at Plaza de la Revolución and the protest plaza (fig. 8.4) built in front of the U.S. Interests Section on the Malecón, political symbolism related to health care is also front and center. Witness, for example, one of the tallest buildings in the city, the Hermanos Ameijeiras Hospital. It was originally designed by the well-known architectural office Moenck and Quintana before the revolution to be the Bank of Cuba but is now a major tertiary facility. A badge of honor for *habaneros* and Cubans is that 5 percent of the occupied beds in this hospital are reserved for nonpaying foreigners. These non-Cubans make their requests through Cuban embassies in their countries as well as political parties, peasant organizations, and labor unions (Scarpaci 1999). Not all those admitted to the hospital affiliate with socialist or Communist parties; the classic example is the eye treatment of the child of a conservative Chilean politician during the hard-line, anti-Communist rule of General Pinochet.

Havana is endowed with a greater number of beds and medical facilities than other Cuban cities because it serves as a national referral center. Hermanos Ameijeiras Hospital reserves up to 70 percent of its beds for patients from other provinces. Of international renown, too, is the Center for Genetic Engineering and Biotechnology, reputed to be one of the largest laboratories in the world. A major high-tech research center, it provides the clinical support for a variety of Cuban medical, agricultural, biotechnological, and veterinary products for domestic consumption and export (Los Naranjos 1984). Yet not all Havana's health care infrastructure is high-tech. On the eastern edge of Havana is the José Martí Pioneer City. It is a seaside youth camp capable of housing 10,000 children and between 3,000 and 4,000 mothers. In 1989, the facility expanded to receive hundreds of children injured by the radiation exposure of the Chernobyl nuclear reactor disaster in the former So-

FIGURE 8.4. Protest plaza (*protestódromo*) erected in front of the U.S. Interests Section in Havana. Located on the Malecón, the plaza shows national hero and martyr José Martí holding a child and pointing accusingly at the U.S. diplomatic office. The structure was erected very quickly in 2000 while Elián González was in Miami and the U.S. courts were reviewing the request by the boy's father and the Cuban government to return him to the island. (Photographs courtesy of Joe Paget)

viet Union. This is just one of the medical diplomacy gestures (Feinsilver 1993) and symbols of Havana's "therapeutic" landscape (Scarpaci 1999).

Throughout the past four decades, the policy and practice of hospital care have functioned at several levels in Havana. First, service tries to broaden and improve existing complexes. This policy focused on the *quintas de salud* in Cerro, the Calixto García Teaching Hospital in Vedado, the cluster of hospitals in Plaza de la Revolución, and the subcenters of Marianao Military Hospital and the National Hospital in Alta Habana. Second, the policy also responded to the massive number of people who frequented the health facilities and whose care was totally free and available to all residents of Havana. A third objective was to build new facilities or rehabilitate existing structures. As noted above, the twenty-five-story Banco Nacional building in Centro Habana was transformed into the Hermanos Ameijeiras Hospital (named after brothers who were martyred in the revolutionary struggle against Batista). Last, numerous smaller facilities were built across the city and took advantage of prefabricated construction models that could be assembled relatively quickly.

In the 1980s, the international success that Cuban medicine and "health tourism" had received led to the construction of highly sophisticated medical services for both nationals and foreigners. Playa municipality today has a good share of these newer facilities: the Center for Medical Surgery, the Institute of Tropical Medicine, and the Iberoamerican Center for Regeneration. In Miramar, a prestigious private clinic was converted into a hospital for foreigners: Cira García. South of Miramar, in La Lisa, the orthopedic hospital Frank País was built. It attracts thousands of Latin Americans annually who receive care gratis even though it serves mainly Cubans. In Boyeros, the National Psychiatric Hospital and the rehabilitation hospital Julio Díaz were converted into general hospitals.

During the first two decades of the revolution, the residents of the city had increasingly used national and provincial hospitals in the city indiscriminately. To rectify that problem, the government tried to tease out the different levels of care more carefully and to shoulder up preventive care. A concerted effort in the 1970s and 1980s placed health care clinics (*policlínicos*) in each municipality. Family Physician Clinics (Consultorios del Médico de la Familia) were also installed in each neighborhood. By the mid-1990s, Havana city boasted a dense network of health care facilities, ranging from primary care (clinics), to secondary care (general hospitals), to tertiary care (specialized medical care facilities) (fig. 8.5 and table 8.3). Havana also has the most favorable ratio of physicians to population in the entire country (1:250); Granma Province in eastern Cuba has just 1:569, a ratio that, although the lowest, is still quite good compared with that of other countries.

Health care specialists are well distributed throughout the nation ("Cuba's Health System" 1994). This contrasts with other Latin American countries, where the capital holds a disproportionate number of specialists (Roemer 1964). Although the distribution of health care personnel and facilities fares relatively well in several respects, the infrastructure is hampered by shortages of anesthetics, sutures, antibiotics, and even aspirin. At present, bed linens, electric lamps, detergents, and basic custodial cleaning supplies are also scarce. These shortages notwithstanding, the government has established a coordinated system that is integrated with the residential layout of the city.

TABLE 8.3. Health Care Facilities in Havana, 1995

---

HOSPITALS

1. Centro de Investigación Médico Quirúrgico
2. Cira García
3. Joaquín Albarrán
4. Clodomira Acosta
5. Ramón González Coro
6. Pediátrico Marfán
7. América Arias
8. Manuel Fajardo
9. Pediátrico Pedro Borrás
10. Ortopédico Fructuoso Rodríguez
11. Calixto García
12. Freyre de Andrade
13. Hermanos Ameijeiras
14. Luis Díaz Soto
15. Ciudad Pioneril Tarará
16. Gineco-Obstétrico Guanabacoa
17. Pediátrico San Miguel del Padrón
18. Materno Infantil de 10 de Octubre
19. Miguel Enríquez
20. Santos Suárez
21. Luis de la Puente Uceda
22. Psiquiátrico Isidro de Armas
23. Centro Quirúrgico de 10 de Octubre
24. Pediátrico de Centro Habana
25. Salvador Allende
26. Neumológico Benéfico Jurídico
27. Pediátrico del Cerro
28. Oftalmológico Pando Ferrer
29. Pediátrico Juan M. Martínez
30. Eusebio Hernández
31. Psiquiátrico Laura Martínez
32. Carlos J. Finlay
33. Psiquiátrico Gustavo López
34. Ortopédico Frank País
35. Antileproso Hernández Vaquero
36. Psiquiátrico Nacional
37. Rehabilitación Julio Díaz
38. Pediátrico Leonor Pérez
39. Enrique Cabrera
40. Pediátrico William Soler
41. Angel A. Aballí
42. Psiquiátrico 27 de Noviembre
43. Julio Trigo
44. Gineco-Obstétrico Lebredo
45. Psiquiátrico de Soregui

FREESTANDING MEDICAL RESEARCH CENTERS

1. Instituto de Medicina Legal
2. Instituto de Cirugía Cardiovascular
3. Instituto de Neurología
4. Instituto de Oncología y Radiobiología
5. Centro de Retinosis Pigmentaria
6. Instituto de Higiene y Epidemiología
7. Instituto de Higiene de los Alimentos Nutrición
8. Instituto de Medicina Tropical Pedro Kourí
9. Instituto de Medicina del Trabajo

PRIMARY HEALTH CARE CLINICS (POLICLÍNICOS)

1. Santa Fé
2. Manuel Fajardo
3. 26 de Julio
4. Docente de Playa
5. Jorge Ruíz Ramírez
6. Primero de Enero
7. Isidro de Armas
8. 15 y 18
9. Puentes Grandes
10. 19 de Abril
11. Héroes del Moncada
12. Plaza
13. Rampa
14. Héroes del Corynthia
15. Van Troi
16. Reina
17. Joaquín Albarrán
18. Marcio Manduley
19. Luis Galván
20. Robert Zulueta
21. Antonio Guiteras
22. Diego Tamayo
23. Angel A. Aballí
24. Tomás Romay
25. Regla
26. Camilo Cienfuegos
27. William Santana
28. Cojímar
29. Docente de Alamar
30. 13 de Marzo
31. E. Betancourt Neninger
32. Campo Florido

TABLE 8.3. (continued)

PRIMARY HEALTH CARE CLINICS (POLICLÍNICOS)

| | |
|---|---|
| 33. Guanabo | 57. Carlos J. Finlay |
| 34. Andrés Ortiz | 58. Aleida Fernández |
| 35. Machaco Amejeiras | 59. Cristobal Labra |
| 36. Docente de Guanabacoa | 60. Elpidio Berovides |
| 37. Hermanos Ruiz Aboy | 61. Pulido Humarán |
| 38. Bernardo Posse | 62. Pedro Fonseca |
| 39. Wilfredo Pérez | 63. Wajay |
| 40. California | 64. Santiago de las Vegas |
| 41. Luis Carbó | 65. Rancho Boyeros |
| 42. 30 de Noviembre | 66. Capdevila |
| 43. Lawton | 67. Mulgoba |
| 44. Luyanó | 68. Salvador Allende |
| 45. 14 de Junio | 69. Calabazar |
| 46. Santos Suárez | 70. Los Pinos |
| 47. Luis de la Puente Uceda | 71. Capri |
| 48. Luis Pasteur | 72. Párraga |
| 49. Luis A. Turcios Lima | 73. Julian Grimau |
| 50. Abel Santamaría | 74. Mantilla |
| 51. Héroes de Girón | 75. Reparto Eléctrico |
| 52. Cerro | 76. Managua |
| 53. Antonio Maceo | 77. Efrain Mayor |
| 54. Portuondo | 78. Rafael Valdés |
| 55. Ramón González Coro | 79. Cuatro Caminos |
| 56. 27 de Noviembre | |

*Source*: Unpublished materials, Ministerio de Salud Pública, n.d.
*Note*: See figure 8.5 for map; numbers here correspond to those on the map in that figure.

These initiatives have given education and health care a significant presence in the fabric of Havana.

There is perhaps no better measure of the health of a community than the infant mortality rate. This measure portrays the ratio of infant deaths (0–365 days) to every 1,000 live births. Havana's mean infant mortality rate was a low 8.73 in 1993 and then fell to around 7.0 in 1999. Two notable geographic patterns emerge. First, all but two municipalities have infant mortality rates less than +1 standard deviation of the mean. These outliers—San Miguel and Arroyo Naranjo municipalities—have large rural tracts where the material conditions of the home and the accessibility to health services are less developed than in the urban parts of the province (fig. 8.6). A large pediatrics hospital in San Miguel may also account for higher levels of infant mortality. Another noteworthy feature is the relatively high infant mortality rate in Habana Vieja (+.06 to +1 standard deviation). The rate reflects the increasingly dete-

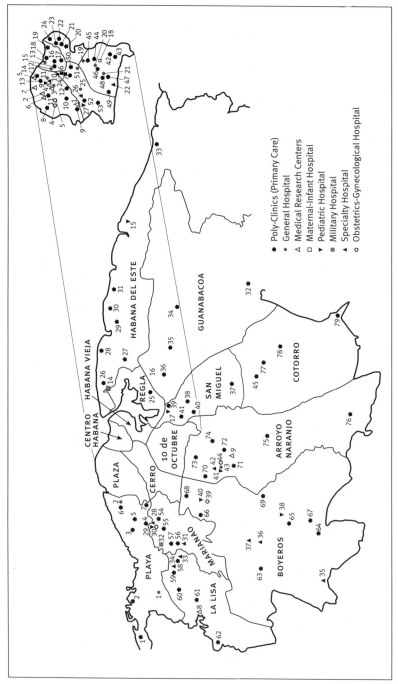

FIGURE 8.5. Health care facilities and medical research centers, Havana, late 1990s. See table 8.3 for key.

- Poly-Clinics (Primary Care)
- General Hospital
△ Medical Research Centers
□ Maternal-Infant Hospital
▼ Pediatric Hospital
■ Military Hospital
▲ Specialty Hospital
○ Obstetrics-Gynecological Hospital

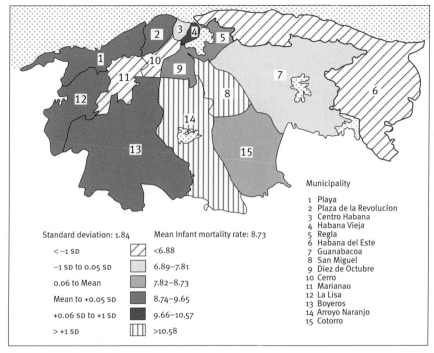

Standard deviation: 1.84    Mean Infant mortality rate: 8.73

| | |
|---|---|
| < –1 SD | <6.88 |
| –1 SD to 0.05 SD | 6.89–7.81 |
| 0.06 to Mean | 7.82–8.73 |
| Mean to +0.05 SD | 8.74–9.65 |
| +0.06 SD to +1 SD | 9.66–10.57 |
| > +1 SD | >10.58 |

Municipality

1  Playa
2  Plaza de la Revolucíon
3  Centro Habana
4  Habana Vieja
5  Regla
6  Habana del Este
7  Guanabacoa
8  San Miguel
9  Diez de Octubre
10 Cerro
11 Marianao
12 La Lisa
13 Boyeros
14 Arroyo Naranjo
15 Cotorro

FIGURE 8.6. Infant mortality rates in Havana, by municipality, 1993

riorated living conditions in this densely settled corner of the city. In the mid-1990s, the City Historian's Office opened a maternity home for high-risk pregnant women, who can receive better food and medical care than in their homes.

## Education

Another policy outcome of the Castro government that characterizes its goal of changing the scale of priorities and hierarchies of urban life is the educational system. Nationally, per capita expenditures for education rose from $11 in 1958 to $42 in 1970 and $175 in 1989 (Jiménez 1990). Even during the Special Period in 1991, when funding plummeted to $92 per capita, Cuba remained in second place in Latin America (behind Venezuela at $117 and ahead of Panama at $82) (*Cuba Va* 1993). Considerable investment has gone into building day care centers, primary schools, high schools, technological institutes, and preuniversity high schools. Most of these new buildings are located in the periphery of Havana as opposed to the traditional centers. Early on in the revolution, old palaces and mansions abandoned by the bourgeoisie were transformed into schools, as were existing buildings in older areas of the city. Miramar, partly emptied by exile migration, became a large educational space in the city. Thousands of children of peasant farmers from the Sierra Maestra came to Miramar for basic literacy training. The Columbia Military Base in Marianao, a sinister representation of military rule in Cuba that in previous decades controlled the political scene, was transformed into a major educational center. Now called Ciudad Libertad (Liberty City), the former barracks contain facilities ranging from primary schools to university classes. Private schools fell under state rule. The huge Catholic school, Belén (or Bethlehem in English, where Fidel Castro studied), previously run by the Jesuits, was turned into the Technical Military Institute. The children of Russian technicians studied at the facilities of the former Colegio de las Ursulinas.

School construction quickened during the early years of the revolution. Between 1959 and 1961, 671 rural primary schools, 339 urban primary schools, and 99 junior high schools were built. Havana played a key role, often immeasurable in the early educational efforts of the revolution. For example, thousands of Havanan families took in student boarders who came from eastern Cuba to study in the capital. Massive scholarship programs have also brought an "overflow" of students to the city. The Rebel Army and adults being trained as teachers, artisans, and other trades also received free, informal lodging in Havana.

Between 1968 and 1973, 475 learning centers of some fashion were built in Cuba. One hundred ninety Basic Rural Secondary Schools (Escuelas Secundarias Básicas en el Campo [ESBECS]) were erected between 1968 and 1973. Each school contained a 500-hectare farm and could hold up to five hundred students (Segre 1978). The ESBECS averaged a cost of half a million pesos and were clustered around the citrus plantations in Ceiba del Agua, Jagüey Grande, and Ciego de Avila. Students boarded there, and life was hard for them. Besides carrying a normal course load, they worked in the fields three hours daily in their gardens as well as in some agricultural production for the nation. Instructors worked there permanently, while the student population rotated (back to their hometowns) every three years. Some schools turned into a rather benign, fenceless prison. Strong children bullied weaker ones, and early sexual activity became a major attraction (including the predominantly young schoolteachers). Personal belongings were to be kept in open lockers because not only were locks scarce, but officials from the Ministry of Education thought they were unnecessary; every youngster bred by the revolution was supposed to be honest.

The counterpart of the ESBECS in the cities were the Basic Urban Secondary Schools (Escuelas Secundarias Básicas Urbanas [ESBURS]). In terms of design, these complexes usually demanded very large lots and introduced considerable visual blight in the cityscape. Even students in the ESBURS are required to leave for forty-five days of agricultural work, usually picking tobacco or coffee. Parents make long, difficult trips on Sundays to see their children and add some extra food to the bland diet.

Two major interventions in the beginning of the 1960s transformed the scale of education in Havana. The first was the creation of small schools that were tied to new housing complexes. The second was a project that portrayed the "moral objectives" of the revolution: the college campus of Ciudad Universitaria José Antonio Echeverría (the campus and university are referred to as CUJAE in Cuba) in Marianao municipality, and the National Schools of Art built on the former golf courses of Country Club in Playa municipality. With contrasting architectural images, these two complexes reflected the enthusiasm of young designers by creating both artistic (Schools of Art) and technical (CUJAE) "cities" with environmental and aesthetic qualities that demonstrated the new values imparted by a socialist society.

In the 1970s and 1980s, practically every neighborhood of Havana received some type of educational facility, made possible largely by the Girón method of prefabricated panels of reinforced concrete (see Chapter 6). Originally developed for junior high schools, Girón was later used for day care centers, high schools, and teacher training centers. The Girón method permitted specialized training centers such as medicine and agronomy to locate in the countryside. Other educational facilities were established throughout the provinces of Havana City and Havana (table 8.4). The exterior finish on the buildings was often poor because of the uneven surfaces of the panels, especially at joints. Because the designs were simple and relatively low in cost, the buildings turned out monotonous and unattractive.

The location of many of these new facilities benefited from the former bourgeoisie's affinity with attractive and bucolic sites. Several biotechnology and genetic engineering research centers were located in the posh residential neighborhoods of Country Club, La Coronela, and San Agustín in the western side of the metropolitan areas. Political parties and workers' organizations also sought the amenities of the countryside. The major labor organization,

TABLE 8.4. New Educational Facilities Placed in and around Havana, 1960s–1970s

| FACILITY NAME | DESCRIPTION | LOCATION |
|---|---|---|
| Escuela de Geografía | Geography faculty, University of Havana | Alamar, eastern Havana City Province |
| Instituto de Ciencias Agropecuarias | Agricultural research and training center | San José de las Lajas, Havana Province |
| Centro de Investigaciones de Sanidad Animal (CENSA) | Veterinary science research and training center | San José de las Lajas, Havana Province |
| Escuela Internacional de Cine y TV | Film school | San Antonio de los Baños, Havana Province |
| Instituto Superior de Dirección de la Economía | Economics research center | La Lisa, Havana City Province |
| Instituto Superior de Relaciones Internacionales | Foreign affairs research and training center | Playa, Havana City Province |
| Instituto Superior de Ciencias Médicas | Medical research and training center | Playa, Havana City Province, in former residence of Sagrado Corazón school |
| Escuela Vocacional Lenin | Vo-tech school | Arroyo Naranjo Municipality, Havana City Province |
| Instituto de Electrónica | Electronics research and training center | Santiago de las Vegas, Havana City Province |
| Instituto de la Construcción | Building construction research and training center | Santiago de las Vegas, Havana City Province |
| Instituto de Ciencias Agropecuarias | Agricultural research and training center | Santiago de Las Vegas, Havana City Province |
| Instituto Superior Pedagógico para la Educación Técnica y Professional | Vo-tech training school | Santiago de las Vegas, Havana City Province |
| Instituto de Economía | Economics research and training center | Cotorro Municipality, Havana City Province |
| Instituto de Geología y Geofísica | Geology research and training center | Cotorro Municipality, Havana City Province |
| Instituto de Transporte Naval | Naval training center | Havana City Province |

*Source*: Authors' field research.

the Central de Trabajadores de Cuba, and the Provincial School of the Cuban Communist Party also opened facilities in these western former urban areas. Even the Communist Party's school Ñico López found a home at Santa Fé beach, Barlovento, where the yachts of U.S. millionaires used to moor before the revolution. Last, each of these complexes created ancillary facilities such as dormitories, cafeterias, libraries, garages, and related support services. Within the contiguous part of Havana, there were also hundreds of preschool and day care facilities built largely in the 1980s, even within Habana Vieja.

The Cuban government controls all educational institutions, since religious and private education has been abolished under the revolution.[4] In so doing, it has striven to promote access to all facets of education without regard for the ability to pay. School attendance is compulsory through the ninth grade, and the state has promoted a wide array of literacy, arts, and cultural programs as part of its massification of public education efforts.

One indelible hallmark left by the Cuban revolution was the literacy campaign in the 1960s. Volunteers pushed into primarily rural parts of the island and helped to increase the literary rate from 53 percent in 1953 to 96 percent in 1988 (Del Aguila 1992). By 1992, the literacy rate had risen to 98.5 percent, giving Cuba the highest literacy rate in Latin America, followed by Argentina (95.5 percent), Uruguay (95.4 percent), and Costa Rica (93.6 percent) ("Demographics" 1993; Provincia de la Ciudad de La Habana 1992). A museum dedicated to this important grassroots effort—El Museo de la Alfabetización in the Marianao district of Havana—displays glimpses of this social movement.

Two public higher education institutions prevailed in 1959: the University of Havana and the University of Santiago de Cuba. In 1996, four universities operated in Havana.

## The Venues of Cuban Tourism

The city of Havana (population 2.2 million) holds several comparative advantages in the south Florida and Caribbean tourist markets. Before the revolution, Havana always offered low per diem costs for the tourists. Multiplier effects in the 1950s from tourism shared common features with tourism in other Caribbean nations. Rum and tobacco sales as well as a broad range of artisan industries benefited from the tourist trade. The 1950s were a time when most of the tourist infrastructure was foreign owned. In Cuba, nationalization of tourist facilities increased after 1961. Although joint ventures in revolutionary Cuba have been permitted since 1982, it would not be until the 1990s that foreign capital would return to the island (Espino 1993).

4. A few private educational programs are offered, though they are sponsored by foreign cultural organizations and embassies. For instance, the Aliance Française offers French classes and adult education.

A BENIGN CLIMATE

Geography has also dealt the island comparative advantages. Although Havana is situated at a lower latitude than Florida, the trade winds produce slightly cooler temperatures in Havana during the summer. In the wintertime, its insular location and a strong maritime influence make it slightly warmer than Florida (table 8.5). Proximity to the largest and most affluent international tourist market in the world has not been lost on Cuban governments throughout the twentieth century (Havanatur 1992).

Tourism in Havana waxed and waned during the past century. Before 1920, it was relatively minor. Marrero (1981a, 316) reported that Cuba grossed $107 million between 1954 and 1956, registering tourism as the third most important source of national wealth behind sugar and tobacco. During prerevolutionary times, Havana functioned as one point in a circuit of North American tourist flows along with Las Vegas and Miami. Hotel ownership and gambling operations among the three points were closely coordinated. Short trips across the Straits of Florida by airplane and boat were especially common allures in the Miami–Key West–Havana link. During the peak years of international tourism between Miami and Cuba, hourly scheduled flights operated between dawn and midnight. In the mid-1950s, an average of 260,000 tourists visited Cuba, and Havana was the main destination (Marrero 1981a, 322). As we discuss below, this figure dropped greatly during the first two decades of the revolution. Comparable levels would not appear until the onset of the economic crisis brought on by the dissolution of the Soviet Union and the socialist bloc in 1989.

In the 1960s and 1970s, tourism was relatively insignificant. Throughout most of the revolution, Havana's standard tourist fare has been colonial Havana, tourism oriented around the accomplishments of the revolution, twentieth-century architecture, the Tropicana nightclub, and the beaches of Habana del Este.

THE RISE AND FALL OF TOURISM

The revolution and the subsequent disruption of diplomatic and trade relations with the United States curtailed international tourism in Cuba. In 1957, 304,711 tourists visited the island. It would take years to reach prerevolutionary levels. Between 1960 and 1975, international tourism practically disappeared in Cuba because the revolutionary government discouraged it. Revo-

TABLE 8.5. Temperature (°C) Comparisons between Selected Florida Cities
and Havana

| CITIES | SUMMER | WINTER |
|---|---|---|
| Jacksonville | 27.3° | 12.5° |
| Saint Augustine | 28.5° | 14.0° |
| Miami | 27.3° | 19.8° |
| Havana | 26.2° | 22.6° |

*Source*: Marrero 1981a, 320.

lutionary leaders considered tourism too closely aligned with the capitalist sins of prostitution, drugs, organized crime, and gambling.[5] In 1976, however, the government created the National Institute of Tourism (Instituto Nacional de Turismo [INTUR]). As a result, international tourism rose from a mere 8,400 visitors in 1974 to 69,500 in 1978 (Espino 1993).

Relative growth of Cuba's tourist trade quickened in the late 1970s and again in the late 1980s. In the 1980s, the rate of international visitors to Cuba increased at an average annual rate of 9.4 percent, greater than the Caribbean's rate as a whole. However, in 1988 Cuba had attracted only 3.2 percent of all Caribbean tourist arrivals and only 2.1 percent of the region's tourist receipts (Espino 1991). By 1990, though, approximately 340,000 tourists visited the island, which increased 82 percent by 1994 (619,000). Figures for 1995 reached nearly three-quarters of a million tourists, and although officials had hoped for some 2.5 million tourists in the year 2000, about 1.6 million had visited Cuba in 1999 (table 8.6). A strong infusion of Spanish capital and joint ventures has bolstered the island's room capacity. Some of the most recent and notable hotel and tourist complexes include the Meliá Las Américas in Varadero and the Meliá-Cohiba in the Vedado district of Havana. The Cuban

5. Prostitution in Cuba has gained worldwide attention. Regrettably, there are sites on the World Wide Web that explain how and where prostitution operates in Havana, Varadero, Cienfuegos, and other cities. A 1995 survey carried out in the Italian tourist magazine *Viaggiare* ranked Cuba as the most popular destination for sex tourists. Although prostitution and pimping are not crimes per se, they fall under Article 62 of the penal code, which classifies "anti-social" behavior. An April 4, 1996, raid on four hundred "bawdy houses" in Havana rounded up residents who worked as prostitutes at "tunnels, bridges, dens, rooftops and public spaces which served as shelter for those who lived from sexual exploitation." In June 1996, *Juventud Rebelde*, a Cuban Communist Party weekly publication, announced that a network of seven thousand prostitutes had been destroyed (See Acosta 1996a).

TABLE 8.6. Leading Origins of Tourists to Cuba, 1995–1999

|  | 1995 | 1996 | 1997 | 1998 | 1999 |
|---|---|---|---|---|---|
| Canada | 143,541 | 162,766 | 169,686 | 215,644 | 276,350 |
| United States | 20,672 | 27,113 | 34,956 | 46,338 | 60,000 |
| Germany | 57,487 | 80,185 | 86,509 | 148,987 | 182,000 |
| Spain | 89,501 | 117,957 | 116,606 | 140,435 | 147,000 |
| France | 34,332 | 62,742 | 93,897 | 101,604 | 133,000 |
| Italy | 114,767 | 192,297 | 200,238 | 186,688 | 161,000 |
| Mexico | 32,069 | 37,229 | 52,742 | 61,589 | 71,000 |
| Total | 745,495 | 1,004,336 | 1,170,083 | 1,415,832 | 1,603,000 |

Source: *Cuba: Evolución económica durante 1999*. Santiago, Chile: CEPAL, 2000, table 22, p. 38.
Note: "Total" includes leading nations as well as all other visitors to the island, but the latter are not included in this table. Also, CEPAL estimated the 1999 data based on preliminary findings.

firm Habagüanex is also undergoing a spate of renovations and building new complexes around Old Havana, which will add to the city's room capacity (Scarpaci 2000b).

Tourism holds great promise for the island and its capital city. Cuba had 40 percent more tourist rooms in 1992 than it did in 1991. A recurrent problem is the gap between gross and net revenues from tourism. In 1992, an estimated $400 million in gross receipts yielded just $240 million in net revenues. This amounts to just 1 percent of the gross social product (GSP). Another obstacle is the relatively low rate of repeat tourism; only 7 or 8 percent of tourists return to Cuba, versus 20 percent elsewhere in the Caribbean. One analyst finds that Cuba attracts tourists who spend very little more than their already low-cost vacation packages. In addition, the multipliers are few because of the high rate of imports in the tourist industry (Mesa-Lago 1994, 19). Espino (2000) estimates that Cuba reached a 37 percent import component on every dollar spent by tourists. Put another way, just 63 cents of every tourist dollar remains in Cuba.

Havana's total capacity in state-operated facilities was 10,700 rooms (31,600 nationwide) in early 2000. In Havana, there are also around 4,500 rooms rented to foreigners, equivalent to twelve to fifteen new hotels. The figure accounts for only those rooms registered and on which taxes are paid, so the actual number should be at least twice that figure. Around 80 percent of the recent construction activity in Cuba is in some way connected with tourism.

The land allocated by the Cuban government and the buildings dedicated to these new projects represent an estimated U.S.$500 million (Núñez, Brown, and Smolka 2000).

Repeat tourism will be key to Havana's success if the U.S. embargo is lifted. Challenges will also lie ahead after the first wave of curiosity seekers pass through the city's streets. Once a tropical destination is "discovered" and promoted appropriately, the allure to such a place should create a tourist flow with its own momentum (Stough and Feldman 1984). In truth, there are an unlimited number of sun, sand, and sea destinations for the North American and European markets (de Albuquerque and McElroy 1992). Although Cuba at one time had an advantage as a getaway spot for U.S. tourists—and had cultivated experience among tourist industry personnel in the international tourist trade—all that vanished with the strengthening of the revolution and the U.S. embargo of the island. Lost, too, was human capital, especially knowledge transferred among generations of tourism workers and business managers.

As Cuba undergoes the transition from a fairly "closed" island to an "open" one, the surge of tourists poses problems. Host population responses to major tourist influxes elsewhere have ranged from outright hostility to overt euphoria (de Albuquerque and McElroy 1992). The mind-set of many Cuban tourism employees must change so that cordiality and attentiveness create repeat tourism. Furthermore, Cuba's eye on the U.S. market would require a special adaptation to Havana's current tourism infrastructure. As de Albuquerque and McElroy note: "Because of the middle-class Americans' penchant for the familiar, this strong U.S. influence in the Caribbean tourist industry is partly responsible for the observed preference for hotel lodging and the relatively large-scale facilities and shorter stays characteristic of mature destinations" (1992, 626). By "mature" destinations the authors mean those with the highest per capita visitor spending in the Caribbean and fewer than half a million inhabitants (Aruba, Bahamas, Barbados, Bermuda, Curacao, St. Maarten, and the U.S. Virgin Islands).

Havana holds its position as the major tourist destination within Cuba. According to a recent United Nations–sponsored publication ("Growth in Tourism" 1994, 20), Havana operates at a 76 percent hotel-room capacity, compared with 94 percent in Holguin, 93 percent in Santiago de Cuba, 62 percent in Varadero, and 75 percent in other principal tourist zones in Cuba. Thus, as the Cuban government seeks to expand its tourist infrastructure throughout the island—and not just in Havana—eastern Cuba (Holguin

FIGURE 8.7. Leading origins of tourists to Cuba, 1996–99 (percentage contribution; data from *Cuba: Evolución económica durante 1999* [Santiago, Chile: CEPAL, 2000], table 22, p. 38)

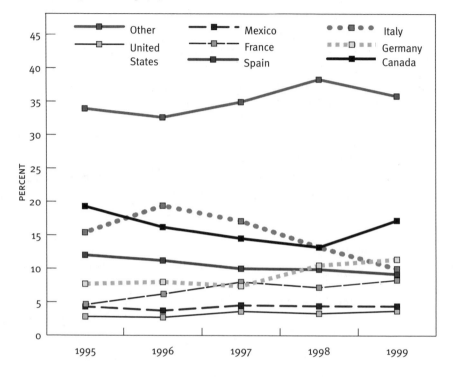

and Santiago de Cuba) approaches maximum capacity while the Havana-Varadero tourist poles have room for growth.

Havana's attraction as an international tourist site stems from the city's architectural beauty and curiosity about the revolution. Data on the island's performance in recent years bode well for Cuba's new role in tourism. Cuba placed fourteenth on the list of the most popular tourist destinations in the Western Hemisphere, which was up from the twenty-fourth spot it held in 1985. During that same time, Cuba rose from twenty-third to ninth among nations with the greatest income from tourism (Acosta 1996b).

The state actively promotes tourism abroad, as do a growing number of joint-venture operations. Handling this travel are 174 Cuban travel representatives outside the country and 38 agencies within Cuba. Although Havana is the primary destination, the entire island boasts seven international airports and enlists three Cuban and thirty-five foreign airlines to handle tourist arrivals (*Business Tips on Cuba*, May 1995, 28). Western Europe is the largest regional market, while Canada provides the largest single national contribution to Cuba's international tourist flow (fig. 8.7). Most Canadians arrive on charter flights departing from the eastern Canadian provinces and book weekly packages. Varadero's airport, Juan Gualberto Gómez International, is 140 kilometers east of Havana, or ninety minutes by road. Measuring 60–80 by 3,000 meters (197–262 by 9,842 feet), its runway can handle large aircraft ("Infrastructure" 1993). Day trips into Havana are common parts of the "ground packages" provided by these flights. A recent trend is that the "official" number of U.S. visitors is almost equal to the relative proportion of Mexicans who make up the international tourist population in Cuba. Other than Canadians, Spanish, German, Italian, and French tourists constitute the major visitors to the island.

The Cuban Ministry of Tourism has identified some sixty-seven "tourist poles" along with more than 7,000 kilometers of coastline. Figure 8.8 reveals four of those poles within Havana City Province (Cojímar, Traditional Center, Vedado, and Monte Barreto). Playa Jibacoa, Playas del Este, and Tarará are the most accessible beaches for tourists and residents within Havana City and Havana Provinces (*Business Tips on Cuba*, May 1995, 27). Hemingway Marina, formerly Barlovento, has undergone major remodeling and hosts an annual fishing competition. Boats from any country—including the United States—can enter the marina for recreational purposes and moor there for seventy-two hours without securing a visa.

## SOLDIERING AND TOURISM

If the shift away from the Soviet Union in a post–Cold War era has been daunting for Cuba, nowhere has this change been more striking than in the role of the island's armed forces. Long gone are the days of armed struggle in Angola and Mozambique. Cuba indeed has been cashing in on this "peace dividend" even though it has the second largest army in Latin America (Brazil leads). The Cuban military had worked in endeavors outside military defense well before the onset of the Special Period. Its presence in tourism is strong and growing.

Gaviota (seagull) is the best-known company of the armed forces. It gained experience in managing recreational centers for Soviet advisers back in the 1960s. That marked the beginning of what has become a multifaceted presence in Cuba's tourist trade. Gaviota now operates bus tours, marinas,

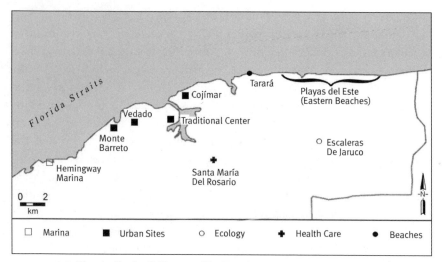

FIGURE 8.8. Tourist "poles," Havana City Province

spas, hunting preserves, fishing excursions, and luxury hotels. It also boasts a large fleet of taxis and airline flights. Gaviota pursues horizontal linkages. It taps into tourists' expendable income through the TRD Caribe chain of department stores. Recall from Chapter 5 that TRD stands for *tiendas de recaudación de divisas*, or foreign-currency collection stores. The Cuban armed forces have reportedly studied China's state-managed economic opening, a process that changed the People's Liberation Army into a major company. Cuba's armed forces have been downsized by some 25 percent (from a maximum of 200,000 men and women during its involvement in Africa in the 1980s). The market, though, has brought problems from which even the Armed Forces are not immune: nepotism and corruption. Despite these dangers, the army has produced a well-disciplined cadre of engineers, managers, agronomists, and technicians. In the words of economist Julio Carranza, former deputy director of the Center for the Study of the Americas in Havana: "The armed forces are trying to generate foreign exchange so as to be able to sustain themselves as a military force without being a load on the state or a burden on the rest of the economy" (Rohter 1995).

## HEALTH TOURISM

As discussed earlier this chapter, principles of equal access to services, an integral approach to health care, and popular participation in health initiatives guide Cuba's health system (Feinsilver 1993, 28). Cuba has generously provided physicians and medical care to developing countries in Africa and Asia. It also provides specialized high-tech medical procedures such as cardiac surgery, eye surgery, and cancer treatment at lower costs than those found in the United States, Europe, or Latin America.

Cuba's renowned system of health care is also available to foreigners provided they purchase services in hard currency. Havana is home to several international tourist hospitals in the Vedado, Miramar, and Centro Habana districts of the city. These facilities provide high-quality tertiary care services. Foreigners unable to pay for certain types of specialized care are also treated on an availability basis for specialized services. For example, Frank País Hospital offers rehabilitation services for war casualties from Nicaragua, El Salvador, and the former Soviet Union. In addition, orthopedic surgical procedures and spinal cord revascularization procedures can be secured there at a fraction of the cost in most advanced industrial countries (Feinsilver 1993, 72).

Cuba also promotes other specialized medical procedures under the label *turismo de salud*. A number of small clinics cater largely to foreigners who seek medical procedures that either do not exist in their country, are too expensive there, or have not been approved (e.g., by the Food and Drug Administration in the United States). These include the Center for Placental Histotherapy, Center for Medical Surgical Research, Cardiology and Cardiovascular Surgery Institute, Gastroenterology Institute, and the Sports Medicine Institute, among others. Foreigners can book complete package trips. Prices include airfare, lodging, ground transportation, nursing and medical care, specified medication and surgical procedures, and designated laboratory work. Patients from the United States can come through third countries (Bahamas, Mexico, Canada, Dominican Republic, and Jamaica).

The Center for Placental Histotherapy, for example, has established a record of accomplishment in evening out skin coloring for thousands of patients who suffer from a pigmentation disorder called vitiligo. Even though the use of human placenta materials for this treatment is illegal in the United States, Cuban physicians and researchers claim that the U.S. embargo and transnational pharmaceutical corporations exert so much pressure that it is difficult to sell Cuban pharmaceutical and biotechnical products outside Cuba. Dr. Carlos Miyares Cao, general director of the Center for Placental Histotherapy, claims that even foreign medical journals in allegedly "sympathetic" countries such as Mexico succumb to pressure about publishing the clinical results of Cuban researchers (personal communication, June 28, 1995).

Many "health tourists" are not daunted by these obstacles. A New Jersey mother, willing to take a risk with Cuba's health tourism and the workings of the Center for Placental Histotherapy, is illustrative. For approximately $2,400, the mother and her son were able to fly from Newark, New Jersey, to Havana (by way of Cancún, Mexico) for the son's medical care. A week's lodging and treatment for vitiligo identified an appropriate dosage and strength. The boy brought back two five-gallon containers of the lotion—a year's supply—which were included in the package. He must return annually for follow-ups and to have the prescription adjusted and refilled. As the mother assessed the health-tourism encounter: "I could easily run up $2,400 in diagnostic work and unproved ultraviolet treatments for the same amount in the Princeton and metropolitan New York areas, without the slightest hope that the vitiligo will dissipate" (personal communication with mother, April 1998). While in Cuba she can purchase special lotions for wrinkles, psoriasis, and aging. She will also find a whole line of placenta-based hair products.

Medical tourists such as this New Jersey mother, though, constitute a small tourist flow. Since Cuban physicians earn just a few dollars a month in real terms, the ratio of labor costs to revenues is fairly low. However, such specialized medical procedures represent years of laboratory work and the purchase of medical equipment manufactured outside Cuba. The key point is that medical tourism in Cuba has moved well beyond the sunshine, tranquillity, and herbal remedies promoted by health spas, mud baths, and mineral springs in other tropical destinations. As the proportion of household expenditures in the United States devoted to health care and well-being continues to rise, this high-tech medical tourism could bolster tourism in Cuba when the economic blockade is lifted.

## CULTURAL TOURISM

The revolution, with its brigades of volunteers, sugar-harvest (*zafra*) campaigns, and international linkages with groups in solidarity with Cuba, is responsible for an undetermined number of "tourists." Instead of visiting for the traditional reasons—"sun and sand"—they come out of curiosity or else are ardent supporters of the Cuban revolution. These visits interject small amounts of hard currency, medicine, and clothing. More important, perhaps, they focus international attention on the blockade.

Afro-Cuban culture also attracts thousands to Havana, and Cubanacán, INTUR, and other state agencies promote trips that focus on *santería*, the island's African-Catholic belief system. *Santeros* (priests and priestesses) meet with tourists. Short presentations explain the role of deities (*orishas*) that blend Yoruba and Roman Catholic symbols. Musical presentations drawing heavily on rumba and other rhythmic interludes make up another important segment of Cuba's "cultural tourism." This is, however, a highly specialized form of tourism. It can easily be accessed in Havana as a primary activity or as a complement to the city's many cultural and physical amenities.

ECOTOURISM

Havana holds little ecological allure for travelers on the ecotourism beat. Although its population density is one of the lowest of all Latin American capitals and it contains about 12 square meters of park and green space per resident, it is far from an ecological haven (GDIC 1990). In fact, Havana Bay is still one of the most polluted waters in the Caribbean (Collis 1995; Díaz-Briquets and Pérez-López 2000), despite some slight improvement in the late 1990s. Nonetheless, those in search of ecotourist experiences usually pass through Havana, which in turn generates multipliers for the Havana tourist market.

In Cuba, 3,200 out of 6,000 species of plants are endemic to the island. The richness of the island's flora and fauna has prompted UNESCO to identify four biosphere reserves, all of them outside Havana.[6] Traditional outdoor recreation activities, however, abound. Fishing, hunting, diving, and bird-watching side trips leave Havana regularly and include tourists who come to Cuba chiefly to experience the capital city.

Ecotourism in Cuba, though, has developed slowly (Collis 1995). Several locations on the island are under consideration for ecotourism development: Sierra Maestra, Pinares de Mayarí, Topes de Collantes, and Ciénaga de Zapata. One of the ecotourist resorts closest to Havana is at Las Terrazas, designated as a Reserve to the Biosphere, about two hours outside Havana in Pinar del Río Province. An ecotourist facility opened in 1994 next to a rural "new town" that was built in the late 1960s, which is considered the best designed of the nearly four hundred built around the country after 1959. Tourists can see some of the island's most varied flora and fauna at Las Terrazas.

6. The four biosphere reserves include the Rosario Sierra at the western edge of the island; a mountainous region known as the Toa River Cuchillas, 970 kilometers from Havana; the Guanahacabibes Peninsula; and Baconao Park, 965 kilometers from the capital.

At present, it is unclear whether Cuba's search for hard currency will allow for a gradual development of these areas, but the implications are dear to Havana's tourist economy as well as the national sector. Cuba's ecotourism appeal in the realm of flora and fauna sightseeing is that the island is the Caribbean's largest and has a high number of endemic species, with no animals dangerous for human beings. These sights will provide "light recreation" such as hiking, boating, camping, photography, and wildlife watching. Although not high on the hard-currency-generating scale, they could provide revenue for environmental trusts to protect some of the island's most pristine natural areas. The recent development of beach resorts in previously wild keys — mostly at the northern central coast, and some with large populations of pink flamingos — has produced concern among environmentalists because of the construction of *pedraplenes* (roads on a rock-filled strip over shallow waters separating the keys from the main island) to large hotels and even airports. Some argue that a better decision would have been to build the hotels on the main island, near an existing town or small city, and then take visitors back and forth to the keys, so as to preserve what makes them more attractive. Inspectors from the Ministry of Science, Technology, and Environment are monitoring the situation closely, looking for signs of dangerous changes in the water and water-based environment due to alterations introduced by the *pedraplenes* in the natural exchange of sea and fresh waters.

JOINT VENTURES

The new strategy in Cuba's tourist industry relies heavily on joint ventures (Dávalos Fernández 1993). A series of legal reforms since the late 1980s have eased the influx of foreign capital to the island. By August 1996, 240 agreements with investments from forty-three countries and in thirty-four sectors of the economy had been signed (Ministry of Economy and Planning 1996). The primary countries of investment are European (especially Spanish) and Canadian (table 8.7).

Land is a critical element the government can contribute in Cuban-foreign joint ventures for tourism and real estate. Tourism grew from 2,000 tourists in 1967 to 1.4 million in 1998. Even though there is no formal land market in Cuba, land has been used to stimulate development and to generate public revenues. In joint ventures — mainly with Spanish, Canadian, Italian, and Israeli associates — the Cuban contribution has been mainly land, construction workers, and some building materials. Since land is the main input, there is a trend for the government to ensure that it amounts to up to 50 percent of the social capital. New projects have often been criticized because of an excessive use of land, with too high densities and little open space. Investors try to explain this because of the high price of land. Land leasing on a twenty-five-year term (which can be extended to another twenty-five if both partners agree) has always been preferred instead of selling.

One of the most controversial projects in Havana in the mid-1990s was the construction of a new five-star hotel. The $70 million Hotel Meliá-Cohiba is located next to the famous Hotel Riviera, on the Malecón, in the Vedado district. It employs 450 workers, a significant number in an urban labor market that must absorb workers from downsized state-run enterprises.

Havana's tourism promotions aim at potential visitors from Canada, Western Europe (especially Spain and Italy), and Mexico. Sol Hotels in Cuba account for a large share of Havana's tourism promotion ("New Five-Star Hotel" 1995, 3). The twenty-two-story Meliá-Cohiba is a Spanish- and Cuban-financed complex that offers 462 rooms, which in 1995 started at $150 per night. Accommodations also include nineteen VIP rooms, convention facilities, and twenty-five presidential suites.

Hotel Meliá-Cohiba towers over the surrounding neighborhood. It dwarfs the Hotel Habana Riviera, set two blocks back, and its huge footprint is set too close to Paseo Street, which is one of the most beautiful promenades in Vedado, ending at the Revolution Square. In the evening, blue-green floodlights cast a powerful glow on the building's modern, gold-colored metal and glass facade. The Meliá-Cohiba surpassed the former Hotel Habana Libre (the Havana Hilton of the late 1950s) as the new symbol of foreign capital in Havana's tourist trade (in the 1990s). Moreover, the quality of the Meliá-Cohíba's architectural design is inferior, and the design is allegedly a copy from a hotel in Japan. As discussed in Chapter 7, Cubans euphemistically referred to this new wave of Spanish investment as the "second conquest" of Cuba. This negative impact on the urban image of the Meliá-Cohiba was followed by a new shopping mall with a blue reflective glass facade facing west into the hot Cuban sun, "repeating the same trick the conquistadors played on the natives by trading small mirrors for golden nuggets" (Coyula 1998).

TABLE 8.7. Selected Joint-Venture Hotel Chains in Cuba, ca. 2001

| HOTEL CHAIN | COUNTRY OF ORIGIN | TOURIST ZONE |
| --- | --- | --- |
| Super-Club | Jamaica | Varadero |
| LTI | Germany | Varadero, Santiago de Cuba |
| Iberostar S.A. | Spain | Havana |
| Sol-Melía | Spain | Havana (Vedado, Miramar), Varadero, Santiago de Cuba |
| RUI Hotels, S.A. | Spain | Varadero |
| Raytur | Spain | Santa Lucía |
| Delta | Canada | Santiago de Cuba |
| Commonwealth | Canada | Marea del Portillo |
| Hospitality, LTD | Canada | Granma |
| Kawama Caribbean | Spain | Varadero |
| Hotels (KCH) | Spain | Havana |
| Golden Tulip | Netherlands | Havana (Habana Vieja) |
| Novotel | France | Havana (Miramar) |

*Sources: Business Tips on Cuba* (July 1994): 21, and authors' field research, 1997–2001.

## Leisure Time, Green Spaces, Sports, and Religion

Havana's climate, briefly described in Chapter 1 and earlier in this chapter, is conducive to year-round outdoor recreation. International appeal derives in good measure from the warm waters (25°C in the winter, 28°C in summer) and beaches within the city limits (Playas del Este) as well as the world-renowned beach of Varadero, 145 kilometers east of the capital.[7] Although all beaches and parks in the city are free of charge to both Cubans and foreign nationals, access to certain tourist facilities for most of the revolution has been limited to foreigners who paid in hard currency. The way some Cubans dress is also used by hotel management to "screen" out certain individuals suspected as "hustlers" who prey on tourists. However, it is also true that Cubans share hotels with foreigners, although the former pay in pesos and

---

7. In 1996 the first toll booths during the revolution opened on the road from Matanzas to Varadero. An estimated five thousand vehicles travel this road daily. Ostensibly, the income from these booths will be used to resurface roads throughout Cuba. Cars pay U.S.$2 and tourist buses U.S.$4. Many say that the toll booths aim to keep prostitutes out of the exclusive beach resort, as well as other Cubans who may not have any legitimate business there. See Napoles 1996c.

the latter in dollars; but this applies to only one chain, Isla Azul, and admittance is strictly controlled by trade unions' quotas. Some hotels also use "Cuban menus" for locals and a separate one for tourists. Cubans can eat freely in a hotel restaurant but cannot sleep there, even if they are willing to pay in dollars.

Because Havana has a relatively low population density and an absence of densely packed apartment buildings, its endowment of green and open areas will come as no surprise. *Habaneros* in 1959 shared only 1 square meter of park space per resident. But by the late 1980s that rate increased tenfold, and by 2001 it was twelvefold. Planners are keenly aware of the need to maintain and increase the amount of green areas, especially in the inner city. Obstacles include a decline in tree nurseries, excessive pruning of trees in constant conflict with the aerial electric and phone networks, a poor maintenance policy, and a need to educate the public about the value of green areas (González 1990, 26).

The heart of the metropolitan area contains Parque Metropolitano; the floodplain of the Almendares River, separating Vedado and Miramar, broadens as it passes through the park. The river shapes the linear park into a rich, green area. Although somewhat difficult to reach, the eastern shore of Havana Bay constitutes another green area and park. Just across the bay lies the Morro-Cabaña Castles, whose grounds afford a striking view of the old city.[8] The creation of the Greenbelt around Havana, begun in the late 1960s (see Chapters 3 and 4), also provides an abundant "green" perimeter around the metropolitan area. Green spaces at the city edge can be reached from downtown Havana (Capitolio building) within 30–45 minutes of driving time (fig. 8.9).

Perhaps the most striking and internationally recognized profiles of Havana includes those paintings, drawings, and photographs that show the Malecón in the foreground and El Morro Castle in the background. To the north of this vista are the tropical waters of the Straits of Florida. The cultural and recreational importance of the Malecón (fig. 8.10) cannot be overstated, but it is important to note other natural lookout points. These points may be forgotten to *habaneros* who have a difficult time securing transportation during the Special Period, and few tourists seek out these vantage points. Nonetheless, the sites noted in fig. 8.11 afford panoramic vistas of the "Pearl of the Antilles."

8. Unfortunately, the bay is one of the ten most polluted bodies of water in the world, according to the UNDP. An oil refinery on the shore dumped 54 tons of hydrocarbons there in 1993 alone (Napoles 1996d).

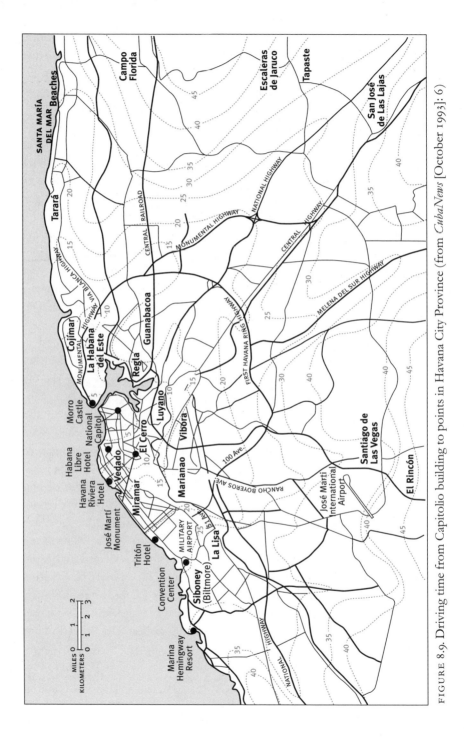

FIGURE 8.9. Driving time from Capitolio building to points in Havana City Province (from *CubaNews* [October 1993]: 6)

FIGURE 8.10. The Malecón, Havana's "social living room" and seaside promenade, with its rhythmic line of *portales* (colonnades), the heart of Centro Habana in the background (Photograph by Roberto Segre)

As we briefly mentioned earlier, a celebrated green space in the heart of the city is Coppelia ice cream parlor at the corner of L and Twenty-third Streets, which represents central aspects of the revolution. Its symbolism is key because the parlor sits under a huge lightweight concrete structure of modern design. Cuba imported some of its ice cream from the U.S. mainland prior to the revolution, and Howard Johnson's, with its 28 flavors, was allegedly the brand of choice. Since the imposition of the embargo, a number of products underwent production in Cuba, and ice cream was no exception. *Helados* (ice cream) *Coppelia* has earned international acclaim on a par with Italian *gelati* and Philippine ice cream (Curtis 1993). Because the city block occupied by Coppelia is thickly canopied by trees, it is an important place of socialization for Cubans. Open from about 11 A.M. until 2 A.M., the ice cream parlor attracts some thousands of visitors daily, most of them *habaneros.*

Coppelia serves as a public space, town square, and point of encounter for what used to be commonly referred to as the revolution's *hombre integrado* (new, integrated person). Occupying the center of the block is a two-story restaurant. The facility functions as the typical stand or kiosk one might find in other Latin American plazas. However, this plaza is different, for unlike the

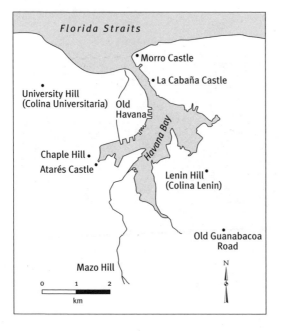

FIGURE 8.11.
Natural lookout points for
panoramic views of Havana

Plaza de Armas or Plaza de la Catedral, present or former institutions of importance (e.g., those of the civil government or the Roman Catholic Church) are absent. Like public spaces in other socialist countries, it is designed to place greater importance on public rather than private or religious interaction (French and Hamilton 1979). In many ways, it is the ultimate democratic ice cream emporium because of the social groups drawn there. Here gather diehard government officials, soldiers, and other *compañeros* of the revolution, as well as *jineteros* (black marketers), high school and college students, and a small concentration of homosexuals who have staked out the park as gathering point for that city's minority. This last image provides the backdrop of the opening scene of Gutiérrez Alea's 1993 film *Strawberries and Chocolate* (*Fresas y Chocolate*). Coppelia, with its steady line (*cola*) of people waiting for ice cream, is, in the words of Curtis (1993, 67), "a social leveler in that everyone must wait his or her respective turn in the ice cream line." But this had changed by the late 1990s: foreigners paying in dollars get quick access to the premises; service is less efficient, and fewer flavors are available; and kiosks selling to people who do not think an ice cream cone is worthy of a long wait are visually disturbing the gardens and pedestrian paths.

Originally built in 1966 on the site of a former hospital, Parque Coppelia is located in the heart of the La Rampa district in Vedado, an important transportation node for the city's buses and taxis that sweep down to the Malecón and to points beyond. The park is surrounded by hotels, airline offices, cafés, cinemas, and government and international agencies. The city block's deep, cool verdant interiors allow for pedestrian circulation to adjacent streets. Even during the Special Period, when many services in Havana have been cut back, the Coppelia (also a brand name) ice cream parlors have managed to provide service at prices (in Cuban pesos) still within reach of *habaneros*.

Havana also possesses a broad array of cultural attractions that are free or very low cost. A survey in 1992 identified some 262 cultural attractions, including theaters (18), movie houses (80), cultural centers (26), art galleries (29), museums (37), and libraries (25) (Poder Popular n.d.). The Special Period closed many of these facilities in the early 1990s, but by 1996 the network of cultural attractions was returning to normalcy. The decrease in movie theaters, related to the availability of films but also to costly repairs needed in many buildings, has been somewhat offset by a program opening new smaller video halls.

Sports installations in Havana were from the outset of the revolution closely bound to existing recreational facilities. The Castro government aspired to achieve world-class status in sports, an objective that has been achieved in regional, international, and Olympic competition. Multiple specialized sports facilities in Havana and throughout the island were required to maintain that level of athletic performance. In the 1960s, the revolution took advantage of the sports complexes "inherited" in the form of "clubs" (Círculos Sociales Obreros [CSOS]) along the coast and in the Ciudad Deportiva (Sports City). But the CSOS dropped from seventeen in 1994 to twelve in 1999.

In the 1970s, several sports complexes were scheduled to be built in municipalities that had never had these kinds of facilities. In doing so, the revolution aimed to provide the same possibilities to all neighborhoods in Havana. Pools and gymnasiums were built in Guanabacoa, San Miguel del Padrón, La Lisa, Arroyo Naranjo, and Diez de Octubre. A few major projects, such as the Sala Polivalente in San José de las Lajas, were constructed in rural Havana. Perhaps the greatest efforts, though, were directed to the Pan American Games in 1991. Olympic stadiums, pools, tennis courts, and other sports facilities were built along the coast of Habana del Este and Alamar. These sports complexes were carefully integrated with the living quarters and services at the Villa Panamericana, which was the last major public housing com-

plex built before the current crisis. By 1992, the city contained 1,206 sport facilities with a seating capacity for 167,000 spectators (Poder Popular n.d.).

Cuba's Special Period has created not only many unanswered economic
questions but also spiritual ones. Therefore, many Cubans have turned to different churches for solace. Although religious expression was never completely outlawed during the revolution, it contracted greatly in the first three
decades of the revolution and was frowned on in revolutionary circles. As
Malone describes it: "Harassment of believers at school and limited access to
higher education have been the most common complaints. In the past, Cuban
children were officially discouraged from believing in God and even mocked
for confessing their faith" (1996, 5). This gradually changed, especially when
Christians were admitted to the Communist Party.

In 1992 and 1993, the Bible was the best-selling title at the Book Fair in Havana. Numerous Protestant denominations are flourishing and, according to
one estimate noted in the *Miami Herald*, may include 18 percent of the Cuban
population. Numerous *casas de culto* (house churches) have been established in
Havana in recent years and are "overflowing with new members" (Malone
1996, 8). Both the Cuban Communist Party and Protestant, Roman Catholic,
and other churches seem to be working toward greater accommodation of
each other. The visit of Pope John Paul II to Cuba in January 1998 also set
about some changes. The pope celebrated a giant mass at the Revolution
Square, and a huge paper billboard with the Sacred Heart covered the same
facade of the National Library where Marx or Lenin was often depicted in the
past. And even though the celebration of Christmas was allowed as a holiday
because of the visit of the pope, it has continued since 1998.

## Whither Social Functions in the Antillean Pearl?

Both residents and tourists highly value the social functions of Havana. The
skyline of Havana has changed little since the highlights of 1958. Unlike other
Latin American cities that display a system of symbols in the built environment such as modern high-rises, giant shopping centers, banks, insurance
companies, luxury hotels, and upscale condominiums, Havana's exterior is
much more modest. In the latter half of the twentieth century and the beginning of the twenty-first, Havana has given priority to indispensable social
functions. Instead of disrupting the built form with commercial and civil
monuments, continuity has prevailed. And instead of abusing resources, the

asceticism of a population that dreamed of the dawn of a real egalitarian society has endured (Loomis 1994).

It is clear today that the disruption of the city's economic base has made reality markedly different from some socialist goals. Social functions that are free of charge—sports, outdoor recreation, and religious practice—have taken on new meanings during the Special Period. Two facets of Havana—one before and the other after the 1959 revolution—are clearly stamped on the city's network of social services. The capital city possesses a large stock of historic buildings, hospitals, clinics, universities and schools, parks, and recreational facilities. Not only is its allure unmatched elsewhere on the island, but its social functions are also unique among major world cities. Perhaps the greatest challenge will be maintaining these amenities before they deteriorate further and preventing new ones from breaking up the built and social fabrics of the city.

# 9

# Habana Vieja
## Pearl of the Caribbean

In the back [of the house] is the carriage entrance, small and shaded. In the front, golden-brown brilliance. A floor of broken tile, stained by unmemorable filth. The patio as if it had just been hosed down. Invisible freshness, unexpected clarity.

—Antón Arrufat, 1981

## Shaping the Urban Roots

The handful of men who accompanied Diego Velázquez could have hardly imagined that the tiny *villa* of Havana would someday be so dramatically transformed. From the time of its settlement on November 16, 1519, Havana has shone against its Antillean landscape and has witnessed crucial events in the Americas and the entire world (Segre 1994a). Havana would form part of the illusory utopian dream of Thomas Moore and would be the first example of an attempt to build a new socialism in the Western Hemisphere. Poets have praised its luminous aura and diaphanous sky (Arrufat 1981): José Lezama Lima, Alejo Carpentier, and Italo Calvino. In what Carpentier (1969) has called the "will of men," Havana's personality has been molded by the sea, hills, and palm groves and by what Alvarez Tabío (2000, 153) describes as being transformed in columns, streets, and squares and a symbiosis of classic and natural order. Over time, Havana has been shaped by a dialectic of geometric abstraction at one extreme and the persistence of an incredible island landscape at the other (Carpentier 1970, 1974a, 1974b). Christopher Columbus eulogized the island: "The Admiral has never seen a more lovely place, full of trees clustered along the river, green and beautiful, so different from our own" (Pichardo 1965). As with other Latin American cities, it is difficult

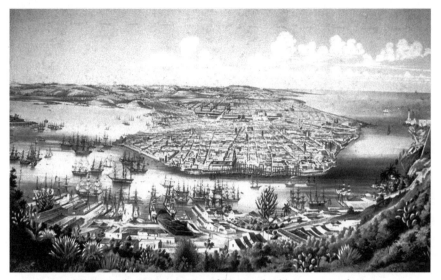

FIGURE 9.1. Nineteenth-century image of Havana looking westward, as seen from the vicinity of what is today Lenin Hill. Regla is in the foreground; El Morro Castle and lighthouse, at the entrance of the bay (right, middle); Old Havana, in midsection followed by Centro Habana; sparsely settled Vedado, just before horizon.

to separate the city from its adjacent physical environment; Buenos Aires from the expansive Pampa; Rio de Janeiro from Corcovado and Sugarloaf Mountain; Caracas from the Avila Valley; Santiago de Chile from the towering Andes; and Havana from its deep and protected bay, which long ago held transparent waters (Segre 1984, 1985a) (fig. 9.1).

Throughout most of its history, government officials, soldiers and sailors, slaves, and merchants circulated throughout Havana's port area, giving the colonial streets and plazas of the port city a clamorous ambience (Sapieha 1990). Thus, Havana was unlike the typical provincial and introverted urban centers found throughout Latin America. The ebb and flow of world travelers ensured that Cuba's main port would not remain a sleepy backwater (Mediz Bolio 1916). Havana's exuberance reached its annual hiatus with the celebration of pre-Lenten carnival each year. The festivity played an essential role in the life of the city because of its changing roles, ambiguous functions, and interjections of new ideas into Havana's culture (Hernández Busto 1992). In the colonial areas, carnival was a time of "psychological liberation" for the slaves. In the revolutionary period, carnival symbolizes the liberation from everyday harshness, as it was moved from February to July so as not interrupt the sugar harvest.

Churches and convents proliferated in the old city, including Santa Clara, Santo Domingo, San Francisco, Santa Catalina, Paula, and La Merced. These were massive inward-looking structures that housed Havana's religious, educational, and public health functions, not to mention some of the wealthiest women in the city. Despite this clearly defined concentration of wealth and architectural symbolism of power, spatial segregation did not prevail. Lezama Lima's (1970, 1988) poetic description of street life filled with plantation owners, slaves, artisans, nuns, merchants, and prostitutes is laced throughout his book *Paradiso* (Paradise). These characters, in his words, gave Havana "an enchanting diversity of minstrels," especially during the pre-Lenten celebrations, carnival, and religious processions and at city markets.

In the second half of the eighteenth century, the city confronted an urban design issue: while neoclassicism was substituting baroque in Europe, Havana grappled with a search of its own style and design (Fernández Miranda 1985). One response was to introduce subtle decorative details into its classical compositions, provoking José Lezama Lima to remark: "that Baroque of ours . . . so firmly friendly to the Enlightenment [of Charles III]" (1988, 494).

The portrait of Havana evident in the Cuban writer Alejo Carpentier's classic book *El siglo de las luces* (The century of lights) joins together three features of colonial Havana. One is the semiregular medieval layout of its narrow labyrinth of streets that alternate with the crisp geometry of the town's renaissance squares. Adorning the squares are the delicate palaces, with their faintly colored doors and windows. A rhythmic sequence of arcades and exterior porticoes as well as shaded courtyards lighten the look of these buildings (fig. 9.2). Shaded courtyards also characterized the formal and spatial continuity of the baroque.

A second feature is the symbiosis among social groups and functions as shown by slaves and colonial masters residing in the same dwelling and rubbing elbows in the same public spaces. The elite residences, called *casa almacén* (warehouse mansion), contained merchandise, such as sacks of sugar or coffee, on the ground floor. Slaves or the administrative quarters were placed on the mezzanine, almost always with low ceilings and engulfed by the double-height porticoed gallery surrounding the central court. The head of the household and his family lived on the *piano nobile* (upper floor; see also Chap-

FIGURE 9.2. Rhythmic sequence of arcades and porticoes facing Plaza Vieja
(Photograph by Roberto Segre)

ter 2). The Havana *casa almacén* combined the home and the workplace and
established a nexus between baroque style and the medieval inheritance of
multifunctional urban space. Havana's special town design fused together different races and social classes (Llanes 1999; García Santana 1999).

A third feature was the concentration of wealth along Havana's narrow
streets. A number of buildings remain from that era, including the mansions
of the Spanish nobility.[1]

Local aristocrats and officials from the Spanish Crown aimed to transform
the precarious image of the city, which for more than two centuries lacked any
sort of monumental center (Venegas and Núñez Jiménez 1986). The governor, the marqués de la Torre, ordered a design for a main town square (Plaza
Mayor) in 1773. The design was targeted for the space occupied by the Plaza
de Armas. It enlisted a continuous stretch of galleries and uniform palaces
surrounding the square in a classical rectangular design that symbolized political power (Sánchez Agusti 1984). Despite the governor's best intentions, the
colonial government carried out only two projects. One was the Captain General's Palace, and the other was the post office (Segundo Cabo). Both buildings served as a model for integrating buildings with the adjacent urban setting, which was characteristic of modern urban baroque. What came to be

1. These include, among others, the conde (count) de Casa Bayona, conde de Casa Barreto,
conde de San Juan de Jaruco, marqués (marquis) de Arcos, marqués de Aguas Claras, and marqués de la Obrapía (Martín Calvo de la Puerta) (Martín Zequeira and Rodríguez Fernández 1993,
1998).

known as "environmental Caribbean syncretism" (Segre 1993) would define the uniqueness of this historic core and would mature and constantly blend artistic and cultural aspects of Havana's built environment.

## The Defining Limits of the Stone Wall

In 1982, Havana joined a select group of world cities that UNESCO declared World Heritage Sites of Humanity (Mahtar M'Bow 1983). It was characterized as a historic center that formed part of a larger metropolitan area (Hardoy and Gutman 1992), and the UN appellation set the spatial limits of the historic district. This included the entire area within the walled city, the network of forts throughout Havana, and the segment of Las Murallas neighborhood that was built during the latter half of the nineteenth century (Hart 1982). To some, this delineation was restrictive because it relied on questionable assumptions about urban culture. Argan (1983), for instance, argues that historic districts often fail to consider three key questions. First, is the mature and expressive period of a city confined only to an ancient relic? Second, do formal and functional attributes of a complex metropolis characterize the traditional core? Last, at what point is there both a qualitative and quantitative break between the historic center and modern city? The UNESCO delineation of Havana's World Heritage Site is too narrow, and the 143 hectares of the old walled center could be easily extended to 1,000 or even 2,000.

Clearly, Havana's historic skyline took shape during the nineteenth century under the architectural and urban-design canons of neoclassicism (see Chapters 1 and 2). It evolved during the early decades of the twentieth century under the figurative and unitary elements of eclectic codes. Despite the encroachment of the modern movement in the city skyline, there appears to be continuity between colonial symbolism (Weiss 1973) and the change of scale and style (Noever 1996). In other words, it makes little sense to speak about a colonial city in Havana in a temporal sense, because time has not been the sole defining feature of the city's old "look." Most Latin American cities, for example, began their republican phase of building construction in the 1820s; clearly, Havana did not (Martín Zequeira and Múscar 1992).

The artificial delineation of UNESCO's historic district beyond where the old city walls stood masks the fact that this area had been incrementally built and blended into the old core area since the late eighteenth century. It is noteworthy that, just as it took many years to complete the wall, the authorities strung out its demolition over many decades. This piecemeal approach deterred major abrupt changes from creeping into the skyline. Another important fact that promised a uniform skyline was a series of building codes and land-use regulations that ensured uniformity in building construction in eighteenth- and nineteenth-century Havana. Thus, in terms of historical periods, the neighborhoods between Paseo del Prado and Infanta were developed before the settlement of the walled city was complete, serving as the last link between old and new Havana (Segre and Baroni 1998).

The timing of urban planning laws and public intervention in Havana made it difficult to alter radically the crowded density of the walled city. The marqués de la Torre, besides his project for the Plaza de Armas, laid out one of the first main boulevards outside the walled city. Originally called the Alameda de Extramuros, this public work was later named Paseo de Isabel II, Paseo del Prado, and ultimately Paseo de Martí. Havana grew from about a hundred thousand inhabitants in 1800 to nearly a quarter of a million by the end of the century. This population pressure forced city governments to focus on a different scale of urban development. Accordingly, between 1818 and 1862, the Urban Planning Laws (Ordenanzas Urbanas) regulated land use and building for new suburban districts (Fernández Simón 1995).

These neighborhoods had to follow the obligatory grid plan. Exceptions were made, however, in some instances. The new streets increased their width from the 6 meters that prevailed in Old Havana to 14 meters in the suburbs. Outlying neighborhoods also differentiated between traditional thoroughfares (*calzadas*) and new avenues, which were characterized by a continuation of portico-covered sidewalks for pedestrian use (Fernández Simón 1959; Préstamo 1995; Zardoya 1999). Urban growth toward the west increased the use of portico-lined roads of major importance located at five-block intervals: Prado, Galiano, Belascoaín, and Infanta. Although conceptualized and laid out in the nineteenth century merely as tree-lined paths, they would become major traffic arteries in the twentieth century.

As noted in Chapter 1, Governor Miguel Tacón began an impressive collection of public works projects between 1834 and 1838 (Chateloin 1989). The construction and expansion of roadways radically transformed Havana. The east-west axis of Reina–Carlos III and the perpendicular road of Paseo de Isabel II (El Prado) assumed social spaces of the highest prestige within the growing city. Projects such as these marked the first time that urban specialists, especially the engineer Mariano Carrillo de Albornoz (Weiss 1967) and local and foreign designers, craftsman, and artists, linked urban design and planning schemata with a concrete project. In 1863, the engineer Manuel Por-tilla undertook the development of a new neighborhood, Las Murallas (The Walls), which would feature large mansions and house about nine hundred residents. The sweeping scale of Havana's mid-nineteenth-century design eliminated much of the desire and need to enter the "old" city, especially given the expanding road network. Municipal architect Saturnino García pro-posed the creation of Serrano Avenue in 1862 to join the port with Príncipe Castle. Authorities destroyed buildings between Obispo and O'Reilly Streets to make way for the new road.

The cultural and aesthetic homogeneity of Havana's landscape is one rea-son why the UNESCO delineation of the historic district should have been broadened beyond Habana Vieja. As Carpentier described it: "A casual stroller can move beyond the port fortresses and walk toward the city's out-skirts, crossing the entire city center and passing along the old *calzadas* of Monte and Reina, and then beyond Cerro and Jesús del Monte *calzadas*, all the while following a continuous string of columns and archways, in which all types of columns are represented, joined, and blended seamlessly" (1982, 51; our translation).

Havana's nineteenth-century urban design reflected elements of the inter-national vanguard, despite internal debates between Spanish-born and Cre-oles and conflicts over various architectural codes and cultural fads of the day. These debates also surfaced in literature, poetry, music, and sculpture. Classi-cists and romantics competed with each other to show that their tastes were cosmopolitan and not strictly parochial. They wanted to show that nascent Cuban society was capable of critically adopting elements of modern design. Indeed, Cuba was not merely a static appendage of Spain (Sabbatini 1967). Elements of good taste and international style among the island's elite ap-peared in several forms: sculpture by the Italian Gaggini (the Lion's Fountain) and paintings by the Frenchman Vermay that adorn the Templete monument complemented the scientific thinking of Tomás Romay, the philosophers Félix Varela and José de la Luz y Caballero, and the literary works of Ger-trudis Gómez de Avellaneda, Domingo del Monte, and José María Heredia (Portuondo 1962; López Segrera 1989; Préstamo 1995).

The elite held social gatherings in the nineteenth century at splendid new *salones* that were adorned by neoclassical columns in the outlying neighbor-hood of Cerro. The great homes of the marquis of Pinar del Río, the country estate (*quinta*) of San José, and the home of the count of Fernandina were the scenes of "high culture" gatherings. Other buildings closer to the historic center of town also held such events: monumental structures (*palazzi*) along the "ring" beyond the old walls such as the Aldama Palace, the home of the marquis of Villalba, and that of the marquis of Balboa. Along the narrower streets of the walled city, we find a few palatial residences of this genre, including the homes of José Ricardo O'Farrill, Joaquín Ríos, Joaquín Gómez, and the marquis of the Royal Proclamation (Pereira 1994).

Another unifying factor of nineteenth-century Havana was the expansion of new services and land uses throughout the city. The constraints of the inner walled city as well as the precariousness of services there made it necessary to spread these services to points beyond. Cemeteries, hospitals, rest homes, markets, leper colonies, parishes, jails, and light industry accompanied Havana's expansion (Rallo 1964). Tobacco factories were scattered throughout Las Murallas neighborhood and precipitated interaction between workers and the elite in the city center (Ortiz 1963). The early introduction (1837) of the Havana-Bejucal railroad line, with the Villanueva station in Havana and its attendant roads and boulevards, firmly established a pattern of housing, workplaces, and services (Le Riverend 1965).

Modernization surfaced yet again in the far corners of nineteenth-century Havana with the construction of Concha railroad station in Marianao and Cristina station at the western edge of the city. Rail expansion into Havana's agricultural hinterland both facilitated the exporting of agricultural commodities and created a demand for port warehouses. For the first time, the southwestern shores of the bay could not accommodate this new growth, and warehouse construction sprang up across the bay in the once sleepy suburbs of Regla and Casablanca.

## Modernity's Symbiosis and Changing Morphogenesis

With the advent of the republic in 1902, which followed four years of U.S. intervention, the historic center of Havana remained the most prestigious corner of the city. Despite the new areas of expansion that attracted most nineteenth-century construction, many building projects also replaced structures in the old city. The nineteenth century witnessed the construction of roughly four hundred buildings in the old city, an amount comparable to all the new construction carried out during the previous two centuries (Capablanca 1982; Judget 1989). The scale of new construction was similar to that of existing buildings, with roughly the same height and building types, thereby ensuring the old city's sober, though sometimes irregular, grid pattern. Indeed, Havana's morphogenesis[2] was unprecedented in the city's history. Neoclassical and decorative refinement replaced the heavy walls and red-tile-covered colonial buildings. By that time the "city of red roofs" had disappeared, even though the colorful tiles characterized other Latin American city centers (Villanueva 1966).

Old Havana still held the aura of Spanish political power and contained the city's elegant shops, which were concentrated along O'Reilly and Obispo Streets (De Fuentes 1916). The historic core of Havana was also being equipped with modern infrastructure such as new sewage lines, water, telephone and telegraph lines, gas pipes, and the like. The Spanish-born who ruled Havana had concerned themselves with sources of fresh water to supply the Albear aqueduct. The U.S. Army occupation (1898–1902) improved the quality of the city life by increasing the frequency and coverage of waste removal as well as paving many streets. The U.S. Army Corps of Engineers expanded Havana's street lighting and telephone system, and replaced the mule-drawn trams with electric streetcars. Modernizing infrastructure in the city center was a strong "pull" factor that kept many elite from moving out to Cerro, a district that had deteriorated during the Independence Wars. Moreover, a modern core helped to prevent many wealthy people in the central area from moving out to lands opening up in Vedado. Consequently, at the beginning of the twentieth century, the new rich were located along the borders of the old city, such as the "ring" area defined by the walls just demolished in the second half of nineteenth century, and along Paseo del Prado. This tree-lined boulevard and pedestrian promenade included such spectacular residences as the homes of the members of Cuban high bourgeoisie: Marta Abreu; the president, José Miguel Gómez; Pedro Estévez and his new wife, Catalina Lasa. Nearby, along Mission Avenue, were built the mansions of Pérez de la Riva (sugar magnate), Conill (landowner), and Dionisio Velasco (Spanish merchant and owner of a drug store chain) (Venegas 1990; Martín Zequeira and Rodríguez Fernández 1993).

In the first two decades of the twentieth century, the image of the historic center changed dramatically. So profound were these changes that during the celebrations of the four hundredth anniversary of the founding of the city,

2. This term follows the usage by Jean Nouvel and Rem Koolhaas and others who use "morphogenesis" in architecture as a process in permanent transformation and renovation. See Rem Koolhaas and Bruce Mau, *Small, Medium, Large, Extra-Large*. New York: Monacelli Press, 1995, p. 928.

speakers commented on the hegemony of many "modern" buildings that "put an end to the melancholic hue of antiquity that Old Havana had . . . and [gave] it the look of a busy North American city" (*La Habana* 1919). Modern was better, and the United States was better still. Nearly forty buildings were constructed during this same period, including banks, office buildings, and warehouses (Llanes 1987). A construction boom stemmed from *peninsulares* who were concerned about losing their historic comparative advantage in Havana's economy, a massive infusion of U.S. capital, and the desire of a rising class of Cuban-born entrepreneurs to take advantage of this growing postcolonial economy. The built environment of Havana's center bore the mark of each of these new and competing business groups. New construction detracted from the aesthetic appeal of Habana Vieja. A new stock market (Lonja de Comercio, 1909) and a customhouse (Aduana del Puerto, 1914) developed along the waterfront.[3] Modernization and an open economy gave rise to new construction on the southern and western sides of the old city too: the train station, the shopping galleries of the Manzana de Gómez (1894–1917) building, and a series of new government administration buildings.

Increasing U.S. imports required support services and facilities in Havana. Ninety percent of U.S. products came through the port, and ample space was devoted to constructing corporate headquarters, warehouses, office buildings, banks, and facilities for related financial services. Some of the older housing stock and building regulations of Habana Vieja were eliminated in order to satisfy this need for suitable space. Although building heights legally could not exceed five stories, several ten-story structures broke through the city's sleepy skyline within the first decade of the republic. Tall new buildings stacked along the narrow colonial streets cast deep shadows like dark canyons across the old quarters. "Efficient" construction companies directed the city's modernization efforts: Purdy and Henderson, Snare and Triest, and Krajewski Pesant were among the important firms. Prestigious architects from the island and abroad also lent a hand: Rafecas y Toñarely, Luis Dediot, José Toraya, Alberto de Castro, Walker and Gillette, Rafael Goyeneche, Moenck y Quintana, and Leonardo Morales figured in this prominent list (Weiss 1950). Because of these designers and builders, Havana assumed a bit of the eclectic look found in New York, Madrid, and Paris. Notable results of these modernization efforts are visible today: the Barraqué Building, Western

3. Both buildings underwent major restoration in 1995 with foreign financial aid as part of broad efforts to revitalize international commerce and selected renovations in Habana Vieja.

Union, the Metropolitana Building, Banco Nacional de Cuba, Royal Bank of Canada, the National City Bank of New York, the Frank Robins Company Building, Banco Mendoza, Banco Pedroso, and Droguería (Pharmacy) Johnson. In tandem with commercial construction arose middle-class apartment buildings and the hotels Ambos Mundos, Cueto, and Lafayette.

What impact did this new construction have on the urban fabric of the colonial city? Although the designs were radically different, they did not diminish the sober monumentality of the old city's columns, porticoes, cornices, and friezes. The canonical use of classic styles coupled with the adoption of free forms of design coming from the United States gave a unique quality to the new construction. In addition, the use of costly building materials such as precious woods, marble and granite, and sophisticated ironwork accented the new craftsmanship inherent in the designs.

Demolitions in Habana Vieja did not always target structures lacking historical and architectural value. Since the 1920s, several organizations monitored urban "revitalization" efforts in the old city. The School of Engineering and Architecture at the University of Havana, certain parts of the press, and professional associations often spoke out when particular projects threatened the city's cultural heritage. For example, the architects Emilio de Soto, Félix Cabarrocas, Pedro Martínez Inclán, and Luis Bay Sevilla lashed out against the speculators Zaldo and Salmón. Real estate investors destroyed the Santo Domingo Convent at the site of the first university in the city. In its place rose banal and nondescript office buildings in the 1950s. This same group of architects spoke out against the first (and useless) heliport of the city. Other atrocities occurred, such as the demolition of Santa Catalina de Siena Convent in order to make way for a bank. As the spire crumbled atop the old Tacón jail, designs were under way to build the Palace of Justice (designed by Luis Bay Sevilla), the artillery school, and the Vapor and Colón markets.

Fortunately, Santa Clara Convent was saved (even though it was turned into the Ministry of Public Works headquarters), thanks to the "Protest of the Thirteen."[4] City officials sold off the area occupied by the old Tacón jail in a public auction, just as was done with the San Francisco Convent (which served as the main post office). Old structures such as these fell into disrepair and eventually deteriorated. Greed on the part of municipal authorities may account for the deterioration of other public spaces. At least three major de-

---

4. This group consisted of intellectuals headed by Rubén Martínez Villena, who in 1923 had also denounced the corrupt practices of governments in power (Le Riverend 1966).

FIGURE 9.3. The underground parking garage at Plaza Vieja as it looked until its demolition in 1995 (Photograph by Roberto Segre)

sign and planning calamities remained indelibly marked in Havana's historic center: the underground parking garage beneath Plaza Vieja (figs. 9.3 and 9.4), which altered the scale of the square by raising it 1 meter above street level (demolished in 1995 by order of Eusebio Leal Spengler, city historian); the neocolonial fortress of the National Police on land of the artillery school; and the apartment buildings constructed next to the cathedral.

The dream of a modern Antillean metropolis preoccupied the government of Gerardo Machado (1925–33). Havana would have its historic district transformed to meet this objective, and the plan of J. C. N. Forestier was pivotal in this regard. Forestier's plan included landscape modification such as lining Teniente Rey Street with palm trees to enhance the view of the Capitolio building, but that project was never implemented. However, authorities restored buildings around the Plaza de Armas and Plaza de la Catedral.

Authorities used historic preservation techniques as envisioned by Eugene Emmanuel Viollet-le-Duc. The search for natural building materials, as postulated by John Ruskin, and the persistence of a classical design ran counter to the natural image of Havana's classic landmarks. For example, resurfacing many old buildings with cement and colored whitewashes covered the fragile seashell-embedded limestone walls. Architects Evelio Govantes and Félix

FIGURE 9.4.
Top of Plaza Vieja's parking garage, 1993. The elevated, treeless, flat slab of concrete on top of the garage served as the new "plaza" after the parking garage was installed in the early 1950s, and it remained until 1995. In this 1993 photograph, neighborhood children are using it for a baseball game. (Photograph by Joseph L. Scarpaci)

Cabarrocas restored the Templete monument on the Plaza de Armas in 1928–30 as well as adjacent mansions (Hernández, Lores, and Méndez 1990). Their work highlighted the stark and sober gray walls, which contrasted with the traditional color schema of the city, as described by historians and chroniclers and as painted by René Portocarrero and Amelia Peláez. Enrique Gil and Luis Bay Sevilla used a similar approach in their restorations of the homes belonging to the count of Casa Bayona and the marqués de Arcos on the Plaza de la Catedral. Taken in its entirety, this concept lent a certain mystery to the history and environment of the colonial city (Capablanca 1982; Cirules 1993; Cohen 1991). Prestigious specialists of the era such as Manuel Pérez Beato (1946) and Pedro Martínez Inclán challenged these restoration efforts. They argued that such interventions violated a major premise of historic architecture: "restore a painting by not painting; restore a sculpture without sculpting; and restore a building without building" (Martínez Inclán 1946).

Despite the bustle of building construction and minor restoration projects during the first decades of the twentieth century, a progressive deterioration of the historic center was visible by the 1930s. Hardly any conservation or restoration had taken place. Colonial buildings were in poor condition. This trend reversed slightly in the 1940s and 1950s because of the efforts of philanthropists, artists, journalists, historians, and architects. Headed by the official city historian Emilio Roig de Leuchsenring (1889–1964)—an indefatigable defender of historic preservation—a team of scholars and celebrities fought to preserve the old city.[5]

In 1928, during the Second Municipal Conference (Segundo Congreso de Municipios), the Plaza de Armas and the Plaza de la Catedral were declared National Historic Monuments. The constitution of 1940 displayed a progressive streak by promulgating Article 58, which referred to the preservation of cultural and artistic heritage sites such as national monuments and landmarks. That same year the mayor approved Roig de Leuchsenring's creation of the Commission on Landmarks, Buildings, Historic Places.

Professional organizations that brought together the youthful vanguard gave new impetus to the preservation of colonial architecture. Pedro Martínez Inclán created the professional forum Patronato Pro-Urbanismo (Urban Patronage) in 1942 and developed courses in Urban Studies within the School of Architecture at the University of Havana. The Urban Studies track examined the design and cultural components of the plazas of Havana. The journal *Arquitectura* published by the Institute of Architects of Havana Province (Colegio Provincial de Arquitectos) published articles almost monthly by Latin American historians and preservationists.[6] These works greatly influenced generations of Cuban architects and planners (Gutiérrez 1992).

The transformation of Havana's commercial base did not alter the essence of the historic core in the early twentieth century. Although modern department stores opened in Centro Habana and offices, hotels, and government buildings gradually moved out to Vedado, Habana Vieja kept its dynamism and multiple land uses. It maintained its rich colonial stock of buildings and di-

5. This cadre of luminous figures, which included Emilio Vasconcelos, Joaquín Weiss, José Bens Arrarte, Domingo Ravenet, Juan José Sicre, Luis Bay Sevilla, and Pedro Martínez Inclán, among others, sought to save the historic city. A force of younger activists also joined the preservationist movement, including Eugenio Batista, Mario Romañach, Nicolás Quintana, Emilio de Junco, Ricardo Porro, Reynaldo Estévez, and Manuel de Tapia Ruano.

6. Contributors included many well-known professionals such as the German Dominican Erwin Walter Palm, the Peruvian Emilo Hart-Terré, and Argentines Angel Guido and Mario Buschiazzo.

versity of social classes, which in literary terms has been depicted by Cuban writers. Lezama Lima, for instance, presents the nuances and character of streets and places that come with a longstanding familiarity with the place (Alvarez Tabío 2000), while the works of Guillermo Cabrera Infante, especially *Tres tristes tigres* (*Three Trapped Tigers*) and *La Habana para un Infante difunto*, highlight the decadent and superficial aspects of rejected Havana Vieja, surpassed in the twentieth century by Vedado (Damade 1994).

Havana took on several contrasting realities. The dock areas had bars and small cafés along San Pedro and Desamparados as well as nightclubs for prostitutes and sailors. In the southern part of Old Havana—Merced, Paula, San Isidro Streets—lay the crowded quarters of poor laborers. Old mansions converted into *ciudadelas* clustered around the small town squares (*plazoletas*) of Belén and El Cristo. Ethnic neighborhoods (composed of Turks, Poles, and Arabs, Jews, and others) were concentrated around the retail and wholesale district of Muralla, Teniente Rey, Luz, and Sol Streets. Amid these very different neighborhoods of Habana Vieja survived the elegant shops on Obispo and O'Reilly Streets. These were located next to banks and offices and frequented perhaps more by intellectuals and waning aristocrats than by the new bourgeoisie, who were too far removed in their protected suburbs. This part of the city was characterized by noise and bitter smells from the stoves of local residents that had survived since the time when Baron von Humboldt described Havana nearly a century before (Alvarez Tabío 1994a; Seguí 1994).

In the 1940s and 1950s Habana Vieja continued as a meeting place and a place of surprise, pleasure, tourists, Hollywood stars, and artists who mixed with drug traffickers, gamblers, pimps, prostitutes, bohemians, and working-class families. This potpourri of colorful characters formed part of the literary recreations by Severo Sarduy (1967). Celebrities helped give the old city its cosmopolitan flavor. For example, Graham Greene and Ernest Hemingway frequented the Ambos Mundos hotel for brief "encounters" and consumed the celebrated local drinks *mojitos* and daiquiris at the Bodeguita del Medio and Floridita restaurants. This depiction of the old city as a place of incredible street life and a wide cast of characters forms part of the "human" scale that the writer Lezama Lima portrays in his silent characters who wander through the narrow streets slowly and enigmatically.

By midcentury, the Habana Vieja of the past had changed considerably. Its characteristic form, carved out by the distinct shapes of its military architecture and exclusionary social spaces of iron, wood, and crystal, was in decline.

In its place stood long shaded streets that gave refuge from a menacing world beyond where the old walls stood. Buicks and Cadillacs, neon signs and night-clubs, casinos, and beaches, all of which expressed another side of the city, circulated through Habana Vieja. Areas of Havana's "rum and sun" scene, cheap sex, and the faraway nightclub Tropicana were dominated by repression and corrupt police terror. Law enforcement waited at the beck and call of politicians and members of organized crime. As discussed in Chapters 2 and 3, the 1950s were replete with contradictions. Havana had become a time bomb whose imminent explosion would chart a new history that would destroy an immediate past in order to search for a renewed future (Fornet 1967; Chaline 1987; Damade 1994).

## Salvation and Amnesia of the Past

Images of Havana in the 1950s, sensationalized by travel agencies and the unforgettable last scene of *Godfather II* with Al Pacino, would be replaced with revolutionary values. These included, perhaps, an overvaluing of manual labor and a desire to compensate those who had suffered hardship and sacrificed under the Batista dictatorship. During the period of revolutionary insurrection (1957–58), Cuba was clearly a highly segregated nation. Magazines and the social pages of daily newspapers carried pictures of cocktail parties, receptions, balls, and dances, drama that was remote from the lives of most Cubans. The massive presence of U.S. tourists and businessmen also portrayed a different view of Cuban reality.

The revolution was going to create a "new" man (to paraphrase Che Guevara), whose place would not be in the cities of Cuba but instead in the countryside and mountains where the struggle for freedom was forged (Lagache 1992; Cabrera Infante 1994). With the benefit of hindsight, viewing Cuba as a schism between city and countryside oversimplified the complexity of social classes and was reductionist. Equally complex was the cultural and economic makeup of the city. Thus, a "ruralist" planning perspective (Baroni 1989) would, in the end, provide little benefit to Havana and its residents.

The inherent features of the formerly walled old city were not promising for a modern city. In the early 1960s, approximately 70,000 residents were crowded into a mere 142.5 hectares laid out in 180 city blocks. As a result, Habana Vieja had a population density ranging from 500 to 1,000 persons per hectare in the early 1980s (Capablanca 1982). In the mid-1990s, planners estimated that about 80,000 residents currently lived there when, ideally, the area should only house about half that number. Crowding is a major problem, and the population density of Habana Vieja is one of the highest in all of Latin America.

At the time of the revolution, only 500 out of roughly 3,000 buildings were in good condition. Of that total, 900 possessed historical value. In the 1950s, 131 buildings had been transformed into ruinous *ciudadelas* (Fernández 1990). The precarious housing conditions carried over well into the late 1970s, when several water-related epidemics arose in the area. Although at one time Habana Vieja had a water supply system that was so sophisticated that it had earned a prize at the World Exposition in Paris in 1889, a lack of maintenance and an excessively large consumer population had rendered the system problematic. In addition, systems of gas, electricity, sewage, and other infrastructure had not been adequately upgraded or maintained during the republican period (1902–58). Public and private motor transport choked the narrow streets of the colonial core. Residents of Habana Vieja had low levels of formal education: 57 percent had graduated from primary school, 40 percent from high school, and 3 percent had some postsecondary training. Black Cubans were in the majority, and they suffered from high unemployment (Judget 1989). With the exception of a few projects already noted, there were no historic restoration plans for buildings in the old city (Segre 1985b). Moreover, the overcrowded buildings housed low-income residents as well as private and public enterprises that invested little in building maintenance. The "natural" deterioration of these structures was aggravated by the annual torrential rains and tropical storms.

Soon after the nationalization of large companies and U.S. banks (1960), the severance of diplomatic relations with the United States (1961), and the beginning of the U.S. blockade against Cuba, the life of the city—especially the center—began declining quickly. The shelves of merchandise in department stores along the popular streets of Muralla and Teniente Rey became bare, as did those of the more elegant stores on Obispo and O'Reilly. Vacancy rates in office buildings increased, and branch offices of internationally renowned banks began closing. Tourism ended abruptly, and only La Bodeguita del Medio, El Patio, and the Floridita restaurants survived; today they are frequented by tourists and those few Cubans with dollars (Paolini 1994).

Erroneous economic decisions also aggravated the deterioration of the historic center. The so-called revolutionary offensive began in 1968 and marked the elimination of all private businesses. Like the historic center of many other Latin American cities (De Tercin 1989; Martín Zequeira and Múscar 1992), Habana Vieja had attracted a large percentage of self-employed merchants, artists, and painters, whose elimination had a negative effect on the historic center (Segre 1992a). Eliminating small entrepreneurs also coincided with a fight against the bureaucracy of city government (Garnier 1971, 1973), which remained in effect until the early 1990s.

For a short time in the late 1970s and early 1980s, Habana Vieja reactivated its functional role as the historic and artistic center (Rivero 1981). The memorable "Saturdays in the Plaza" entailed the authorized selling of artwork and handicrafts by talented artists in two improvised markets located in the Plaza de Armas and Plaza de la Catedral. Within a short time, however, the crafts fair was abruptly shut down by the government because of "illicit enrichment" on the part of the artists and craftspersons.[7] In 1993, in the old governor's summer home—Quinta de los Molinos—just below the University of Havana, the same artisan fair was reinstated. By 1996, street vendors of old books, popular art, and handicrafts had once again saturated the Plaza de Armas and the Plaza de la Catedral, though the activity at the latter site was later moved to the nearby Avenida del Puerto to clear the views of the cathedral, only to be partially replaced by tables covered by colorful umbrellas and filled with tourists while loud salsa music blasts through the plaza.[8]

At the same time, the demise of the old city meant a gradual loss in the old building trades, which, since colonial times, had achieved high levels of craftsmanship (Coyula 1991b). Not only did masons, stone cutters, carpenters, blacksmiths, and bricklayers disappear, but also a whole generation of young apprentices was interrupted, creating a huge gap in the transfer of traditional building techniques. The myth surrounding prefabrication—long considered to be a universal panacea—also surfaced in the historic core in the form of buildings with standardized designs such as schools and health clinics (De la Nuez 1991; Segre 1994a).

7. The shutdown of the crafts fair was reflected with biting humor in Gutiérrez Alea's film *Death of a Bureaucrat.*

8. It is generally believed that the merchandise in the 1990s is of lesser quality than in the previous era. In addition, in the 1970s and 1980s, there were few tourists in these markets, and the sales were almost entirely in pesos. In the 1990s, tourists were the main clients, and they paid in dollars.

## Dreaming of the Future Form of Habana Vieja

Urban and regional planning strategies worked in tandem to achieve their respective goals. As identified in Chapter 4, a clear manifestation of that coordination appeared in the 1968 Greenbelt plan (Plan del Cordón de La Habana), which had three goals. First, it sought to integrate *habaneros* into the agricultural push toward the unattained 1970 sugar-harvest goal of 10 million tons. Second, the Greenbelt would enable Havana to become self-sufficient in food (Gutelman 1967). Third, the new farm belt at the city's edge would absorb idle labor stemming from the drastic reduction in small businesses from the revolutionary offensive and clerical workers in the antibureaucracy campaign. Although the plan completed the construction of around thirty water reservoirs and several agricultural-worker settlements, few of the massive coffee and bean plantations survived, and only mango fruit orchards remain as witnesses to that effort. Priority given to rural productive infrastructure throughout Cuba at that time left few resources available for urban housing initiatives (Segre 1985b).

The housing shortage in the historic center forced the government to allow local residents to convert vacant stores into private residences. Such commercial-to-residential conversion was a radical measure that made it difficult to reactivate retail activity in the streets of the old city while also disrupting the look of the place. In the absence of building code enforcement, new occupants adapted these new spaces as they pleased, which many times resulted in radically changing the facade of buildings and arbitrarily replacing the original large transparent store windows with bricks and concrete blocks. At the same time, the high ceilings of the old residences made it possible for the new occupants to build a loft-style mezzanine (called *barbacoa*) to maximize the number of occupants per dwelling. However, the weight of these makeshift lofts and the furniture they held often weakened the load-bearing walls of these old structures. Makeshift partitions replaced the iron grillwork around the windows and distorted the exterior of these nineteenth-century buildings (Coyula 1985a, 1985b; Mathéy 1994).

The two master plans elaborated for Havana during the 1960s (see Chapter 4) did not make special reference to Habana Vieja (Casal and Sánchez 1984). Even though a good deal of attention was placed on the road network and industrial complexes at the city's edge, the plans revealed concern about returning to some of the roots of the historic center in a way that clearly emanated from the ideas of the Congrés Internationale d'Architecture Moderne (CIAM).

These master plans emphasized the role of the pedestrian and sought to revive functions of the city center that would include workplaces and local labor markets. Cultural activities also held a priority in the new plans, as did a concern over reducing population densities and increasing the amount of open spaces in Havana. In essence, these strategies sought to push the city beyond its original compact layout and toward a more dispersed metropolis. Without a doubt, though, the most significant proposal of the master plan regarding Habana Vieja focused on land use around the port and the elimination of the warehouses in order to open up the view of the bay from the old colonial streets (Padrón and Cuervo 1988).[9] In doing so, the port could still be modernized with container systems for sea-land transfer and break-in-bulk points. However, the new container facilities would lie in the back bay, to the south and east of the old city. The relocation of the warehouses and siting of the new container facilities would free up the original shoreline along the bay to accommodate the shipping of noncontainerized merchandise, the circulation of heavy vehicles along the waterfront, and the habitual disorder caused by the movement of ships, trains, and trucks. Most of this initiative, however, including plans for cleaning up the highly polluted bay, was postponed because of its high cost, and then later the progressive decline in public resources made the port's revitalization efforts virtually impossible.

It was not easy in the early years of the revolution to give a great deal of attention to architectural and historic preservation. Only Alejo Carpentier (1979), in his book *La consagración de la primavera*, saw the necessity within the revolution to restore colonial structures. A small team called the National Landmarks Commission formed within the National Council of Culture in 1963. Its charge was to develop a national plan for restoring Cuba's principal landmarks (López Castañeda 1971). Scant resources available for these endeavors led them to concentrate efforts around the Catedral, Armas, and San Francisco plazas because of their coherent and homogeneous nature. Of particular importance was increasing sensitivity about preserving the city's built cultural heritage. This was further strengthened through international connections Cuba began making with both Western and Eastern Europe during the 1960s and 1970s. Historic preservation and the safekeeping of national landmarks received great impetus after the dissemination of the 1964 Venice Charter (Carta de Venecia) and the 1965 meeting in Warsaw, Poland, of the

---

9. This was the vision of Martínez Inclán in the 1930s and the way the road running along Havana Bay and the eastern edge of the old city—Alameda de Paula—had existed originally.

International Commission on the Protection of Landmarks and Historic Places (López Casteñeda 1963; Rigol 1978).

The exodus of the Cuban bourgeoisie also meant some loss of the city's concern with urban architecture. A growing political class in Cuba consisting of the urban proletariat and farmers gave the revolution a pragmatic approach. City administration in Havana became more concerned about satisfying immediate needs and less about inheriting contaminated bourgeoisie values, including architectural ones. During the "hard years" (Sánchez 1989), the Department of Demolitions had more power in carrying out its annual goals than did those who tried to restore national landmarks. Sometimes local politicians and bureaucrats were more concerned about getting rid of a historic building (out of fear of collapse or squatter invasion) than restoring it. Such local sentiment ran against national-level attempts to implement strict guidelines on how to treat historic properties. On the one hand, the former Aldama Palace was restored to its original condition, a complicated task because it had been converted into a tobacco factory. On the other hand, the architectural integrity of the Segundo Cabo Palace on the Plaza de Armas — one of the best examples of Cuban colonial architecture — was marred by widening windows to accommodate air-conditioning units. Another insensitive modification occurred in 1995 with the Lonja de Comercio (stock market building). There, a modern steel structure clad in dark reflective glass was installed around the original cupola as part of a Spanish joint venture's efforts to convert the building into a modern office complex that contained a radio station, a foreign press office, and business offices (Villegas 2000, 158).

Despite its emphasis on technical studies, the School of Architecture at the University of Havana played an important role in the struggle to save the city's cultural heritage. Young professors and students of architectural history revived the writings and ideas of Joaquín Weiss and Pedro Martínez Inclán, which led them to study building restoration in Habana Vieja. In the 1970s, a team called the Architecture and Urban Studies Historic Research Group (Grupo de Investigaciones Históricas de la Arquitectura y el Urbanismo [GIHAU]), directed by Roberto Segre, organized a series of studies, including drawing the facades of every building in the old city. The idea to recuperate the city with drawings of streets and buildings was later developed by the architect Francisco Bedoya (a sort of Cuban Piranesi) in his re-creation of the colonial center. Moreover, images of some important buildings done by a team from the School of Architecture of Barcelona (1995), as well the images of a new guide of Havana (Curbelo Castellanos 1999), provided a visual template of what a revitalized city might look like.

## The Historic Roots Syndrome

The new socialist constitution of 1976 ushered in a new stage in the life of Cuban institutions. It greatly strengthened provincial and local powers. These new local institutions reduced the excessive and centralized powers of many government functions. Key elements of the 1940 constitution addressing historic districts were embraced. In 1977, the National Assembly of Poder Popular (People's Power) passed two executive laws that embraced the principles of the new constitution: the Cultural Heritage Protection Law and the National and Local Landmark Protection Law. Since 1978, the national legislation has protected fifty-seven historic urban centers, sites, and buildings throughout the country, including the seven original *villas* of Baracoa, Bayamo, Santiago de Cuba, Camagüey, Sancti Spíritus, Trinidad, and La Habana. Designations by UNESCO as World Heritage Sites include Old Havana (the originally walled precinct plus the nineteenth-century extension in Las Murallas district and the whole system of colonial fortresses annexed to the city [1982]); the colonial town of Trinidad and the Valle de los Ingenios (valley of the sugar mills [1988]); the castle of San Pedro de la Roca (El Morro in Santiago de Cuba) in 1997; the Viñales Valley in Pinar del Río (1999); and the ruins from 191 coffee farms in the eastern provinces of Guantánamo and Santiago de Cuba that were started by French farmers fleeing from the Haitian revolution in late eighteenth century (2000). In 1980, two entities were given direct responsibility for aspects in the old city: the National Center for Conservation, Restoration, and Museum Studies (Centro Nacional de Conservación, Restauración y Museología [CENCREM]), which is sponsored by the national Ministry of Culture; and the City Historian's Department of Architecture office, which is part of the City Museum and Havana's local government. Last, the Grupo para el Desarrollo Integral de la Capital was created in 1987 to strengthen a singular vision of the city.

Old Havana's master plan includes two levels of action: transforming the district's social and economic functions, and architectural and urban planning projects. An essential premise behind government actions is community participation and raising people's awareness about the cultural value of Habana

Vieja. Eusebio Leal, the city historian, has acted as a major catalyst in disseminating information about the city's rich history. At the same time, Leal has widely promoted the objectives and achievements of the historic restoration efforts within the old city. Headquartered in the Office of the City Historian, created in 1938 by Emilio Roig de Leuchsenring, Leal has the freedom and energy to intervene in the UNESCO-declared district, based on the statutes in Law 143-93, passed by the Council of State. In 1995, the Council of Ministers approved Accord 2951, which declared the historic center a zone of "Great Significance for Tourism" (Zona de Alta Significación para el Turismo) (Leal 1986, 1988). In the early 1990s, Leal created Habagüanex, a joint-venture for-profit firm.[10] Habagüanex attracts hard currency for historic preservation (Pattullo 1996, 192–194). The company brought in $4 million in the first year of operation (Luis 1995, 38). By using conferences, workshops, street fairs, mass media, and the City Museum, Leal educated both the local community and politicians about the value of Habana Vieja. Revitalization efforts have also counted on a blend of specialists who serve as technical advisers and local "sweat equity" by the residents. Combining local residents with outside experts ensures that gentrification will not displace the local population from its old housing stock. Although population displacement because of urban revitalization is common in other Latin American historic districts such as Old San Juan, Puerto Rico, it has been policy in Havana to avoid such outcomes.

The vision for reducing population densities in Habana Vieja relied on voluntary actions among residents who would be attracted by better living and work conditions elsewhere in the city (Capablanca 1982). Increasing jobs in Habana Vieja has benefited women, who have found employment in services, nonpolluting light industry, crafts, and artisan workshops. On the other side, the existing social problems of Habana Vieja, including lower levels of schooling, unemployment, crime, and delinquency, were not fully taken into account initially. Nevertheless, several social programs such as kindergartens, schools, old-age centers, pharmacies, and community centers have been spun

10. Habagüanex S.A. (whose corporate slogan in English is "The future world of Old Havana") is probably the most powerful state agency in the old city today. This new state firm seeks to generate hard currency through tourism and related services in Habana Vieja and then use those funds for historic preservation. Among its many tasks, the firm operates and manages a series of restaurants in and around the area including El Patio, La Mina, Hostal Valencia, Don Giovanni, La Zaragozana, Hanoi, La Torre de Marfil, Al Medina, Puerto de Sagua, and Castillo de Farnes. It also negotiates with foreign investors who wish to invest in Habana Vieja. See also Pattullo (1996).

off directly from the hard currency that Habagüanex generates (PNUD 2000). The extent to which the office can balance tourist demands, on the one hand, with the expectations of local residents, on the other hand, is a historic preservation challenge that many revitalized districts confront (Barthel 1996; Scarpaci 2000b).

Moreover, these social problems were especially aggravated by overcrowding, *solares*, and *cuarterías*. Pockets of these residents were not factored into redevelopment efforts, and they differed markedly from artists and intellectuals in the old quarters. Although these latter two groups formed an essential component in Eastern Europe, they did not automatically increase the standard of living in Habana Vieja. Planning directives also failed to implement measures to improve run-down housing gradually or provide relief for thousands of residents (fig. 9.5). With the benefit of hindsight, an incremental approach to housing improvement would have been more effective given the impossibility of completely restoring the entire historic district all at once.

State ownership of land and the disappearance of private property made it impossible for the costly restoration operation to be profitable. If other Latin American cities relied on investors who could recuperate their investment by charging higher rents once restoration was completed, comparable investments in Havana went into a "black hole" because issues of social justice and equity outweighed services, and rents paid by residents of restored buildings represented a minimal portion of real costs.

Resource availability from a variety of government agencies and local and foreign firms enabled the government to support financially various projects in the historic center. For example, the Spanish bank Grupo Argentaria financed the restoration of the Lonja de Comercio for renting office spaces at a cost of $13 million. Costa Line, an Italian shipping company, restored the customs piers for $35 million. Regularly scheduled ships leaving out of ports in Jamaica now bring tourists to Havana. The strengthening of tourism through hotels and restaurants and the location of cultural institutions in Habana Vieja helped to rejuvenate the old city partially (Fernández 1981; Heine 1991). Habana Vieja hosts a wide array of tourist attractions and government offices that bring a distinct vibrancy to these quarters.

What is the contemporary land use of the old city? In 1992, one of the authors directed a research project that documented the ground level land use of 4,747 buildings and lots in Habana Vieja. The purpose of the land-use survey, part of a larger comparative land-use study of eight other Latin historic inner-city neighborhoods, was to document land uses, building height, and

FIGURE 9.5.
Modern building in Habana Vieja. Modern buildings built in Habana Vieja during the revolution respected the low skyline of most buildings. The structures relied heavily on precise geometric features but still contrasted with the more traditional structures adjacent to them. This structure was built by a Microbrigade and serves as a family physician office and home. (Photograph by Joseph L. Scarpaci)

building conditions (Scarpaci forthcoming). Land uses included residences, parks, restaurants, and grocery stores (*bodegas*, in Havana), institutional buildings (government and religious), parks, parking garages or lots, and demolished or abandoned lots and buildings. Building height was measured by the number of floors and building condition by a curbside assignment of the facade and entrance (as "poor," "fair," and "good"). The 1992 survey of Habana Vieja found that three of four street-level land uses were residential, giving it a higher residential profile than either Montevideo or Buenos Aires (other cities in the study with more than one million inhabitants). The second defining land use was "institutional," attesting to Habana Vieja's large number of government buildings, offices, and, most of all, warehouses used for food and other goods. The small circulation of automobiles in Havana produces a low percentage of urban space devoted to garages and parking lots (fig. 9.6). In the old quarters, just 1 percent of the lots and buildings were used for parking (versus 5 percent in Buenos Aires and 3 percent each in Montevideo

FIGURE 9.6. Land uses in Old Havana, 1992 (Data from Scarpaci, fieldwork)

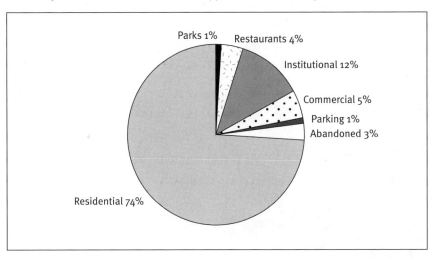

(Uruguay), Cuenca (Ecuador), and Santa Fé de Bogotá (Colombia). In short, these land uses characterize the highly pedestrian and residential nature of Habana Vieja, which seems to be frozen in time.

## Innovation and Tradition

Ambitious plans coming with Havana's designation as a World Heritage Site carried a hefty price tag. As a result, restoration efforts were initially confined to a few streets, plazas, buildings, and interiors of city blocks. In the 1980s, emphasis was placed on historic areas as opposed to building-specific projects that characterized the previous decade. A series of "development axes" guided restoration efforts. These axes centered on the streets of Oficios and Mercaderes and Obispo and O'Reilly as well as the plazas of Catedral, Armas, Cristo, and Vieja (figs. 9.7 and 9.8).

Until the 1980s, the predominant policy approach in historic preservation was the so-called passive one. This meant reviving, restoring, and recycling valuable old buildings, retaining the open spaces left by building demolitions in order to open the tightly packed center, and not building new structures. Key features of the passive policy approach were relaxed because of the need for social services and housing. New terms of the preservation debate cen-

FIGURE 9.7. New buildings in Old Havana. This apartment complex, designed by Emma Alvarez Tabío in the late 1980s, blends well with surrounding facades yet is clearly modern. (Photograph by Roberto Segre)

tered on aesthetic and design principles such as a "constructive management" policy of urban renewal (Hardoy and Gutman 1992).

The debate between the "old" and the "new," such as that which arose in the 1950s, resurfaced in the 1980s. State agencies represented the traditional "essentials" approach, which argued for a strict and faithful compliance with the formal and decorative features of the past. Some individuals favoring this position included Marta Arjona of the Cultural Heritage National Office, Antonio Núñez Jiménez of the National Commission of Landmarks (succeeded after his death by Arjona), and, at the beginning, Eusebio Leal. Embracing this strict adherence to past design required artisan and technical ability for the reproduction of complex details, which was often done with shabby "modern" materials. In this sense, forgotten were the teachings of the great Italian masters such as Franco Albini (in Cuba in the 1950s), Carlo Scarpa, and Ernesto N. Rogers.

On the other side, at the end of the eighties, city historian Leal and CENCREM (led by Isabel Rigol and Luis Lápidus, who died in 1995) tried to integrate some young architects of the "Generation of the 1980s," who pro-

FIGURE 9.8. Restored buildings on Calle Obispo, Habana Vieja (Photograph by Roberto Segre)

moted innovations and novel applications of formal codes of interior design and the filling in of empty lots with structures that blended harmoniously with their settings.[11] These young architects brought new ideas about the presence of modern architecture in the historical context. Evidence of their work is the project for the parking lot in Plaza Vieja done by Patricia Rodríguez Alomá and Felicia Chateloin; the hotel Cueto restoration by Emilio Castro; and the hotel Lancaster in Paseo del Prado by Oscar García and Teresa Martín (Anderton 1999).

The myth that the planning and design practices could solve many of Havana's problems shifted radically from the bureaucratic paradigm of the revolution (dealing with widespread urban problems) to myths about colonial architecture (Segre 1994d; González Mínguez 1991). Several factors accounted

11. Advocates of this approach were Eduardo Luis Rodríguez, Emma Alvarez Tabío, Felicia Chateloin, Patricia Rodríguez Alomá, Abel Rodríguez, Ricardo Fernández, Emilio Castro, Rafael Fornés, Francisco Bedoya, Juan Luis Morales, Rosendo Mesías, and Jorge Tamargo. Despite the generation gap, the ideas of these young professionals found support among certain older government officials (Mario Coyula, director of architecture, Poder Popular) and well-established professionals who were identified with the postulates of the modern movement (Sergio Baroni, Roberto Gottardi, Antonio Quintana, Fernando Salinas, Roberto Segre).

for this paradigmatic shift. One was the collapse of the socialist world, which in turn created greater political isolation for Cuba. Another was the dire economic rout in which Cuba found itself in the 1990s. Yet another stems from an insecurity about the future. Taken in their entirety, these factors help explain why officials have looked back in time for planning and design solutions. History lent a sense of legitimization and social order in a system that, in Choay's words, "cannot overcome its own changes nor the acceleration of those changes" (1992, 188). The heritage-site syndrome and narcissism of historic preservation move in tandem with the "mummification and fetishization of architecture" (Dorfles 1965). In other words, the acritical reproduction of historic landscapes meant reviving some buildings that, to paraphrase Filarete and Mario Botta, really should have been helped to die. Brilliant forms and spaces derive from these restoration efforts, with their modern pastel colors that lack historic meanings (Rodríguez 1991, 1992, 1994). Images from the mass media zoomed in immediately on the new "colonial" restoration, especially the film industry. Nevertheless, the problem not only was one of color but also concerned issues of historic veracity given that such banal and picturesque perfection never registered in the collective memory of *habaneros* (Herrera Ysla 1991). An example of this thinking is the proposal to turn back the clock and demolish the present Ministry of Education building and replace it with a replica of the Santo Domingo Convent.

New housing in Habana Vieja is established three ways: (1) converting large mansions into apartments, such as the compact units proposed by Carlos Dunn in the Plaza Vieja; (2) the official use of the "loft" (*barbacoa*) as put forth by Rafael González de la Peñas in the units at 402 Oficios Street; and (3) the use of flat roofs for building new living spaces in the old city. Juan Luis Morales, Rosendo Mesías, Teresa Ayuso, and Lourdes León earned a prize in the Third Iberoamerican Competition at the Torroja Institute in Madrid. This award-winning design included the use of characteristic designs and the participation of the residents.

Four-story apartment complexes arose in the empty lots of the old city. They had unique facades and included traditional inner courtyards and patios. Good examples of these apartments can be found in the structure designed by Emma Alvarez Tabío on Oficios Street, Eduardo Luis Rodríguez's work on Velasco, and Francisco Bedoya's structure attached to the Aldama Palace. One might imagine that the innovators triumphed over the "essentialists" in this design and planning polemic. However, the cityscape revealed evidence

FIGURE 9.9.
Microbrigade project halted. The need for simple building maintenance and historic preservation existed well before the Special Period and remains in parts of Habana Vieja. Here a Microbrigade project on Mercaderes, photographed in 1992, remained idle, and part of the scaffolding had deteriorated. By 2001, many precarious buildings were being restored by the City Historian's Office. (Photograph Joseph L. Scarpaci)

to the contrary. Several projects were greatly exaggerated and of low quality in the formal sense. Others built by unskilled Microbrigade workers with low levels of technical training had extremely poor finishings. Of course, preservationists feared that an opening in the approach of how far a historic structure can be changed could lead to a "free for all" of imitators who might spin out of control. Some "modern" structures aged prematurely in striking contrast to the detailed perfection of the older ones. In some cases, veteran work crews had to be brought back to rescue some of the Microbrigade projects.

The disintegration of the socialist world in 1989 and the ensuing Special Period in Cuba curtailed restoration efforts in Habana Vieja (fig. 9.9). Funds destined for restoring national landmarks dried up. In 1994, San Francisco Convent opened a historic preservation school, and the following year a new wing of the restored Santa Clara Convent was inaugurated as a postgraduate center. Perhaps the most painful fact is realizing that it will be nearly impossi-

TABLE 9.1. City Historian's Office, Approximate Income and Investment after Decree-Law 143 in 1993

| YEAR | INCOME (U.S.$, MILLIONS) | INVESTMENT (MILLION PESOS) | INVESTMENT (U.S.$, MILLIONS) |
|---|---|---|---|
| 1994 | 3.0 | | |
| 1995 | 11.2 | | |
| 1996 | 21.7 | | |
| 1997 | 33.0 | | |
| 1998 | 40.8 | | |
| 1999 | 51.3 | | |
| 2000 (estimated) | 62.0 | 120 | 53 |

*Source*: Unpublished materials by City Historian's Office.

ble to create a multifunctional space in the heart of the colonial city (Segre 1992b). Except for a few celebrated restaurants, the decline in commercial activity and deterioration of food services have made the narrow streets and plazas silent once nightfall sets in (Paolini 1994). In the second half of the 1990s, the City Historian's Office very much increased its work and also extended it to cover social needs of the local residents, such as in the San Isidro neighborhood and Havana's celebrated seaside promenade, the Malecón.

The structure of the City Historian's Office led by Eusebio Leal grew more complicated as the scope of businesses (table 9.1) and tasks increased (fig. 9.10). By the end of 2000, it included the Master Plan Office (fig. 9.11, "Master Plan") and the San Isidro project, which restores a historically poor neighborhood in the southern tip of Habana Vieja (Collado et al. 1998). San Isidro is also the most notorious red-light district of Havana, and "business" boomed there in the early 1900s. Another division in the office is in charge of restoring the first fourteen blocks of Havana's landmark waterfront promenade, the Malecón (García et al. 1998). Other functions include a mass media group and a radio station. Also under the City Historian are the departments of Cultural Heritage, Architectural Heritage, Housing, and Architectural Projects and a workshop-school to train youngsters to become skilled rehabilitation workers. Because of its large business operations, it also has an Economics department, which includes accounting, investments, taxes, donations and cooperation, imports/exports, employment, and commercial. Its business activities encompass several enterprises: Puerto de Carena Con-

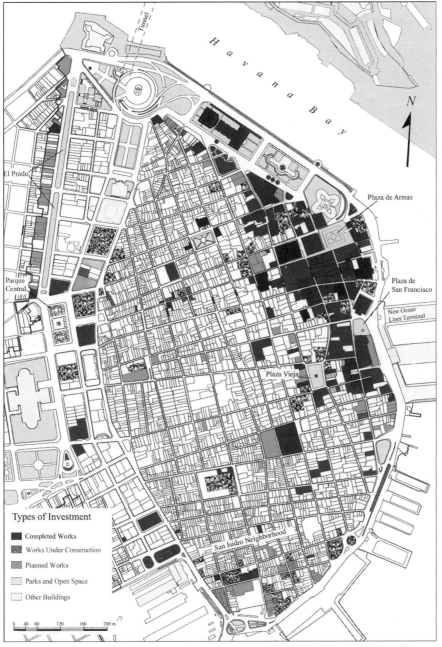

FIGURE 9.10. Master plan, Habana Vieja (Modified and translated from original map from City Historian's Office, 1999)

FIGURE 9.11. Organizational chart, City Historian's Office (Simplified and modified after chart from City Historian's Office)

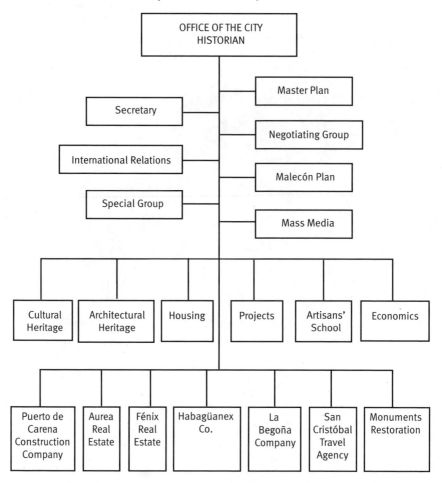

struction Company, two real estate agencies (Aurea and Fénix), Habagüanex (the initial commercial enterprise under the City Historian's Office and still the most important), La Begoña, a travel agency (San Cristóbal), and the Restoration of Monuments company that grew from the initial one that laid the basis for the preservation of historic landmarks in Old Havana in the 1980s (fig. 9.10; Rodríguez 1999, 13).

Private spaces have increasingly replaced public spaces as meeting places and areas of community exchange in Habana Vieja. Individual activities pre-

TABLE 9.2. Rehabilitation Works at Old Havana by the City Historian's Office, 1999–2000

| | |
|---|---|
| • Seat of the municipal government of Old Havana (original seat of the House of Representatives, 1909–11) | • Johnson Drugstore, at Obispo Street |
| | • Park La Bacaladera |
| • Museo del Ron (Rum Museum, former mansion of the counts of Mortera) | • Public lighting of the Avenida del Puerto |
| | • Park Obispo |
| • Hostel Tejadillo | • Angela Landa School, at Plaza Vieja |
| • Hostel Comendador | • Mi Casita Colonial |
| • Casa del Niño Discapacitado (Home for Handicapped Children) | • Horchatería |
| | • Aquarium |
| • Monuments to generals from the Independence Wars Antonio Maceo and Calixto García* (rehabilitation and reposition of the statue of Gómez that had been removed in the 1960s for political reasons). Construction of a new monument to Simón Bolívar on G Street* and rehabilitation of the Villalón Park*. Rehabilitation of the monument to El Quijote, on J at 23rd Street*. Construction of a monument to the Mexican composer Agustín Lara on Alameda de Paula, Old Havana. | • Sundial in La Cabaña fortress (1763–74) |
| | • Casa de los Combatientes (Home of the Revolutionary Veterans) |
| | • La Fuerza fortress / Ceramics Museum |
| | • The House of the count of Casa Bayona |
| | • Colonial Art Museum |
| | • The Oficios and Obrapla Palace |
| | • Valencia Hostal |
| | • The House of Juana Carvajal / The Archeological Cabinet of the City Historian |
| • Casa Balear*, on 23rd Street at G. | • The House of the conde of San Juan de Jaruco / Cuban Fund for Cultural Works (Fondo Cubano de Bienes Culturales) |
| • Synagogue Beth Shalom | |
| • Cafeteria La Volanta at Manzana de Gómez, facing the Central Park | |
| • Saldos store | • House of the conde de Casa Barreto / Provincial Center of Art and Design |
| • Habana 1791 parfumerie, at Mercaderes Street and Compostela | • Santa Clara Convent (headquarters of CENCREM) |
| • Hostel San Miguel, at Cuba Street | |
| • Hostel Los Frailes, at Muralla Street between Oficios and Mercaderes | • Mateo Pedroso Palace / Crafts Palace |
| | • Segundo Cabo Palace / Cuban Book Institute |
| • La Moderna Poesía library, at Obispo Street (rehabilitation) | • House of the count of Casa Lombillo / Education Museum |
| • Rehabilitation of Iglesia de Paula (Paula Church) (1745) and of the Alameda de Paula promenade (1772) | • House of the Cárdenas Sisters / Center for the Development of Visual Arts of the Ministry of Culture |
| • Esplanade and surrounding open space at Castillo de la Punta (La Punta Castle) (1589–ca. 1600) | |

Source: City Historian's Office; Martin and Rodríguez 1993; authors' field research.
Note: Asterisk indicates that it is located in Vedado, showing the scope of the City Historian's Office's projects.

vail over gatherings of friends around restaurant tables. Recently, the home restaurants (*paladares*) in the living rooms and small kitchens have become the new "public" gathering points. Only tourists in Habana Vieja wander in search of urban history, trying to decipher in the old stones the enigmas of the present and future. The new uses of buildings and private spaces reflect the changing economic conditions. Magnificent exterior balconies, for instance, which once looked "like elegant chariots in the air" (García 1992, 93), have lost their splendor. Far off in the distance of "ruralized" Old Havana today, one hears the cackling of caged roosters and hens that now own the balconies and rooftops. "And suddenly you realize that the roosters don't call the families together, dispersed as they are by a Biblical wind, and that there are no longer dogs in the streets nor flying cockroaches" (Alvarez Tabío 1994a, 16; our translation).

Habana Vieja's transformation in the 1990s is expansive and unprecedented. Although tourism is alien to local residents, they learn to profit from it directly or indirectly. Since the second half of the 1990s, part of the profits obtained from these operations now go to improve the living condition of local residents. Moreover, many locals find jobs in these new renovation projects and tourist-based services. Restored patrician mansions that were abandoned by their original owners almost two centuries ago are being turned into museums, hostels, or art galleries. These buildings coexist with slums (*cuarterías*) and a dilapidated streetscape where interior poverty and neglect increasingly pop up. Overcrowding and poor living conditions push residents into the streets, creating a noisy but lively environment that is more vibrant and authentic the farther away residents are from the flow of tourists.

Tourism generates its own externalities in Habana Vieja. Painstakingly restored historic public spaces are being occupied by dollar-based retailing and services at a quick pace. The commerce distorts the views of these historic public spaces and makes pedestrian circulation difficult at times. Parking is becoming a problem in Old Havana as more cars and tourist buses arrive. At times, there is a continuous "metal wall" of tourist bases along Avenida del Puerto that blocks the views of the bay and the fortresses that crown its eastern hill. Despite the commercial success of the City Historian's Office, the long-term solution for nearly three thousand buildings in Habana Vieja must eventually rely on empowering as many people as possible to pay for the repairs in the places in which they live. However, gainful employment and a strong economy should not lessen the oversight of makeshift modifications.

While owner-occupied and owner-maintained dwellings mean severing the reliance on funds from the state, the City Historian's Office, or joint-venture projects, it cannot permit ad hoc changes to spring up throughout the historic zone. Residents of Habana Vieja remain hopeful that the future will both heal its wounds and revive the glories of the past.

# Havana's Future

## Risks and Opportunities

It's beautiful to be a communist, even though it gives you lots of headaches. And the thing is that communist headaches are supposed to be historical, that is to say, they don't go away with aspirins, but only by creating paradise on earth.... Under capitalism our heads ache and they decapitate us. In the struggle for the revolution the head is a time bomb.... Communism will be, among other things, an aspirin the size of the sun.

—Roque Dalton, *On Headaches*

If the Cuban revolution thwarted efforts to change Havana into just another Antillean Miami, we might assess the events after 1959 according to what might have occurred had an unfettered market prevailed. This closing chapter considers such a scenario. The tension surrounding the city's uncertain future permeates daily life, and the chapter begins with an overview of those anxieties and tensions. We then summarize some of the paramount features, risks, and opportunities in different aspects of city life (population, housing, social services, education, communications, transport, road network, water supply, energy, and household fuel). Last, we analyze the trade-offs that exist between rescuing the city from its economic quagmire and slowly transforming its built environment in the twenty-first century.

## Saving Havana: Anxieties and Uncertainties for the "Pearl of the Caribbean"

Havana faced its most pressing problems of the twentieth century in the 1990s and enters the twenty-first with incertitude that is both internal and external. The greatest challenge concerns the ability to boost its economy, improve its governance, and empower its population without losing social equity and achievements. In addition, all future scenarios will be conditioned based on Cuba's relationship with the United States. Like other modern metropolises, its "urban kingdom" (Mongin 1995), with its sprawling territory, has definitively replaced the concept of the compact city that has been "blown to pieces" (Fernández Galiano 1994). Change in urban structure in many cities is attributable not only to the now universally diffused U.S. suburban model but also to warfare, terrorism, and civil strife. These conflicts have ranged from Berlin, Stalingrad, Nagasaki, and Hiroshima to Hanoi, Sarajevo, Beirut, Grozny, Los Angeles, and Oklahoma City (Lang 1995; Enzensberger 1995). In Latin America, guerrilla conflict hurt city residents more than it changed the makeup of the city. Fighting between state authorities and the Tupamaros, Montoneros, and Sendero Luminoso (Shining Path) inflicted the greatest toll against individuals as opposed to buildings.

Modernity and markets have also threatened the great world cities. Since the 1950s explosion in real estate speculation, Latin American cities have changed in profound ways. Little remains of the colonial heritage of Buenos Aires, Montevideo, Rio de Janeiro, or Caracas. Similarly, Mexico City and São Paulo today retain few of the monumental eclectic palaces that once graced their historic centers. Some art deco or rationalist designs still remain in Santo Domingo, La Paz, or Quito. A yearning for the modernity of glass-wrapped skyscrapers, sumptuous apartment buildings, and giant shopping centers has replaced this historic memory (Rama 1985; Sarlo 1994).

Havana is an anomaly in contemporary urban history. Its image in the 1950s as an Antillean metropolis that was destined to become another nexus in the Las Vegas and Miami triangle of gambling and tourism was frozen in time on January 1, 1959 (Benítez Rojo 1989; Michener and Kings 1989). This event derailed multimillion-dollar investments by tourist companies and organized crime. Nevertheless, the revolution also benefited from expensive projects started by the local bourgeoisie and foreign investors. Buildings as well as the city layout have withstood the encroachment of urbanization until today, despite the "macondian" rains (García Márquez 1979), hurricanes, obsolescence, and lack of maintenance that have beaten the city for nearly four decades.

Prioritizing provincial capital investment meant fewer resources for Havana. What little new construction that has been carried out in Havana between 1959 and the mid-1990s was confined to the periphery. Practically nothing of significance was built in inner-city Havana since 1959 because of the elimination of the private sector and the evening out of land values. Design and construction patterns favored public buildings that did not blend in with the built environment. To some extent, not building in the city center contributed to the unconscious and parochial rejection by decision makers who associated big cities with corruption and social unrest. Soon after the triumph of the revolution, the commercial value of land in Havana was reduced to $4 per square meter. This measure stopped speculation but also fostered an excessive use of land—something suicidal in a small agricultural island nation. Revolutionary ideology gave Havana a predictable character through the construction of houses, schools, hospitals, hotels, and shops at the edge of the traditional city, but the real imprint of the revolutionary economic and social changes happened in the change of land uses and occupants of existing buildings (Scarpaci 2000a). For decades, the "myth of the new" prevailed (Segre 1995), influenced by the same spirit of modernity prevalent in the 1950s. Havana's architectural heritage reflects several styles, ranging from the colonial to the International Style and a whole array of paradigms within each design. Like a "rusty oasis" (Fernández Alba 1995) that has heroically withstood the march of time, this variety of design stands out within the squalid extension of the urban fabric. However, what was once a product of little resources and shifting priorities may prove to be a source of wealth. The devolution and financial autonomy of what the City Historian's Office has accomplished may be a harbinger of things to come. Simply stated: Is it possible to profit from Havana's valuable built heritage without distorting it, while also satisfying residential demand for shelter? A related challenge is to empower local residents to "pay for themselves" while lessening their dependence on a paternalistic state that lacks the means to perform many tasks. Accordingly, is it possible to spread the model put forth by the City Historian's Office to other parts of the city? The extent to which that example can be generalized will lead Havana closer to a much touted sustainability model (Scarpaci and Coyula, forthcoming). Another big question is who will establish a pattern of streetscapes and behavior in the public spaces of a city whose look and vitality was once defined by a very large lower middle class, which is now absent.

Cuba lost its solid economic support with the collapse of the Soviet world, and with it went the possibility of giving its residents the quality of education, medical care, and housing found in the First World. Since the onset of the Special Period in 1990, daily living has slipped to conditions found in the Fourth World. Havana became the main victim of this situation. Power blackouts darkened the city's streets into irregular and dangerous tunnels while the gasoline shortage precipitated ecologically correct and sweaty bicycle travel. City services suffered, especially street cleaning and waste removal. Strict food rationing and shortages ended the few bars and restaurants that had previously graced Havana's streets. State construction projects and the overworked Microbrigade efforts also came to a grinding halt. Residents, already cramped into smaller quarters, could do little to preserve or repair their dwellings. City government fell into fiscal straits, unable to provide even a modicum of services. As dire as these symptoms may be, urban planners and administrators around the world confront growth management, urban policy and scale, and privatization daily (Kirby 1995). Havana, alas, is not immune. In the late 1990s there was a steady recovery, mainly addressed at the macroeconomic level. The gross domestic product (GDP) grew by 5.5 percent in 2000, but that sill represents 85 percent of the 1989 level, the last year before the Special Period was declared.

As we have documented throughout this book, the gravity of the economic quagmire opened doors to foreign investment. Ironically, the development of joint-venture tourist and real estate installations has brought negative consequences. One has been visual and functional, with too big and often banal new buildings that distort the surrounding scale and character of valuable urban places. Another is social, creating a rising inequality that had long ago been wiped away by the revolution. This, in turn, ignited a frantic search for the dollar (once the persecuted and prohibited symbol of *yanqui* domination), which circulates freely throughout Cuba. A new free-market wave prevails in Havana and already pervades the urban image. It includes farmers' markets, the sale of craft goods, and the private in-house *paladar* restaurant. Piecemeal initiatives have partially renewed urban life but in different ways. Social relations, for instance, once concentrated in public spaces, are now confined to the private spaces of homes or garages. Front porches have been increasingly closed to make way for an extra bedroom, thus distorting the streetscape. Changes such as these may prove to be profound, but they also reflect a change in the way of life that started with the advent of television and the massive incorporation of women into the workforce. Socializing on the porch may become an "old-time memory" along the same lines as the corner grocery. Not to be outdone, the state jumped into the market frenzy by opening numerous dollar-run stores, changing the tranquil residential flavor of Miramar into a string of retail outlets, now mostly used by Cubans.

The rush of new opportunity is everywhere, and with it comes a challenge to urban design and planning in Havana. Foreign investment ushers in tourists, a few cruise ships are now docking in Havana Bay, and new hotels and condominiums for foreigners are springing up across the city. Together they represent hope for Havana as well as a serious threat to the architectural treasures of the city. Yet the pace of this investment is still slow. It is hoped that awareness about the danger of losing the city's architectural heritage to globalization will continue to rise. There is a need for a public consciousness about the banal and generic architecture that creeps into new projects for hotels, real estate joint ventures for foreigners, cheap fast-food restaurants, and shopping centers (Coyula 1999a). These is some evidence that this message has reached the top Cuban decision makers, especially following the historic Sixth Congress of the Cuban National Union of Artists and Writers (Unión Nacional de Escritores y Actores de Cuba [UNEAC]).

A genuine concern over the city's safeguarding is evident even in Miami, where the prestigious Cuban American architect Andres Duany and the Cuban National Heritage organization are committed to the preservation of the built environment of Havana and have expressed concern about the need for a uniform planning law that would regulate zoning in this new rush of foreign investment. A 1996 *New York Times* article highlighted the activities and hopes of these Cuban Americans in south Florida (Wise 1996), and an article in the *New Yorker* in early 1998 discusses preservation issues and actors in Havana (Goldberger 1998). A scholarship for a graduate to study Vedado was created at the University of Miami in 2000. A focus on preserving a common heritage, which actually belongs to all of humanity (according to UNESCO), could help in healing the wounds of political resentment that during forty years have clouded reasonable arguments from both sides (Segre 2000, 113).

The passion of these expatriates and their desire to preserve the city's historic heritage are laudable. Pumping public and private investment into former Communist countries is a policy goal argued by many. The argument rests on the premise that the collapse of Communism affords a special opportunity for liberal and capitalist nations to reassert their leadership (Skidelsky 1996). Nonetheless, two distorted points emerge in the case of the Cuban expatriates who wish to save Havana's built form. In their stating that "things are falling down, everything is disappearing," one might assume that the socialist government did nothing in the past few decades to protect the city. In fact, scarce resources and considerable personal sacrifice went into the creation and maintenance of the Landmarks Commission, the Center for Restoration, Conservation, and Museum Science, and the Office of the City Historian. At the same time, a late show of love for the city appeared with the creation of the Grupo para el Desarrollo Integral de la Capital in 1987. Solidarity for Havana's well-being also comes from UNESCO and governments in Europe, Mexico, Venezuela, and Argentina. These countries have financed numerous building, restoration, and conservation efforts in the historic center. Spain in particular has played a vital role in this regard. The High Technical School of Architecture of Barcelona (Escuela Técnica Superior de Arquitectura de Barcelona [ETSAB]) has compiled drawings of the eclectic buildings constructed at the turn of the twentieth century (Masides i Serracant 1995) and is conducting another study in Vedado. The town council of Andalucia published a seminal guide to colonial and modern architecture in Havana (Martín Zequeira and Rodríguez Fernández 1998). In Asturias, an architectural organization (Colegio de Arquitectos del Principado de Asturias) is joining efforts with Havana to restore the Malecón and is preparing to publish an exhaustive work on the modern architecture of Havana (Sambricio and Segre 2000).

The rather apocalyptic remarks made in Miami by the Cuban National Heritage group and the well-known architect Nicolás Quintana (Quintana 2000, 151) must be tempered and placed into context. It is also important to note that had the socialist project not ended the development efforts of the 1950s, even less might be left today of Old Havana, the residences of Vedado, or the art deco in Víbora or Marianao. Would Habana Vieja have qualified as a World Heritage Site if the 1956 master plan of José Luis Sert had been implemented? And would the Malecón, despite its dilapidated state, retain that look so identified with the beginning of the twentieth century, or would it rather be dominated by high-rise condominiums and hotels? This scenario should help to prevent repeating the mistake. It remains, for example, a concern in many design reviews for proposed buildings such as the case of siting a high-rise apartment complex in nearly every empty lot along the Paseo thoroughfare in Vedado. The argument leading to the rejection of that project was: "Why do you want to build here? Because it's beautiful. And why is it beautiful? Because there are no high rises." Shortly after, the Landmarks Commission established a protection zone in Vedado and Miramar. One strategy to resist the pressure of some ill-oriented investors has been uniting forces around preservation by different organizations and commissions.

Speculators, builders, real estate moguls, and others have been anxiously waiting for forty years to retake Havana and to restore the lost value of the city's property. As a recent conference on global cities sponsored by the Lincoln Institute of Land Policy concluded, spatial planning techniques in market economies are increasingly rendered powerless. In their wake arise "new rules of property and politics that de facto make city governments subordinate to powers outside their control" (Lincoln Institute of Land Policy 1996, 7).

Will Havana succumb to this same fate? Leading Cuban economists still argue that social property is the sine qua non of a socialist project (Carranza, Gutiérrez, and Monreal 1995, 9). Without a command economy, social property, and the state's control over the means of production, the term "socialism" loses its original meaning (Przeworski 1989, 1992). Classical socialist models have tried to allocate resources through an economic system in which central planning was absolute. Some Cuban scholars contend that "the construction of socialism does not require the elimination of the market but the suppression of the hegemony of capital, which is different" (Carranza, Gutiérrez, and Monreal 1995, 14; our translation); it is unclear whether such a goal is possible, or whether the conceptual premises are sharply elucidated. As this chapter suggests, there is good reason to question the romantic notion of Havana as it withers before us. Instead, there may be a middle course of action that is both prudent and possible.

## Arresting Urban Decline: A Sectoral Assessment

What future direction should the city take? Which of the two faces of this beautiful Antillean metropolis should shine more brightly in the twenty-first century—the living museum of the past, or a ubiquitous, modern, and placeless skyline? As one of us commented in a *New York Times* article about Cuban Americans in south Florida who wish "to safeguard the Cuban National Heritage . . . which has been threatened by an accelerating process of deterioration" (Cuba National Heritage n.d.): "What people [in Havana] resent is to think of Cuban-Americans sitting in Miami, putting in pins [in maps] and placing Burger Kings and McDonalds in Havana" (Wise 1996). Perhaps, but as we discussed in chapter 8, a Cuban fast-food chain, El Rápido, is imposing its stamp on the cityscape without outside help. To be sure, the revolution stopped the "Miamization" of Havana's waterfront and made both Cuba and Havana "a different America" (Chaffee and Prevost 1992). However, it also overlooked important gaps in the financing of urban services and the maintenance of the city's built environment.

An opportunity to identify what *habaneros* perceive as the city's major challenges arose when Havana became a member of the Ibero-American Strategic Development Center. This agency tried to stimulate the development of strategic urban plans that counted on a participatory methodology and a sensitivity to local culture. As such, it sought to integrate citizen, public, and private initiatives for harmonious urban development and to promote the exchange of experiences in economic and trade cooperation among city members. All of this took place as part of certain initiatives that commenced in the 1980s in which cities participated in the kind of strategic planning characteristic of large companies and corporations that function in a competitive marketplace. As a result of this initiative, Havana developed a strategic plan for the period 1998–2000 and a second one for 2001–3. The plan has been adopted by the city government as a frame for all its work.

Havana's risks and opportunities vary across sectors. Population, housing, social services, education, culture, transportation, road networks, water supply, communications, and energy and household fuel all pose distinct challenges (table 10.1). At the same time, however, underlying each problem is a basis for improvement and lessons to be learned about Havana's future.

## Lessons Learned, Lessons Forgotten

Havana's two faces have vacillated from a free-market economy, to central planning, and now back to a moderate mixed economy under strong state control. Radical changes such as these suggest that there are models to be copied and lessons to be learned. The experience of the former Soviet Union and Eastern bloc nations should be telling in the case of Cuba and Havana. Havana's microenterprises must cope with pricing, advertising, return business, buying in bulk, and access to credit. A new business class plods along, building its firms and incrementally improving its entrepreneurial learning curve. *Paladar* owners welcome their newfound occupational independence and may desire less of what the government wishes to impose over all self-employed: "greater discipline and control" ("Si de cuenta propia se trata" 1995; our translation). Perhaps the only obstacle in their horizon will be a battery of new government guidelines and taxes in the event that *paladares* and self-employment—as past experience has shown—should prove to be too profitable in the eyes of Cuban authorities (Peters and Scarpaci 1998). On the other hand, some of these poor nouveaux riches may use their new economic

TABLE 10.1. Sectoral Assessment of Havana's Physical and Human Resources, 2001

| SECTOR | CHARACTERISTICS |
|---|---|
| Population | • low population density<br>• life expectancy of 75 years<br>• growth below fertility replacement level—population is aging<br>• 56% of population is working age |
| Housing | • 60% of the nation's precarious housing stock is in Havana<br>• 100,000 uninhabitable housing units<br>• half of city's stock is in average or poor condition<br>• irregular and slow pace of construction |
| Social services | • central planning, lack of individual incentives, and full employment have produced shortages, long lines, high prices, and poor services<br>• high-quality health care and educational services<br>• state strives to maintain socialist establishment |
| Education | • 10 billion pesos invested nationally in higher education since 1959<br>• high concentration of skilled workers in Havana labor force<br>• rote memorization of facts in high schools despite good texts<br>• understaffed schools |
| Culture | • high concentration of theaters, art galleries, and internationally renowned artists and events |
| Transport | • bus system by *ruteros* is no longer the main transportation mode in absence of metro or street-car system<br>• 1 million bicycles (about one for every two *habaneros*)<br>• point-to-point bicycle bus transfers for precarious roads (e.g., tunnel under bay) |

| RISKS | OPPORTUNITIES |
|---|---|
| • downsizing (*compactación*) state firms will increase unemployment<br>• top-heavy state bureaucracy may hinder citizen participation | • many mass organizations can be used to mobilize community projects<br>• no threat of "hyperurbanization"<br>• "perfeccionamiento" process of state enterprises will improve efficiency and also income of the workers |
| • further deterioration<br>• potential displacement of residents through joint ventures or foreign investment or through housing swaps involving money under the table | • good original construction quality favors conservation<br>• self-help with self-employed workers complements state provisions and allows individuals to make repairs that the state cannot assume |
| • widening gap in quality of services between center and suburbs<br>• worsening of physical condition of schools and health care facilities<br>• access to dollars producing dual-class system and dual markets | • Special Period can be used to phase in adequate tax policies to nurture entrepreneurs yet finance essential social services |
| • rising unemployment for high school and college graduates<br>• disparity between formal education and gainful employment | • good potential for retraining skilled laborers who have been displaced from downsizing public agencies |
| • deterioration of national landmarks and monuments<br>• low cultural values of hustlers (*macetas*) are becoming a success model even though they promote local culture in sordid and unauthentic ways<br>• lack of urban culture: disparity between formal culture and street culture | • neighborhood-based music, theater, cultural, or dance events hold potential for small businesses and local tourism<br>• small bed-and-breakfast establishment potential in city's neighborhoods could tap into local cultural allures<br>• recent government priority to community work and massive dissemination of culture |
| • increase of private cars and return to high consumption of fossil fuels and discontinuance of conservation practices once Special Period ends<br>• poor integration of bicycle lanes and safety measures and lack of shaded bicycle routes<br>• must improve taxi and jitney services | • unprecedented introduction of conservation practices and the creation of a culture of bicycling has produced a "greening" of the city<br>• revive and improve service connections between city center, suburbs, and interprovincial points |

TABLE 10.1. (continued)

| SECTOR | CHARACTERISTICS |
|--------|-----------------|
| Road network | • dense network of primary and secondary arteries with major sectors in need of repair<br>• ramps for elderly, invalids, baby carriages, and bicycles, as well as bike lanes, in short supply |
| Water supply | • Ample water reserves exist to meet present and future demands<br>• more than half of pumped water is lost through leakage<br>• low water pressure requires electric pumps for building cisterns |
| Communications | • telephone service deficient because of obsolete and damaged technology; overloaded switchboards in poor condition<br>• one of lowest telephone indexes in Latin America (8.73 per 100 inhabitants)<br>• rains disrupt phone service<br>• tightly controlled access to Internet, e-mail, and World Wide Web |
| Energy and household fuels | • scheduled and nonscheduled power blackouts peaked in 1993 but by 2001 were rare<br>• high-sulfur and polluting petroleum for power plants is purchased on spot market |

*Source*: Authors' field research.

power to bribe inspectors and officials and construct tasteless buildings that distort the urban image of Havana.

Recent structural changes in Havana's political economy raise more questions about the nature of the socialist state than our theoretical tools can answer. Many theorists have long been disenchanted with the nature of the state in Eastern Europe, the former Soviet Union, and Cuba before the socialist camp collapsed. Far from withering away in those societies as envisioned by Marx, the state took on an almost Orwellian role in its management of everyday life. Today, though, new free-market regulations provide minute detail

| RISKS | OPPORTUNITIES |
| --- | --- |
| • continuation of spotty and low-quality road repairs will prove costly in long term unless public works commence soon<br>• economic recovery may revive private automobile and taxi travel and increase noise and air pollution and greater demand for parking facilities | • development of pedestrian malls could be modeled after existing examples (San Rafael, Obispo, Prado)<br>• circular cement speed bumps separating cars from cyclists permanent part of road system |
| • leakage threatens road and building foundations by dissolving limestone rock<br>• saltwater intrusion in aquifer<br>• decline in chlorinization and treatment of drinking water increases intestinal ailments | • technical aspects of water problems concerning treatment and distribution well known to professional personnel (problem is lack of money for solving problems) |
| • continued neglect of telecommunications system will lead to greater deterioration and greater costs when/if ultimately repaired<br>• nondigital dialing is incompatible with many telephone, FAX, local area network (LAN) systems | • new foreign investments will improve a broad gamut of hardware services<br>• educated population capable of using Internet resources for education and small business |
| • public-street lighting still insufficient and some dates from 1890s; needs repair and maintenance<br>• obsolete and highly polluting thermoelectric plants, though mainly used as support during peak hours, pose health and environmental risks<br>• household fuel sources expensive, unevenly distributed, and polluting | • *habaneros* now well schooled in energy conservation<br>• neighborhood vegetable garden program has benefited more than 26,000 families by mid-1996, potential exists to expand community gardens that use mainly organic inputs<br>• government investment policy has provided 47% of households with gas service and improves public lighting |

about who can become self-employed. *Perestroika* and *glasnost* in the former Soviet Union ushered in rapid change, as have market liberalization reforms in post-Mao China. As Kay posited: "Whether these herald a new phase in the transition to socialism or a new variant of capitalism only time will tell" (1994, 208). The unanswered theoretical question is whether the introduction of the dollar has derailed the revolution and, if so, whether it can get back on track. At the dawn of the new millennium, the answer may be that changes have not altered significantly the basic goals of the revolution. However, in Marxist theory, changes in the economic base are not reflected immediately in the "superstructure." The question is whether a mixed economy will ultimately produce a mixed ideology. That combination might be seen by some as desirable, but it could also trigger greater inequity, social unrest, moral deterioration, and chaos.

The sudden shift toward limited capital accumulation in Havana—historically a process confined to the capitalist mode of production—is changing Cuba's transition to socialism. No longer is socialism the antisystemic force theorists once considered it to be (Polanyi 1977; Taylor 1985). While the Eastern Europe experience shows that it is not alarming to find inequalities under state socialism (Szelenyi 1982), we can only hope that the Cuban experience can avoid the pitfalls that have plagued the former socialist alliance (Tismaneanu 1992; Clawson 1992; Murrell 1992; Ickes and Ryterman 1992). Because of forty-two years of "pure" socialism, Havana is ill prepared to support a market economy easily. Socialist Budapest, Prague, Warsaw, and other Eastern European cities always permitted limited private ownership of businesses, self-employment in certain services, and farmers' markets alongside their centrally planned economies (Pérez-López 1994a, 249). To many Cubans and students of development studies around the globe, Cuba was going to provide a missing ingredient in Marx's incomplete theory of the state's role in making a transition to socialism.

## Rescuing Havana's Cultural Meanings: From Lenin to Lennon in the New Millennium

The triumph of the revolution in 1959 produced an out-migration of many artists and intellectuals. It automatically divided Cuban culture into a "before and after 1959" mind-set and between ideas and works made in Cuba versus those created abroad (Campuzano 2000). From a purely stylistic approach, the division produced by this diaspora proved to be arbitrary in architecture and urban design. The modern movement that produced many important buildings after the Second World War did not end in 1959 but actually was extended with several fine works well into the late 1960s. Many leading architects who left Cuba were identified as opponents of the revolution. As a result, many of them were excluded from the island's cultural media and historic anthologies until the 1970s.

The First Congress on Education and Culture in 1971 set the rules for this policy, and it was articulated in the "Padilla case," when an award-winning poet was harassed as a "dissenter." The episode ended in a pathetic public repentance. This period was known within the cultural milieu as "the gray decade." In architecture, this policy was reinforced with functional and economic arguments that were used by the state design and construction officials against designers who could be labeled as elitists. The implication was that the "elitists" had no concern for sound building technology or—even worse—showed disregard for the needs of the people. The unfinished complex of the five Schools of Arts (1960–65; fig. 10.1) at the former Country Club golf links became the center of a polemic that ended with a victory of the "builders over the artists." Ironically, those same builders were eventually replaced in decision making by makeshift builders. Emphasis in heavy-panel prefabrication of a few standardized building types, allegedly to allow mass production, ended in the predictable loss of beauty as well as the loss in construction quality and output levels. Yet some rare cases of good design in fully prefabricated buildings demonstrated that the real threat to the building trades was a "prefabricated" mentality (Segre 1999c, 64).

Gradually, a historic rehabilitation of the outcasts began to spread, starting with those farther in time or distance. Julián del Casal (1863–93), considered a founder of Cuban modern poetry together with the national hero José Martí (1853–95), had been regarded as an exotic homosexual. His importance in the humanities was stressed in 1981 by the influential poet Roberto Fernández Retamar, who also promoted the major Argentinean poet Jorge Luis Borges, long considered an opponent of the Cuban revolution. Eventually, some exiled writers such as Severo Sarduy were published in Cuba. Another almost excluded poet who never left, Dulce María Loynaz, won the National Prize for Literature in 1987 and in 1992 received the Cervantes Prize, which is considered the most important prize in Spanish literature. Other artists and writers such as Eliseo Diego, Raúl Martínez, Alfredo Sosabravo, César López, and Antón Arrufat, who might not be classified as "mainstream," also received top national prizes.

This trend in recognizing the merits and detriments of the revolution reached a high point in 1993 when the leading Cuban film director, Tomás Gutiérrez Alea, made *Fresa y Chocolate*. Ostensibly, his was a story about the revindication of an excluded homosexual intellectual. Its subtext, however, explored the more general theme of intolerance in Cuban society. Later, in 1999, the City Historian's Office rehabilitated a prominent monument and re-

FIGURE 10.1. School of Arts complex, Cubanacán, Havana City Province.
The School of Arts complex was built in the early 1960s on the site of a former
golf course and represents some of the finest design in Havana's post-1959 era.
(Photographs by Joseph L. Scarpaci)

placed the statue of General José Miguel Gómez, a hero in the Independence Wars and one of the first Cuban presidents (1908–12). The statue had been removed in the 1960s because of the bitter criticism of Gómez and other politicians during the republican period (1902–58), who were accused of corruption and acceptance of U.S. influence.

During the 1980s, a movement of young intellectuals and professionals began questioning the rigidity and stereotypes held by the previous generation in the fields of art and architecture. A painting exhibition titled "Volumen I," held at the Galeria Habana in 1981, signaled a departure from some of this rigidity and coalesced what came to be know as the "Generation of the 1980s" (Mosquera 1999, 24). In architecture, the new works that were carried out by young architects were financed by the Poderes Populares (People's Power organizations) in various cities across the country. The Department of Architecture of the Poder Popular in Havana, headed by Mario Coyula, directed these initiatives. These city governments allotted a greater degree of flexibility in allowing these young architects to incorporate their designs into the local urban fabric than in Havana. Typical projects conducted by these younger architects included apartment buildings, restaurants, cafeterias, family physician offices, and gas stations. The majority of these projects were done for the Microbrigades or the People's Power organizations. These designers and their works culminated in the exhibition "Young Cuban Architecture" (Arquitectura Joven Cubana) at the Havana Center for the Development of Visual Arts (Centro de Desarrollo de las Artes Visuales de La Habana) in 1990. Some of these architects and painters from the "Generation of the 1980s" established themselves in Mexico, Spain, and the United States.

Ricardo Porro, the chief architect of the Schools of Arts, returned to Cuba after more than thirty years of living in Paris. Porro and his two Italian collaborators — Vittorio Garatti and Roberto Gottardi — the latter the only one who had remained in Cuba — met again for the first time in Havana in late 1999. That same year, the Cuban government decided to allocate an estimated amount of U.S.$18 million to finish the buildings that were paralyzed in the 1960s and to rehabilitate the whole complex.

The Sixth Congress of UNEAC, celebrated in November 1998, was also important in many ways to architecture and urban design. For the first time, architecture was discussed in a UNEAC congress. The whole morning session of the first day was devoted to the threat posed by globalization and banal designs used in new projects (Coyula 2000c). The congress addressed issues about culture and society. It called for a wider dissemination of culture that included community cultural work, culture and tourism, the economy of culture, the teaching of art, the international image projected by the Cuban culture, young writers and artists, and cultural promotion.

Efforts to reach out to creative voices outside the island have continued slowly through the mass media, specialized publications, meetings, workshops, and seminars. Leading international architects such as the Cuban American Andres Duany and the Puerto Rican Jorge Rigau visited the island as outward signs of that creative embrace. The two architects participated in a workshop in December 1998 that explored the redevelopment of the mouth of Havana's main river, the Almendares. In late 1999, a large exhibition was opened at the 1600s Convento de Santa Clara in Old Havana, showing the visionary proposals of the group Manifestos. The projects were made by several leading world avant-garde architects: the Austrians Wolf Prix, from Coop Himmelblau, Carl Pruscha, and Peter Noever; the Americans Thom Mayne, from Morphosis, Eric Owen Moss, and Lebbeus Woods; and the Spaniard Carme Pinós. A book collecting the projects as well as texts by the architects and the conference proceedings of a 1995 meeting in Havana, *The Havana Project*, was also presented in its Spanish version. Yet little public discussion stemmed from these very provocative and controversial projects, which may reflect the lack of a broader conceptualization of culture among practicing architects, academics, and even critics.

Joint Cuban-foreign design studios were carried in the late 1990s with undergraduate and graduate students from Harvard, the University of Washington at Seattle, Köln, Weimar, Darmstadt, Humboldt University in Berlin, High Technical School of Architecture of Madrid (Escuela Técnica Superior de Arquitectura de Madrid [ETSAM-Madrid], Oslo, and Paris-Villemin and Paris-Versailles. Meetings and workshops have also attracted professors from Milan, Venice, Florence, Naples, La Sapienza, Rome; IUAV, Venice; Simón Bolívar, Caracas; Ryerson University, Toronto; Bartlett, London; Newcastle-upon-Tyne and Hudderston; Bucaramanga, Colombia; Guadalajara, Mexico; and others. Several of these design studios were coordinated by the Grupo para el Desarrollo Integral de la Capital (GDIC), which also organized an international seminar on waterfronts (City by the Water) in 1998. This waterfront conference enlisted design projects from many of the universities, noted above, as well as Virginia Tech in the United States. Another conference was hosted by the GDIC in October 1999 that explored historic preservation as a driving force in urban rehabilitation. It attracted top Cuban experts and officials—including Ricardo Alarcón, president of the Cuban National Assembly—as well as three American mayors from Baltimore, Charleston, and Knoxville, plus the vice president of the National Trust for Historic Preservation in the United States. A similar international seminar was organized by the GDIC in 2000 on sustainable habitat. The U.S. Committee of ICOMOS also made its first visit to Cuba in early 1998, coordinated through the Cuban Committee; and the City Historian's Office and the National Center for Conservation, Restoration and Museum Studies (Centro Nacional de Conservación, Restauración y Museología [CENCREM]) hosted many international seminars on historic preservation issues, plus others coordinated by the National Union of Cuban Architects, Engineers, and Builders (Unión Nacional de Arquitectos, Ingenieros y Constructores [UNAICC]). In 2000, the GDIC also hosted an urban design studio, Havana I, with the Graduate School of Design from Harvard University, led by Lee Cott. The following year, the same groups put on Havana II, and publications are expected from both meetings. These Harvard-Cuban encounters sought to discover ways of combining urban redevelopment with preservation in relevant but underused sites of the Cuban capital. The two studios offer a historic revindication for Harvard given the disruptive master plan generated by José Luis Sert in 1956–58, discussed earlier in this book.

The desire to revive local culture and the cultural significance of architecture is evident, too, by the works of local architects and state companies. On the Paseo del Prado, Roberto Gottardi, one of the designers of the Schools of Art, succeeded in preserving the external look of a new restaurant, while refurbishing a historic building. He did so without falling victim to the habitual tackiness that undermines such projects. At the same time, José Antonio Choy synthesized the modern tradition of the 1950s with the high-tech and deconstructivism styles of the contemporary period in his work at the new branch of the Banco Financiero Internacional, on Quinta Avenida in Miramar (fig. 10.2). This building creatively blends with the sober classicist existing bank, built in the 1940s. It achieves what seemed to be impossible for the designers of the new Parque Central Golden Tulip Hotel (fig. 10.3). New aesthetic values emerge in this bank through the dialogue between designers, painters, and muralists such as Rita Longa, Zaida del Río, and Eduardo Rubén, among others. This is also evident in the Hotel Meliá-Habana (fig. 10.4) by Abel García.

Construction of condominiums for foreigners by real estate joint ventures has increased quickly in Havana. More than 100 hectares are dedicated to those projects, mostly through in-fill in prime locations along the Malecón

FIGURE 10.2. Banco Financiero Internacional. Originally a commercial structure, the building was modified and redesigned by José Antonio Choy, on Fifth Avenue, Miramar. (Photograph by Roberto Segre)

and Fifth Avenue in Miramar. By early 2001, only one building with twenty-nine apartments had been finished, an unimaginative complex named Monte-carlo Palace (fig. 10.5). The quality of design in most of these buildings is low, with a sort of "lite" architecture that resembles public-housing blocks (Microbrigade buildings)—vaguely postmodernized and with more space and bigger windows than conventional residences for Cubans. These design elements are odd considering that the buildings are destined for clients whose basic needs call for a bed, shower, an air-conditioner, and a space to park their Hyundais (Coyula 2000c). One foreign investor called for a preposterous mixture of styles: neoclassical, Mediterranean, and Cuban colonial. In one case, the architect solved the problem by putting three different layers, one on top of the other.

In 2000, the Cuban government decided not to sell the flats anymore. Buildings under construction and deals already closed were given a green light. However, the next condominiums for foreigners will be property of the Cuban government and only for rent. Even though preventing the sale of national property to foreigners is a rational decision, this approach tends to look at real estate businesses as a one-time source of income, without capturing

FIGURE 10.3.
Parque Central Hotel,
located on the town
square of the same
name. In the mid-1990s,
a Dutch corporation
(Golden Tulip) devel-
oped this site at the busy
intersection of Prado
and Neptuno, in Habana
Vieja. The only original
remnant of the building
is the light-colored cor-
ner facade in the lower
left-hand corner of the
building. The remainder
of the structure is dis-
proportionate in size, as
shown by the exagger-
ated size of the columns
and porticoes at ground
level. (Photograph by
Mario Coyula)

land value increments. On the other hand, the government set the price of
land without using it as a planning tool to create incentives or disincentives
for building at certain locations. Moreover, the price of land is not systematically updated. This leads to efforts to seek short-run profits, with buildings as
big as possible—many times bigger than they should be—and structures that
fit badly in large vacant lots within the existing urban fabric composed of
much smaller lots and buildings. Neighbors do not recognize direct benefits
from the newcomers and their condominiums. Rather, residents of Miramar
see additions to a public infrastructure that is already critically overloaded.

The Monte Barreto area consists of a large tract of land with more than 40
hectares that remained barren up to the mid-1970s. Today, the development
of the area is in the hands of a joint-venture Cuban-Italian enterprise called
Inmobiliaria Monte Barreto, S.A. This complex is situated in an ideal location
and in one of the last open spaces of this size in Havana: between Third Ave-

FIGURE 10.4. Hotel Meliá-Habana. Designed by Abel García, the hotel is located on the oceanfront at the periphery of a larger commercial hotel complex in Miramar, Monte Barreto. (Photograph by Roberto Segre)

nue and the beautiful Fifth Avenue, between Seventieth and Eightieth Streets (fig. 10.6). The complex is anchored by the Miramar Trade Center. The locational decision proved to be shortsighted. Buildings run parallel to the shore, starting with those that came first. Four hotels (Tritón, Neptuno, Meliá-Habana, and Panorama, the last under construction) occupy that front line, leaving pedestrians and the rest of the new buildings without access or even ground-level views of the sea (fig. 10.7). Behind that first row will be two strips of buildings that will contain cubic buildings (see figs. 10.8 and 10.7D) of Miramar Trade Center. The center will have 180,000 square meters of offices and shops, plus 70,000 square meters for a two-thousand-car garage. By early 2001, two of these buildings had been finished. Farther away from the sea and across Fifth Avenue will be three more hotels, one of which (Miramar-Novotel) is already built (fig. 10.9) and two others are projected. Even farther south is an open space with some natural caves and unique vegetation that serve as a public park.

A much wiser layout and urban design would have been leaving a lineal central park running all the way into the sea, lined with buildings that provide two exceptional views: of the park and the ocean. This public space could also

FIGURE 10.5.
Foreign resident condominiums, Miramar. One of the few units completed for the foreign business community in Havana. These condominiums will be available for foreigners to own, after a stop-and-go decision by the Cuban government. In 2000, the government decided that it would allow the sale of units to foreigners in those cases in which deals had already been made, but it then stated that it would only lease units on the market after the year 2000. (Photograph by Mario Coyula)

perform as a social leveler, bringing together foreigners and Cubans. Herein lies another lesson than can be learned from Monte Barreto: not only is diversity good to preserve nature, but it offers broader societal value as well. The entire complex of more than 40 hectares is dollar oriented, with no room for a badly needed mixed development that might include other urban functions and different levels of income and social strata. Such a highly segregated area offers insight about what might become a car-oriented consumer pattern of suburban development. That image could reshape Havana and change the traditional way both tourists and Cubans interact in public spaces.

The Seventh Havana Art Biennial celebrated in November–December 2000 displayed a strong architectural focus, a harbinger of what we hope will be a new concern for the built environment in Havana. Some public art was done, recalling the almost forgotten days of the "urban revitalization" or

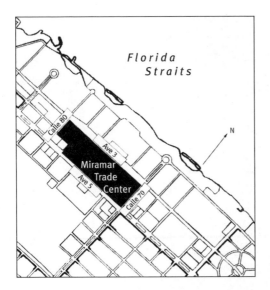

FIGURE 10.6.
Relative location of
Miramar Trade Center

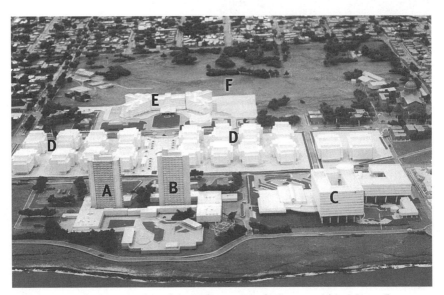

FIGURE 10.7. Architectural model of Miramar Trade Center within Monte Barreto development project. The model reveals the preexisting hotels near the Ocean: The Tritón (A), Neptuno (B), and Meliá-Habana (C). In the middle will be built other office buildings (D), while the background contains the already completed Novotel Hotel (E) with a park at the southern tip (F).

FIGURE 10.8. One of eighteen business and office complexes being built at the Miramar Trade Center (Photograph Roberto Segre)

"townscaping" (*reanimación urbanística*) projects that sharply improved the image of important corners in Havana during the 1970s and early 1980s. A seminar, La Habana 2000: Diseño, Cultura y Ciudad (Havana 2000: Design, Culture, and City) was organized by UNEAC for the city's 481st anniversary, and several exhibitions and theoretical seminars were devoted to the recovery of the historic city, the transformation of the present city, the future of Havana, the architecture of the 1960s, strategic planning, community development, and urban design projects to create a new streetscape for Aramburu (a dilapidated street in Centro Habana). In late 2000, the internationally renowned architect Frank Gehry visited Havana for the first time and talked to an enthusiastic crowd of architects, students, and artists. Some were surprised to learn about his current project for public housing in Portland, Oregon—a far cry from the titanium glitz of the Guggenheim Museum in Bilbao, Spain, which may have obscured the public image of his great talent.

A political campaign in the streets of Havana and throughout the island

FIGURE 10.9. Novotel Miramar, anchoring the southern end of Monte Barreto complex. See also figure 10.7 (E) for relative location. (Photograph by Mario Coyula)

began with a seemingly endless series of daily political rallies in late 1999. The protests continued into most of 2000 and gradually evolved into an ideological war. The crusade demanded that the U.S. administration return the six-year-old Elián González to his father in Cuba. The boy was kept by distant relatives in Miami after he survived the dramatic sinking of a small boat while trying to reach the United States, which cost his mother and several other travelers their lives. As noted in Chapter 8, a special plaza and stage to house the open-air rallies were quickly built at the Malecón in front of the U.S. Interests Section (fig. 8.4). The complex includes an elongated bronze sculpture of Cuba's national hero, José Martí, holding a small boy in one arm, while the other points accusingly at the U.S. Interests Section. After Elian's return, the mobilization campaign was kept in place, gradually incorporating cultural as well as political issues. This gave rise to a deeper, longer-term movement calling for a massive dissemination of culture, as opposed to mass culture (Paneque 2000).

This new statue of Martí is seen by many as alien to the Cuban national hero's physical image and charisma, as is the broad-shouldered giant statue placed at the former Plaza Cívica (currently Revolution Square) in 1953. Both monuments differ from the first monument of Martí at Parque Central (1905), done by the leading Cuban sculptor from the turn of the past century, José Vilalta de Saavedra. Figurative sculptures of revolutionary heroes in commemorative monuments, including Che Guevara, have often become banal, conventional artifacts that failed to grasp in contemporary terms the historic dimension and specific aura of their personalities. Some few exceptions in Havana were the first large monument done after the revolution came to power in 1959, the park monument to the university martyrs (designed by Escobar, Coyula, Domínguez, and Hernández, 1965–67), which covered a full city block close to Havana University (fig. 10.10); the mausoleum of the Heroes of March 13 at Colón Cemetery in Havana (designed by Escobar, Coyula, and Villa, 1981–82; fig. 10.11); and Che and the Children (Fernández and Villa, 1982) at Lenin Park.

On December 5, 2000, a statue of John Lennon by José Villa was inaugurated in the park at Seventeenth and Sixth Streets, in Vedado. The event marked a turning point for several reasons (fig. 10.12). The statue shows a life-sized image of the former Beatle sitting naturally on a bench. It is not only homage to a great musician of the twentieth century but also an act of historic justice. In the late 1960s and through the 1970s, the Beatles were banned as ideologically alien to the revolutionary ideals. This attitude reflected the official rejection of the young men's fashion of long hair, beards, and beaded necklaces, without realizing that it was the look of a counterculture opposing the establishment in capitalist countries. Moreover, one could argue that the Cuban mountain guerrilla rebels had started the fashion in the 1950s. The statue was inaugurated in the presence of the minister of culture and writer Abel Prieto—longhaired himself—and Fidel Castro. In a way, this closes a thirty-year span that ranges from Lenin Park to Lennon Park.

## An Ambiguous Destiny?

As we have attempted to show throughout this book, Havana is unique among Latin American cities for several reasons. Its population is small compared with that of other capitals, and its growth rate remains among the lowest in the region, the city having increased its population from just over 1 million residents in 1959 to 2.2 million in the mid-1990s, and with little immigration. By the late 1990s, its population growth had even dipped into the negative range, highlighting the problems that an aging population and its at-

FIGURE 10.10. University Martyrs Park-Monument, Centro Habana. Designed by Emilio Escobar, Mario Coyula, Sonia Domínguez, and Armando Hernández, 1965–67, the work is one of the first pieces of civic art built after 1959 that recognizes almost a century of student struggles against Cuban governments. It was designed to encourage interaction in the town square. Pedestrians can walk through the park, and children can play on the concrete mounds that carry burlap-impressed images of students who were martyred as far back as the nineteenth century. (Photograph by Joseph L. Scarpaci)

tendant planning concerns portend in the areas of labor force participation, social security, long-term care, and housing. The city's skyline changed little, and the neighborhoods, streets, blocks, and houses have not significantly altered the look of the capital since 1959, except for the ever lingering sight of construction cranes over Habana Vieja. Nevertheless, a visitor returning to Havana after an absence of nearly half a century will find changes in the people and the land uses of the city. The facades of many buildings are tired and distorted by makeshift modifications, car porches, vendors' stands, and fencing, the last three quickly ignited by the Special Period. Streets are dark, potholes are large, and neighborhoods are quiet except for the sound of passing bicyclists or blasting stereos. But that same visitor would be struck by the persistence of the city and the tenacity of its urban heritage. Everything, or almost everything, remains in the same place. Despite the steady pounding of

FIGURE 10.11. Heroes of March 13, Colón Cemetery, designed by Escobar, Coyula, and Villa, 1981–82 (Photograph by Joseph L. Scarpaci)

salt spray, rains, hurricanes, little maintenance, and a poor national economy, Havana survives (*pa'lante* in local vernacular), albeit more run down than ever before.

The city also continues to be quite exceptional in Latin America because the old colonial homes and the eclectic palaces built by the sugar aristocracy ("sugarocracy" as Moreno Fraginals called them) remain, as do the creative art deco buildings and the modest and widespread examples of the modern movement. Remarkable, too, is that the street layout of Old Havana remains relatively unchanged over these past centuries. Moving westward comes Centro Habana, which, despite its debilitated state, has held on to the continuous protection afforded by its famous *portales*. Adjacent Vedado retains a dense tree canopy over its streets and its majestic beaux arts mansions. West of Vedado is Miramar. Although it is rapidly becoming a major retail center for upscale stores and foreign residents, it has not lost its residential charm and is still home to many working-class *habaneros*. South of the city center is Lawton and Vibora, where one can easily see the creative interior subdivisions and remodeling of homes, gardens, and *portales* built by a middle class decades before.

FIGURE 10.12.
John Lennon statue. Designed by José Villa, the statue is located in a park in a residential neighborhood of Vedado. The highest authorities attended the December 2000 dedication of the statue. Ironically, the music of the Beatles was forbidden in Cuba during the 1960s and 1970s. However, Lennon's popular lyric "You can say that I'm a dreamer, but I'm not the only one" is translated into Spanish on the ground next to the statue. Within six months of the unveiling of the work, the "granny glasses" were yanked off the bronze image three times, even though there is twenty-four-hour security at the site.

Let us imagine what might have happened had the revolution of January 1, 1959, not arrived. To be sure, the proposals of José Luis Sert and his Harvard associates would have been carried out by the National Planning Board. Havana today would easily have 3 or 4 million residents. A strip of high-rise luxury hotels, country clubs, condominiums, and offices would form a waterfront barrier from Guanabo in the east to Santa Fe in the west: a 40-kilometer ribbon of steel-and-glass towers. Havana's shoreline would resemble nothing more novel than parts of Miami Beach, Isla Verde in San Juan, Puerto Rico, or Copacabana and Botafogo in Rio de Janeiro. Real estate speculation would have boomed in two clusters: apartments and offices in the central areas (Habana Vieja, Centro Habana, and Vedado) and a suburban extension of high-income neighborhoods to the west, in Country Club and La Coronela. This kind of suburbanization would have brought urban sprawl in the form of shopping malls and large supermarkets along with private universities and schools. The road axis along Rancho Boyeros might have spurred "garden neighborhoods." Along the Central Highway we could easily envision improvised shanties and the small homes of manual laborers. Squatters would fill in every poorly accessible vacant area, including high-risk ones prone to flooding. Squatters and low-income residents would occupy vacant lots dotted throughout the city. Those spaces would become the "gray areas" of the city, so common in the 1950s, and so ripe for the rise of *solares* and *cuarterías*. A speculative real estate market would generate the "gray areas" that would most likely serve as homes for the urban poor as well as migrants from the *campo*. This is not to suggest that Havana does not have pockets of poverty. Rather, we suggest a scenario that would have been much more pervasive throughout the cityscape.

Habana Vieja, Centro Habana, and Vedado would have lost their original shape. It may have been revived by new administrative functions and stores, but it would also have included the visual blight of the large plastic signs and icons of McDonalds, Pizza Hut, and Burger King. The concentration of retail functions would have brought functional and visual blight to main roads and central places: Prado, Parque Central, Reina, Galiano, Belascoaín, Infanta, La Rampa, and Zanja. Many fine old buildings would have been torn down to make room for large parking lots, breaking the spatial coherence of the city. Sert's plan to widen all these roads would have been carried out with limited-access roads, which would have only compounded traffic jams. They would have crisscrossed the fabric of the city, reaching even into the depths of Habana Vieja, as discussed in Chapter 9.

We would find a different Havana. Some of the contradictions that tourism and the free market have brought would be sharpened. The scarcity of building materials in socialist Cuba is well known. It has arrested architectural development as surely as Vesuvius arrested Pompeii (Livingston 1996). Nonetheless, the majority of *habaneros* wait patiently for the chance to improve their homes, while a social class with significant resources has been able to improve its housing in Havana's many neighborhoods. Cristina García captures the sentiment of those who had to wait, in her fictitious account of contemporary Havana: "Last fall, the line at the hardware store snaked around the block for the surplus paint, left over from a hospital project on the other side of Havana. Felicia bought the maximum amount allowed, eight gallons, and spent two Sundays painting the house with borrowed brushes and ladders. . . . 'After all,' she said, 'you could die waiting for the right shade of blue'" (1992, 39–39). Shiny buildings would tower over the city, designed, no doubt, by internationally renowned architects. Yet those same structures would have dismissed the cultural glimmer of the past and the traces of history etched into its landscape, as well as the amenities that make Havana a special place. The questions to be asked are: How can a vibrant future be achieved without losing all that has been conserved? How can we balance the changes that are soon to come with the urban heritage maintained so laboriously despite the absence of resources to execute such a Herculean task? Can the wishes of the Cuban National Heritage in Miami be accommodated with the aspirations of the Grupo para el Desarrollo Integral de la Capital in Havana and with the rapid real estate and speculation boom that would transform Havana? Is it possible to reconcile the dreams of many 90 miles away with those who sleep in the city every night? With a rush by some to make up for more than forty years of "lost" time, the end result will be a series of buildings that look more like the Meliá-Cohiba Hotel next to the Hotel Riviera on the Malecón than a more balanced approach to urban growth might reveal. Other Miami-Havana ties are more subtle but just as real, nonetheless. There is even rising interest in burying Cuban Americans, now entombed in south Florida, in Cuba, once legal barriers dissolve (De Córdoba 1996).

The incipient challenge facing Havana is how to handle changes that will prepare the city for a competitive economic market so as not to jeopardize the notability of its built environment or undermine its social accomplishments. Even the business-minded British publication the *Economist* devoted a special supplement to Havana, noting: "Old Havana, if it can be rescued before it crumbles, is a jewel of Spanish colonial architecture, and has a certain risqué chic spiced up with smoking and sex. Cuba has a highly educated work force and a sophisticated consumer market. And, most tantalising of all, Americans are debarred from trading there" ("Survey Havana" 1996, 12). While substituting the traditional rigid nature of city government for other forces could be advantageous from some points of view, it is important not to succumb to other extremes. Such a perilous situation might result when, for instance, the power of money overshadows the collective will of *habaneros* who would be removed from participating in how the city is administered. Having said that, we are acutely aware that current government administrative problems plague the city (see Chapter 5). A vibrant city, we contend, must take into account the wishes of its citizens.

The only way to obtain the $10 billion to $14 billion necessary to restore Havana is to act swiftly at both macro and micro levels (Coyula 1995). At one level, careful attention must be given to establishing guidelines about new investment, settlements, and economic activities. At another level, community participation should be encouraged that will help restore public spaces, buildings, and empty shops for starting small firms and other initiatives. Havana's streets, stores, plazas, and colonnades need to be revived in a way that integrates the present, albeit cautious, drive toward a market economy with ways of the past and with the social accomplishments of the revolution. These goals are not incompatible. As the exiled Cuban poet René Vázquez (born 1952, in Caibarién) observed at a conference on Cuban "bi-polarity" in Stockholm, which included Cuban writers from the island and in exile, "It's time to start forgiving and understanding ourselves, or at least to tolerate and acknowledge the other's rights *to exist* as a Cuban. . . . Nothing is more similar to a Cuban Communist than a Cuban anti-Communist. Our call [to this meeting] appealed to moderation, analysis, prudence and respect for the true protagonist of this meeting: the suffering Cuban people" (Vázquez 1994, 7–8; original emphasis, our translation). At the same conference, Miguel Barnet (born 1940, in La Habana) remarked: "Only those who transcend the limits of time shall win the battle, no matter in which pole they are. . . . The journey will be forever if it is committed to eternity. The dialogue between us cannot suffer from cracks or divergence. We can live with them, even if they are painful. . . . One way or another, we are the heirs of a nation forged in its own contradictions. . . . Time will erase personal discrepancies. . . . I see everyone in Cuba because a Cuban cannot be assimilated and because no one has really left, whether in a dream or in a nightmare" (Barnet 1994, 20).

Two faces emerge in the Antillean skyline of San Cristóbal de la Habana after nearly five hundred years of urbanization: one before the revolution—with colonial relics, twentieth-century housing stock, and ostentatious highrises of the 1950s—and one after the revolution that directed construction to public housing and schools and to even out the disparities with the rest of the island. Time and neglect are etched into both faces. The utopian ideal of restoring Havana will not only depend on lifesaving foreign investment, real estate developers, multinational corporations, or joint ventures. It will take more than skyscrapers, shiny hotels, and luxurious condominiums to revive a lackluster Havana and to restore its original radiance. Only by reviving the economy, guaranteeing modest levels of individual well-being, and orchestrating some aspect of the city's new private initiatives toward a common goal will the shining face of Havana's streets and plazas reappear. When every house can be repaired, painted, and rejuvenated by its occupants, Havana will once again become the "Antillean Pearl" it longs to be.

# Bibliography

Acosta, D. 1996a. "Cuba: Pimps and Prostitutes Expelled from 'Blue Paradise.'" InterPress Service. Worldwide distribution via the APC networks. June 11.

———. 1996b. "Cuba: Public and Private Spheres Must Come to Grips on Tourism." InterPress Service. Worldwide distribution via the APC networks. June 26.

———. 1996c. "Labour-Cuba: Change of Attitudes Needed along with Reforms." InterPress Service. Worldwide distribution via the APC networks. April 29.

Acosta, M. 1995. "Entrevista con Carlos Lage en el NTV." *Granma*, December 22, p. 4.

Acosta León, M., and J. E. Hardoy. 1971. *Reforma urbana en Cuba revolucionaria*. Caracas: Síntesis Dosmil.

———. 1972. "La urbanización en Cuba." *Demografía y Economía* (Mexico City) 6:41–59.

ACU (Agrupación Católica Universitaria). 1957. *¿Por qué la reforma agraria?* Havana: Universidad Católica.

Alonso, A. 1950. "La injusticia y el privilegio." *Propiedad Urbana* (Havana), no. 166: 9.

Alonso, Y. 1995. "Castro Only Wishes Embargo Was the Problem." *Houston Chronicle*, July 25, p. 17.

Alupez, M. 1993. "Bicycles Overtake Bus Travel in Cuba." *Urban Age* 2:16–17.

Alvarez Estévez, R. 1988. *Azúcar e inmigración, 1900–1940*. Havana: Ciencias Sociales.

Alvarez Tabío, E. 1989. *Vida, mansión y muerte de la burguesia cubana*. Havana: Letras Cubanas.

———. 1992. "Cocina al minuto: Acerca de la alquimia, la gula y la improvisación pp.15/20." *Arquitectura Cuba* 41:3–5.

———. 1994a. "La Habana hablada a tres." *3ZU* (ETSAB, Barcelona) 3:16–21.

———. 1994b. "El sueño despues." In *Y el perro ladra y la luna enfría: Fernando Salinas: Diseño, ambiente y esperanza*, edited by C. Véjar Pérez-Rubio, 15–20. Mexico City: Universidad Autónoma de México.

———. 2000. *Invención de La Habana*. Barcelona: Editorial Casiopea.

Amaral, A., ed. 1994. *Arquitectura neocolonial: América Latina, Caribe, Estados Unidos*. Mexico City: Fondo de Cultura Económica.

"Análisis del mercado de la vivienda." 1955. *Propiedad Urbana* (Havana), no. 254: 21.

Anderton, F. 1999. "In Cuba, Seeds of a Design Renaissance." *New York Times*, The Living Arts: New York, October 7, pp. B1–B14.

Angotti, T. 1989. "Microbrigades and the Spirit of Rectification." *Frontline* (Oakland, Calif.) 6, no. 14: 13.

"Approximate Driving Times in the Havana Area." 1993. *CubaNews* (Miami Herald Publishing Co.) (October): 6.

Aranda, S. 1968. *La revolución agraria cubana*. Mexico: Siglo XXI.

Arce, L. 1997. "La Habana como un laboratorio: An interview with Wolf Prix." *Arquitectura-Cuba* (UNAICC, Havana), Nueva Epoca, no. 376: 36–39.

Argan, G. C. 1983. *Storia dell'arte Come storia della Cittá*. Rome: Editori Riuniti.

Arnold, A. 1999. *Democracy in Cuba and the 1997–98 Elections.* Havana: Editorial José Martí.

Aroca, S. 1995. "2,500 Cubans a Year Kill Selves; Rate Called Highest in Hemisphere." *Miami Herald,* May 31, p. 10-A.

Arrate, J. M. F. 1762. *Llave del Nuevo Mundo: Antemural de las Indias Occidentales: La Habana descrita: Noticias de su fundación, monumentos Y estados.* Havana, 1830.

Arrinda, A. 1964. "El problema de la vivienda en Cuba." *Cuba Socialista* 40:11.

Arrufat, A. 1981. "La ciudad que heredamos." *Revolución y Cultura* 107 (July): 10–19.

Aruca, L. 1985. "Los portales de La Habana." *Arquitectura y Urbanismo* 5, no. 3: 24–29.

Aymonino, C. 1965. *Origini e sviluppo della citta moderna.* Padua: Marsilio.

Bähr, J., and G. Mertins. 1982. "A Model of the Spatial Differentiation of Latin American Metropolitan Cities." *Applied Geography and Development* 19:22–45.

Banco Nacional de Cuba s/f. N.d. *Informe económico 1999.* Havana: Banco Nacional de Cuba.

Bancrofft, R. 1994. "Alternative Building Materials and Technologies for Housing Construction in Cuba." In *Phänomen Cuba: Alternativewege in Architektur Stadetenwicklung und Ökologie,* edited by K. Mathéy, 196–202. Karlsruhe: Lehurstuhl für Städtedau und Entwerfern Orl Fakultät Für Architektur.

Bancrofft, R., A. Rojas, and V. Marín. 1999. "La formación del arquitecto: Recorrido en la evolución del pensamiento arquitectónico en la Facultad de Arquitectura de La Habana." *Arquitectura y Urbanismo* 20, no. 2: 62–64.

Barba, R., and A. E. Avella. 1996. "Cuba's Environmental Law." *Association for the Study of the Cuban Economy Newsletter* (Winter): 35–36.

Barclay, J. 1993. *Havana: Portrait of a City.* London: Cassel.

Bardach, A. L. 1995. "Letter from Havana: Casablanca on the Caribbean." *Vanity Fair,* March, 56–72.

Barkin, D. 1974. "La redistribución del consumo." In *Cuba: Camino abierto,* edited by D. Barkin and N. Manitzas, 186–223. Mexico City: Siglo XXI.

Barnet, M. 1994. "Estocolmo 1994." In *Bipolaridad de la cultura cubana,* edited by R. Vázquez, 19–21. Stockholm: Olof Palme International Center.

Barnou, P. 1951. *Breve historia de Holanda.* Buenos Aires: España-Calpe.

Baroni, S. 1989. "Territorio y modo de vida." *Planificación Física* (Havana) 2:5.

———. 1992–93. "Rapporto dall'Avana." *Zodiac: Rivista Internazionale di Architettura* (Milan) 8 (September–February): 161–77.

———. 1994a. "La Habana y su país (en sus tres tiempos)." *Carta de La Habana* (Grupo para el Desarrollo Integral de la Capital, Havana), no. 5: 1.

———. 1994b. "Report from Havana." In *Phänomen Cuba: Alternativewege in Architektur Stadetenwicklung und Ökologie,* edited by K. Mathéy, 21–30. Karlsruhe: Lehurstuhl für Städtedau und Entwerfern Orl Fakultät Für Architektur..

———. 1999. "La arquitectura y las ideas." *Arquitectura y Urbanismo* 20, no. 2: 5–12.

———. 2000. "Havana's Architecture." *Cuba Update* (Center for Cuban Studies, New York) 19, nos. 2–3: 5–12 (updated and enlarged English version of the original text, "Rapporto dall'Avana," 1992–93).

Barthel, D. 1996. *Historic Preservation.* New Brunswick, N.J.: Rutgers University Press.

Bastlund, K., and J. L. Sert. 1967. *Architecture, City Planning, Urban Design.* London: Thames & Hudson.

Bay Sevilla, L. 1924. *La vivienda del pobre.* Havana: Imprenta Montalvo, Cardenas y Cía.

Bedoya, F. 1992. "Edificio de comercio, servicios y viviendas en Reina y Aguila, Centro Habana: Primer premio Concurso Poder Popular, Habana 1989." *Arquitectura Cuba* 375:22.

Bejerano, D. 1992. "Conjunto habitacional 'Buen Retiro,' calle 45 entre 106 y 108. Marianao." *Arquitectura Cuba* 375:24.

Bengelsdorf, C. 1985. "Between Vision and Reality: Democracy in Socialist Theory and Practice." Ph.D. diss., Massachusetts Institute of Technology.

Benítez Rojo, A. 1989. *La isla que se repite: El Caribe y la perspectiva postmoderna.* Hanover, N.H.: Ediciones del Norte.

Benjamin, W. 1962. *Saggi e frammenti: Angelus Novus.* Turin: Einaudi.

Bens Arrarte, J. M. 1931. "La grande Habana de 1950." *Colegio de Arquitectos* (Havana) 5 (May): 18.

———. 1956. "La Habana republicana: Desarollo urbanístico." *Revista Nacional de la Propiedad Urbana* (Havana) 274 (February): 14.

———. 1959. "Las oportunidades de La Habana." *Revista Nacional de la Propiedad Urbana* (Havana) 300 (February): 10.

———. 1960a. "La evolución de la ciudad de La Habana desde mediados del siglo XIX hasta las primeras décadas del XX." *Arquitectura Cuba* 327–29:437.

———. 1960b. "La grande Habana: Los problemas de la zonificación." *Arquitectura Cuba* 322:323–24.

———. 1960c. "La grande Habana de 1980." *Arquitectura Cuba* 322:273.

Berg, A. 1973. *The Nutrition Factor: Its Role in National Development.* Washington, D.C.: Brookings Institution.

Bergad, L. W. 1989. "The Economic Viability of Sugar Production Based on Slave Labor in Cuba, 1859–1878." *Latin American Research Review* 24. no. 1: 95–114.

Bettelheim, C. 1969. "On the Transition between Capitalism and Socialism." *Monthly Review,* March, 9.

Bode Hernández, G. 1972. *Hacia la industrialización del sector de la construcción.* Havana: Ciencia y Técnica, Instituto Cubano del Libro.

Boorstein, E. 1968. *The Economic Transformation of Cuba.* New York: Monthly Review Press.

Browder, J., J. Bohland, and J. Scarpaci. 1995. "Patterns of Development on the Metropolitan Fringe: Peri-urban Expansion in Jakarta, Bangkok, and Santiago." *Journal of the American Planning Association* 61:310–27.

Brundenius, C., and A. Zimbalist. 1985a. "Cuban Economic Growth One More Time: A Response to Imbroglios." *Comparative Economic Studies* 27 (Spring): 3.

———. 1985b. "Cuban Growth: A Final Word." *Comparative Economic Studies* 27 (Winter): 4.

———. 1985c. "Recent Studies on Cuban Economic Growth: A Review." *Comparative Economic Studies* 27 (Spring): 1.

———. 1989. *The Cuban Economy: Measurement and Analysis of Socialist Performance.* Baltimore: Johns Hopkins University Press.

Bugeda Lanzas, J. 1954. *La propiedad horizontal.* Havana: Cultural.

Bühler-Oppenheim, K. 1949. *Datos históricos sobre el tabaco.* Havana: Actas Ciba.

Burgess, E. W. 1925. "The Growth of the City: An Introduction to a Research Project." In *The City,* edited by R. E. Park, E. W. Burgess, and R. D. McKenzie, 47–62. Chicago: University of Chicago Press.

*Business Tips on Cuba.* 1995. Volume 2, no. 4. Havana: Oficina Nacional de TIPS en Cuba.

Cabrera Infante, G. 1971. *Three Trapped Tigers.* Translated from the Cuban novel *Tres tristes tigres* by Donald Gardner and Suzanne Jill Levine in collaboration with the author. New York: Harper & Row.

———. 1985. *La Havane pour un infante défunt.* Paris: Seuil.

———. 1991. *Tres tristes tigres.* Barcelona: Seix Barral.

————. 1992. "La Habana para los fieles difuntos." In Cabrera Infante, *Mea Cuba.* Barcelona: Plaza & Janes.

————. 1994. *Mea Cuba.* Barcelona: Plaza & Janes.

————. 1999. *El libro de las ciudades.* Madrid: Alfaguara.

Callinicos, A. 1991. *The Revenge of History: Marxism and the East European Revolutions.* Oxford: Polity Press.

Campuzano, L. 2000. "Raúl Hernández Novás: El encuentro de Casal y Martí." *Revolución y Cultura* 5 (September–October): 16–20.

Capablanca, E. 1982. "Habana Vieja: Anteproyecto de restauración." *Arquitectura Cuba* 353–54:4.

————. 1983. "La Plaza Vieja: Propuesta de restauración." *Arquitectura Cuba* 34:355–56.

Cárdenas, E. 1991. *En la búsqueda de una arquitectura nacional.* Havana: Letras Cubanas.

————. 1999a. "El Art Deco o la entrada a la modernidad." *Arquitectura y Urbanismo* 2, no. 99: 15–26.

————. 1999b. "Uso y significado del espacio público." *Arquitectura y Urbanismo* 3, no. 99: 10–19.

————. 2000. "En el cambio de milenio: Polémicas y realidades en la arquitectura cubana." *AAA: Archivos de Arquitectura Antillana* (Santo Domingo) 5, no. 10: 128–33.

Cardoso, H., and E. Faletto. 1979. *Dependency and Development in Latin America.* Berkeley: University of California Press.

Carley, R., and A. Brizzi. 1997. *Cuba: Four Hundred Years of Architectural Heritage.* New York: Whitney.

Carneado, J. F. 1962. "El problema de la vivienda y la Ley de Reforma Urbana." *Cuba Socialista* 14:10–30.

Carpentier, A. 1966. *Tientos y diferencias.* Havana: UNEAC.

————. 1969. *Los pasos perdidos.* Havana: UNEAC.

————. 1970. *La ciudad de las columnas.* Barcelona: Editorial Lumen.

————. 1974a. "Problemática de la actual novela latinoamericana." In *Tientos y diferencias,* Havana: Unión de Escritores y Artistas de Cuba.

————. 1974b. *El siglo de las luces.* Havana: Editorial Arte y Literatura.

————. 1979. *La consagración de la primavera.* Havana: Letras Cubanas.

————. 1982. *La ciudad de las columnas: Fotografías de Grandal.* Havana: Letras Cubanas.

Carranza, J., L. Gutiérrez, and P. Monreal. 1995. *Cuba: La restructuración de la economía.* Havana: Editorial de Ciencias Sociales.

Casal, F. T., and M. Sanchez. 1984. "Planes directores de la ciudad de Havana: Análisis post-revolucionario." *Universidad de La Habana* 222 (January/September): 289.

Castells, M. 1974. *Estructura de clases y política urbana en América Latina.* Buenos Aires: SIAP.

Castex, P. 1986. *La politique de production-distribution du logement à Cuba.* Paris: Groupe de Recherche et d'Echanges Technologiques.

Castro, F. 1964. *La historia me absolverá.* Havana: Editora Política.

————. 1965a. "Constitución del Partido Comunista de Cuba." Speeches from September 30 and October 1, 1965. *Cuba Socialista* 51.

————. 1965b. "Discurso del Comandante Fidel Castro en la reunión de los secretarios de los Servicios Generales de las 25 sindicatos nacionales, (21/01)." In "Cronología de la Revolución Cubana referida a la arquitectura (1953–1969)," *Ensayos sobre arquitectura e ideologia en Cuba revolucionaria,* edited by Roberto Segre, 122. Havana: Universidad de La Habana, 1970.

————. 1970. "Discurso [speech]." Clausura Congreso UIA (September–October 1963). In

*Ensayos sobre arquitectura e ideología en Cuba revolucionaria*, edited by Roberto Segre, 104–10. Havana: Centro de Información Científico-Técnica, University of Havana.

———. 1975. "Informe Central al Primer Congreso del Partido Comunista de Cuba." *Granma*, December 20, p. 2.

———. 1977. "Discurso [speech]." Clausura en el segundo período de la Asamblea Nacional del Poder Popular (December 24). *Bohemia* (Havana), December 30, p. 2.

———. 1978. "Discurso [speech]." Clausura del XIV Congreso de la Central de Trabajadores de Cuba (December 2). *Granma*, December 4, p. 2.

———. 1980. "Informe Central al Segundo Congreso del Partido Comunista." *Bohemia* (Havana), December 26, p. 2.

———. 1984a. "Discurso [speech]." Clausura del Primer Fórum Nacional de Energía (December 4). *Granma*, December 6, p. 2.

———. 1984b. *La historia me absolverá*. Havana: Editorial Política.

———. 1987. "Pleno extraordinario del Partido Comunista de Cuba en la ciudad de La Habana." *Granma*, June 15, p. 3.

———. 1989. "Discurso [speech]." El Teatro "Karl Marx." *Granma*, October 2, p. 3.

———. 1990. "Discurso [speech]." July 26. *Bohemia* (Havana), August 3, p. 50.

———. 1995. "Seguimos creyendo en los enormes beneficios del socialismo." Speech given at the National Assemby. *Granma*, December 30, pp. 4–6.

———. 2000. "Cuba ni negocia ni vende su revolución, que ha costado la sangre y el sacrificio de muchos de sus hijos." *Granma*, June 22, p. 3.

Castro, R. 1996. "Maintaining Revolutionary Purity: Excerpts from a Report Presented by the General of the Army, Raul Castro, to the Central Committee of the Communist Party of Cuba, March 23, 1996." Reprinted from *Granma*, March 27, 1996. Cited in Free Cuba Center of Freedom House, *Cuba: Political Pilgrims and Cultural Wars*, 31–37. Washington, D.C.: Free Cuba Center of Freedom House.

CEA (Centro de Estudios de las Américas). 1995. *Los consejos populares, la gestión de desarrollo y la participación popular en Cuba: Conclusiones preliminares*. Havana: Centro de Estudios de las Américas.

CED (Centro de Estudios Demográficos). 1976. *La población de Cuba*. Havana: Ciencias Sociales.

CEE (Comité Estatal de Estadísticas). 1983. *Censo de población y viviendas de 1981: Evolución de la urbanización en Cuba, 1907–1981*. Havana: Instituto de Demografía y Censos.

Chaffee, W., and G. Prevost. 1992. "Cuba: A Background." In *Cuba: A Different America*, edited by W. Chaffee and G. Prevost. Totowa, N.J.: Rowman & Littlefield.

Chailloux, J. M. 1945. *Síntesis histórica de la vivienda popular (los horrores del solar habanero)*. Havana: Editorial J. Montero.

Chaline, C. 1987. "La Havane: Urbanisme de rupture ou de ratrappage?" *Annales de Geographie* 534:171–85.

Chateloin, F. 1989. *La Habana de Tacón*. Havana: Letras Cubanas.

Chauvin, L. O. 1996. "The Many Struggles of Cuban Academics." *Chronicle of Higher Education*, May 31, pp. A-33, 35.

Choay, F. 1992. *L'allegorie du patrimonine*. Paris: Seuil.

Chomsky, A. 1994. "Recent Historiography of Cuba." *Latin American Research Review* 29, no. 3: 220–36.

Chowdhury, A., and C. Kirkpatrick. 1994. *Development Policy and Planning*. London: Routledge.

Choy, J. A., and J. León. 1997. "El arquitecto y su obra: Pensamiento, obras y proyectos." *Arquitectura-Cuba* (UNAICC, Havana), Nueva Epoca, 376:5.

Cirules, E. 1993. *El imperio de La Habana.* Havana: Casa de las Américas.

Ciudad de La Habana. N.d. *Datos socioeconomicos* [pamphlet]. Havana: Poder Popular, Ciudad de la Habana.

Clawson, P. 1992. "Understanding the Post-Soviet Wasteland." In *Uprooting Leninism, Cultivating Liberty,* edited by Vladimir Tismaneanu and Patrick Clawson, 49–58. Lanham, Md.: University Press of America and Foreign Policy Research Institute.

Cohen, J. L. 1991. "Sulle traccie di Henard." *Casabella* (Milan) 34:531–32.

Collado, R., et al. 1998. "San Isidro: La nueva imagen: Proyecto social para la rehabilitación integral de un barrio habanero." In *Ciudad/City.* Pamplona: Ediciones Boloña.

Collis, D. 1995. *Environmental Implications of Cuba's Economic Crisis.* Cuba Briefing Paper Series No. 8 (July). Washington, D.C.: Cuba Project, Center for Latin American Studies, Georgetown University.

Comité Cubano de Asentamientos Humanos. 1976. *Los asentamientos humanos en Cuba.* Havana: Editorial de Ciencias Sociales.

Comité Estatal de Construcción. 1977. *La vivienda y su desarrollo en Cuba: Seminario Internacional de Arquitectura. 6 al 18 de noviembre.* Havana: Ministerio de Construcción, CEDITEC.

———. 1978. *Arquitectura y desarrollo nacional, Cuba, 1978.* Havana: Ministerio de Construcción, CEDITEC.

Consejo Nacional de Economía. 1958. *El empleo, el subempleo y el desempleo.* Havana: Consejo Nacional de Economía.

Cott, L. 2000. "Housing, Historic Preservation, and Community: A Design Workshop." *DRCLAS News* (Harvard University, David Rockefeller Center for Latin American Studies) (Winter): 29–30.

Coyula, M. 1984. "Por una noción más amplia de monumento." *Arquitectura y Urbanismo* 2:8–14.

———. 1985a. "Housing, Urban Renovation, and Popular Power: Some Aspects Concerning Havana." *Trialog* (Darmstadt, Germany) 6:35.

———. 1985b. "Vivienda, renovación urbana, y poder popular: La Habana (primera parte)." *Arquitectura y Urbanismo* 7, no. 2: 12.

———. 1987. "Materia y espíritu de lo ecléctico urbano." *Arquitectura y Urbanismo* 1:38–43.

———. 1990. "Planeando el futuro de Havana: Una entrevista con Mario Coyula." *Cuba Update* (Center for Cuban Studies, New York) 4, no. 11: 22.

———. 1991a. "Al reencuentro de la ciudad perdida." *Arquitectura y Urbanismo* 91, no. 1: 23–31.

———. 1991b. "Dandole taller al barrio." *Casa de las Américas* (Havana) 185 (October/December): 132–40.

———. 1992. "El veril entre dos siglos: Tradición e innovación para un desarrollo sustentable." *Casa de las Américas* (Havana) 189 (October/December): 94–101.

———. 1993a. "Para aprender del pasado: Una guía de La Habana." In *Guía de arquitectura: La Habana colonial (1519–1898),* edited by M. E. Martín Zequeira and E. L. Rodríguez Fernández, 11–14. Seville: Junta de Andalucia.

———. 1993b. "Vivienda accesible y desarrollo sustentable." *Carta de La Habana* (Grupo para el Desarrollo Integral de la Capital, Havana), año 1, #2.

———. 1995. "La Habana siempre, siempre La Habana." *ArquiAméricA* (San José, Costa Rica), 2.

———. 1998. "Arquitectura y ciudad en la cultura cubana contemporánea." *Revolución y Cultura* 6 (November–December).

————. 1999a. "Arquitectura y entorno: La ciudad como entorno en movimiento." *Arquitectura y Urbanismo* 2, no. 99: 61–62.

————. 1999b. "Dos paradigmas urbanos, un mismo cumpleaños." *Carta de La Habana* (Grupo para el Desarrollo Integral de la Capital, Havana), #18–19:21–25.

————. 1999c. "En defensa del Vedado." *Revolución y Cultura* 5 (September–October): 4–5.

————. 2000a. "Architecture and City in Contemporary Cuban Culture." *Cuba Update* (Center for Cuban Studies, New York) 19, nos. 2–3: 13–14, 16–18.

————. 2000b. "Architecture, Sex, and Revolution." *La Gaceta de Cuba* (UNEAC, Havana) 4 ( July–August).

————. 2000c. "La arquitectura habanera en el 2000 vista desde el futuro." *Revista Bimestre Cubana* (Havana) 87, epoca 3, #12 ( January–June): 200–209.

————. 2000d. "El futuro de la ciudad: Desarrollo en equilibrio." *Revista de Occidente* (Madrid) 230–31 ( July–August): 89–104.

————. 2000e. "Havana Always: Preserving the Soul of a City." *DRCLAS News* (Harvard University, David Rockefeller Center for Latin American Studies) (Winter): 27–28.

————. 2000f. "Housing in Cuba: Part II." *Designer/Builder* (Santa Fe, N.Mex.) 7, no. 7: 29–35.

————. 2000g. "Influencias cruzadas Cuba/EEUU en el medio construido: Carril Dos, o autopista en dos sentidos?" *AAA: Archivos de Arquitectura Antillana* (Santo Domingo), 5, no. 10: 118–23; also in *Arquitectura y Urbanismo* 2, no. 99: 8–14.

————. 2000h. "Un parque, un río, una ciudad." *Siempre Verde* (Parque Metropolitano de La Habana) no. 1 (April 2000): 2–4.

————. 2000i. "Sobre diversidad, escala, carácter . . . y otras sutilezas." *Carta de La Habana* (Grupo para el Desarrollo Integral de la Capital, Havana), año 7, #22: 1.

Coyula, M., M. Cabrera, and R. Oliveras. 1995. *Los talleres de transformación integral del barrio: Una experiencia de planeamiento sustentable y participativo en La Habana.* Havana: Grupo para el Desarrollo Integral de lo Ciudad.

Coyula, M., G. González, and A. T. Vincentelli. 1993. *Participación popular y desarrollo en los municipios.* Havana: CEA.

Coyula, M., Miren Uriarte, and María Caridad Cruz. 1995. *Medio ambiente urbano y participación popular en Cuba: Marco conceptual.* Havana: Grupo para el Desarrollo Integral de la Capital.

Cuba. 1976. *Constitución de la República de Cuba.* Havana: Ministerio de Justicia, Editorial Orbe.

Cuba National Heritage. N.d. *Cuba National Heritage* [brochure]. Miami: Cuba National Heritage.

"Cuba's Health System: Tested in Hard Times." 1994. *CubaNews* (Miami Herald Publishing Co.) (November): 11.

"Cuba's Self-Employed Continue to Dwindle As Government Measures Prompt Many to Quit." 2001. *CubaNews (Target Research,* Washington, D.C.) (March): 7.

"Cuba's Water Resources." 1995. *CubaNews* (Miami Herald Publishing Co.) (April): 9.

*Cuba Va.* 1993. (Coordinador Estatal de Solidadarid con Cuba, Havana) 5 (December).

Curbelo Castellanos, J. L. 1999. *Cuba y La Habana.* Madrid: Límite Visual.

Curtis, James. 1993. "Havana's Parque Coppelia: Public Space in Socialist Cuba." *Places* 8, no. 3: 62–69.

D'Acosta-Calheiros, H. 1964. "La investigación y el desarrollo técnico en las construcciones de Cuba, después de la revolución." *Arquitectura Cuba* 332:37.

Damade, J. 1994. "Les villes de La Havane: En Jacobo Machover." In *La Havane, 1952–1961: D'un dictateur l'autre: Explosion des sens et morale révolutionnaire,* 42–48. Serie Memoires 31. Paris: Editions Autrement.

Dávalos Fernández, R. 1990. *La nueva ley general de la vivienda.* Havana: Editorial Ciencias Sociales.

―――. 1993. *Las empresas mixtas: Regulación jurídica.* Havana: Consultoria Jurídica Internacional.

de Albuquerque, K., and J. L. McElroy. 1992. "Caribbean Small-Island Tourism Styles and Sustainable Strategies." *Environmental Management* 16:619–32.

De Armas, M., and M. Robert. 1975. "Vivienda de los estratos populares en la seudo-república." Thesis, Escuela de Arquitectura, Facultad de Tecnología, Havana.

De Armas, R. 1975. *La revolución pospuesta.* Havana: Ciencias Sociales.

De Córdoba, J. 1996. "Grave Issue: Exiles, Even in Death, Seek to Return to Cuba." *Wall Street Journal,* March 26, pp. 1, 9.

de Fuentes, W. 1916. *Por el arte.* Havana: Arquitectura, Pintura, Escultura, La Moderna Poesía.

Del Aguila, J. 1992. "Cuba." In *The Software Toolworks Multimedia Encyclopedia.* Novato, Calif.: Software Toolworks.

De la Nuez, I. 1990. "La arquitectura posible." *La Gaceta de Cuba* (UNEAC, Havana) 2 (February): 10.

―――. 1991. "El espejo cubano de la posmodernidad: Más allá del bien y del mal." *Plural* (Mexico City) 238 (July): 21.

De las Cuevas Toraya, J. 1993. *La industria cubana de materiales de construcción.* Havana: Ministerio de la Industria de Materiales de Construcción.

"Demographics: Cuba's Education Levels." 1993. *CubaNews* (Miami Herald Publishing Co.) (November): 14.

De Soto, H. 1989. *The Other Path: The Invisible Revolution in the Third World.* New York: Harper & Row.

De Tercin, F., ed. 1989. *La ciudad hispanoamericana: El sueño de un orden.* Madrid: CEHOPU.

Díaz Acosta, A., and S. Guerra. 1982. *Panorama histórico literario de nuestro América, 1900–1943.* Havana: Casa de Las Américas.

Díaz-Briquets, S. 1994. "Cuba." In *Latin American Urbanization: Historical Profiles of Major Cities,* edited by M. G. Greenfield, 173–87. Westport, Conn.: Greenwood Press.

Díaz-Briquets, S., and J. Pérez-López. 2000. *Conquering Nature: The Environmental Legacy of Socialist Cuba.* Pittsburgh: University of Pittsburgh Press.

Dilla, H. 1995. "Los municipios cubanos y los retos del futuro." *Comunidad* (Instituto de Planficación Física, Havana) 4, no. 95: 69–72.

Dilla, H., G. González, and A. T. Vincentelli. 1993. *Participación popular y desarrollo en los municipios cubanos.* Havana: Centro de Estudios sobre América.

Dirección de Planificación Física. 1984. Plan Director (map). Havana: Instituto de Planificación Física.

Dirección Provincial de Planificación Física. 2000. "Esquema de ordenamiento territorial y urbanismo." Havana: Dirección Provincial de Planificación Física.

Donato, E. 1972. "Sert, 1929–1959." *Cuadernos de Arquitectura y Urbanismo* (Barcelona) 93:2.

Dorfles, G. 1965. *Nuovi miti, Nuovi riti.* Turin: Einaudi.

Duany, A. 1997. "The Future of Havana." In *One World: Shared Cultural Influences in the Architecture of the Americas.* Miami: Association of Collegiate Schools of Architecture, University of Miami. Also published in *Cuba Update* (Center for Cuban Studies, New York) 19, nos. 2–3 (2000):35–36.

Dunlop, B. 1999. *Havana: The Photography of Hans Engels.* Munich: Prestel.

Durán, M. 1992. "Edificio de apartamentos en calle 11 entre 4 y 6, Vedado." *Arquitectura Cuba* 375:30.

Duverger, H. 1993a. "Acapite." In *Guía de arquitectura: La Habana colonial (1519–1898)*, edited by M. E. Martín Zequeira and E. L. Rodríguez Fernández, 15–32. Seville: Junta de Andalucia.

———. 1993b. "Los orígenes: La villa de San Cristobal de La Habana." In *Guía de arquitectura: La Habana colonial (1519–1898)*, edited by M. E. Martín Zequeira and E. L. Rodríguez Fernández, 17. Seville: Junta de Andalucía.

———. 1994. "El maestro francés del urbanismo criollo para La Habana." In *Jean Claude Nicolas Forestier (1861–1930): Du jardin du paysage urbain*, edited by Bénédicte Leclerc, 221–40. Paris: Picard Editeur.

Eckstein, S. 1977. "The Debourgeoisment of Cuban Cities." In *Cuban Communism*, edited by I. L. Horowitz, 443–74. New Brunswick, N.J.: Transaction Books.

Eliash, H., and M. Moreno. 1989. *Arquitectura y modernidad en Chile, 1925–1965*. Santiago, Chile: Universidad Católica de Chile.

Elinson, H. 1999. *Cuba's Jineteros: Youth Culture and Revolutionary Ideology*. Cuba Briefing Paper Series No. 20 (March). Washington, D.C.: Cuba Project, Center for Latin American Studies, Georgetown University.

Entenza y Jova, P. 1953. "Algunas consideraciones sobre la legislación de alquileres." *Propiedad Urbana* (Havana), no. 230: 11.

Enzensberger, H. M. 1995. *Guerra civil*. São Paulo: Companhia das Letras.

Espino, D. 1991. "International Tourism in Cuba." Paper presented at the First Annual Meeting of the Association for the Study of the Cuban Economy, Miami, August 15–17.

———. 1993. "Tourism in Socialist Cuba." In *Tourism Marketing and Management in the Caribbean*, edited by D. J. Gayle and J. N. Goodrich, 111–19. London: Routledge.

———. 2000. "Cuban Tourism during the Special Period." In *Cuba in Transition*, 10:360–80. Washington, D.C.: ASCE (Association for the Study of the Cuban Economy).

Estévez, R. 1953. "El forum del Colegio de Arquitectura sobre la Plaza Cívica y Monumento de Martí." *Espacio* (Havana) 9, no. 2: 36.

———. 1977. *Los poderes populares y el plan de viviendas: Formas de ampliar los recursos para incrementar la construccion de viviendas: VII Seminario de Viviendas y Urbanismo*. Havana: CEDITEC.

———. 1984. "Análisis de la realizaciones de viviendas en Cuba y en otros paises socialistas." Paper presented at the XI Seminario de Vivienda y Urbanismo, Havana, March. Mimeo.

Estévez, R., and J. A. Pereda. 1990. *Situación, demanda, y política de vivienda y urbanización en Cuba desde 1959: Ciudad '4, IV Congreso Iberoamericano de Urbanismo*. Havana: Congreso Iberoamericano de Urbanismo.

"Facts and Statistics." 1996a. *CubaNews* (Miami Herald Publishing Co.) (March): 4.

"Facts and Statistics." 1996b. *CubaNews* (Miami Herald Publishing Co.) (June): 4.

Fagen, R. 1986. "The Politics of Transition." In *Transition and Development*, edited by R. Fagen, C. D. Deere, and J. L. Coraggio, 249–63. New York: Monthly Review Press.

Feinsilver, J. 1993. *Healing the Masses: Cuban Health Politics at Home and Abroad*. Berkeley: University of California Press.

———. 1994. "Cuban Biotechnology: A First World Approach to Development." In *Cuba at a Crossroads: Politics and Economics after the Fourth Party Congress*, edited by J. F. Pérez-López, 167–89. Gainesville: University of Florida Presses.

———. 1995. "From Healing the Masses to Healing the Classes: Scenarios for the Reform of the Cuban Health Sector." Paper presented at the conference "Toward a New Cuba? Revolutionary Legacy and Market Imperative in the Age of Globalization," Princeton University, April 7–8.

Fernández, E. 1990. *Las zonas residenciales en ciudad de La Habana: Ciudad '4. IV.* Congreso Iberamericano de Urbanismo, Comisión 2. Renovación Urbana. Havana: IV Congreso Iberamericano de Urbanismo.

Fernández, J. M. 1995. "Sobre la necesidad del establecimiento de un sistema jurídico sobre el ordenamiento urbano en Cuba." *Comunidad* (Instituto de Planificación Física, Havana) 4, no. 95: 90–94.

————. 1996. *Regulaciones y desarrollo urbano en la ciudad de La Habana.* Havana: Grupo para el Desarrollo Integral de la Capital.

Fernández, M. 1999. "Diagnósticos ambientales participativos: Carmelo, Ceiba, Palatino, Pogolotti, Puentes Grandes." *Parque Metropolitano de La Habana.* August. Havana: CIERI.

Fernández, O. 1981. "La Habana Vieja: Renace una ciudad." *Cuba Internacional* (Havana) 1 (January): 33.

Fernández, P. 1987. "La vivienda obrera durante el machadato: El Reparto Ludgarita." In *Arte: Cuba, república,* edited by P. Fernández and L. Merino, 125. Colección de lecturas, Facultad de Artes y Letras. Havana: Universidad de La Habana.

Fernández Alba, A. 1995. "Metrópolis de oasis oxidados." *Astrálago* (Madrid) 2 (March): 3–7.

Fernández Cox, C. 1990. "Hacia una modernidad apropiada: Obstáculos y tareas internas." In *Nueva arquitectura en América Latina: Presente y futuro,* edited by A. Toca, 71–79. Mexico City: G. Gili.

Fernández Figueroa, E. J. 1993. *Cuba: La historia como condicionante del territorio.* Madrid: Principado de Asturias-Asociación Rubén Darío.

Fernández Font, M. 1998. "Algunas reflexiones sobre el período especial." *Revista Bimestre Cubana* (Havana) 83, epoca 3, #8 (January–June): 13–25.

Fernández Galiano, L. 1994. "Metrópolis." *Arquitectura Viva* 35 (March/April): 3.

Fernández Miranda, M. 1985. *La Habana, ciudad de América, La Habana Vieja: Mapas y planos en los archivos de España.* Madrid: Ministerio de Cultura de Espana.

Fernández Núñez, J. M. 1976. *La vivienda en Cuba.* Havana: Arte y Literatura.

Fernández Simón, A. 1950. *Memoria história técnica de los acueductos de la ciudad de La Habana.* Havana: Colegio Provincial de Arquitectos.

————. 1959. "Los distintos tipos de urbanizaciones que fueron establecidos en la ciudad de La Habana en su época colonial." *Revista de la Propiedad Urbana* (Havana) 3 (February): 39–44.

————. 1995. "Los distintos tipos de urbanizaciones fueron establecidas en la ciudad de la Habana durante su época colonial." In *Cuba: Arquitectura y urbanismo,* edited by F. J. Préstamo Hernández, 163–80. Miami: Ediciones Universal.

Fields, G. 1985. "Economic Development and Housing Policy in Cuba." *Berkeley Planning Journal* (Berkeley, Calif.) 3, nos. 1–2 (Spring–Fall).

Figueras, M. A. 1994. *Aspectos estructurales de la economía cubana.* Havana: Editorial de Ciencias Sociales.

Fitzgerald, E. V. 1986. "Notes on the Analysis of the Small Underdeveloped Economy." In *Transition and Development,* edited by R. Fagen, C. D. Deere, and J. L. Coraggio, 28–53. New York: Monthly Review Press.

Forbes, D., and N. Thrift. 1987. *The Socialist Third World: Urban Development and Territorial Planning.* Oxford: Blackwell.

Forestier, J. C. N. 1928. *Gardens: A Note-book of Plans and Sketches.* New York: Charles Scribner and Sons.

Fornet, A. 1967. *En blanco y negro.* Havana: Instituto del Libro.

Freixa, J. 1973. *José Luis Sert.* Barcelona: G. Gili.

French, R., and F. E. Hamilton. 1979. *The Socialist City.* Chichester, England: John Wiley and Sons.

Fuentes, N. 1987. *Ernest Hemingway retrouvé.* Paris: Gallimard.

Fuller, L. 1985. "The Politics of Workers' Control in Cuba, 1959–1983." Ph.D. diss., University of California, Berkeley.

García, C. 1992. *Dreaming in Cuban.* New York: Ballantine Books.

García, E., et al. 1998. "El Malecón de La Habana: Un proceso de transformación y cooperación." In *Ciudad/City.* Pamplona: Ediciones Boloña.

García Márquez, G. 1979. *Cien años de soledad.* Bogotá: La Oveja Negra.

García Pleyán, C. 1986. *La transformación de la estructura de las ciudades principales de Cuba.* Havana: Instituto de Planficación Física and Instituto Superior Politécnico José Antonio Echeverría.

———. 1994. *Convocatoria al Simposio sobre Planeamiento y Gestión Territorial en los Municipios Cubanos.* October. Havana: Instituto de Planificación Física.

———. 1995a. "Gestión del suelo y disciplina urbanística: Resultados del primer taller de derecho urbanístico." *Comunidad* (Instituto de Planificación Física, Havana) 4, no. 95: 36–44.

———. 1995b. "Planeamiento urbano y gestión local en los municipios cubanos: Desafíos y perspectivas en un contexto cambiante." *Comunidad* (Instituto de Planificación Física, Havana) 4, no. 95: 77–89.

García-Saiz, M. C. 1990. "Antillas: Audiencia de Santo Domingo." In *Historia urbana de Iberoamérica: La ciudad Barroca, análisis regionales, 1573/1750,* edited by Francisco de Solano, 2:2. Madrid: Consejo Superior de Colegios de Arquitectura de España, Comisión Nacional Quinto Centenario, Junta de Andalucia, Consejería de Obras Públicas y Transportes.

García Santana, A. 1999. *Contrapunteo cubano del arco y el horcón.* Havana: Instituto Cubano del Libro.

García Vázquez, F. J. 1968. *Aspectos del planeamiento y la vivienda en Cuba.* Buenos Aires: Editorial Jorge Alvarez.

Garnier, J. P. 1971. "Une ville et une révolution: La Havane." *Espaces et Sociétés* (Paris) 3 (July): 147.

———. 1973. *Une ville, une revolution: La Havane, de l'urbaine à la politique.* Paris: Editions Anthropos.

GDIC (Grupo para el Desarrollo Integral de la Capital). 1990. *Estrategia.* Havana: Ediciones Plaza Vieja.

———. 1991. *Problemática de las urbanizaciones en las zonas de desarrollo de viviendas en la ciudad de La Habana.* Havana: Grupo para el Desarrollo Integral de la Capital.

———. 1994. *Prediagnóstico.* Havana: Grupo para el Desarrollo Integral de la Capital (October).

Gelabert-Navia, J. A. 1994. "Havana in the 1920s." In *Phänomen Cuba: Alternativewege in Architektur Stadetenwicklung und Ökologie,* edited by K. Mathey, 43. Karlsruhe: Lehurstuhl für Städtedau und Entwerfern Orl Fakultät Für Architektur.

Gilbert, A. 1994. *Latin America.* London: Routledge.

Ginsberg, N. 1961. *Atlas of Economic Development.* Chicago: University of Chicago Press.

Glazer, H. 2000. "Housing in Cuba: Part I." *Designer/Builder* (Santa Fe, N.Mex.) 7, no. 6.

Gobierno de Cuba. 1899. *Censo de población.* Havana: Gobierno de Cuba.

Goldberger, P. 1998. "Bringing Back Havana." *New Yorker,* January 26.

Gomila, S. 2000. "Una política sustentable para la vivienda y los asentamientos humanos."

Paper presented at a conference titled "Towards a Sustainable Habitat: Challenges for the New Millennium." Grupo para el Desarrollo Integral de la Capital, Havana, May 22–24.

Gomila, S., J. Portuondo, M. López, and R. Estévez. 1984. "Intervención del Centro Técnico de la Vivienda y el Urbanismo en el Seminario Internacional de Arquitectura y Remodelación de Ciudades." Havana. Mimeo.

González, D. 1997. *Economía y calidad en la vivienda: Un enfoque cubano*. Havana: Ciencia y Técnica.

González, G. 1995. "Cambios económicos y descentralización municipal en Cuba: Los retos del futuro." *Comunidad* (Instituto de Planficación Física, Havana) 4, no. 95: 61–68.

González, M. 1990. "Sobre areas verdes en la capital." *Boletín Informativo* (Centro de Documentación, Poder Popular, Havana) 7:18–26.

———. 1993. *Sobre planos, esquemas y planes directores de la ciudad de La Habana*. Havana: Grupo para el Desarrollo Integral de la Capital.

———. 1999. "1959–1999: Dos Habanas que se juntaban y eran una sola hermosa Habana." *Carta de La Habana* (Grupo para el Desarrollo Integral de la Capital, Havana), #18–19.

———. 2000. *10° encuentro sobre las areas verdes en la ciudad de La Habana* (Proceedings). Havana: Grupo para el Desarrollo Integral de la Captial.

González, P., and E. Cabrera. 1996. "Todas las tonalidades del arco iris: Parque Lenin, convergen naturaleza, cultura y recreación." *Sol y Son* (La Revista Internacional de Cubana de Aviación, Havana) 36, no. 3:39–42.

González Manet, E. 1976. "El Vedado: Anatomía de un barrio." *Boletín de la Comisión Nacional Cubana de la UNESCO* (Havana) 64:16.

———. 1983. "Historia y presencia de la vieja Habana." *Boletín de la Comisión Nacional Cubana de la UNESCO* (Havana) 91:22.

González Mínguez, N. 1991. "La ciudad cubana en 1990: Perspectivas." *Ciudad y Territorio* (Madrid) 86–87:9.

Goodrich, J. N. 1993. "Socialist Cuba: A Study of Health Tourism." *Journal of Travel Research* 12 (Summer):36–41.

Griffin, L., and L. Ford. 1980. "A Model of Latin American City Structure." *Geographical Review* 37:397–422.

"Growth in Tourism." 1994. *Business Tips on Cuba*, vol. 1, no. 5. Havana: Oficina Nacional de TIPS en Cuba.

Gunn, G. 1995. *Cuba's NGOs: Government Puppets or Seeds of a Civil Society?* Cuba Briefing Paper Series No. 7 (February). Washington, D.C.: Cuba Project, Center for Latin American Studies, Georgetown University.

Guselnikov, V. 1976. *Economía de la construcción*. Havana: CEDITEC.

Gutelman, M. 1967. *L'agriculture socialiste a Cuba*. Paris: F. Maspero.

Gutiérrez, P. J. 1998. *Trilogía sucia de La Habana*. Barcelona: Anagrama.

Gutiérrez, R. 1983. *Arquitectura y urbanismo en Iberoamérica*. Madrid: Ediciones Cátedra.

———. 1992. *Buenos Aires: Evolución histórica*. Buenos Aires: Fondo Editorial Escala.

Gwynne, R. 1986. *Industrialisation and Urbanisation in Latin America*. Baltimore: Johns Hopkins University Press.

"Habana 1." 1971. *Arquitectura Cuba* 340.

"Habana 2." 1973. *Arquitectura Cuba* 341–42.

*La Habana y sus grandes edificios modernos*. 1919. Obra conmemorativa del IV Centenario de su fundación. Havana: Pernas y Figueroa.

Hamberg, J. 1986. *Under Construction: Housing Policy in Revolutionary Cuba*. New York: Center for Cuban Studies.

————. 1990. "Cuba." In *Housing Policies in the Socialist Third World*, edited by Kosta Mathéy, 35–70. London: Mansell.

————. 1994. "The Dynamics of Cuban Housing Policy." Ph.D. diss., Columbia University.

Hamilton, N. 1992. "The Cuban Economy: Dilemmas of Socialist Construction." In *Cuba: A Different America*, edited by W. Chaffee and G. Prevost. Landham, Md.: Rowman & Littlefield.

Hardoy, J. E. 1974. "Estructura espacial y propiedad." In *Cuba: Camino abierto*, 2d ed., edited by D. Barkin and N. Manitzas, 274–311. Mexico City: Siglo XXI.

————. 1992. "Theory and Practice of Urban Planning in Europe, 1850–1930: Its Transfer to Latin America." In *Rethinking the Latin American City*, edited by J. E. Hardoy and R. Morse, 20–49. London: Johns Hopkins University Press.

Hardoy, J. E., and C. Aranovich. 1969. "Urbanización en América hispánica entre 1580 y 1630." *Boletin del Centro de Investigaciones Históricas y Estéticas* (Caracas) 11 (May): 35.

Hardoy, J. E., and M. Gutman. 1992. *Impacto de la urbanización en los centros históricos de Iberoamérica*. Madrid: Mapfre.

Harms, H., P. Pfeiffer, and W. Ludeña, eds. 1996. *Vivir en el "centro": Vivienda de inquilinato en los barrios céntricos de las metrópolis de América Latina*. Hamburg: Technische Universität Hamburg-Harburg.

Hart, A. 1979. "Discurso pronunciado en la cuarta conferencia intergubernamental sobre políticas culturales en Latinoamérica y el Caribe, auspiciada por la UNESCO" (Bogotá, November 1, 1978). Del Trabajo cultural. Selección de discursos Editorial de Ciencias Sociales: 309. La Habana. Mimeographed.

————. 1982. "La declaración de La Habana Vieja como Patrimonio de la Humanidad es un reconocimiento a la defensa del patrimonio cultural de Cuba." *Granma*, December 16, p. 4.

Havanatur. 1992. *Cuba: Body and Soul: Technical Information for Tourism Professionals*. Panama: Creative Printing.

Heine, J. 1991. "Habana Vieja: La ciudad de las columnas." *Mundo* (Santiago, Chile) 10B, no. 9: 16.

Hernández, E. 1994. "Sustentable, alternativo, progresivo . . . bajo consumo." *Carta de La Habana* (Grupo para el Desarrollo Integral de la Capital, Havana), no. 5: 2.

Hernández, T., R. Lores, and L. Méndez. 1990. *La nueva Habana Vieja*. Lima: Cambio y Desarrollo, Instituto de Investigaciones.

Hernández Busto, E. 1992. "Los otros signos de la isla." *Plural* (Mexico City) 250 (July): 22.

Herrera, L. 1976. "Plan de normalización para la Construcción." *Revista Normalización*, no. 111 (January–March): 3.

Herrera Ysla, N. 1991. "La Habana de mi corazón." *Excelsior* (Mexico City), Sección Metropolitana, 2, no. 3: 1.

Herring, H. 1966. *The History of Latin America*. New York: Knopf.

Hoyt, H. 1939. "The Pattern of Movement of Residential Rental Neighborhoods." In *The Structure and Growth of Residential Neighborhoods in American Cities*, 114–22. Washington, D.C.: Federal Housing Administration.

Huerta, T. 2000a. "Resultados y razones" (interview of Carlos Lage, pt. 1). *El Economista de Cuba* (Havana) (July–August).

————. 2000b. "Resultados y razones" (interview of Carlos Lage, pt. 2). *El Economista de Cuba* (Havana) (September–October).

*Human Development Report 2000*, <<http://www.undp.org/hdro.htm>>.

Ibarra, J. 1985. *Un análisis psicosocial del cubano: 1898–1925*. Havana: Ciencias Sociales.

————. 1992. *Cuba, 1898–1921: Partidos políticos y clases sociales*. Havana: Ciencias Sociales.

ICGC (Instituto Cubano de Geodesia y Cartografía). 1979. *Atlas demográfico de Cuba*. Havana: ICGC.

Ickes, B., and R. Ryterman. 1992. "Credit Should Flow to Entrepreneurs." In *Uprooting Leninism, Cultivating Liberty*, edited by Vladimir Tismaneanu and Patrick Clawson, 69–84. Lanham, Md.: University Press of America and Foreign Policy Research Institute.

INAV (Instituto Nacional de Ahorro y Vivienda). 1962. "Presencia del INAV en la Revolución Cubana." Havana: INAV.

"Informe Central al XIV Congreso de la Central de Trabajadores de Cuba." 1978. *Granma*, December 2, p. 3.

Informe Nacional de Cuba. 1996. *Conferencia Mundial de Naciones Unidas para los Asentamientos Humanos. Habitat II*. Havana-Istanbul: Instituto Nacional de Vivienda.

"Infrastructure." 1993. *CubaNews* (Miami Herald Publishing Co.) (October): 9.

Inmobiliaria Monte Barreto, SA. N.d. Miramar Trade Center, Havana [brochure].

InterPress. 1996a. "Cuba: Peso gana terreno al dolar en casas de cambio." InterPress Third World News Agency (IPS), Montevideo. Distributed electronically through the APC network, August 21.

InterPress. 1996b. "Cuba: Zonas francas, nuevo paso en apertura al capital extranjero." InterPress Third World News Agency (IPS), Montevideo. Distributed electronically through the APC network, September 13.

IPF (Instituto de Planificación Física). 1973. "La Habana Metropolitana, un instrumento para el desarrollo de Cuba socialista." *Arquitectura Cuba* 341–42:3.

———. 1992. "El problema de la vivienda en Cuba: Algunas consideraciones para su solución." *Arquitectura Cuba* 41.

Izquierdo, R., and M. Liz. 1984. "Vivienda en La Habana." Paper presented before the meetings of Remodelación de Ciudades, Havana, November. UNAICC.

Izquierdo, T., and M. Quevedo. 1972. "Elementos para la historia de un barrio residencial habanero." Thesis. Escuela de Arquitectura, Facultad de Tecnología, Havana.

James, P. 1959. *Latin America*. London: Cassell.

Jenkins, R. 1987. *Transnational Corporations and the Latin American Automobile Industry*. Pittsburgh: University of Pittsburgh Press.

Jiménez, G. 1990. "29 años sin analfabetismo." *Granma*, March 1, p. 2.

———. 1997. "La Banca Cubana en vísperas de la revolución." *Revista Bimestre Cubana* (Havana) 81, epoca 3, #6 (January–June): 53–69.

———. 1998. "Nivel de vida de los cubanos anterior a 1959." *Revista Bimestre Cubana* (Havana) 83, epoca 3, #8 (January–June): 41–62.

Joe, B. E. 1995. "Yndamiro Restano: Recently Released POC Thanks AI, Plans to Return to Cuba." Amnesty International. November. Mimeo.

Johnson, W. F. 1920. *The History of Cuba*. New York: B. F. Buck and Co.

*Journal of Decorative and Propaganda Arts, 1875–1945*. 1996. (Wolfson Foundation, Miami) 22. Theme issue on Cuba.

Judget, J. 1989. "The Many Lives of Old Havana." *National Geographic* (August): 278–300.

Junta Central de Planificación. 1976. *La situación de vivienda en Cuba en 1970 y su evolución prospectiva*. Junta Central de Planificación, Dirección Central de Estadística. Havana: Orbe.

Kavafis, K. 1978. *Poesías completas*. Madrid: Ediciones Peralta.

Kay, C. 1994. *Latin American Theories of Development and Underdevelopment*. London: Routledge.

Kirby, A. 1995. "A Research Agenda for the Close of the Century." *Cities* 12:5–11.

Klak, T. 1994. "Havana and Kingston: Mass Media and Empirical Observations of Two Caribbean Cities in Crisis." *Urban Geography* 15:318–44.

Kuethe, A. J. 1986. *Cuba, 1753–1853: Crown, Military, and Society.* Knoxville: University of Tennessee Press.

Labatut, J. 1957. "Experiencias en la práctica y la enseñanza de la planificación urbana." *Arquitectura* (Havana) 290, no. 25: 446.

Lagache, E. 1992. "La Havane expectativa." *Lumières de la Ville* (Paris) 5 (June): 177.

Lane, P. 2000. "*Au naturel*: Buscando una solución para el Río Almendares mediante la biotecnología." *Siempre Verde* (Parque Metropolitano de La Habana), no. 2 (October).

Lang, P. 1995. *Mortal City.* New York: Princeton Architectural Press.

Laprade, A. 1931. "Parques y jardines de J. C. N. Forestier." *Colegio de Arquitectura de la Habana* 3, no. 15: 9.

Latin American Center, University of California at Los Angeles. 1968. "Cuba." *Supplement to Statistical Abstract of Latin America.* Los Angeles: Latin American Center, University of California at Los Angeles.

Leal, E. 1986. *Regresar en el tempo.* Havana: Letras Cubanas.

———. 1988. *La Habana, ciudad antigua.* Havana: Letras Cubanas.

Le Corbusier. 1947. "Plan director de Buenos Aires." *Número Monográfico de la Arquitectura de Hoy* 4. Buenos Aires.

Lee, S. 1994. "Entrevista a Carlos Lage." *Granma,* October 31.

———. 1995a. "Batallas priorizadas: Ordenar el trabajo por cuenta propia garantizar el cobro de impuestos y eliminar toda ilegalidad." *Granma,* December 28, p. 3.

———. 1995b. "Se presentarán 29,131 candidatos para los 14,229 escaños municipales." *Granma,* June 27, p. 1.

———. 1996a. "A comienzos del 96: Hablemos de presupuesto y de impuesto." *Granma,* January 5.

———. 1996b. "La ayuda familiar y otras respuestas." *Granma,* May 23, p. 2.

———. 2000a. "Analizan producción y distribución de los productos normados." *Granma,* November 25.

———. 2000b. "Incrementar las exportaciones y disminuir las importaciones innecesarias." *Granma,* March 18, p. 8.

———. 2000c. "Lo que hagamos tenemos que hacerlo bien." Presentation by Carlos Lage on the Comisión Gubernamental de Apoyo a la Ciudad de La Habana (Governmental Commission of Support of Havana City). *Granma,* February 19.

Leff, C., ed., and Narciso G. Menocal, guest ed. 1996. Cuba theme issue. *Journal of Decorative and Propaganda Arts, 1875–1945* (Wolfson Foundation, Miami) 22.

Le Riverend, J. 1960. *La Habana: Biografía de una provincia.* Havana: Academia de la Historia de Cuba.

———. 1965. *Historia economica de Cuba.* Havana: Editora Universitaria.

———. 1966. *La república: Dependencia y revolución.* Havana: Editora Universitaria.

———. 1992. *La Habana, espacio y vida.* Madrid: Mapfre.

Levine, R. 1993. *Tropical diaspora: The Jewish experience in Cuba.* Gainesville: University of Florida Presses.

Lezama Lima, J. 1970. *La ciudad hechizada.* Havana: UNEAC.

———. 1988. *Confluencias: Selección de ensayos.* Prólogo, Abel Prieto. Havana: Letras Cubanas.

———. 1994a. "Pasajes inéditos de un diario íntimo." *La Gaceta de Cuba* (UNEAC, Havana) 3 (May–June): 14.

———. 1994b. *La visualidad infinita.* Havana: Letras Cubanas.

———. 1998. *La Habana caleidoscópica.* Madrid: Bartleby Editores.

Linares, M. T., and C. Vitier. 2000. "Un fructífera centuria." *Juventud Rebelde Dominical* (Havana), December 31.

Lincoln Institute of Land Policy. 1996. "Global City Regions: Searching for Common Ground." *Landlines* (Newsletter of the Lincoln Institute of Land Policy, Cambridge, Mass) 8, no. 1: 1–7.

Livingston, M. 1996. "Houses That Dream in Cuban: The Crumbling of Habana Vieja." University of Tennessee, Department of Building Construction. Mimeo.

Livingston, R. 1990. *Cirugía de casas*. Buenos Aires: Editorial CP 67.

Llana, M. E. 1983. *Casas del Vedado*. Havana: Letras Cubanas.

Llanes, L. 1978. "Los marginados de la arquitectura (1902–1919)." *Universidad de La Habana* 207 (January/March): 89–100.

———. 1985. *Apuntes para una historia sobre los constructores cubanos*. Havana: Letras Cubanas.

———. 1987. "Las actividades comerciales y financieras y su influencia sobre las construcciones." In *Arte: Cuba, república*, edited by P. Fernández and L. Merino, 49–53. Colección de lecturas, Facultad de Artes y Letras. Havana: Universidad de La Habana.

———. 1988. *La transformación de La Habana*. Havana: Letras Cubanas.

———. 1993. *1898–1921: La transformación de La Habana a través de su arquitectura*. Havana: Letras Cubanas.

Llanes, L. 1999. *The Houses of Old Cuba*. New York: Thames & Hudson.

Lobo Montalvo, M. L. 2000. *Havana: History and Architecture of a Romantic City*. New York: Monacelli Press.

Locay, L. 1995. "Institutional Requirements for Successful Market Reforms." In *Cuba in Transition*, vol. 5. ASCE (Association for the Study of the Cuban Economy). Online at <<http://lanic.utexas.edu/la/cb/cuba/asce/cuba5>>.

Loomis, J. A. 1994. "Architecture or Revolution: The Cuban Experiment." *Design Book Review* 32–33 (Spring/Summer): 71–80.

———. 1999. *Cuba's Forgotten Art Schools: Revolution of Forms*. New York: Princeton Architectural Press.

López, A. 1987. "Las obras oficiales durante el período de gobierno de Ramón Grau San Martín (1944–1948)." In *Arte: Cuba, república*, edited by P. Fernández and L. Merino, 269. Colección de lecturas, Facultad de Artes y Letras. Havana: Universidad de La Habana.

López, F. 2000a. "Cumplir con el pueblo, un reto permanente de la agricultura." *Granma*, January 5.

———. 2000b. "No hay ley capaz de doblegar la dignidad de un pueblo." *Granma*, July 12.

López Castañeda, F. 1963. "Labor de restauración realizada por la Comisión Nacional de Monumentos durante el año 1963." *Arquitectura/Cuba* 332:6–17.

———. 1971. "Conservación y restauración de monumentos." *Constructores* (Havana) 1 (January): 19–25.

López Rangel, R., and R. Segre. 1986. *Caos urbano y nuevas tendencias en la arquitectura latinoamericana*. Mexico City: G. Gili.

López Segrera, F. 1972. *Cuba: Capitalismo dependiente y subdesarrollo (1510–1959)*. Havana: Casa de las Américas.

———. 1980. *Raíces históricas de la Revolución Cubana (1868–1959)*. Havana: Ediciones Unión.

———. 1989. *Cuba: Cultura y sociedad, 1510–1985*. Havana: Letras Cubanas.

Los Naranjos. 1984. *Creación y desarrollo de una empresa pecuaria genética modelo: Empresa pecuaria genética "Los Naranjos."* Havana: Editorial Científico-Técnica.

Luis, R. 1995. "¿Se salvará La Habana?" *Prisma* (Havana), no. 271, año 21 (September/October): 33–38.

Luxner, L. 1995. "Cuba as Future Client and Competitor." *CubaNews* (Miami; a publication of the Miami Herald Publishing Co.) (June): 8.

Lynch, K. 1972. *What Time Is This Place?* Cambridge: MIT Press.

Machado Ventura, O. 1960. *Comunidades pesqueras.* Havana: Departamento de Desarrollo Social.

———. 1969. "Discurso [speech]." *Clausura al seminario de viviendas* (March). Havana: Ministerio de Construcción.

———. 1976. "La Habana: DESA: La industrialización de la construcción de la vivienda. El sistema I.M.S. en Cuba." Mimeo.

Mahtar M'Bow, A. 1983. *La Plaza Vieja.* Ministerio de Cultura. Havana: Ediciones Plaza Vieja.

Malone, S. T. 1996. *Conflict, Coexistence, and Cooperation: Church-State Relations in Cuba.* Cuba Briefing Paper Series No. 10 (August). Washington, D.C.: Cuba Project, Center for Latin American Studies, Georgetown University.

Manitzas, N. 1974. "El marco de la revolución." In *Cuba: Camino abierto,* 2d ed., edited by D. Barkin and N. Manitzas, 13–59. Mexico City: Siglo XXI.

Maribona, A. 1957. "El fantástico crecimiento de la propiedad urbana en la Gran Habana." *Revista de la Propiedad Urbana* (Havana), no. 284 (October): 13.

Marquetti, H. 2000. "El proceso de reanimación del sector industrial en Cuba: Principales resultados y problemas." *Revista Bimestre Cuba de la Sociedad de los Amigos del País,* epoca 3, no. 13: 5–30.

Marrero, L. 1956. *Historia económica de Cuba: Guía de estudio y documentación.* Havana: Universidad de Havana, Instituto Superior de Estudios e Investigaciones Económicas.

———. 1975a. *Cuba: Economía y sociedad: El siglo XVII (I).* Madrid: Playor.

———. 1975b. *Cuba: Economía y sociedad: El siglo XVII (II).* Madrid: Playor.

———. 1976. *Cuba: Economía y sociedad: El siglo XVII (III).* Madrid: Playor.

———. 1981a. *Cuba: Economía y sociedad.* San Juan, Puerto Rico: Editorial San Juan.

———. 1981b. *Geografía de Cuba.* San Juan, Puerto Rico: Editorial San Juan.

Martín Zequeira, M. E. 1999. "Una ciudad con vista al mar: Conversación con Andres Duany." *La Gaceta de Cuba* (UNEAC, Havana) 2 (March–April): 10–13.

Martín Zequeira, M. E., and E. Múscar. 1992. *Proceso de urbanización en América del Sur.* Madrid: Mapfre.

Martín Zequeira, M. E., and E. L. Rodríguez Fernández. 1992. *La Habana: Map and Guide to 337 Significant Architectural Monuments in the Cuban Capital and Surroundings.* Darmstadt, Germany: Trialog.

———. 1993. *Guía de arquitectura: La Habana colonial (1519–1898).* Seville: Selección y Catálogo, Junta de Andalucia.

———. 1998. *La Habana: Guía de arquitectura. Havana, Cuba. An Architectural Guide.* Havana and Seville: Ciudad de La Habana, Junta de Andalucía.

Martínez, O. 2000. "Entramos al siglo XXI con la economía creciendo, pero aún más importante, con la dignidad multiplicada." Presentation to the sixth period of the National Assembly. *Granma,* December 22.

Martínez Inclán, P. 1925. *La Habana actual: Estudio de la capital de Cuba desde el punto de vista de la arquitectura de ciudades.* Havana: Imprenta P. Fernández.

———. 1946. *Algunas nociones de estética urbana.* Havana: Imprenta P. Fernández.

———. 1949. *Código de urbanismo: Carta de Atenas, Carta de La Habana.* Havana: Imprenta P. Fernández.

Masides i Serracant, M. 1995. *La Habana I: Laminarios del patrimonio arquitectónico cubano.* Barcelona: ACCIC.

Mathéy, K. 1992a. "Self-Help Housing Policies and Practices in Cuba." In *Beyond Self-Help Housing*, edited by K. Mathéy, 181–216. London: Mansell.

———, ed. 1992b. *Beyond Self-Help Housing*. London: Munsell.

———. 1994. "Informal and Substandard Neighbourhoods in Revolutionary Cuba." In *Phänomen Cuba: Alternativewege in Architektur Stadetenwicklung und Ökologie*, edited by K. Mathéy, 123–32. Karlsruhe: Lehurstuhl für Städtedau und Entwerfern Orl Fakultät Für Architektur.

Medin, T. 1990. *Cuba: The Shaping of Revolutionary Consciousness*. Boulder, Colo.: Lynee Rienner.

Mediz Bolio, A. 1916. *Palabras al viento: Crónicas de Cuba*. Mexico City: Ateneo Peninsular.

Mena, C., and A. Cobelo. 1992. *Historia de la medicina en Cuba: Hospitales y centros benéficos en Cuba colonial*. Miami: Ediciones Universales.

Menéndez, M. 1992. "Entrevista con Nisia Agüero." In *El desarrollo del país y las políticas urbanas: Barrios céntricos de inquilinato para sectores de bajos ingresos en metrópolis latinoamerianas: Procesos de formación, dinámica de desarrollo y planificación deficiente en la restructuración urbanas: Estudio de Caso: La Habana*, edited by M. Coyula, 17–22. Havana: Instituto Superior Politécnico José Antonio Echeverría.

Mesa-Lago, C. 1988. "The Cuban Economy in the 1980s: The Return of Ideology." In *Cuba: Past Interpretations and Future Challenges*, edited by S. Roca, 59–100. Boulder, Colo.: Westview Press.

———. 1994. *Are Economic Reforms Propelling Cuba to the Market?* Coral Gables, Fla.: University of Miami, North-South Center.

Mesías, R., and J. L. Morales. 1985. "Arquitectura al servicio del usuario: Creadores de su vivienda." XI Seminario de Vivienda y Urbanismo. Havana: Centro Técnico de la Vivienda y el Urbanismo. Mimeo.

Michener, J. A., and J. Kings. 1989. *Six Days in Havana*. Austin: University of Texas Press.

Ministry of Economy and Planning. 1996. "Cuba Economic Report: First Semester, 1996." Havana: Ministry of Economy and Planning.

MINSAP (Ministerio de Salud Pública). 1994. Unpublished health, morbidity, and mortality data gathered by the Geography Section, MINSAP, Vedado, Havana City.

Mongin, O. 1995. *Vers la troisième ville?* Paris: Hachette.

Montoulieu y de la Torre, E. 1953. "El crecimiento de La Habana y su regularización (1923)." *Ingeniería Civil* (Havana) 8, no. 4: 567.

Moreno Fraginals, M. 1964. *El ingenio: El complejo económico social cubano del azúcar*. Vol. 1, *1760–1860*. Havana: Comisión Nacional Cubana de la UNESCO.

———. 1976. *The Sugar Mill: The Socioeconomic Complex of Sugar in Cuba, 1760–1860*. New York: Monthly Review Press.

———. 1978. *El Ingenio*. Vols. 1–3. Havana: Ciencias Sociales.

———. 1995. *Cuba/España, España/Cuba: Historia común*. Barcelona: Grijalbo Mondadori.

Mosquera, G. 1999. "The Infinite Island: Introduction to Contemporary New Cuban Art." In *Contempary Art from Cuba: Irony and Survival on the Utopian Island*, 23–29. Arizona State University Art Museum. New York: Delano Greenidge Editions.

Munford, E. 2000. *The CIAM Discourse on Urbanism, 1928–1960*. Cambridge: MIT Press.

Murrell, P. 1992. "Privatization versus the Fresh Start." In *Uprooting Leninism, Cultivating Liberty*, edited by Vladimir Tismaneanu and Patrick Clawson, 59–68. Lanham, Md.: University Press of America and Foreign Policy Research Institute.

Napoles, R. 1996a. "Cuba: Cattle Rustlers and Illicit Butchers Devastate Herds." InterPress Service. Worldwide distribution via the APC networks. May 17.

————. 1996b. "Cuba: Government Limits Private Profit Making." InterPress Service. Worldwide distribution via the APC networks. June 6.

————. 1996c. "Cuba-Economy: Taxes Hit Free Market Sales." InterPress Service. Worldwide distribution via the APC networks. May 7.

————. 1996d. "Cuba-Environment: Havana Bay—The Island's Most Polluted Ecosystem." InterPress Service. Worldwide distribution via the APC networks. May 30.

"New Five-Star Hotel." 1995. *CubaNews* (Miami Herald Publishing Co.) (January): 3.

"New Police in Havana." 1996. *CubaNews* (Miami Herald Publishing Co.) (February): 3.

"New Rules, Taxes Hit Self-Employed Workers." 1996. *CubaNews* (Miami Herald Publishing Co.) (June): 2.

Niddrie, D. 1971. "The Caribbean." In *Latin America: Geographical Perspectives*, edited by H. Blakemore and C. T. Smith, 73–120. London: Methuen.

Noceda, J. M. 1984. "Las formulaciones teóricas del Movimiento Moderno en la arquitectura y el urbanismo en Cuba: 1928–1958." Tesis de grado. Escuela de Arquitectura, Facultad de Artes y Letras, Havana.

Nochteff, H. 1984. *Desindustrialización y retroceso en Argentina, 1976–1982: La industrial electronica de consumo*. Buenos Aires: Facultad Latinoamericano de Ciencias.

Noever, P., ed. 1996. *The Havana Project: Architecture Again*. Munich: Prestel.

Novick, A. 1991. "Arbitros, pares, socios: Técnicos locales y extranjeros en la génesis del urbanismo porteño." *Arquitectura Sur* (Mar del Plata, Argentina) 4, no. 2: 44.

Núñez, R. 1996. *Land Planning and Development in Havana City: Two Study Cases: The New Investment Context Regarding Land*. Havana: Grupo para el Desarrollo Integral de la Capital.

Núñez, R., H. J. Brown, and M. Smolka. 2000. "Using Land Value to Promote Development in Cuba." *Land Lines* (Lincoln Institute of Land Policy, Cambridge, Mass.) (March): 1, 4–5.

Núñez, R., and C. García Pleyán. 1999. "Regeneration in Old Havana and the Role of Value Capture." Working paper (English and Spanish), Lincoln Institute, Cambridge, Mass. (available free downloading at www.lincolninst.edu).

"Official Says Cuban Unemployment Is 7 Percent." 1996. *CubaNews* (Miami Herald Publishing Co.) (June): 2.

Oficina del Historiador de la Ciudad de La Habana. 1998. *El Malecón de La Habana: Un proceso de transformación y de cooperación. The Havana Malecón: A Transformation and Co-operation Process*. Havana and Pamplona: *Ciudad/City*, Oficina del Historiador de la Ciudad de La Habana, Colegio Oficial de Arquitectos Vasco-Navarro.

————. 1999. *Desafío de una utopía: Una estrategia integral para la gestión de salvaguardia de La Habana Vieja. Challenge of a Utopia: A Comprehensive Strategy to Manage the Safeguarding of the Old Havana*. Havana and Pamplona: *Ciudad/City*, Oficina del Historiador de la Ciudad de La Habana, Colegio Oficial de Arquitectos Vasco-Navarro.

Oliver, P. 1970. *Shelter and Society*. London: Cresset Press.

Ortega, L. 1993. "Junto al barrio: Rehabilitación de Atarés." *Arquitectura y Urbanismo* 14:9–14.

————. 1996. "Barrio de Atarés." In *Vivir en el "centro." Vivienda e inquilinato en los barrios céntricos de las metrópolis de América Latina*, edited by H. Harms, W. Ludeña, and P. Pfeiffer, 95–134. Hamburg-Harburg: Technische Univeristât.

Ortiz, F. 1963. *Contrapunteo cubano del tabaco y el azúcar*. Havana: Consejo Nacional de Cultura.

Otero, R. 1940. "Obras de embellecimiento que proyectaba J. C. N. Forestier para La Habana." *Arquitectura* (Havana) 86, no. 8: 208.

Padrón Lotti, M., and H. Cuervo Masoné. 1988. "La ciudad de La Habana: Una nueva voluntad urbanística en marcha." Paper delivered at the III Congreso Iberoamericano de Urbanismo. Barcelona.

————. 1991. "La ciudad de La Habana: Una nueva voluntad urbanistica." *Ciudad y Territorio* (Madrid), nos. 86–87: 107

Palm, E. W. 1955. *Los monumentos arquitectónicos de La Española*. Santo Domingo: Universidad de Santo Domingo.

Paneque, A. 2000. "Cuba vive hoy día un proceso pleno de desarrollo cultural." Interview with the UNEAC president, Carlos Martí. *Granma*, December 29, p. 6.

Paolini, R. 1994. "La Habana Vieja: Víctima de la guerra fría." *El Diario de Caracas*, May 29, p. 30.

Park, R. E., W. W. Burgess, and R. D. McKenzie. 1925. *The City*. Chicago: University of Chicago Press.

"Participatory Planning and Preservation in Havana: Q & A with Mario Coyula." 1997. *Land Lines* (Lincoln Institute of Land Policy, Cambridge, Mass.) (July) (available free downloading at www.lincolnsinst.edu).

Partido Comunista de Cuba. 1976. *Plataforma programática del Partido Comunista de Cuba*. Havana: Departamento de Orientación Revolucionaria del Comité del Partido Comunista de Cuba.

Pastor, M. A., and A. Zimbalist. 1995. "Waiting for Change: Adjustment and Return in Cuba." *World Development* 23: 705–20.

Pattullo, P. 1996. *Last Resorts: The Cost of Tourism in the Caribbean*. London: Cassell and Latin American Bureau.

Payne, S. 1995. "Cuba's Garden Revolution." *Permaculture International Journal* 54:14–24.

Pendle, G. 1978. *A History of Latin America*. New York: Pendle.

Pereira, M. A. 1985. "El monumento a Jose Martí en la Plaza de la Revolución." In *Memorias del 3er simposio de la cultura en la ciudad de La Habana*, 20–22. Havana: Dirección Provincial de la Cultura, Poder Popular.

————. 1994. "La producción monumentaria conmemorativa en Cuba, 1959–1993." Ph.D. diss., Facultad de Artes y Letras, Universidad de La Habana.

Pérez, F., and M. Fernández. 1996. *A Strategy to Improve Water Supply and Sanitation in Havana*. Havana: Grupo para el Desarrollo Integral de la Capital.

Pérez, H. 1975. *El subdesarollo y la vía del desarrollo*. Havana: Ciencias Sociales.

Pérez, L. 1988. *Cuba: Between Reform and Revolution*. New York: Oxford University Press.

Pérez, M. 1995a. *Autoconstrucción con participación popular: Una alternativa válida*. Havana: Grupo para el Desarrollo Integral de la Capital.

————. 1995b. *Condición y estructura de la vivienda en La Habana*. Havana: Grupo para el Desarrollo Integral de la Ciudad.

————. 1996. *Hacia una política local de mejoramiento ambiental con participación comunitaria*. Havana: Grupo para el Desarrollo Integral de la Capital.

Pérez Beato, M. 1936. *Habana antigua: Apuntes históricos*. Havana: Fernández y Co.

Pérez de la Riva, J. 1946. *Origen y regimen de la propiedad horizontal*. Havana: Moderna Poesía.

————. 1963. *Correspondencia reservada del Capitán General don Miguel Tacón con el gobierno de Madrid: 1834–1836*. Havana: Departamento de Coleccion Cubana, Biblioteca Nacional "José Marti."

————. 1965. "Desarrollo de la población habanera." *Bohemia* (Havana), November 14, pp. 100–101.

————. 1975. "Los recuresos de Cuba al comenzar el siglo: Inmmigración, economía y nacionalidad (1899–1906)." In *La república neocolonial: Anuario de estudios cubanos*, 1:5–35. Havana: Ciencias Sociales.

Pérez-López, J. 1994a. "Economic Reform in Cuba: Lessons from Eastern Europe." In *Cuba at a Crossroads: Politics and Economics after the Fourth Party Congress*, edited by J. F. Pérez-López, 238–63. Gainesville: University of Florida Presses.

——. 1994b. "Islands of Capitalism in an Ocean of Socialism: Joint Ventures in Cuba's Development Strategy." In *Cuba at a Crossroads: Politics and Economics after the Fourth Party Congress*, edited by J. F. Pérez-López, 190–219. Gainesville: University of Florida Presses.

——. 1995. *Cuba's Second Economy*. New Brunswick, N.J.: Transaction Books.

Pérez Montás, E. 1998. *La ciudad del Ozama: 500 años de historia urbana*. Santo Domingo: Patronato de la Ciudad Colonial de Santo Domingo, Centro de Altos Estudios Humanísticos y del Idioma Español.

Peters, P. 2000. *The Farmer's Market: Crossroads of Cuba's New Economy*. Arlington, Va.: Lexington Institute.

Peters, P., and J. L. Scarpaci. 1998. *Cuba's New Entrepreneurs: Five Years of Small-Scale Capitalism*. Arlington, Va.: Alexis de Tocqueville Institution.

Peyrerea, C. 1929. *Las huellas de los conquistadores*. Madrid: Aguilar.

Pezuela, J. 1868. *Historia de Cuba*. Vol. 1. Madrid: N.p.

Pichardo, H. 1965. *Documentos para la historia de Cuba epoca colonial*. Havana: Editorial Nacional de Cuba.

Pichardo-Moya, F. 1943. "La edad media cubana." *Revista Cuba* (Havana).

Piñera, T. 1998. "Bellas artes: Una nueva dimensión." *Granma*, July 25.

Pino-Santos, O. 1973. *El asalto a Cuba por la oligarquía financiera yanqui*. Havana: Casa de las Américas.

Pita, F. 1995. "Las propiedades confiscadas hay que reclamarlas aquí." *Granma*, April 29, p. 4.

PNUD. 2000. *Programa para el desarrollo humano a nivel local*. Havana: Programa de las Naciones Unidas para el Desarrollo, Cuba.

Poder Popular. N.d. *Datos socioeconomicos: Ciudad de La Habana* [brochure]. Havana: Poder Popular.

Polanyi, K. 1957. *The Great Transformation*. Boston: Beacon Press.

Pollock, P. 2000. "Exploring Cuba's Urban and Environmental Heritage." Working paper (English), Lincoln Institute, Cambridge, Mass. (available free downloading at www.lincolnsinst.edu).

Pons, P. 1994. "La Habana: ¡Abajo con el Malecón!" *Ajoblanco* (Barcelona) 69 (December): 38–41.

Portela, A. 1994. "Oil Search." *CubaNews* (Miami; a publication of the Miami Herald Publishing Co.) (April): 7.

Portuondo, F. 1965. *Historia de Cuba, 1492–1898*. Havana: Editorial Pueblo y Educación.

Portuondo, J. A. 1962. *Bosquejo histórico de las letras cubanas*. Havana: Editora del Ministerio de Educación.

Poumier, M. 1975. *Apuntes sobre la vida cotidiana en Cuba en 1898*. Havana: Ciencias Sociales.

Pradilla, E. 1982. *Ensayos sobre el problema de la vivienda en América Latina*. Mexico City: Unidad Xochimilco.

Prensa Latina. 1996. "Cuba: Economic Report, First Semester, 1996." Ministry of Economy and Planning. Electronic posting from presal@blythe.org, July 24.

Presno, P. R. 1952. "Factor de progreso para la república ha sido y es la colonia española." *Album del cinquentenario de la asociación de reporters de La Habana. 1902–1952*, 109. Havana: Editorial Lex.

Préstamo, F. 1995. *Cuba: Arquitectura y urbanismo*. Miami: Ediciones Universal.

Programa de Cooperación Internacional. "Cooperación con Cuba." 47–60. *Conserjería de obras públicas y transporte 2000*. Seville: Junta de Andalucía.

Provincia de Ciudad de La Habana. 1992. *Características generales de la ciudad de La Habana.* Havana: Provincia de Ciudad de La Habana.

Przeworski, A. 1989. "Class, Production, and Politics: A Reply to Burawoy." *Socialist Review* 19, no. 2: 87–112.

———. 1992. *Democracy and Markets: Political and Economic Reforms in Eastern Europe and Latin America.* Cambridge: Cambridge University Press.

Quintana, A. 2000. "Cuba en su arquitectura y urbanismo: Pasado: Los años 50: Presente y futuro." *AAA: Archivos de Arquitectura Antillana* (Santo Domingo) 5, no. 10: 146–55.

Quintana, N. 1974. "Evolución histórica de la arquitectura en Cuba." In *Enciclopedia de Cuba,* Tomo 5:91. Madrid: Playor.

Rallo, J. 1964. "Transformación de La Habana desde 1762 hasta 1830." *Cuba en la UNESCO* (Havana) 3–5 (March): 6.

Rallo, J., and R. Segre. 1978. *Evolución histórica de las estructuras territoriales y urbanas de Cuba, 1519–1959.* Havana: Facultad de Arquitectura, Instituto Superior Politécnico José Antonio Echeverría.

Rama, A. 1985. "La ciudad letrada." In *Cultura urbana latinoamericana,* edited by R. Morse and J. E. Hardoy, 12–29. Buenos Aires: CLACSO 5.

Ramón, F. 1967. *Miseria de la ideología urbanística.* Madrid: Ciencias Sociales.

———. 1991. "La Habana: Por una ciudad más humana, bella, y funcional." In *Actas del XVI Congreso Anual de la Asociación de Estudios del Caribe.* Havana: Asociación de Estudios del Caribe.

"Resolución conjunta no. 3/95 de los Ministerios de Finanzas y Precios y de Seguridad Social sobre actividades y oficios por cuenta propia." *Granma,* June 13, p. 2.

Rigau, J., and N. Stout. 1994. *Havana.* New York: Rizzoli.

Rigol, I. 1978. "Protección de monumentos." *Arquitectura/Cuba* 347–348:90.

Rivero, A. 1981. "Una vieja ciudad rejuvenece." *Revolución y Cultura* 107 (July): 76.

Rivero, N. 1994. "Cuba's Oil Predicament." *CubaNews* (Miami; a publication of the Miami Herald Publishing Co.) (April): 7.

Roberts, W. A. 1953. *Havana: The Portrait of a City.* New York: Coward-McMann.

Roca Calderío, B. 1973. "Prólogo." *Seis leyes de la revolución.* Havana: Editorial de Ciencias Sociales.

Roca, S. G. 1994. "Reflections on Economic Policy: Cuba's Food Program." In *Cuba at a Crossroads: Politics and Economics after the Fourth Party Congress,* edited by J. F. Pérez-López, 94–117. Gainesville: University of Florida Presses.

Rodríguez, A., G. Riofrío, and E. Welsh. 1973. *Segregación y desmemorización política: El caso de Lima.* Buenos Aires: SIAP.

Rodríguez, A. A., and F. Cabrera. 1995. "La problemática de la legislación urbanística en la capital." *Comunidad* (Instituto de Planificación Física, Havana) 4, no. 95: 95–97.

Rodríguez, E. L. 1991. "Arquitectura joven cubana: Solamente una propuesta." *Excelsior* (Mexico City), Sección Metropolitana, 14, no. 12: 1.

———. 1992. "Hacia una realización alternativa o el arquitecto en crisis." *Arquitectura/Cuba* 375, no. 41: 64–71.

———. 1994. "Entrevista." *El Nuevo Herald* (Miami) 6, no. 7: 1–2.

———. 1996. "The Architectural Avante-garde: From Art Deco to Modern Regionalism." *Journal of Decorative and Propaganda Arts, 1875–1945* 22:255–76.

———. 1998. *La Habana: Arquitectura del siglo XX.* Barcelona: Blume.

———. 2000a. *The Havana Guide: Modern Architecture, 1925–1965.* New York: Princeton University Press.

———. 2000b. "Modern Architecture in Cuba." *Cuba Update* (Center for Cuban Studies, New York) 19, nos. 2–3.

Rodríguez, J. A. 2000. "¿Por qué no bajan los precios?" *Juventud Rebelde* (Havana), December 3.

Rodríguez, J. L. 2000. "Solo el abnegado esfuerzo y la enorme capacidad de resistencia de nuestro pueblo nos ha permitido obtener alentadores resultados." Report on economic results in 2000 and plan for 2001 to the 6th period of the National Assembly. *Granma*, December 23.

Rodríguez, L. 2000. "Bioinsecticidas vs. Plagas." *Juventud Técnica* (Havana), no. 297 (April).

Rodríguez, P. 1999. "Desafío de una utopía/Challenge of a Utopia." Plan Maestro de La Habana Vieja. In *Ciudad/City*. Pamplona: Ediciones Boloña.

Rodríguez Alomá, P. 1996. *Viaje en la memoria: Apuntes para un acercamiento a La Habana Vieja*. Havana and Pamplona: *Ciudad/City*, Oficina del Historiador de la Ciudad de La Habana, Colegio Oficial de Arquitectos Vasco-Navarro.

Rodríguez Feo, J. 1994. "Carta desde La Habana." *La Gaceta de Cuba* (UNEAC, Havana) 1:94.

Roemer, M. 1964. *Medical Care in Latin America*. Washington, D.C.: Pan American Health Union.

Rogers, E. N., J. L. Sert, and J. Tyrwhitt. 1961. *El corazón de la ciudad: Para una vida más humana de la comunidad (CIAM)*. Barcelona: Editora Científico Médica.

Rohter, R. 1995. "In Cuba, Army Takes on Party Jobs, and May Be Only Thing That Works." *New York Times*, June 8, p. A-12.

———. 1996. "Cuba's Nuclear Plant Project Worries Washington." *New York Times*, February 25, p. A-18.

Roig de Leuchsenring, E. 1952. "Transformación de La Habana en medio siglo, 1902–1952." In *Album del cincuentenario de la asociación de reporteros de La Habana, 1902–1952*, 163. Havana: Editorial Lex.

———. 1964. *La Habana, apuntes históricos*. Vols. 1-3. Havana: Consejo Nacional de Cultura.

Rorick, H., and S. Gomila. 1984. *Las Arboledas Sketchbook: Design for a New Community in Cuba*. Havana: Centro Técnico de la Vivienda y el Urbanismo and Groundwork Institute.

Rosenberg, R. 1992. "Cuba's Free-Market Experiment: Los Mercados Libres Campesinos, 1980–1986." *Latin American Research Review* 27, no. 3: 51–89.

Rosete, H., and J. C. Guanche. 2000. "La ciudad cuesta pero vale." Interview with Mario Coyula. *Alma Mater* (Havana) no. 369 (October): 8–9.

Rossi, A. 1966. *L'architettura della citta*. Padua: Marsilio.

Sabbatini, M. 1967. "La formazione della societá neocoloniale cubana." Rome: *Ideologie* 1:54.

Sagebien, J., and R. Coto-Ojeda. 2000. *Cuba and Puerto Rico: From Cold Warriors to Business Associates*. Cuba Briefing Paper Series No. 23 (January). Washington, D.C.: Cuba Project, Center for Latin American Studies, Georgetown University.

Salinas, F. 1963a. "La arquitectura en los países en vias de desarrollo." Informe del Relator General. VII Congreso de la Unión Internacional de Arquitectos. Havana, September, p. 29. Mimeo.

———. 1963b. "La industrialización de la vivienda: Una proposición." *Arquitectura Cuba* 336:33.

———. 1967. "La arquitectura revolucionaria del Tercer Mundo." *Tricontinental* (Havana) 1 (July–August): 93–102.

———. 1971. "Descolonización de la ciudad." *Arquitectura Cuba* 340:2–3.

———. 1988. *La cultura de la vivienda cubana: De la arquitectura y el urbanismo a la cultura ambiental*. Guayaquil, Ecuador: Facultad de Arquitectura Universidad de Guayaquil.

Sambricio, C., and R. Segre. 2000. *Arquitectura en la ciudad de La Habana: Primera modernidad.* Spain: Electa.

Sánchez, O. 1989. "Tras el rastro de los fundadores: Un panorama de la plástica cubana." Trajectoire Cubaine, Centre d'Art Contemporain, Corbeil Essones, 8–17.

Sánchez Agusti, M. 1984. *Edificios públicos de La Habana en el siglo XVIII.* Valladolid, Spain: Universidad de Valladolid.

Sánchez-Albornoz, N. 1974. *The Population of Latin America.* Berkeley: University of California Press.

San Martín, J. 1947. *Memoria del plan de obras del gobierno del Dr. Ramón Grau San Martín.* Havana: Ministerio de Obras Públicas.

Santovenia, E. 1943. *Historia de Cuba.* Vol. 2. Havana: Trópico.

Santovenia, E., and R. Shelton. 1964. *Cuba y su historia.* Miami: Rema Press.

Sapieha, N. 1990. *Old Havana, Cuba.* London: Tauris Parke Books.

Sarduy, S. 1967. *Ecrit en dansant.* Paris: Seuil.

Sarlo, B. A. 1994. "Cidade real, cidade imaginária, cidade reformada." *Revista do Patrimônio Histórico e Artístico Nacional* (Rio de Janeiro) 23:167–77.

Sartor, M. 1992–93. "La città latinoamericana tra antecedenti precolobiani, leggi di fondazione e tradizione." *Zodiac 8: Rivista Internazionale di Architettura* (Milan) 93 (September–February): 15.

Scarpaci, J. L. 1989. "Theory and Practice of Privatization." In *Health Services Privatization in Industrial Societies,* edited by J. L. Scarpaci, 1–24. New Brunswick, N.J.: Rutgers University Press.

———. 1994. "Chile." In *International Handbook of Latin American Urbanization,* edited by Gerald Greenfield, 37–69. Westport, Conn.: Greenwood Press.

———. 1996a. "Back to the Future: The Sociopolitical Dynamics of Miramar's Real-Estate Market." In *Cuba in Transition,* edited by José Alonso, 6:196–201. Washington, D.C.: Association for the Study of the Cuban Economy.

———. 1996b. "Industrial Analysis: Havana's Real Estate." *CubaNews* (Miami; a publication of the Miami Herald Publishing Co.) (December): 9.

———. 1999. "Healing Landscapes: Revolution and Health Care in Havana." In *Therapeutic Landscapes: The Dynamic between Place and Wellness,* edited by A. Williams, 201–20. Lanham, Md.: University Press of America.

———. 2000a. "On the Transformation of the Socialist Cities." *Urban Geography* 21:659–69.

———. 2000b. "Reshaping Habana Vieja: Revitalization, Historic Preservation, and Restructuring in the Socialist City." *Urban Geography* 21:724–44.

———. Forthcoming. *Plazas and Skyscrapers: The Transformation of the Latin American Centro Histórico* [title tentative].

Scarpaci, J. L., and M. Coyula. Forthcoming. "Urban Sustainability, Built Heritage, and Globalization in the Cuban Capital." In *Sustainability in the Developing Realm,* edited by Saskia Sassen. Geneva: United Nations Press.

Scarpaci, J. L., A. Gaete, and R. Infante. 1988. "Planning Residential Segregation: The Case of Santiago de Chile." *Urban Geography* 9:19–36.

Scarpaci, J. L., and A. Z. Hall. 1995. "Havana Peddles through Hard Times." *Sustainable Transport* 4 (Winter): 4–5, 15.

Scarpaci, J. L., and I. Irarrázaval. 1994. "Decentralizing a Centralized State: Local Government Finance in Chile within the Latin American Context." *Public Budgeting and Finance* 14, no. 4: 120–36.

Segre, R. 1968a. "Significación de Cuba en la evolución tipológica de las fortificaciones coloniales de América." In *Lectura Crítica del Entorno Cubano*, edited by Roberto Segre, 23–65. Havana: Letras Cubanas.

———. 1968b. "Vivienda y prefabricación en Cuba." *AUCA* (Santiago, Chile), no. 12: 37–41.

———. 1970a. "Cronologia de la Revolución Cubana referida a la arquitectura, 1953–1969." In *Ensayos sobre arquitectura e ideologia en Cuba revolucionaria*, edited by Roberto Segre, 67–155. Havana: Universidad de La Habana, Centro de Información Científico y Técnico.

———. 1970b. *Diez años de arquitectura en Cuba revolucionaria*. Havana: Ediciones Unión.

———. 1974. *Transformación urbana en Cuba*. Barcelona: G. Gili.

———. 1975. "Contenido de clase en la arquitectura cubana de los años 50." *Revista de la Biblioteca Nacional José Martí* 3 (September–December): 97.

———. 1978. "Las transformaciones ambientales en Cuba." In *Las estructuras ambientales en América Latina*, edited by Roberto Segre, 217–81. Havana: Departamento de Cultura, Universidad de La Habana.

———. 1984. "Architecture in the Revolution." In *The Scope of Social Architecture*, edited by R. Hatch, 349–60. New York: Van Nostrand Reinhold.

———. 1985a. *Historia de la arquitectura y el urbanismo: Países desarollados: Siglo XIX y XX*. Madrid: Instituto de Estudios de Administración Local.

———. 1985b. *La vivienda en Cuba: República y revolución*. Havana: Departamento de Actividades Culturales, Universidad de La Habana.

———. 1989. *Arquitectura y urbanismo de la Revolución Cubana*. Havana: Pueblo y Educación.

———. 1990. *Lectura crítica del entorno Cubano*. Havana: Letras Cubanas.

———. 1992a. "La Plaza de Armas: Simbolísmo originario y figuras del poder." *DANA (Documentos de Arquitectura Nacional y Americana)* (Instituto Argentino de Investigación de Historia de la Arquitectura y del Urbanismo, Resistencia, Argentina) 31–32:113–116.

———. 1992b. "Savia nueva en odres viejos: La continuidad del talento." *Arquitectura Cuba* 375:7–14.

———. 1993. "Sincretismo en la arquitectura centroamericana: Trayectoria de Bruno Stagno." *Revolución y Cultura*, epoca 4, 1 (January–February): 43–47.

———. 1994a. "Architektur und Städtebau im revolutionären Kuba: Das historische Erbe und der Mythos des Neuen." In *Phänomen Cuba: Alternativewege in Architektur Stadetenwicklung und Ökologie*, edited by K. Mathéy, 1–19. Karlsruhe: Lehurstuhl für Städtedau und Entwerfern Orl Fakultät Für Architektur.

———. 1994b. *Arquitectura antillana del siglo XX*. Xochimiloc: Universidad Autonóma de Mexico.

———. 1994c. "Preludio a la modernidad: Convergencias y divergencias en el contexto caribeño (1900–1950)." In *Arquitectura neocolonial: América Latina, Caribe, Estados Unidos, memorial*, edited by A. Amaral, 95. San Pablo, Mexico: Fondo de Cultura Económica.

———. 1994d. "Tres décadas de arquitectura cubana: La herencia histórica y el mito de lo nuevo." *Revolución y Cultura* 33 (May/June): 36–45.

———. 1996a. "La Habana siglo XX: Espacio dilatado y tiempo contraído." *Ciudad y Territorio* (Madrid), no. 110: 713–31.

———. 1996b. *La Plaza de Armas de La Habana: Sinfonía urbana inconclusa*. Havana: Editorial Arte y Literatura.

———. 1999a. *América Latina fin de milenio: Raíces y perspectivas de su arquitectura*. Havana: Editorial Arte y Literatura.

———. 1999b. "L'Avana postmoderna." *Capitolium* (Rome) 3, no. 7: 83–87.

———. 1999c. "Encrucijadas de la arquitectura en Cuba: Realismo mágico, realismo socialista y realismo crítico." *AAA: Archivos de Arquitectura Antillana* (Santo Domingo) 4, no. 9: 56–76.

———. 2000. "40 años, 90 millas y una cubanía" (40 years, 90 miles, but one sole cubanhood). Introduction to the special number of *AAA: Archivos de Arquitectura Antillana* (Santo Domingo) 5, no. 10: 11–113.

Segre, R., and S. Baroni. 1998. "Cuba y La Habana: Historia, población y territorio." *Ciudad y Territorio* (Madrid), no. 116: 351–79.

Segre, R., E. Cárdenas, and L. Aruca. 1981. *Historia de la arquitectura y el urbanismo: América Latina y Cuba*. Havana: Pueblo y Educación.

Segre, R., and R. López Rangel. 1982. *Architettura e territorio nell'America Latina*. Milán: Electa Editrice.

Segre, R., and C. Sambricio. 2000. *Arquitectura en la ciudad de La Habana: Primera modernidad*. Madrid: Electa España.

Segui, G. 1994. "Les odeurs de la rue." In *La Havane, 1952–1961: D'un dictateur a l'autre: explosion des sens et morale révolutionnaire*, edited by Jacobo Machover, 27–38. Série Mémoires 31. Paris: Editions Autrement.

Séneca, J. C. 1976. *Ordenamiento urbano*. Havana: Instituto de Planificación Física.

Serraino, P., and J. Shulman. 2000. *Modernism Rediscovered*. Cologne: Taschen.

"Si de cuenta propia se trata." 1995. *Granma*, June 15, p. 2.

Skidelsky, R. 1996. *The Road from Serfdom: The Economic and Political Consequences of the End of Communism*. New York: Allen Lane, Penguin Press.

Slater, D. 1982. "State and Territory in Postrevolutionary Cuba: Some Critical Reflections on the Development of Spatial Policy. *International Journal of Urban and Regional Research* 6:1–33.

Sotillo, A., and L. Ayllón. 2000. "La Unión Europea cambiará su ayuda a Cuba para lograr reformas económicas y políticas." *ABC Internacional* (Madrid), December 4.

Soto, L. 1977. *La revolución del 33*. Vols. 1–3. Havana: Ciencias Sociales.

Stallings, B. 1986. "External Finance and the Transition to Socialism in Small Peripheral Societies." In *Transition and Development*, edited by R. Fagen, C. D. Deere, and J. L. Coraggio, 54–78. New York: Monthly Review Press.

*The Statesman's Yearbook, 1982–83*. 1982. 19th ed. New York: St. Martin's Press.

Stix, G. 1995. "Ban That Embargo: Physicians Advocate Lifting Sanctions against Cuba." *Scientific American* (March): 32–34.

Stough, R., and M. Feldman. 1984. "Tourism Development Models: Public Policy Management Implications." Paper presented at the Caribbean Studies Association Meetings, June 30–May 2, St. Kitts, West Indies. Mimeo.

Stout, N., and J. Rigau. 1994. *Havana. La Habana*. New York: Rizzoli.

Stretton, H. 1978. *Urban Planning in Rich and Poor Countries*. Oxford: Oxford University Press.

"Survey Havana." 1996. *Economist*, April 6 (supplement).

Szelenyi, I. 1982. *Urban Inequities under State Socialism*. London: Oxford.

Tabares del Real, J. A. 1971. *La revolución del 30: Sus dos ultimos años*. Havana: Arte y Literatura.

Taller. 1995. *Los consejos populares, la gestión de desarrollo y la participación popular en Cuba: Conclusiones preliminares*. Havana: Centro de Estudios de América.

Taylor, P. 1985. *Political Geography: World-Economy, Nation-State, and Locality*. London: Longman.

Tejeira-Davis, E. 1987. *Roots of Modern Latin American Architecture*. Heidelberg: University of Heidelberg.

Thomas, H. 1998. *Cuba or the Pursuit of Freedom*. New York: Da Capo Press.

Tingle, V. R., and A. Montenegro. 1923. *La Gran Vía de La Habana*. Havana: J. E. Barlow.

Tismaneanu, V. 1992. "Between Liberation and Freedom." In *Uprooting Leninism, Cultivating Liberty*, edited by Vladimir Tismaneanu and Patrick Clawson, 1–48. Lanham, Md.: University Press of America and Foreign Policy Research Institute.

"Tourism: Guitart out of Cuba." 1995. *CubaNews* (Miami Herald Publishing Co.) (November): 4.

Turner, J. F., and R. Fichter. 1972. *Freedom to Build: Dweller Control of the Housing Process*. New York: Macmillan.

UIA (Unión Internacional de Arquitectura). Cuban Section. 1963. *Informe de Cuba al VII Congreso de la UIA*. Havana: UIA.

Ullman, C. D., and E. L. Harris. 1945. "The Nature of Cities." *Annals of the American Academy of Political and Social Sciences* 242:7–17.

UNEAC (Unión Nacional de Escritores y Actores de Cuba). 1998. *Síntesis de los acuerdos y recomendaciones del VI Congreso en plenarias y comisiones de trabajo: Dictámenes*. Havana: Editorial Unión.

"Unions in Cuba Fight Social Inequities." 2001. *Militant* 65, no. 17: 5.

United Nations. 1995a. "Havana." In *The Challenge of Urbanization: The World's Large Cities*, 96–98. New York: United Nations, Department for Economic and Social Information and Policy Analysis, Population Division.

———. 1995b. *United Nations Development Survey, 1995*. New York: United Nations.

United Nations Development Program. 2000. *Human Development Report*. New York: UNDP.

Uriarte, M., G. González, J. E. Fornés, and M. Fernández. 1997. *El reto de todos: Una estrategia de revitalización para el parque de la población habanera: Parque Metropolitano de La Habana*. Havana: Canadian Urban Institute.

Valladares y Morales, A. 1947. *Urbanismo y construcción*. Havana: P. Fernández y Cia.

Vázquez, R. 1994. "Prólogo." In R. Vázquez, *Bipolaridad de la cultura cubana*, 7–18. Stockholm: Olof Palme International Center.

Vázquez Raña, M. 1993. "Entrevista con Carlos Lage: El sol de México." *Bohemia* (Havana), June 11.

Vega Vega, J. 1963. *La reforma urbana de Cuba y otras leyes en relación a la vivienda*. Havana: Ministerio de Construcción.

Véjar, C. 1994. *Y el perro ladra y la luna enfría: Fernando Salinas: Diseño, ambiente y esperanza*. Mexico City: Universidad Autónoma de México.

Venegas, C. 1989. "Las fábricas de tabaco habaneras." *Arquitectura y Urbanismo* 3, no. 10: 14.

———. 1990. *La urbanización de las murallas: Dependencia y modernidad*. Havana: Letras Cubanas.

———. 1996. "Havana between Two Centuries." Cuba theme issue. *Journal of Decorative and Propaganda Arts* (Wolfson Foundation, Miami) 22:13–34.

———. 1999. "Mis amores por La Habana: Una entrevista con Mario Coyula." *La Gaceta de Cuba* (UNEAC, Havana) 2 (March–April): 15, 17–18. English excerpts: "My Loves for Havana: An Interview with Mario Coyula." *Cuba Update* (Center for Cuban Studies, New York) (Summer) 2000.

Venegas, C., and A. Núñez Jiménez. 1986. *La Habana: Fotografías de Manuel Méndez Guerrero*. Madrid: Instituto de Cooperación Iberoamericana.

Vilas, C. M. 1989. *State, Class, and Ethnicity in Nicaragua: Capitalist Modernization and Revolutionary Change on the Atlantic Coast*. Boulder, Colo.: Lynne Reinner.

Villanueva, C. R. 1966. *Caracas en tres tiempos*. Caracas: Ediciones Comisión Asuntos Culturales del Cuatricentenario de Caracas.

Villegas, E. 2000. "Lonja de comercio de La Habana." *AAA: Archivos de Arquitectura Antillana* (Santo Domingo) 5, no. 10: 158–60.

Violich, F. 1987. *Urban Planning for Latin America*. Boston: Oelgeschlager, Gunn & Hain.

Vivas, F. 1966. "Hacia una arquitectura de masas." *Boletín de la Escuela de Arquitectura* (Havana) 5–6:4–8.

———. 1983. *Reflexiones para un mundo mejor*. Caracas: Edición del Autor.

Walker, P. G. 1996. *Challenges Facing the Cuban Military*. Cuba Briefing Paper Series No. 12. Washington, D.C.: Cuba Project, Center for Latin American Studies, Georgetown University.

Wall, D. 1990. "The Political Economy of Industrialization in Sandinista Nicaragua." Ph.D. diss., University of Iowa.

Walton, J. 1987. "Urban Protest and the Global Political Economy: The IMF Riots." In *The Capitalist City*, edited by M. P. Smith and J. R. Feagin, 364–86. London: Blackwell.

Weil, C., and J. Scarpaci. 1992. *Health and Health Care in Latin America during the "Lost Decade": Insights for the 1990s*. Minneapolis: Prisma Institute, University of Minnesota Press.

Weiss, J. 1947. *Arquitectura cubana contemporanea*. Colegio Nacional de Arquitectos. Havana: Letras Cubanas.

———. 1950. *Medio siglo de arquitectura de Cuba*. Havana: Universidad de La Habana, Facultad de Arquitectura, Imprenta Universitaria.

———. 1966. *La arquitectura colonial cubana: Siglos XVI al XIX*. Havana and Seville: Instituto Cubano del Libro and Junta de Andalucía.

———. 1967. "Un urbanista olvidado." *Arquitectura Cuba* 337:69.

———. 1972. *La arquitectura colonial cubana: Siglos XVI/XVII*. Havana: Editorial de Arte y Literatura.

———. 1973. *La Arquitectura Colonial Cubana*, Tomo I. Havana: Siglos XVI/XVII, Editorial de Arte y Literatura.

———. 1978. *Techos coloniales cubanos*. Havana: Editorial Arte y Literatura.

———. 1996. *La arquitectura colonial cubana. Siglos XVI al XIX*. Havana and Seville: Instituto Cubano del Libro and Junta de Andalucía

Wernstedt, F. 1961. *World Climatic Data: Latin America and the Caribbean*. Ann Arbor, Mich.: Edwards Brothers.

West, R., and J. Augelli. 1966. *Middle America: Its Lands and Peoples*. Englewood Cliffs, N.J: Prentice-Hall.

White, T. 1898. *Our War with Spain for Cuba's Freedom*. New York: Freedom Publishers.

Whitefield, M. 1994. "Cuba May Be Able to Dance around the Trade Embargo." *Fort Worth Star-Telegraph*, April 22, p. 3.

Wiener, P. L., J. L. Sert, and P. Schulz. 1960. "La Havane: Plan pilote et directives generales." *L'architecture d'aujourd'hui* (Paris) 88:62.

Williams, S. 1994. *Cuba: The Land, the History, the People, the Culture*. Philadelphia: Running Press.

Wise, M. Z. 1996. "The Challenge of a Crumbling Havana." *New York Times*, January 15, p. 38-H.

Wright, I. A. 1916a. *The Early History of Cuba*. New York: Macmillan.

———. 1916b. *Los orígenes de la minería en Cuba*. Havana: A. Muñiz y Hermano.

———. 1927. *Historia documentada de San Cristóbal de La Habana en el siglo XVI*. Havana: Imprenta El Siglo XX.

Zardoya, M. V. 1999. "Las calzadas, arterias vitales de La Habana." *Arquitectura y Urbanismo* 2, no. 99.

Zimbalist, A. 1989. "Incentives and Planning in Cuba. *Latin American Research Review* 24:65–94.

———. 1993. "Teetering on the Brink: Cuba's Current Economic and Political Crisis." *Latin American Studies* 24:407–18.

Zschaebitz, U., and F. Lesta. 1990. *Actas de Atarés: Rehabilitación urbana de darrios en La Habana, Cuba.* Hamburg, Germany: Hamburg Technical University.

# Index

Abbott, 77
Abnegation, 257
Abolition, 41. *See also* Slavery
Aborigines, 11
Abreu, Marta, 318
Academia de Música de Santa Cecilia, 30
*Ácana*, 22
*Accesoria*, 100
*Acopio*, 250
ACOREC, 192
Acropolis, 68, 117
Administration of Physical Planning and
    Architecture (Planificación Física y Arqui-
    tectura), 193
Administrative Councils (Consejos de Admi-
    nistración), 174
Adobe, 29
Aduanas, 59
Aerolíneas Q, 98
Africa, 90, 96, 231, 297
Afro-Cuban religion, 129
Agricultural Command Outposts (Puestos de
    Mando Provincial de la Agricultura), 140,
    151, 275
Agricultural Development (Desarrollo
    Agropecuario), 141
Agricultural Markets, 250
Agriculture: diversification in, 139; and pro-
    duction, 139
Aguada del Cura, 104
Aguirre, Mirta, 116n
Airlines, 294
Air pollution, 242, 271
Airport, 159
Alamar, 213, 218–20, 225, 307
Alameda: definition of, 33; Alameda de
    Extramuros, 315; Alameda de Isabel II, 35;
    Alameda de Paula, 28, 97, 106

Alarcón, Ricardo, 133, 362
*Albañilería*, 31
Albear, 104
Albear aqueduct, 104, 318
Albergues, 223
Albers, Joseph, 82n
Albini, Franco, 83, 197, 336
Aldama Palace, 31, 55, 59, 317, 330, 338
Alea, Gutiérrez, 306, 327n
Alexander, Christopher, 206n, 225
*Algarrobo* trees, 107
Alger, 29
Alhambra, 60
Allende, Salvador, 33, 216, 255
*Alma Mater* statue, 117
Al Medina restaurant, 333n
Almendares, 5, 12, 54, 99, 362
Almendares Park, 107
Almendares River, 17, 23, 56–57, 69, 103, 107,
    109, 120, 121, 153, 303; Basin, 181; pollu-
    tion, 182
Almendares-Vento Basin, 181
Alonso Alicia, 116n
Alta Habana, 197, 218, 225, 280
Alturas de Almendares, 54
Alturas de Belén, 119
Alturas de Biltmore, 121
Alturas de Coronela, 119
Alturas de Miramar, 119, 121
Aluminum, 208
Alvarez, Mercedes, 207n 204
Alvarez Tabio, Emma, 223n, 337n, 338
Ameijeiras, Efigenio, comandante, 133
America, continental, 18
American Club, 108
American Tobacco Company, 61
Americas, 168
Amerindian settlement and culture, 11, 15

Amnesty International, 173
Andalucian associations, 108
Andalucians, 46
Andaluz, 46
Andean America, 11
Andes, 8, 311
Anesthetics, 281
Angola, 295
Angotti, Tom, 217n
Annés folles, 63
Antibiotics, 281
Anti-Communist sentiment, 279; Cuban, 377;
    guerrillas, 138
Antigua and Barbuda, 261
Antilles, 3, 14, 16, 21; and "Antillean Pearl,"
    308, 377; Greater, 14–15; Lesser, 14, 20
Arabs, 45, 324
Archdiocese of Santo Domingo 19
Architects, 151n, 163, 221
Architectural Departments (Direcciones de
    Arquitectura), 222
Architecture. *See names of specific styles*
Architecture and Urban Studies Historic
    Research Group (GIHAU), 330
Argentina, 69, 93, 216, 260–61, 289, 351
Ariguanabo, 104
Arimao River, 15
Arjona, Marta, 336
Aróstegui Hill, 49
Arquitecto de la Comunidad, 231
*Arquitectura*, 323
*Arrobas*, 31n
Arroyo Arenas, 72
Arroyo Bermejo, 276
Arroyo Naranjo, 243, 275–76, 282, 307
Arrufat, Antón, 359
Art deco style, 123, 129
Article 58, 323
Artists, 221
Art noveau, 129
Arts, 205
*Arts and Architecture*, 124
Aruba, 293
Asia, 90, 297
Asians, 46
Askhenazic Jews, 46
Aspirin, 281
Assassins, 33, 37

Association of Caribbean States, 255
Association of Tourist Agents, 274
Asturians, 46
Asturias, 351
Atabey. *See* Alturas de Biltmore
Atarés, 47, 98, 112, 136, 162, 166, 223n, 232
Atarés Castle, 24, 49
Atarés fortress. *See* Atarés Castle
Athens Charter (*Carta de Atenas*), 82, 205
Atlanta, Ga., 111
*Atlas Demográfico de Cuba*, 11
Atomization, 196, 216
*Audiencia*, 16
Audiencia de Santo Domingo, 16, 19–20
Auditorium, 122, 132
Augustinians, 118
Aula Magna, 117
Aurea and Fénix, 342
Australia: and investment, 240
Autoconsumos estatales, 183
Automobiles, 59, 235, 242, 302n, 334; BMWs,
    188; Buicks, 325; buses, 235, 242, 268, 277,
    302n; car-orientation, 367; Cadillacs, 325;
    Chevrolets, 275; Fords, 275; Hyundais, 188,
    364; Nissans, 188; Plymouths, 247; Toyotas,
    188
Autopista del Mediodía, 97, 104
Autopista Nacional, 156, 275
*Avenidas*: Avenida de Acosta, 72; Avenida
    de Bolívar, 33; Avenida de las Palmas, 68;
    Avenida de los Presidentes, 56, 69, 118;
    Avenida del Puerto, 72, 97, 112, 327, 344;
    Avenida Paseo, 69; Avenida 31, 104; defini-
    tion of, 41
Avila Valley, 311
Avilés, marquis, 57n
Ayuso, Teresa, 338
Azcue, Eusebio, 155
Azores, 23
Aztec, 11

Bacuranao, 14, 275–76; and Bacuranao mine,
    21
Bacuranao River, 182
Bahamas, 237, 261, 293, 297
Bahamian Channel, 13
Bahía, 197, 202
Bahía de la Habana. *See* Havana Bay

Bähr and Mertins, 85
Baile Rojo, 111
Balboa, marquis of, 317
Ballesté, Joel, 159n
Ballet, 132
Ballet Nacional de Cuba, 115
Balneario de la Concha, 109
Balneario Hijas de Galicia, 109
Balneario Universitario, 109, 111
*Balseros*, 149
Banco Financiero Internacional (BFI), 192, 363
Banco Internacional de Comercio S.A. (BICSA), 192
Banco Mendoza, 320
Banco Nacional, 280
Banco Nacional de Cuba, 190, 192, 320
Banco Pedroso, 320
Banes, 25
Bank of Cuba, 279
Bantu, 16
Baquero, Max, 155
Baracoa, 11–12, 331
*Barbacoa*, 232, 328, 338
Barbados, 261, 293
Barcelona, Spain, 56, 273
Barces y López, 60
Bardet, Gastón, 73
Barlovento. *See* Hemingway Marina
Barnet, Miguel, 377
Baró, Juan Pedro, 57n
Baroni, Sergio, 162n, 224, 337n
Baroque style, 29, 67, 126, 129
Barraqué Building, 319
Barriadas, 21n
Barrios, 24; Angel, 24; Barrio Chino, 113, 123; Dragones, 24; Estrella, 24; Monserrate, 24; Paula, 24; San Francisco, 24; San Isidro, 24; Residencial Obrero de Luyanó, 76; Santa Teresa, 24; Sur, 82
*Barrios insalubres*, 100, 223, 227
Bars, 188, 324
Bartlett, London, 362
Basic Agricultural Production Units (UBPA), 149
Basic Rural Secondary Schools. *See* Escuelas Secundarias Básicas en el Campo
Basque, 46, 108

Batabanó, gulf of, 12
*Bateyes*, 11, 93, 239
Batista, Eugenio, 323n
Batista, Fulgencio, 67, 72–73, 83, 109, 111, 112, 115, 131, 152, 200, 273, 281; and 1935 coup d'état, 66, 75, 95; government of, 73, 81, 91, 96, 102, 128, 199, 325
Batistianos, 133
Bauhaus school, 208n
Bauta, 72
Bautista Antonelli, Juan, 14, 26
Bayamo, 11, 15, 331
Bay of Pigs invasion, 127, 135, 138, 274
Bay Sevilla, Luis, 320, 322, 323n
Beatles, 371
Beaudoin, Eugene E., 65
Beaux arts styles, 69
Bedoya, Francisco, 223n, 330, 337n, 338
Bedroom community, 205
Beer, 250
Beet sugar, 41
Beggars, 37
Beijing, China, 273
Bejerano, Daniel, 223n, 224
Bejucal, 40
Belascoaín, 67, 79, 315, 375
Belén, 286, 324
Belize, 260–61
Belot oil refinery, 97
Benéfica, 60
Benetton, 188
Bens Arrarte, José, 323n
Berlin, Germany, 347, 362
Berlin Wall, 222
Bermuda, 293
Bernaza Street, 46
Bettelheim, Charles, 140
Bible, 308
Bicycles, 242–43, 269–71, 277, 349
Big Five, 111
Biltmore country club, 111, 112, 121, 196
Biltmore subdivision, 118
Biotechnology, 148, 240, 287, 297
Bishop, Maurice, 255
*Bisneros*. See *Maceteros*
Black market, 251, 259, 306
Board of Technical Research, 202
*Bodegas*, 68, 78, 241, 249–50, 272, 334

Bodeguita del Medio restaurant, 324
Bogotá, 82
*Bohíos*, 9, 30, 94
Bola de Nieve, 132
Bolívar, Simón, 52
*Bolsa de valores*, 126
*Bombonera*, 118
Bonet, Antonio, 82
Book Fair, 308
Bordello, 114
Borges, Jorge Luis, 359
Borges, Max, 116n
Borrego, Orlando, 141
Botafogo, 374
Botanical Gardens, 212
Botanical Park, 153
Boullée and Ledoux, 203
Bourgeois, 54–55, 61, 64, 83, 112, 129, 131, 318
Boutiques, 188
Boyeros, 79, 98, 170, 201, 243, 275–76, 281
Brando, Marlon, 123
Brasília, 82
Brazil, 216, 295; and architects, 124
Breuer, 123
Brick, 29
Brigade 2506, 135
Brisas del Mar, 275
British New Towns, 204n
Broa Inlet, 12
Brunner, Karl, 73
Brutalism, 129
Bucharest, Romania, 273
Budapest, Hungary, 214, 358
Buenos Aires, Argentina, 43, 52, 69, 82, 84, 208, 246, 311, 334, 347
Building components, 149
Building Ordinances of 1861, 160
Bungalows, 57
Bureaucratism, 206
Burger King, 352, 375
Burrus grain towers, 97
Buschiazzo, Mario, 323n

Caballero, Roberto, 225
Cabaña fortress, 83
Cabarrocas, Félix, 71, 320, 321
*Cabildo*, 20, 22–23

Cabrera, Lydia, 116n
Cabrera Infante, Guillermo, 122, 324
CADECA S.A., 187
Cádiz, 23, 29, 46
Cafés, 31n, 123, 132–33, 188, 324; Café de la Dominica, 32n; Café de la Paloma, 32n; Café de la Taverna, 32n; Café de las Copas, 32n; Café de los Franceses, 32n; as public gathering places, 32n
Calabazar, 72
California mission style, 124
California-style chalets, 196
Calixto García Teaching Hospital, 117, 280
Calixto López, 60
Callampas, 217n
*Calles*, 41, 97, 100, 153, 275; Calle Veintitres, 56–57, 118
Calthorpe, Peter, 225
Calvino, Italo, 310
*Calzadas*, 8, 21, 41, 53, 97, 273, 315, 316; Calzada Belascoáin, 41; Calzada Caliano, 41; Calzada Cristina, 41; Calzada de Cerro, 8, 41, 67, 316; Calzada de Infanta, 118, 213; Calzada de Luyanó, 8, 67; Calzada de Monte, 8, 41, 58, 67, 127, 213, 316; Calzada de Puentes Grandes, 41, 67; Calzada de Rancho Boyeros, 102; Calzada de Reina, 316; Calzada Diez de Octubre/Calzada Jesús del Monte, 8, 41, 53, 67, 113, 316; Calzada Güines, 41, 67; Calzada Street, 123; Calzada Zapata, 41
Camagüey, 11–12, 79, 221, 239, 331
Camagüey Province, 176
Camellos, 268
Campeche, 24
Campesinos, 183
Campo de Marte, 32n, 59
Campo Florido, 112
Canada, 237, 295, 297, 300–301; and invest-ment, 240; tourists from, 277, 300
Canada Dry, 77
Canadians, 188
Canal tax, 18
Canary Islanders, 46
Canary Islands, 15
Cañas Abril, Eduardo, 81n
Cancún, Mexico, 298
Candado soap, 198

Candela, Félix, 203
Candilis, George, 206n
Candler College, 116
Cao, Carlos Miyares, 297
Capitolio, 59–60, 68–69, 106, 246, 279
Capri, 202
Captain General's Palace, 33, 59, 64, 313
Carabalí, 16
Caracas, 19, 311, 347
Cárdenas, Agustín, 116n
Cárdenas, Eliana, 162n
Cardiology and Cardiovascular Surgery Institute, 297
Cardoso, Onelio Jorge, 116n
Caretakers, 137. See also *Tías*
Caribbean Islands, 129, 235, 255, 292; and tourist markets, 289, 293; and "Pearl of the Caribbean," 51, 346; and planning, 219. *See also* Antilles: and "Antillean Pearl!"
Caribbean Sea, 3–4, 12, 18, 32, 35
Carlos III. *See* Charles III
Carme Pinós, Spaniard, 362
*Carmen*, 56
Carnival, 277, 311, 312
Carob tree. See *Algarrobo* trees
Carpentier, Alejo, 67, 115, 116n, 132, 310, 312, 316
Carranza, Julio, 296
Carrazana, Roberto, 204n
Carreño, Bartolomé, 14
Carreño Building, 135
Carrera de Indias, 13
Carretera Central, 66–67, 72, 97, 102, 197, 245, 274, 375
Carrillo de Albornoz, Mariano, 315
Carta de La Habana, 73
Cartagena, 14
Cartesian scheme, 205
*Casa almacén*, 55, 312, 313
Casablanca, 53, 97, 112, 317
*Casa de citas*, 111
Casa de las Américas, 132
*Casas de culto*, 308
*Casas de vecindad*, 76
Casiguagua, 12
Casinos, 108; Casino Deportivo, 99, 109; Casino Español, 60, 108, 110, 111
Castilians, 46

Castillo de Farnes, 333n
Castro, Emilio, 223n, 337, 337n
Castro, Fidel, 91, 95, 96, 116, 141, 149, 151, 155, 158, 159, 169, 173, 179, 199, 206–7, 211, 213, 218, 239, 241, 248, 274n, 286, 371; government of, 33, 278, 285, 307; "History Will Absolve Me" speech, 96; speech of 26 July 1999, 248
Castro, Lenin, 204n
Castro, Raul, 165n
Catalán, 108
Catholicism, 112, 116. *See also* Roman Catholicism
Catholic schools, 286
Cayo Cruz, 98, 153, 181
Cayo Hueso, 64, 162, 166, 213, 214; neighborhood of, 142
CEDEM (Centro de Estudios Demográficos/ Center of Demographic Studies), 242
Ceiba del Agua, 151, 286
Cell panel: in Cuba, 207
Cement: for building trades, 139
CENCREM, 331, 336, 363
Center for Genetic Engineering and Biotechnology, 279
Center for Medical Surgery, 281
Center for Medical Surgical Research, 297
Center for Placental Histotherapy, 297–98
Center for Restoration, Conservation, and Museum Science, 350
Center of Demographic Studies, 242
Center of the Study of the Americas, 296
Central Administration of the State (OACE), divisions of, 143
Central America, 126. *See also names of specific countries*
Central de Trabajadores de Cuba (CTC), 288
*Centrales. See* Sugar: and sugar mill
Central Highway. *See* Carretera Central
Planning Board (JUCEPLAN), 150
Centro Asturiano, 60, 108
Centro de Dependientes, 60
Centro de Desarrollo de las Artes Visuales de La Habana (Havana Center for the Development of Visual Arts), 361
Centro de Estudios Demográficos (CEDEM) (Center of Demographic Studies), 242

Centro Gallego, 60, 108, 246, 250, 278, 280, 297

Centro Habana neighborhood, 42, 46, 47, 48, 58, 62, 99, 100, 102, 105, 106, 112, 113, 121, 127, 128, 137, 174, 189, 197, 213, 224, 311, 323, 373–75

Centro Nacional de Conservación, Restauración, y Museología. *See* CENCREM

*Ceratonia siliqua.* See *Algarrobo* trees

Cerro, 30, 42, 46–47, 53, 55–56, 99, 102, 105, 121, 278, 280, 316, 318

Cervantes Prize, 359

Céspedes and Machado, 64

Cha-cha-cha musical style, 115

Chamber of Commerce, 190

Chandigarh, 82

Chaple Hill, 98

Charles II (king of Spain), 23

Charles III (king of Spain), 24, 30, 33, 37

Charrasqueado, Juan, 133

Chateau Miramar, 122

Chateloin, Felicia, 337, 337n

Chernobyl disaster, 279

Chibás, Eduardo, 95, 202

Chicago, Ill., 126

Chile, 73, 126, 216, 236, 255, 260–61

Chimbote, Peru, 84

China, 242, 255, 296; imports from, 248, indentured workers from, 25; post-Mao, 357

Chinatown (Barrio Chino), 113, 123

*Chinos*, 46

Cholera, 52

*Choteo*, 129

Choy, José Antonio, 363; Popular Power, 223n

Christians, 308

Christmas, 308; and Christmas Day Tea Party, 111

Christ of Havana, 97

Churches, 312

CIAM. *See* Congrés International de Architecture Moderne

*Ciclón*, 115

Ciego de Avila, 239, 286

Ciénaga, 54

Ciénaga de Zapata, 299

Cienfuegos, 4, 25, 73, 239, 247

Cienfuegos, Camilo, 274n

CIMEX, 271

Cinemateca, 132

Cintas, Oscar, 115

Cira García, 281

Círculo Militar y Naval, 109

Círculos Sociales Obreros, 307

Circunscripciones, 174

Cité des Affaires, 83

City Beautiful movement, 69

City by the Water, 362

City Historian's Office, 158, 185, 277, 285, 333, 340, 342, 344–45, 348, 351, 359, 363; and Department of Architecture, 331; and Department of Cultural Heritage, 340

City Model (Maqueta de la Ciudad), 167

City Museum, 331, 333

City of Alchemy, 233

City of Columns, 42

Ciudad Camilo Cienfuegos, 202

Ciudad de La Habana, 239

Ciudad Deportiva, 307

*Ciudadelas*, 76, 100, 101, 216, 223, 324

Ciudad Libertad, 99, 286

Ciudad Universitaria José Antonio Echeverría, 287

Civic Center, 121

Civil engineers, 155

Civil society, 176

Cleansing of Escambray, 138

Club Cubaneleco, 109

Club de Ferreteros, 109

Club de Profesionales, 109

Club Náutico, 110, 119

CMEA. *See* Council of Mutual Economic Assistance

Cobalt, 4

Coca-Cola, 77

Coffee, 25, 31, 40, 249, 312, 331; and coffee bean, 31n; and coffeehouse, 132; *Tres quilos*, 122

Cojímar, 295

Cojímar River, 182; pollution of, 182

Colegio de Arquitectos, 81, 125

Colegio de Arquitectos del Principado de Asturias, 351

Colegio de Belén, 116–18, 122

Colegio de La Salle, 116

Colegio de las Ursulinas, 286

Colegio Provincial de Arquitectos de La

Habana (Institute of Architects of Havana Province), 102, 323
Colgate toothpaste, 198
Colina, 68
Colina Universitaria, 82, 96
Colombia, 73, 99, 216, 236, 335
Colón, 113
Colón Cemetery, 107, 371
Colonial Center, 85
Colonial style, 348
Colonnaded portico, 42
Columbia Military Base, 104, 136, 286
Columbia University, 117
Columbus, Christopher, 2, 8, 310
Comités para la Defensa de la Revolución. *See* Committees for the Defense of the Revolution
Commission on Landmarks, Buildings, and Historic Places, 323
Committees for the Defense of the Revolution (CDR), 134, 176–77
Communism, 248, 279, 350
Communist Party, 96, 115, 288, 308
Communist Party of Cuba (PCC), 141, 169, 173n, 177, 273, 308; Central Committee of, 165n; first Central Committee of, 169; First Congress of, 143, 212. *See also* Communist Party
Communist Youth Union, 177
Community participation, 175–76, 186
Community Strategic Plans, 166
Comodoro, 109, 122
*Compañeros*, 306
Compañía Cubana de Electricidad, 109
Comprehensive Workshop for Neighborhood Change, 177
Concentric Zone Model, 85
Concha railroad station, 317
Concrete, 208
Condominium Law, 121, 197
Coney Island, 111
Congo River, 16
Congrés International de Architecture Moderne, 50, 74, 80, 82, 82n, 203, 213, 328
Congress of Education and Culture, First, 219
Congress of the Communist Party, Fourth, 239

Congress of the Cuban National Union of Artists and Writers. *See* UNEAC
Congress of the International Union of Architects, Seventh, 206–7
Congress on Education and Culture, First, 358
Conill, Enrique, 54, 64–65, 318
Conquistadors, 301
Consejo de Estado, 247
Consejo Popular de Barrio, 163
Consejo Provincial de Cuencas Hidrográficas, 181
Consejos Populares, 176–77
Constitutional reform, 172
Construction industry, 142
Construction of ExpoCuba, 158
Constructive management, 336
Constructivism, 210
Consultorios del Médico de la Familia, 281
Contingentes, 161, 221
Contraband, 24n
Contract labor, 41
Convento de Santa Clara, 362
Convents, 312
Cooking oil, 250
Coolidge, Calvin, 63
Coordination, Administration, and Executive Boards (JUCEIS), 169
Copacabana, 109, 122, 374
Coppelia, 305–7
Coppelia ice cream parlor, 132
Copper, 4, 21, 40
Coppola, Francis Ford, 121
Corcovado, 311
Córdoba, 46
Cordón de La Habana, 140. *See also* Greenbelt
Coro 19
Coronela, 196
"Corner of Sin," 127n. *See also* Galiano Street; San Rafael Street
Correction of Mistakes, Process of, 138, 145–46, 161, 218, 223
Corridos, 133
Cortázar, Julio, 133
Cortés, Hernán, 12, 15
Cortina, José Manuel, 54
Cosculluela, 104
Costa, Lucio, 82

Costa Line, 332
Costanera, 69
Costa Rica, 289
Cotorro, 72, 102, 197, 243
Cott, Lee, 363
Council of Ministers, 333
Council of Mutual Economic Assistance
 (CMEA), 145, 189, 236–37, 255
Council of State, 333
Country Club, 49, 54, 57, 99, 105, 119, 121,
 192, 196, 287, 299, 359, 374
Country Club de la Habana, 111
Country Club Park, 99
Covadonga, 60
Coyula, Mario, 151, 162n, 224, 337n, 361
Creole, 26, 32–33, 35, 37, 42, 55, 59, 128, 132
Cretaceous period, 3
Criadas, 101
*Criollo*, 110, 129
Cristina station, 317
Crystal, 324
CSOS (Círculos Sociales Obreros), 307
CTC, 239; and Secretary General, 256
Cuartel de los Bomberos, 59
*Cuarterías*, 80, 100, 101, 222, 227, 232, 332,
 344, 375
Cuartro Caminos, 102
Cuba, 2–5, 24, 35, 64, 89, 109, 123, 129, 172,
 204n, 234, 241, 295, 298, 347, 353, 356, 358,
 359, 361, 363, 370, 376, 377; agriculture in,
 139, 182, 250; Armed Forces of, 258, 295–
 96; architectural history of, 210; biodiver-
 sity in, 299–300; bourgeoisie of, 134, 200,
 214; as built environment, 184; and cession
 to England, 277; colonial, 316; and commercialism, 124; and confiscation, 133; and
 contextualism, 203; copper production in,
 21; and credibility, 176; Creoles of, 37; currency of, 91; economy of, 39, 40, 89, 145,
 146, 150, 188, 213, 221, 222, 235, 237–38,
 239–40, 248, 255, 258–59, 338, 348–49;
 education in, 89, 90, 285; emigration to, 45;
 and energy source, 148; exports from, 91;
 farms in, 243; and foreign capital, 192, 289;
 and foreign trade, 192, 238; foreigners in,
 273; French immigration to, 30–31; and
 General Comptroller's Office, 83; geography of, 4–6; gold production in, 15–16;

government of, 364; health system in, 89,
 93, 94, 278, 297; housing in, 94, 95, 143,
 199, 200, 204, 214; human development in,
 260; and imports, 79, 91, 305; industry in,
 92, 247; joint ventures in, 193; labor force
 of, 79, 91, 256; literacy rate in, 289; markets
 in, 91; and maritime trade, 23; and military
 rule, 286; municipalities of, 174; and
 National Assembly, 133; national income
 of, 134, 187; national policy of, 139; and
 nationalization, 134; per capita income of,
 89, 93; and political class, 330; population
 of, 26; pre-Columbian, 2, 8, 11; rationing
 in, 249–50; and restoration, 339; and segregation, 325; settlement in, 16; services in,
 116, 244; and socialist democracy, 176;
 social mobilization in, 274; sugar revenues
 in, 25; toursim in, 244–45, 248, 250, 259,
 290–95, 300, 302; transportation in, 274;
 unemployment rate in, 91; urban development in, 89, 138, 210; and urban environment and public participation, 179–82; and
 urban planning, 151n, 177–78
—ministries of: Economy Minister of, 253;
 Ministry of Agriculture, 271; Ministry of
 Communications, 83; Ministry of Construction (MICONS), 206–7, 209, 211, 217, 222;
 Minister of Culture, 371; Ministry of Education, 287, 338; Ministry of Finances and
 Prices, 190; Ministry of Foreign Investment
 and Economic Collaboration (MINVEC),
 189–90; Ministry of Public Health, 243;
 Ministry of Public Works, 65, 73, 83, 135,
 150, 202, 320; Ministry of Science, Tech-
 nology, and Engineering, 300; Ministry of
 Social Welfare, 135; Ministry of Tourism
 and Hotels, 192, 295; Ministry of Work and
 Social Security, 190
Cubalse, 193
Cubanacán. *See* Country Club
Cuban Americans, 194, 350, 352, 362, 376
Cuban colonial style, 364
Cuban Committee, 363
Cuban Federation of Women (FMC), 176
Cuban missile crisis, 138, 274
Cuban National Assembly, 362
Cuban National Heritage 336, 350, 351, 352,
 356

Cuban peso, 187
Cuban revolutions, 203
Cuban Telephone Company, 134
Cubelas, Rolando (comandante), 133
Cuenca, 335
Cuenca Sur, 104
*Cuentapropistas*, 253
Cueto, 320
Cueva del Humo, 76
Cuidadelas, 227
CUJAE (Ciudad Universitaria José Antonio
    Echeverría), 287
Cultural Heritage Protection Law, 331
Culture, 205
Cumaná, 16
Cumberland, duke of 23
Curaçao, 25, 293
Currency, hard, 148n
Czarnikow-Rionda, 141
Czechoslovakia: imports from, 248

D'Acosta-Calheiros, Hugo, 204n, 207
Darié Sandú, 277
Dauval Guerra, Luis, 74
de Aguas Claras, marqués, 313n
de Arcos, marqués, 313n, 322
*Death of a Bureaucrat*, 327n
de Avilés, Menéndez, 22
De Beche, 119
de Carlo, Giancarlo, 206n
de Casa Barreto, conde, 313n
de Casa Bayona, conde, 313n, 322
de Castro, Alberto, 319
Decentralization, 175, 222
de Céspedes, Carlos Miguel, 63
Decree-Law 50, 189
Decree-Law No. 211, 229
Decree No. 217, 230
Dediot, Luis, 319
de Fuentes, Walfrido, 54
de Junco, Emilio, 323n
del Alamo, J.I., 65
de la Luz y Caballero, José, 316
de la Obrapía, marqués, 313n
de la Puerta, Martín Calvo. *See* de la Obrapía,
    marqués
de la Riva, Pérez, 318
de la Torre, marqués, 25, 313, 315

del Casal, Julián, 359
del Castillo Jr., Orestes, 223n
del Cueto, José Ramón, 57n
del Monte, Domingo, 316
del Río, Zaida, 363
Democratization, 171
Demographers, 151n, 155
de Narváez, Pánfilo, 12
de Ocampo, Sebastián, 12
Department of Architecture and Urbanism of
    the city of Havana, 143
Department of Demolitions, 330
Department stores, 127
Dependientes, 60
Deregulation, 175
de Revilla-Camargo, Condesa, 57n
de Roda, Cristóbal, 26
Desamparados, 324
de San Juan de Jaruco, conde, 313n
Deserters, 37
*Desmerengamiento*, 161
Desnoes, Edmundo, 132
de Sores, Jacques, 14, 26
de Soto, Emilio, 320
de Tapia Ruano, Manuel, 81n, 323n
Deurbanization, 140
Diego, Eliseo, 116n, 359
Diez, Carlos Jorge, 160n
Diez de Octubre, 42, 79, 98, 105, 170, 173,
    201, 213, 224, 307
Diezmero, 72, 197
*Diplotiendas*, 137
Directorio Revolucionario, 95, 131
*Dirigentes*, 151, 248
Disinvestment, 149
Disneyland, 84
*Distritos*, 176
Docks, 324
Dollar: legalization of, 187
Dominican Republic, 261, 297
Don Giovanni restaurant, 333n
Doric columns, 36
Drake, Sir Francis, 20, 21
Droguería Johnson, 320
Duany, Andres, 350, 362
Dunn, Carlos, 338
Du Pont, 77
Duty-free zones, 247

Dwellings, 228–30
Dysentery, 52

East Basin, 182
Eastern Europe, 140, 145, 204n, 214, 221, 237–38, 271n, 329, 332, 356, 358; and Eastern European bloc, 186, 353
Eastern European bloc, 186, 353
East Germany, 278
East-West Highway, 160
*Echar sisa*, 17
Echeverría, José Antonio, 95
Eclecticism, 129
Economic Society of Friends of the Country, 30–31
*Economist*, 376
*Economist Intelligence Unit*, 240
Economists, 151n
Ecosystem, 184
Ecuador, 335
Education, 205, 285–86. *See also* Cuba: education in; Havana: education in
Egido Street, 19
Eightieth Street, 366
Ejército Rebelde, 275
Ekloh, 78
El Acoso, 132
El Bloqueo, 219
El Bosque de la Habana, 107
El Caballero de París, 133
El Cano, 72
El Carmelo, 56, 123
El Carmelo de Calle Calzada, 132
El Chori, 123
El Cristo, 324
Elections, 173
Electric streetcar, 52
El Encanto, 78, 127
El Mégano, 276
El Morro. *See* Morro Castle
El Museo de la Alfabetización, 289
El País, 198
El Patio, 333n
El Patio restaurant, 326
El Romerillo neighborhood, 136
El Salvador, 276, 297
El Sevillano, 197
*El siglo de las luces*, 312

El Templete, 13
*El tiempo muerto*, 74
El Vedado. *See* Vedado
El Wajay, 197
*Embalses*, 5
Embil, 119, 202
Employment and pay: regulation of, 190
Energy production, 139
Engels, 268
Engineers, 151n, 163
England, 214; exports to, 39; and railway design, 35–36; and United Kingdom, 240
Enríquez, Carlos, 116n
Ensanche de la Habana, 54
Ensenada de la Chorrera, 12
Entrepreneurs, 251, 253
Entresols, 26
Environmental design: concept of, 208n
Eproyiv, 193
ESBEC. *See* Escuelas Secundarias Básicas en el Campo
Escaleras de Jaruco, 275
Escambray Mountains, 4, 138
Escambray River, 15
Escuela Técnica Superior de Arquitectura de Barcelona (ETSAB), 351
Escuela Técnica Superior de Arquitectura de Madrid (ETSAM), 362
Escuelas Secundarias Básicas en el Campo, 142, 286–87
Espada, Bishop, 30
Espino, Juan, 56
Espinosa, Luis, 152
Esposizione Universale di Roma. *See* L'EUR
Esso, 97
Estación Central de Ferrocarriles, 19, 59, 65
Estévez, Pedro, 318
Estévez, Reynaldo, 204n, 323n
Estrada Palma, Tomás, 59
*Estrategia*, 166
ETSAB (Escuela Técnica Superior de Arquitectura de Barcelona), 351
ETSAM (Escuela Técnica Superior de Arquitectura de Madrid), 362
Europe, 115, 161, 208n, 351; and health care, 297; and design, 204n, 213; and rationalism and art deco, 75; and tourism, 277. *See also* Eastern Europe; Western Europe

Executive Committee of the Council of Ministers, 190
Executive Committes (Comités Ejecutivos), 174
ExpoCuba, 146
*Extramuros*, 41
Extremeños, 46

Fab laundry detergents, 198
Faculty of Architecture, the University of Havana, 232
Falla-Gutiérrez family, 115
Family Physician Clinics (Consultorios del Médico de la Familia), 281
Farmers' markets, 250
*Favelas*, 217n
Fernández, Cesáreo, 202
Fernández, Enrique, 159n
Fernández, José M., 159n
Fernández, Oriente (captain), 150
Fernández, Ricardo, 337n
Fernández Retamar, Roberto, 359
Fernandina, count of, 316
Fertilizer, 139, 149, 238
Fifth Avenue. *See* Quinta Avenida
Fifth International Congress of International Architects, 204n
*Fílin*, 115
Fin de Siglo, 78
Firestone, 77
First Agrarian Reform Law, 134, 138
First annual economic plan, 139
First Five-Year Plan, 138, 141, 144
First Havana Master Plan (1963–64), 152–54, 170
First Physical Planning Seminar, 194
First Republican Center, 85
First World, 205, 211, 231
*Fleteras*, 114
Flogar, 78
Floral Park, 119
Flores, 196
Florida, 19, 24, 73, 289–90, 350, 352, 376
Florida, Straits of, 3, 12, 16, 83, 303
*Florida* (steamship), 97
Floridita restaurant, 324, 326
Focsa, 109
Focsa building, 205

Fodder, 149
Fontanar, 197
Food: as biggest social problem, 148n; and food supply, 159; processing of, 139
Foreign exchange, 148
Foreign investment, 187, 189
Forensic Medicine Institute of Havana, 261
Forestier, J. C. N., 50, 65, 69, 71, 97, 128, 268, 321
Fornés, Rafael, 337n
Fornet, Ambrosio, 133
*Fotingos*, 112
Fraginals, Moreno, 39–40, 373
France, 25, 214; exports to, 39; and investment, 240; tourists from, 295
Frank País Hospital, 297
Frank Robins Company Building, 320
Free Farmers' Market, 149
French Revolution, 203
*Fresas y Chocolate*, 306, 359
Friedmanism, 256
*Fritas*, 122
Fuerza, 18

*G. Bombax*, 13
Gaggini, 316
Galeria Habana, 113
Galiano Street, 67, 79, 113, 127, 127n, 361 315, 375
Galicians, 46; and Galician colony, 109
Gallo rice, 198
Gambling, 33, 77, 347
Garatti, Vittorio, 155
García, Abel, 363
García, Aracelis, 160n
García, Oscar, 337
García, Saturnino, 316
García de Castro, Camilo, 54, 64
García de Mesa, Josefina, 57n
García Oliveras, Julio (comandante), 150
Garden City, 69; concept of, 57, 73
Garneray, 31
Gasoline stations, 188
Gastón, Miguel, 83, 116n
Gastroenterology Institute, 297
Gaviota, 295–96
GDIC (Grupo para el Desarrollo de la Capi-

tal), 126, 166, 223, 228, 331, 351, 362–63, 376

Gehry, Frank, 369

*Gelati*, 305

Gelats, Juan, 57n

*Gemelas*, 58

General Housing Law (Ley General de la Vivienda), 144, 222, 229

Generation of the 1980s (Generación de los 80), 223n

Geographers, 151n, 155

George III (king of England), 23

German measles, 52

Germany; exports to, 39; tourists from, 295

Gibraltar, Straits of, 16

GIHAU, 330

Gil, Enrique, 322

Girón, prefabrication model, 142

Girón method, 287

*Glasnost*, 357

Glidden, 77

Globalization, 259, 273, 350

Global market, 254

*Godfather II, The*, 121, 325

Gómez, José (general), 318, 361

Gómez, Joaquín, 317

Gómez, José Miguel, 58, 60

Gómez de Avellaneda, Gertrudis, 316

Gómez Mena, María Luisa, 115

González, Elián, 370

González, Mario, 151, 152, 159n, 162n, 204n

González de la Peñas, Rafael, 338

González de Mendoza, Antonio, 54

González de Mendoza, Pablo, 57n

González Lobo, Carlos, 224

González Romero, Raúl, 203, 204

Good Year, 77

Gottardi, Roberto, 337n, 361, 363

Govantes, Evelio, 71, 321

Govantes y Cabarrocas, 57

Gaviota tourist group, 192

Goyaneche, Rafael, 319

*Gracias Fidel*, 133, 151, 155

Gramatges, Harold, 116n

Granada, 29

Granma Province, 239, 281

Grau San Martín, Ramón, 72–74, 76

Great Depression, 71, 110, 120

Greater Havana, 120

Great Harvest, 138

Great Panel 70, 142

Greco-Roman columns, 117

Greco-Roman styles, 30

Greek Orthodox, 45

Greenbelt, 98, 140, 153, 206, 303, 328; planning for, 151

Greene, Graham, 133, 324

Green Spaces, 302

Grenada, 255

Grenoble-Echirolles, 209

Gropius, Walter, 77n, 82n, 123

Gross domestic product, 236–37, 349

Gross national product, 90, 93, 235, 260

Gross social product (GSP), 142, 236–37, 244, 292

Group for the Comprehensive Development of the Capital (GDIC), 162, 228

Group of Eleven (Los Once), 115

Growth Pole Theory, 239

Grupo Argentiaria, 332

Grupo de Investigaciones Históricas de la Arquitectura y el Urbanismo (GIHAU), 330

Grupo Domos, 240

Grupo Negociador, 190

Grupo para el Desarrollo Integral de la Capital. *See* GDIC

GSP. *See* Gross social product

Guanabacoa, 53, 170, 245, 275, 307

Guanabo, 112, 374

Guanabo River, 182

Guanajatabeyes, 8

Guantánamo, 239, 331

*Guayacán*, 22

Guerrillas, 51, 96, 151

Guevara, Ernesto "Che," 140, 210, 274n, 325, 371

Guggenheim Museum (Bilbao, Spain), 369

Guido, Angel, 323n

Guillén, Nicolás, 116n

Guillermo de Zéndegui, 115

Güira de Melena, 275

Gulf of Mexico, 3, 16

Gulf Stream, 14

Gumá, Joaquín, 115

Gunn, Gillian, 165n

Gutiérrez, Ramón, 224
Gutiérrez Alea, Tomás, 132, 359
Gymnasiums, 307

Habagüanex, 13, 193, 292, 332, 333, 333n, 342
Habana del Este, 83–84, 146, 170, 192, 197, 202, 213, 225, 275–76, 290, 307; buildings of, 209; and high-rise structures, 205; and housing and planning, 204; municipality of, 218; neighborhood units for, 203; population density of, 204; Unit No. 1, 202–4; Unit No. 2, 203
Habana Libre. *See* Havana Hilton
Habana Libre-Guitart. *See* Havana Hilton
Habana-Pinar del Río Highway, 73
Habana Vieja, 8, 13, 19, 44–47, 51, 59, 62, 64, 67–68, 80, 84, 97–99, 100, 102, 103, 105, 106, 112, 117, 126, 127, 158, 185, 222, 245, 250, 275, 282, 289, 292, 311, 315, 316, 319n, 318–20, 323–32, 333–35, 333n, 338–40, 342, 344–45, 351, 362, 372–76
Habana Yacht Club, 109, 110
*Habaneros*, 1, 17, 23, 26, 30–31, 54, 62, 66, 75–76, 79, 98, 100, 108, 111, 116, 136, 149, 159, 179, 183, 187, 189, 197, 199, 223, 242, 244, 247–48, 256, 275, 277–79, 303, 305, 307, 328, 338, 353, 373, 375, 376
Habitat-Cuba, 231
Hacendados dock, 97
Haiti, 24–25, 30–32; revolution in, 331
Hamberg, Jill, 217n
Hamburgers, 122
Hanoi, 273, 347
Hapsburg kings, 23
Hardware Clerks' Club (de Ferreteros), 109
Hart-Terré, Emilio, 323n
Harvard University, 362, 374; Graduate School of Design, 363
Hatch, Richard, 217n
Haussmann, Baron, 37, 62, 65
Havana, 1–6, 8, 14, 21, 24–25, 35, 45, 53, 55, 57–58, 71, 77–79, 82, 89, 90, 93, 96–98, 100, 104, 105, 112, 124–26, 129, 130, 131, 159, 160, 184, 199, 201, 208, 213, 222, 225, 239–40, 242, 244, 246–48, 256, 267, 270–71, 274, 276, 291, 294–96, 298, 301, 307–8, 311, 331, 337, 340, 346–49, 351–54, 356, 358, 361–63, 365, 367, 369, 371–77; admin-istration of, 186; Afro-Cuban culture in, 299; agriculture in, 159, 182–83, 328; air and noise pollution in, 180–81; American presence in, 42; architecture in, 331, 351; back-bay district of, 232; bourgeois in, 188; building codes in, 41, 54; built environment of, 223, 314–15; built heritage of, 123, 167, 348, 350; *cabildo* of, 16–17, 19; Central Business District, 77; city administration of, 330; and City Hall, 83; climate of, 302; commerce in, 60; crime in, 249; decentral-ization of, 153; design and construction of, 36, 142, 214, 316, 350; design and style in Colonial, 29; economy of, 187, 235–36, 240, 249, 255, 257–58, 286–87; education in, 116, 289, 312; environment of, 184; ethnic composition of, 45; expansion of, 37, 47, 49; fortifications in, 18–19; geography of, 290; government of, 168; and Greenbelt, 276, 303; growth of, 153, 241; health care in, 116, 118, 261, 266, 278, 281, 283; hinter-land of, 206; historic center of, 84, 321; housing in, 94, 99, 136, 196, 218, 221, 224; infant mortality in, 278; investment in, 41, 332; labor force of, 101, 245; landscape of, 280; land use in, 177; and maritime trade, 16–17, 311; master plan of, 65; mayor of, 169, 213; and modernization, 74, 268; neighborhoods of, 162, 226; quality of life in, 261; and planning, 136, 167, 177–78; plazas in, 323; population density and land area of, 43, 119, 120, 153, 155, 228, 303, 329, 371; port of, 39; and public health, 312; public housing in, 267; public works in, 52; rail lines in, 40; real estate in, 193–94, 197–98; and rehabilitation, 194–95; residents of, 186; and retail network, 273; and rural to urban migration, 278; services in, 267, 317; skyline of, 207; social strata of, 200; status of, 18, 26; street patterns of, 198; suburban, 46, 49–50, 219, 324; tourism in, 121n, 261, 266, 289–93, 299, 308, 350; tourist hospitals in, 297; trans-portation in, 180, 275; urban revitalization in, 333; and vice, 77; and wages, 187; zon-ing laws in, 56
Havana Art Biennial, Seventh, 367
Havana Bay, 5, 12, 17, 34, 54, 63, 65, 82–83,

103, 153, 180–81, 246, 299, 303, 311, 350; and Basin, 182; southern part of, 158
Havana-Bejucal railroad, 317
Havana Biltmore Yacht and Country Club, 111
Havana Center for the Development of Visual Arts, 361
Havana City Province, 169, 169n, 176, 185, 275, 295
Havana Hilton, 121, 121n, 132, 240, 301
Havana In-Bond, 192
*Havana Project, The*, 362
Havana Province, 40, 241, 169, 169n, 173
Havana Province Institute of Architects (Colegio Provincial de Arquitectos de La Habana), 102
Health care clinics. *See* Policlínicos
Health farms (*Quintas de salud*), 278, 280
Health tourism, 281
*Heart of the City*, 83
"Heat island," 105
*Helados*, 305
Helms-Burton bill, 133, 240
Hemingway, Ernest, 122, 324
Hemingway Marina, 122, 196, 275, 288, 295
Hénad, Eugéne, 65
Heredia, 31
Heredia, José María, 316
Hermanos Ameijeiras Hospital, 279, 281
Hernández, Oscar, 224
Hershey sugar mill, 112
Hietzler, Louis, 65
High Technical School of Architecture of Barcelona (ETSAB), 351
High Technical School of Architecture of Madrid (ETSAM), 362
Hilton, 240
Hilton, Conrad, 240
Himmelblau, Coop, 362
Hispaniola, 3, 9–10, 15–16, 19
Holguín, 239, 246, 293
Holguín River, 15
Hollywood revival, 84
*Hombre integrado*, 305
Homeowners, 199, 200
Honey, 40
Hornos, 113
Hospital Antigue, 277

Hostal Valencia, 333n
Hotels, 63, 274; Ambos Mundos hotel, 320, 324; Flamingo hotel, 121; Havana Biltmore, 119; Hotel Capri, 121; Hotel Colina, 121; Hotel Cueto, 337; Hotel Habana Libre (Havana Hilton), 121, 121n, 132, 240, 301; Hotel Lancaster, 337; Hotel Meliá-Cohiba, 301, 376; Hotel Meliá-Habana, 363, 366; Hotel Miramar-Novotel, 366; Hotel Nacional, 64–65, 68, 122; Hotel Neptuno, 366; Hotel Panorama, 366; Hotel Plaza, 122; Hotel Riviera, 121, 301, 376; Hotel Sevilla, 122; Hotel Tritón, 366; Lincoln hotel, 63; Parque Central Golden Tulip Hotel, 363; St. John hotel, 121; Saratoga hotel, 63; Sol Hotels, 301; Telégrafo Hotel, 60
Housing, 186, 196, 199–203, 210, 230,; as main problem in late 1990s, 148n; socialist, 214; stock, 226; styles of, 55; units for, 209
Housing Division, the Ministry of Construction, 225
*Huertos intensivos*, 183
Humboldt University, 362
Hurricanes, 126, 347; Flora, 211; Santa Teresa, 24
Husillo Dam, 154
Hydroelectric energy, 5
Hygienists, English and German, 69
Hyperurbanization, 241

Iacocca, Lee, 239
Iberian Peninsula: Moorish domination of, 18
Iberoamerican Center for Regeneration, 281
Iberoamerican Competition, Third, 338
Ibero-American Strategic Development Center, 353
Ice cream, 132, 305
*Iglesia*, 22
Ihosvanys, 138
IIT (Instituto de Investigacíon del Transporte), 182, 271
Ildefons Cerdá, 56
Import-substitution industrializations, 256
IMS, 142
INAV. *See* National Institute for Savings and Housing
Inca, 11

Independence Wars, 25, 42–44, 51, 53, 56–57, 60, 110, 318, 361
*Independendista*, 32
India fountain, 106
Indies Route. *See* Carrera de Indias
Industrialists, 133
Industrialization, 93, 139
Industrial parks, 247
Infanta, 67, 315, 375
Informal economy, 68, 241
Infrastructure, 196n, 139
ING Bank, 188, 192, 240
*Ingenio. See* Sugar: and sugar mill
Inglaterra, 60, 63. *See also* England
Inmobiliaria Monte Barreto, S. A., 365
Institute of Architects (Colegio de Arquitectos), 81, 125
Institute of Architects of Havana Province, 323
Institute of Physical Planning (IPF), 150, 155
Institute of Research on Transportation (IIT, Instituto de Investigacíon del Transporte), 182, 271
Institute of Tropical Medicine, 281
Institutionalization, 143, 171; process of, 170
Instituto de Investigacíon del Transporte, 182, 271
Instituto Nacional de Turismo, 291, 299
Instituto Técnico Militar, 117
Institutos de Segunda Enseñanza, 59, 75
Intercompany Cooperation Councils (Consejos de Cooperación Interempresarial), 186
International Commission on the Protection of Landmarks and Historic Places, 330
International Seminar of City Architecture, 222
International Style, 67, 76, 78n, 196, 213, 220, 348
International Union of Architects (UIA), 208
INTUR (Instituto Nacional de Turismo), 291, 299
Inversion a riesgo, 190
IPF, 152
Irijoa, 60
Iron, 4, 324
Iron bridge (Puente de Hierro), 180
*Isla*, 115
Isla Azul, 303

Isla de Cuba, 63
Isla de la Juventud, 173
Isla Verde, 374
Isle of Pines, 103, 173
Istanbul (Turkey) Habitat, 166
Itabo River, 182
Italians, 188, 301
Italy: and Italian models, 205; and tourism and business, 295, 300
Izquierdo, Raúl, 223n

Jacobs, Jane, 206n
Jagua gold mine, 16
Jaimanitas River, 182, 196
Jamaica, 3, 16, 25, 237, 261, 297, 332
Japan, 301
Jardines de la Tropical (Brewery), 107
Jenkins Hill, 36
Jesuits, 21, 116, 286; schools of, 116; Spanish, 118
Jesús María neighborhood, 58, 64, 202
Jews, 45–46, 324; Askhenazic Jews, 46; Jewish merchants, 127; Sephardic Jews, 46
*Jineteras*, 114, 188
*Jineteros. See* Black market
John Paul II (pope), 308
Jorrín, Enrique, 116n
José Antonio Echeverría University (CUJAE), campus, 153, 212
José Gener, 60
José Luís Rodríguez, 253
José Martí district, 211
José Martí International Airport, 245, 247
José Martí Monument, 81–82, 114, 128, 279, 370–71
José Martí Pioneer City, 279
Juan Gualberto Gómez International, 295
Juan Manuel Márquez, 202
Jugüey Grande, 286
July Movement, 26th of, 131
Junta Nacional de Planificación. *See* National Planning Board
Juraguá, 247
Justice Palace, 128, 273

Kay, Ken, 225
Keppel, Sir George, 23
Kerosene, 250

Keynesian economics, 257
Key West, 97, 290
Kholy, Pedro Pablo, 54
Knowles, George (admiral), 23
Kohly, 107, 119, 121
Koolhaas, Rem, 318n
Korea, 274n
Krajewski Pesant, 319

La Avenida de la Univérsidad, 68
Labatt, 240
Labatut, Jean, 65, 75
Labrador Ruíz, Enrique, 116n
La Begoña, 342
La Benéfica, 75
La Bodeguita del Medio restaurant, 122, 326
La Cabaña, 97
La Cabaña ridge, 24
La Chorrera, 14
La Coca, 275
La Concha, 111
*La consagración de la primavera,* 329
La Copa, 78
La Corbata neighborhood, 136
La Corona, 61
La Coronela, 79, 218, 287, 374
Lacret, 72
La Cueva del Humo, 100, 135
Ladas, 137
La Esperanza, 75
Lafayette, 320
La Floridita, 122
La Fuerza fortress, 14, 22
Lage, Carlos, 187, 256
La Gran Vía de La Habana, 64
La Güinera, 136, 162, 166
La Habana, 170, 239, 331
*La Habana para un Infante difunto,* 324
La Habana 2000: Diseño, Cultura y Ciudad
    (seminar), 369
La Lisa, 72, 281, 307
Lam, Wilfredo, 115, 116n
La Merced, 312
La Meridiana, 60
La Mina, 15
La Mina restaurant, 333n
Lamparilla, 64
Landholders, 133

Landlords, 134
Landmarks Commission, 350, 351
Land speculation, 134
Land use, local, 152
Land-use regulations, 134
Lansky, Meyer, 77, 121
La Paz, 347
Lápidus, Luis, 336
La Playa, 119
La Punta, 18, 24, 45
La Punta Castle, 21, 26, 33, 65
La Punta fort. *See* La Punta Castle
La Quinta de los Molinos, 33
La Rampa, 67, 78, 113, 122, 127, 128, 274, 307,
    375
Lasa, Catalina, 57n, 318
Las Animas, 75
Las Arboledas, 224–25
La Sierra, 99, 230
Las Murallas, 314, 316, 317, 331
Las Ruina, 277
Las Terrazas, 299
Las Tunas, 239
Las Vegas, 77, 290, 347
Las Villas, 239
Las Yaguas, 76, 100, 135
La Tambora, 76
*Latifundistas,* 134
La Timba, 76
Latin America, 32, 35, 52, 92, 93, 95, 96, 116,
    177, 179, 200, 204n, 208n, 216, 235–36, 241,
    260–61; countries of, 231; guerilla warfare
    in, 347; health care in, 297; housing debate
    in, 215–16; and planning, 219; poverty of,
    196; and self-help housing, 201; squatter
    communities in, 217n. *See also names of specific
    countries*
La Torre de Marfil restaurant, 333n
Lavasol, 198
La Victoria, 113
Law, September 1995, 190
Law 33, 180
Law 35, 134
Law 73, 192
Law 86, 201
Law 135, 199
Law 691, 134
Law Decree 165, 247

Law for the State Budget of 1995, 149–50
Law No. 77, 189
Law of Foreign Investment, 190
Laws of the Indies, 8, 18, 20, 105, 177
Lawton, 64, 99, 373
La Zaragozana restaurant, 333n
Leal Spengler, Eusebio, 321, 333, 336, 340
Le Corbusier, 50, 65, 69, 80, 82–83, 123, 203, 215, 219
Lecuona, Ernesto, 116n
Legal reforms, of 1992, 173
Leisure time, 302
L'Enfant, Pierre, 32, 36–37
Lenin, Vladimir I., 210, 271, 308, 358
Lenin Hill, 311
Lenin Park, 153, 212, 271, 275–77, 371
Lenin Vocational School, 142, 212, 221
Lennon, John, 56, 358, 371
Lennon Park, 371. *See also* Lennon, John
León, Lourdes, 338
León, Luis, 162n
L'EUR (Esposizione Universale di Roma), 42, 128
Leveau, Theo, 65
Ley de Propiedad Horizontal, 121
Lezama Lima, José, 116n, 310, 324
*Libreta*, 188, 249–50, 272
Life expectancy, 260
Lima, Peru, 216n, 241
Lima-Callao metropolitan area, 246
Lincoln Institute of Land Policy, 352
Línea Street, 8, 56, 103
Lion's Fountain, 316
Literacy rate, 260
Llega y Pon, 100, 135
Local Power (Poder Local), 169
Locomotive, 34
*Lo cubano*, 134
Loma de los Catalanes, 54, 64, 65, 66
Longa, Rita, 363
Lonja de Comercio, 59, 330, 332
López, César, 359
Lorenzo, Marta, 159n
*Losa hueca* (LH), 213
*Los nortes*, 16
Los Once, 115
Louisiana, 25, 31
L'Ouverture, Toussaint, 24

Low Countries: exports to, 39
Loynaz, Dulce María, 359
L Street, 118
Luciano, Charles "Lucky," 77
Lugano I/II, 216
*Lunes de Revolución*, 132
Lutgardita, 71, 76
Luyanó, 5, 49, 58, 98, 245
Luyanó River: basins of, 182; pollution in, 182
Luz Street, 324
Lyceum Lawn Tennis Club, 109
Lynch, Kevin, 194, 206n

*Macetas*, 188
*Maceteros*, 248
Machado, Gerardo, 63, 66, 71–72, 75, 77, 321
Machine repair parts, 149
Machinery, 238
Macondian rains, 347
Madrid, Spain, 160, 319, 338
Mafia, 82
Mafiosi, 77
Magazines, 199
Mahogany, 22
*Maine*, USS, 63
*Maine* Monument, 68
Málaga, 46
Malecón, 6, 8, 44, 49, 53, 64, 68–69, 79–80, 83–84, 99, 103, 109, 121, 122, 132, 149, 167, 277, 279, 301, 303, 307, 340, 351, 363, 370, 376
*Mambises*, 52
Mambo, 115
Mambo Club, 114
*Mampostería*, 6, 30
Mañach, Jorge, 116n
Manganese, 4
Manifestos, 362
Mantilla, 197
Mantilla, Jorge, 82n
Manzana de Gómez, 60, 135, 319
*Maqueta*, 167
Margarita, 16
Marianao, 53–54, 57–58, 69, 72, 75, 79, 99, 103, 104, 109, 111, 119, 170, 201, 224, 278, 286–87, 289, 317, 351
Marianao Beach, 111
Marianao Military Hospital, 280

Mariel, 4, 103, 247
Mariel Harbor, 6
Marina, 113
Marine terrace, 8
Markets, 211
Market socialism, 140
Marquesa, 133
Mart neighborhood, 135
Martí, José, 128, 271n, 359, 370
Martín, Teresa, 337
Martínez, Frank, 116n
Martínez, Raúl, 359
Martínez Inclán, Pedro, 54, 63–64, 73, 76, 80, 268, 320, 322–23, 323n, 330
Martínez Pedro, Luis, 116n
Martínez Villena, Rubén, 320n
Martín Pérez River: basins of, 182; pollution in, 182
Marty, Francisco, 34n
Marx, Karl, 254, 268, 308, 356–58
MasterCard, 192
Master Plan of 1971, 155–58; emphasis of, 156; and road plan, 156
Master Plan of 1984, 159
Master Plan of 1990, 160
Master Plan Office, 340
Master plans, 152
Matanzas, 4, 17, 73, 80, 103, 112, 239, 246, 275, 302n
Matanzas Province, 40
Matanzas Harbor, 6
Maternidad Obrera, 75
Mathéy, Kosta, 217n
Mausoleum of the Heroes of March 13, 371
Maximo Gómez, 221
Maya, 11
Mayne, Thom, 362
Maza, Aquiles, 75
McDonald's, 273, 352, 375
McKim, Mead, and White, 64
Medina, 56
Mediodía Highway, 275
Mediterranean Spanish style, 47
Mediterranean Style, 74, 364
Meliá, 188
Meliá-Cohiba, 291
Meliá Las Américas, 291
Melones, 98, 246

Méndez, José Antonio, 116n
Menéndez, Cecilia, 151
Menocal, Mario G., 59, 65
Menocal hills, 275
Mercaderes Street, 335
*Mercedazgo*, 19
*Mercedes*, 19
Merced Street, 324
Merchants, 133
Merici Academy, 116
Merril, 197
Mesías, Rosendo, 162n, 223n, 337n, 338
Mesoamerica, 8, 11
*Mestizaje*, 129
Metrobus, 268
Metropolitana Building, 320
Metropolitan Administration of Havana, 170
Metropolitan Havana, 213
Metropolitan Park (Parque Metropolitano), 153–54, 246, 275
Mexican revolutions, 203
Mexicans, 295
Mexico, 12, 13, 18, 52, 126, 216, 237, 297, 301, 351, 361; architects of, 124; and investment, 240
Mexico City, 43, 246, 347
Miami, Fla., 77, 97, 290, 346, 347, 350–52, 370, 376; and Miamization, 352
Miami Beach, Fla., 374
Miami–Havana–San Juan axis, 77
*Miami Herald*, 308
Microbrigade, 141, 143–44, 146, 156, 161, 207, 213, 215, 217–20, 230, 339, 349, 361; and buildings, 364; and Microbrigade movement, 141–42
Microbrigadistas. *See* Microbrigade
Middle class, 135
Mies, 123
Military Hospital, 75
Ministries. *See* Cuba—ministries of
Miramar, 5, 44, 49, 54, 57, 64, 69, 78, 99, 103, 105, 111, 121, 126, 128, 131, 187–89, 224, 230, 271, 273, 275, 277, 281, 286, 297, 303, 349, 351, 363–65, 373; and Forty-First Street, 78; and Forty-Second Street, 78; and land use, 137; neighborhood of, 137
Miramar Trade Center, 366
Miramar Yacht Club, 109

Miscegenation, 129
Misleidys, 138
Mission Avenue, 318
Modern monumental movement, 123, 129
Modern movement, 50, 123, 124
Módulo, 204n
Moenck y Quintana, 279, 319
*Mogotes*, 4
*Mojitos*, 324
*Mona Lisa*, 115
Moncada, 96, 95; declaration of, 199
Money launderers (*maceteros*), 248
Mongolia, 237
Monreal, Pedro, 247
Monserrate-Egido Avenues, 37
Monserrate Street, 52
Monte Barreto, 224, 295, 365, 367
Montecarlo Palace, 364
Montenegro, Amado, 64
Monte Street, 132
Montevideo, 334, 347
*Montoneros*, 347
Montoulieu, Eduardo, 81n, 82n
Montoulieu, Enrique J., 64
Monumental Highway, 275
Monument to the university martyrs, 371
Moonlighting, 248
Moore, Thomas, 310
Moorish design, 24
Morales, Juan Luis, 223n, 337n, 338
Morales, Leonardo, 57, 319
Moré, Benny, 116n
Morphosis, 362
Morro, 18
Morro-Cabaña Castles, 303
Morro Castle, 21, 23, 39, 45, 69, 83, 97, 103, 279, 303, 311, 331
Moscow, 204n, 212, 214, 248, 273
Moskvichs, 137
Moss, Eric Owen, 362
Mozambique, 295
Mudejar tradition, 105
Muliutin, 160
Multiflex system, 208
Multiple Nuclei Model, 85
Municipal Conference, Second, 323
Municipalities, 172
*Municipios*, 72, 96, 99, 162

Murallas neighborhood, 39
Muralla Street. *See* Ricia Street
Music, 31
Mussolinesque, 128
Mutual Aid program, 135

Nacional theater, 59
Napoleon III (emperor of France), 37
Narcotics, 77
Naroca building, 205
National and Local Landmark Protection Law, 331
National Assembly, 133, 173n, 179, 185, 189; Deputies of, 173; secretary of, 174
National Botanical Garden, 275–76
National Center for Conservation, Restoration, and Museum Studies. *See* CENCREM
National City Bank of New York, 320
National Commission of Landmarks, 336
National Conference of Architects, First, 82n
National Conference on Housing and Urbanism, Eleventh, 144
National Council of Culture, 329
National Historic Monuments, 323
National Hospital, 280
National Institute of Agrarian Reform, 139
National Institute of Culture, 115
National Institute of Savings and Housing (INAV), 150, 201, 202, 203
National Institute of Tourism. *See* Instituto Nacional de Turismo
National Landmarks Commission, 329
National Library, 81, 308
National Lottery, 202
National Observatory, 4
National Physical Plan, 151
National Planning Board, 82n, 83, 103, 374
National Planning Conference, First, 82n
National Police, fortress of, 321
National Poll of Internal Migrants, 242
National Prize for Literature, 359
National Psychiatric Hospital, 281
National Revolutionary Militias, 134
National Revolutionary Police, 243
National School of Art, 287
National Theater, 83
National Trust for Historic Preservation: vice-president of, 363

National Union of Cuban Architects, Engineers, and Builders (UNAIC), 363
National Zoo, 275–76
Nazareno, village of, 151
Nazareno hill, 275
Nazis, 212
Negro, 26, 32
Neighborhood Popular Councils, 176
Neighborhoods, 136–37, 163, 184. *See also names of specific neighborhoods*
Neoclassical style, 29–32, 126, 364
Neocolonial style, 129
Neptuno Street, 113, 127
Nercesián, Norald, 159n
Neruda, Pablo, 132
Nervi, Pier Luigi, 203
Nestle's, 78n
Netherlands: and investment, 240
Neutra, 123
Neutra, Richard, 77n, 82n
Newark, N.J., 298
New Deal, 74–75
New Havana. *See* Centro Habana neighborhood
New Jersey, 298
New Jewel Movement, 255
Newspapers, 199
New Year's Eve, 111
New York, 126, 298, 319
New York City, 117
*New Yorker*, 350
*New York Times*, 350, 352
New Zoo, 153
NGOs (nongovernmental organizations): Cuban, 165, 165n; foreign, 165–66, 172, 231
Nicaragua, 297; Sandinista, 254–55
Nickel, 4
Nico López, 288
Niemeyer, Oscar, 204n
Nipe, 4, 25
Noever, Peter, 362
Nombre de Díos, Panama, 14
North American blockade, 138; and property, 133
North Atlantic countries, 224
North Korea: imports from, 248
Northern America, 161

Nouvel, Jean, 318n
Nuclear reactor, 247
Nuevitas, 4, 25
Nuevitas Bay, 12
Nuevo Biltmore, 119
Nuevo Miramar, 224
Nuevo Vedado, 49, 75, 105, 107, 121; Twentieth Street, 78
Núñez, Pastorita, 202
Núñez Jiménez, Antonio, 336

Oak, 22
Obispo Street, 37, 39, 127, 316, 318, 324, 326, 335
Observatory, 97
October Revolution, 203
O'Donnell, Leopoldo, 39
O'Farrill, José Ricardo, 317
Office of Physical Planning, 150
Office of the City Historian. *See* City Historian's Office
Offices of Architecture and Urbanism (DAU), 152
Oficios Street, 32n, 335, 338
Oil, 4, 90, 97, 149, 235, 238, 245, 274, 303n; and imports, 146; and oil refineries, 134; and shipments from United States, 138; shortages of, 232
Old Havana. *See* Habana Vieja
Old San Juan, Puerto Rico, 333
Old World, 90
Oliveras, Rosa, 159n, 160n
Olmsted, Frederick Law, 57
Olympic competition, 307
Operation Peter Pan, 135
*Ordenanzas*, 41
Ordenanzas de la Construcción de 1862, 41
O'Reilly Street, 37, 39, 316, 318, 324, 326, 335
Organic architecture, 129
Organized crime, 248, 325, 347
*Organopónicos de alto rendimiento*, 183
*Organopónicos populares*, 183
Oriente, 239, 241
*Orígenes*, 115
*Orishas*, 299
Orthodox Marxist, 140
Orthodox Party, 95, 202
Otero, Lisandro, 132

Otero, Raúl, 54, 57, 64–65, 75
Ottoman Empire, 45
Owings, 197

Pabellón Cuba, 128
Pacino, Al, 325
Padilla case, 359
Padrón, Juan, 194
Painters, 221
País, Frank, 281
Palace, 64
Palace of Justice, 81–82, 320
Palacio de la Revolución, 128
*Paladares*, 245, 250, 344, 349, 353
*Palazzi*, 317
Palermo, 69
Palestinos (Palestinians), 179
Palm, Erwin Walter, 323n
Pampa, 311
Panama, 237, 260–61, 285
Pan-American Conference, Sixth, 63
Pan-American Conference of Architects,
     Eighth, 82n
Pan American Games, 307; in Havana, 225
Pan American Highway, 73
*Papel Periódico de la Habana*, 39
*Paradiso*, 312
Paraguay, 261
Parcelación Zayas, 119
*Parcelas*, 183
Paris, 62, 65, 319; boulevards of, 37; and
     Parisian School, 65
Parke-Davis, 77
Parking lots, 205
Parks, 132, 153
Parque Central, 60, 64, 99, 106, 108, 114, 371,
     375
Parque Coppelia, 306
Parque de Fraternidad, 68, 106
Parque Metropolitano, 128, 303
Parque Villalón, 123
Parroquial Mayor, 21
Partagás Tobacco Factory, 60–61
*Parterres*, 56, 106
Partido Socialista Popular. *See* Communist
     Party
*Pasaje*, 63, 100
*Paseo a pie*, 28

Paseo Avenue, 8
Paseo de Carlos III, 68, 113, 118
Paseo de Isabel II, 33, 315
Paseo de la Infanta, 315
Paseo de la Reina, 33
Paseo del Prado, 106, 108, 112, 315, 318, 337,
     363
Paseo de Martí, 315
Paseo de Tacón, 33
*Paseo en carruaje*, 28
Paseo Extramural, 28
*Paseos*, 106
Paseo Street, 56, 301, 351
Paso Seco, 104
Paso Superior railroad yards, 98
Pastry shops, 188
Patronato Pro-Urbanismo, 73, 323
Paula Street, 312, 324
Payret, 60
Peace dividend, 295
*Pedraplenes*, 300
Peláez, Amelia, 116n, 322
*Peninsulares*, 26, 32, 65
People's Liberation Army, 296
People's Powers, 152
Pepsi Cola, 77
*Perestroika*, 357
Pérez Beato, Manuel, 322
Pérez Benitoa, José, 128
Pérez Prado, Dámaso, 116n
Periódo especial, 213
Perla neighborhood, 135
*Permutas*, 229
Pernod Ricard, 240
Perry, Clarence, 204n
Persian rugs, 33
Peru, 126, 216, 261; pre-Fujimori, 258
Pesticides, 149, 238
Petroleum. *See* Oil
Pharmaceutical industry, 148
Pharmaceuticals, 297
Phillip II (king of Spain), 17, 18
Phillip III (king of Spain), 23
Phillip IV (king of Spain), 23
Phillips, 116
Physical framework, 136
Physical planning, 139
Physical Planning Departments, 229

Piedrabuena, 216
Pila Street, 112
Pilotis, 215
Pimps, 114
Pinar del Río, 169, 331; and marqués, 316; province of, 73, 239, 275, 299
Pinares de Mayarí, 299
Piñera, Virgilio, 116n
Pinochet, Augusto, 279
Pitt, William the Elder, 24
Pizza Hut, 375
Plan del Cordón de La Habana, 328
Planners and the Greenbelt, 151
Plaster, 6, 30
Playa, 121, 224, 281, 287
Playa de Marianao, 54
Playa Girón, 135. *See also* Bay of Pigs invasion
Playa Jibacoa, 295
Playa Miramar, 119
Playa Municipality, 276
Playas del Este, 270, 295, 302
Plaza Cívica, 65, 68, 74–75, 81–82, 84–85, 128, 203, 273, 301, 308, 370; forum of, 77
Plaza de Armas, 13, 21–22, 28, 33, 106, 306, 313, 315, 321–23, 327, 329, 330, 335
Plaza de la Catedral. *See* Plaza de la Ciénaga
Plaza de la Ciénaga, 21–22, 27, 59, 64, 306, 321–23, 327
Plaza de la Revolución, 54, 201–4, 206, 213, 214, 218, 250, 273, 279–80, 329, 335
Plaza del Cristo, 28, 335
Plaza del Vapor, 113
Plaza de Marianao, 123
Plaza de San Francisco, 22, 28, 329
Plaza Finlay, 75
Plaza Mayor, 313
Plazas, 60, 63, 99, 105, 106, 305, 323, 327, 335
Plaza Vieja, 22, 28, 32n, 158, 321, 335, 337, 338
*Plazoletas*, 324
Pleyán, Carlos García, 162n
Poder Popular, 143, 173–77, 337n, 361; National Assembly of, 331. *See also* People's Powers
Poéte, Marcel, 65
Pogolotti, 58, 76
Polar brewery, 107
Poles, 324

*Policlínicos*, 211, 278, 281; and public health, 205
Politeama, 60
Pools, 307
Popular Councils, 166; in Havana, 162
Popular Neighborhood Councils (Consejos Populares de Barrios), 175
Population, 136
Porro, Ricardo, 323n, 361
Port: development of, 158; and port installations, 139
*Portales*, 30–31, 41, 54–55, 105, 197, 213, 373
Porticoes, 68
Portilla, Manuel, 316
Portillo, César, 116n
Portland, Oreg., 369
Portobelo, 14
Portocarrero, René, 116n, 322
*Posada*, 114
Post–Cold War era, 295
Postmodernism: in Cuba, 224
Poverty, 52; and beggars, 37; and shantytowns, 80, 100, 101, 154; in Latin America, 196
Pozos Dulces, Count, 56
Prado, 47, 59–61, 68, 103, 109, 241, 315, 375
Prado boulevard, 33
Prague, 214, 358
Prebaroque, 126, 129
Precipitation, 5; annual, 4
Presidentes Avenue, 8, 64
Presidential Palace, 59, 61, 68, 83, 95
Prieto, Abel, 371
Prieto, Alberto, 81n
Príncipe Castle, 24, 33, 49, 54, 68, 316
Privatization, 175
Prix, Wolf, 362
Profesionales, 111
Proletariat, 54, 64
Prost, Henri, 65
Prostitution, 77, 112, 114
Protestantism, 308
Protestant schools, 116
Protest of the Thirteen, 320
Provincial Assembly of the City of Havana, 173
Provincial Department of Architecture and Urbanism, 162
Provincial Physical Planning Office, 159, 160n

Provincial planning departments (Dirección Provincial de Planificación Fisica, DPPF), 152
Provincial plans, 151
Provincial School of the Cuban Communist Party, 288
Pruscha, Carl, 362
Public health, 205
Public transportation, 268
*Pueblos jóvenes*, 217n
Puentes Grandes, 53
Puerta de la Tenaza 19
Puerto Cortés, 14
Puerto de Carena Construction company, 340
Puerto de Safua restaurant, 333n
Puerto Príncipe, 11
Puerto Rico, 3, 16, 19, 90
Puestos de Mando de la Agricultura, 140, 275
Punta Brava, 72
Purdy and Henderson, 319
Purísima Concepción, 60
Pyrenees, 46

Querejeta, 119
Quibú River, 182; pollution of, 182
*Quinquenio gris*, 219
*Quinta*, 316
Quinta Avenida, 57, 80, 99, 103, 111, 131, 137, 188, 363, 364, 366
Quinta de los Molinos, 49, 82, 117, 327
Quintana, Antonio, 76, 116n, 209, 337n
Quintana, Nicolás, 81n, 82n, 116n, 152, 323n, 351
Quintas, 105
*Quintas de salud*, 278, 280
Quito, 347
*Quitrines*, 28

Rafacas y Toñarely, 319
Railroad, 31n, 35–36, 40, 90, 245, 274
Raleigh, Sir Walter 21
Rampa, 121
Rancho Boyeros, 4, 197, 218, 247, 374
Rancho Boyeros Avenue, 71–72, 271
Rápido, 273, 352
Rationalism, 129
Ravenet, Domingo, 323n
Rayneri, Eugenio, 57

Real estate, 193–194, 197–98, 200
*Reanimción urbanistica*, 369
Rebel Army, 131, 133, 139, 286; Corps of Engineers, 150
*Reconcentración*, 52
Register of Economic Associations, 190
Regla, 33, 45, 47, 53, 97, 245, 311, 317
Reina, 67, 375
Reina Mercedes Hospital, 274
Religion, 302, 312; Catholicism, 112, 116; Protestantism, 308; and religious expression, 308; Roman Catholicism, 261, 299, 308. *See also* Jews
Renaissance, 8
Reparto Aranguren, 76
Reparto Bahía, 218
Reparto Flores, 276
Reparto Náutico, 196
*Repartos*, 54, 56, 202
Republican period, 168, 326
Republican style, 106
Reserve to the Biosphere, 299
Residencial Wajay, 202
Restaurants, 188. *See also names of specific restaurants*
Restoration of Monuments company, 342
*Retretas*, 28
Revitalization, 137
Revolution, 89, 95, 121, 126, 131, 133–34, 137–38, 168, 241, 248, 251, 266–67, 274, 286, 288, 298, 302, 305, 308–9, 325, 346, 357, 374; Cuban, 210, 221; French, 30
Revolutionary Directorate (Directorio Revolucionario), 95, 131
Revolution Square. *See* Plaza Cívica
Rey, Gina, 159n
Ricia Street, 39, 46, 127, 324, 326
Rigau, Jorge, 362
Rigol, Isabel, 162n, 336
Rimac River, 241
Rina, 198
Rio de Janeiro, 43, 311, 347, 374
Río de la Plata, 69, 83
Ríos, Joaquín, 317
Riverside, Ill., 57
Roads, 268; and investment for road network, 156
Roanoke Island, 21

Rodríguez, Abel, 337n
Rodríguez, Alberto, 209
Rodríguez, Eduardo Luis, 162n, 204n, 223n,
  337n, 338
Rodríguez, José Luis, 149
Rodríguez, Mariano, 116n
Rodríguez Alomá, Patricia, 337, 337n
Rogers, Ernesto N., 336
Roig de Leuchsenring, Emilo, 323, 333
Rojas, Angela, 162n
Romañach, Mario, 76, 82n, 116n, 152, 323n
Roman Catholic Church, 306
Roman Catholicism, 261, 299, 308. *See also*
  Catholicism
Romay, Tomás, 316
Roosevelt, Franklin D., 74
Rorick, Huck, 225
Ross, Pedro, 256
Royal Bank of Canada, 320
Royal Crown, 77
Royal Proclamation, marquis of the, 317
Rubén, Eduardo, 363
Rum, 40, 250, 289, 325
Rumba, 299
Rural Housing Department (Viviendas
  Campesinas), 139
Ruralization, 201
Ruskin, John, 321
Russia, 238; exports to, 39; and technicians,
  286
Ruston, 116

*Sabana*, 13
Sacred Heart, 308
Sagrado Corazón, 116
Sagua de Tánamo, 4
St. Augustine, 20–21
St. Dominigue, Haiti. *See* Haiti
St. Maarten, 293
Saladrigas, René, 151
Sala Polivalente, 307
Salas, Julián, 217n
Salinas, 224
Salinas, Fernando, 162n, 203, 204, 207–10,
  208n, 232, 337n
Salinas, Rosa M., 224
Salmona, Rogelio, 224
Salsa, 327

Salvador Gomila, 225
San Antonio de los Baños, 104
San Augustín, 218, 287
San Cristóbal, 342
San Cristóbal de la Habana, 1, 11, 13, 21, 377
Sancti Spíritus, 11, 239, 331
San Francisco Convent, 312, 320, 339
San Francisco de Paula, 26, 53, 72, 102, 197,
  312
San Ignacio Street, 39
San Isidro, 112, 340
San Isidro Street, 324
Sanitarium, 75
San José de las Lajas, 72, 102, 307
San Juan, Puerto Rico, 19, 58, 83, 374
San Lázaro, 44, 67, 113, 118
San Lorenzo, 42
San Martín, José R., 74
San Miguel, 282
San Miguel del Padrón, 307
San Pedro, 324
San Pedro de la Roca, castle of. *See* Morro
  castle
San Rafael Street, 127, 127n
San Salvador de la Punta, 14
Santa Catalina, 72, 197, 312
Santa Catalina de Siena Convent, 312, 320
Santa Clara, 96, 131, 239, 312
Santa Clara Convent, 320, 339
Santa Fé, 196, 374
Santa Fé beach, 288
Santa Fé de Bogotá, 335
Santa María del Mar, 112, 144
Santa Marta, Colombia, 14
*Santería*, 299
*Santeros*, 299
Santiago, Chile, 12, 311
Santiago de Cuba, 4, 21, 73, 79, 95, 96, 117,
  135, 146, 176, 211, 239, 246, 293, 331, 331;
  and investment opportunities, 41
Santiago de las Vegas, 53, 72
Santo Domingo, Dominican Republic, 17, 21,
  58, 83
Santo Domingo Convent, 312, 320, 338, 347
Santos Suárez, 49, 58, 99, 105
São Paulo, 43, 52, 347
Sarduy, Severo, 359
Sarrá, Ernesto, 57n

Scandinavia: satellite cities of, 204n
Scarpa, Carlo, 336
Schenley Whiskey, 128
School of Architecture of Barcelona, 330
School of Engineering and Architecture, 320
Schools, 211; Protestant, 116
Schools of Arts, 359, 361, 363
Schulthess, Alfred, 78n
Schultz, Paul, 82, 152
Schumann, Tony, 217n
Sculptors, 221
Sears and Roebuck, 77
Second Agrarian Reform Law, 134, 138
Second Five-Year Plan, 144
Second Republican Center, 85
Sector Model, 85
Segre, Roberto, 162n, 208n, 330, 337n
Segundo Cabo, 313
Segundo Cabo Palace, 30, 330
Segundo Congreso de Municipios (Second
    Municipal Conference), 323
Seguro Médico building, 205
Self-governance, 176
Self-help, 135; and mutual aid, 201; and self-
    help housing, 201, 211
Semiassembled products, 149
Sendero Luminoso, 347
*Se Permuta*, 241
Serrano Avenue, 64, 316
Sert, José Luis, 73, 77n, 81n, 82–86, 121, 152,
    268, 351, 363, 374
Service, 101
Seventeenth Street, 371
Seventieth Street, 366
Sevilla Biltmore, 60, 63
Seville, 14, 20, 29, 46; and Sevillan monopoly,
    15; and Sevillian tradition, 105
Sex industry, 112, 114
Sex tourism, 189
Shangai, 113, 123
Shantytowns, 80, 100, 101, 154
Sheffield, 209
Shell, 97
Sherritt, 240
Sherwin Williams, 77
Shoes, 249
Siboney. *See* Biltmore country club
*Siboneyes*, 8, 9

Sicre, Juan José, 75, 323n
Sierra, 254
Sierra de los Organos, 4
Sierra Maestra, 4, 151, 202, 286, 299
Sierra Maestra building, 271
Simón Bolívar, Caracas, 362
Siporex, 209
*Sisa de la zanja* (canal tax), 18
Sixth Street, 371
Skidmore, 197
Skidmore, Owings, and Merril, 83
Slaves, 25, 31–32, 41; freed, 37; and slavery, 40
Sliding Scaffolding Model, 142
Sloppy Joe's Bar, 122
Smithson, Peter and Alison, 206n
Snare and Triest, 319
Soap, 249–50
Social and Agricultural Development Group
    (Grupo de Desarrollo Social y Agropecua-
    rio) (DESA), 141
Social diversity, 55
Socialism, 175
*Socialism and Man in Cuba*, 140
Socialist housing: in Havana, 214
Social security expenditures, 150
Social services, 205
Social workers, 162
Sociedad Económica de Amigos del País
    (Economic Society of Friends of the Coun-
    try), 30–31
Sociedad Nuestro Tiempo, 115
Sociologists, 151n, 155, 163
Soil, 32, 40; clay, 29; miry, 30
*Solares*, 76, 80, 222, 332, 375
Sol Street, 46, 324
Soria y Mata, 160
Sorugue, M., 65
Sosabravo, Alfredo, 359
South America, 13
Southern Watershed Basin (Cuenca Sur), 104
South Havana Aquifer, 6
Soviet bloc, 148n; and trading arena, 146
Soviet Union, 204n, 211, 222, 234–35, 237–
    38, 271n, 274, 295; aid from, 255; collapse
    of, 138, 213; former, 2, 145, 221, 246, 279,
    297, 353, 356–57; and planning, 212
Spain, 3, 13, 51, 89, 90, 301, 316, 351, 361;
    colonial rule of, 90; Crown of, 313; exports

to, 39; immigrants from, 53; independence from, 90; and investment, 121n, 240; and nobility, 313; tourists from, 295, 300
Spaniards, 10, 46, 52, 188
Spanish-American War, 46, 63
Spanish Armada, 23
Spanish Colonial Style, 74, 129
Spanish Liberating Army, 52
Special Period, 138, 158, 161–62, 167, 181, 183, 186, 209, 223, 225–31, 234–35, 236–38, 244, 248–51, 259–61, 274, 278, 285, 295, 303, 307–9, 339, 348–49, 372; first phase of, 148
Sporting complexes, 211
Sports, 266, 302
Sports City (Ciudad Deportiva), 307
Sports Medicine Institute, 297
Squibb, 77
Stalin, Joseph, 212
Stalingrad, 160, 214, 347
State construction, 201
State Council (Consejo de Estado), 247
State Group for the Cleaning, Conservation, and Development of the Havana Bay, 182
State investment, 144
State quotas (*acopio*), 250
Statistical yearbook, 236
Steel, 149, 208; and enamel, 208
Steinhart, Frank, 60
Stockholm, 377
Stores, 188
*Strawberries and Chocolate*, 306
Suburbanization, 44, 120, 201
Sugar, 25, 29, 33–35, 37, 66, 72, 79, 89, 120, 139, 235, 237–38, 290, 312; bagasse, 235; *guarapo*, 122; harvest of, 91, 92, 140, 211, 212, 298, 312, 328; and economy, 41; exports of, 40, 71; market for, 34; plantations for, 93; prices of, 57, 63, 72, 91; production of, 25, 40, 45, 90–92, 139, 274; and sugar barons, 3, 35, 63, 318, 373; and sugar boom, 2, 24, 51, 90; and sugarcane, 16, 74, 235; and sugar industry, 93; and sugar mill, 3, 40–41, 93, 112, 133–34, 235, 239, 331; and sugar quota, 91, 138; trade in, 39
Sugarloaf Mountain, 311
Suicide, 261
*Supergráficas*, 221

Super Graphics, 143
Supermarkets, 272
Sustainability, 183–84
Sutures, 281
Swapping (*permutas*), 144. See also *Se Permuta*
Synagogue, 46
Syphilis, 18
System of Economic Planning and Management (SDPE), 143, 171

Tacón, Francisco, 32
Tacón, Governor Miguel, 3, 32, 34n, 35–37, 45, 315
Tacón jail, 320
Tacón Theater, 28
Tadeo Creek, 182
Taínos, 8–10
Tallapiedra, 203, 246
Tallapiedra power plant, 98
*Talleres*, 177; neighborhood of, 162–65
Talleres de Transformación Integral del Barrio (TTIBS), 162
Tallet, José Z., 116n
Tamargo, Jorge, 223n, 337n
Tarará, 112, 276, 295
Tarará River, 182
Tariff, regulations, 190
Taxes, 248, 254, 256, 353
Tax Law, 190
Team X, 206n, 220
Technical Military Institute, 286
Technical University of Hamburg, Germany, 232
Technology, 211
Tejas corner, 213
Television: and home prototypes, 199
Temperatures, monthly, 4, 5
Templete, 316, 322
Ten Cents, 77
Teniente Rey Street, 39, 46, 321, 324, 326
Ten Years' War, 41
Terraza de Cojímar, 122
*Teteras*, 180
Texaco, 97
Texeda, Governor, 22
Thailand, 189
Thamesmead, 209
Thieves, 33, 37

Third Avenue, 365

Third Five-Year Plan, 145

Third Republican Center, 85

Third Style, 67

Third World, 90, 129, 216; countries of, 207

*Three Trapped Tigers* (*Tres Tristes Tigres*), 122, 324

*Tías*, 137

TIBBS, 166; and Advisory Council, 166; and Consultant Council, 166

Tiendas Caracol, 192

Tiendas CUBALSE, 192

Tiendas de Recaudación de Divisas (TRDS), 188

Tiendas Panamericanas, 192

Tiendas TRD, 192

Tiendas Universal, 192

Tile, 208

Titón, 132

Tobacco, 37, 40, 238, 289–90; and cigar factories, 52; and cigarettes, 250; and factories 39, 42, 60, 61, 317, 330; *rapé*, 33

Toll booths, 302n

Tonel, Antonio Eligio, 219

Toothpaste, 249

Topes de Collantes, 299

Toraya, José, 319

Torricelli Track Two law, 165n

Torroja Institute, 338

Toulouse-le-Mirail, 209

Tourism, 77, 91, 96, 112, 113, 121, 148, 161, 289–90, 295, 326, 327n, 332, 333, 344, 347, 350; cultural, 298; ecotourism, 299; health, 296–97; and "sin in the sun," 113; and tourist hotels, 60

Town Planning Associates, 82

Traditional Center, 295

Trafficante, Santos, 77, 121

Transportation, 271; public, 268

TRD (Tiendas de Recuperación de Divisas), 188

TRD Caribe, 296

Tres Reyes del Morro, 14

*Tres Tristes Tigres*, 122, 324

Trigo, Domingo, 56

Trinidad, 4, 11–12, 25, 103, 331

Tropical Brewery, 107

Tropical Gardens, 107

Tropicana, 78, 122, 290, 325

Tropic of Cancer, 4, 23

Trujillo, 14

Tunis, 29

Tupamaros, 347

*Turcos*, 45–46

Turks, 46, 324

Turner, Ted, 239

Turquino Peak, 4

26 de Julio, 95, 96

Twenty-third Street, 122

Typhus, 52

UNAIC, 363

UNDP. *See* United Nations Development Program

UNEAC, 350; Sixth Congress of, 361

UNESCO, 84, 126, 158, 299, 314, 316, 331, 333, 350–51

Unilever, 240

Union Club, 109

Unión Nacional de Arquitectos, Ingenieros, y Constructores (UNAIC), 363

Unión Nacional de Escritores y Actores de Cuba. *See* UNEAC

Unit 1, 204, 204n

United Hebrew Congregation, 46

United Kingdom: and investment, 240

United Nations, 293, 314

United Nations Development Programme (UNDP), 182, 260–61, 303n

United States, 52, 57, 76, 93, 124, 148, 274, 295, 326, 347, 361–63, 370; administration of, 133, 370; architects of, 123; and Army Corps of Engineers, 318; banks of, 192; and blockade, 206, 237, 326; and capital, 60; and Capitol building, 36; and Committee of ICOMOS, 363; Congress, 150; design principles of, 204n; exports to, 39–40; and embargo, 148, 201, 211, 268n, 293, 297–98; and Food and Drug Administration, 297; and functionalism of public buildings, 75; health care in, 278, 297; and hierarchy of settlements, 169n; imports from, 89, 91, 237; influence of, 90, 91, 293, 361; and Interests Section, 279, 370; and intervention, 63, 91, 134, 317; and invasion, 135; and investment, 36, 40, 50, 77, 90, 239; markets of, 25; military of, 51, 114; and millionaires, 288; and neighborhood unit, 204n; occupation by, 43, 318; and railway design, 35; spending by, 298; and suburbanization, 347; and sugar quota, 91; and tourism, 122, 237, 274, 293, 325; trade relations with, 290; visitors from, 295

U.S. Rubber, 77

U.S. Virgin Islands, 293

Universidad Católica de Villanueva, 118

Universidad de Las Villas in Santa Clara, 117

Universidad de Oriente, 117

University Bathing Resort (Balneario Universitario), 109, 111

University Hill, 118

University of Havana, 49, 82, 95, 116–18, 190, 320, 327; School of Architecture, 208, 323, 330; Urban Planning Chair, 80; Urban Studies, 323

University of Miami, 350

University of Santiago de Cuba, 289

Urban design: in Latin America, 203

Urban Forecast System and Project Zones for the year 2000, 151

Urban Housing Department, 207

Urban husbandry, 243

Urbanism: Cuban, 202; World Day of, 82n

Urbanization, 8, 43, 93, 119

Urban Land-Use and Zoning Regulations (*Regulaciones Urbanísticas*), 178

Urban master plans, 151

Urban morphology, 29

Urban planning: in Cuba, 162

Urban Planning Laws, 315

Urban Reform Law, 218

Urban Revitalization, 143

Urban sprawl, 129

Uruguay, 93, 260–61, 289, 335

Vagrants, 33

Valdés, Governor, 22

Valhalla, 68

Valle de los Ingenios, 331

Valle del Perú, 151

*Vampires in Havana* (*Vampiros en La Habana*), 194

Van der Rohe, Ludwig Mies, 77n

Van Eyck, Aldo, 206n

Vapor, 113

Vapor and Colón markets, 320

Varadero, 98, 103, 291, 293–94, 302, 302n

Varatti, Vittorio, 361

Varela, Enrique Luis, 75, 81

Varela, Félix, 316

Vargas Llosa, Mario, 133

*Vascos. See* Basque

Vasoncelos, Emilio, 65, 323n

Vázquez, René, 377

*Vecinos*, 16

Vedado, 5–6, 8, 21, 42, 44, 46, 49, 52, 54, 56–57, 57n, 60, 64, 67, 69, 75, 78, 82, 96, 100, 103, 105, 106, 109, 111, 113, 121, 127, 128, 132, 167, 187, 197, 203, 213, 275, 278, 280, 291, 295, 297, 301, 303, 307, 311, 318, 323, 324, 350, 351, 371, 373–75; corner of L and Twenty-third Streets, 274, 305; Seventeenth Street, 78; Velasco y Sarrá, Dionisio, 83

Vedado Tennis Club, 109, 110, 132, 133

Velasco, 338

Velasco, Dionisio, 318

Velázquez de Cuéllar, Diego, 11, 310

Venezuela, 19, 93, 124, 216, 237, 261, 285, 351

Venice Charter, 329

Vento underground aquifer, 182

Vento Watershed Basin, 154, 158–59

Venturian axion, 84

Veracruz, 14, 18

Vermay, 31, 316

Vía Blanca, 72, 98, 102, 270

Vía Monumental, 97, 103

Vía Tunel, 197

Víbora, 49, 58, 64, 75, 99, 105, 351, 373

Vietnam, 237, 254–55, 274n; imports from, 248

Vilalta de Saavedra, José, 371

Villa, José, 371

Villa (Bola de Nieve), Ignacio, 116n

Villaba, marquis of, 317

Villanueva, Carlos Raúl, 124

Villanueva, Count, 32

Villanueva Station, 30, 35, 317

Villa Panamericana, 146, 224–27, 307

*Villas*, 11–12, 15–16, 20, 28–30, 33, 56, 310, 331

*Villas miseries*, 217n

Villa Soldati, 216

Viñales Valley, 331
Viollet-le-Duc, Eugene Emmanuel, 321
Visa credit card, 192
Vitier, Cinto, 116n
Vivas, Fruto, 207
Viviendas de bajo Consumo, 228
*Volantas*, 28
Volodia School, 142, 221
Von Humboldt, Alexander (baron), 11, 324
Von Klenze, 68

Wajay, 208
Walker and Gillette, 319
Wall Street, 126
Warehouses, 139
Warsaw, Poland, 329, 358
Warsaw Pact, 278
Washington, D.C., 32, 36–37
Water pollution, 104, 299
Water quality, 28
Wax, 40
Weiner, Paul Lester, 82
Weiss, Joaquín, 323n, 330
Welfare, 231
West Basin, 182
Western Europe, 295, 329
Western Mining, 240
Western Union, 319
West Germany, 214
Weyler, Captain General Valeriano, 52
*What Time Is This Place?*, 194
White Creoles, 26, 46
White House, 37
Wiener, Paul Lester, 152
Windward Passage, 3
Wood, 324; precious, 40
Wood, General Leonard, 45
Woods, Lebbeus, 362

Woolworth, 77
Workers' Central Union of Cuba, 238
Workshop on Housing Policy: First, 228; Second, 229
Workshops, 163–64. See also *Talleres*
World Day of Urbanism, 82n
World Exposition, Paris, 104, 326
World Heritage Site, 84, 126, 158, 222, 224, 314, 331, 335, 351. *See also* UNESCO
World's Fair, New York, 128
World War II, 72, 77, 113, 212, 255; post–, 204n
World Wide Web, 189n
Wright, Frank Lloyd, 124, 203
Writers, 221

Xerophylic, 4
Xifré Street, 113

Yacht, 111
Yacht Club, 132
*Yaguas*, 52
Yarini y Poncé de León, Alberto, 112
Yoruba, 299
Yucatán, 73
Yucatán Channel, 16
Yucatán Peninsula, 3
Yugoslavia, 142

*Zafra. See* Sugar: harvest of
Zaldo y Salmón, 54, 320
Zamora neighborhood, 135
Zanja, 375
*Zanja*, 17; Zanja Real, 17, 29, 33
Zanja Street, 113
Zarza, 275
Zona Congelada, 137
Zoo, 75, 212